DATA FILES FOR STUDENTS

To complete the activities in this book, students will need data files, which are available online.

To access the data files, follow these instructions:

1. Open your browser and access the companion website at NGL.Cengage.com/AdobeAi

2. For data files to complete each activity within a chapter, select the chapter number from the drop-down box (below the book title), then click "Student Downloads" in the Book Overview section on the left panel. ·

3. For ACP Prep Guide data files, select "Student Downloads" in the Book Resources section on the left panel.

T0198228

Adobe
Illustrator
REVEALED

CHRIS BOTELLO

Acknowledgments

Grateful acknowledgment is given to the authors, artists, photographers, museums, publishers, and agents for permission to reprint copyrighted material. Every effort has been made to secure the appropriate permission. If any omissions have been made or if corrections are required, please contact the Publisher.

Cover Image Credit:

Jason Treat/National Geographic

Adobe® Photoshop®, Adobe® InDesign®, Adobe® Illustrator®, Adobe® Flash®, Adobe® Dreamweaver®, Adobe® Edge Animate®, Adobe® Creative Suite®, and Adobe® Creative Cloud® are trademarks or registered trademarks of Adobe Systems, Inc. in the United States and/or other countries. Third party products, services, company names, logos, design, titles, words, or phrases within these materials may be trademarks of their respective owners.

Adobe product screenshot(s) reprinted with permission from Adobe Systems Incorporated.

For product information and technology assistance, contact us at Customer & Sales Support, 888-915-3276

For permission to use material from this text or product, submit all requests online at
www.cengage.com/permissions

Further permissions questions can be emailed to
permissionrequest@cengage.com

National Geographic Learning | Cengage
200 Pier 4 Boulevard, Suite 400
Boston, MA 02210

National Geographic Learning, a Cengage company, is a provider of quality core and supplemental educational materials for the PreK–12, adult education, and ELT markets. Cengage is a leading provider of customized learning solutions with employees residing in nearly 40 different countries and sales in more than 125 countries around the world. Find your local representative at **NGL.Cengage.com/RepFinder.**

Visit National Geographic Learning online at **NGL.Cengage.com.**

ISBN: 978-0-357-54177-7

Printed in the United States of America.

Print Number: 02
Print Year: 2022

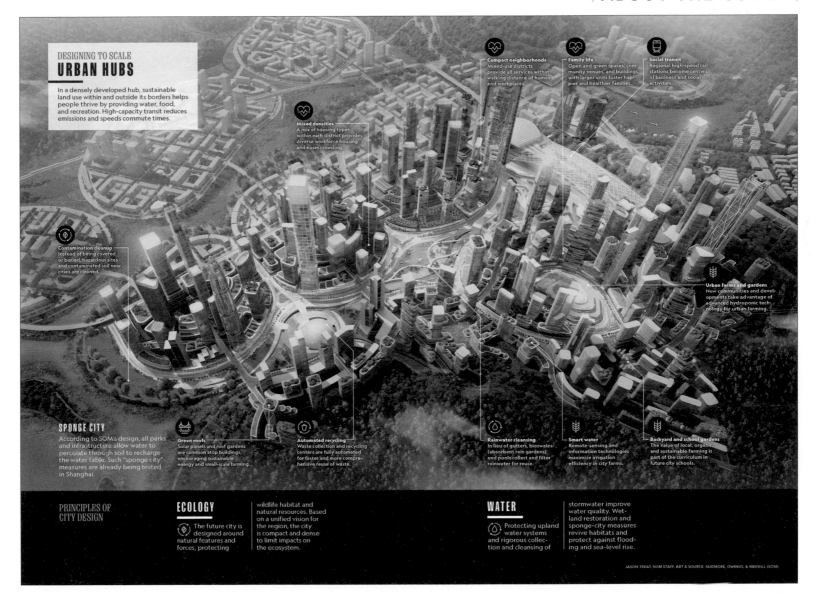

DESIGNING TO SCALE
URBAN HUBS

In a densely developed hub, sustainable land use within and outside its borders helps people thrive by providing water, food, and recreation. High-capacity transit reduces emissions and speeds commute times.

Mixed densities
A mix of housing types within each district provides diverse workforce housing and eases crowding.

Compact neighborhoods
Mixed-use districts provide all services within walking distance of homes and workplaces.

Family life
Open and green spaces, community venues, and buildings with larger units foster happier and healthier families.

Social transit
Regional high-speed rail stations become centers of business and social activities.

Contamination cleanup
Instead of being covered or buried, hazardous sites and contaminated soil near cities are cleaned.

Urban farms and gardens
New communities and developments take advantage of advanced hydroponic technology for urban farming.

SPONGE CITY

According to SOM's design, all parks and infrastructure allow water to percolate through soil to recharge the water table. Such "sponge city" measures are already being tested in Shanghai.

Green roofs
Solar panels and roof gardens are common atop buildings, encouraging sustainable energy and small-scale farming.

Automated recycling
Waste collection and recycling centers are fully automated for faster and more comprehensive reuse of waste.

Rainwater cleansing
In lieu of gutters, bioswales (absorbent rain gardens) and pools collect and filter rainwater for reuse.

Smart water
Remote-sensing and information technologies maximize irrigation efficiency in city farms.

Backyard and school gardens
The value of local, organic, and sustainable farming is part of the curriculum in future city schools.

PRINCIPLES OF CITY DESIGN

ECOLOGY
The future city is designed around natural features and forces, protecting wildlife habitat and natural resources. Based on a unified vision for the region, the city is compact and dense to limit impacts on the ecosystem.

WATER
Protecting upland water systems and rigorous collection and cleansing of stormwater improve water quality. Wetland restoration and sponge-city measures revive habitats and protect against flooding and sea-level rise.

JASON TREAT, NGM STAFF. ART & SOURCE: SKIDMORE, OWINGS, & MERRILL (SOM)

Sustainability was a key factor in designing this futuristic city, resulting in a clean, green, and livable urban hub.

CONTENTS

UNIT 1 PROJECT

NATIONAL GEOGRAPHIC STORYTELLER

UNIT 2 EXPLORING OPTIONS

CHAPTER 5 WORKING WITH LAYERS

CHAPTER 6 WORKING WITH PATTERNS AND BRUSHES

NATIONAL GEOGRAPHIC CREATIVE

CHAPTER 7 WORKING WITH DISTORTIONS, GRADIENT MESHES, ENVELOPES, AND BLENDS

CONTENTS

CHAPTER 8 WORKING WITH TRANSPARENCY, EFFECTS, AND GRAPHIC STYLES

UNIT 2 PROJECT

NATIONAL GEOGRAPHIC CREATIVE
SEA SURVIVORS: INFORMATION CURATION

UNIT 3 INCORPORATING ADVANCED TECHNIQUES

CHAPTER 9 DRAWING WITH SYMBOLS

CHAPTER 10 CREATING 3D OBJECTS

NATIONAL GEOGRAPHIC CREATIVE
KATIE SLOVICK: DESIGN PROJECT

CHAPTER 11 CREATING AND DESIGNING GRAPHS

CHAPTER 12 PREPARING FILES FOR PREPRESS, PRINTING, AND THE WEB

CHAPTER 13 CREATING COMPLEX ILLUSTRATIONS

UNIT 3 PROJECT

ABOUT THE AUTHOR

Chris Botello began his career as a print production manager for *Premiere* magazine. He designed and produced movie and TV campaigns for Miramax Films and NBC Television and was the art director for Microsoft's launch of sidewalk.com/boston. Chris is the author of the *Revealed* Series of books on Photoshop, Illustrator, and InDesign, and the co-author of *YouTube for Dummies*. He lives in Los Angeles where he teaches graphic design and Adobe software classes. Chris uses his own Revealed books as the text for his classes.

REVIEWERS

Andrea Batts-Latson
Frederick Community College
Frederick, Maryland

Jessica Campbell
Buchholz High School
Gainesville, Florida

Eric Cornish
Miami Dade College
Miami, Florida

Emmalee Pearson
Madison Area Technical
College
Madison, Wisconsin

Alison Spangler
John Paul Stevens High School
Northwest Vista College
San Antonio, Texas

Odemaris Valdivia
Santa Monica College
Santa Monica, California

CREATIVE STORYTELLING | *THE REVEALED SERIES VISION*

The Revealed Series is your guide to today's best-selling multimedia applications. These comprehensive books teach the skills behind the application, showing you how to apply smart design principles to multimedia products such as dynamic graphics, animation, and websites.

A team of design professionals including multimedia instructors, students, authors, and editors worked together to create this series. We recognized the unique learning environment of the multimedia classroom and produced a series that:

- Gives you comprehensive step-by-step instructions.
- Offers in-depth explanation of the "Why" behind a skill.
- Includes creative projects for additional practice.
- Explains concepts clearly using full-color visuals.
- Keeps you up to date with the latest software upgrades so you can always work with cutting edge technology.

It was our goal to create a book that speaks directly to the multimedia and design community—one of the most rapidly growing computer fields today. We think we've done just that, with a sophisticated and instructive book design.

AUTHOR'S VISION

I am thrilled to have revisited this book on Adobe Illustrator Creative Cloud. Illustrator was the first Adobe program I learned—back in 1988! Since then, it's always been, secretly, my favorite program, even though I seem to spend most of my time in Photoshop. With this update, I'm particularly excited about the advanced exercises we've created for Chapter 13, which we refer to in-house as the "wow" chapter. These are comprehensive and challenging projects that teach you to create complex illustrations from scratch. Many cross-reference with Adobe Photoshop or employ continuous-tone effects in Illustrator to achieve some eye-popping results. When I think back to the earliest days of Adobe Illustrator, I'm quietly amazed at how far this program has come.

Thank you to Ann Fisher for her intelligence, dedication, and friendship as the developmental editor on this title. Thank you to Karen Caldwell for guiding this project to completion and always keeping us informed and on track. Thank you to the reviewers for their invaluable real-world feedback. Thank you to Chris Jaeggi for her clarity and consistent leadership. Thank you to Raj Desai for his vision and the latitude for making what's best in this new series possible. And thank you to Jessica Livingston and Allison Katen Lim for creating the National Geographic features that compliment this series of books so well.

—Chris Botello

INTRODUCTION TO
ADOBE® ILLUSTRATOR CREATIVE CLOUD

Welcome to *Adobe Illustrator Creative Cloud—Revealed*. This book offers creative projects, concise instructions, and complete coverage of basic to advanced Illustrator skills, helping you to create polished, professional-looking artwork. The book is designed to be used as content for the classroom and as a general reference for the software.

This 13-chapter text begins with fundamental concepts and progresses to in-depth exploration of the software's full set of features.

Chapter Opener

Each chapter opens with an impactful, full-page image to engage students visually with what they will be learning. The lesson topics and the Adobe Certified Professional Exam Objectives covered in the chapter are clearly laid out so students and instructors can easily track their progress in acquiring skills and preparing for the exam.

What You'll Do

A What You'll Do figure begins every lesson. This figure gives you an at-a-glance look at what you'll do in the chapter, either by showing you a reference figure from the project or a feature of the software.

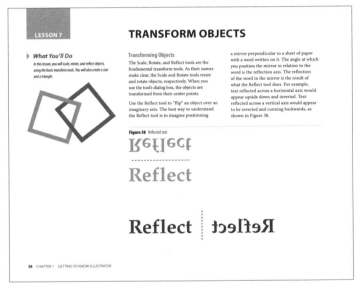

Comprehensive Conceptual Lessons

Before jumping into instructions, in-depth conceptual information tells you "why" skills are applied. This book provides the "how" and "why" through the use of clear and concise narrative instruction. Also included in the text are tips and sidebars to help you work more efficiently and creatively, or to teach you a bit about the history or design philosophy behind the skill you are learning.

Step-by-Step Instructions

This book combines in-depth conceptual information with concise steps to help you learn Illustrator Creative Cloud. Each set of steps guides you through a lesson where you will create, modify, or enhance an Illustrator Creative Cloud file. Steps reference large colorful images and quick step summaries round out the lessons.

Skills Review

A Skills Review at the end of each chapter contains hands-on practice exercises that mirror the progressive nature of the lesson material.

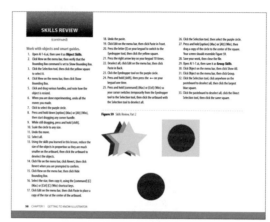

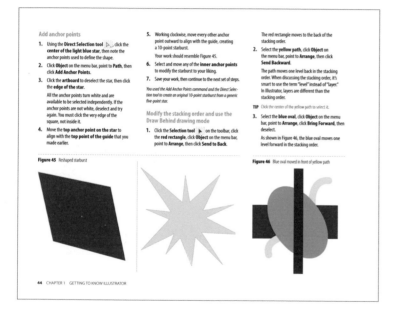

Chapter Projects

This book contains a variety of end-of-chapter materials for additional practice and reinforcement. Each chapter concludes with two Project Builders and one or two Design Projects. Together, these projects provide a valuable opportunity for students to practice and explore the concepts and techniques learned in the chapter. For the instructor, they are an opportunity to evaluate students' abilities to utilize taught skills as they work independently.

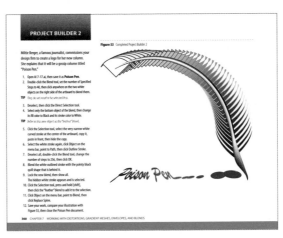

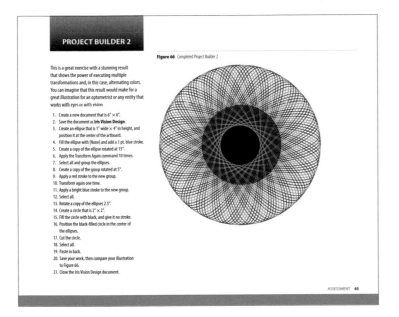

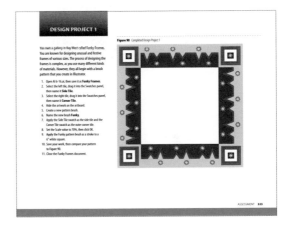

| PREVIEW |

NATIONAL GEOGRAPHIC | CREATIVES

This edition of *Adobe Illustrator Creative Cloud—Revealed* provides six opportunities for students to discover the work of National Geographic Creatives and be inspired to pursue their own artistic careers.

Three mid-unit features are based on in-depth interviews and images designed by the Creatives. These features give students a window into their career development, creative processes, and passion for their work. Students learn firsthand how accomplished creative professionals use their skill and

talent to create impactful, meaningful works that bring their projects to life. The projects encourage students to create their own work based on the design featured in the career profile they have just studied. Students are guided to create pieces that relate to their lives; to research local and community issues; and to incorporate photographs, data, or copy that tie directly to their school, community, and interests.

Three end-of-unit features incorporate longer creative projects that allow students to explore designing for impact, with an emphasis on visual storytelling, to create infographics and posters inspired by the featured National Geographic examples.

NATIONAL GEOGRAPHIC STORYTELLER **NIRUPA RAO**

DEVELOPING AN APPRECIATION

Growing up in Bengaluru, India, Nirupa Rao spent much of her childhood exploring the nearby jungle with her family. Their walks through the wild, tropical forest cultivated Nirupa's fondness for and appreciation of nature. Her granduncle, a field botanist, collected plant specimens from the jungle surrounding her grandfather's farm. Her mother's stories of this research inspired an air of adventure and excitement. A storyteller at heart, Nirupa enjoyed putting on plays for her family and also took an interest in creating handcrafted items, such as toys and books. Nirupa has carried her artistic talent and passion for nature into her career as a botanical illustrator. Her detailed works depict impactful stories about the unique behaviors of plants in India.

EDUCATION AND EARLY CAREER

With the exception of one online course, Nirupa is mostly a self-taught artist. While studying in Singapore, Nirupa had the opportunity to learn from other creatives and experiment with different mediums. Her interest grew when her cousin, a botanical researcher, shared photographs of plants and flowers with her. This inspired Nirupa to begin painting. She then took an internship in the children's division of a publishing house in the United Kingdom. While there, she learned about media research and further developed her creative skills using software programs such as Adobe Creative Suite. This helped Nirupa visualize her next step—providing children in India with similar content, so they, too, could learn about plants native to India.

CREATIVE PROJECTS AND PUBLICATIONS

In 2016, *National Geographic* awarded Nirupa a Young Explorers Grant to create an illustrated book of plant life in the Western Ghats of India. Published in 2019, *Hidden Kingdom—Fantastical Plants of the Western Ghats* sets Nirupa's colorful and intricately detailed illustrations to rhyme and helps open children's minds to the magical plants that exist in their own backyard. In addition to publishing other pieces, Nirupa's work has been displayed in the museum at Harvard's Dumbarton Oaks Museums. She collaborates with botanists and naturalists to ensure scientific accuracy in every illustration.

In Nirupa's book, *Hidden Kingdom*, she shares this watercolor painting titled *Strangler Fig*. The painting shows a tropical wild fig tree, which is part of the Ficus genus. This particular fig is often referred to as a strangler fig because of its unique behavior. This keystone species produces fruit throughout the year, providing food for birds, bats, and small mammals. In turn, birds drop strangler fig seeds on the branches of grown trees. The seeds germinate upon existing trees as a means to access sunlight more quickly. Over time, the roots of the strangler fig engulf the host tree, cutting off its access to sunlight and eventually strangling it to death with its roots.

Looking to capture this unique plant behavior, Nirupa created a watercolor painting of the strangler fig. Sitting low on the ground, she sketched the fig from below to capture the shapes of the branches, which she has described as "a tough grasping for sunlight." Nirupa often uses notes, photographs, and detailed sketches of the plants, which she then brings back to her studio to paint, scan, and manipulate using different software. Nirupa's process is very detail-oriented and thorough. She believes if you take the time to comprehend the complexity of an ecosystem, you can begin to understand how individual plants evolve, and what that communicates about the ecology of a place as a whole.

UNIT 1 PROJECT **229**

| DESIGN PROJECT |

PROJECT DESCRIPTION

In this project, you will explore a plant within your community. Using pencil, paper, paints, or any art supplies available to you, you will create an illustration. Focus on capturing the details of the plant, such as the colors and textures. Include elements of the environment in which it grows. The goal of this project is to create a detailed botanical illustration of a plant and its environment within your community.

SKILLS TO EXPLORE

- Scribbling
- Smoothing and Shading
- Hatching and Cross-Hatching
- Creating Highlights
- Rough Sketching
- Finger Blending
- Stippling
- Working with Pencil, Pen, Paint
- Observation and Patience

SOFT SKILLS CHALLENGE

Host a round-table discussion with at least three classmates. The roundtable should focus on plant life in your community and the local environment as a whole. You will need to recruit classmates to take part in the discussion, write a script introducing the round-table topic and the people participating, and create an outline of the questions and talking points. It will be your job to facilitate the discussion, keep the conversation moving, and ensure everyone's opinion is being respected. The goals of this challenge are to think critically about the plant life in your community and connect it to a bigger picture. Find out what your peers think about the topic and use collaboration and conversation as a way to better understand the complexities of the topic.

ROUND-TABLE CHECKLIST

1. Group of three or more peers
2. Written script introducing the topic and each participant
3. Outline of questions and talking points
4. Safe space to facilitate respectful conversation

FOLLOW NIRUPA'S EXAMPLE

One of the many reasons Nirupa enjoys sketching is that it slows down your eye and helps you pick out small details of the subject you are looking at. This is very important when grasping the complexity of a plant and understanding how it behaves and interacts with other plants and wildlife in its natural environment.

Once you've chosen a plant to sketch, walk around it and look at it from different angles. Think about how much of the plant is visible and which vantage point gives you the best view. Keep your focus on the plant, but make sure you capture relevant surrounding plants and wildlife. Incorporate your prior knowledge about the plant as well. For example, if you were illustrating a purple coneflower, you might wait for a bee to land on the flower and sketch that as well, as the purple coneflower is a favorite for many pollinators.

Create a note-taking system. Consider a grid of notes so you can organize your observations and keep track of important details. Some categories could include: colors, textures, surrounding plant life, observed wildlife, movement over time, etc.

230

The end-of-unit features also incorporate a "Soft Skills Challenge" that provides an opportunity to collaborate and engage with peers about each project.

- **Design Projects** give students hands-on practice creating their own artifacts, inspired by the featured theme or topic. Using their own research, students build their own composition, illustration, or layout. Design Projects include examples of pre-work to encourage student planning and preparation.

- **Portfolio Projects** allow students to build on the design project, to create a more complex piece, and incorporate more advanced skills from the current unit. Students have the freedom to be creative and choose from a list of recommended skills and tools to use in their projects. These projects encourage students to provide information about a given topic, incorporating both visual and textual elements.

PROJECT DESCRIPTION

In this project, you will use your plant illustration from the Design Project to create an infographic describing the different parts of the plant. You will need to either photograph and upload, or scan your illustration to your computer. Once you have your botanical illustration available on your computer, you will use Adobe Illustrator to refine, enhance, and add information to it. The goal of this project is to create a comprehensive infographic that educates viewers about the appearance, behavior, and environment of a local plant.

SKILLS TO EXPLORE

- Work with Basic Shapes
- Apply Fill and Stroke Colors to Objects
- Make Direct Selections
- Create Point Text
- Manipulate Text with the Touch Type Tool
- Create Gradients
- Draw Straight and Curved Lines
- Draw Elements of an Illustration
- Apply Attributes to Objects
- Use Image Trace
- Use the Live Paint Bucket Tool
- Transform Objects
- Offset and Outline Paths
- Create Compound Paths
- Work With the Pathfinder Panel
- Apply Round Corners to Objects
- Use the Shape Builder Tool
- Create Clipping Masks

SOFT SKILLS CHALLENGE

Write a blog post about the work you created and share it to a social media account. In your blog, include basic background information about your chosen plant, such as its behavior and characteristics. You will also want to write about why you chose the plant, what your creative process was when creating your composition, and some details of your illustration that a viewer might miss upon first glance. This is a great opportunity to explain your work to a wider audience and tell why you made some of your creative choices.

Don't forget to keep the conversation going. Respond to comments and interactions with your post. The goal of this challenge is for you to present your designs and use your work as a steppingstone to bigger conversations.

FOLLOW NIRUPA'S EXAMPLE

Take photographs. It can be hard to capture every detail in a sketch and even harder to remember the details once you've left the scene. Photographs are a great way to record a moment and refer back to it later. Sometimes photographs can even document elements you did not notice initially; for example, a nearby ant hill or the plant's shadow on the ground.

Use your resources. It can be helpful to know what you are looking for before you get there. Research local plants online, or better yet, find someone in your community to talk to. You might interview your science teacher or a friendly neighbor who enjoys gardening. Plants often have small details, such as colors and textures, that go unnoticed but communicate a lot about their behavior and health. If you do your research ahead of time, you will know what types of organisms are commonly found in your environment, and which are not. This will help you determine whether the plants you are seeing naturally occur in this ecosystem.

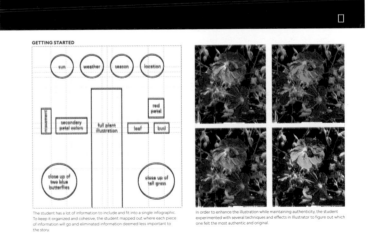

GETTING STARTED

The student has a lot of information to include and fit into a single infographic. To keep it organized and cohesive, the student mapped out where each piece of information will go and eliminated information deemed less important to the story.

In order to enhance the illustration while maintaining authenticity, the student experimented with several techniques and effects in Illustrator to figure out which one felt the most authentic and original.

RESOURCES

A FULL SUITE OF SUPPORTING RESOURCES

Instructor Companion Site

Everything you need for your course in one place! This collection of product-specific lecture and class tools is available online via the instructor resource center. You'll be able to access and download materials such as PowerPoint® presentations, data and solution files, Instructor's Manual, Industry-Aligned Credential correlations, and more.

- Download your resources at **companion-sites.cengage.com**.

Instructor's Manual

The Instructor's Manual includes chapter overviews and detailed lecture topics for each chapter, with teaching tips.

Syllabus

A sample Syllabus includes a suggested outline for any course that uses this book.

PowerPoint Presentations

Each chapter has a corresponding PowerPoint presentation to use in lectures, distribute to your students, or customize to suit your course.

Solutions to Exercises

Solution files are provided to show samples of final artwork. Use these files to evaluate your students' work or distribute them electronically so students can verify their work.

Test Bank and Test Engine

Cognero®, Customizable Test Bank Generator is a flexible, online system that allows you to import, edit, and manipulate content from the text's test bank or elsewhere, including your own favorite test questions; create multiple test versions in an instant; and deliver tests from your LMS, your classroom, or wherever you want.

- K12 Teachers, log on at **nglsync.cengage.com**, or **companion-sites.cengage.com**.

- Higher Education Teachers, log on at **www.cengage.com**.

THE ONLINE SOLUTION FOR CAREER AND TECHNICAL EDUCATION COURSES

MindTap for *Adobe Revealed Creative Cloud* is the online learning solution for career and technical education courses that helps teachers engage and transform today's students into critical thinkers. Through paths of dynamic assignments and applications that you can personalize, real-time course analytics, and an interactive eBook, MindTap helps teachers organize and engage students. Whether you teach this course in the classroom or in hybrid/e-learning models, MindTap enhances the course experience with data analytics, engagement tracking, and student tools such as flashcards and practice quizzes. MindTap for Adobe Illustrator also includes:

- an Adobe Professional Certification Prep Guide
- Career Readiness Module for the Arts, A/V Tech & Communications Career Cluster
- a bonus Module for Adobe Illustrator on the iPad

K-12 teachers and students who have adopted MindTap can access their courses at **nglsync.cengage.com**.

Don't have an account? Request access from your Sales Consultant at **ngl.cengage.com/repfinder**.

Higher education teachers and students can access their courses at **login.cengage.com**.

ACCESS RESOURCES ONLINE, ANYTIME

Accessing digital content from National Geographic Learning, a part of Cengage has never been easier. Through our new login portal, NGLSync, you can now easily gain access to all Career & Technical Education digital courses and resources purchased by your district, including: MindTap, Cognero Test Bank Generator, and Teacher/Student Companion Sites.

Log on at **nglsync.cengage.com** or **www.cengage.com**.

SUBJECT MATTER EXPERT CONTRIBUTORS

Adobe Certified Professional Test Prep Guide
Debbie Keller
Director Career & Technical Education
Adobe Education Leader
Medina Valley Independent School District
Castroville, Texas

Adobe Illustrator on the iPad
Chana Messer
Artist, Designer, Educator
Adobe Education Leader
University of Southern California (USC), FIDM
Los Angeles, California

GETTING STARTED

INTENDED AUDIENCE

This text is designed for the beginner or intermediate user who wants to learn how to use Adobe Illustrator Creative Cloud. The book provides comprehensive, in-depth material that not only educates, but also encourages you to explore the nuances of this exciting program.

APPROACH

The text allows you to work at your own pace through step-by-step tutorials. A concept is presented, and the process is explained, followed by the actual steps. To learn the most from the use of the text, you should adopt the following habits:

- Proceed slowly: Accuracy and comprehension are more important than speed.
- Understand what is happening with each step before you continue to the next step.
- After finishing a skill, ask yourself if you could do it on your own, without referring to the steps. If the answer is no, review the steps.

GENERAL

Throughout the initial chapters, students are given precise instructions regarding saving their work. Students should feel they can save their work at any time, not just when instructed to do so.

Students are also given precise instructions regarding magnifying/reducing their work area. Once the student feels more comfortable, he/she should feel free to use the Zoom tool to make their work area more comfortable.

ICONS, BUTTONS, AND POINTERS

Symbols for icons, buttons, and pointers are shown in the step each time they are used. Once an icon, button, or pointer has been used on a page, the symbol will be shown for subsequent uses on that page *without* showing its name.

FONTS

The data files contain a variety of commonly used fonts, but there is no guarantee these fonts will be available on your computer. If any of the fonts in use are not available on your computer, you can make a substitution, realizing that the results may vary from those in the book.

WINDOWS AND Mac OS

Adobe Illustrator CC works virtually the same on Windows and Mac OS operating systems. In those cases where there are significant differences, the abbreviations (Win) and (Mac) are used.

SYSTEM REQUIREMENTS

For a Windows operating system:

- Processor: Intel® Pentium® 4 processor or AMD Athlon® 64 processor (2 GHz or faster)

- Operating System: Microsoft® Windows 7 (with Service Pack 1), 8, or 8 .1

- Memory: 1 GB of RAM

- Storage space: 2.5 GB of available hard-disk space

- Monitor: 1024 × 768 resolution (1280 × 800 recommended)

- Video: 16-bit or higher OpenGL 2.0 video card; 512 MB RAM (1 GB recommended)

- Broadband Internet connection required for activation, Creative Cloud membership validation, and access to online services

For a MacOS operating system:

- Processor: Multicore Intel® processor with 64-bit support

- Operating System: Mac OS X 10.7, v10.8, or v10.9

- Memory: 1 GB of RAM

- Storage space: 3.2 GB of available hard-disk space

- Monitor: 1024 × 768 or greater monitor resolution (1280 × 800 recommended)

- Video: 16-bit or greater OpenGL 2.0 video card; 512 MB of VRAM (1 GB recommended)

- Broadband Internet connection required for software activation, Creative Cloud membership validation, and access to online services

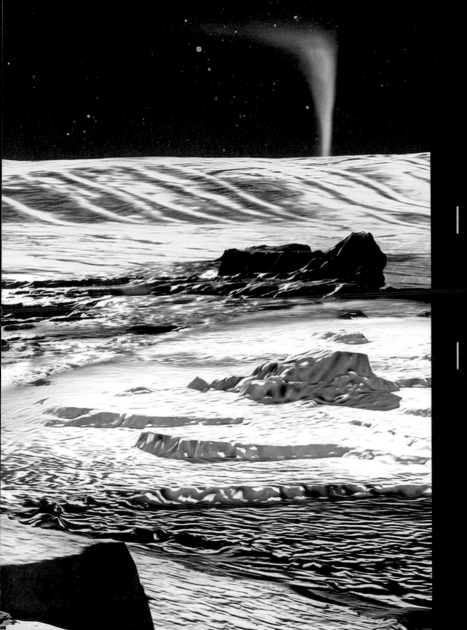

CREATING OBJECTS

A scientific illustration provides a model to suggest what the surface of Pluto might look like. This "Plutoscape" show Pluto's largest moon, Charon, in the distance.

Illustration by John Tomanio. From "Pluto at Last." *National Geographic Magazine*, Vol. 228, No. 1, July, 2015

CHAPTER 1

GETTING TO KNOW
ILLUSTRATOR

Adobe Certified Professional in Graphic Design and Illustration Using Adobe Illustrator

2. Project Setup and Interface

This objective covers the interface setup and program settings that assist in an efficient and effective workflow, as well as knowledge about ingesting digital assets for a project.

2.1 Create a document with the appropriate settings for mobile, web, print, film and video, or art and illustration.

   A Set appropriate document settings for printed and onscreen artwork.

   B Create a new document preset to reuse for specific project needs.

2.2 Navigate, organize, and customize the application workspace.

   A Identify and manipulate elements of the Illustrator interface.

   B Organize and customize the workspace.

   C Configure application preferences.

2.3 Use nonprinting design tools in the interface to aid in design or workflow.

   A Navigate a document.

   B Use rulers.

   C Use guides and grids.

   D Use views and modes to work efficiently with vector graphics.

2.4 Manage assets in a project.

   A Open artwork.

   B Place assets in an Illustrator document.

2.5 Manage colors, swatches, and gradients.

   A Set the active fill and stroke color.

4. Creating and Modifying Visual Elements

This objective covers core tools and functionality of the application, as well as tools that affect the visual appearance of document elements.

4.3 Make, manage, and manipulate selections.

   A Select objects using a variety of tools.

   B Modify and refine selections using various methods.

   C Group or ungroup selections.

4.4 Transform digital graphics and media.

   A Modify artboards.

   B Rotate, flip, and transform individual layers, objects, selections, groups, or graphical elements.

EXPLORE THE ILLUSTRATOR WORKSPACE

▶ *What You'll Do*

In this lesson, you will start Adobe Illustrator and explore the workspace.

Looking at the Illustrator Workspace

The arrangement of windows and panels that you see on your monitor is called the **workspace**. The Illustrator workspace features the following areas: artboard, pasteboard, menu bar, Control panel, toolbar, and a stack of collapsed panels along the right side of the document window. Figure 1 shows the default workspace, which is called Essentials Classic.

Illustrator offers predefined workspaces that are customized for different types of tasks. Each workspace is designed so that panels with similar functions are grouped together. For example, the Typography workspace shows the many type- and typography-based panels that are useful for working with type. You can switch from one workspace to another by clicking Window on the menu bar, pointing to Workspace, and then choosing a workspace. Or you can click the Switch Workspace button on the menu bar.

Figure 1 Essentials Classic workspace

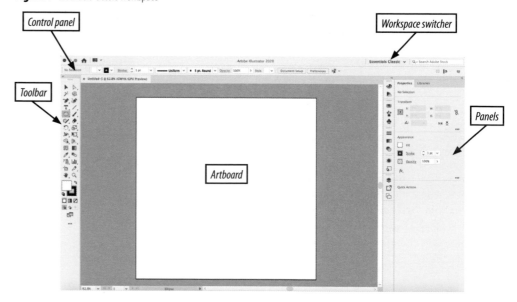

You can customize the workspace to suit your working preferences. For example, you can open and close whatever panels you want and group them as you like and in a way that makes sense for you and your work. You can save a customized workspace by clicking Window on the menu bar, pointing to Workspace, then clicking New Workspace. Once the new workspace is named, it will appear in the Workspace menu.

Exploring the Toolbar

As its name implies, the toolbar houses all the tools that you will work with in Illustrator. The first thing you should note about the toolbar is that not all tools are visible; many are hidden. Look closely and you will see that some tools have small black triangles, indicating that other tools are hidden behind them. To access hidden tools, point to the visible tool on the toolbar, then press and hold the mouse button. This will reveal a menu of hidden tools. The small black square to the left of a tool name in the submenu indicates which tool is currently visible on the toolbar, as shown in Figure 2.

When you expose hidden tools, you can click the small triangle to the right of the menu and create a separate panel for those tools.

You can view the toolbar as a single column or a double column of tools. Simply click the Collapse/Expand panels button at the top of the toolbar to toggle between the two setups. In this book, we will show you the toolbar in double columns.

Figure 3 identifies essential tools that you'll use all the time when you're working with Illustrator. To choose a tool, simply click it. You can also press a shortcut key to access a tool. For example, pressing the letter [P] on your keypad selects the Pen tool. To learn the shortcut key for each tool, point to a tool until a tool tip appears with the tool's name and its shortcut key in parentheses. **Tool tips** are small windows of text that identify various elements of the workspace, such as tool names, buttons on panels, or names of colors on the Swatches panel, for example. Tool tips appear when they are activated in the General preferences dialog box. Click Illustrator (Mac) or Edit (Win) or on the menu bar, point to Preferences, then click General.

Figure 2 Viewing hidden tools

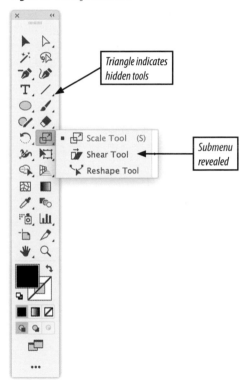

Figure 3 Essential tools

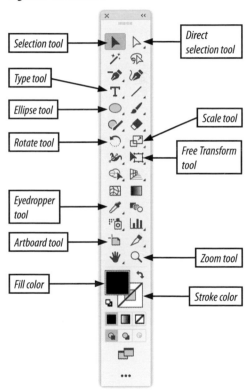

Working with Panels

Working in Illustrator is not only about using tools and menus. Many essential Illustrator functions are grouped into panels. For example, the Paragraph panel is the central location for paragraph editing functions, such as text alignment and paragraph indents. The Swatches panel houses colors that you can access to apply fills and strokes to objects.

You access all panels from the Window menu. You never have to wonder where to find a panel, because all panels are on the Window menu. Some panels are placed within categories on the Window menu. For example, all the text-related panels, such as the Character panel and the Paragraph panel, are listed in the Type category.

When you choose a panel from the Window menu, the panel is displayed in its expanded view. Panels themselves have menus. You can display a panel's menu by clicking the panel menu button at the top right of the panel. Figure 4 shows the Paragraph panel and its menu.

To better manage available workspace, you can reduce the size of a panel by clicking the Collapse to Icons button, which displays a panel only by its name and an icon. Even better, you can group panels strategically to save space and to combine specific functions into one area. Figure 5 shows two essential typography panels grouped together. The Paragraph panel is the active panel—it is in front of the

Character panel in the group and available for use. To activate the Character panel, you would simply click its tab. With this simple grouping, you can do nearly all the text formatting you're likely to do, all in one place. To group panels, drag one by its name onto the name of the other.

Docking panels is another way to organize panels. When you dock panels, you connect the bottom edge of one panel to the top edge of another panel so that both move together. To dock panels, first drag a panel's name tab to the bottom edge of another panel. When the bottom edge of the other panel is highlighted in bright blue, release the mouse button, and the two panels will be docked.

Figure 4 The Paragraph panel menu

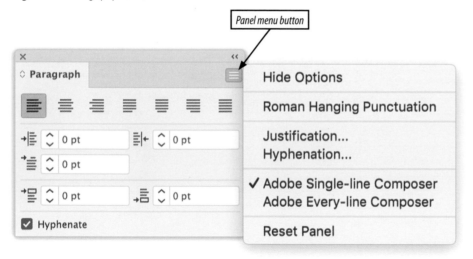

Figure 5 Character and Paragraph panels grouped

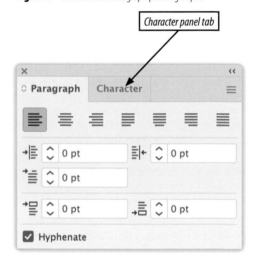

Figure 6 shows an entire dock of panels minimized on the right side of the document window. Clicking a panel thumbnail, or icon, opens the panel as well as any other panels with which it is grouped. In the figure, the Color panel icon has been clicked, and the panel is showing. Docking panels in this manner is a great way to save space on your screen, especially if you're the type of designer who likes to have a lot of panels available at all times.

Figure 6 Multiple panels docked together and minimized as icons

TIP You can hide all open panels, including the toolbar, by pressing [tab]. Press [tab] again to show the panels. This is especially useful when you want to view artwork and the entire document window without panels in the way.

Creating Customized Toolbars

The ability to create alternative, customized toolbars is a great feature in Illustrator. Over the years, as Illustrator has become more complex and able to do more and more things, the toolbar has become quite crowded. You can create multiple toolbars specified for different functions. For example, you could customize a toolbar just for your favorite drawing tools or just for transforming objects.

To create additional toolbars, click the Window menu, point to Toolbars, then click New Toolbar. Once you've named the toolbar, it appears on the artboard beside the main toolbar. To add tools to the new toolbar, click the three dots at the bottom, then drag and drop tools from the menu. Note that all toolbars you create are listed and accessible on the Window menu.

Explore the Toolbar

1. Start Adobe Illustrator.

2. Click **File** on the menu bar, click **Open**, navigate to the drive and folder where your Chapter 1 Data Files are stored, then open **AI 1-1.ai**.

3. Click **Window** on the menu bar, point to **Workspace**, then click **Essentials Classic**.

4. Click **Window** on the menu bar, point to **Workspace**, then click **Reset Essentials Classic**.

   Your window should resemble Figure 7.

5. Click the **small double arrow** at the top of the toolbar, then click it again to switch between the two toolbar setups.

6. Point to the **Type tool** $\boxed{\text{T}}$, then press and hold the mouse button to see the **Type on a Path tool** $\boxed{\text{◁}}$.

7. View the **hidden tools** behind the other tools with small black triangles.

8. Click **Illustrator (Mac)** or **Edit (Win)** on the menu bar, point to **Preferences**, click **General**, verify that **Show Tool Tips** is checked, then click **OK**.

9. Position your mouse pointer over the **Selection tool** $\boxed{\blacktriangleright}$ until its tool tip appears.

All of the figures in this book that show the toolbar will display the panel in two columns.

10. Press the following keys, and note which tools are selected with each key: **[A]**, **[P]**, **[V]**, **[T]**, **[I]**, **[H]**, and **[Z]**.

11. Press **[tab]** to temporarily hide all open panels, then press **[tab]** again.

    The panels reappear.

12. Keep this file open, and continue to the next set of steps.

You explored different views of the toolbar, revealed hidden tools, used shortcut keys to access tools quickly, hid the panels, and then displayed them again.

OPENING ILLUSTRATOR FILES IN PREVIOUS VERSIONS

Illustrator is "backwards compatible," meaning that Illustrator CC can open files from previous versions. The reverse, however, isn't true; earlier versions can't open newer versions. For example, Illustrator CS6 cannot open Illustrator CC documents. This can become an issue if you send an Illustrator CC file to another designer, client, or vendor who is using an older version. To accommodate, you can "save down" to a previous version when you save the file. When you name the file and click Save, the Illustrator Options dialog box opens. Click the Version list arrow to choose the version to which you want to save it. Note that any new CC features used in your file may be lost when the file is converted to the older format.

Figure 7 The document window

Image courtesy of Chris Botello

Work with panels

1. At the right-hand side of the window, drag the **Properties panel** by its name to the center of the window, then click the **small x** at the upper-left corner of the panel to close it.

2. Drag the **Libraries panel** by its name to the center of the window, then close it.

3. Click the **Swatches panel icon** 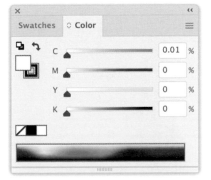 in the dock of collapsed panels to the right of the pasteboard to open the Swatches panel.

   The panel opens but does not detach from the stack of collapsed panels. The Swatches panel is grouped with the Brushes and Symbols panels in this workspace.

4. Drag the **Swatches panel name tab** to the left so it is ungrouped from the stack.

5. Click the **Color panel icon** in the dock of collapsed panels, then drag the **Color panel name tab** to the left so it is ungrouped from the stack.

6. Drag the **Color panel name tab** onto the **Swatches panel name tab**, then release the mouse button.

   The Color panel is grouped with the Swatches panel, as shown in Figure 8.

TIP If you do not see the CMYK sliders on the Color panel, click the Color panel menu button ≡, then click Show Options.

7. Click **Window** on the menu bar, then click **Align**.

   The Align panel appears and is grouped with the Transform and Pathfinder panels.

8. Drag the **entire panel group** to the bottom edge of the Swatches and Color panels group; then, when a blue horizontal line appears, release the mouse button.

   The panel is docked, as shown in Figure 9.

9. Click and drag the **gray bar** at the top of the Swatches and Color panels group around the document window.

Figure 8 Grouped panels

The Align, Transform, and Pathfinder panels group moves with the Swatches and Color panels group because it is docked.

Figure 9 Docked panels

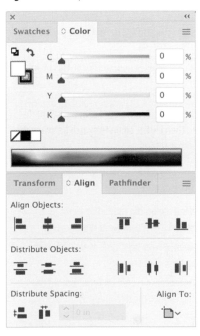

10. Keep this file open, and continue to the next set of steps.

You explored methods for grouping and ungrouping panels, then you docked two panel groups together.

Create and save a customized workspace

1. Using the same methods, create the dock of panels shown in Figure 10.

2. Close all the other panels at the far-right edge of the window.

3. Minimize the dock of panels you created so they appear as icons.

4. Position the dock of icons at the far-right edge of the window.

The right edge of your window should resemble Figure 11.

5. Click **Window** on the menu bar, point to **Workspace**, then click **New Workspace.**

6. In the **Name text box**, type **your last name** in all caps, then click **OK**.

A new workspace is created representing the current layout of the document window.

You docked panels, minimized them to small icons at the right side of the window, and then created a new workspace with the new arrangement.

Figure 10 Seven panels grouped and docked

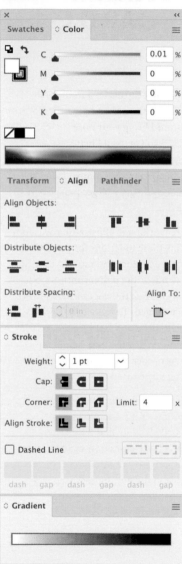

Figure 11 Dock of seven minimized panels

VIEW AND MODIFY ARTBOARD ELEMENTS

What You'll Do

In this lesson, you will explore various methods for viewing the document and document elements, such as rulers, guides, grids, and selection marks.

Using the Zoom Tool

Imagine creating a layout on a traditional pasteboard—not on your computer. For precise work, you would bring your nose closer to the pasteboard so you could better see what you're doing. At other times, you would hold the pasteboard away from you at arm's length so you could get a larger perspective of the artwork.

When you're working in Illustrator, the Zoom tool performs these functions for you. When you click the Zoom tool and move it over the document window, the pointer shows a plus sign. When you click the document, the area you click is enlarged. To reduce the view of the document, press and hold [option] (Mac) or [Alt] (Win). When the plus sign changes to a minus sign, click the document, and the document size is reduced.

Using the Zoom tool, you can reduce or enlarge the view of the document from 3.13% to 64,000%. Note that the current magnification level appears in the document tab near the filename and in the Zoom Level text box at the bottom-left corner of the window.

Accessing the Zoom Tool

As you work, you can expect to zoom in and out of the document more times than you can count. The most basic way of accessing the Zoom tool is to click it on the toolbar, but this can get very tiring if you need to access it often.

A better method for accessing the Zoom tool is to use keyboard shortcuts. When you are using other tools, don't switch to the Zoom tool by selecting it from the toolbar. Instead, press and hold [command] [space bar] (Mac) or [Ctrl] [space bar] (Win) to temporarily change the Selection tool into the Zoom tool. When you release the keys, the Zoom tool changes back to whichever tool you were using. To access the Zoom-minus tool, press and hold [command] [option] [space bar] (Mac) or [Ctrl] [Alt] [space bar] (Win).

TIP Double-clicking the Zoom tool on the toolbar changes the document view to 100% (actual size). In addition to the Zoom tool, Illustrator offers other ways to zoom in and out of your document. One of the quickest and easiest ways is to press [command] [+] (Mac) or [Ctrl] [+] (Win) to enlarge the view, and [command] [−] (Mac) or [Ctrl] [−] (Win) to reduce the view. You can also use the Zoom In and Zoom Out commands on the View menu.

Using the Hand Tool

When you zoom in on a document to make it appear larger, eventually the document will be too large to fit in the window. Therefore, you will need to scroll to see other areas of it. You can use the scroll bars along the bottom and the right sides of the document window or you can use the Hand tool to scroll through the document.

The best way to understand the concept of the Hand tool is to think of it as your own hand. Imagine that you could put your hand up to the document on your monitor and move the document left, right, up, or down like a paper on a table or against a wall. This is similar to how the Hand tool works.

Using the Hand tool is often a better choice for scrolling than using the scroll bars because you can access the Hand tool using a keyboard shortcut. Regardless of whatever tool you are using, simply press and hold [space bar] to access the Hand tool. Release [space bar] to return to whatever tool you were using.

TIP Double-clicking the Hand tool on the toolbar changes the document view to fit the page (or the spread) in the document window.

Working with Rulers, Grids, and Guides

Many illustrations involve positioning and aligning objects precisely. Illustrator is well equipped with many features that help you with these tasks.

Rulers are positioned at the top and left sides of the pasteboard to help you align objects. To display or hide the rulers, you can click View on the menu bar, point to Rulers, then click Hide Rulers or Show Rulers, or you can use the keyboard shortcuts [command] [R] (Mac) or [Ctrl] [R] (Win). Rulers can display measurements in different **units**, such as inches, picas, or points. You determine the units with which you want to work in the Preferences dialog box. On the Illustrator (Mac) or Edit (Win) menu, point to Preferences, then click Units to display the dialog box.

TIP In this book, all exercises use inches as the unit of measurement.

Hiding and Showing Selection Marks

All objects you create have visible selection marks or selection edges, and when an object is selected, those edges automatically highlight to show anchor points.

While you're designing your illustration, you might want to work with selection marks hidden so all you see is the artwork. To hide or show selection marks, click the Hide Edges or Show Edges command on the View menu.

Figure 12 shows artwork with selection marks visible and hidden. In both examples, the artwork is selected, but the selection marks are not visible in the example on the right.

Figure 12 Selection marks visible on the left star

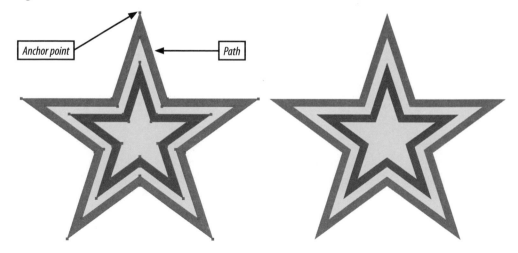

Choosing Screen Modes

Screen modes are options for viewing documents. The two basic screen modes in Illustrator are Preview and Outline. You'll work in Preview mode most of the time. In **Preview** mode, you see all your objects with fills and strokes and effects.

Outline mode displays all your objects as only hollow shapes, with no fills or strokes. Working in Outline mode can sometimes be helpful for selecting various objects that are positioned close together.

Figure 13 shows the motorcycle artwork in Outline mode.

To select objects in Preview mode, simply click anywhere on the object's fill or stroke. In Outline mode, however, you need to click the edge of the object.

Figure 13 Artwork in Outline mode

Understanding Preferences

All Adobe software products come loaded with preferences. **Preferences** are specifications you can set for how certain features of the application behave. The Preferences dialog box houses the multitude of Illustrator preferences. Getting to know available preferences is a smart approach to mastering Illustrator. Many preferences offer important choices that will have significant impact on how you work.

Working with Multiple Open Documents

On many occasions, you'll find yourself working with multiple open documents. For example, let's say you're into scrapbooking. If you're designing a new illustration to highlight a recent trip to Italy, you might also have another file open of an illustration you created last year when you went to Hawaii. Why? For any number of reasons. You might want to copy and paste art elements from the Hawaii document into the new document. Or you might want the Hawaii document open simply as a reference for typefaces, type sizes, image sizes, and effects that you used in the document.

When you're working with multiple open documents, you can switch from one to the other simply by clicking on the title bar of each document.

Illustrator offers a preference for having multiple open documents available as tabs in the document window. This can be useful for keeping your workspace uncluttered. With this preference selected, a tab will appear for each open document, showing the name of the document. When you click the tab, that document becomes active.

Working with tabbed documents can sometimes be inhibiting, because the tabbed option allows you to view only one document at a time. That issue is easily solved, however. All you need to do is drag a tabbed document by its name out of the window, and it will be become a floating window.

The User Interface preferences dialog box is where you specify whether you want open documents to appear as tabs. Click Illustrator (Mac) or Edit (Win) on the menu bar, point to Preferences, then click User Interface. Click to activate the Open Documents As Tabs option, then click OK.

Using Shortcut Keys to Execute View Commands

The most commonly used commands in Illustrator list a shortcut key beside the command name. Shortcut keys are useful for quickly accessing menu commands without stopping work to go to the menu. Make a mental note of helpful shortcut keys and incorporate them into your work. You'll find that using them becomes second nature.

See Table 1 for shortcut keys you will use regularly for manipulating the view of your Illustrator screen.

TABLE 1: SHORTCUT KEYS FOR VIEWING COMMANDS		
	Mac	**Windows**
Hide/Show Guides	command-;	Ctrl-;
Hide/Show Edges	command-H	Ctrl-H
Hide/Show Rulers	command-R	Ctrl-R
Activate/Deactivate Smart Guides	command-U	Ctrl-U
Fit Page in Window	command-0	Ctrl-0
Fit Spread in Window	option-command-0	Alt-Ctrl-0
Toggle Preview and Outline Screen Modes	command-Y	Ctrl-Y
Hide/Show Grid	command-"	Ctrl-"

Use the Zoom tool and the Hand tool

1. Press the **letter [Z]** on your keypad to access the **Zoom tool** 🔍 .

2. Position the **Zoom tool** 🔍 over the **document window**, click twice to enlarge the document, press **[option] (Mac)** or **[Alt] (Win)**, then click twice to reduce the document.

3. Click the **Zoom Level list arrow** in the lower-left corner of the document window, then click **800%**.

   Note that 800% is now listed in the document tab beside the file name.

4. Double-click **800%** in the Zoom Level text box, type **300**, then press **[return] (Mac)** or **[Enter] (Win)**.

5. Click the **Hand tool** 🖐 on the toolbar, then click and drag the **document window** to scroll.

6. Double-click the **Zoom tool** 🔍 .

   Double-clicking the Zoom tool 🔍 changes the view of the document to 100% (actual size).

7. Click the **Selection tool** ▶, point to the **center of the document window**, then press and hold **[command] [space bar] (Mac)** or **[Ctrl] [space bar] (Win)**.

   The Selection tool ▶ changes to the Zoom tool 🔍 .

8. Click **three times**, then release **[command] [space bar] (Mac)** or **[Ctrl] [space bar] (Win)**.

9. Press and hold **[space bar]** to access the **Hand tool** 🖐, then scroll around the image.

10. Press and hold **[command] [option] [space bar] (Mac)** or **[Ctrl] [Alt] [space bar] (Win)**, then click the **mouse button** multiple times to reduce the view to 25%.

    Your document window should resemble Figure 14.

11. Keep this file open, and continue to the next set of steps.

You explored various methods for accessing and using the Zoom tool for enlarging and reducing the document. You also used the Hand tool to scroll around an enlarged document.

Figure 14 Viewing the document at 25%

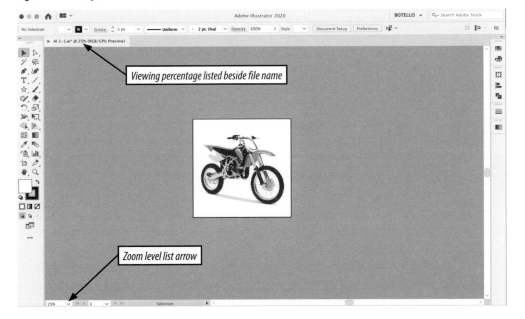

Viewing percentage listed beside file name

Zoom level list arrow

Hide and show rulers and set units and increments preferences

1. Click **View** on the menu bar, note the shortcut key for the **Fit All in Window command**, then click **Fit Artboard in Window**.

2. Click **View** on the menu bar, point to **Rulers**, then note the **Hide/Show Rulers command** and its shortcut key.

   The Rulers command is listed as either Hide Rulers or Show Rulers depending on the current status.

3. Leave the View menu, then press **[command] [R] (Mac)** or **[Ctrl] [R] (Win)** several times to hide and show rulers, finishing with rulers showing.

4. Note the units on the rulers.

   Depending on the preference you have set, your rulers might be showing inches, picas, or another unit of measure.

5. Click **Illustrator (Mac)** or **Edit (Win)** on the menu bar, point to **Preferences**, then click **Units**.

6. Click the **General list arrow** to see the available measurement options, then click **Picas**.

7. Click **OK**.

   The rulers change to pica measurements. Picas are a unit of measure used in layout design long before the advent of computerized layouts. One pica is equal to 1/6 inch. It's important that you understand that the unit of measure you set as ruler units will affect all measurement utilities in the application, such as those on the Transform panel, in addition to the ruler increments.

8. Reopen the **Units Preferences dialog box**, click the **General list arrow**, then click **Inches**.

   Your dialog box should resemble Figure 15.

9. Click **OK**.

10. Keep this file open and continue to the next set of steps.

You used shortcut keys to hide and show rulers in the document. You used the Units Preferences dialog box to change the unit of measure for ruler units.

Figure 15 Units preferences set to Inches

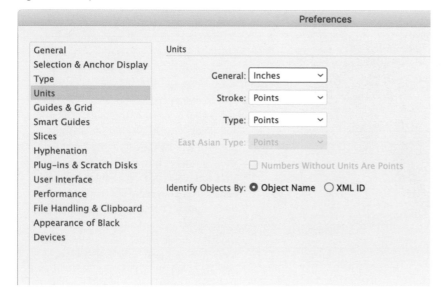

ARRANGING DOCUMENTS

When you're working with multiple documents, you can use the Arrange Documents button on the menu bar. If you have three separate documents open, for example, the 3-UP options in the Arrange Documents panel will tile and display all three documents in a column or a row. The Tile All In Grid option positions all open documents in a single window, allowing you to compare artwork from one file to another and even drag objects across documents.

Hide and show guides, selection marks, and the document grid

1. Click **Select** on the menu bar, then click **All**.

2. Click **View** on the menu bar, then note the **Hide/Show Edges command** and its shortcut key.

   The command is listed as either Hide Edges or Show Edges, depending on the current status.

3. Leave the View menu, then press **[command] [H] (Mac)** or **[Ctrl] [H] (Win)** several times to switch between hiding and showing selection marks, finishing with marks showing.

TIP The Hide Edges shortcut key is easy to remember if you think of *H for Hide*. Remember, though, that this shortcut key only hides and shows selection marks— not other elements, like ruler guides, which use different shortcut keys.

4. Click the **Select** menu, then click **Deselect**.

5. Click **View** on the menu bar, point to **Guides**, then note the **Hide/Show Guides command** and its shortcut key.

   The Guides command is listed as either Hide Guides or Show Guides depending on the current status.

6. Leave the View menu, then press **[command] [;] (Mac)** or **[Ctrl] [;] (Win)** several times to hide and show guides, finishing with guides showing.

   Four guides are shown in Figure 16.

TIP Make note of the difference between the Hide/Show Guides shortcut key and the Hide/Show Edges shortcut key.

7. Click **View** on the menu bar, then click **Show Grid**.

8. Leave the View menu, then press **[command] ["] (Mac)** or **[Ctrl] ["] (Win)** several times to hide and show the grid.

TIP Notice the difference between the Hide/Show Guides shortcut key and the Hide/Show Grid shortcut key—they're just one key away from each other.

9. Hide the grid and the guides.

10. Keep this file open and continue to the next set of steps.

You used shortcut keys to hide and show selection marks, ruler guides, and the document grid.

Figure 16 Four guides showing

Guides

Toggle screen modes and work with multiple documents

1. Click the **View menu**, note the shortcut key command for **Outline mode**, then escape the View menu.

2. Press **[command] [Y] (Mac)** or **[Ctrl] [Y] (Win)** repeatedly to toggle between Outline and Preview mode, finishing in Preview mode.

3. Click **Illustrator (Mac)** or **Edit (Win)** on the menu bar, point to **Preferences**, then click **User Interface.**

4. Verify that the **Open Documents As Tabs check box** is checked, then click **OK**.

5. Click **File** on the menu bar, click **Save As**, type **Motocross** in the File name box, then click the **Save button** to save the file with a new name.

TIP Each time you save a data file with a new name, the Illustrator Options dialog box will open. Click OK to close it.

6. Open AI 1-2.ai, then click the **tabs** of each open document several times to toggle between them, finishing with Motocross.ai as the active document.

7. Drag the **Motocross.ai tab** straight down approximately ½ **inch**.

   When you drag a tabbed document down, it becomes a "floating" document.

8. Position your mouse pointer **over the title bar of Motocross.ai**, click and drag to position it at the **top of the window beside the AI 1-2.ai tab**, then release the mouse button when you see a horizontal blue bar.

   The document is tabbed once again.

9. Close AI 1-2.ai without saving changes if you are prompted.

10. Close Motocross.ai without saving changes if you are prompted.

You verified that the Open Documents As Tabs option in the User Interface Preferences dialog box was activated. You removed the document from its tabbed position, resized it, moved it around, then returned it to its tabbed status.

USING THE DOCUMENT INFO PANEL

The Document Info panel, listed on the Window menu, contains useful information about the document and objects in the document. Along with general file information such as filename, ruler units, and color space, the panel lists specific information like the number and names of graphic styles, custom colors, patterns, gradients, fonts, and placed art. To view information about a selected object, choose Selection Only from the panel menu. Leaving this option deselected lists information about the entire document. To view artboard dimensions, click the Artboard tool, choose Document from the panel menu, and then click to select the artboard you want to view.

DEACTIVATING CORNER WIDGETS WHEN USING THE DIRECT SELECTION TOOL

When you select the Direct Selection tool and select an object on the page, it is likely that you will see small icons beside the selected object. These are corner widgets, and they are a new feature in Illustrator Creative Cloud that allows you to modify the corners of objects into round and pointed corners. We cover this extensively in Chapter 4. When doing the many exercises in this book that involve using the Direct Selection tool, it is best that you deactivate corner widgets so they don't distract from your work. To do so, click the View menu, then click Hide Corner Widget.

WORK WITH OBJECTS AND SMART GUIDES

Working with Preferences

Illustrator features several Preferences dialog boxes. Preferences affect many aspects of the Illustrator interface, including guides, smart guides, and rulers. You can think of preferences as the "ground rules" that you establish before doing your work. For example, you might want to specify your preferences for guide and grid colors or for hyphenation if you're doing a lot of type work.

One tricky thing about preferences is that, if you're just learning Illustrator, preferences refer to things you don't really know about. That's OK. Illustrator's preferences default to a paradigm that makes most of the work you do intuitive. But as you gain experience, it's a good idea to go back through the available preferences and see if there are any changes you want to make or with which you want to experiment.

One more thing about preferences: remember that they're there. Let's say you want to apply a 2 pt. stroke to an object, but the Stroke panel is showing stroke weight in inches. First, you click the Stroke panel options button to show the Stroke panel menu, but you soon find that the menu holds no command for changing the readout from inches to points. That's when you say to yourself, "Aha! It must be a preference."

Resizing Objects

Individual pieces of artwork that you create in Illustrator—such as squares, text, or lines—are called **objects**. All objects you create in Illustrator are composed of paths and anchor points. When you select an object, its paths and anchor points become highlighted.

Figure 65 Final Project Builder 1

Linda's Starburst Cafe

You have many options for changing the size and shape of an object. One of the most straightforward options is to use the **bounding box**. Select any object or multiple objects, then click Show Bounding Box on the View menu. Eight handles appear around the selected object, as shown in Figure 17. Click and drag the handles to change the shape and size of the object.

When you select multiple objects, a single bounding box appears around all the selected objects. Manipulating the bounding box will affect all the objects. Illustrator offers basic keyboard combinations that you can use when dragging bounding box handles. See Table 2.

Figure 17 Bounding box around selected object

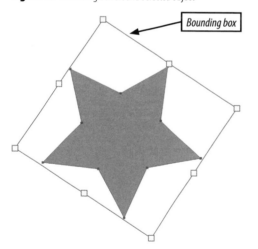

Bounding box

TABLE 2: OBJECT RESIZING COMBINATIONS		
Mac	**Windows**	**Result**
Shift-drag a corner handle	Shift-drag a corner handle	The object is resized in proportion; its shape doesn't change
Option-drag a handle	Alt-drag a handle	Resizes the object from its center point
Option-shift-drag a handle	Alt-shift-drag a handle	Resize the object from its center and in proportion

Copying Objects

At any time, you can copy and paste an object. When you paste, the object is pasted at the center of the artboard—regardless of the position of the original. When designing, you'll often find it more desirable for the copy to be pasted in the exact same location as the original. The **Paste in Front** command pastes the copy directly in front of the original. The **Paste in Back** command pastes the copy directly behind the original. Both have quick keys that are easy to remember. The command for Paste in Front is [command] [F] (Mac) or [Ctrl] [F] (Win) and Paste in Back is [command] [B] (Mac) or [Ctrl] [B] (Win).

Be sure to make a note that you can copy objects while dragging them. Press and hold [option] (Mac) or [Alt] (Win), then drag to create a copy of the object. This behavior is referred to as **drag and drop a copy**, and it's something you'll do a lot of in Illustrator and in this book.

TIP In this book, you'll be asked numerous times to paste in front and paste in back. The direction will read, "Copy, then paste in back," or "Copy, then paste in front." It would be a good idea for you to remember the quick keys.

Hiding, Locking, and Grouping Objects

The Hide, Lock, Group, and Ungroup commands on the Object menu are essential for working effectively with layouts, especially complex layouts with many objects. Hide objects to get them out of your way. They won't print, and nothing you do will change the location of them as long as they are hidden. Lock an object to make it immovable—you will not be able to select it. Lock your objects when you have them in a specific location and you don't want to accidentally move or delete them. Don't think this is being overly cautious. Accidentally moving or deleting objects and being unaware that you did so happens all the time in complex layouts. Having objects grouped strategically is also a solution for getting your work done faster.

You group multiple objects with the Group command on the Object menu. Grouping objects is a smart and important strategy for protecting the relationships between multiple objects. When you click on grouped objects with the Selection tool, all the objects are selected. Thus, you can't accidentally select a single object, move it, or otherwise alter it independently from the group. However, you *can* select individual objects within a group with the Direct Selection tool—that's how the tool got its name. Even if you select and alter a single object within a group, the objects are not ungrouped. If you click on any of them with the Selection tool, all members of the group will be selected.

Working with Smart Guides

When aligning objects, you will find **smart guides** to be very effective and, well, really smart. When the Smart Guides feature is activated, smart guides appear automatically when you move objects in the document. They give you visual information for positioning objects precisely in relation to the artboard or other objects. For example, you can use smart guides to align objects to the edges and centers of other objects, and to the horizontal and vertical centers of the artboard.

You can change settings for smart guides using the Smart Guides section of the Preferences dialog box. You use the View menu to turn them on and off. Figure 18 shows smart guides at work.

Figure 18 Smart guides indicate relationships between objects

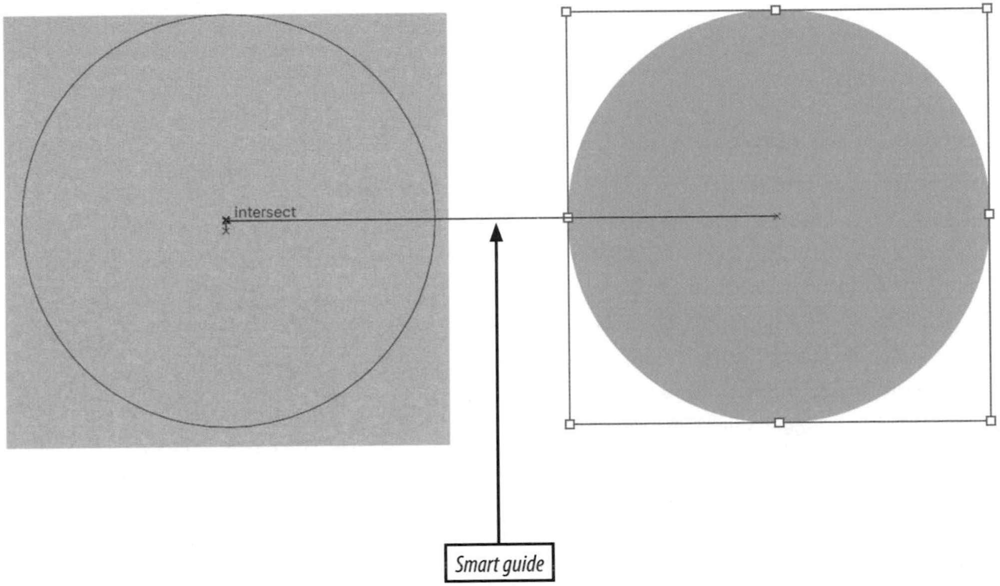

intersect

Smart guide

Set essential preferences

1. Check to make sure you have closed all open documents.

   When changing preference settings, no documents should be open.

2. Click **Illustrator (Mac)** or **Edit (Win)** on the menu bar, point to **Preferences**, then click **General**.

3. Set your General preferences to match Figure 19, then keep the dialog box open until the end of the exercise. You will be making changes to other preference categories.

   The keyboard increment determines the distance a selected object moves when you click an arrow key on your keypad. The measurement entered, .0139" is equivalent to 1 pt. The Show Tool Tips option will reveal a tool's name when you position your cursor over it.

TIP If you press and hold [shift] while pressing the arrow keys, a selected object moves a distance that is 10× the keyboard increment.

4. Click **Guides & Grid** on the left side of the Preferences dialog box, then verify that your settings match those shown in Figure 20.

TIP Note that you have options for showing your guides as dots.

Figure 19 General preferences

Figure 20 Guides & Grid preferences

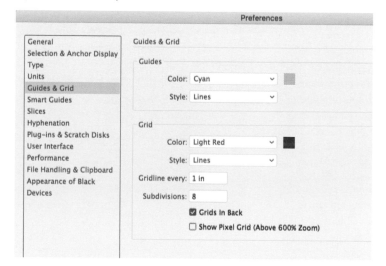

5. Click **Smart Guides** on the left side of the Preferences dialog box, then enter the settings shown in Figure 21.

TIP It's a good idea for your smart guides to be a distinctly different color than your ruler guides and artboard grid.

6. Click **User Interface** on the left side of the Preferences dialog box, then make sure your settings match those shown in Figure 22.

7. Click **OK.**

You specified various essential preferences in different Preferences dialog boxes.

Figure 21 Smart Guides preferences

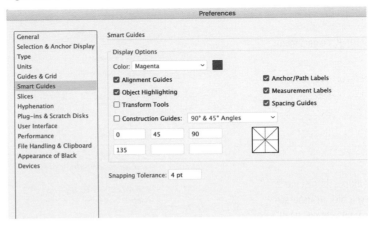

Figure 22 User Interface preferences

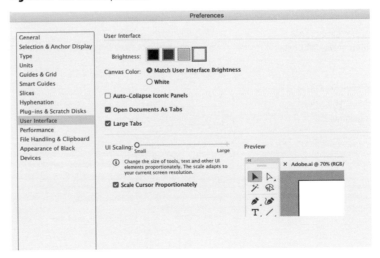

Resize objects

1. Open A1-2.ai, then save it as **Objects**.

2. Click the **Selection tool** 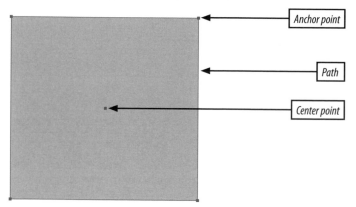, then click the **pink square** to select it.

   As shown in Figure 23, the paths and the anchor points that draw the square are revealed, as is the object's center point.

3. Click **View** on the menu bar, then click **Show Bounding Box**.

   Eight handles appear around the rectangle.

TIP Make it a point to remember the quick key for showing and hiding the bounding box: [shift] [command] [B] (Mac) or [shift] [Ctrl] [B] (Win).

4. Click and drag **various handles**, and note how the object is resized.

5. When you are done experimenting, undo all the moves you made to the bounding box.

   The Undo command is at the top of the Edit menu.

6. Press and hold down **[shift]** while dragging the **top-left corner handle** toward the edge of the document.

   The object is resized proportionately.

7. Undo the move.

8. Click the **green circle** to select it.

9. Press and hold **[option]** **(Mac)** or **[Alt] (Win)**, then start dragging **any corner handle**.

   As you drag, the object is resized from its center.

10. While still holding down **[option]** **(Mac)** or **[Alt] (Win)** and dragging, press and hold **[shift]**.

    The object is resized in proportion from its center.

11. Scale the **circle** to any size.

12. Undo the move.

13. Click **Select** on the menu bar, then click **All**.

    All the objects on the artboard are selected. The bounding box appears around all three objects. Make it a point to remember the quick

key for Select All: [command] [A] (Mac) or [Ctrl] [A] (Win).

14. Using the skills you learned in this lesson, experiment with resizing all the objects.

15. Click **File** on the menu bar, click **Revert**, then click **Revert** when you are prompted to confirm.

    Reverting a file returns it to its status when you last saved it. You can think of it as a "super undo."

16. Keep this file open and continue to the next set of steps.

You explored various options for resizing objects, then you reverted the file.

Copy and duplicate objects

1. Click **View** on the menu bar, then click **Hide Bounding Box**.

2. Select the **star**, then copy it, using the **[command] [C] (Mac)** or **[Ctrl] [C] (Win)** shortcut keys.

3. Click **Edit** on the menu bar, then click **Paste in Front**.

   The copy is pasted directly in front of the original star.

4. Press the **letter [I]** on your keypad to switch to the **Eyedropper tool** 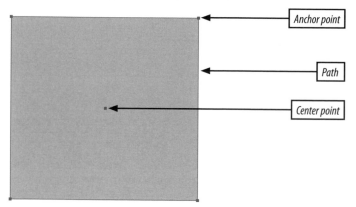.

   The star remains selected.

5. Click the **pink square**.

   The star takes on the same fill and stroke colors as the square.

6. Press the right arrow key [→] on your keypad 10 times.

   The star moves 10 keyboard increments to the right.

Figure 23 Paths, anchor points, and center point on an object

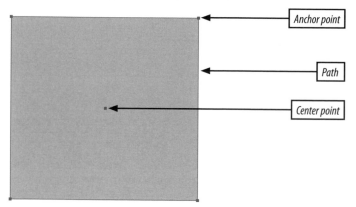

Anchor point

Path

Center point

7. Deselect all, click **Edit** on the menu bar, then click **Paste in Back**.

A copy of the orange star is pasted directly behind the original orange star that was copied.

8. Click the **Eyedropper tool**  on the **green circle**.

9. Press and hold **[shift]**, then press ← on your keypad one time.

Pressing and holding [shift] when pressing an arrow key moves the selected object(s) 10 keyboard increments.

10. Press and hold **[command] (Mac)** or **[Ctrl] (Win)** so your cursor switches temporarily from the **Eyedropper tool** to the **Selection tool** , then click the **artboard** with the **Selection tool** to deselect all.

Pressing [command] (Mac) or [Ctrl] (Win) is a quick way to switch temporarily to the Selection tool .

11. Compare your artboard to Figure 24.

12. Click the **Selection tool** , then select the **green circle**.

13. Press and hold **[option] (Mac)** or **[Alt] (Win)**, then drag a **copy of the circle** to the **center of the pink square**.

Your artboard should resemble Figure 25.

TIP This method for creating a copy is referred to as "drag and drop a copy."

14. Save your work, then close the file.

You copied and pasted an object, noting that it pasted by default in the center of the artboard. You used the Paste in Front and Paste in Back commands along with arrow keys to make two offset copies of the star. You duplicated the circle with the drag and drop technique.

Figure 25 Dragging and dropping a copy of the circle

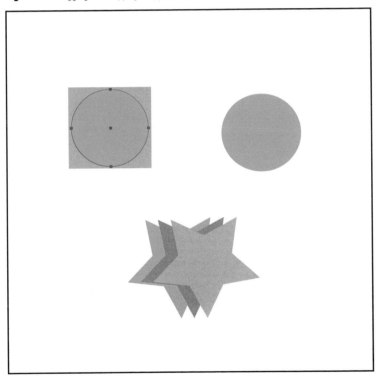

Figure 24 Three stars

Hide, lock, and group objects

1. Open AI 1-3.ai, then save it as **Groups**.

2. Click **Object** on the menu bar, then click **Show All**.

   This document was originally saved with hidden objects. Three objects appear. They are all selected.

3. Click **Object** on the menu bar, then click **Group**.

4. Click the **Selection tool** , click **anywhere on the pasteboard** to deselect all, then click the **pink circle**.

   All three objects are selected because they are grouped.

5. Click the **pasteboard** to deselect all, click the **Direct Selection tool**, then click the **pink circle**.

   Only the circle is selected, because the Direct Selection tool selects individual objects within a group.

6. Select all, click **Object** on the menu bar, then click **Ungroup**.

7. Click the **Selection tool**, select the **small square**, click **Object** on the menu bar, point to **Lock**, then click **Selection**.

   The object's handles disappear, and it can no longer be selected.

8. Click **Object** on the menu bar, then click **Unlock All**.

   The small square is unlocked.

9. Select all, click **Object** on the menu bar, point to **Hide**, then click **Selection**.

   All selected objects disappear.

10. Click **Object** on the menu bar, then click **Show All**.

    The three objects reappear in the same location that they were in when they were hidden.

    TIP Memorize the shortcut keys for Hide/Show, Group/Ungroup, and Lock/Unlock. They are easy to remember and extremely useful. You will be using these commands a lot when you work in Illustrator.

11. Hide the **pink circle** and the **small square**.

12. Save your work, then continue to the next set of steps.

You revealed hidden objects, grouped them, then used the Direct Selection tool to select individual objects within the group. You ungrouped, locked, unlocked, and hid objects.

Work with smart guides

1. Click **View** on the menu bar, then click **Smart Guides** if it is not already checked.

2. Click the **large blue square**, then try to center it visually on the page.

3. Release the mouse button when the word **center** appears, as shown in Figure 26.

   Smart guides use the word center to identify when the center point of an object is in line with the center point of the artboard.

4. Show the **hidden objects**, then hide the **small square**.

Figure 26 Smart guide aligning square with center of artboard

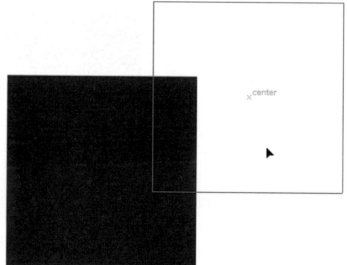

5. Using smart guides, align the **center of the pink circle** with the **center of the large blue square**.

6. Show the **hidden small square**.

7. Use smart guides to align the **top of the small square** with the **top of the large square**, as shown in Figure 27.

8. Position the **small square** as shown in Figure 28.

9. Save your work, then close the Groups document.

You aligned an object at the center of the document and created precise relationships among three objects using smart guides.

Figure 27 Aligning the tops of two squares

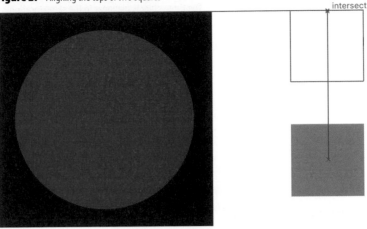

intersect

Figure 28 Aligning the bottoms of two squares

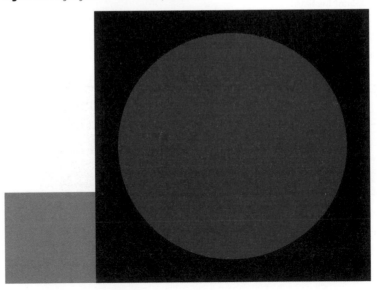

CREATE BASIC SHAPES

▶ What You'll Do

In this lesson, you will examine the differences between bitmap and vector graphics. Then you will use the Rectangle tool to examine Illustrator's various options for creating simple vector graphics.

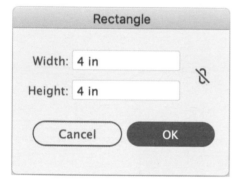

Understanding Bitmap Images and Vector Graphics

Before you begin drawing, you should become familiar with some basic information about computer graphics.

For starters, computer graphics fall into two main categories—bitmap images and vector graphics. **Bitmap images** are created using a square or rectangular grid of colored squares called **pixels**. Because pixels (a contraction of "picture elements") can render subtle gradations of tone, they are the most common medium for continuous-tone images—what you perceive as a photograph.

All scanned images are composed of pixels, and all "digital" images are composed of pixels. Adobe Photoshop is the leading graphics application for working with digital "photos." Figure 29 shows an example of a bitmap image.

Figure 29 Bitmap graphics

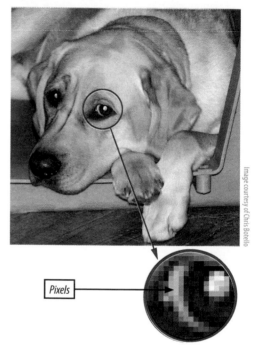

Image courtesy of Chris Botello

Pixels

The number of pixels in each inch is referred to as the image's **resolution**. To be effective, pixels must be small enough to create an image with the illusion of continuous tone. Thus, bitmap images are termed **resolution-dependent**.

The important thing to remember about bitmap images is that any magnification of the image—resizing the image to be bigger—essentially means that fewer pixels are available per inch (the same number of pixels is now spread out over a larger area). This decrease in resolution will have a negative impact on the quality of the image. The greater the magnification, the greater the negative impact.

Graphics that you create in Adobe Illustrator are vector graphics. **Vector graphics** are created with lines and curves and are defined by mathematical objects called vectors.

Vectors use geometric characteristics to define the object. Vector graphics consist of anchor points and line segments, together referred to as paths. Figure 30 shows an example of a vector graphic.

Computer graphics rely on vectors to render bold graphics that must retain clean, crisp lines when scaled to various sizes. Vectors are often used to create logos or "line art," and they are the best choice for typographical work, especially small and italic type.

As mathematical objects, vector graphics can be scaled to any size. Because they are not created with pixels, there is no inherent resolution. Thus, vector graphics are termed **resolution-independent**. This means that any graphic that you create in Illustrator can be output to fit on a postage stamp or on a billboard!

Figure 30 Vector graphics

Use the Rectangle tool

1. Click **File** on the menu bar, click **New**, create a new document that is 8" wide by 8" in height, name the file **Basic Shapes**, then click **OK**.

2. Click **File** on the menu bar, click **Save As**, navigate to the drive and folder where your Data Files are stored, then save the file.

3. Click the **Default Fill and Stroke button** 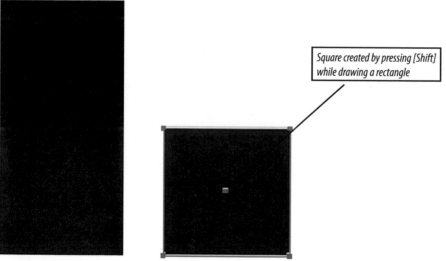 on the toolbar.

4. Click the **Swap Fill and Stroke button** on the toolbar to reverse the default colors.

   Your fill color should now be black, and your stroke color white. The **fill color** is the inside color of an object. The **stroke color** is the color of the object's border or frame.

5. Click the **Rectangle tool** on the toolbar.

6. Click and drag the **Rectangle tool pointer** on the artboard, then release the mouse button to make a rectangle of any size.

7. Press and hold **[shift]**, then create a **second rectangle**.

   As shown in Figure 31, pressing and holding [shift] while you create a rectangle constrains the shape to a perfect square.

8. Create a **third rectangle** drawn from its center point by pressing and holding **[option] (Mac)** or **[Alt] (Win)** as you drag the **Rectangle tool pointer.**

TIP Use [shift] in combination with [option] (Mac) or [Alt] (Win) to draw a perfect shape from its center.

9. Save your work, then continue to the next set of steps.

You created a freeform rectangle, then you created a perfect square. Finally, you drew a square from its center point.

Use the Rectangle dialog box

1. Click **Select** on the menu bar, then click **All** to select all the objects.

2. Click **Edit** on the menu bar, then click **Cut** to remove the objects from the artboard.

3. Verify that the **Rectangle tool** is still selected, then click **anywhere on the artboard**.

   When a shape tool is selected, clicking once on the artboard opens the tool's dialog box, which allows you to enter precise information for creating the shape. In this case, it opens the Rectangle dialog box.

4. Type **4** in the Width text box, type **4** in the Height text box, as shown in Figure 32, then click **OK**.

5. Save your work, then continue to the next lesson.

You clicked the artboard with the Rectangle tool, which opened the Rectangle dialog box. You entered a specific width and height to create a perfect 4" square.

Figure 31 Creating a rectangle and a square

Square created by pressing [Shift] while drawing a rectangle

Figure 32 Rectangle tool dialog box

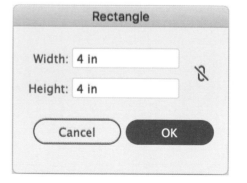

APPLY FILL AND STROKE COLORS TO OBJECTS

▶ *What You'll Do*

In this lesson, you will use the Swatches panel to add a fill color to an object and apply a stroke as a border. Then you will use the Stroke panel to change the size of the default stroke.

Activating the Fill or Stroke

The Fill and Stroke buttons are on the toolbar. To apply a fill or stroke color to an object, you must first activate the appropriate button. You activate either button by clicking it, which moves it in front of the other. When the Fill button is in front of the Stroke button, the fill is activated. The Stroke button is activated when it is in front of the Fill button.

As you work, you will often switch back and forth, activating the fill and the stroke. Rather than using the mouse to activate the fill or the stroke each time, simply press [X] to switch between the two modes.

Applying Color with the Swatches Panel

The Swatches panel is central to color management in the application and a main resource for applying fills and strokes to objects.

The Swatches panel has several preset colors, along with gradients, patterns, and shades of gray. The swatch with the red line through it is called [None] and is used as a fill for a "hollow" object. Any object without a stroke will always have [None] as its stroke color.

When an object is selected, clicking a swatch on the panel will apply that color as a fill or a stroke, depending on which of the two is activated on the toolbar. You can also drag and drop swatches onto unselected objects. Dragging a swatch to an unselected object will change the color of its fill or stroke, depending upon which of the two is activated.

Apply fill and stroke colors

1. Verify that the **4" × 4" square** is still selected.

2. Click the **fill color** on the toolbar to verify that it is the active color.

   See Figure 33.

3. Click **any blue swatch** on the Swatches panel to fill the square.

   Note that the Fill button on the toolbar is now also blue.

TIP When you position the mouse pointer over a color swatch on the Swatches panel, a tool tip appears that shows the name of that swatch.

4. Click the **Selection tool** ▶, then click **anywhere on the artboard** to deselect the blue square.

5. Drag and drop a **yellow swatch** from the Swatches panel onto the blue square on the artboard.

The fill color changes to yellow because the fill button is activated on the toolbar.

6. Press the **letter [X]** to activate the **Stroke button** on the toolbar.

7. Click any **red swatch** on the Swatches panel.

   A red stroke is added to the square because the Stroke button is activated on the toolbar.

8. Open the **Stroke panel**, increase the Weight to **8 pt.**, then compare your artwork to Figure 34.

TIP By default, Illustrator positions a stroke equally inside and outside an object. Thus, an 8 pt. stroke is rendered with 4 pts. inside the object and 4 pts. outside.

9. Note the **Align Stroke section** on the Stroke panel.

10. Click the **Align Stroke to Inside button** ⌐.

    The entire stroke moves to the inside of the square.

11. Click the **Align Stroke to Outside button** ⌐.

    The entire stroke moves to the outside of the square.

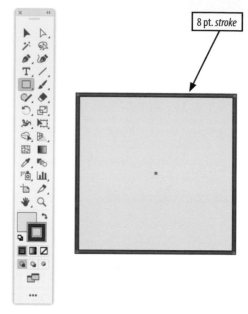

8 pt. *stroke*

Figure 34 8 pt. red stroke on yellow square

12. Click the **Align Stroke to Center button** ⌐.

    The stroke is returned to the default position, equally inside and outside the object.

13. Click ✎ **(None)** on the Swatches panel to remove the stroke from the square.

14. Save your work, then continue to the next set of steps.

You filled the square with blue by clicking a blue swatch on the Swatches panel. You then changed the fill and stroke colors to yellow and red by dragging and dropping swatches onto the square. You used the Stroke panel to increase the weight and change the alignment of the stroke, then removed it by choosing [None] from the Swatches panel.

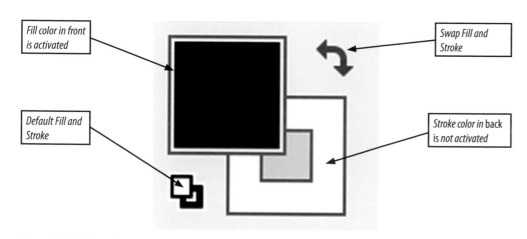

Fill color in front is activated

Default Fill and Stroke

Swap Fill and Stroke

Stroke color in back is *not* activated

Figure 33 Fill color in front and activated on the toolbar

SELECT, MOVE, AND ALIGN OBJECTS

▶ *What You'll Do*

In this lesson, you will use the Selection tool in combination with smart guides to move, copy, and align four squares.

Selecting Objects

Before you can move or modify an Illustrator object, you must select it. When working with simple illustrations that contain few objects, selecting is usually simple, but it can become very tricky in complex illustrations, especially those containing many small objects positioned closely together.

By now you're familiar with using the Selection tool to select objects. You can also use the Selection tool to create a marquee selection, which is a dotted rectangle that disappears as soon as you release the mouse button. Any object that the marquee touches before you release the mouse button will be selected. Marquee selections are useful for both quick selections and precise selections. Make sure you practice and make them part of your skills set.

Moving Objects

When it comes to accuracy, consider that Illustrator can move objects incrementally by fractions of a point—which itself is a tiny fraction of an inch! That level of precision is key when moving and positioning objects.

Two basic ways to move objects are by clicking and dragging or by using the arrow keys, which by default move a selected item in 1 pt. increments. Pressing [shift] when you press an arrow key moves the object in increments of 10 pts. in that direction.

Pressing [shift] when dragging an object constrains the movement to horizontal, vertical, and 45° diagonals. Pressing [option] (Mac) or [Alt] (Win) while dragging an object creates a copy of the object.

Move and position objects with precision

1. Click **View** on the menu bar, then click **Fit Artboard in Window**.

2. Click **View** on the menu bar, then verify that both **Smart Guides** and **Snap to Point** are activated.

   Snap to Point automatically aligns anchor points when they get close together. When dragging an object, you'll see it "snap" to align itself with a nearby object or guide.

TIP There will be a check next to each if it is activated. If it is not activated, click each option to make it active.

3. Click the **Selection tool** ▶ on the toolbar, then click the **yellow square**.

4. Position the pointer over the **top-left anchor point**; click and drag so that the anchor point aligns with the **top-left corner of the artboard**, as shown in Figure 35; then release the mouse button.

   The smart guide changes from "anchor" to "intersect" when the two corners are aligned.

You used the Selection tool in combination with smart guides to position an object exactly at the top-left corner of the artboard.

Figure 35 Intersecting two points

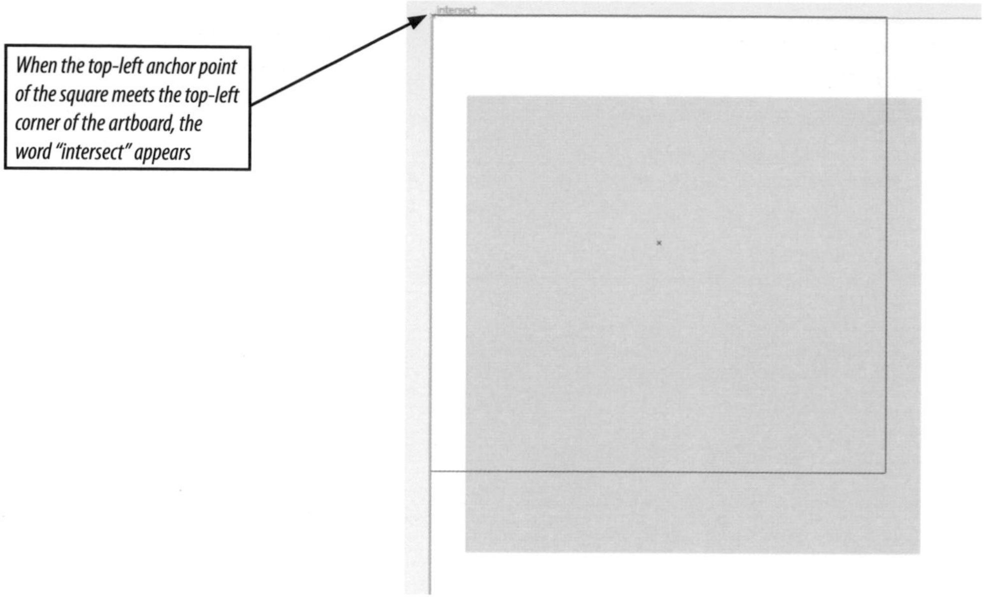

When the top-left anchor point of the square meets the top-left corner of the artboard, the word "intersect" appears

Duplicate objects using drag and drop

1. Press and hold **[shift] [option] (Mac)** or **[shift] [Alt] (Win)**, then click and drag a **copy of the yellow square** immediately below itself, as shown in Figure 36.

   When moving an object, pressing and holding [shift] constrains the movement vertically, horizontally, or on 45° diagonals. Pressing [option] (Mac) or [Alt] (Win) while dragging an object creates a copy of the object.

   TIP When you press [option] (Mac) or [Alt] (Win) while dragging an object, the pointer becomes a double-arrow pointer.

2. With the bottom square still selected, press and hold **[shift]**, then click the **top square** to select both items.

3. Press and hold **[shift] [option] (Mac)** or **[shift] [Alt] (Win)**, then drag a **copy of the two squares** immediately to the right.

4. Change the **fill color** of **each square** to match the colors shown in Figure 37.

5. Save your work, then continue to the next lesson.

You moved and duplicated the yellow square using [shift] to constrain the movement and [option] (Mac) or [Alt] (Win) to duplicate or "drag and drop" copies of the square.

Figure 36 Duplicating the square

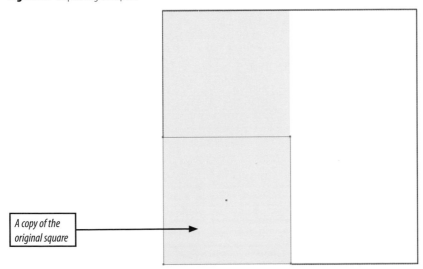

A copy of the original square

Figure 37 Four squares with different fills

TRANSFORM OBJECTS

▶ *What You'll Do*

In this lesson, you will scale, rotate, and reflect objects, using the basic transform tools. You will also create a star and a triangle.

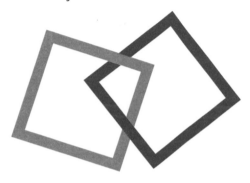

Transforming Objects

The Scale, Rotate, and Reflect tools are the fundamental transform tools. As their names make clear, the Scale and Rotate tools resize and rotate objects, respectively. When you use the tool's dialog box, the objects are transformed from their center points.

Use the Reflect tool to "flip" an object over an imaginary axis. The best way to understand the Reflect tool is to imagine positioning a mirror perpendicular to a sheet of paper with a word written on it. The angle at which you position the mirror in relation to the word is the reflection axis. The reflection of the word in the mirror is the result of what the Reflect tool does. For example, text reflected across a horizontal axis would appear upside down and inverted. Text reflected across a vertical axis would appear to be inverted and running backwards, as shown in Figure 38.

Figure 38 Reflected text

Reflect

- - - - - - - - - - - - - - - - -

Reflect

Reflect | Reflect

Each transform tool has a dialog box where you enter precise numbers to execute the transformation on a selected object. You can access a tool's dialog box by double-clicking the tool. Click the Copy button in the dialog box to create a transformed copy of the selected object. Figure 39 shows the Scale dialog box.

Repeating Transformations

One of the most powerful commands relating to the transform tools is Transform Again, found on the Object menu. Whenever you transform an object, selecting Transform Again repeats the transformation. For example, if

you scale a circle 50%, the Transform Again command will scale the circle 50% again.

The power of the command comes in combination with copying transformations. For example, if you rotate a square 10° and copy it at the same time, the Transform Again command will create a second square rotated another 10° from the first copy. Applying Transform Again repeatedly is handy for creating complex geometric shapes from basic objects.

Use the Scale and Rotate tools

1. Select the **green square**, double-click the **Scale tool** 🔲 , type **50** in the Scale text box, then click **OK**.

2. Click **Edit** on the menu bar, then click **Undo Scale**.

   TIP You can also undo your last step by pressing [command] [Z] (Mac) or [Ctrl] [Z] (Win).

3. Double-click the **Scale tool** 🔲 again, type **50** in the Scale text box, then click **Copy**.

   The transformation is executed from the center point; the center points of the original and the copy are aligned.

4. Fill the **new square** created in Step 3 with **blue**.

5. Double-click the **Rotate tool** ↻ , type **45** in the Angle text box, click **OK**, then deselect.

6. Apply a **22 pt. yellow stroke** to the rotated square, deselect, then compare your screen to Figure 40.

7. Save your work, then continue to the next set of steps.

You used the Scale tool to create a 50% copy of the square, then filled the copy with blue. You rotated the copy 45°. You then applied a 22 pt. yellow stroke.

Figure 39 Scale dialog box

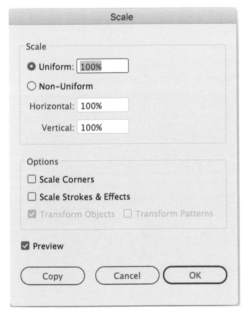

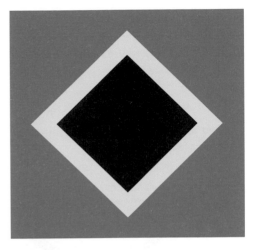

Figure 40 Rotated square

Use the Transform Again command

1. Click the **Ellipse tool** ⬭ on the toolbar.

   TIP The Ellipse tool ⬭ is located behind the Rectangle tool ▢ .

2. Click the **artboard** to open the Ellipse tool dialog box, type **3** in the Width text box and **.5** in the Height text box, then click **OK**.

3. Change the **fill color** to **[None]**, the **stroke color** to **blue**, and the **stroke weight** to **3 pt**.

4. Click the **Selection tool** ▶ , click the **center point of the ellipse**, then drag it to the **center point of the yellow square**.

   TIP The center smart guide appears when the two centers meet.

Continued on next page

5. Double-click the **Rotate tool** , type **45** in the Angle text box, then click **Copy**.

6. Click **Object** on the menu bar, point to **Transform**, then click **Transform Again.**

TIP You can also access the Transform Again command by pressing [command] [D] (Mac) or [Ctrl] [D] (Win).

7. Press **[command] [D] (Mac)** or **[Ctrl] [D] (Win)** to create a **fourth ellipse**.

   Your screen should resemble Figure 41.

8. Select the **four ellipses**, click **Object** on the menu bar, then click **Group**.

9. Save your work, then continue to the next set of steps.

You created an ellipse, filled and stroked it, and aligned it with the yellow square. You then created a copy rotated at 45°. With the second copy still selected, you used the Transform Again command twice, creating two more rotated copies. You then grouped the four ellipses.

Create a star and a triangle, and use the Reflect tool

1. Select the **Star tool** ☆, then click **anywhere on the artboard**.

   The Star tool ☆ is hidden beneath the current shape tool.

2. Type **1** in the **Radius 1 text box**, type **5** in the **Radius 2 text box**, type **5** in the **Points text box**, then click **OK**.

   A star has two radii; the first is from the center to the inner point, and the second is from the center to the outer point. The **radius** is a measurement from the center point of the star to either point.

TIP When you create a star using the Star dialog box, the star is drawn upside down.

3. Double-click the **Scale tool** , type **25** in the **Scale text box**, then click **OK**.

4. Fill the star with **white**, then apply a **5 pt. blue stroke** to it.

5. Click the **Selection tool** ▶, then move the star so that it is completely within the red square.

6. Double-click the **Reflect tool** ▷◀, click the **Horizontal option button**, then click **OK**.

   The star "flips" over an imaginary horizontal axis.

TIP The Reflect tool ▷◀, is located behind the Rotate tool ↻.

7. Use the **Selection tool** ▶ or the **arrow keys** to position the star roughly in the **center of the red square**.

   Your work should resemble Figure 42.

8. Click the **Polygon tool** ⬡ on the toolbar.

   The Polygon tool is hidden beneath the current shape tool on the toolbar.

9. Click **anywhere on the blue square** to open the tool's dialog box.

10. Type **1.5** in the **Radius text box**, type **3** in the **Sides text box**, then click **OK**.

11. Fill the **triangle** with **red**.

12. Change the **stroke color** to **yellow** and the **stroke weight** to **22 pt**.

13. Position the **triangle** so that it is centered within the **blue square**.

    Your completed project should resemble Figure 43.

14. Save your work, then close Basic Shapes.

You used the shape tools to create a star and a triangle, then used the Reflect tool to "flip" the star over an imaginary horizontal axis.

Figure 41 Using the Transform Again command

Figure 42 The star with a white fill and blue stroke

Figure 43 The finished project

MAKE DIRECT SELECTIONS

▶ **What You'll Do**

In this lesson, you will use the Direct Selection tool and a combination of menu commands, such as Add Anchor Points and Paste in Front, to convert existing shapes into new designs.

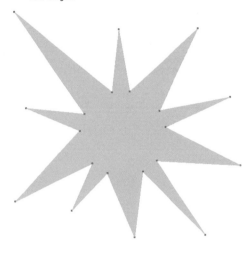

Using the Direct Selection Tool

The Direct Selection tool selects individual anchor points or single paths of an object. Using [shift], you can select multiple anchor points or multiple paths. You can also select multiple points or paths by dragging a direct selection marquee. The tool also selects individual objects within a group, which can be useful for modifying just one object in a complex group.

Clicking the center of an object with the Direct Selection tool selects the entire object. Clicking the edge selects the path segment only; the anchor points on the object all appear white, which means they are not selected.

The Direct Selection tool gives you the power to distort simple objects such as squares and circles into unique shapes. Don't underestimate its significance. While the Selection tool is no more than a means for selecting and moving objects, the Direct Selection tool is in itself a drawing tool. You will use it over and over again to modify and perfect your artwork.

Adding Anchor Points

As you distort basic shapes with the Direct Selection tool, you will often find that to create more complex shapes, you will need additional anchor points.

The Add Anchor Points command creates new anchor points without distorting the object. To add anchor points to an object, click the Object menu, point to Path, then click Add Anchor Points. The new points are automatically positioned exactly between the original anchor points. You can create as many additional points as you wish.

Turning Objects into Guides

Guides are one of Illustrator's many features that help you work with precision. Any object you create can be turned into a guide. With the object selected, click the View menu, point to Guides, then click Make Guides. Guides can be locked or unlocked in the same location. It is a good idea to work with locked guides so they don't interfere with your artwork. Unlock guides only when you want to select them or delete them.

When an object is turned into a guide, it loses its attributes, such as its fill, stroke, and stroke weight. However, Illustrator remembers the original attributes for each guide. To transform a guide back to its original object, first unlock and then select the guide. Click the View menu, point to Guides, then click Release Guides.

Working with the Stacking Order

The **stacking order** refers to the order of how objects are arranged in front and behind other objects on the artboard. Every time you create an object, it is created in front of the existing objects. (Note that this discussion does not include any role of layers and the Layers panel.) You can manipulate the stacking order with the Arrange commands on the Object menu. See Table 3 for descriptions of each Arrange command.

You can also use the **Draw Behind drawing mode** to create an object behind a selected object or at the bottom of the stacking order.

Make guides and direct selections

1. Open AI 1-4.ai, then save it as **Direct Selections**.

2. Click **View** on the menu bar, then deactivate the **Smart Guides feature**.

3. Click the **Selection tool** ▶, then select the **green polygon**.

4. Click **View** on the menu bar, point to **Guides**, then click **Make Guides**.

   The polygon is converted to a guide.

   TIP If you do not see the polygon-shaped guide, click View on the menu bar, point to Guides, then click Show Guides.

5. Convert the **purple starburst** to a guide.

6. Click **View** on the menu bar, point to **Guides**, click **Lock Guides**, then click the **pasteboard** to close the menu.

If you see Unlock Guides on the Guides menu, the guides are already locked.

7. Click the **Direct Selection tool** ▷, then click the **edge of the red square**.

   The four anchor points turn white. If the four anchor points are not white, deselect and try again. You must click the very edge of the square, not inside it.

8. Click and drag the **anchor points** to the **four corners of the guide** to distort the square.

   Your work should resemble Figure 44.

You converted two objects to guides. You then used the Direct Selection tool to create a new shape from a square by moving anchor points independently.

TABLE 3: ARRANGE COMMANDS			
Command	Result	quick key (Mac)	quick key (Win)
Bring Forward	Brings a selected object forward one position in the stacking order	[command] [right bracket]	[Ctrl] [right bracket]
Bring to Front	Brings a selected object to the very front of the stacking order—in front of all other objects	[shift] [command] [right bracket]	[shift] [Ctrl] [right bracket]
Send Backward	Sends a selected object backward one position	[command] [left bracket]	[Ctrl] [left bracket]
Send to Back	Sends a selected object to the very back of the stacking order—behind all the other objects	[shift] [command] [left bracket]	[shift] [Ctrl] [left bracket]

Figure 44 Reshaped red square and guides

Add anchor points

1. Using the **Direct Selection tool** , click the **center of the light blue star**, then note the anchor points used to define the shape.

2. Click **Object** on the menu bar, point to **Path**, then click **Add Anchor Points**.

3. Click the **artboard** to deselect the star, then click the **edge of the star**.

   All the anchor points turn white and are available to be selected independently. If the anchor points are not white, deselect and try again. You must click the very edge of the square, not inside it.

4. Move the **top anchor point on the star** to align with the **top point of the guide** that you made earlier.

5. Working clockwise, move every other anchor point outward to align with the guide, creating a 10-point starburst.

   Your work should resemble Figure 45.

6. Select and move any of the **inner anchor points** to modify the starburst to your liking.

7. Save your work, then continue to the next set of steps.

You used the Add Anchor Points command and the Direct Selection tool to create an original 10-point starburst from a generic five-point star.

Modify the stacking order and use the Draw Behind drawing mode

1. Click the **Selection tool** on the toolbar, click the **red rectangle**, click **Object** on the menu bar, point to **Arrange**, then click **Send to Back**.

   The red rectangle moves to the back of the stacking order.

2. Select the **yellow path**, click **Object** on the menu bar, point to **Arrange**, then click **Send Backward**.

   The path moves one level back in the stacking order. When discussing the stacking order, it's smart to use the term "level" instead of "layer." In Illustrator, layers are different than the stacking order.

TIP Click the center of the yellow path to select it.

3. Select the **blue oval**, click **Object** on the menu bar, point to **Arrange**, click **Bring Forward**, then deselect.

   As shown in Figure 46, the blue oval moves one level forward in the stacking order.

Figure 45 Reshaped starburst

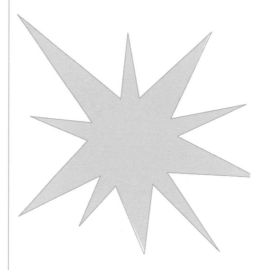

Figure 46 Blue oval moved in front of yellow path

4. Verify that the **toolbar** is displayed in two columns.

When the toolbar is displayed in two columns, the three drawing modes are visible as icons at the bottom. When the panel is displayed in a single column, you need to click the Drawing Modes icon to display the tools in a submenu.

5. Note the **four objects** in the bottom-left quadrant of the artboard.

The blue oval is at the back, the purple rectangle is in front of the blue oval, the curvy yellow path is in front of the purple rectangle, and the red rectangle is at the front.

6. Select the **purple rectangle**, then click the **Draw Behind button** 〇 at the bottom of the toolbar.

There are three available drawing modes: Draw Normal, Draw Behind, and Draw Inside.

7. Click the **Ellipse tool** 〇 on the toolbar, then draw a **circle** at the **center of the blue oval**.

The circle is created behind the purple rectangle, though it still appears to be in front while it is selected. With the Draw Behind drawing mode activated, an object you draw will be positioned one level behind any selected object on the artboard. If no object is selected, the new object will be positioned at the back of the stacking order.

8. Click the **Eyedropper tool** 🖊, click the **red rectangle**, then compare your artboard to Figure 47.

The Eyedropper tool 🖊 samples the fill and stroke colors from the red rectangle and applies them to the selected object.

9. Click the **Draw Normal button** 〇, then save your work.

10. Continue to the next set of steps.

You arranged objects on the artboard, used the Draw Behind feature, then changed the color of the circle you created.

Figure 47 Red circle drawn behind the purple rectangle

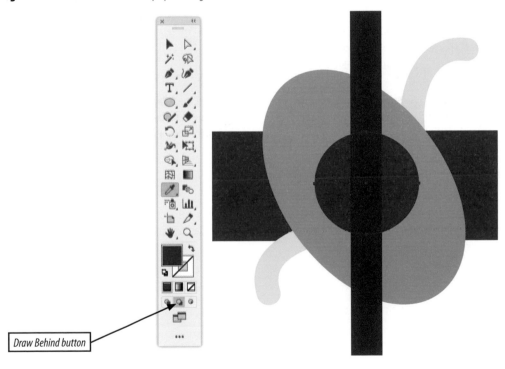

Draw Behind button

Create a simple special effect utilizing the Direct Selection tool

1. Click the **Selection tool** ![selection tool icon], overlap the **large orange** and **blue squares** so that they resemble the small orange and blue squares, then deselect.

2. Click the **Direct Selection tool** ![direct selection tool icon], then select the **top path segment** of the orange square.

   It will look like the whole square is selected, but you will see white anchor points in the four corners.

3. Copy the **path**.

4. Select the **intersecting path segment** on the blue square.

5. Click **Edit** on the menu bar, click **Paste in Front**, then compare your result to Figure 48.

6. Save your work, then close the Direct Selections document.

You performed a classic Illustrator trick using the Direct Selection tool. Selecting only a path, you copied it and pasted it in front of an intersecting object to create the illusion that the two objects were linked.

Figure 48 Illusion of linked squares

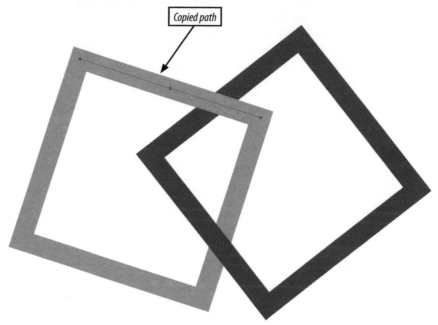

Copied path

WORK WITH MULTIPLE ARTBOARDS

In this lesson, you will explore various options when working with multiple artboards.

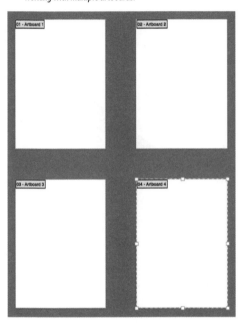

Understanding Multiple Artboards

The artboard is your workspace in an Illustrator document. Sometimes the size of the artboard will be important to your design; sometimes it won't. For example, let's say that you're designing a logo that will be used for a variety of items such as letterhead, business cards, a poster, and a building sign. When you are creating the logo, you're just designing artwork. The size at which you're creating the artwork isn't really important because you can resize it later to use in these different types of layouts.

At other times, the work you do in Illustrator will be at a specific size. Let's say, for example, that you're designing layouts for letterhead, business cards, and promotional postcards for the company for which you made the logo. In this case, you would need to set up your document, or the size of the artboard, at specific sizes, such as 8.5" × 11" for the letterhead, 3" × 2.5" for the business card, and 4" × 6" for the postcard.

Illustrator allows you to have anywhere from one to 100 artboards in a single document, depending on the size of the artboards. Using the previous example, this means that you could design all three pieces in one document—no need to switch between documents for the letterhead, business card, and postcard.

Beyond this basic convenience, working with multiple artboards offers many important benefits. You won't have to recreate unique swatch colors or gradients in different files; you'll only need to create them once.

Paste commands on the Edit menu allow you to paste an object on multiple artboards in exactly the same location—another example of the consistency that can be achieved by working in a single document.

Managing Multiple Artboards

Creating multiple artboards can be the first thing that you do when beginning a design or one of the last things you do. The New Document dialog box, shown in Figure 49, is where you define the specifics of a document, including the number of artboards.

The Width and Height values define the size of all the artboards you create at this stage, whether single or multiple, but you can resize artboards any time after creating them.

Once you specify the number of artboards, you have controls for the layout of the artboards. The four buttons to the right of the Number of Artboards text box offer basic layout choices—grid by row, grid by column, arrange by row, and arrange by column. The Spacing text box specifies the physical space between artboards, and the Rows value defines the number of rows of artboards in a grid.

When you click the OK button in the New Document dialog box, the document window displays all the artboards you've specified. Regardless of the number, the top-left artboard will be highlighted with a black line. This identifies the artboard as "active." As such, all View menu commands you apply affect this

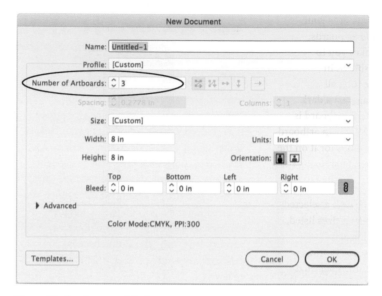

Figure 49 New Document dialog box

artboard. In other words, if you click the Fit Artboard in Window command, the active artboard is resized to fit in the document window. You can also click the Fit All in Window command to view all artboards.

When you create a new document, you can use a preset document profile in the New Document dialog box. The Document Profile menu lists preset values for size, color mode, units, orientation, transparency, and resolution. This can help you set up the basic orientation for your document quickly. For example, the Web profile automatically creates an RGB document with pixels as units. By default, all new document profiles use one artboard, but you can add more in the Number of Artboards text box.

The **Artboard tool** on the toolbar is your gateway to managing multiple artboards. Clicking the Artboard tool takes you to "artboard editing mode." As shown in Figure 50, when you click the tool, all artboards appear numbered against a dark gray background. The "selected" artboard is highlighted with a marquee. When an artboard is selected, you can change settings for it on the Control panel beneath the menu bar, using the following options:

- Click the Presets menu to change a selected artboard to any of the standard sizes listed, such as Letter, Tabloid, or Legal.
- Click the Portrait or Landscape buttons to specify the orientation for the selected artboard.
- Click the New Artboard button to create a duplicate of the selected artboard.
- Click the Delete Artboard button to delete the selected artboard.
- Click the Name text box to enter a name for the selected artboard. This could be useful for managing your own work and for adding clarity when you hand your Illustrator file over to a printer or some other vendor.
- Click the Width and Height text boxes to enter different values and resize the selected artboard.

To exit edit artboards mode, press the Escape key or click any other tool on the toolbar.

Figure 50 Artboard tool selected; artboards can be edited

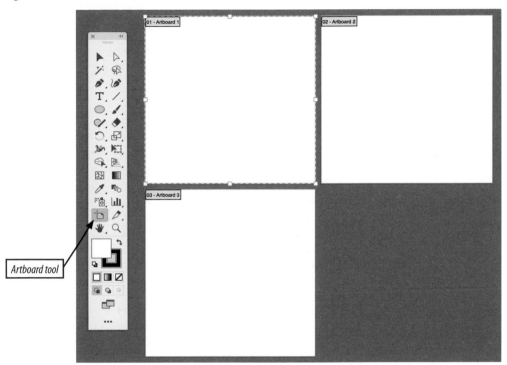

Artboard tool

Creating, Editing, and Arranging Artboards

Once you click the Artboard tool, you have many options for creating, editing, and arranging artboards.

You can click the New Artboard button on the Control panel. When you do, move your cursor over the other artboards and you'll see a transparent artboard moving with the cursor. If you have smart guides activated, green lines will appear to help you align the new artboard with the existing artboards. Click where you want to position the new artboard. Using this method, the new artboard button will create a new artboard at the size specified in the New Document dialog box.

As an alternative, you can simply click and drag with the Artboard tool to create a new artboard. Once you "drag out" the new artboard, you can enter a specific height and width for the artboard on the Control panel. To resize an existing artboard, first select the artboard, then enter values in the Width and Height text boxes.

You can manipulate the layout and positioning of artboards simply by clicking and dragging them as you wish.

Printing Multiple Artboards

When you work with multiple artboards, you can print each artboard individually, or you can compile them into one page. Usually, you'll want to print them individually, and this is easy to do in the Print dialog box. Use the forward and backward arrows in the print preview window to click through each artboard. In the Artboards section, if you click All, all artboards will print. To print only specific artboards, enter the artboard number in the Range field. To combine all artwork on all artboards onto a single page, select the Ignore Artboards option. Depending on how large your artboards are, they'll be scaled down to fit on a single page or tiled over a number of pages.

Using the Artboards Panel

You can use the Artboards panel to perform artboard operations. You can add or delete artboards, reorder and renumber them, and navigate through multiple artboards. When you create multiple artboards, each is assigned a number and is listed with that number on the Artboards panel. If you select an artboard, you can click the up and down arrows to reorder the artboards in the panel. Doing so will renumber the artboard but will not change its name.

Pasting Artwork on Multiple Artboards

The ability to paste copied artwork on multiple artboards is an important function and critical to maintain consistency between layouts. The Edit menu offers two powerful commands: Paste in Place and Paste on All Artboards. Use the Paste in Place command to paste an object from one artboard to the same spot on another. Even if the two artboards are different sizes, the pasted logo will be positioned at exactly the same distance from the top-left corner of the artboard.

The Paste on All Artboards command goes a giant step further, pasting artwork in the same position on all artboards.

Create a new document with multiple artboards

1. Verify that no documents are open and that smart guides are activated.

TIP The Smart Guides command is on the View menu.

2. Click **File** on the menu bar, then click **New**.

The New Document dialog box opens.

3. Type **Winning Business Collateral** in the **Name text box**.

4. Set the number of artboards to **3**, then click the **Grid by Row button** ☒ .

5. Set the **Spacing** and **Columns text boxes** to **2**.

6. Verify that the **Units** are set to **Inches**.

7. Set the Width to **6** and the Height to **8.5**, then compare your dialog box to Figure 51.

8. Click **OK**.

When you click OK, the three artboards fit in your document window.

9. Click the **Selection tool** ▶ , then click **each artboard** to make each active.

A thin black line highlights each artboard when it is selected.

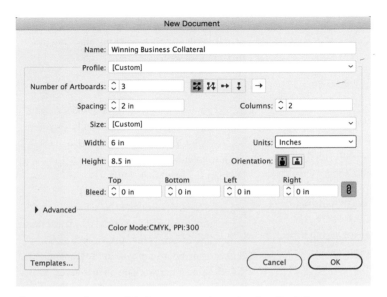

Figure 51 New Document dialog box set to create three artboards at 6" × 8.5"

10. Click the **top-right artboard** to make it the active artboard, click **View** on the menu bar, then click **Fit Artboard in Window**.

11. Click **View** on the menu bar, then click **Fit All in Window**.

12. Continue to the next set of steps.

You specified settings for a new document with three artboards in the New Document dialog box. You clicked artboards in the document to activate them. You used the Fit in Window and Fit All in Window commands to view artboards.

Create and name artboards

1. Click the **Artboard tool** ⬚ on the toolbar.

    Clicking the Artboard tool ⬚ switches the interface to the editing artboards mode. The top-right artboard is selected. All the artboards are numbered.

2. Click the **New Artboard button** ⊞ on the Control panel.

    A new artboard with the number 4 is added. The New Artboard button ⊞ creates a new artboard at the specified document size (in this case, 6" × 8.5").

3. Click and drag to position the **new artboard** as shown in Figure 52.

4. Click the **top-right artboard** to select it, then click the **Delete Artboard button** 🗑 on the Control panel.

5. Click the **Artboard tool** ⬚ on the toolbar, then click and drag to create a **new artboard** approximately the size of a standard business card.

Figure 52 Positioning the new artboard

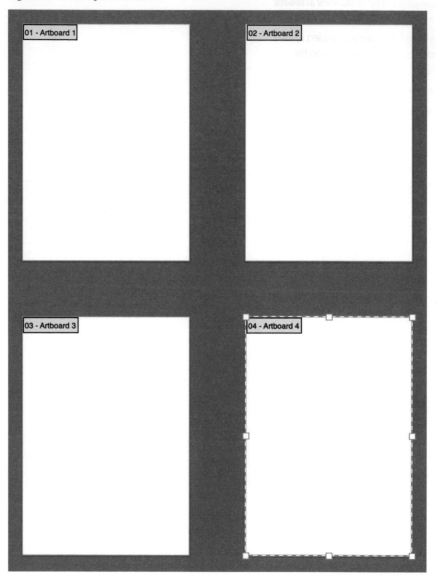

6. Press and hold **[option] (Mac)** or **[Alt] (Win)**, then drag and drop a **copy of the new artboard** in the space beneath it, as shown in Figure 53.

7. Click the **bottom-left artboard** to select it, then type **Bookmark** in the Name text box on the Control panel.

   The artboard is renamed.

8. Name the **bottom-right artboard Buckslip**.

9. Name the **top-left artboard Letterhead**.

10. Name the **two new artboards Biz Card Front** and **Biz Card Back**, respectively.

11. Save your work, then continue to the next set of steps.

You created a new artboard using three different methods: using the New Artboard button, using the Artboard tool, and dragging and dropping. You named all artboards.

Figure 53 New artboard created by dragging and dropping

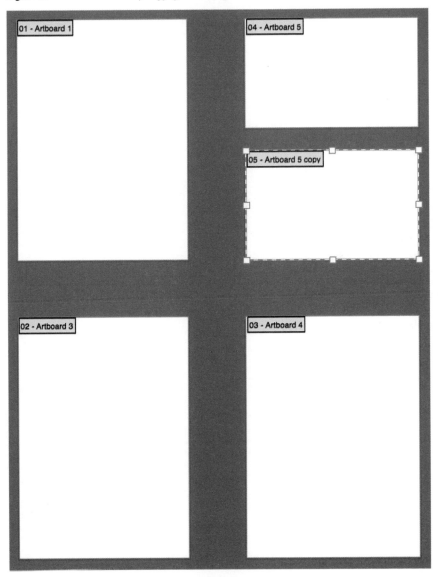

Resize and arrange artboards

1. Click the **artboard named Bookmark** to select it, type **2** in the **W Value (width) field** on the Control panel, then press or **[return] (Mac)** or **[Enter] (Win)**.

   The artboard is resized.

2. Resize the artboard named **Buckslip** to **4" wide × 6" high**.

3. Resize the **two business cards** to **3.5" × 2"**.

4. Click the **Letterhead artboard**, click the **Select Preset menu** on the Control panel, then click **Letter**.

   The artboard is resized to 8.5" × 11".

5. Click and drag the **artboards** to arrange them as shown in Figure 54.

6. Click the **Selection tool** 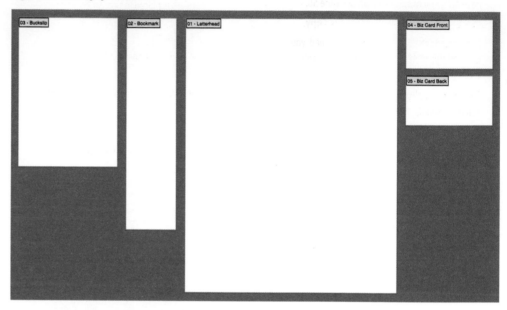 to escape edit artboards mode, then save your work.

7. Continue to the next set of steps.

You resized, renamed, and arranged artboards.

Paste artwork on multiple artboards

1. Open the file named Winning Logo.ai.

2. Click **Select** on the menu bar, click **All**, click **Edit** on the menu bar, then click **Copy.**

3. Close Winning Logo.ai.

4. In the Winning Business Collateral document, click the **Artboard Navigation menu list arrow** in the lower-left corner of the document window, as shown in Figure 55, then click **1 Letterhead**.

   The Letterhead artboard is centered in the window.

TIP The Artboard Navigation menu list arrow is at the lower-left corner of the document window.

Figure 54 Rearranging the artboards

Figure 55 Choosing 1 Letterhead from the Artboard Navigation menu

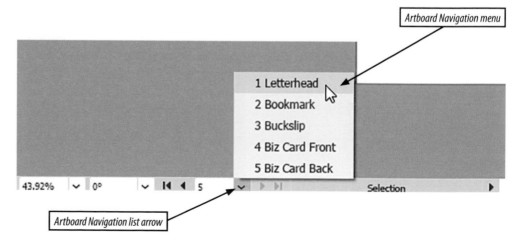

5. Click **Edit** on the menu bar, click **Paste**, then position the artwork as shown in Figure 56.

6. Click **Edit** on the menu bar, then click **Copy**.

   Even though the artwork is already copied, you need to copy it again so it is copied from this specific location.

7. Click the **Buckslip artboard** to make it the active artboard.

8. Click **Edit** on the menu bar, then click **Paste in Place**.

   The artwork is placed in the same location, relative to the top-left corner of the artboard, on the Buckslip artboard.

9. Click **Edit** on the menu bar, then click **Undo Paste in Place**.

10. Click **Edit** on the menu bar, then click **Paste on All Artboards**.

11. Click **View**, click **Fit All in Window**, then compare your screen to Figure 57.

12. Save and close the Winning Business Collateral document.

You copied artwork, then pasted it in a specific location on one artboard. You used the Paste in Place command to paste the artwork in the same location on another artboard. You then used the Paste on All Artboards command to paste the artwork on all artboards.

Figure 56 Positioning the logo

Figure 57 Artwork pasted on all artboards

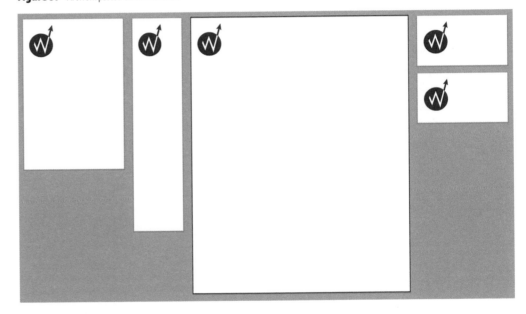

Explore the Illustrator workspace

1. Click File on the menu bar, click Open, navigate to the drive and folder where your Chapter 1 Data Files are stored, click AI 1-5.ai, then click Open.
2. Click Window on the menu bar, point to Workspace, then click Essentials.
3. Click the double arrows on the toolbar to see two setups for the toolbar.
4. Point to the Type tool, then press and hold the mouse button to see the Type on a Path tool.
5. View the hidden tools behind the other tools with small black triangles.
6. Click Illustrator (Mac) or Edit (Win) on the menu bar, point to Preferences, click General, verify that Show Tool Tips is checked, then click OK.
7. Position your mouse pointer over the Direct Selection tool until its tool tip appears.
8. Click the Selection tool, then press the following keys and note which tools are selected with each key: [P], [V], [T], [I], [H], [Z], [A].
9. Press [tab] to temporarily hide all open panels, then press [tab] again.
10. Click the Color panel icon in the stack of collapsed panels to the right of the pasteboard to open the Color panel.
11. Click the Collapse panels button at the top of the panel to minimize the panel, then click Color to open the panel again.
12. Drag the Color panel name tab to the left so it is ungrouped.

13. Click the Swatches panel icon in the stack of collapsed panels to the right of the pasteboard to open the Swatches panel.
14. Drag the Swatches panel name tab to the left so it is ungrouped.
15. Drag the Swatches panel name tab to the blank space next to the Color panel name tab, then release the mouse button.
16. Click Window on the menu bar, then click Info.
17. Drag the Info panel name tab to the bottom edge of the Color and Swatches panels group until you see a blue horizontal line appear, then release the mouse button to dock the Info panel.
18. Click and drag the dark gray bar at the top of the panel group, found above the Color and Swatches panel name tabs, to move the docked panels.
19. Click the Info panel name tab, then drag it away from the other two panels.
20. Click Window on the menu bar, point to Workspace, then click Reset Essentials.
21. Press the letter [Z] on your keypad to access the Zoom tool.
22. Position the Zoom tool over the document window, click twice to enlarge it, press [option] (Mac) or [Alt] (Win), then click twice to reduce the document.
23. Click the Zoom Level list arrow in the lower-left corner of the document window, then click 600%.
24. Note that 600% is now listed in the document tab.
25. Double-click 600% in the Zoom Level text box, type **300**, then press [return] (Mac) or [Enter] (Win).
26. Click the Hand tool on the toolbar, then click and drag the document window to scroll.

27. Double-click the Zoom tool.
28. Click the Selection tool, point to the center of the document window, then press and hold [command] [space bar] (Mac) or [Ctrl] [space bar] (Win).
29. Click three times, then release [command] [space bar] (Mac) or [Ctrl] [space bar] (Win).
30. Press and hold [space bar] to access the Hand tool, then scroll around the image.
31. Press and hold [command] [option] [space bar] (Mac) or [Ctrl] [Alt] [space bar] (Win), then click the artboard multiple times to reduce the view to 25%.

View and modify artboard elements

1. Click View on the menu bar, then click Fit Page in Window.
2. Click View on the menu bar, then note the Rulers command and its shortcut key.
3. Leave the View menu, then press [command] [R] (Mac) or [Ctrl] [R] (Win) several times to hide and show rulers, finishing with rulers showing.
4. Note the units on the rulers.
5. Click Illustrator (Mac) or Edit (Win) on the menu bar, point to Preferences, then click Units.
6. Click the General list arrow to see the available measurement options, then click Picas.
7. Click OK.
8. Reopen the Units Preferences dialog box, click the General list arrow, then click Inches.
9. Click OK.
10. Select all the objects on the artboard.
11. Click View on the menu bar, then note the Hide/Show Edges command and its shortcut key.

12. Leave the View menu, then press [command] [H] (Mac) or [Ctrl] [H] (Win) several times to switch between hiding and showing selection marks, finishing with selection marks showing.

13. Click the View menu, point to Guides, then note the Guides commands and their shortcut keys.

14. Escape the View menu, then press [command] [;] (Mac) or [Ctrl] [;] (Win) several times to hide and show guides, finishing with guides showing.

15. Click View on the menu bar, then click Show Grid.

16. Press [command] ["] (Mac) or [Ctrl] ["] (Win) several times to hide and show the grid.

17. Hide guides and the grid.

18. Click View on the menu bar, then note the quick key command for Outline mode.

19. Enter [command] [Y] (Mac) or [Ctrl] [Y] (Win) repeatedly to toggle between Outline and Preview modes, finishing in Preview mode, as shown in Figure 58.

20. Click Illustrator (Mac) or Edit (Win) on the menu bar, point to Preferences, then click User Interface.

21. Verify that the Open Documents As Tabs check box is checked, then click OK.

22. Save AI 1-5.ai as **Tiger**.

23. Open AI 1-2.ai, then click the tabs of each document several times to toggle between them, finishing with Tiger.ai as the active document.

24. Drag the Tiger.ai tab straight down approximately ½ inch.

25. Position your mouse pointer over the upper-right or bottom-right corner of the document, then click and drag toward the center of the monitor window to reduce the window to approximately half its size.

Figure 58 Skills Review, Part 1

26. Position your mouse pointer over the title bar of the document, then click and drag to move Tiger.ai halfway down toward the bottom of your monitor.

27. Position your mouse pointer over the title bar of Tiger.ai, click and drag to position it at the top of the window beside the AI 1-2.ai tab, then release the mouse button when you see a horizontal blue bar.

28. Close AI 1-2.ai without saving changes if you are prompted.

29. Close Tiger.ai without saving changes if you are prompted.

Shutterstock/Bibadash

(continued)

Work with objects and smart guides.

1. Open AI 1-6.ai, then save it as **Object Skills**.
2. Click View on the menu bar, then verify that the Bounding Box command is set to Show Bounding Box.
3. Click the Selection tool, then click the yellow square to select it.
4. Click View on the menu bar, then click Show Bounding Box.
5. Click and drag various handles, and note how the object is resized.
6. When you are done experimenting, undo all the moves you made.
7. Click to select the purple circle.
8. Press and hold down [option] (Mac) or [Alt] (Win), then start dragging any corner handle.
9. While still dragging, press and hold [shift].
10. Scale the circle to any size.
11. Undo the move.
12. Select all.
13. Using the skills you learned in this lesson, reduce the size of the objects in proportion so they are much smaller on the artboard, then click the artboard to deselect the objects.
14. Click File on the menu bar, click Revert, then click Revert when you are prompted to confirm.
15. Click View on the menu bar, then click Hide Bounding Box.
16. Select the star, then copy it, using the [command] [C] (Mac) or [Ctrl] [C] (Win) shortcut keys.
17. Click Edit on the menu bar, then click Paste to place a copy of the star at the center of the artboard.

18. Undo the paste.
19. Click Edit on the menu bar, then click Paste in Front.
20. Press the letter [I] on your keypad to switch to the Eyedropper tool, then click the yellow square.
21. Press the right arrow key on your keypad 10 times.
22. Deselect all, click Edit on the menu bar, then click Paste in Back.
23. Click the Eyedropper tool on the purple circle.
24. Press and hold [shift], then press the ⬅ on your keypad one time.
25. Press and hold [command] (Mac) or [Ctrl] (Win) so your cursor switches temporarily from the Eyedropper tool to the Selection tool, then click the artboard with the Selection tool to deselect all.

26. Click the Selection tool, then select the purple circle.
27. Press and hold [option] (Mac) or [Alt] (Win), then drag a copy of the circle to the center of the square. Your screen should resemble Figure 59.
28. Save your work, then close the file.
29. Open AI 1-7.ai, then save it as **Group Skills**.
30. Click Object on the menu bar, then click Show All.
31. Click Object on the menu bar, then click Group.
32. Click the Selection tool, click anywhere on the pasteboard to deselect all, then click the largest blue square.
33. Click the pasteboard to deselect all, click the Direct Selection tool, then click the same square.

Figure 59 Skills Review, Part 2

34. Select all, click Object on the menu bar, then click Ungroup.
35. Deselect all.
36. Click the Selection tool, select the smallest square, click Object on the menu bar, click Lock, then click Selection.
37. Click Object on the menu bar, then click Unlock All.
38. Select the three blue squares, click Object on the menu bar, then click Hide.
39. Click Object on the menu bar, then click Show All.
40. Click View on the menu bar, then verify that Smart Guides is checked.
41. Click the large blue square, then drag it by its center point toward the center of the artboard.
42. Release the mouse button when the word center appears.

43. Using the same steps, align all the squares so that your artboard resembles Figure 60.
44. Save your work and close the file.

Create and basic shapes and apply color.

1. Open AI 1-8.ai, then save it as **Flag**.
2. Select the black rectangle, then change its fill to a dark blue swatch on the Swatches panel.
3. Select the gray rectangle, then change its fill to a light blue swatch.
4. Select the two blue rectangles, press and hold [option] (Mac) or [Alt] (Win), then drag copies of the squares immediately above them.

5. Select all four squares, copy them, click Edit on the menu bar, then click Paste in Front.
6. Drag the new squares immediately to the right of the existing four squares.
7. With the four new squares still selected, double-click the Reflect tool, click the Horizontal option button, click Copy, then deselect the squares.
   Your artboard should resemble Figure 61.
8. Save your work.

Make direct selections.

1. Select the four light blue squares, then lock them.
2. Click the Direct Selection tool.

Figure 60 Skills Review, Part 3

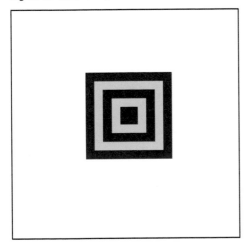

Figure 61 Positioning four squares

3. Select only the top-right corner of the top-left dark blue rectangle, then drag the point straight up to the top edge of the artboard.

4. Select only the bottom-left corner of the bottom-right dark blue rectangle, then drag the point straight down to the bottom edge of the artboard.

Your artboard should resemble Figure 62.

5. Save your work.

Stroke and transform shapes

1. Click the Rectangle tool, click the artboard to open its dialog box, then create a rectangle that is 2.5" × 2.5".

2. Center the rectangle on the artboard.

3. Apply a None  fill to the rectangle and a 2 pt. black stroke.

4. Double-click the Rotate tool to open its dialog box, type **12** in the Angle text box, then click Copy.

5. Enter [command] [D] (Mac) or [Ctrl] [D] (Win) 13 times to repeat the transformation 13 times.

6. Select all of the black rectangles, click Object on the menu bar, then click Group.

7. Deselect all, then set the fill color to the dark blue color and the stroke color to None.

8. Click the Ellipse tool, then position the crosshair exactly at the center of the artboard.

9. Press and hold [option] (Mac) or [Alt] (Win), begin dragging out an ellipse from its center, add the [shift] key to constrain it to a perfect circle, then size the circle so that extends out to the exact edge of the shape created by the rectangles.

10. Change the stacking order so the dark blue circle is behind all the black rectangles.

Your artboard should resemble Figure 63.

11. Save your work, then close Flag.ai.

Figure 62 Changing the shape of two rectangles

Figure 63 The final flag artwork

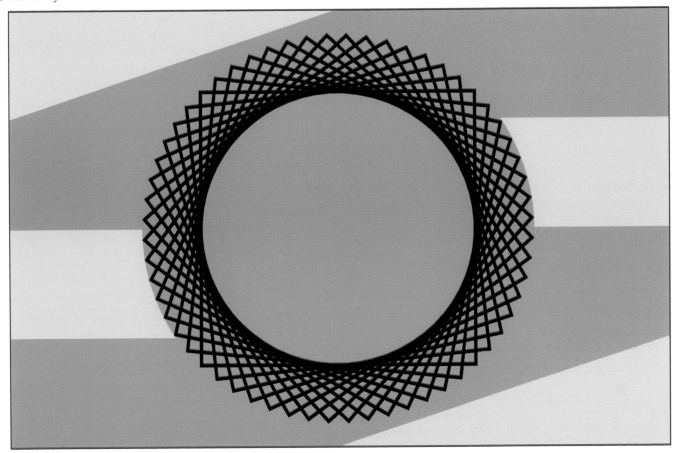

(continued)

Work with multiple artboards.

1. Open AI 1-9. ai, then save it as **Artboard Skills**.
2. Click the Artboard tool.
3. Click the New Artboard button on the Control panel.
4. Float your cursor over the artboard, then position the new artboard to the right of the original.
5. Scroll to the right of the newest artboard.
6. Click and drag with the Artboard tool to create a new artboard of any size to the right of the new artboard.
7. Click the original artboard and name it **Stationery**.
8. Type **8** in the W Value (width) text box on the Control panel, type **10** in the H Value (height) text box, then press [return] (Mac) or [Enter] (Win).
9. Name the second artboard **Envelope**, then resize it to 9" wide × 3" high.
10. Name the third artboard **Business Card**, then resize it to 3.5" × 2".
11. Click View on the menu bar, then click Fit All in Window.
12. Click and drag the artboards to arrange them as shown in Figure 64.
13. Save your work, then close the Artboard Skills document.

Figure 64 Completed Skills Review

This project builder will reinforce making stars and using the Direct Selection tool to modify basic shapes. Rather than work with a conventionally shaped star, you will create something original. This exercise is also very instructive for using copies as shadows and overlapping fills in a way that creates the look of one object from many. If you like, you can imagine that the exercise is for a logo for a restaurant.

1. Open AI 1-10.ai, then save it as **Window Sign**.
2. Click the Direct Selection tool, then click the edge of the star.
3. Move two of the outer anchor points of the star farther from its center.
4. Move four of the inner points toward the center.
5. Select the entire star.
6. Reflect a copy of the star across the horizontal axis.
7. Fill the new star with an orange swatch, and reposition it to your liking.
8. Group the two stars.
9. Copy the group, then paste in back.
10. Fill the copies with black.
11. Using your arrow keys, move the black copies five increments to the right and five increments down.
12. Select only the orange star using the Direct Selection tool.
13. Copy the orange star, then paste in back.
14. Fill the new copy with black.
15. Rotate the black copy 8°.
16. Apply a yellow fill to the orange star, then apply a 1 pt. black stroke to both yellow stars.
17. Remove the black stroke from the front-most star.
18. Save your work, then compare your illustration to Figure 65 on the following page.
    What's interesting about the result is that there's a black shadow between the two yellow stars. You would expect both black stars to be behind the two yellow stars, performing the role of shadows. In that case, the two yellow stars would overlap in a way that they would appear as a single star. In this case, the black star between them is unexpected and creates a more complex effect for the illustration.
19. Close the Window Sign document.

PROJECT BUILDER 2

This is a great exercise with a stunning result that shows the power of executing multiple transformations and, in this case, alternating colors. You can imagine that this result would make for a great illustration for an optometrist or any entity that works with eyes or with vision.

1. Create a new document that is 6" × 6".
2. Save the document as **Iris Vision Design**.
3. Create an ellipse that is 1" wide × 4" in height, and position it at the center of the artboard.
4. Fill the ellipse with [None] and add a 1 pt. blue stroke.
5. Create a copy of the ellipse rotated at 15°.
6. Apply the Transform Again command 10 times.
7. Select all and group the ellipses.
8. Create a copy of the group rotated at 5°.
9. Apply a red stroke to the new group.
10. Transform again one time.
11. Apply a bright blue stroke to the new group.
12. Select all.
13. Rotate a copy of the ellipses 2.5°.
14. Create a circle that is 2" × 2".
15. Fill the circle with black, and give it no stroke.
16. Position the black-filled circle in the center of the ellipses.
17. Cut the circle.
18. Select all.
19. Paste in back.
20. Save your work, then compare your illustration to Figure 66.
21. Close the Iris Vision Design document.

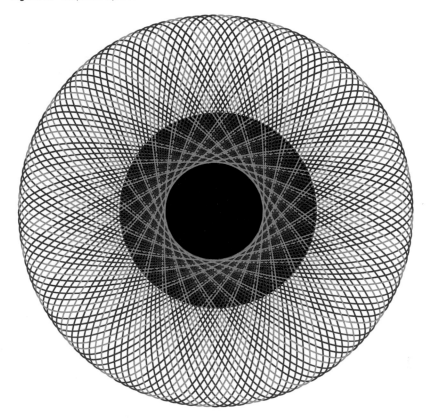

Figure 66 Completed Project Builder 2

The owner of Emerald Design Studios has hired you to design an original logo for her new company. She's a beginner with Illustrator, but has created a simple illustration of what she has in mind. She tells you to create something "more sophisticated." The only other information she offers about her company is that they plan to specialize in precise, geometric design.

1. Open AI 1-11.ai, then save it as **Emerald Logo**.
2. Select all four diamonds and group them.
3. Use the Scale tool to create a copy at 75%.
4. Use the Transform Again command five times.
5. Use smart guides or Outline mode to help you identify each of the seven groups.
   Smart guides will appear as you mouse over each group. Outline mode will show you the black outlines of all seven groups.
6. Rotate all the groups in relation to one another so that no two groups are on the same angle.
7. Apply a dark green stroke to all groups.
   Figure 67 shows one possible result of multiple transformations. Your illustration may differ.
8. Save your work, then close the Emerald Logo document.

Figure 67 One result for the Design Project

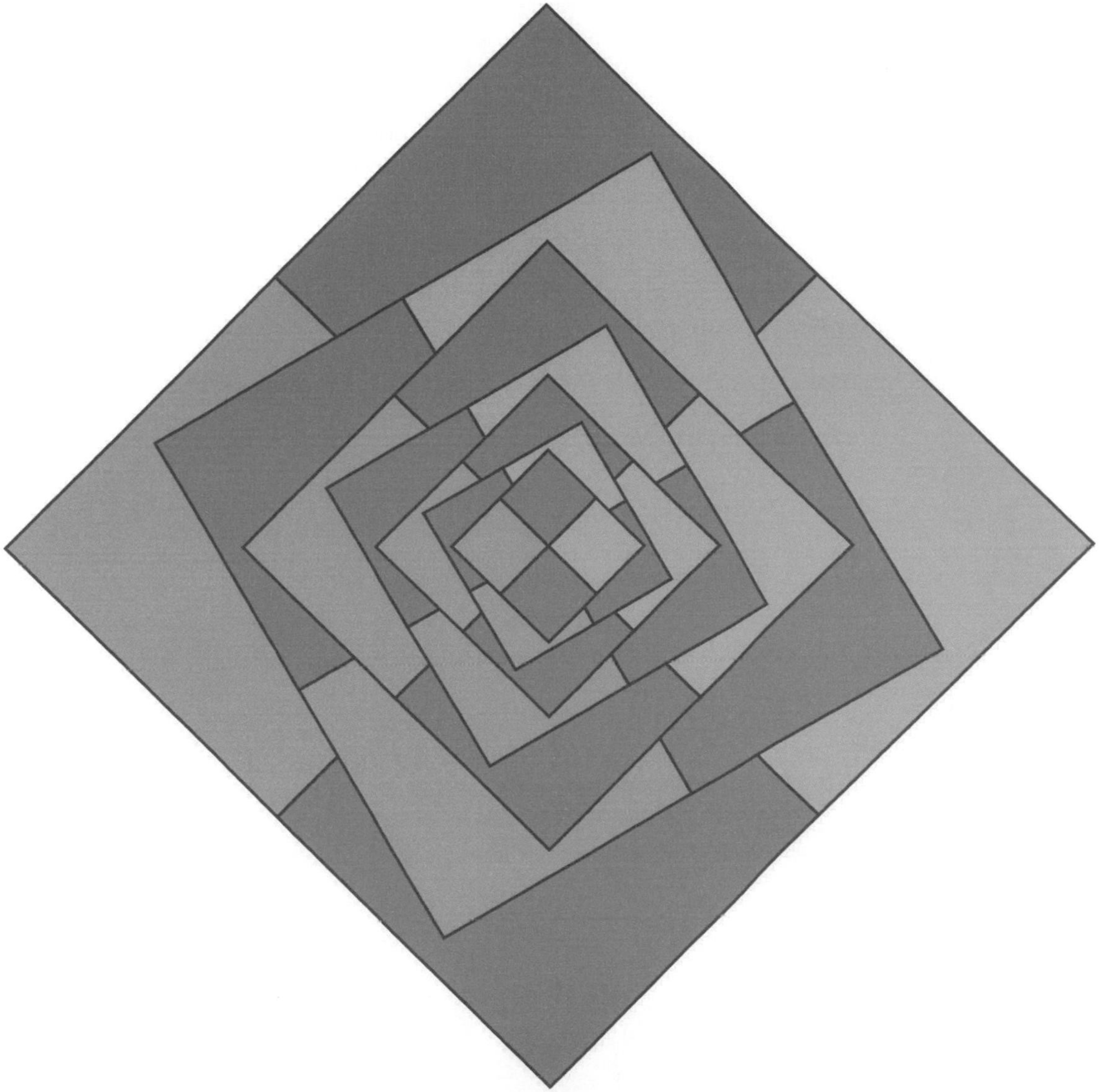

CHAPTER 2

CREATING TEXT AND GRADIENTS

1. Create Point Text
2. Flow Text into an Object
3. Position Text on a Path
4. Manipulate Text with the Touch Type Tool
5. Create Gradients
6. Adjust Gradients in Text and Objects
7. Apply Gradients to Strokes

Adobe Certified Professional in Graphic Design and Illustration Using Adobe Illustrator

1. Working in the Design Industry

This objective covers critical concepts related to working with colleagues and clients, as well as crucial legal, technical, and design-related knowledge.

1.5 Demonstrate knowledge of basic design principles and best practices employed in the design industry.
    B Identify and use common typographic adjustments to create contrast, hierarchy, and enhanced readability/legibility.

2. Project Setup and Interface

This objective covers the interface setup and program settings that assist in an efficient and effective workflow, as well as knowledge about ingesting digital assets for a project.

2.2 Navigate, organize, and customize the application workspace.
    C Configure application preferences.
2.4 Manage assets in a project.
    B Place assets in an Illustrator document.
2.5 Manage colors, swatches, and gradients.
    B Create and customize gradients.
    C Create, manage, and edit swatches and swatch libraries.

4. Creating and Modifying Visual Elements

This objective covers core tools and functionality of the application, as well as tools that affect the visual appearance of document elements.

4.2 Add and manipulate text using appropriate typographic settings.
    A Use type tools to add typography.
    B Use appropriate character settings.
    C Use appropriate paragraph settings.
    D Convert text to graphics.
    E Manage text flow.

CREATE POINT TEXT

▶ What You'll Do

In this lesson, you will use the Type tool to create the word BERRY as display text. You will use the Character panel to format the text and perfect its appearance. You will also create a vertical version of the text.

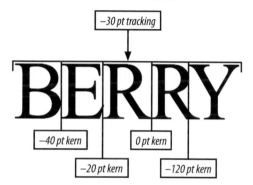

Creating Text

You can create text anywhere on the artboard. Select the Type tool, click the artboard, then begin typing. You can enter text horizontally or vertically. The ability to type vertically is rather unusual; most text-based applications don't offer this option.

Text generated by the Type tool is positioned on a path called the **baseline**. You can select text by clicking anywhere on the text or by clicking on the baseline, depending on how your Type preferences are set.

Formatting Text

The Character and Paragraph panels neatly contain all of the classic commands for formatting text. Use the Character panel to modify text attributes such as font and type size, tracking, and kerning. You can adjust the **leading**, which is the vertical space between baselines, or apply a horizontal or vertical scale, which compresses or expands selected type, as shown in Figure 1. The Paragraph panel applies itself to more global concerns, such as text alignment, paragraph indents, and vertical spaces between paragraphs.

Figure 1 Examples of text formatting

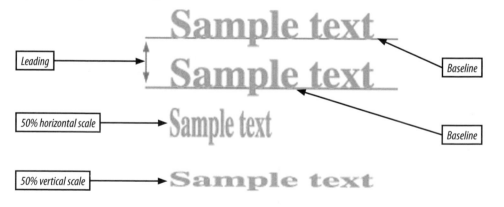

Tracking and kerning are essential, but often overlooked, typographic operations. **Tracking** inserts uniform spaces between characters to affect the width of selected words or entire blocks of text. **Kerning** is used to affect the space between any two characters and is particularly useful for improving the appearance of headlines and other display text. Positive tracking or kerning values move characters farther apart; negative values move them closer together.

Illustrator can track and kern type down to 1/1000 of a standard em space. The width of an em space is dependent on the current type size. In a 1-point font, the em space is 1 point. In a 10-point font, the em space is 10 points. With kerning units that are 1/1000 of an em, Illustrator can manipulate a 10-point font at increments of 1/100 of 1 point! Figure 2 shows examples of kerning and tracking values.

Figure 2 Examples of kerning and tracking

kern

−30/1000

kern

0/1000

kern

30/1000

staying on **track**

−30/1000

staying on **track**

0/1000

staying on **track**

30/1000

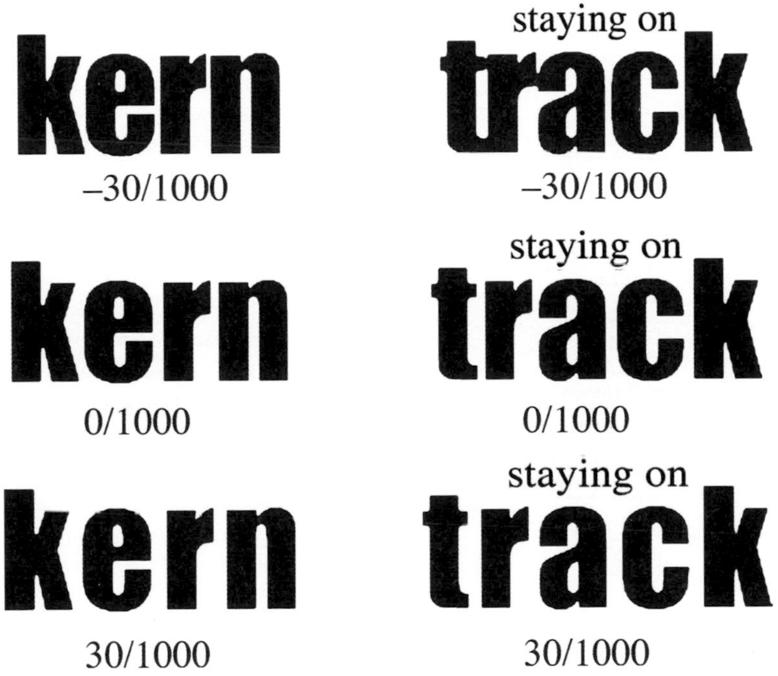

Adjusting and Applying Hyphenation

When working with large blocks of text, you can decide whether or not you want to hyphenate the text. Illustrator has a Preferences panel dedicated to hyphenation. Click Illustrator (Mac) or Edit (Win) on the menu bar, point to Preferences, then click Hyphenation. Hyphenation in Illustrator is applied automatically based on the language dictionary that is in use. You can turn automatic hyphenation on and off or change the hyphenation default settings in the Hyphenation dialog box. To access the Hyphenation dialog box, click the Paragraph panel menu button, then click Hyphenation. To turn hyphenation off, remove the check mark in the Hyphenation check box.

Hiding Objects While Working with Text

Two factors that make selecting text and other objects difficult are the number and proximity of objects in the document. When you have many objects positioned closely together, selecting an individual object can sometimes be tricky.

Hiding objects is a simple way to avoid this problem, just don't forget they are there—they won't print if they are hidden.

The Hide Selection command is on the Object menu—as is the Show All command, which reveals all hidden objects. When hidden objects are revealed, they are all selected.

Create text

1. Open AI 2-1.ai, then save it as **Berry**.

2. Click **View** on the menu bar, then click **Hide Bounding Box** if the bounding box is showing.

   If the bounding box is already hidden, you won't see the Hide Bounding Box command.

3. Click the **Type tool** T , then click **anywhere on the artboard**.

   When you click, type is created. The type is 12 pt. by default and is selected, so you can type over it.

4. Type **BERRY** using all capital letters.

   The word BERRY will be interesting for you to work with because the letter combinations will require you to kern them in relation to one another.

TIP By default, new text is generated with a black fill and no stroke. Text you create by clicking the artboard is called point text.

5. Click the **Selection tool** , then drag the **text** to the center of the artboard.

TIP Verify that Smart Guides are not activated.

6. Click **Window** on the menu bar, point to **Type**, then click **Character** to show the Character panel.

7. Click the **Character panel menu button** ≡ , then click **Show Options** to view the entire panel as shown in Figure 3.

8. Save your work, then continue to the next set of steps.

You used the Type tool to create the word BERRY, showed the Character panel, then expanded the view of the Character panel.

Figure 3 Character panel with all options showing

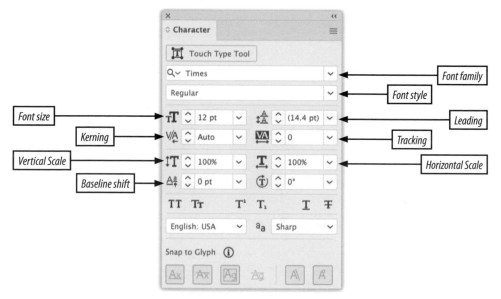

TRACKING AND KERNING

Typography, the art of designing letterforms, has a long and rich history that extends back to the Middle Ages. With the advent of desktop publishing in the mid-1980s, many conventional typographers and typesetters declared "the death of typography." They claimed that unskilled computer users would be careless with type and that computers would reduce typography to ugly, bitmap fonts. More optimistic mindsets have since prevailed. The personal computer and software, such as Adobe Illustrator, have made available libraries of typefaces that are far more extensive than what has ever been available before. Contrast this with the days when the typewriter ruled, with its single typeface and two point sizes as the standard for literally millions of documents, and you get a sense of the typographic revolution that has occurred in the last 30 years.

Many designers are so eager to tackle the "artwork" that they often overlook the type design in an illustration. Tracking and kerning, which are the manipulation of space between words and letters, are essential elements to good type design and are often woefully ignored.

Illustrator's precise tracking and kerning abilities are of no use if they are ignored. One good way of maintaining awareness of your tracking and kerning duties is to take note of others' oversights. Make it a point to notice tracking and kerning, or the lack thereof, when you look at magazines, posters, and especially billboards. You'll be amazed at what you'll see.

Format text

1. On the Character panel, click the **Font family list arrow**, point to **Times New Roman** or a similar font, then click **Regular** from the Font style list arrow.

2. Click the **Font size text box** 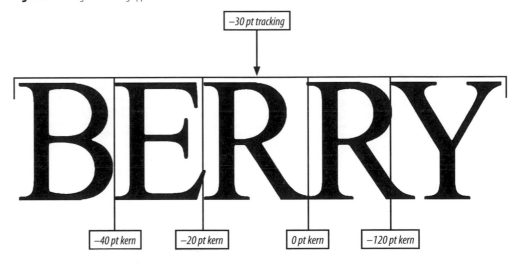, type **142**, then press **[return] (Mac) or [Enter] (Win)**.

3. Click the **Horizontal Scale text box** , type **90**, then press **[return] (Mac) or [Enter] (Win)**.

4. Deselect the text.

5. Save your work, then continue to the next set of steps.

You used the Character panel to modify the font, font size, and horizontal scaling of the word BERRY.

Track and kern text

1. Compare your text to Figure 4.

   The spatial relationships between the letters are inconsistent and challenging. The two Rs are the only two letters that are almost touching. The E is closer to the first R than it is to the B, and the Y is too far away from the second R.

2. Select the **text** with the **Selection tool** .

3. On the Character panel, enter **–30** in the **Tracking text box** .

4. Click the **Type tool** , then click **between the B and the E**.

5. On the Character panel, click the **up and down arrows** in the **Kerning text box** to experiment with higher and lower kerning values, then change the Kerning value to **–40**.

6. Using Figure 5 as a guide, change the Kerning values to **–20**, **0**, and **–120** between the next three letter pairs.

   The two Rs are kerned so they are touching. When two letters touch in this way, it is called a **ligature** in typography lingo.

Continued on next page

Figure 4 Formatted text

BERRY

Figure 5 Kerning and tracking applied to text

–30 pt tracking

BERRY

–40 pt kern   *–20 pt kern*   *0 pt kern*   *–120 pt kern*

7. Click the **Selection tool**, open the **Paragraph panel**, then click the **Align center button**, as shown in Figure 6.

   When text is center aligned, its anchor point is centered on its baseline. This can be handy for aligning its center with the center of other objects.

8. Click **Object** on the menu bar, point to **Hide**, then click **Selection**.

9. Save your work, then continue to the next set of steps.

You used the Character panel to change the tracking of the word BERRY, then you entered different Kerning values to affect the spacing between the four letter pairs. You center-aligned the text, then hid the text.

Create vertical type

1. Click the **Vertical Type tool**, then click **anywhere on the artboard**.

   TIP The Vertical Type tool is hidden beneath the Type tool.

Align center button

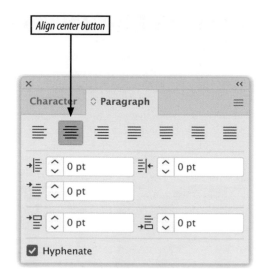

Figure 6 Paragraph panel

2. Type the word **BERRY** using all capital letters.

   TIP The Type tools retain the formatting attributes that were previously chosen. Therefore, the new text has the same Tracking value of −30, and the Horizontal Scale is set to 90%.

3. Click the **Selection tool**, select the **text**, then move it to the center of the artboard.

   TIP When any tool other than the Selection tool is selected on the toolbar you can press [command] (Mac) or [Ctrl] (Win) to switch to the Selection tool. When you release [command] (Mac) or [Ctrl] (Win), the last chosen tool will be active again.

4. Change the **font size** to **84 pt**.

5. Change the **Tracking value** to **−160**.

6. Verify that both the **Horizontal** and **Vertical Scales** are set to **100%**, then deselect the text.

Your screen should resemble Figure 7.

7. Save your work, then close the Berry document.

You used the Vertical Type tool to create a vertical alternative to the first word you typed. You adjusted the tracking to better suit a vertical orientation.

Figure 7 Vertical text

FLOW TEXT INTO AN OBJECT

▶ *What You'll Do*

In this lesson, you will explore options for formatting text flowed into objects.

Filling an Object with Text

Using the Area Type tool, you can flow text into any shape you can create, from circles to birds to bumblebees! Text in an object can be formatted as you would format text in a basic rectangular box. You can change such attributes as fonts, font size, and alignment, and the text will reflow in the object as you format it. Text that you create inside an object is called **area text**.

Figure 8 shows an example of an object filled with text. Note the blue background in the figure. When you first flow text into an object using the Area Type tool, the object loses any fill or stroke color applied to it. However, you can add different colors to the object and the text after you enter the text. When you select the object with the Selection tool, any fill or stroke you choose will be applied to the text. When you select the object with the Direct Selection tool, the fill or stroke will be applied to the object.

Figure 8 An object filled with text

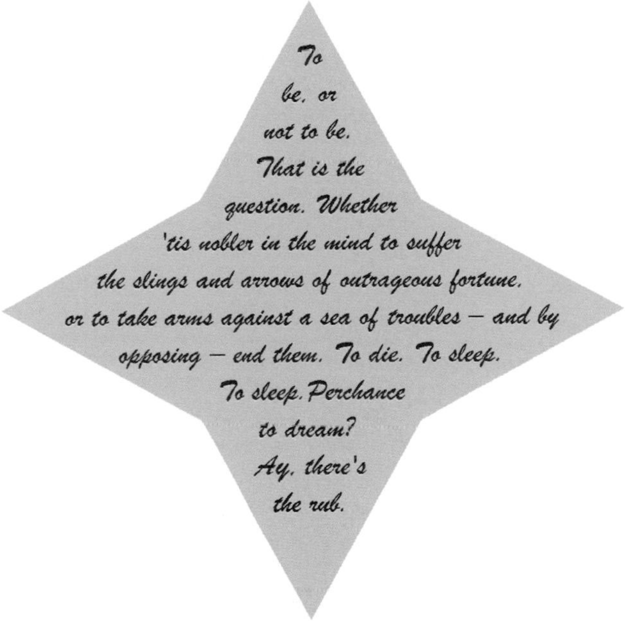

After the text is flowed into the object, you can use the Direct Selection tool to modify the object; the text will reflow within the modified shape.

You'll often find that centering text in an object is the best visual solution. Figure 9 shows text aligned left and flowed into an odd-shaped object. In Figure 10, the same text is centered and fills the object in a way that is more visually pleasing.

TIP You can underline text and strike through text using the Underline and Strikethrough buttons at the bottom of the Character panel.

Figure 9 Text aligned left

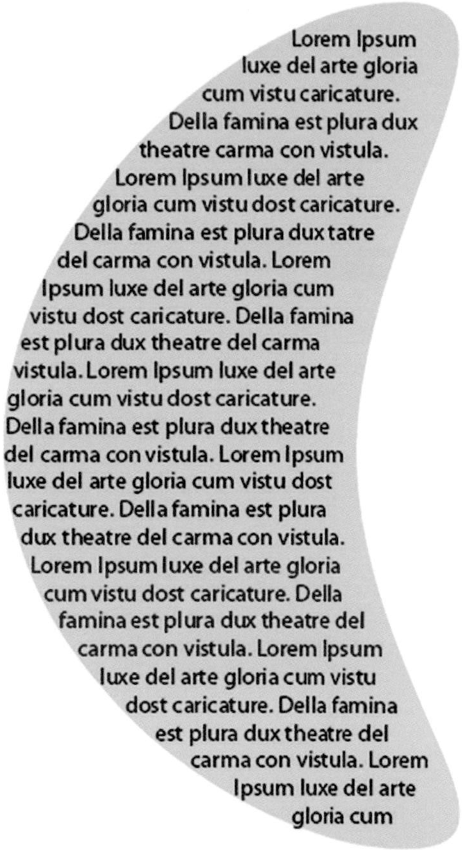

Lorem Ipsum
luxe del arte gloria
cum vistu caricature.
Della famina est plura dux
theatre carma con vistula.
Lorem Ipsum luxe del arte
gloria cum vistu dost caricature.
Della famina est plura dux tatre
del carma con vistula. Lorem
Ipsum luxe del arte gloria cum
vistu dost caricature. Della famina
est plura dux theatre del carma
vistula. Lorem Ipsum luxe del arte
gloria cum vistu dost caricature.
Della famina est plura dux theatre
del carma con vistula. Lorem Ipsum
luxe del arte gloria cum vistu dost
caricature. Della famina est plura
dux theatre del carma con vistula.
Lorem Ipsum luxe del arte gloria
cum vistu dost caricature. Della
famina est plura dux theatre del
carma con vistula. Lorem Ipsum
luxe del arte gloria cum vistu
dost caricature. Della famina
est plura dux theatre del
carma con vistula. Lorem
Ipsum luxe del arte
gloria cum

Figure 10 Text centered in the object

Lorem Ipsum
luxe del arte gloria
cum vistu caricature.
Della famina est plura dux
theatre carma con vistula.
Lorem Ipsum luxe del arte
gloria cum vistu dost caricature.
Della famina est plura dux tatre
del carma con vistula. Lorem
Ipsum luxe del arte gloria cum
vistu dost caricature. Della famina
est plura dux theatre del carma
vistula. Lorem Ipsum luxe del arte
gloria cum vistu dost caricature.
Della famina est plura dux theatre
del carma con vistula. Lorem Ipsum
luxe del arte gloria cum vistu dost
caricature. Della famina est plura
dux theatre del carma con vistula.
Lorem Ipsum luxe del arte gloria
cum vistu dost caricature. Della
famina est plura dux theatre del
carma con vistula. Lorem Ipsum
luxe del arte gloria cum vistu
dost caricature. Della famina
est plura dux theatre del
carma con vistula. Lorem
Ipsum luxe del arte
gloria cum

FORMATTING A STORY

You can use any of the shapes you create as text boxes, and you can thread, or flow, text from one object to another. When you add text to an object, it becomes a text object with an in port and an out port. To thread text, click the out port of an object that contains text; then click the in port of the object to which you want to thread the text. If the object isn't already defined as a text object, click on the path of the object.

You can also thread text by selecting an object that has type in it and then selecting the object or objects to which you want to thread the text. Click Type on the menu bar, point to Threaded Text, then click Create. You will see icons representing threads. To view threads, choose View on the menu bar, point to Show Text Threads, then select a linked object.

Fill a rectangle with text

1. Open AI 2-2.ai, then save it as **Newspaper Column**.

2. Open the file named Dummy text.ai.

3. Click the **Type tool** T , click anywhere in the text, then press **[command] [A] (Mac)** or **[Ctrl] [A] (Win)** to select all the text.

4. Copy the text, then close the Dummy text file.

5. In the Newspaper Column file, click the **Rectangle tool** .

6. Draw a **rectangle** that corresponds exactly to the blue guides.

   It doesn't matter if your rectangle has a fill or a stroke.

7. Click the **Area Type tool** .

8. Position the **Area Type tool** on the **top path of the rectangle**, then click.

   The rectangle automatically fills with dummy placeholder text that is selected and highlighted. It's important to understand that this is not the text you copied from the other file. It is default text that fills an object whenever you click the Area Type tool on the object.

TIP This default placeholder text feature is a preference that can be disabled. To do this, go to the Type Preferences dialog box, then disable the Fill New Type Objects With Placeholder Text option.

9. Click **Edit** on the menu bar, then click **Paste**.

   The text you copied replaces the default placeholder text.

10. Select all the **text**, then change the font to **Times New Roman** on the Character panel.

    If your computer doesn't have Times New Roman, use something similar.

11. Set the **font size** to **12**, then set the **leading** to **13.5**.

12. On the Paragraph panel, set the **Space after paragraph value** to **5 pt**.

13. Set the **First-line left indent** to **8 pt**.

14. Click the **Justify with last line aligned left button** .

    Your Paragraph panel should resemble Figure 11.

Continued on next page

Figure 11 Settings on the Paragraph panel

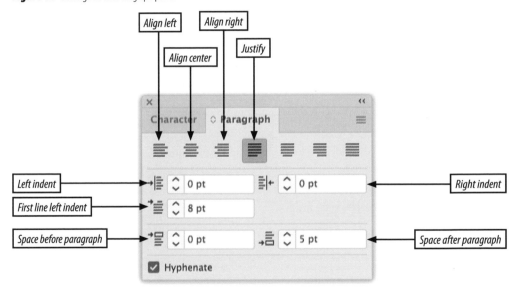

15. Deselect the text, hide guides, then compare your results to Figure 12.

TIP To hide guides, click View on the menu bar, point to Guides, then click Hide Guides.

16. Save your work, then close the Newspaper Column document.

You drew a rectangle, then used the Area Type tool to fill the rectangle with copied text. You used the Character and Paragraph panels to modify the text to fit the rectangle to the format of a traditional newspaper column.

Fill an irregular shaped object with text

1. Open AI 2-3.ai, then save it as **California**.

2. Open the file named Dummy text.ai, click the **Type tool** T , then click and drag to select only the **first two paragraphs**.

3. Copy the selected text, then close the Dummy text file.

4. Click the **Selection tool** , then click the **outline of California** to select it.

5. Click the **Area Type tool** .

6. Position the **Area Type tool** on the **top of the path**, then click.

The outline of the California graphic loses its black stroke.

7. Click **Edit** on the menu bar, then click **Paste**.

The copied text replaces the default placeholder text.

8. Select all the text.

9. On the Character panel, set the **font size** to **12**, then set the **leading** to **13**.

10. On the Paragraph panel, set the **Space after paragraph value** to **7 pt**.

11. Click the **Align center button** .

12. Set the **Left indent** and the **Right indent** to 8 pt.

13. Click the **type cursor** before the **letter S** in the first line of text.

14. Press **[return] (Mac)** or **[Enter] (Win)**.

15. Click the **Selection tool** , then click a **gold or yellow swatch** on the Swatches panel.

The text changes to the color you click.

16. Click the **artboard** to deselect.

17. Click the **Direct Selection tool** , then click the **edge of the outine of California**.

Since the object has no fill or stroke, you can't see the edge when it's not selected. You can guess where the edge is to select it, or you can switch to Outline mode to see it and select it.

18. Verify that the **fill color** is active on the toolbar, then click a **dark red swatch** on the Swatches panel.

19. Activate the **stroke color** on the toolbar, then apply a **black stroke** to the object.

20. Show the Stroke panel, then change the **Weight** to **3 pt**.

21. Deselect.

Figure 12 Newspaper column formatted

Newspaper headline goes here in 24 point bold text

by J. Q Reporter

Sed ut perspiciatis unde omnis iste natus error sit voluptatem accusantium doloremque laudantium, totam rem aperiam, eaque ipsa quae ab illo inventore veritatis et quasi architecto beatae vitae dicta sunt explicabo. Nemo enim ipsam voluptatem quia voluptas sit aspernatur aut odit aut fugit, sed quia consequuntur magni dolores eos qui ratione voluptatem sequi nesciunt. Neque porro quisquam est, qui dolorem ipsum quia dolor sit amet, consectetur, adipisci velit, sed quia non numquam eius modi tempora incidunt ut labore et dolore magnam aliquam quaerat voluptatem. Ut enim ad minima veniam, quis nostrum exercitationem ullam corporis suscipit laboriosam, nisi ut aliquid ex ea commodi consequatur? Quis autem vel eum iure reprehenderit qui in ea voluptate velit esse quam nihil molestiae consequatur, vel illum qui dolorem eum fugiat quo voluptas nulla pariatur?

At vero eos et accusamus et iusto odio dignissimos ducimus qui blanditiis praesentium voluptatum deleniti atque corrupti quos dolores et quas molestias excepturi sint occaecati cupiditate non provident, similique sunt in culpa qui officia deserunt mollitia animi, id est laborum et dolorum fuga. Et harum quidem rerum facilis est et expedita distinctio. Nam libero tempore, cum soluta nobis est eligendi optio cumque nihil impedit quo minus id quod maxime placeat facere possimus, omnis voluptas assumenda est, omnis dolor repellendus. Temporibus autem quibusdam et aut officiis debitis aut rerum necessitatibus saepe eveniet ut et voluptates sint et molestiae non recusandae. Itaque earum rerum hic tenetur a sapiente delectus, ut aut reiciendis voluptatibus maiores alias consequatur aut perferendis doloribus asperiores repellat.

Nemo enim ipsam voluptatem quia voluptas sit aspernatur aut odit aut fugit, sed quia consequuntur magni dolores eos qui ratione voluptatem sequi nesciunt. Neque porro quisquam est, qui dolorem ipsum quia dolor sit amet, consectetur, adipisci velit, sed quia non numquam eius modi tempora incidunt ut labore et dolore magnam aliquam quaerat voluptatem. Ut enim ad minima veniam, quis nostrum exercitationem ullam corporis suscipit laboriosam, nisi ut aliquid ex ea commodi consequatur? Temporibus autem quibusdam et aut officiis debitis aut rerum necessitatibus saepe eveniet ut et voluptates repudiandae sint et molestiae non recusandae.

22. Click the **Selection tool** ▶, click the **text** to select it, then click the **white swatch** on the Swatches panel.

Your artwork should resemble Figure 13.

23. Save your work, then close the California document.

You used the Area Type tool to paste text into an object the shape of the state of California. You used the Character and Paragraph panels to format the text to fit the object in a way that was most visually appealing. You then changed the color of the text and applied a fill and stroke to the object.

Figure 13 Completed California artwork

Sed ut perspiciatis unde omnis iste natus error sit voluptatem accusantium doloremque laudantium, totam rem aperiam, eaque ipsa quae ab illo inventore veritatis et quasi architecto beatae vitae dicta sunt explicabo. Nemo enim ipsam voluptatem quia voluptas sit aspernatur aut odit aut fugit, sed quia consequuntur magni dolores eos qui ratione voluptatem sequi nesciunt. Neque porro quisquam est, qui dolorem ipsum quia dolor sit amet, consectetur, adipisci velit, sed quia non numquam eius modi tempora incidunt ut labore et dolore magnam aliquam quaerat voluptatem. Ut enim ad minima veniam, quis nostrum exercitationem ullam corporis suscipit laboriosam, nisi ut aliquid ex ea commodi consequatur? Quis autem vel eum iure reprehenderit qui in ea voluptate velit esse quam nihil molestiae consequatur, vel illum qui dolorem eum fugiat quo voluptas nulla pariatur?

At vero eos et accusamus et iusto odio dignissimos ducimus qui blanditiis praesentium voluptatum deleniti atque corrupti quos dolores et quas molestias excepturi sint occaecati cupiditate non provident, similique sunt in culpa qui officia deserunt mollitia animi, id est laborum et dolorum fuga. Et harum quidem rerum facilis est et expedita distinctio. Nam libero tempore, cum soluta nobis est eligendi optio cumque nihil impedit quo minus id quod maxime placeat facere possimus, omnis voluptas assumenda est, omnis dolor repellendus. Temporibus autem quibusdam et aut officiis debitis aut rerum necessitatibus saepe eveniet ut et voluptates repudiandae sint et molestiae non recusandae. Itaque earum rerum hic tenetur a sapiente delectus, ut aut reiciendis voluptatibus maiores alias consequatur aut perferendis doloribus asperiores repellat.

CALIFORNIA

POSITION TEXT ON A PATH

▶ *What You'll Do*

In this lesson, you will explore the many options for positioning text on a path.

Using the Path Type Tools

Using the Type on a Path tool or the Vertical Type on a Path tool, you can type along a straight or curved path. This is the most compelling of Illustrator's text effects, and it opens up a world of possibilities for the designer and typographer.

You can move text along a path to position it where you want. You can "flip" the text to make it run in the opposite direction, on the opposite side of the path. You can also change the baseline shift to modify the distance of the text's baseline in relation to the path. A positive value "floats" the text above the path, and a negative value moves the text below the path. You can modify text on a path in the same way you would modify any other text element. Figure 14 shows an example of text on a path, whereas Figure 15 shows an example of text flipped across a path.

Figure 14 Text on a path

Figure 15 Text flipped across a path

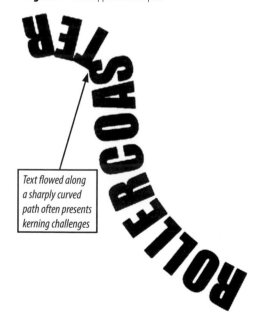

Text flowed along a sharply curved path often presents kerning challenges

Flow text on a path

1. Open AI 2-4.ai, then save it as **Type on a Path Intro**.

TIP Turn off the Bounding Box when you work with the Type tools.

2. Click the **Selection tool** ▶, then select the **path**.

3. Click the **Type on a Path tool** ✎, click the **path** close to the leftmost anchor point.

4. Type **ROLLERCOASTER** in all caps.

5. Click **the Selection tool** ▶, change the **typeface** to **Impact**, then change the **font size** to **22 pt**.

Three light blue brackets appear on the path, as shown in Figure 16. The brackets are used for dragging the text along the path. The left and right brackets represent the space in which the text is visible on the panel. In other words, the text can be visible on the path only in the space between the two outer brackets.

Continued on next page

Figure 16 Identifying the three brackets on the path

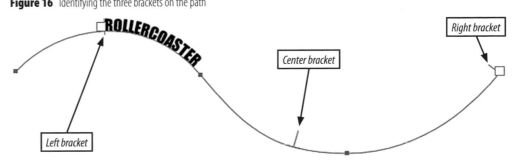

6. Click and drag the **left bracket** to the right to move the type along the entire path.

7. Click and drag the **left bracket** to the left to return the type to the beginning of the path.

8. On the Paragraph panel, click the **Align center button** ≡ .

   The center bracket indicates the center point between the two other brackets. The text is now centered at the center bracket.

9. Click and drag the **center bracket** down across the path so your text flips onto the other side of the path, as shown in Figure 17.

10. Click and drag the **left bracket** to the right to move the text along the bottom side of the path.

11. Click and drag the **left bracket** to the left to return the text to the center of the path.

12. Click and drag the **center bracket** across the path again so the text is once again positioned on the top of the path and reads right to left.

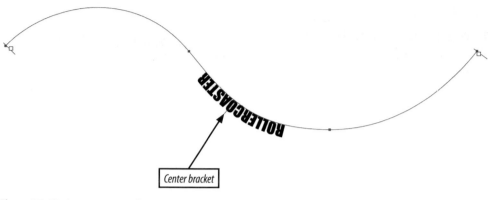

Center bracket

Figure 17 Flipping text across a path

13. On the Character panel, enter **–18** in the **baseline shift text box** A̲ᵃ̲ .

    The baseline shift value indicates the distance between the baseline of the text and the path. At a value of 0, the bottom of the text sits on the path. With a negative value, the text moves below the path. In this case, with a –18 baseline shift, the text is completely below the path.

14. Save your work, then close the Type on a Path Intro document.

You used the Type on a Path tool to type on a path. You formatted the text, then used the left bracket to move the type along the path. You used the center bracket to flip the type back and forth across the path. You then changed the baseline shift to move the text in relation to the path.

Flow text on a path

1. Open AI 2-5.ai, then save it as **Type on a Circle**.

2. Click the **Selection tool** ▶, select the **inner circle**, then copy it.

   You will paste the copy of the inner circle in a later step.

3. Select **both circles**, then **lock** them.

4. Enter **[command] [F] (Mac)** or **[Ctrl] [F] (Win)** to paste in front.

   The copied circle pastes in front the original. When you put type on a path, the path loses its fill and stroke. Therefore, you will place the type on this copied path.

5. Click the **Type on a Path tool** ⤳, position it at **10 o'clock on the small circle**, then click.

6. Type **MELROSE AVENUE** in all caps.

7. Click the **Align center button** ≡ on the Paragraph panel.

8. On the Character panel, set the **font** to **Impact**, set the **font size** to **45**, then verify that all other text boxes on the Character panel are set to their default settings (0 or 100%).

   As shown in Figure 18, the left and right brackets are very close together.

   Continued on next page

Figure 18 Preparing to drag handles

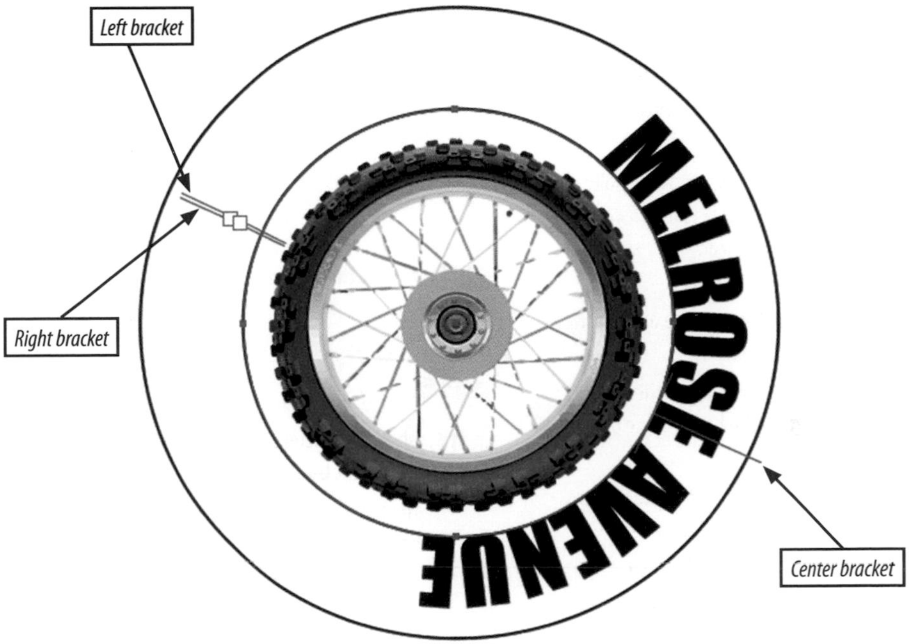

Left bracket

Right bracket

Center bracket

Shutterstock/dashadima

9. With the **Selection tool** ▶, position the **left bracket** and **right bracket** at **9 o'clock** and **3 o'clock**, respectively.

The text needs to be positioned vertically between the two circles.

10. On the Character panel, enter **7 pt**. in the baseline shift text box ⒜.

Your artwork should resemble Figure 19.

11. Click **Object** on the menu bar, then click **Lock**.

The path and the text on the path are locked.

12. Click **Edit** on the menu bar, then click **Paste in Front**.

A third circle is pasted. You will use this new circle to place the text at the bottom of the illustration.

13. Position the **left bracket** at **3 o'clock** and the **right bracket** at **9 o'clock**.

Your artwork should resemble Figure 20.

14. Drag the **center bracket** straight across the circle path so the type flips across the path. On the Character panel enter **–44** in the baseline shift text box, then enter **–140** in the tracking text box.

Because the baseline shift and tracking values are so extreme, the text requires kerning between the letter pairs in many instances. Particularly problematic is that the space between "MOTORCYCLE" and "SHOP" needs to be increased so they appear as two separate words.

15. Kern character pairs as you see fit to best improve the appearance of the text.

16. Click the **Rectangle tool** ▢, create a **small rectangle**, then rotate it to make a diamond shape positioned at **9 o'clock**.

TIP Rotate the rectangle using the Rotate tool ↻, or show the bounding box and rotate using a handle.

17. Create a copy of the **diamond**, position it at **3 o'clock**, then compare your results to Figure 21.

18. Save your work, then close the Type on a Circle document.

You created artwork with text wrapping over and under the same circle. You used two circles to achieve the effect—one for the text at the top and another for the text at the bottom. You changed the baseline shift to position the text vertically centered in the space between the two circles. You flipped the bottom text across the path so it reads left to right. You then adjusted the baseline shift, tracking, and kerning values to perfect its appearance.

Figure 19 Positioning the text on the circle

Figure 20 Text at the bottom is upside down

Figure 21 Final artwork

MANIPULATE TEXT WITH THE TOUCH TYPE TOOL

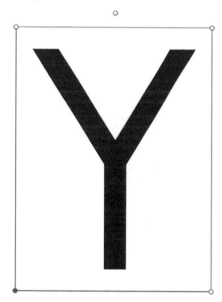

Using the Touch Type Tool

The Touch Type tool has the power to truly allow designers to do what they want do with type in Illustrator. Illustrator has long held the unofficial but widely accepted title of best application for designing and manipulating type—but, nevertheless, there were limitations. To best understand the benefits of the Touch Type tool, it helps first to examine those limitations.

Figure 22 shows the word "bounce" set in Illustrator text. Note by the selection marks that the word is a single object. If you wanted to manipulate the text to appear as shown in Figure 23, you'd have to use the Character panel and apply baseline shifts and rotations to each character. If you then wanted to manipulate the space between the characters, as shown in Figure 24, you'd need to kern each letter pair. Because of the tedious and time-consuming challenges of working with individual characters, many designers instead choose to set each character as a single object, as shown in Figure 25.

Figure 22 A single text object

Figure 23 Text characters manipulated individually

Figure 24 Kerning manipulated individually

Figure 25 A work-around; each character is an individual object

The Touch Type tool allows you to scale, rotate, and move each character in a type object independently of the other characters. Rather than have to input values in the Character panel, you can manipulate individual characters by hand, scaling and repositioning by hand. It is truly revolutionary to Illustrator.

Working with the Touch Type Tool

After you've typed a word, click the Touch Type tool, then click a letter. When you do, a rectangle with five points—one on each corner and one centered at the top—appears around the character. Clicking and dragging these five points, you can scale the character uniformly, scale vertically, scale horizontally, rotate, and move the character. Figure 26 identifies what each point does to the type.

TIP You can use the Touch Type tool to quickly select and change the color of each character in a type object.

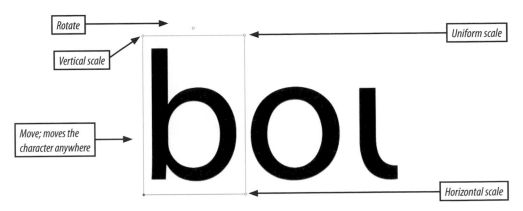

Figure 26 Transform options with the Touch Type tool

What's truly brilliant about the Touch Type tool is that the other letters in the word move to accommodate any transformation you make. What's more, you can freely move type characters closer together or farther apart as you transform them. The Touch Type tool brings enormous freedom for working with type and opens the door to new possibilities and new ideas for typographical illustrations.

Use the Touch Type tool

1. Open AI 2-6 save it as **Touch Type**, then verify that the Swatches panel is showing.

2. Click the **Touch Type tool** ⊞ , then click the **first letter T**.

   A bounding box appears around the letter.

TIP The Touch Type tool ⊞ is located behind the Type tool **T**, with the other type tools.

3. Click and drag the **top-right handle** of the bounding box.

   As you drag, the letter is scaled in proportion.

4. Drag until the type resembles Figure 27.

   As you drag, notice that the space between the bounding box around the letter T and the letter o next to it does not change.

5. Position the **Touch Type tool** ⊞ over the left center of the **letter T** then drag.

   The letter moves independently from the other letters. No matter how far you drag the letter T vertically, the horizontal space between the letter T and the o is maintained.

6. Undo your steps as necessary so the type still resembles Figure 27.

7. Select the **letter o** with the **Touch Type tool** ⊞ , then drag it closer to the **letter T**, as shown in Figure 28.

   Now that both the letter T and the letter o have been manipulated by the Touch Type tool ⊞ , you are able to move the letter o as close or as far apart to the letter T as you like—even overlap them.

8. Click the **letter u**, then click and drag the **lower-right handle**.

   The character is scaled on the horizontal axis only.

9. Click the **letter c**, then click and drag the **upper-left handle**.

   The character is scaled on the vertical axis only.

10. Click the **letter h**, then click and drag the **point centered above it**.

    The character is rotated as you drag.

11. Select the **letter T** with the **Touch Type tool** ⊞ , then change its **fill color** on the Swatches panel to a color of your choice.

12. Use the **Touch Type tool** ⊞ to re-create the illustration shown in Figure 29.

13. Save your work, then close the Touch Type document.

You used the Touch Type tool to scale, rotate, and change the color of individual characters on a text object.

Figure 27 Scaling the "T"

Figure 28 Moving the "o" closer to the "T"

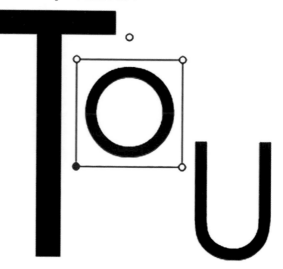

Figure 29 The final illustration

CREATE GRADIENTS

▶ *What You'll Do*

In this lesson, you will use the Color panel, Gradient panel, and Swatches panel to create, name, modify, and save gradients.

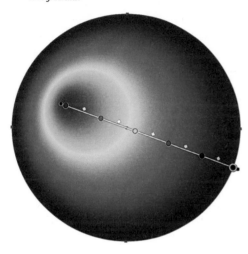

Using the Gradient Panel

A **gradient** is a graduated blend between colors. The Gradient panel is the command center for creating and adjusting gradients. In the panel, you will see a slider that represents the gradient you are creating or using. The slider has at least two colors. The leftmost color is the starting color, and the rightmost color is the ending color.

The colors used in a gradient are represented on the Gradient panel by small circle icons called **color stops**. The Gradient panel shown in Figure 30 shows a two-color gradient.

The point at which two colors meet in equal measure is called the **midpoint** of the gradient. The midpoint is represented by the diamond above the slider. The midpoint does not necessarily need to be positioned evenly between the starting and ending colors. You can change the appearance of a gradient by moving the midpoint.

Figure 30 Gradient panel

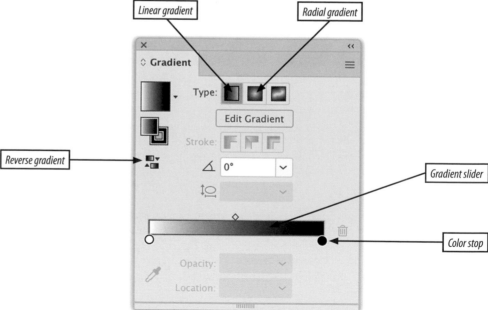

The Swatches panel contains standard gradients that come with the software. To create your own original gradients, start by clicking an object filled with an existing gradient. You can then modify that existing gradient on the Gradient panel. You can change either or both the beginning and ending colors. You can change the location of the midpoint. You can also add additional colors into the gradient or remove existing colors.

> **TIP** As you work to perfect a gradient, you can see how your changes will affect the gradient by filling an object with the gradient you are modifying. As you make changes on the Gradient panel, the changes will be reflected in the object.

You can define a gradient as linear or radial. A linear gradient can be positioned left to right, up and down, or on any angle. You can change the angle of the gradient by entering a new value in the Angle text box on the Gradient panel.

Think of a radial gradient as a series of concentric circles. With a radial gradient, the starting color appears at the center of the gradient. The blend radiates out to the ending color. By definition, a radial gradient has no angle ascribed to it.

Using the Color Panel

The Color panel, shown in Figure 31, is where you move sliders to mix new colors for fills, strokes, and gradients. You can also use the panel to adjust the color in a filled object.

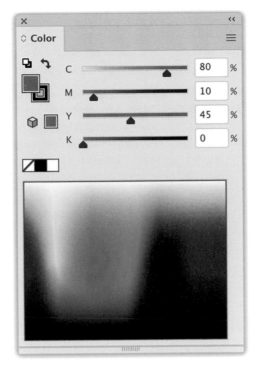

Figure 31 Color panel

The panel has five color modes: CMYK, RGB, Grayscale, HSB, and Web Safe RGB. The panel will default to CMYK or RGB, depending on the color mode you choose when creating a new document.

Rather than use the sliders, you can also type values directly into the text boxes. For example, in CMYK mode, a standard red color is composed of 100% Magenta and 100% Yellow. The notation for this callout would be

100M/100Y. Note that you don't list the zero values for Cyan (C) and Black (K)—you don't list the color as 0C/100M/100Y/0K. In RGB mode (0–255), a standard orange color would be noted as 255R/128G.

Changing Color Stops

The best way to change a color stop on the Gradient panel is to double-click the color stop. Doing so opens a dual Color/Swatches panel that allows you to toggle between the two by clicking the appropriate panel icon on the left edge. Choose the Color panel icon to create a new color or adjust an existing color. Use the Swatches panel icon to choose an already-named color.

Adding Colors and Gradients to the Swatches Panel

Once you have defined a color or a gradient to your liking, it's a smart idea to save it by dragging it into the Swatches panel or click the Color panel menu button and select Create New Swatch. Once a color or gradient is moved into the Swatches panel, you can name it by double-clicking it and then typing a name in the Swatch Options dialog box. You cannot modify it, however. For example, if you click a saved gradient and adjust it on the Gradient panel, you can apply the new gradient to an object, but the original gradient on the Swatches panel remains unaffected. You can save the new and altered gradient to the Swatches panel for future use.

Create a gradient

1. Open AI 2-7.ai, then save it as **Gradient fills**.

2. Create a **4" circle** at the center of the artboard, then apply a **yellow fill** to the circle.

3. Click the **Swatches panel menu button** ☰, point to **Open Swatch Library**, point to **Gradients**, then click **Spectrums**.

   The Spectrums panel opens.

4. Click the **swatch named Spectrum**.

   The yellow fill changes to the Spectrum fill.

5. Open the **Gradient panel**.

6. Click the **Gradient panel menu button** ☰, then click **Show Options** if they are not already showing.

7. Click the **yellow color stop** on the gradient slider, and drag it straight down off the panel to delete it.

8. Delete all the **color stops** *except* for the first and last color stops.

TIP The changes you make to the gradient slider are reflected in the selected circle.

9. Click the **leftmost color stop** to select it, press and hold **[option] (Mac)** or **[Alt] (Win)**, then click the **red swatch** in the top row of the Swatches panel.

10. Double-click the **rightmost color stop**.

    The Color/Swatches panel opens at the bottom of the Gradient panel.

11. Click a **purple swatch** on the Swatches panel.

    It's not necessary to press and hold [option] (Mac) or [Alt] (Win) when using *this* Swatches panel to change a color stop. For that reason, this is the easiest and fastest way to change a color stop.

12. Float the **mouse pointer** just below the **bottom edge of the gradient slider** on the Gradient panel until a **white arrowhead with a plus sign** appears, then click to add a **new color stop** between the red and purple stops.

13. Double-click the **new color stop**, change its color to **orange**, then drag it to the immediate right of the red color stop.

14. Click to add a **new color stop** between the orange and purple stops.

15. Change its color to **yellow**.

16. Add a **new color stop** between the yellow and purple stops, then change its color to **green**.

17. Add a **blue color stop** between the green and purple stops.

18. Spread the **color stops** out evenly so your Gradient panel resembles Figure 32.

Figure 32 Six color stops on the Gradient panel

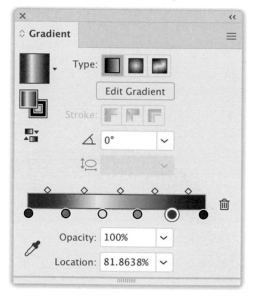

19. Click the **Selection tool** ▶ , then click the **Radial Gradient button** 🔘 on the Gradient panel.

As shown in Figure 33, the fill in the circle becomes a radial gradient from red in the center to purple at the outer edge.

20. Click the **Color panel menu button** ☰ , then click **Create New Swatch**.

21. Name the new swatch **Custom Rainbow**, then click **OK**.

The Custom Rainbow swatch is added to the Gradients section of the Swatches panel.

22. Click the **Gradient tool** 🔲 on the toolbar.

The Gradient tool is used to manipulate gradient fills that are already applied to objects. The gradient control bar appears directly on the selected circle. You can change the length, angle, and direction of the gradient by dragging the gradient control bar. You can manipulate the color stops to position them exactly where you want them on the circle.

23. Click the **black button** on the far left of the **gradient control bar**, then drag it in any direction to any length.

Figure 34 shows one possibility.

24. Save your work, then continue to the next lesson.

You applied the Spectrum gradient to the yellow circle. You modified the gradient by deleting color stops and adding new color stops. You changed the color of the new stops, then applied the gradient as a radial gradient. You clicked the Gradient tool, then moved the gradient control bar to modify how the radial gradient fills the circle.

Figure 33 Gradient applied as a radial gradient

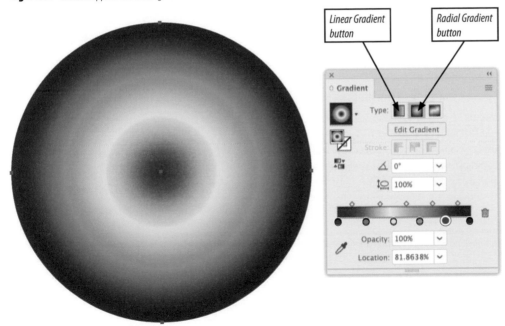

Figure 34 Modified gradient fill

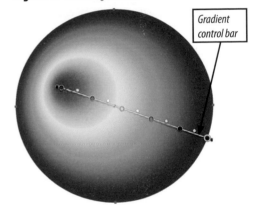

Gradient control bar

Linear Gradient button

Radial Gradient button

ADJUST GRADIENTS IN TEXT AND OBJECTS

▶ **What You'll Do**

In this lesson, you will use the Gradient tool to adjust how gradients fill text and objects and fill the objects with a gradient.

GRADIENT

GRADIENT

GRADIENT

Applying Fills and Strokes to Text

Regardless of the fill and stroke colors shown on the toolbar, new text is generated by default with a black fill and no stroke. To change the color of text, you must select the text with a Selection tool or by highlighting it with a Type tool. When you switch to a Selection tool, the text is selected as a single object (a blue baseline and anchor point are revealed), and any color changes you make will affect the text globally. If you want to change the fill or the stroke of an individual character, you must select that character with a Type tool.

Converting Text to Outlines

About the only thing you can't do to Illustrator text is fill it with a gradient. To create that effect, you first need to convert the text into objects. You can do this by selecting the text, then using the Create Outlines command on the Type menu. The letterforms, or outlines, become standard Illustrator objects with anchor points and paths that you can modify like any other object. Figure 35 shows an example of text converted to outlines.

Create Outlines is a powerful feature. Beyond allowing you to fill text with a gradient, it allows you to modify the letter forms as you would any other object. It also makes it possible to create a document with text and without fonts. This can save you time in document management when sending files to a printer by circumventing potential problems with missing fonts or font conflicts.

Once text is converted to outlines, you can no longer change the typeface. Also, the type loses its font information, including sizing "hints" that optimize letter shape at different sizes. Therefore, if you plan to scale type substantially, change its font size on the Character panel before converting it to outlines.

Figure 35 Text converted to outlines

Using the Gradient Tool with Linear Gradient Fills

As you saw with the radial gradient in the previous lesson, the Gradient tool is used to manipulate gradient fills that are already applied to objects, and it only affects the way a gradient fills an object.

To use the Gradient tool, you first select an object with a gradient fill. When you click the Gradient tool, the **gradient control bar** appears in the object itself, as shown in Figure 36. For linear gradients, the gradient control bar begins at the left edge and ends at the right edge by default.

You can change the length, angle, and direction of the gradient by dragging the gradient control bar.

Figure 36 Gradient control bar

Figure 37 shows the gradient control bar starting outside the object at the top and ending below it. Where you begin dragging and where you end dragging determine the length of the gradient from the beginning color to the ending color, even if it's outside the perimeter of the object.

You can further modify how the gradient fills the object by modifying the gradient control bar itself. Click and drag the diamond-shaped endpoint of the bar to lengthen or shorten the gradient. You can also click and drag the

Figure 37 Changing the position of the gradient control bar

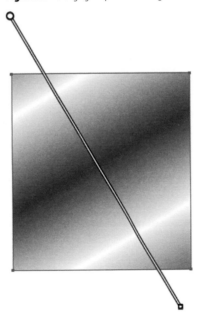

circle-shaped starting point to move the entire bar to a different location.

When you click the gradient control bar, the color stops that compose the gradient appear, as shown in Figure 38. You can click and drag the color stops right there, on the object, for precise control of how the gradient fills the object. You can change the color of the stops on the gradient control bar and even add or delete color stops. To change the color of a stop, simply double-click it; the Color/Swatches panel will appear at the bottom of the Gradient panel.

Figure 38 Color stops on the gradient control bar

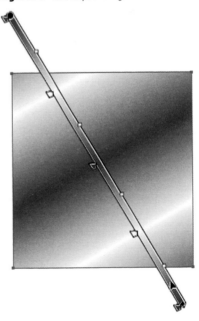

Perhaps the best method for working with the gradient control bar is to first click and drag the Gradient tool as close as possible to where you want it to begin and end. Then use the gradient control bar for tweaking the position of the gradient and the position of the color stops within the object.

When you float the cursor near the endpoint of the gradient control bar, the rotate icon appears, as shown in Figure 39. Click and drag to rotate the gradient control bar and the gradient within the object.

Applying Gradient Fills to Multiple Objects

If you select multiple objects and then click a gradient swatch on the Swatches panel, the gradient will fill each object individually. However, with all the objects selected, you can use the Gradient control bar to extend a single gradient across all of them.

When you convert text to outlines and apply a gradient fill, the gradient automatically fills each letter individually. In other words, if you fill a five-letter word with a rainbow gradient, each of the five letters will contain the entire spectrum. To extend the gradient across all the letters, drag the Gradient tool from the left edge of the word to the right edge, or vice versa.

Using the Gradient Tool with Radial Gradient Fills

With radial gradients, the gradient control bar shows the length of the gradient from the center of the circle to the outermost circle. Figure 40 shows the gradient control bar for three radial gradients.

Figure 40 Three radial gradients

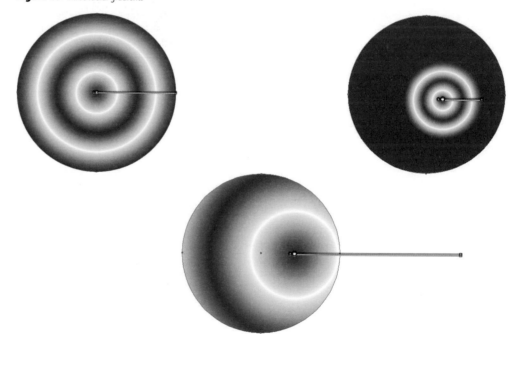

Figure 39 Rotating the gradient control bar

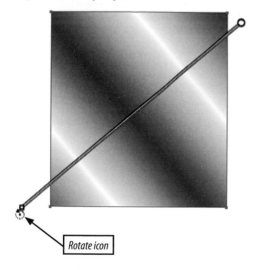

Rotate icon

When you click the gradient control bar on a radial gradient, a dotted line appears, showing you the perimeter of the gradient, whether that's within or outside the actual object. In Figure 41, the dotted line indicates that more of the gradient is actually outside of the object than visible within the object.

Radial gradients are not limited to concentric circles: You can also create radial gradients with concentric ellipses. To do so, click and drag the black circle on the dotted line of the radial gradient. As shown in Figure 42, doing so will distort the concentric circles into ellipses.

Figure 41 Dotted line shows the perimeter of the radial gradient

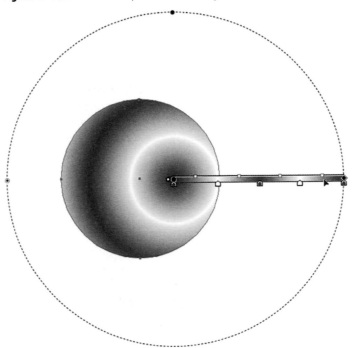

Figure 42 Distorting the gradient

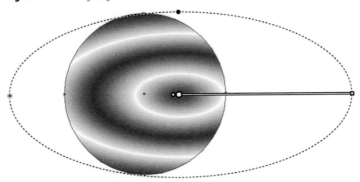

Apply a gradient fill to text

1. Open the Gradient fills.ai document from the previous lesson, if necessary.

2. Click **Object** on the menu bar, then click **Show All**.

3. Click the **Selection tool** ▶, select the **circle with the gradient**, click **Object**, point to **Hide**, then click **Selection**.

4. Select all **six lines of text**, click **Type** on the menu bar, then click **Create Outlines**.

   The type is converted to shapes and is no longer editable as type.

5. Click **View** on the menu bar, then click **Hide Edges**.

6. Click the **Custom Rainbow swatch** you created and saved to the Swatches panel.

7. On the Gradient panel, click the **Linear Gradient button** ▢.

   The gradient fills each letter form individually. In other words, the gradient runs from red to violet from left to right in each letterform on the page.

8. Click the **Selection tool** ▶, then click to select the **second word from the top**.

   Because selection edges are hidden, you won't see selection marks.

9. Click the **Gradient tool** ▦ on the toolbar.

When you select the Gradient tool ▦, gradient control bars appear on each letter. You will use the Gradient tool ▦ on the toolbar to manipulate the gradient fills.

10. Press and hold **[shift]**, then click and drag the **Gradient tool** ▦ from the **top of the letter T to the bottom of the letter T**.

TIP Introducing the [shift] key constrains the drag to a straight line.

11. Select the **third word**, then click and drag the **Gradient tool** ▦ from the left edge of the letter G to the right edge of the letter T.

12. Select the **fourth word**, then click and drag the **Gradient tool** ▦ from the left edge of the artboard to the right edge of the artboard.

13. Select the **fifth word**, then click and drag the **Gradient tool** ▦ from the left edge of the letter D to the right edge of the letter D.

14. Select the **sixth word**, then click and drag the **Gradient tool** ▦ from the top-left corner of the letter A diagonally down to the bottom-right edge of the letter I.

   Your artwork should resemble Figure 43.

15. Save your work, then close the Gradient fills document.

You filled the same text objects six different ways using the Gradient tool at different lengths and angles.

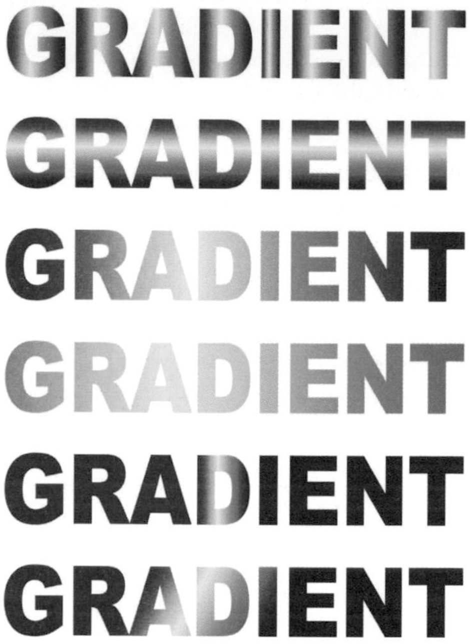

Figure 43 Six different gradient fills

Adjust a radial gradient fill

1. Open AI 2-8.ai, then save it as **Motorcycle Radial**.

2. Select the **small circle**, then change its **stroke color to red**.

3. On the Stroke panel, change the **Weight** to **12 pt**.

4. On the Stroke panel, click the **Align Stroke to Outside button** .

   Your Stroke panel should resemble Figure 44.

5. Increase the **stroke weight** to **51 pt**.

   At 51 pt., the stroke is the same size as the space between the two circles, no larger.

6. Click **Object** on the menu bar, point to **Path**, then click **Outline Stroke**.

The Outline Stroke command converts a stroked path into an object at the current size of the stroke. The object is now like a donut: a large circle with a smaller circle cut out of its center.

7. Verify that the **fill color** is activated on the toolbar.

8. On the Gradient panel, click the **black and white gradient square** directly under the panel name.

   The linear gradient fills the selected object.

9. On the Gradient panel, click the **Radial Gradient button** .

   The object is filled with a radial gradient. The result is a bit tricky, because it appears mostly black. With a radial gradient, the start color (in this case, white) is at the center of the object. This object's center is a negative space, so we can't see the

white color at its center. Nevertheless, the gradient is radiating from white at the object's center to black at its outer edge.

10. On the Gradient panel, drag the **white color stop** to the right to the midpoint of the gradient slider.

11. Add a **new color stop** to the left of the gradient slider.

12. Change the color of the **leftmost color stop** and the **rightmost color stop** to **green**.

   Your Gradient panel should resemble Figure 45.

TIP Note that the rightmost color stop represents the outer edge of the circular object.

Continued on next page

Figure 44 Stroke panel set to Align Stroke to Outside

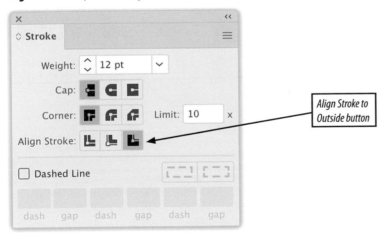

Align Stroke to Outside button

Figure 45 Three color stops on the Gradient panel

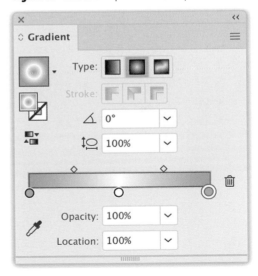

13. Reposition the **color stops** as shown in Figure 46.

With the three color stops in this far-right position, the three-color gradient is visible at the outer edges of the object.

14. Click **Object** on the menu bar, point to **Arrange**, then click **Send to Back**.

15. Deselect, then compare your artwork to Figure 47.

16. Save your work, then close the Motorcycle Radial document.

You applied a heavy weight stroke to the outside of a circle then converted the stroke to an object. You then applied a radial gradient to the object and moved the color stops so the gradient was visible inside the object.

Figure 46 Positioning the color stops so the gradient is visible in the object

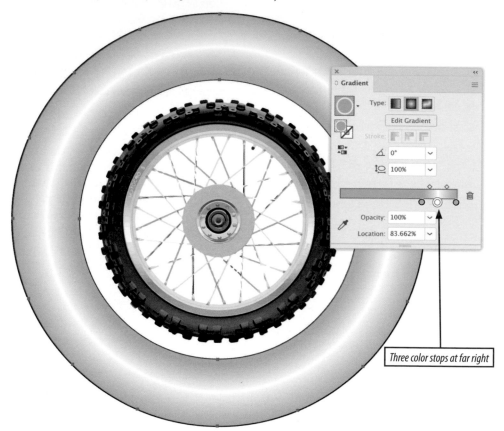

Three color stops at far right

Figure 47 Final artwork

APPLY GRADIENTS TO STROKES

▶ *What You'll Do*

In this lesson, you will apply gradients to strokes on objects and use the Gradient panel to determine how the gradient strokes the object.

Applying a Gradient to a Stroke

You can use the Gradient panel to apply a gradient to a stroked object and to determine how the gradient is applied. To apply the stroke, simply select the object and, with the Stroke icon activated, choose a gradient to apply to the object.

The Gradient panel offers three buttons you can use to determine how the gradient is applied to the stroke. The three options are as follows:

Within Stroke: As shown in Figure 48, the gradient moves left to right across the object.

Figure 48   The within stroke option for the gradient

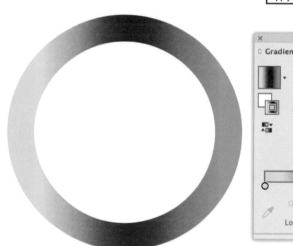

Apply gradient within stroke

Along Stroke: As shown in Figure 49, the gradient moves clockwise around the object.

Across Stroke: As shown in Figure 50, the gradient radiates from the outside to the inside of the stroke.

If you want to specify how the stroke aligns to the object—inside, center, or outside—use the align stroke options on the Stroke panel before using the Gradient panel to apply a gradient to the stroke.

You cannot apply a gradient to a stroke on live type. You must first convert the type to outlines, then you will be able to apply a gradient to the stroke.

Figure 49 The along stroke option for the gradient

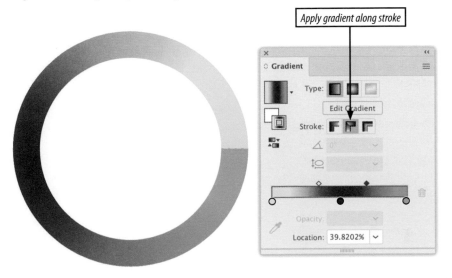

Figure 50 The across stroke option for the gradient

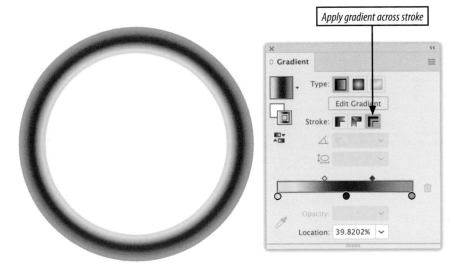

Apply gradients to strokes

1. Open AI 2-9.ai, then save it as **Gradient Strokes**.

2. Select the **triangle**, then verify that the **stroke icon** is activated on the toolbar.

3. Click the **Yellow**, **Orange**, **Blue gradient swatch** on the Gradient panel.

   The gradient is applied to the triangle.

4. Note the **three stroke buttons** on the Gradient panel.

   By default, the first button—Apply gradient within stroke—is selected. As shown in Figure 51, the gradient moves from left to right across the triangle.

TIP In the figure, the selection marks on the triangle are hidden.

5. Click the **second** of the **three stroke buttons**.

   As shown in Figure 52, the Apply gradient along stroke option is applied, and the gradient moves clockwise around the stroke.

Figure 51 Gradient applied within stroke

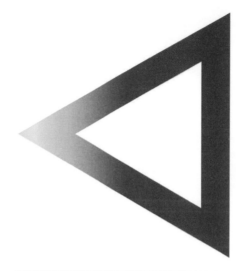

Apply gradient within stroke

Figure 52 Gradient applied along stroke

Apply gradient along stroke

6. Click the **third** of the **three stroke buttons**.

   As shown in Figure 53, the Apply gradient across stroke option is applied, and the gradient radiates outward from the center of the stroke.

7. Click the **Reverse Gradient button**  on the Gradient panel, then compare your screen to Figure 54.

8. Save your work, then close the Gradient Strokes document.

   You applied a gradient to the stroke on an object, then applied two different options for how the stroke is applied. You clicked the Reverse Gradient button to reverse how the across stroke option applied the gradient.

Figure 53 Gradient applied across stroke

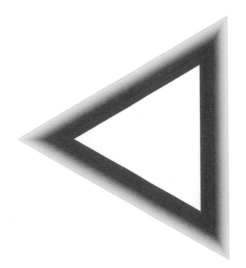

Apply gradient across stroke

Figure 54 Reversing the gradient on the stroke

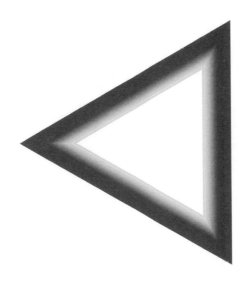

Reverse gradient

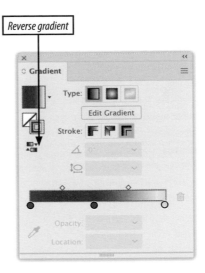

Create point text

1. Open AI 2-10.ai, then save it as **Restaurant Logo**.
2. Using a bold font, type **NOW OPEN** on two lines anywhere on the artboard, using all capital letters.

TIP The font used in Figure 55 is Impact.

3. Change the font size to 29 pt. and the leading to 25 pt.
4. Verify that the baseline shift is set to 0.
5. Change the alignment to center and the horizontal scale to 75%.
6. Position the text in the center of the white circle.
7. Hide the text.
8. Save your work.

Flow text into an object

1. Copy the beige circle.
2. Paste the copy in front of it.
3. Click the Type tool, then select all of the green text at the bottom of the artboard, with the Type tool.
4. Copy the green text.
5. Click the Selection tool, then click the top beige circle.
6. Click the Area Type tool, click the edge of the top beige circle, then paste.
7. Center-align the text in the circle.
8. Change the baseline shift to −4 pt.
9. Fill the selected text with the same fill color as the beige circle (50% Orange).
10. On the Color panel, drag the Magenta slider to 40% to darken the text.
11. Hide the text.
12. Save your work.

Figure 55 Completed Skills Review

Position text on a path

1. Select the dark gray circle.
2. Click the Type on a Path tool, then click the top of the circle.
3. Using a bold font, type **THE HOLE-IN-ONE** in all capital letters across the top of the circle

TIP The font in Figure 55 is Arial Black. If your type appears at the bottom of the circle, drag the start or end bracket to position the type at the top of the circle. Zoom in so you can clearly see the brackets. If you move the circle instead of the type, undo your last step and try again.

4. Change the font size to 36 pt., and set the horizontal scale to 75% and the fill color to White.

TIP You may need to use a different font size, depending on the font you choose.

5. Click the Selection tool, click Edit on the menu bar, click Copy, click Edit on the menu bar, click Paste in Front, then move the center bracket clockwise to position the copied text across the bottom of the circle.
6. Select the copied text with the Type tool, then type **RESTAURANT**.
7. Drag the RESTAURANT text across the path to flip its direction.
8. Apply a negative baseline shift to move the text below the path.

TIP The baseline shift used in Figure 55 is −26 pt.

9. Copy both text objects, click Edit on the menu bar, then click Paste in Back.
10. Fill the back copies of the text with Black, then move them 2 pt. up and 2 pt. to the right.
11. Save your work.

Create and apply gradients

1. Apply the White, Black Radial gradient to the small white circle.
2. Change the ending color stop on the gradient slider to Smoke.
   Each swatch has a color name that you will see when you hover the mouse pointer over the swatch.

TIP Press [option] (Mac) or [Alt] (Win) while you select Smoke from the Swatches panel.

3. Save the new gradient to the Swatches panel.
4. Name it **Golf Ball**.
5. Fill the large green circle with the Golf Ball gradient.
6. Change the starting color stop to Pure Yellow.
7. Change the ending color stop to Little Sprout Green.
8. Move the midpoint to the 80% location on the gradient slider.
9. Save the new gradient as **The Rough**.
10. Apply a 2 pt. black stroke to the large circle and the smaller peach circle.
11. Save your work.

Adjust a gradient and create a drop shadow

1. Click Object on the menu bar, then click Show All.
2. Deselect all by clicking the artboard.
3. Select NOW OPEN and convert the text to outlines.
4. Fill the text with the white to black linear gradient.
5. Change the starting color stop to Black.
6. Create an intermediary white color stop at the 50% mark on the gradient slider.
7. Drag the Gradient tool starting at the top of the word NOW to the bottom of the word OPEN.
8. Change the middle color stop of the gradient to Latte.

9. Save the new gradient as **Flash**.
10. Deselect the text.
11. Delete the green text from the bottom of the artboard.
12. Convert the remaining text objects into outlines.
13. Apply a 2 pt. black stroke to the two circles in the illustration.
14. Select all, then lock all objects.
15. Save your work, compare your illustration to Figure 55, then close the Restaurant Logo document.

Apply gradients to strokes

1. Open AI 2-11.ai, then save it as **Gradient Strokes to Text**.
2. Select the letter Z with the Selection tool, then verify that the stroke icon is activated on the toolbar.
3. Click Type on the menu bar, then click Create Outlines.
4. Click the White to Cyan gradient swatch on the Swatches panel.
   The gradient is applied to the stroke.
5. Note the three stroke buttons on the Gradient panel.
6. Click the third of the three stroke buttons.
7. Click the Reverse Gradient button on the Gradient panel.
8. Save your work, then close the Gradient Strokes to Text document.

An eccentric California real-estate mogul hires your design firm to "create an identity" for La Mirage, his development of high-tech executive condominiums in Palm Springs. Since he's curious about what you'll come up with on your own, the only creative direction he'll give you is to tell you that the concept is "a desert oasis."

1. Create a new 6" × 6" document, then save it as **Desert Oasis**.
2. Using a bold font and 80 pt. for a font size, type **LA MIRAGE** in all capitals.

TIP The font shown in Figure 56 is Impact.

3. Change the horizontal scale to 80%.
4. Change the baseline shift to 0.
5. Apply a −100 Kerning value between the two words.
6. Convert the text to outlines, then click the linear gradient swatch on the Swatches panel that fades white to black.
7. Using the Color panel, change the first color stop to 66M/100Y/10K.
8. Create an intermediary color stop that is 25M/100Y.
9. Position the intermediary color stop at 70% on the slider.
10. Save the gradient on the Swatches panel, and name it **Desert Sun**.
11. Drag the Gradient tool from the exact top to the exact bottom of the text.
12. Create a rectangle around the text, and fill it with the Desert Sun gradient.
13. Drag the Gradient tool from the bottom to the top of the rectangle.
14. Send the rectangle to the back of the stack.
15. Apply a 1 pt. black stroke to LA MIRAGE.
16. Type the tagline, a **desert oasis**, in 14 pt. lowercase letters.
17. Apply a Tracking value of 500 or more to the tagline, then convert it to outlines.
18. Save your work, compare your image to Figure 56, then close the Desert Oasis document.

Figure 56 Completed Project Builder 1

Your friend owns Loon's Balloons. She stops by your studio with a display ad that she's put together for a local magazine and asks if you can make all the elements work together better. Her only direction is that the balloon must remain pink.

1. Open AI 2-12.ai, then save it as **Balloons**.
2. Save the pink fill on the balloon to the Swatches panel, and name it **Hot Pink**.
3. Fill the balloon shape with the White, Black Radial gradient from the Swatches panel.
4. Change the black color stop on the gradient slider to Hot Pink.
5. Using the Gradient tool, change the highlight point on the balloon shape so it is no longer centered in the balloon shape.
6. Copy the balloon, then paste it in front.
7. Click the Selection tool on the block of text that begins with "specializing in . . ." and then cut the text.
8. Click the top balloon with the Selection tool, then switch to the Area Type tool.
9. Click the top edge of the top balloon, then paste.
10. Center the text and apply a −4 baseline shift.
11. Adjust the layout of the text as necessary.

TIP You can force a line of text to the next line by clicking before the first word in the line you want to move, then pressing [shift] [return] (Mac) or [shift] [Enter] (Win).

12. Move the headline LOON'S BALLOONS so each word is on a different side of the balloon string.
13. Apply a 320 Kerning value between the two words.
14. Save your work, compare your screen to Figure 57, then close the Balloons document.

Figure 57 Completed Project Builder 2

You work in the marketing department of a major movie studio, where you design movie posters and newspaper campaigns. You are respected for your proficiency with typography. Your boss asks you to come up with a "teaser" campaign for the movie *Vanishing Point*, a spy thriller. The campaign will run on billboards in 10 major cities and will feature only the movie title, nothing else.

1. Create a new 6" × 6" document, then save it as **Vanish**.
2. Type **VANISHING POINT**, using 100 pt. and a bold font.

TIP The font used in Figure 56 is Impact.

3. Change the Horizontal Scale to 55%.
4. Convert the text to outlines.
5. On the Swatches panel, click the white to black linear gradient swatch.
6. Drag the Gradient tool from the exact bottom to the exact top of the letters.
7. Copy the letters, then paste them in front.
8. Fill the copied letters in front with White.
9. Using your arrow keys, move the white letters 2 pt. to the left and 8 pt. up.
10. Save your work, then compare your text with Figure 58.
11. Close the Vanish document.

Figure 58 Completed Design Project

NATIONAL GEOGRAPHIC LEARNING

ALEX VON DALLWITZ
ART DIRECTOR

Alex von Dallwitz has been drawing for as long as he can remember. His love of cityscapes and design initially propelled him into architecture. But after experiencing the restrictive codes and regulations of the field, Alex decided to switch gears and study graphic design.

As a student, Alex drew inspiration from his art and design teachers, as well as professional graphic artists like Saul Bass and Armin Hofmann. Studying and emulating their work helped Alex find his own unique style. After working in various design studios, Alex took on the role of Art Director at National Geographic Learning. In addition to providing artistic direction for both print and digital education products, Alex designs page layouts and covers, combining imagery and typography to create engaging user experiences. Along with his team, Alex sees a project through every stage of the process, from research and prototyping to final publication.

This role often comes with a busy schedule and looming deadlines. Even so, Alex sees the value in taking short breaks to clear his head. For Alex, nature is more than just rejuvenating—it's inspiring.

Hiking, biking, and kayaking help Alex get his creative juices flowing. In addition, with many people working remotely, the interaction between colleagues and vendors is critical and often helps Alex to see his project from a new perspective. Alex shares, "Whether you're collaborating with a colleague or you're engaged with a National Geographic Explorer, there are such great interactions that happen... these are the people that help bring the story to life."

PROJECT DESCRIPTION

In this project, you will create a new or updated logo for a school club or team. You will have the opportunity to think through the different aspects of the organization and reflect on its goals and mission. You will then decide which elements of the club or team are most important to capture in the revised logo. The goal of this project is to create or enhance a logo to capture people's attention and visually represent the personality and culture of the organization.

QUESTIONS TO CONSIDER

- What stands out to you?
- What questions would you ask?
- What is important to convey in the logo?

WORK-BASED LEARNING
Powered by MindTap

Supervised Agricultural Experience logo
© Cengage Learning, Inc.

GETTING STARTED

A logo should clearly communicate the mission of an organization. It should also grab the reader in an instant. Research the dos and don'ts of logo design. Look at examples of logos for businesses you admire. Are they simple or more elaborate? How many colors are used in the design? How do the visual elements interact with the typography?

Then talk to some members of the school club or team you have chosen. What do they feel are the most important aspects of their organization? What colors, symbols, or images would best represent this group? As you reflect on the logos you are drawn to and the mission of the organization, draw simple sketches of your ideas and refine your design. Does your sketch clearly represent the club or team? Would an outsider to the organization know what this logo represents?

CHAPTER 3

DRAWING AND COMPOSING AN ILLUSTRATION

1. Draw Straight Lines
2. Draw Curved Lines
3. Draw Elements of an Illustration
4. Apply Attributes to Objects
5. Assemble an Illustration
6. Stroke Objects for Artistic Effect
7. Use Image Trace
8. Use the Live Paint Bucket Tool
9. Explore Alternate Drawing Techniques

Adobe Certified Professional in Graphic Design and Illustrations Using Adobe Illustrator

2. Project Setup and Interface

This objective covers the interface setup and program settings that assist in an efficient and effective workflow, as well as knowledge about ingesting digital assets for a project.

2.4 Manage assets in a project.

    B Place assets in an Illustrator document.

    C Use the Links panel.

4. Creating and Modifying Visual Elements

This objective covers core tools and functionality of the application, as well as tools that affect the visual appearance of document elements.

4.1 Use core tools and features to create visual elements.

    A Create graphics or artwork to create visual elements.

4.3 Make, manage, and manipulate selections.

    B Modify and refine selections using various methods.

4.5 Use basic reconstructing and editing techniques to manipulate digital graphics and media.

    A Apply basic autocorrection methods and tools.

    B Repair and reconstruct graphics.

    D Use Image Trace to create vectors from bitmap images.

DRAW STRAIGHT LINES

▶ *What You'll Do*

In this lesson, you will create three new views, then explore basic techniques for using the Pen tool as you prepare to draw a complex illustration.

Drawing in Illustrator

You can create any shape using the Pen tool, which is why it's often called "the drawing tool." More precisely, the pen is a tool for drawing straight lines, curved lines, polygons, and irregularly shaped objects. It is, however, no *more* of a drawing tool than any of the shape tools but, rather, simply more versatile. Make note that *to master Illustrator, you must master the Pen tool.*

The challenges of the Pen tool are finite and can be grasped with no more than 30 minutes' study. As with many aspects of graphic design (and of life!), mastery comes with practice. So make it a point to learn Pen tool techniques. Don't get frustrated. Use the Pen tool often, even if it's just to play around making odd shapes.

All artists learn techniques for using tools such as brushes, chalk, and palette knives. Once learned, those techniques become second nature, subconscious and unique to the artist. Much the same goes for Illustrator's Pen tool. When you are comfortable and confident, you will find yourself effectively translating design ideas from your imagination straight to the artboard, without even thinking about the tool!

Viewing Objects on the Artboard

If you are drawing on paper and you want to see your work up close, you move your nose closer to the paper. Computers offer more effective options. As you have already seen, the Zoom tool is used to enlarge areas of the artboard for easier viewing. When you are working with the Pen tool, your view of the board becomes more critical as anchor points are tiny, and you will often move them in 1-point increments.

Instead of clicking the Zoom tool to enlarge the artboard, you can click and drag a marquee around the specific area you want to enlarge. The **marquee,** which is a dotted rectangle surrounding the area, will disappear when you release the Zoom tool, and whatever was in the marquee will be magnified as much as possible while still fitting in the window.

The New View command allows you to save any view of the artboard. Let's say you zoom in on an object. You can save that view and give it a descriptive name, using the New View command. The name of the view is then listed at the bottom of the View menu, so you can return to it at any time by selecting it. Saving views is an effective way to increase your productivity.

Drawing Straight Segments with the Pen Tool

You can use the Pen tool to make lines, also known as **paths**. You can also use it to create a closed shape, such as a triangle or a pentagon. When you click the Pen tool to make anchor points on the artboard, straight segments are automatically placed between the points. When the endpoints of two straight segments are united by a point, that point is called a **corner point**. Figure 1 shows a simple path drawn with five anchor points and four segments.

Perfection is an unnecessary goal when you are using the Pen tool because you can move and reposition anchor points and segments, as well as add and delete new points. You can use the Pen tool to create the general shape you have in your mind. Once the object is complete, you can use the Direct Selection tool to perfect or tweak the points and segments. Tweaking a finished object is always part of the drawing process.

TIP When the Pen tool is positioned over an anchor point on a selected path, the Delete Anchor Point tool appears. To remove a point from a path, use the Delete Anchor Point tool . If you select a point and cut it, the path becomes broken.

Aligning and Joining Anchor Points

Often, you will want to align anchor points precisely. For example, if you have drawn a diamond-shaped object with the Pen tool, you may want to align the top and bottom points on the same vertical axis and then align the left and right points on the same horizontal axis to perfect the shape.

The **Average** command is a simple and effective choice for aligning points. With two or more points selected, you can use the Average command to align them on the horizontal axis, on the vertical axis, or on both the horizontal and vertical axes. Two points aligned on both the horizontal and vertical axes are positioned one on top of the other.

Why is this command named "Average"? The name is appropriate because when the command moves two points to line them up on a given axis, that axis is positioned at the average distance between the two points. Thus, each point moves the same distance.

Figure 1 Elements of a path composed of straight segments

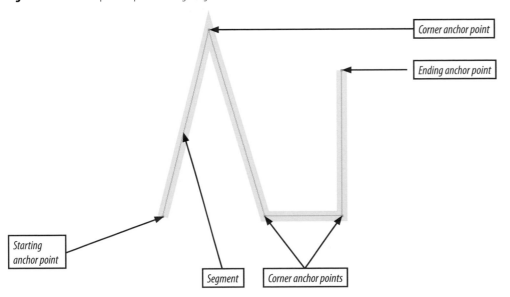

Corner anchor point

Ending anchor point

Starting anchor point

Segment

Corner anchor points

The **Join** command unites two anchor points. When two points are positioned in different locations on the artboard, the Join command creates a segment between them. When two points are aligned on both the horizontal and vertical axes and are joined, the two points become one. Applying the Join command always results in a corner point.

You will often use the Average and Join commands in tandem. Figure 2 shows two pairs of points that have each been aligned on the horizontal axis, then joined with the Join command.

Create new views

1. Open AI 3-1.ai, then save it as **Straight Lines**.

2. Choose the **Essentials workspace**, click the **Zoom tool** 🔍 on the toolbar, then position it at the **upper-left corner of the artboard**.

3. Click and drag a **marquee** that encompasses the **entire yellow section**, as shown in Figure 3.

   The area within the selection box is now magnified.

   TIP If the Zoom tool does not offer a marquee selection, click Illustrator (Mac) or Edit (Win) on the menu bar, click Preferences, click the Selection & Anchor Display, then remove the check mark next to Zoom to Selection.

4. Click **View** on the menu bar, then click **New View**.

5. Name the new view **yellow**, then click **OK**.

6. Press and hold **[space bar]** to access the **Hand tool** ✋, then drag the **artboard** upward until you have a view of the **entire pink area**.

7. Create a **new view** of the **pink area**, and name it **pink**.

   TIP If you need to adjust your view, you can quickly switch to a view of the entire artboard by pressing [command] [0] (Mac) or [Ctrl] [0] (Win), then create a new marquee selection with the Zoom tool 🔍 .

8. Create a **new view** of the **green area**, named **mint**.

Figure 2 Join command unites open points

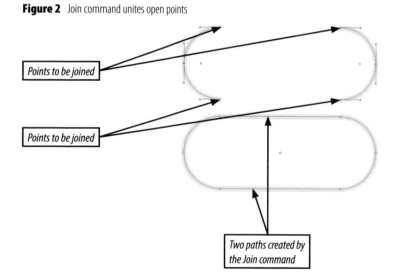

Points to be joined

Points to be joined

Two paths created by the Join command

Figure 3 Drag the Zoom tool to select what will be magnified

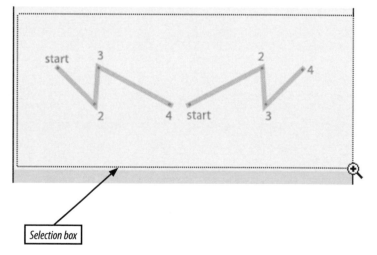

Selection box

9. Click **View** on the menu bar, then click **yellow** at the bottom of the menu.

The Illustrator window changes to the yellow view.

TIP You can change the name of a view by clicking View on the menu bar, then clicking Edit Views.

You used the Zoom tool to magnify an area of the artboard. You named the view yellow and then made two more views named pink and mint.

Draw straight lines

1. Verify that you are still in the **yellow view**, then click the **Pen tool** .

2. Open the **Swatches panel**, set the **fill color** to **[None]** and the **stroke color** to **Black**, then open the **Stroke panel** and set the **stroke weight** to **1 pt**.

3. Using Figure 4 as a reference, click **position 1 (start)**.

4. Click **position 2**, then note how a segment is automatically drawn between the two anchor points.

5. Click **position 3**, then click **position 4**.

TIP If you become disconnected from the current path you are drawing, undo your last step, then click the last anchor point with the Pen tool and continue.

6. Press and hold **[command] (Mac)** or **[Ctrl] (Win)** to switch to the **Selection tool** , then click the **artboard** to stop drawing the path and to deselect it.

You need to deselect one path before you can start drawing a new one.

7. Release **[command] (Mac)** or **[Ctrl] (Win)**, click **position 1 (start)** on the next path, then click **position 2**.

8. Skip over position 3 and click **position 4.**

9. Using Figure 5 as a guide, position the **Pen tool** anywhere on the segment **between points 2 and 4**, then click to add a **new anchor point**.

TIP When the Pen tool is positioned over a selected path, the Add Anchor Point tool appears.

10. Click the **Direct Selection tool** , then drag the new anchor point to **position 3**, as shown in Figure 6.

Using the Pen tool, you created two straight paths.

Figure 4 Four anchor points and three segments

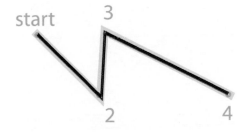

Figure 5 Click the path with the Pen tool to add a new point

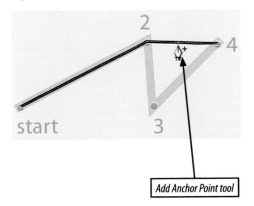

Add Anchor Point tool

Figure 6 Move an anchor point with the Direct Selection tool

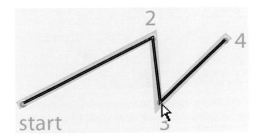

Close a path and align the anchor points

1. Click **View** on the menu bar, then click **pink**.

2. Click the **Pen tool** , click the **start/end position** at **the top of the polygon**, then click **positions 2 through 6**.

3. Position the **Pen tool** over the **first point** you created, then click to close the path, as shown in Figure 7.

4. Switch to the **Direct Selection tool** , click **point 3**, press and hold **[shift]**, then click **point 6**.

TIP You use the [shift] key to select multiple points. Anchor points that are selected appear as solid blue squares; anchor points that are not selected are white or hollow squares.

5. Click **Object** on the menu bar, point to **Path**, then click **Average**.

6. Click the **Horizontal option button** in the Average dialog box, then click **OK**.

   The two selected anchor points align on the horizontal axis, as shown in Figure 8.

7. Select both the **start/end point** and **point 4**.

8. Use the **Average command** to align the points on the vertical axis.

Figure 7 Close a path at its starting point

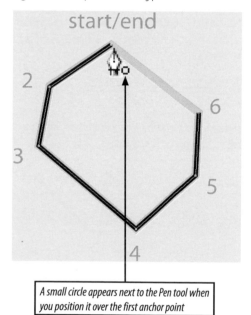

A small circle appears next to the Pen tool when you position it over the first anchor point

Figure 8 Two points aligned on the horizontal axis

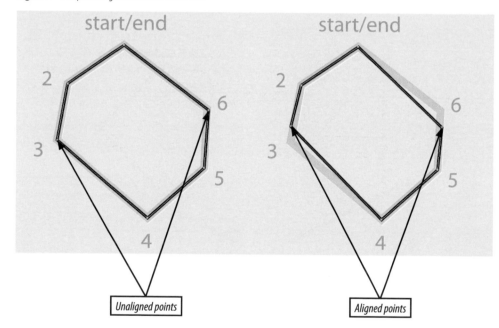

Unaligned points

Aligned points

9. Select both **point 2** and **point 5**, then use the **Average command** to align the points on both axes, as shown in Figure 9.

You drew a closed path, then used the Average command to align three sets of points. You aligned the first set on the horizontal axis, the second on the vertical axis. You aligned the third set of points on both axes, which positioned them one on top of the other.

Join anchor points

1. Switch to the **mint view** of the artboard.

2. Use the **Pen tool** to trace the **two diamond shapes**.

TIP Remember to deselect the first diamond path with the Selection tool before you begin tracing the second diamond.

3. Click the **left anchor point** of the **first diamond** with the **Direct Selection tool**, click **Edit** on the menu bar, then click **Cut**.

Cutting points also deletes the segments attached to them.

4. Cut the **right point** on the **second diamond**.

Your work should resemble Figure 10.

Continued on next page

Figure 9 Averaging two points on both the horizontal and vertical axes

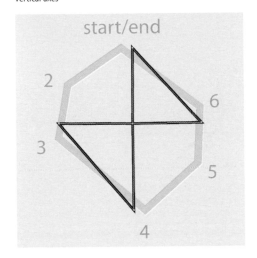

Figure 10 Cutting points also deletes the segments attached to them

5. Select the **top point** on each path.

6. Click **Object** on the menu bar, point to **Path**, then click **Join**.

   The points are joined by a straight segment, as shown in Figure 11.

TIP The shortcut key for Average is [command] [option] [A] (Mac) or [Ctrl] [Alt] [A] (Win). The shortcut key for Join is [command] [J] (Mac) or [Ctrl] [J] (Win).

7. Join the **two bottom points**.

8. Apply a **yellow fill** to the object, then save your work.

   Your work should resemble Figure 12.

9. Close the Straight Lines document.

You drew two closed paths. You cut a point from each path, which deleted the points and the segments attached to them, creating two open paths. You used the Join command, which drew a new segment between the two top points and the two bottom points on each path. You then applied a yellow fill to the new object.

Figure 11 Join command unites two distant points with a straight segment

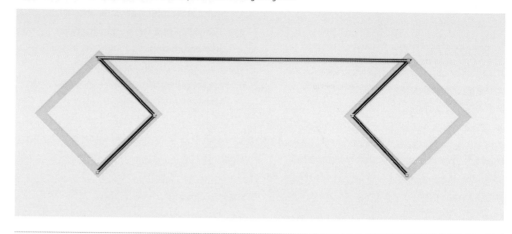

Figure 12 Joining the two open anchor points on an open path closes the path

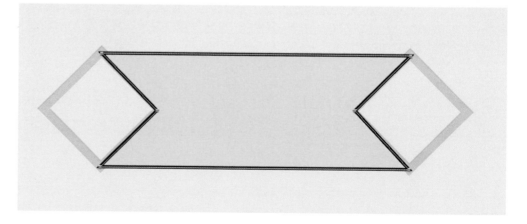

DRAW CURVED LINES

▶ *What You'll Do*

In this lesson, you will use the Pen tool to draw and define curved paths, and you will learn techniques to draw lines that abruptly change direction.

Defining Properties of Curved Lines

When you click to create anchor points with the Pen tool, the points are connected by straight segments. You can "draw" a curved path between two anchor points by *clicking and dragging* the Pen tool to create the points instead of just clicking. Anchor points created by clicking and dragging the Pen tool are known as **smooth points**.

When you use the Direct Selection tool to select a point connected to a curved segment, you will expose the point's **direction lines**, as shown in Figure 13. The angle and length of the direction lines determine the arc of the curved segment. Direction lines are editable. You can click and drag the **direction points**, or handles, at the end of the direction lines to reshape the curve. Direction lines function only to define curves and do not appear when a document is printed.

Figure 13 Direction lines define a curve

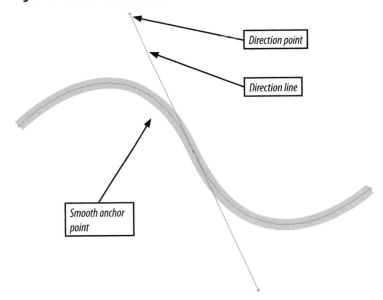

Direction point

Direction line

Smooth anchor point

A **smooth point** always has two direction lines that move together as a unit. The two curved segments attached to the smooth point are both defined by the direction lines. When you manipulate the direction lines on a smooth point, you change the curve of both segments attached to the point, always maintaining a *smooth* transition through the anchor point.

TIP You can change the appearance of anchors and handles in the Selection & Anchor Display section of the Preferences dialog box. One key preference is "Highlight anchors on mouse over." With this activated, anchor points are enlarged when you float a selection tool over them, making them easier to select.

When two paths are joined at a corner point, the two paths can be manipulated independently. A corner point can join two straight segments, one straight segment and one curved segment, or two curved segments. That corner point would have zero, one, or two direction lines, respectively. Figure 14 shows examples of smooth points and corner points.

When a corner point joins one or two curved segments, the direction lines are unrelated and are often referred to as "broken." When you manipulate one, the other doesn't move.

Converting Anchor Points

The Anchor Point tool changes corner points to smooth points and changes smooth points to corner points.

To convert a corner point to a smooth point, you click and drag the Anchor Point tool on the anchor point to *pull out* direction lines. See Figure 15.

Figure 14 Smooth points and corner points

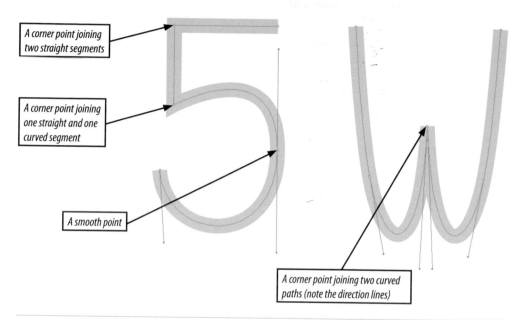

A corner point joining two straight segments

A corner point joining one straight and one curved segment

A smooth point

A corner point joining two curved paths (note the direction lines)

Figure 15 Converting a corner point to a smooth point

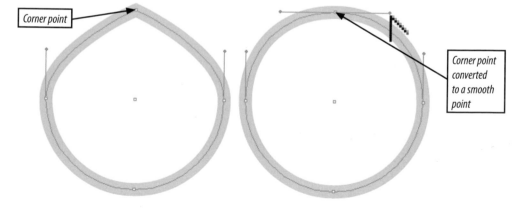

Corner point

Corner point converted to a smooth point

The Anchor Point tool works two ways to convert a smooth point to a corner point, and both are very useful when drawing.

When you click directly on a smooth point with the Anchor Point tool, the direction lines disappear. The two attached segments lose whatever curve defined them and become straight segments, as shown in the middle circle in Figure 16.

You can also use the Anchor Point tool on one of the two direction lines of a smooth point. The tool "breaks" the direction lines and allows you to move one independently of the other, as shown in the third circle in Figure 16. The smooth point is converted to a corner point that now joins two unrelated curved segments. Once the direction lines are broken, they remain broken. You can manipulate them independently with the Direct Selection tool; you no longer need the Anchor Point tool to do so.

Toggling Between the Pen Tool and Selection Tools

Drawing points and selecting points go hand in hand, and you will often need to switch back and forth between the Pen tool and one of the selection tools. Clicking from one tool to the other on the toolbar is unnecessary and will impede your productivity. To master the Pen tool, you must incorporate the keyboard command for "toggling" between the Pen tool and the selection tools. With the Pen tool selected, press [command] (Mac) or [Ctrl] (Win), which will switch the Pen tool to the Selection tool or the Direct Selection tool, depending on which tool you used last.

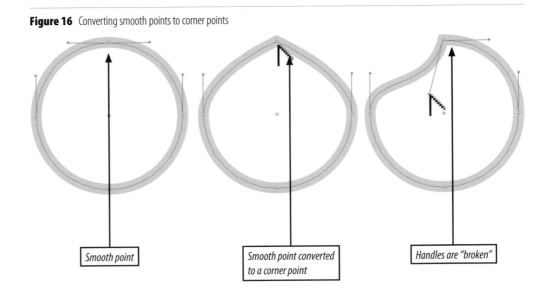

Figure 16 Converting smooth points to corner points

Smooth point

Smooth point converted to a corner point

Handles are "broken"

Draw and edit a curved line

1. Open AI 3-2.ai, then save it as **Curved Lines 1**.

2. On the toolbar, verify that the **fill color** is **[None]** and the **stroke color** is **Black**.

3. Click the **Pen tool** , then position it over the **first point position** on the line.

4. Click and drag upward until the pointer is at the **center of the purple star**, then release the mouse button.

5. Position the **Pen tool** over the **second point position.**

6. Click and drag down to the **red star**, then release the mouse button.

7. Using the same method, trace the remainder of the **blue lines**, as shown in Figure 17.

8. Click the **Direct Selection tool** on the toolbar.

9. Select the **second anchor point.**

   When you click an anchor point with the Direct Selection tool , the anchor points' two direction lines with direction handles appear. Direction handles can be dragged to manipulate the path.

10. Click and drag the **direction handle** of the **top direction line** to the **second purple star**, as shown in Figure 18, then release the mouse button.

   The move changes the shape of both segments attached to the anchor point.

11. Select the **third anchor point** with the **Direct Selection tool** .

12. Drag the **bottom direction handle** to the **second red star**, as shown in Figure 19, then release the mouse button.

13. Manipulate the direction lines to restore the curves to their appearance in Figure 17.

14. Save your work, then close the Curved Lines 1 document.

You traced a curved line by making smooth points with the Pen tool. You used the Direct Selection tool to manipulate the direction lines of the smooth points and adjust the curves. You then used the direction lines to restore the line to its original curves.

Figure 17 Smooth points draw continuous curves

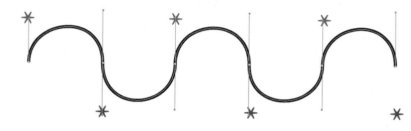

Figure 18 Moving one direction line changes two curves

Click the Direct Selection tool on any smooth point to expose its direction lines

---

Figure 19 Round curves are distorted by moving direction lines

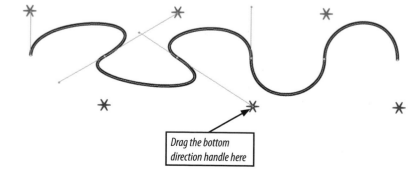

Drag the bottom direction handle here

Convert anchor points

1. Open AI 3-3.ai, then save it as **Curved Lines 2**.

2. Click **View** on the menu bar, then click **View #1**.

3. Click the **Direct Selection tool** ▷, anywhere on the **black line**.

    Make note of the location of the six existing anchor points that become visible.

4. Click **Object** on the menu bar, point to **Path**, then click **Add Anchor Points**.

    Five anchor points are added. They do not change the shape of the line.

5. Click the **Anchor Point tool** ▷, then click **each of the five new anchor points**.

    The smooth points are converted to corner points, as shown in Figure 20.

TIP The Anchor Point tool ▷, is hidden beneath the Pen tool ✐,.

6. Click the **six original anchor points** with the **Anchor Point tool** ▷,.

7. Position the **Anchor Point tool** ▷, over the **sixth anchor point** from the left.

8. Click and drag the **anchor point** to the **purple star**.

    The corner point is converted to a smooth point.

9. Using Figure 21 as a guide, convert the **corner points** to the left and right of the new curve.

You added five new anchor points to the line, then used the Anchor Point tool to convert all 11 points from smooth points to corner points. You then used the Anchor Point tool to convert three corner points to smooth points.

Figure 20 Smooth points converted to corner points

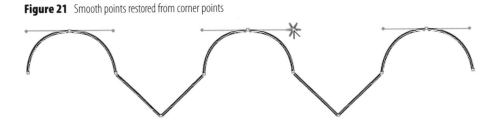

Figure 21 Smooth points restored from corner points

Draw a line with curved and straight segments

1. Click **View** on the menu bar, then click **View #2**.

2. Click the **Pen tool** 🖊, position it over the **first point position**, then click and drag down to the **green star**.

3. Position the **Pen tool** 🖊 over the **second point position**, then click and drag up to the **purple star**, as shown in the top section of Figure 22.

4. Click the **second anchor point** with the **Pen tool** 🖊.

   The direction line you dragged is deleted, as shown in the lower section of Figure 22. Deleting the direction line allows you to change the direction of the path.

5. Click the **third point position** to create the third anchor point.

6. Position the **Pen tool** 🖊 over the **third anchor point**, then click and drag a **direction line** up to the **green star**.

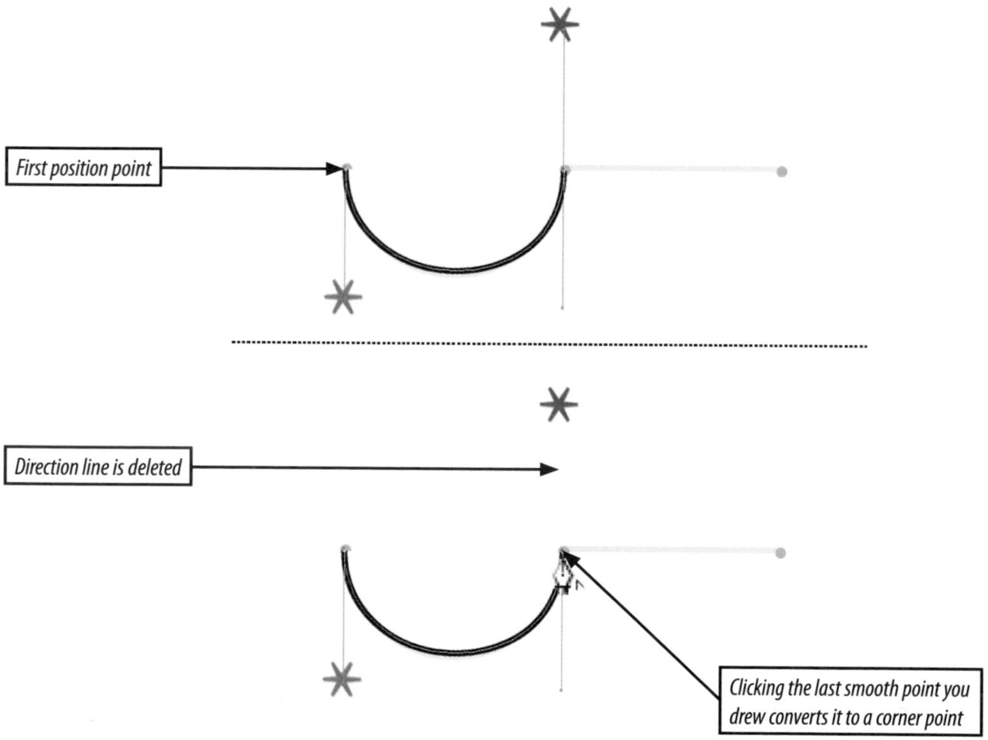

7. Position the **Pen tool** 🖊 over the **fourth point position**, then click and drag down to the **purple star**.

8. Click the **fourth anchor point**.

9. Position the **Pen tool** 🖊 over the **fifth position**, then click.

10. While the **Pen tool** 🖊 is still positioned over the **fifth anchor point**, click and drag a **direction line** down to the **green star.**

11. Finish tracing the line, then deselect the path.

12. Save your work, then continue to the next set of steps.

You traced a line that has three curves joined by two straight segments. You used the technique of clicking the previous smooth point to convert it to a corner point, allowing you to change the direction of the path.

Figure 22 Click to convert an open smooth point to a corner point

First position point

Direction line is deleted

Clicking the last smooth point you drew converts it to a corner point

THE PENCIL, SMOOTH, AND PATH ERASER TOOLS

When drawing paths, be sure to experiment with the Pencil, Smooth, and Path Eraser tools, which are grouped together on the toolbar. You can draw freehand paths with the Pencil tool and then manipulate them using the Direct Selection tool, the Smooth tool, the Path Eraser tool, or the Path Reshape feature on the Pen tool or Anchor Point tool. The Smooth tool is used to smooth over line segments that are too bumpy or too sharp. The Path Eraser tool looks and acts just like an eraser found at the end of a traditional pencil; dragging it over a line segment erases that part of the segment from the artboard. The Pencil tool draws freehand lines or straight lines. Press and hold [shift] while dragging the Pencil tool to draw horizontal and vertical straight lines and diagonal lines with a 45° angle.

Reverse direction while drawing

1. Click **View** on the menu bar, then click **View #3**.

2. Click the **Pen tool** , position it over the **first point position**, then click and drag down to the **purple star**.

3. Position the **Pen tool** over the **second point position**, then click and drag up to the **red star**, as shown in the top section of Figure 23.

4. Press and hold **[option] (Mac)** or **[Alt] (Win)** to switch to the **Anchor Point tool**, then click and drag the **direction handle** on the **red star** down to the **second purple star**, as shown in the lower section of Figure 23.

TIP Press [option] (Mac) or [Alt] (Win) to toggle between the Pen tool and the Anchor Point tool.

5. Release **[option] (Mac)** or **[Alt] (Win)**, then continue to trace the line using the same method.

TIP If you switch between the Pen tool and the Anchor Point tool using the toolbar instead of using [option] (Mac) or [Alt] (Win), you will disconnect from the current path.

6. Save your work, then close the Curved Lines 2 document.

You used the Anchor Point tool to break the direction lines of a smooth point, converting it to a corner point in the process. You used the redirected direction line to define the next curve in the sequence.

Figure 23 Use the Anchor Point tool to "break" the direction lines and redirect the path

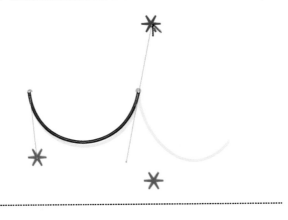

DRAW ELEMENTS OF AN ILLUSTRATION

▶ ## *What You'll Do*

In this lesson, you will draw 14 elements of an illustration. By tracing previously drawn elements, you will develop a sense of where to place anchor points when drawing a real-world illustration.

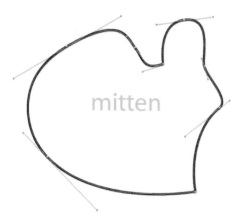

Starting an Illustration

Getting started with drawing an illustration is often the hardest part. Sometimes the illustration will be an image of a well-known object or a supplied sketch or a picture. At other times, the illustration to be created will exist only in your imagination. In either case, the challenge is the same: How do you translate the concept from its source to the Illustrator artboard?

Drawing from Scratch

Drawing from scratch means that you start with a new Illustrator document and create the illustration, using only the Illustrator tools. This approach is common, especially when the goal is to draw familiar items such as a daisy, fish, or sun.

Illustrator's shape tools (such as the Ellipse tool) combined with the transform tools (such as the Rotate tool) make the program powerful for creating geometric designs from scratch. The Undo and Redo commands allow you to experiment and create surprising designs.

Typographic illustrations—even complex ones—are often created from scratch.

Many talented illustrators and designers can create complex graphics off the cuff. It can be an astounding experience to watch an illustrator start with a blank artboard and, with no reference material, produce sophisticated graphics with attitude, expression, and emotion, as well as unexpected shapes and subtle relationships between objects.

Tracing a Scanned Image

Using the Place command, it is easy to import a scanned image into Illustrator. For complex illustrations—especially those of people or objects with delicate relationships, such as maps or blueprints—many designers find it easier to scan a sketch or a photo and import it into Illustrator as a guide or a point of reference.

Tracing a scanned image is not "cheating." An original drawing is an original drawing, whether it is first created on a computer or on a piece of paper. Rather than being a negative, the ability to use a computer to render a sketch is a fine example of the revolutionary techniques that illustration software has brought to the art of drawing. Figure 24 shows an illustration created from scratch in Illustrator, and Figure 25 shows a scanned sketch that will be the basis for the illustration you will create throughout this chapter.

Figure 24 An illustration created from scratch

Figure 25 Place a scanned sketch in Illustrator, and you can trace it or use it as a visual reference

Draw a closed path using smooth points

1. Open AI 3-4.ai, then save it as **Snowball Parts**.

2. Click **View** on the menu bar, then click **Arm**.

3. Verify that the **fill color** is set to **[None]** and the **stroke color** is set to **Black**.

4. Click the **Pen tool** , position it over **point 1**, then click and drag a **direction line** to the **green star on the right side of the 1**.

5. Go to **position 2**, then click and drag a **direction line to the next green star**.

TIP Watch the blue preview of the new segment fall into place as you drag the Pen tool . This will help you understand when to stop dragging the direction line.

6. Using the same method, continue to draw **points 3 through 6**, then compare your screen to Figure 26.

7. Position the **Pen tool** over **point 1.**

8. Press and hold **[option] (Mac)** or **[Alt] (Win)**, then click and drag to position the **ending segment** and close the path.

You drew a curved path. To close the path, you used a corner point, which allowed you to position the ending segment without affecting the starting segment.

Figure 26 Points 1 through 6 are smooth points

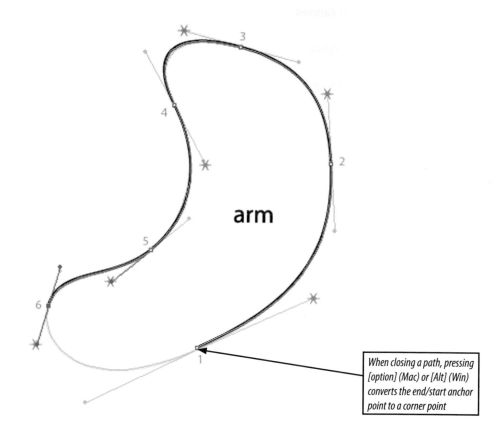

When closing a path, pressing [option] (Mac) or [Alt] (Win) converts the end/start anchor point to a corner point

Begin and end a path with a corner point

1. Click **View** on the menu bar, then click **Hatband** at the very bottom of the menu.

2. Verify that the **fill color** is set to **[None]** and the **stroke color** is set to **Black**.

3. Click the **Pen tool** 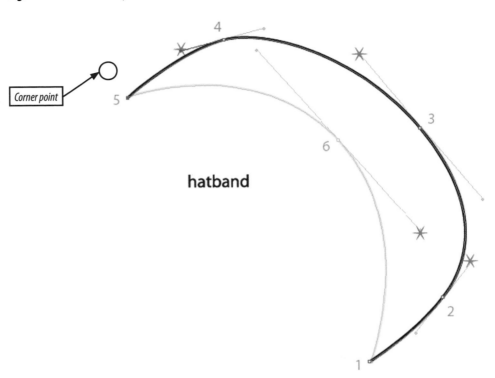, then click **position 1** to create a corner point.

4. Draw the next two curved segments for **positions 2** and **3**, using the green stars as guides.

5. Position the **Pen tool** over **position 4**, then click and drag to the **green star**.

6. Click **position 5** to create a corner point, as shown in Figure 27.

7. Position the **Pen tool** over **position 6**, then click and drag to the **green star**.

8. Click **position 1** to close the path with a corner point.

9. Click the **Selection tool**, then deselect the path.

You began a path with a corner point. When it was time to close the path, you simply clicked the starting point. Since the point was created without direction lines, there were no direction lines to contend with when closing the path.

Figure 27 Point 5 is a corner point

Corner point

hatband

Redirect a path while drawing

1. Click **View** on the menu bar, then click **Nose**.

   The Nose view includes the nose, mouth, eyebrow, and teeth.

2. Click the **Pen tool** , then click **point 1** on the nose to start the path with a corner point.

3. Create smooth points at **positions 2** and **3**.

The direction of the nose that you are tracing abruptly changes at point 3.

4. Press and hold **[option] (Mac)** or **[Alt] (Win)** to switch to the **Anchor Point tool** , then move the **top direction handle** of **point 3** down to the **red star**, as shown in Figure 28.

5. Release **[option] (Mac)** or **[Alt] (Win)** to switch back to the **Pen tool** , click and drag **position 4** to finish drawing the path, click the **Selection tool** , then deselect the path.

The nose element, as shown in Figure 29, is an open path.

6. Save your work, then continue to the next set of steps.

Tracing the nose, you encountered an abrupt change in direction, followed by a curve. You used the Anchor Point tool to redirect the direction lines on point 3, simultaneously converting point 3 from smooth to corner and defining the shape of the curved segment that follows.

Figure 28 Use the Anchor Point tool to redirect the path

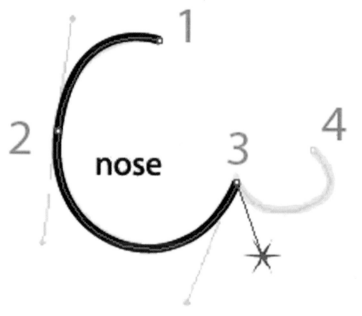

Figure 29 Nose element is an open path

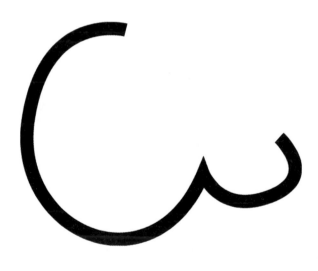

Place a scanned image

1. Click **View** on the menu bar, then click **Fit All in Window**.

2. Click **File** on the menu bar, then click **Place**.

3. Navigate to the drive and folder where your Chapter 3 Data Files are stored.

4. Click **Snowball Sketch.tif**, then click **Place**.

5. Click anywhere on the artboard to place the file.

6. Use the **Scale tool** 🔲, to scale the placed file **115%**.

TIP You can apply all the transform tools to placed files.

7. Click the **Selection tool** ▶, move the placed file to the right of the artboard, then lock it.

8. Draw the remaining elements of the illustration, using the sketch or Figure 30 as a reference. Save your work after you complete each element.

TIP The mouth, eyebrow, and teeth are in the Nose view.

You placed a file of a scanned sketch to use as a reference guide. You scaled the object, dragged it to the right of the artboard, locked it, and then drew the remaining elements of the illustration.

Figure 30 Use a scanned sketch as a reference or for tracing

APPLY ATTRIBUTES TO OBJECTS

▶ *What You'll Do*

You will create four new colors on the Color panel and apply each to one of the illustration elements. Using the Eyedropper tool, you will paint the remaining items quickly and easily.

Using the Eyedropper Tool

In Illustrator, **attributes** are formatting that you have applied to an object to affect its appearance. Typographic attributes, for example, would include font, leading, and horizontal scale. Artistic attributes include the fill color, stroke color, and stroke weight.

The Eyedropper tool is handy for applying *all* attributes of an object to another object. Its icon is particularly apt. The Eyedropper tool "picks up" an object's attributes, such as fill color, stroke color, and stroke weight.

> **TIP** You can think of the Eyedropper tool as taking a sample of an object's attributes.

The Eyedropper tool is particularly useful when you want to apply one object's attributes to another. For example, if you have applied a blue fill with a 3.5 pt. orange stroke to an object, you can easily apply those attributes to new or already-existing objects. Simply select the object that you want to format, then click the formatted object with the Eyedropper tool.

This is a simple example, but don't underestimate the power of the Eyedropper tool. As you explore more of Illustrator, you will find that you are able to apply a variety of increasingly complex attributes to objects. The more complex the attributes, the more the Eyedropper tool reveals its usefulness.

You can also use the Eyedropper tool to copy type formatting and effects between text elements. This can be especially useful when designing display type for headlines.

Adding a Fill to an Open Path

You can think of the letter O as an example of a closed path and the letter U as an example of an open path. Although it seems a bit strange, you can add a fill to an open path just as you would to a closed path. The program draws an imaginary straight line between the endpoints of an open path to define where the fill ends. Figure 31 shows an open path in the shape of a U with a red fill. Note where the fill ends. For the most part, avoid applying fills to open paths. Though Illustrator will apply the fill, an open path's primary role is to feature a stroke. Any effect that you can create by filling an open path you can also create with a more effective method by filling a closed path.

Figure 31 A fill color applied to an open path

Apply new attributes to closed paths

1. Verify that nothing is selected on the artboard.
2. Open the **Color panel**, then create a **royal blue color** on the Color panel.
3. Fill the **arm** with the royal blue color, then change its **stroke weight** to **6 pt**.

TIP Use the views at the bottom of the View menu to see and select each element with which you need to work. The mouth, eyebrow, and teeth are in the Nose view.

4. Deselect the arm, then create a **deep red color** on the Color panel.
5. Fill the **hatband** with the **deep red color**, then change its **stroke weight** to **3 pt**.

Figure 32 New attributes applied to five elements

6. Deselect the **hatband**, then create a **flesh-toned color** on the Color panel that is **20% Magenta** and **56% Yellow**.
7. Fill the **head** with the **flesh tone**; don't change the stroke weight.
8. Fill the **pom-pom** with **White**; don't change the stroke weight.
9. Fill the **mouth** with **Black**; don't change the stroke weight.
10. Compare your work with Figure 32.
11. Save your work, then continue to the next set of steps.

You applied new attributes to five closed paths by creating three new colors, using them as fills, then changing the stroke weight on two of the objects.

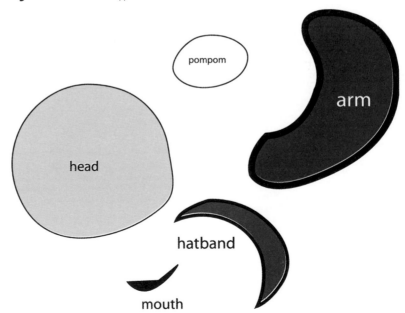

Copy attributes with the Eyedropper tool

1. Select the **torso**.

2. Click the **Eyedropper tool** ✐, then click the **blue arm**.

   As shown in Figure 33, the torso takes on the same fill and stroke attributes as the arm.

3. Switch to the **Selection tool** ▶, select the **hat**, click the **Eyedropper tool** ✐, then click the **hatband**.

4. Using any method you like, fill and stroke the remaining objects using the colors shown in Figure 34.

5. Save your work, then continue to the next set of steps.

   You applied the attributes of one object to another by first selecting the object to which you wanted to apply the attributes, then clicking the object with the desired attributes using the Eyedropper tool.

Figure 33 Use the Eyedropper tool to apply the attributes of one object to another with one click

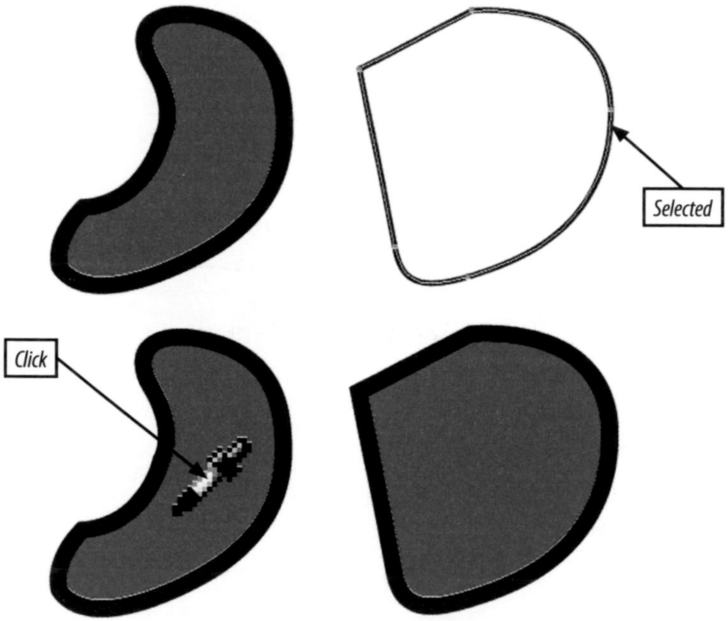

Selected

Click

Figure 34 All elements ready to be assembled

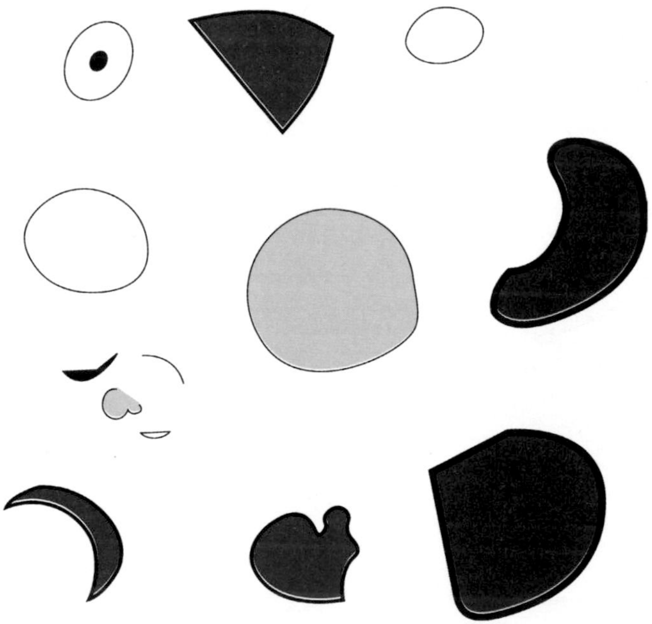

ASSEMBLE AN ILLUSTRATION

What You'll Do

In this lesson, you will arrange the elements you drew in Lesson 4 to create a composed illustration.

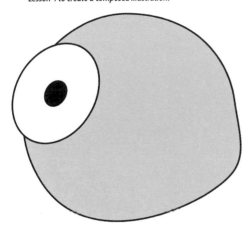

Assembling an Illustration

Illustrator's basic stacking order design is sophisticated enough to compose any illustration. Assembling an illustration with multiple objects will test your fluency with the stacking order commands: Bring to Front, Send to Back, Bring Forward, Send Backward, Paste in Front, Paste in Back, Group, Lock, Unlock All, Hide, and Show All. The sequence in which you draw the elements determines the stacking order (newer elements are in front of older ones), so you'll almost certainly need to adjust the stacking order when assembling the elements. Locking and hiding placed elements will help you to protect the elements when they are positioned correctly.

Assemble the illustration

1. Select and copy **all the elements** on the artboard.

2. Create a **new CMYK Color document** that is **9" × 9"**, then save it as **Snowball Assembled**.

3. Paste the **copied elements** into the Snowball Assembled document.

4. Deselect all objects, select the **head**, click **Object** on the menu bar, point to **Arrange**, then click **Send to Back**.

5. Group the **eye and the iris**, then position the **eye on the head** as shown in Figure 35.

6. Click the **eye**, press **[option] (Mac)** or **[Alt] (Win)**, then drag to create a copy of it, as shown in Figure 36.

Continued on next page

Figure 35 Eye positioned on the head

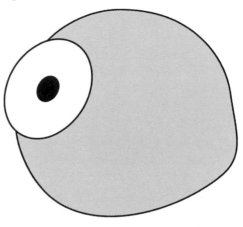

Figure 36 Second eye is a copy of the first

7. Position the **nose on the face**, cut the **nose**, select the **left eye**, then paste in front.

   The nose is pasted in the same position, but now it is in front of the eye, as shown in Figure 37.

8. Select the **teeth**, then bring them to the front.

9. Position the **teeth over the mouth**, then group them.

10. Position the **mouth and the teeth on the head**, and the **eyebrow over the right eye**, as shown in Figure 38.

11. Finish assembling the illustration, using Figure 39 as a guide.

12. Save your work, then continue to the next set of steps.

TIP Use the Arrange commands on the Object menu to change the stacking order of objects as necessary.

You assembled the illustration utilizing various commands to change the stacking order of the individual elements.

Figure 37 Nose pasted in front of the left eye

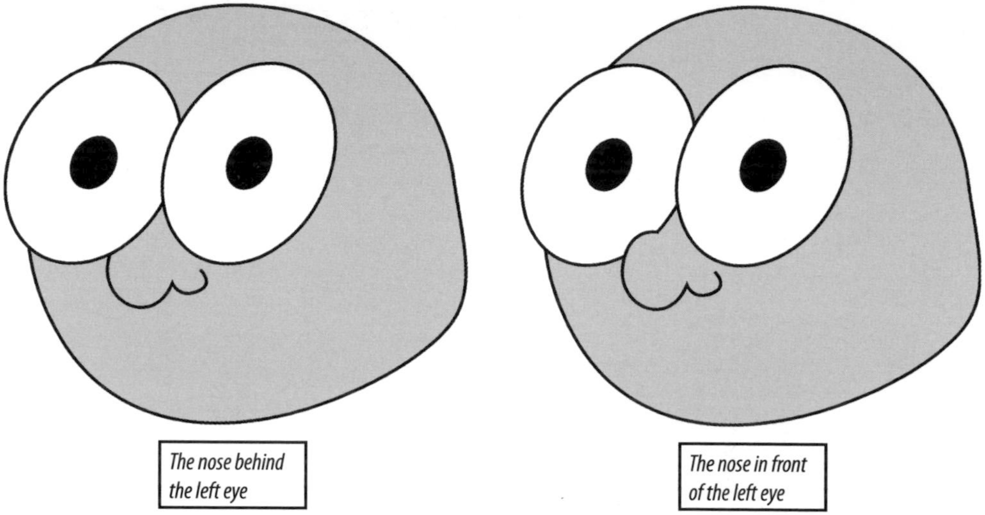

The nose behind the left eye

The nose in front of the left eye

Figure 38 Eyebrow positioned over the right eye

Figure 39 All elements in position

STROKE OBJECTS FOR ARTISTIC EFFECT

▶ *What You'll Do*

In this lesson, you will experiment with strokes of varying weight and attributes using options on the Stroke panel. You will then apply pseudo-strokes to all of the objects to create dramatic stroke effects.

Defining Joins and Caps

In addition to applying stroke weights, you use the Stroke panel to define other stroke attributes, including joins and caps, and whether a stroke is solid or dashed. Figure 40 shows the Dashed Line utility and Cap options on the Stroke panel.

Caps are applied to the ends of stroked paths. The Stroke panel offers three choices: Butt Cap, Round Cap, and Projecting Cap. Choose Butt Cap for squared ends and Round Cap for rounded ends. Generally, rounded caps are more appealing to the eye.

Figure 40 Stroke panel

Cap options

Dashed line options

○ Stroke

Weight: 1 pt

Cap:

Corner: Limit: 4 x

Align Stroke:

☑ Dashed Line

12 pt	7 pt				
dash	gap	dash	gap	dash	gap

Arrowheads:

Scale: 100% 100%

Align:

Profile: Uniform

The Projecting Cap applies a squared edge that extends the anchor point at a distance that is one-half the weight of the stroke. With a Projecting Cap, the weight of the stroke is equal in all directions around the line. The Projecting Cap is useful when you align two anchor points at a right angle, as shown in Figure 41.

When two stroked paths form a corner point, **joins** define the appearance of the corner. Miter Join is the default join and produces stroked lines with pointed corners. The Round Join produces stroked lines with rounded corners, and the Bevel Join produces stroked lines with squared corners. The greater the weight of the stroke, the more apparent the join will be, as shown in Figure 42.

Defining the Miter Limit

The **miter limit** determines when a miter join will be squared off to a beveled edge. The miter is the length of the point from the inside to the outside. The length of the miter is not the same as the stroke weight. When two stroked paths are at an acute angle, the length of the miter will greatly exceed the weight of the stroke, which results in an extreme point that can be very distracting.

| **TIP** You can align a stroke to the center, inside, or outside of a path using the Align Stroke buttons on the Stroke panel.

The default miter limit is 4, which means that when the length of the miter reaches 4 times the stroke weight, the program will automatically square it off to a beveled edge. Generally, you will find the default miter limit satisfactory, but you should remain conscious

of it when you draw objects with acute angles, such as stars and triangles. Figure 43 shows the impact of a miter limit on a stroked star with acute angles.

Figure 41 Projecting caps are useful when segments meet at right angles

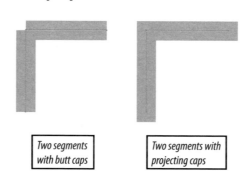

Two segments with butt caps

Two segments with projecting caps

Figure 42 Three types of joins

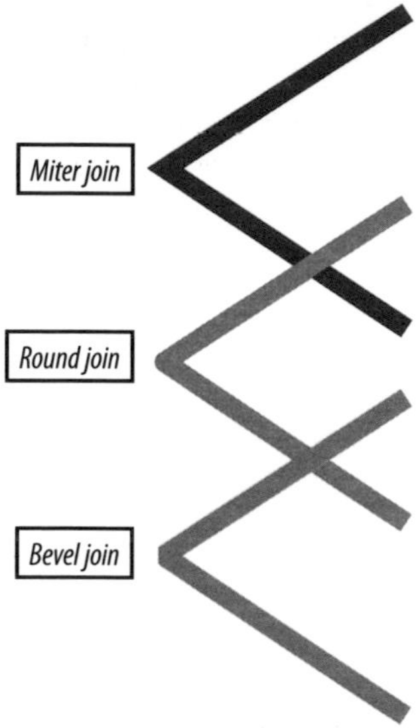

Miter join

Round join

Bevel join

Figure 43 Miter limit affects the length of stroked corner points

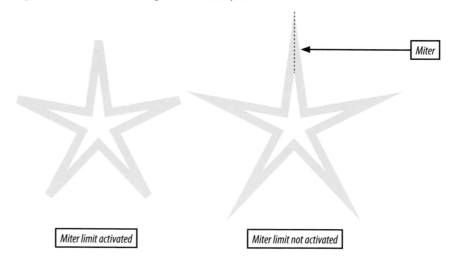

Miter

Miter limit activated

Miter limit not activated

Creating a Dashed Stroke

A dashed stroke is like any other stroked path in Illustrator, except that its stroke has been broken up into a sequence of dashes separated by gaps. The Stroke panel offers you the freedom to customize dashed or dotted lines by entering the lengths of the dashes and the gaps between them in the six dash and gap text boxes. You can create a maximum of three different sizes of dashes separated by three different sizes of gaps. The pattern you establish will be repeated across the length of the stroke.

When creating dashed strokes, remain conscious of the cap choice on the Stroke panel. **Butt caps** create familiar square dashes, and **round caps** create rounded dashes.

Creating a dotted line requires round caps. Figure 44 shows three dashed lines using the same pattern but with different caps applied. The red line is formatted with butt caps. The blue line is formatted with round caps. The green line is a dotted path. Dotted paths are formatted with round caps and a dash width of 0 pts.

Improving the Appearance of a Dashed Stroke

The Stroke panel offers two helpful settings for working with dashed lines—"Preserves exact gap and dash lengths" (Exact dashes) and "Aligns dashes and corners to path ends, adjusting lengths to fit" (Adjust dashes). These settings affect how dashes are distributed along a stroked path or the edge of a stroked object. Figure 45 shows each option. The red rectangle is an

example of the Exact dashes option. The dashes are distributed around the edge of the rectangle with the exact measurements input in the Stroke panel, regardless of the resulting appearance. In this case, the appearance leaves a bit to be desired. Each of the four corners looks different from the others, which is a bit disconcerting.

The blue rectangle is an example of the Adjust dashes option. Though the measurements for the dashed stroke are the same as those input for the red rectangle, here the Adjust dashes option automatically adjusts the position and gaps of the dash so the corners all look the same and the overall dashed effect is balanced.

Creating Pseudo-stroke Effects

Strokes around objects, especially black strokes, often contribute much to an illustration in terms of contrast, dimension, and dramatic effect. A classic technique that designers have used since the early versions of Illustrator is the "pseudo-stroke," or false stroke. Basically, you place a black-filled copy behind an illustration element, then distort the black element with the Direct Selection tool so it "peeks" out from behind the element in varying degrees.

This technique, as shown in Figure 46, is relatively simple to execute and can be used for dramatic effect in an illustration.

Figure 44 Caps are an important factor in determining the appearance of a dotted line

Figure 45 Gap and dash options applied to a stroke

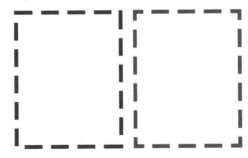

Figure 46 The "pseudo-stroke" effect

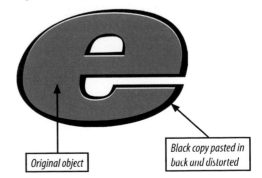

Original object

Black copy pasted in back and distorted

Modify stroke attributes

1. Select the **eyebrow**, the **nose**, and the **mouth**.

2. Click **Select** on the menu bar, then click **Inverse**.

   The selected items are now deselected, and the deselected items are selected.

3. Hide the selected items, then open the **Stroke panel**.

4. Select all, then change the **stroke weight** to **3 pt**.

5. Click the **Stroke panel menu button** , click **Show Options** if options are hidden, then click the **Round Cap button** .

   The caps on open paths are rounded.

6. On the Stroke panel, click the **Bevel Join button** .

   The miter joins on the mouth and nose change to bevel joins, as shown in Figure 47.

7. On the **Stroke panel**, click the **Round Join button** .

The bevel joins on the mouth and nose change to round joins, as shown in Figure 48.

8. Remove the stroke from the teeth.

TIP Use the Direct Selection tool  to select the teeth, since they are grouped with the mouth.

You hid elements so you could focus on the eyebrow, nose, and mouth. You applied round caps to the open paths and round joins to the corner points.

Figure 47 Bevel joins applied to paths

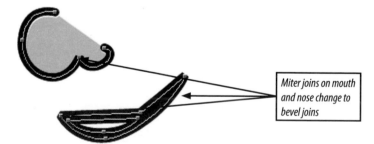

Miter joins on mouth and nose change to bevel joins

Figure 48 Round joins applied to paths

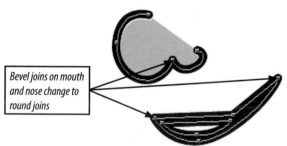

Bevel joins on mouth and nose change to round joins

Create a dashed and dotted stroke

1. Show all objects, then select all.
2. Deselect the snowball, then hide the selected items.

   The snowball should be the only element showing.
3. Select the **snowball**, then change the **stroke weight** to **4 pt**.
4. Click the **Dashed Line check box** on the Stroke panel.
5. Experiment with different dash and gap sizes.
6. Toggle between Butt and Round Caps.

   The dashes change from rectangles to ovals.
7. Enter **1 pt. dashes** and **4 pt. gaps**.
8. Click the **Round Cap button** , verify that the **Adjust dashes option** is activated, then compare your snowball to the one shown in Figure 49.
9. Show all the objects that are currently hidden.
10. Save your work, then continue to the next set of steps.

You applied a dashed stroke to the snowball object and noted how a change in caps affected the dashes.

Figure 49 Creating a dotted stroke using the Stroke panel

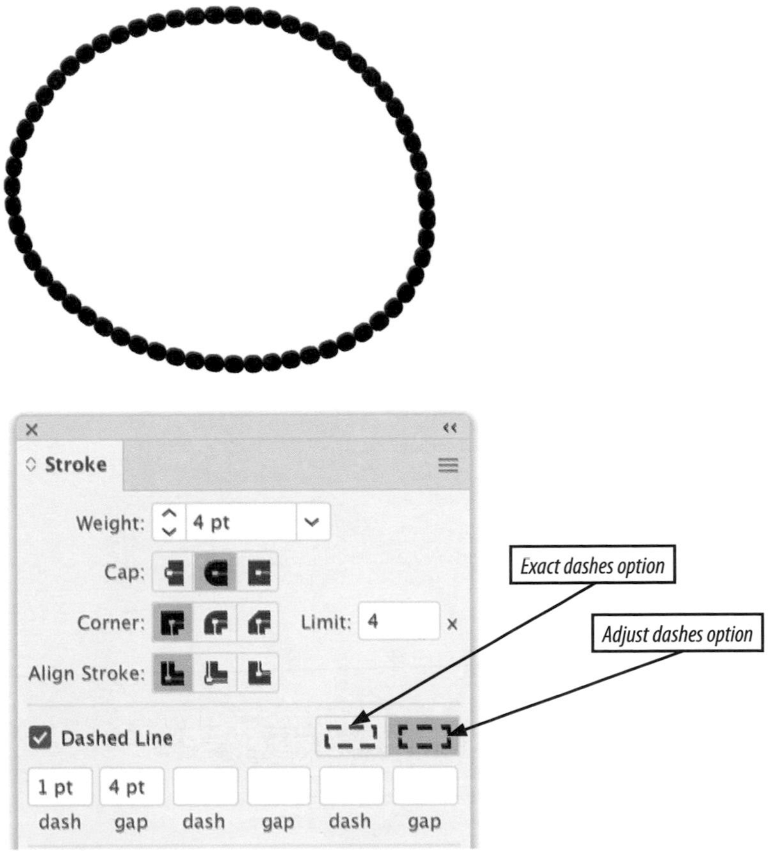

Exact dashes option

Adjust dashes option

Create pseudo-strokes

1. Select the **pom-pom**, copy it, then paste in back.

2. Apply a **black fill** to the copy.

TIP The copy is still selected behind the original white pom-pom, making it easy to apply the black fill.

3. Click the **white pom-pom**, then remove the stroke.

4. Lock the **white pom-pom**.

5. Using the **Direct Selection tool** 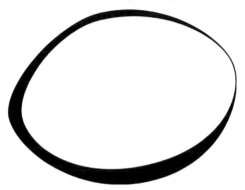, select the **bottom anchor point** on the black copy.

6. Use the **arrow keys** on your keypad to move the **anchor point 5 pts. down**.

   More and more of the black copy is revealed as its size is increased beneath the locked white pom-pom.

7. Move the **left anchor point 4 pts. to the left**.

8. Move the **top anchor point 2 pts. up**, then deselect.

   Your work should resemble Figure 50.

9. Using the same methods and Figure 51 as a reference, create distorted black copies behind all the remaining elements except the torso, the mouth, and the eyebrow.

10. Save your work, then close the Snowball Assembled document.

You created black copies behind each element, then distorted them, using the Direct Selection tool and the arrow keys, to create the illusion of uneven black strokes around the object.

Figure 50 Pom-pom with the pseudo-stroke effect

Figure 51 Completed illustration

USE IMAGE TRACE

What You'll Do

In this lesson, you will use Image Trace.

Using Image Trace

Image Trace is a feature that converts a bitmap image into a vector image so you can modify it as you would a vector graphic. When you place and select an image, the Image Trace button becomes available on the Control panel. Click the triangle beside the Image Trace button to expose the Image Trace menu, shown in Figure 52. Image Trace offers many tracing presets that give you different results. These presets include Line Art, Sketched Art, Black and White Logo, and 16 Colors.

In addition to the options in the Image Trace menu, you can use the Image Trace panel, shown in Figure 53. Here you can click the Preset list arrow to choose which type of preset you want to use to trace the bitmap. Click the Preview check box to see a preview of your image as you click on different presets.

Figure 52 Tracing presets in the Image Trace menu

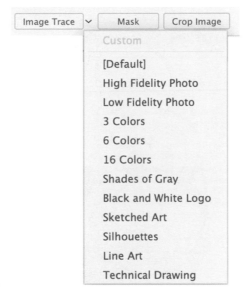

Figure 53 Image Trace panel

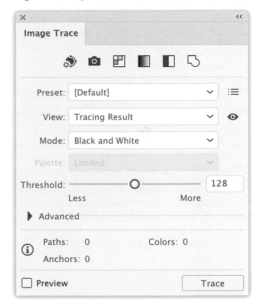

The Image Trace panel is dynamic if the Preview option is activated. The selected image will update with any changes you make in the panel. Click the View menu to see the Tracing Results, or switch to Outline view to see just the paths being created by the tracing utility. Drag the Colors slider to increase or decrease the number of colors available for the resulting trace. Figure 54 shows the traced image reduced to six colors.

| **TIP** The Colors slider is called the Threshold slider when you are working with black and white only.

Tracing a Line Art Sketch

Figure 55 shows a magic marker sketch of a dog that has been scanned into Photoshop and placed in Illustrator. Figure 56 shows the artwork after it has been traced using the Sketched Art preset in the Image Trace panel. Not much difference, you say? Images can be deceiving. Though the images in Figures 55 and 56 appear to be similar, they couldn't be more different because the artwork in Figure 56 is a vector graphic that has been traced from the bitmap graphic shown in Figure 55.

Figure 54 Traced image

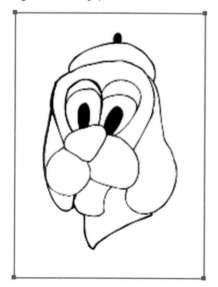

Figure 55 Bitmap graphic placed in Illustrator

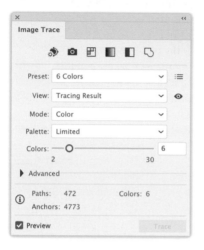

Figure 56 Traced graphic

Tracing a Photograph

You use Image Trace to trace a bitmap photo the same way you trace a sketch. With photographic images especially, the presets list can be used to create some really interesting illustration effects. Figure 57 shows four different vector graphics, each traced with a different preset and with different color settings.

Expanding a Traced Graphic

After Image Trace has been executed, the Expand button becomes available on the Control panel. To select and modify the paths and points that make up the new vector graphic, you must first click the Expand button. Once expanded, the illustration is available to be selected and modified, as shown in Figure 58.

Especially when tracing photographs, the Image Trace utility creates illustrations with complex relationships between different paths. Working with expanded tracing results will often test your skills for working with paths.

Figure 57 Four traced graphics

Figure 58 Expanded artwork with selectable components

Whenever you link to or embed artwork from another file, such as a TIF file from Photoshop, that file will be listed on the Links panel along with any metadata that has been saved with the file. The Links panel shows a thumbnail of the artwork and the filename to help you identify the file. The Links panel also uses icons to indicate the artwork's status, such as whether the link is up to date, the file is missing, or the file has been modified since you placed it. You can use the Links panel to see and manage all linked or embedded artwork. To select and view a linked graphic, select a link and then click the Go To Link button, or choose Go To Link on the Links panel menu. The file will appear centered in the window.

When you place an image, the Control panel lists the name of the placed file, its color mode (usually RGB, CMYK, or Grayscale), and its resolution in PPI (pixels per inch). The resolution listing is the effective resolution—in other words, the resolution of the file as its size in Illustrator. If you scale up a placed image, its effective resolution goes down, and the resolution listing on the Control panel will update to show the decrease. In the converse, if you scale down a placed image, its effective resolution increases.

Click on the filename on the Control panel to reveal a menu of options, shown in Figure 59. These commands help you to manage the link to the placed file. For example, click Go To Link, and the placed file will be centered in your window; this can be very helpful when working with many images. Click Edit Original to open the placed file in its native application. Click Relink to reestablish the link to the placed image if you've moved it to a different location on your computer or server.

These commands are all available on the Links panel, shown in Figure 60. Note the yellow triangle with the exclamation point, which indicates that the placed file has been modified in its native application since being placed. In other words, the original is different from the placed file. Click the Update Link icon on the Links panel or on the Control panel to update the link and bring the placed file in sync with the original file.

Figure 59 Link options on the Control panel

BW photo.tif   CMYK   PPI: 625   Unembed

Relink from CC Library...
Relink...
Go To Link
Edit Original
Update Link
Placement Options...

Embedding Placed Images

Another important option on the Control panel is the **Embed** button. When you place a file, that file is not automatically a part of the Illustrator file. Instead, a link is created from Illustrator to that file. If you were to move the Illustrator file to a different computer—or email it to a friend—the placed image would not be available when the file is opened on the

Figure 60 Links panel

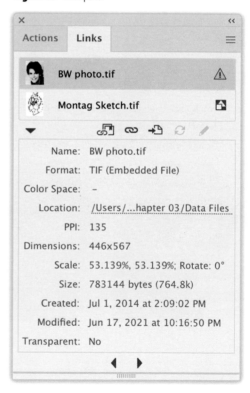

other computer. The link would be broken. For this reason, many designers choose to click the Embed button; doing so is like copying and pasting the placed file into the Illustrator document. The placed image no longer links to an original; it is in the Illustrator document and saved with the Illustrator document.

TIP To unembed an image, click Unembed on the Control panel or click the Links panel menu button, then click Unembed. You will be prompted to save the image to your hard drive.

Use Image Trace to trace a sketch

1. Open Al 3-5.ai, then save it as **Image Trace Sketch**.

   The file contains a placed marker sketch that was scanned in Photoshop.

2. Click the **Selection tool** ▶ , then click the **placed graphic**.

   When the placed graphic is selected, the Image Trace button on the Control panel becomes visible.

3. On the Control panel, click **Image Trace**.

   A progress bar appears while the placed image is being traced. Once completed, the Expand button appears on the Control panel.

4. On the Control panel, click **Expand**.

   As shown in Figure 61, the traced graphic is expanded into vector objects.

5. Deselect all; then, using the **Direct Selection tool** ▷ , select and fill the illustration with whatever colors you like. Figure 62 shows one example.

6. Save your work, then close the Image Trace Sketch document.

You used the Image Trace utility on the Control panel to convert a placed sketch into vector objects.

Figure 61 Expanded artwork

Use Image Trace to trace a photo

1. Open Al 3-6.ai, then save it as **Image Trace Photo**.

   The file contains a placed image that was scanned into Photoshop.

2. Zoom in on the photo, click the **Selection tool** ▶ , select the **graphic**, then open the **Image Trace panel** from the Window menu.

3. Click the **Preset list arrow**, then click **Line Art**.

   Continued on next page

Figure 62 One example of the painted illustration

4. Click the **Mode list arrow**, then click **Grayscale**.

5. Click the **Preview check box** if necessary.

   Your panel and image should resemble Figure 63.

6. Click the **Mode list arrow**, then click **Color**.

7. Drag the **Colors slider** to **4**, then compare your result to Figure 64.

8. Click **Expand** on the Control panel, then deselect all.

9. Click the **Direct Selection tool** , then select and fill the objects that make up the illustration. Figure 65 shows one example.

10. Save your work, then close Image Trace Photo.

You used the Image Trace panel to explore various tracing and color options, watching the result update dynamically.

Figure 63 Previewing the Image Trace results

Figure 64 Changing the results to four colors only

Figure 65 Coloring the expanded artwork

USE THE LIVE PAINT BUCKET TOOL

▶ What You'll Do

In this lesson, you will use the Live Paint Bucket tool and the Live Paint Selection tool, learn about regions and edges, and paint live paint groups

Using the Live Paint Features

When Adobe launched the Live Paint Bucket tool, they called it "revolutionary," and that was not an overstatement. The Live Paint Bucket tool breaks all the fundamental rules of Illustrator and creates some new ones. For that reason, when you are working with the Live Paint Bucket tool, it's a good idea to think of yourself as working in Live Paint mode because Illustrator will function differently with this tool than it will with any other. Essentially, the Live Paint Bucket tool is designed to make painting easier and more intuitive. It does this by changing the basic rules of Illustrator objects. In Live Paint mode, the concept of "objects" no

longer applies—you can fill and stroke negative spaces. The Live Paint Bucket tool uses two object types called regions and edges. **Regions** and **edges** are comparable to fills and strokes, but they are "live." As shown in Figure 66, where two regions overlap, a third region is created and can be painted with its own color.

Adobe likes to say that Live Paint is intuitive—something that looks like it should be able to be filled with its own color can indeed be filled with its own color. As long the Live Paint Bucket tool is selected, selected objects can be filled using the new rules of Live Paint mode. Once you leave Live Paint mode, the paint that you have applied to the graphic remains part of the illustration.

Figure 66 Identifying regions and edges in an illustration

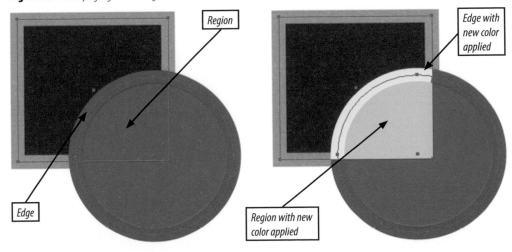

Live Painting Regions

Figure 67 shows three selected rectangles that overlap each other. The selection marks show various shapes created by the overlap. As stated earlier, these overlapping areas or shapes are called regions. To fill the regions, you must first select all the objects that you want to paint. Click the Live Paint Bucket tool, click a color on the Swatches panel, then click a region that you want to fill. As shown in Figure 68, when you position the Live Paint Bucket tool pointer over a region, that region is highlighted. Then when you click the Live Paint Bucket tool, the region is filled, as shown in Figure 69.

As shown in Figure 70, each region can be filled with new colors. But that's not all that the Live Paint Bucket tool has to offer. The "live" part of Live Paint is that these regions are now part of a **Live Paint group**, and they maintain a dynamic relationship with each other. This means that when any of the objects is moved, the overlapping area changes shape and fill accordingly. For example, in Figure 71, the tall, thin rectangle has been moved to the left. Note how the overlapping regions have been redrawn and how their fills have updated with the move.

TIP To select multiple regions in a Live Paint group, click the **Live Paint Selection tool** ⬚⬚ on the toolbar, click the first region, press and hold [shift], then click the remaining regions. The selected regions appear with a gray dotted fill pattern until you click a new color on the Swatches panel and deselect the artwork.

Figure 67 Three overlapping selected rectangles

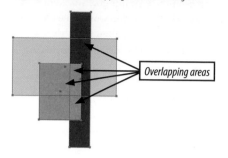

Overlapping areas

Figure 68 Positioning the Live Paint Bucket tool pointer

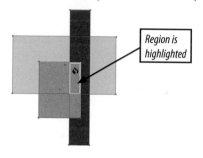

Region is highlighted

Figure 69 Filling a region with a new color

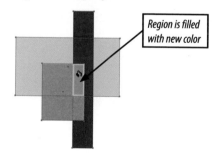

Region is filled with new color

Figure 70 Filling multiple regions

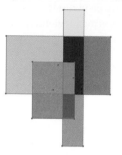

Figure 71 Moving an object in a Live Paint group

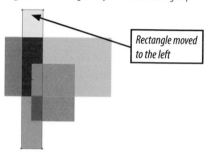

Rectangle moved to the left

Painting Virtual Regions

The intuitive aspect of Live Paint mode goes one step further with virtual regions. Figure 72 shows six Illustrator paths; each path is selected and has a 1 pt. black stroke and no fill. This simple illustration provides a perfect example of the powers of the Live Paint Bucket tool.

Imagine trying to fill the four center polygons created by the overlapping strokes in "classic"

Illustrator without the Live Paint Bucket tool. This seemingly simple goal would be a very tough challenge. You would need to create four polygons that align perfectly with the shapes created by the overlapping strokes because without the shapes, you'd have nothing to fill. And because the strokes are so thin, you'd need those polygons to align exactly with the strokes. Finally, if you moved any of the strokes, you'd need to modify the polygons to match the new layout.

With the Live Paint Bucket tool, the regions that are created by the intersection of the paths can be filled as though they were objects. Figure 73 shows four regions that have been filled with the Live Paint Bucket tool.

In this case, as in the case of the overlapping rectangles, the dynamic relationship is maintained. Figure 74 shows the paths moved, the filled regions redrawn, and their fills updated.

Figure 72 Six paths

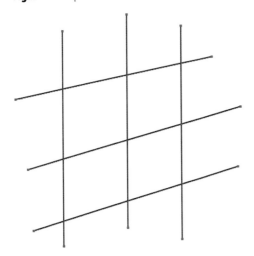

Figure 73 Four filled regions between paths

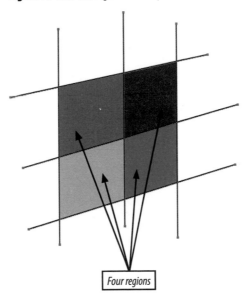

Four regions

Figure 74 Moving paths in a Live Paint group

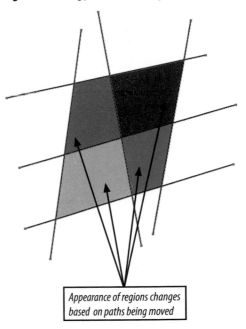

Appearance of regions changes based on paths being moved

Inserting an Object into a Live Paint Group

New objects can be inserted into a Live Paint group. To do so, switch to the Selection tool, then double-click inside any of the regions of the group. As shown in Figurc 75, a gray rectangle appears around the group, indicating that you are in insertion mode. Once in **insertion mode**, you can then add an object or objects to the group.

As shown in Figure 76, another tall rectangle has been added to the group. It can now be painted with the Live Paint Bucket tool as part of the Live Paint group. Once you've added all that you want to the Live Paint group, exit insertion mode by double-clicking the Selection tool outside of the Live Paint group.

Expanding a Live Paint Group

When you are done colorizing a Live Paint group, you have the option of using the Expand command to release the Live Paint group into its component regions. Simply select the Live Paint group, then click the Expand button on the Control panel. Each region will be converted to an ordinary Illustrator object.

Figure 75 Viewing the art in insertion mode

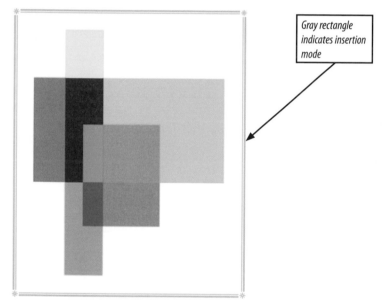

Gray rectangle indicates insertion mode

Figure 76 Adding an object to the Live Paint group

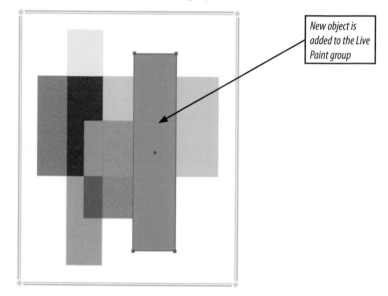

New object is added to the Live Paint group

Live Painting Edges

In Live Paint mode, just as regions are akin to fills, edges are akin to strokes. With the Live Paint Bucket tool, you can paint edges as well as regions.

Figure 77 shows two overlapping objects, each with a 6 pt. stroke. To paint edges (strokes), you must first double-click the Live Paint Bucket tool, then activate the Paint Strokes check box in the Live Paint Bucket Options dialog box, as shown in Figure 78. When activated, the Live Paint Bucket tool will paint either regions or edges, depending on where it's positioned.

When you position the Live Paint Bucket tool over an edge, its icon changes to a paintbrush icon. The edge is highlighted and paintable as though it were its own object, as shown in Figure 79.

Figure 77 Two overlapping rectangles

Figure 78 Choosing the Paint Strokes option

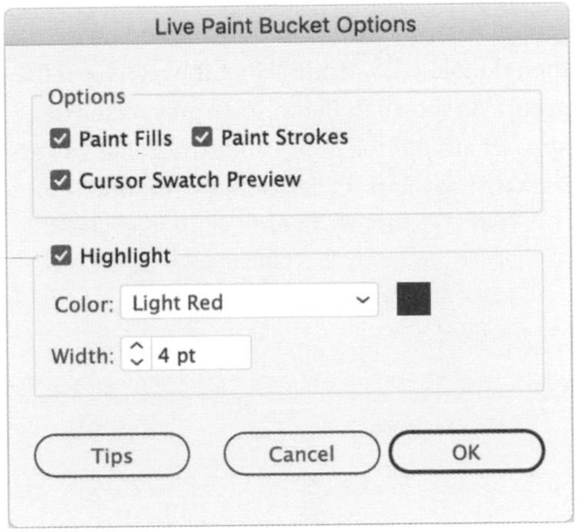

Figure 79 Painting edges

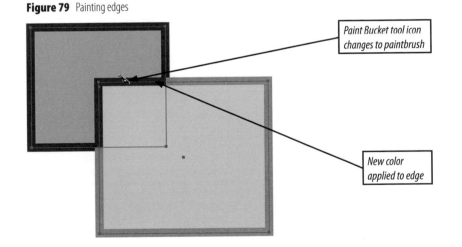

Paint Bucket tool icon changes to paintbrush

New color applied to edge

Use the Live Paint Bucket tool

1. Open AI 3-7.ai, then save it as **Live Paint Circles**.

2. Open the **Swatches panel**, fill the **top circle** with **red**, fill the **left circle** with **green**, then fill the **right circle** with **blue**.

3. Select all, double-click the **Live Paint Bucket tool** 🪣, to open the Live Paint Bucket Options dialog box, verify that both the **Paint Fills** and **Paint Strokes check boxes** are checked, then click **OK**.

TIP The Live Paint Bucket tool 🪣, is located behind the Shape Builder tool 🔧,.

4. Click any of the **orange swatches** on the Swatches panel.

   Note that because you are in Live Paint mode, none of the selected objects change to orange when you click the orange swatch.

5. Position the **Live Paint Bucket tool pointer** over the **red fill of the red circle**, then click.

6. Click any **pink swatch** on the Swatches panel, position the **Live Paint Bucket tool pointer** over the area where the **orange circle overlaps the blue circle**, then click.

   As shown in Figure 80, the region of overlap between the two circles is filled with pink.

7. Using any colors you like, fill all seven regions so your artwork resembles Figure 81.

8. Click the **stroke button** on the toolbar to activate the stroke, then choose any **purple swatch** on the Swatches panel, position the **Live Paint Bucket tool pointer** over any of the **black strokes** in the artwork, then click.

   When positioned over a stroke, the Live Paint Bucket tool pointer changes to a paintbrush icon.

9. Using any color you like, change the color of all 12 edges, then deselect all so your artwork resembles Figure 82.

Figure 80 Painting the region that is the overlap between two circles

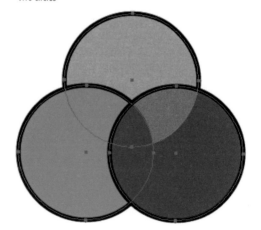

Figure 81 Viewing seven painted regions

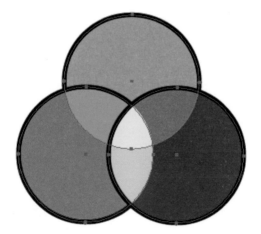

Figure 82 Viewing 12 painted edges

10. Deselect all; click the **Direct Selection tool** 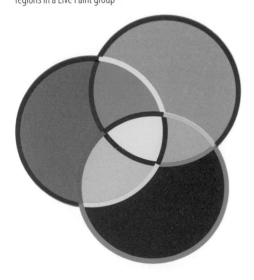 ; then, without pulling them apart, drag the **circles** in different directions, noting that the components of the Live Paint group maintain a dynamic relationship as shown in Figure 83.

11. Select all, click **Expand** on the Control panel, deselect all, then pull out all the regions so your artwork resembles Figure 84.

The illustration has been expanded into multiple objects.

12. Save your work, then close the Live Paint Circles document.

You used the Live Paint Bucket tool to fill various regions and edges of three overlapping circles. You then moved various components of the Live Paint group, noting that they maintain a dynamic relationship. Finally, you expanded the Live Paint group, which changed your original circles into multiple objects.

Figure 83 Exploring the dynamic relationship between regions in a Live Paint group

Figure 84 Dissecting the expanded Live Paint group

Use the Live Paint Bucket tool to paint an illustration

1. Open AI 3-8.ai, then save it as **Live Paint Dog**.

2. Click the **Selection tool** , then click the **different colored strokes** so you understand how the illustration has been drawn.

   The illustration has been created with a series of open paths. The only closed path is the nose.

3. Select all, then change the **stroke color** of all the **paths** to **Black**.

4. Click the **Live Paint Bucket tool** , then click a **red swatch** on the Swatches panel.

   Note that because you are in Live Paint mode, none of the selected objects changes to red when you click the red swatch.

5. Press **[command] (Mac)** or **[Ctrl] (Win)** to switch to the **Selection tool** , click the **artboard** to deselect all, then release **[command] (Mac)** or **[Ctrl] (Win)** to return to the **Live Paint Bucket tool** .

6. Fill the **hat** and the **knot** at the top of the hat with **red**, then click **Black** on the Swatches panel.

7. Click the **Live Paint Selection tool** , click the **nose**, press and hold **[shift]**, click the **left eye**, then click the **right eye**.

   Your illustration should resemble Figure 85.

   TIP When you select multiple areas with the Live Paint Selection tool , the areas are filled with a dot pattern until you apply a color.

Figure 85 Using the Live Paint Selection tool

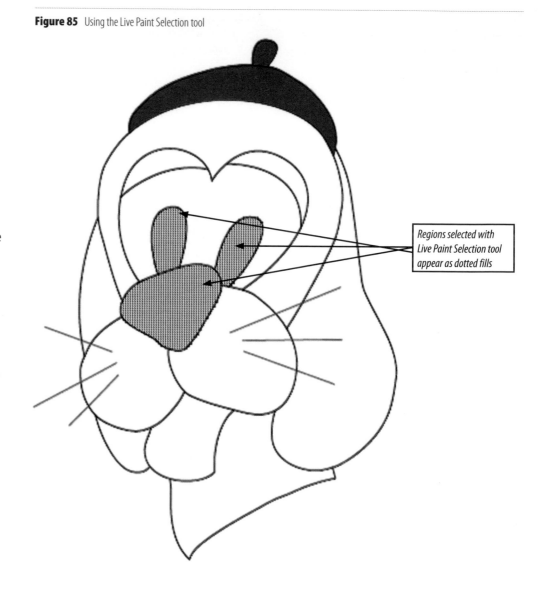

Regions selected with Live Paint Selection tool appear as dotted fills

8. Click **Black** on the Swatches panel.

9. Using the same method, select **both eyelids**, then fill them with a **lavender swatch**.

10. Click the **Live Paint Bucket tool** , click a **yellow swatch** on the Swatches panel, then paint the illustration so your illustration resembles Figure 86.

    Note the small areas between the whiskers that must be painted yellow.

11. Using the **Live Paint Bucket tool** , paint the **right jowl light brown**, paint the **left jowl a darker brown**, then paint the **tongue pink**.

12. Click the **stroke button** on the toolbar to activate the stroke, then click a **gray swatch** on the Swatches panel.

13. Double-click the **Live Paint Bucket tool** , click the **Paint Stroke check box** in the Live Paint Bucket Options dialog box if it is not already checked, then click **OK**.

14. Click the **Live Paint Bucket tool**  on **each line segment that makes up the dog's whiskers**.

    TIP You will need to click 14 times to paint the six whiskers because each whisker is made from more than one line segment.

Continued on next page

Figure 86 Painting the yellow regions

15. Deselect, compare your work to Figure 87, save your work, then close the Live Paint Dog document.

You used the Live Paint Bucket tool to fill regions created by the intersection of a collection of open paths. You also used the tool to paint edges.

Figure 87 Viewing the finished artwork

EXPLORE ALTERNATE DRAWING TECHNIQUES

▶ *What You'll Do*

In this lesson, you will learn some new and fun drawing techniques including how to reshape a path with the Anchor Point tool and how to change Pencil tool settings to draw the way you want to.

Reshaping Path Segments with the Anchor Point Tool

Along with its ability to convert smooth anchor points to corner anchor points and vice versa, the Anchor Point tool can also convert path segments from straight to curved. In fact, the Anchor Point tool is so powerful that you can use it as an alternate to dragging directional handles to modify a curve. Instead, you can click and drag any segment with the Anchor Point tool to reshape it and position it as you like.

Figure 88 shows a shape created from a simple rectangle. No directional handles were manipulated to create these curves. Instead, the original straight segments were curved and reshaped using the Anchor Point tool.

When you're creating paths with the Pen tool, you can access the Anchor Point tool and the path segment reshape function simply by pressing [option] (Mac) or [Alt] (Win).

In practice, you'll likely use a combination of both methods—dragging directional handles

and dragging path segments—but you'll find that the Anchor Point tool adds a more freehand, intuitive option.

Drawing with the Pencil Tool

With the widespread use of tablets and pen styluses, advances in Illustrator's Pencil tool are making the tool a great option for drawing by hand. For many designers, it's become a real alternative to the Pen tool.

Figure 88 A curved object reshaped from a simple rectangle

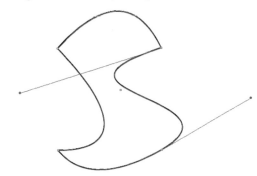

Setting specific options is important for making the tool practical for drawing. In Figure 89, note that the Fidelity slider is set to Smooth. At this setting, relatively uneven lines you draw using your stylus and tablet will smooth out automatically.

Figure 90 shows a relatively uneven line being drawn with the Pencil tool. Figure 91 shows

the same path once the Pencil tool is lifted. The path is automatically smoothed out and anchor points are added at necessary locations.

Note the Keep selected option in Figure 89. When this option is activated, you can add to a path you've already drawn by floating over an open anchor point and continuing your drawing with the Pencil tool. Essentially, this

allows you to draw on your screen with the Pencil tool as you would draw on a piece of paper with a real pencil.

The Edit selected paths option is a critical one that has a big effect on how the Pencil tool works. It's one you might have to activate and deactivate to draw certain types of artwork.

Figure 89 Pencil Tool Options dialog box

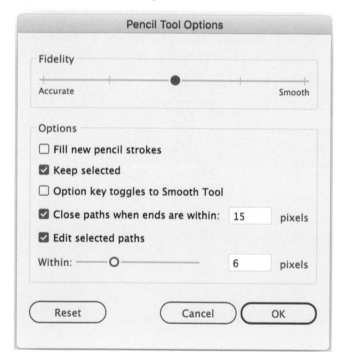

Figure 90 Rough line being drawn

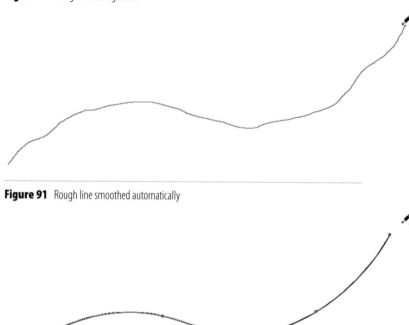

Figure 91 Rough line smoothed automatically

Figure 92 shows a simple, hand-drawn circle done with the Pencil tool. If you want to draw a line across the circle, as shown in Figure 93, you must do so with the Edit selected paths option *deactivated*. If the Edit selected paths option is activated, drawing the line across the circle will edit the circle and redraw it with the new line, as shown in Figure 94.

On the other hand, the Edit selected paths option can be very useful for doing just that—editing paths while you draw. If you want to tweak a line, simply draw over it and the path will redraw with the new line.

| **TIP** Press [shift] while drawing with the Pencil tool to draw in straight lines.

Figure 92 Simple circle

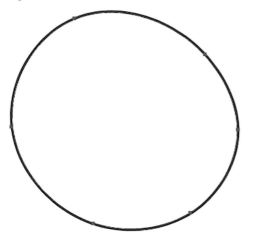

Figure 93 Circle with line drawn across it

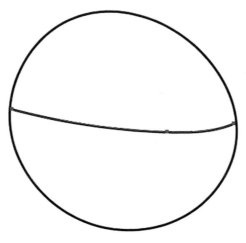

Figure 94 Circle redrawn with new line

Reshape path segments with the Anchor Point tool

1. Open AI 3-9.ai, then save it as **Reshape Path**.

2. Click the **Anchor Point tool** .

   The Anchor Point tool is behind the Pen tool .

   TIP You can access the Anchor Point tool by pressing [shift] [C] on your keypad. If you are drawing with the Pen tool , you can press [option] (Mac) or [Alt] (Win) to quickly switch to the Anchor Point tool .

3. Drag the **bottom black path segment** as many times as necessary to align it to the blue line.

   In this exercise, you will drag only path segments; don't drag any anchor points or any directional handles. This exercise is intended to show that you can use the Anchor Point tool alone to reshape any path. Depending on where you click, you can eventually modify a path into any shape.

4. Drag the **right black segment** to align it to the blue line.

5. Using Figure 95 as a reference, drag the **top black segment** up then, as you're dragging, press the **[shift] key** and keep dragging to make the **arc** shown in the figure.

   With the [shift] key pressed, the directional handles are even and the arc is balanced on both sides.

6. Drag the **arc** left so it aligns with the top blue path.

7. Reshape the remaining paths to match the blue shape.

8. Save your work, then close Reshape Path.

You used the Anchor Point tool to reshape an object.

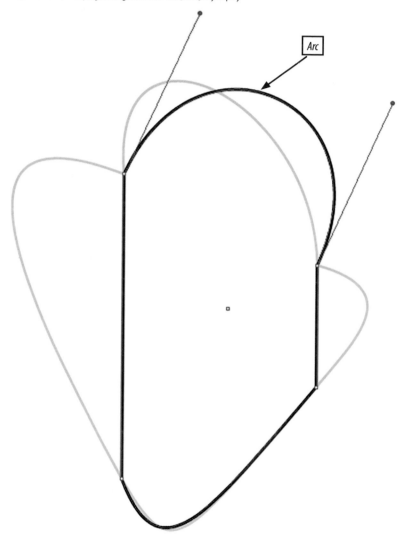

Figure 95 Reshaping the segment with the [shift] key in play

Arc

Draw with the Pencil tool

1. Open AI 3-10.ai, then save it as **Pencil Tool**.

2. Set the **fill color** to **[None]**, set the **stroke color** to **Black**, then set the **stroke weight** to **2 points**.

3. Double click the **Pencil tool** , then compare your Pencil Tool Options dialog box to Figure 96.

   Note that Fidelity is set to Smooth and that the Keep selected and Edit selected paths options are both activated.

Continued on next page

Figure 96   Pencil Tool Options dialog box

4. Click **OK**, then zoom in on the **top path** on the artboard.

5. Trace the **first half-circle** slowly, then release the mouse button.

   As you draw, the path is very jagged and rough, but when you release the mouse button, the path is smoothed out. As shown in Figure 97, the path is created with the minimum number of anchor points necessary.

6. Float over the **end point**, then draw the **second half-circle**.

   Because the Keep selected option is activated, the second segment you draw is connected to the first to create a single path.

7. Finish drawing the **top path**.

8. Zoom in on the **middle path** on the artboard.

9. Trace the **first half-circle**, then, *without releasing your finger from the mouse pointer*, press and hold **[shift]**, then trace the **straight horizontal line** so your path resembles Figure 98.

Figure 97 Smooth path created with Pencil tool

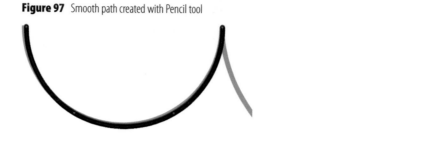

Figure 98 Straight segment added to curved segment

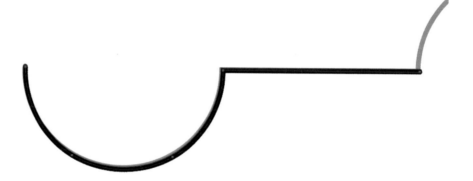

10. Using the same method, complete the trace in one move.

11. Zoom in on the path at the **bottom of the artboard**, then select it with the **Selection tool** 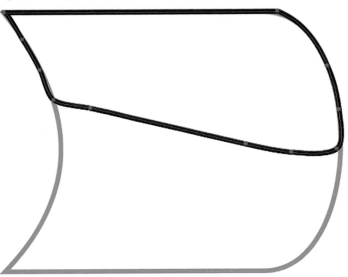.

    The path was drawn with the Pencil tool.

12. Click the **Pencil tool**, then draw a **path** from a point on the left segment to a point on the right segment.

    As shown in Figure 99, because the Edit selected paths option is activated, the object is edited and redrawn with the new path.

13. Save your work, then close the Pencil Tool document.

You used the Pencil tool to trace different paths. You introduced the [shift] key to trace straight paths along with curved paths. With the Edit selected paths option activated, you edited a path by drawing a segment across an existing object.

Figure 99 Editing the path with the Pencil tool

Draw straight lines

1. Open AI 3-11.ai, then save it as **Mighty Montag**.
2. Place the Montag Sketch.tif into the Mighty Montag document; you will need to navigate to the drive and folder where your Chapter 3 Data Files are stored to find it.
3. Position the sketch in the center of the artboard, then lock it.
4. Set the fill color to [None] and the stroke to 1 pt. Black.
5. Click the Pen tool, then starting with the two lines that represent the dog's neck, create a 4-sided shape for the neck.
   Don't worry that the shape is in front of the dog's tongue, ears, and jowls. It will eventually be placed behind them when you assemble the illustration.
6. Draw six whiskers.
7. Save your work.

Draw curved lines

1. Using the Pen tool, draw an oval for the eye.
2. Draw a crescent moon shape for the eyelid.
3. Draw an oval for the iris.
4. Save your work.

Draw elements of an illustration

1. Trace the left ear.
2. Trace the hat.
3. Trace the nose.
4. Trace the left jowl.
5. Trace the right jowl.
6. Trace the tongue.
7. Trace the right ear.
8. Trace the head.
9. Save your work.

Apply attributes to objects

1. Unlock the placed sketch and hide it.
2. Fill the hat with a red swatch.
3. Fill the right ear with 9C/18M/62Y.
4. Fill the nose with Black.
5. Fill the eye with White.
6. Fill the tongue with Salmon.
7. Using Figure 100 as a guide, use the colors on the Swatches panel to finish the illustration.
8. Save your work.

Assemble an illustration

1. Send the neck to the back of the stacking order, then lock it.
2. Send the head to the back, then lock it.
3. Send the left ear to the back, then lock it.
4. Bring the hat to the front.
5. Bring the right ear to the front.
6. Select the whiskers, group them, then bring them to the front.
7. Select the tongue, then cut it.
8. Select the right jowl, then apply the Paste in Back command.
9. Bring the nose to the front.
10. Select the eye, the eyelid, and the iris; then group them.
11. Drag and drop a copy of the eye group.

TIP Press and hold [option] (Mac) or [Alt] (Win) as you drag the eye group.

12. Select the right jowl.
13. On the Color panel add 10% K to darken the jowl.
14. Use the Color panel to change the fills on other objects to your liking.
15. Save your work.

Stroke objects for artistic effect

1. Make the caps on the whiskers round.
2. Change the whiskers' stroke weight to .5 pt.
3. Unlock all.
4. Select the neck and change the joins to round.
5. Apply pseudo-strokes to the illustration.

TIP Copy and paste the elements behind themselves, fill them with black, lock the top objects, then use the Direct Selection tool to select anchor points on the black-filled copies. Use the arrow keys on the keyboard to move the anchor points. The black copies will peek out from behind the elements in front.

6. Click Object on the menu bar, then click Unlock All.
7. Delete the Montag Sketch file behind your illustration.
8. Save your work, compare your illustration to Figure 100, then close the Mighty Montag document.

Figure 100 Completed Skills Review, Part 1

Use Image Trace

1. Open AI 3-12.ai, then save it as **Skills Trace Photo**.
2. Zoom in on the photo, click the Selection tool, select the graphic, then open the Image Trace panel.
3. Click the Preset list arrow on the Image Trace panel, then click Line Art.
4. Click the Mode list arrow, then click Grayscale.
5. Click to activate the Preview option if necessary.
6. Click the Mode list arrow, then click Color.
7. Drag the Colors slider to 6.
8. Click the Expand button on the Control panel, then deselect all.
9. Click the Direct Selection tool, then select and fill the objects that make up the illustration.
10. Figure 101 shows one example.
11. Save your work, then close the Skills Trace Photo document.

Figure 101 Completed Skills Review, Part 2

Morguefile

Use the Live Paint Bucket tool

1. Open AI 3-13.ai, then save it as **Live Paint Skills**.
2. Open the Swatches panel, fill the top circle with any orange swatch, fill the left circle with any blue swatch, then fill the right circle with any purple swatch.
3. Select all, then double-click the Live Paint Bucket tool to open the Live Paint Bucket Options dialog box, verify that both the Paint Fills and Paint Strokes check boxes are checked, then click OK.
4. Click any yellow swatch on the Swatches panel.
5. Position the Live Paint Bucket tool pointer over the orange fill of the orange circle, then click.
6. Click any pink swatch on the Swatches panel, position the Live Paint Bucket tool pointer over the area where the yellow circle overlaps the purple circle, then click.
7. Using any colors you like, fill the remaining five regions with different colors.
8. Click the stroke button on the toolbar, click any blue swatch on the Swatches panel, position the Live Paint Bucket tool pointer over any of the black strokes in the artwork, then click.
9. Using any color you like, change the color of all 12 edges, then deselect all.
10. Click the Direct Selection tool; then, without pulling them apart, drag the circles in different directions noticing that they stay grouped, as shown in Figure 102.
11. Save your work, then close the Live Paint Skills document.

Figure 102 Completed Skills Review, Part 3

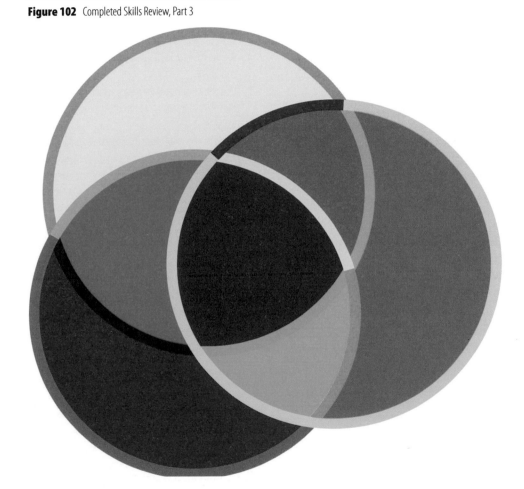

The owner of The Blue Peppermill Restaurant has hired your design firm to take over all its marketing and advertising, saying it needs to expand its efforts. You request all The Blue Peppermill's existing materials, such as slides, prints, digital files, brochures, and business cards. Upon examination, you realize that the restaurant has no vector graphic version of its logo. Deciding that this is an indispensable element for future design and production, you scan in a photo of its signature peppermill, trace it, and apply a blue fill to it.

1. Create a new 6" × 6" document, then save it as **Peppermill**.
2. Place the Peppermill.tif file into the Peppermill document.

The Peppermill.tif file is in the Chapter 3 Data Files folder.

3. Scale the placed image 150%, then lock it.
4. Set the fill color to [None] and the stroke to 2 pt. Black.
5. Using the Zoom tool, create a selection box around the round element at the top of the peppermill to zoom in on it.
6. Using the Pen tool, trace the peppermill, adjusting your view as necessary to see various sections of the peppermill as you trace, then fill it with a blue swatch.
7. When you finish tracing, tweak the path, if necessary, then save your work.
8. Unlock the placed image and cut it from the document.
9. Save your work, compare your illustration to Figure 103, then close the Peppermill document.

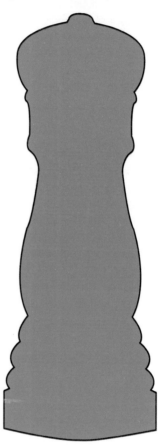

Figure 103 Completed Project Builder 1

You work at a children's library that has recently been remodeled. The staff has asked you to create a mural theme with interesting shapes of bright colors for the freshly painted walls. You create a sample in Illustrator to present to the staff—a single theme that can be modified to create multiple versions of the artwork.

1. Open AI 3-14.ai, then save it as **Tic Tac Toe**.
2. Select all, then change the stroke colors to Black.
3. Click the Live Paint Bucket tool, select a fill color, then click in any of the squares.
4. Fill each of the squares with a different color, then deselect all.
5. Click the Direct Selection tool, then change the angles of the black paths. Figure 104 shows one possible result.
6. Save your work, then close Tic Tac Toe.

Figure 104 Completed Project Builder 2

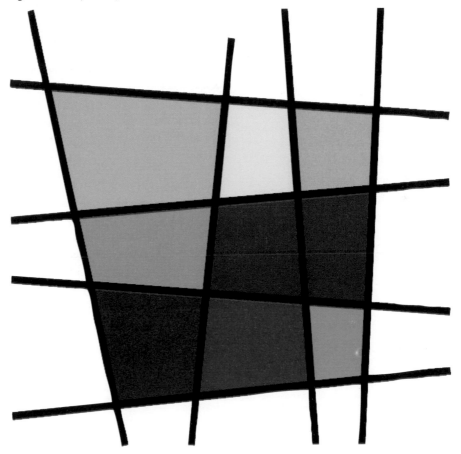

Your design firm is contacted by a company called Stratagem with a request for a proposal. Stratagem manufactures molds for plastic products. The terms of the request are as follows: You are to submit a design for the shape of the bottle for a new dishwashing liquid. You are to submit a single image that shows a black line defining the shape. The line art should also include the nozzle. The size of the bottle is immaterial. The design is to be "sophisticated, so as to be in visual harmony with the modern home kitchen." The name of the product is "Sleek."

1. Go to the grocery store and purchase bottles of dishwashing liquid whose shape you find interesting.

2. Use the purchases for ideas and inspiration.
3. Sketch your idea for the bottle's shape on a piece of paper.
4. Take a picture of the sketch or scan it and save it as a TIF file.
5. Create a new Illustrator document, then save it as **Sleek Design**.
6. Place the scan in the document, then lock it.
7. Trace your sketch, using the Pen tool.
8. When you are done tracing, delete the sketch from the document.
9. Tweak the line to define the shape to your specifications.
10. Use the Average dialog box to align points to perfect the shape.
11. Save your work, compare your illustration to Figure 105, then close the Sleek Design document.

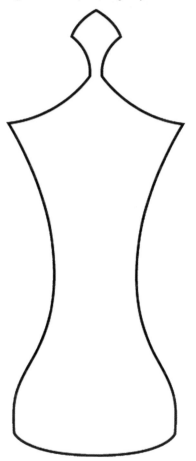

Figure 105 Completed Design Project 1

The classic sci-fi movie, *2001: A Space Odyssey*, includes a 20-minute "Dawn of Man" sequence that begins millions of years ago with a group of apes, presumably on the African plains. One day, *impossibly*, a tall, black, perfectly rectangular slab appears out of nowhere on the landscape. At first the apes are afraid of it, afraid to touch it. Eventually, they accept its presence.

Later, one ape looks upon a femur bone from a dead animal. With a dawning understanding, he uses the bone as a tool, first to kill for food and then to kill another ape from an enemy group. Victorious in battle, the ape hurls the bone into the air. The camera follows it up, up, up, and—in one of the most famous cuts in film history—the image switches from the white bone in the sky to the similar shape of a white spaceship floating in space.

1. How do you feel upon first seeing the "monolith" (the black rectangular slab)? Were you frightened? Do you sense that the monolith is good, evil, or neutral?
2. How would you describe the sudden appearance of the straight-edged, right-angled monolith against the landscape? What words describe the shapes of the landscape in contrast to the monolith?
3. Do you think perfect shapes exist in nature, or are they created entirely out of the imagination of human beings?
4. If perfect shapes exist—if they are real—can you name one example? If they are not real, how is it that humankind has proven so many concepts in mathematics that are based on shapes, such as the Pythagorean theorem?
5. What advancements and achievements of humankind have their basis in peoples' ability to conceive of abstract shapes?
6. Can it be said legitimately that the ability to conceive abstract shapes is an essential factor that distinguishes humankind from all the other species on the planet?
7. Create a new document, then save it as **Shape**.
8. In Adobe Illustrator, draw any shape you remember from the opening sequence, except the monolith.

Figure 106 A stamp printed in Great Britain for the Great British Film series shows 2001: *A Space Odyssey*; circa 2014

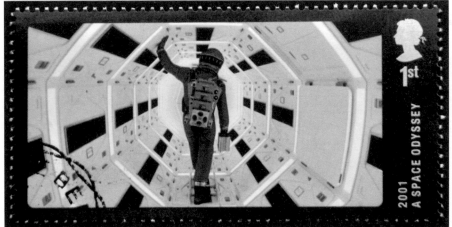

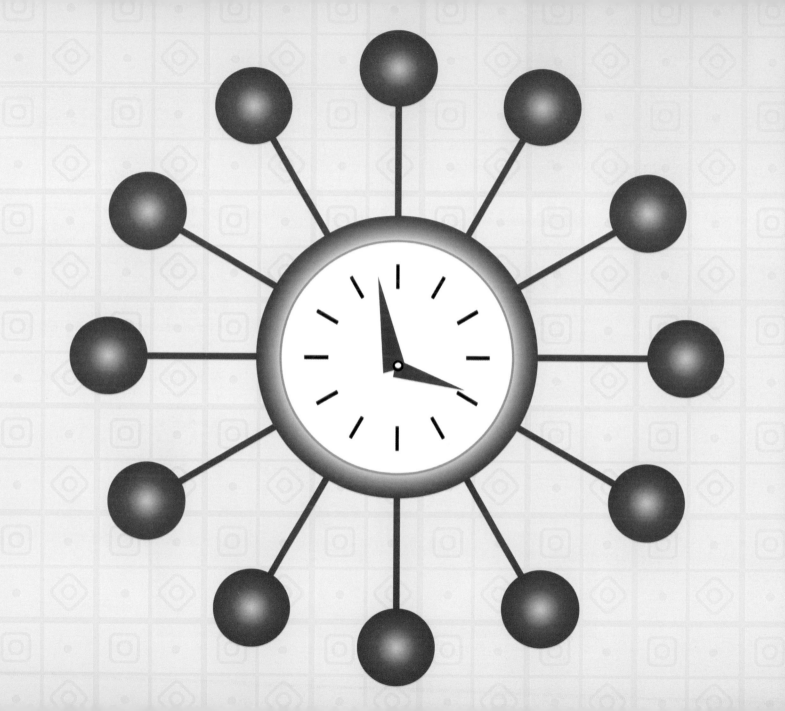

CHAPTER

4

TRANSFORMING AND DISTORTING OBJECTS

1. Transform Objects
2. Offset and Outline Paths
3. Create Compound Paths
4. Work with the Pathfinder Panel
5. Apply Round Corners to Objects
6. Use the Shape Builder Tool
7. Create Clipping Masks

CERTIFIED PROFESSIONAL

Adobe Certified Professional in Graphic Design and Illustration Using Adobe Illustrator

3. Organize Documents

This objective covers document structure such as layers and tracks, for efficient workflows.

3.2 Modify layer visibility using opacity and masks.

    B Create, apply, and manipulate clipping masks.

4. Creating and Modifying Visual Elements

This objective covers core tools and functionality of the application, as well as tools that affect the visual appearance of document elements.

4.4 Transform digital graphics and media.

    B Rotate, flip, and transform individual layers, objects, selections, groups, or graphical elements.

4.5 Use basic reconstructing and editing techniques to manipulate digital graphics and media.

    B Repair and reconstruct graphics.

    C Evaluate or adjust the appearance of objects, selections, or layers.

TRANSFORM OBJECTS

What You'll Do

In this lesson, you will explore options for transforming objects with the transform tools.

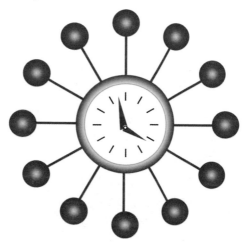

Mastering Illustrator Tools

Think about a conventional toolbox. You've got a hammer, nails, a few different types of screwdrivers, screws, nuts, bolts, a wrench, and probably some type of measuring device. That set of tools could be used to build anything from a birdhouse to a dollhouse to a townhouse to the White House.

A carpenter uses tools in conjunction with one another to create something, and that something is defined far less by the tools than by the imagination of the carpenter. But even the most ambitious imagination is tempered by the demands of knowing which tool to use and when.

Illustrator offers many sophisticated transform "tools" on the toolbar, and the metaphor is apt. Each tool provides a basic function, such as a rotation, scale, reflection, precise move, or precise offset. It is you, the designer, who uses those tools in combination with menu commands and other features to realize your vision. And like the carpenter, your ability to choose the right tool at the right time will affect the outcome of your work.

This is one of the most exciting aspects of working in Illustrator. After you learn the basics, there's no blueprint for building an illustration. It's your skills, your experience, your smarts, and your ingenuity that lead you toward your goal. No other designer will use Illustrator's tools quite the same way you do. People who appreciate digital imagery understand this significant point: Although the tools are the same for everyone, the result is personal—it's *original*.

Defining the Transform Tools

When you change an object's size, shape, or position on the artboard, Illustrator defines that operation as a transformation. Transforming objects is a fundamental operation in Illustrator, one you will perform countless times.

Because transformations are so essential, Illustrator provides a number of methods for doing them. As you gain experience, you will naturally adopt the method that you find most comfortable or logical.

The toolbar contains five transform tools: Rotate, Scale, Reflect, Shear, and Free Transform. The Rotate tool rotates an object or a group of objects around a fixed point. The Scale tool enlarges and reduces the size of objects. The Reflect tool "flips" an object across an imagined axis, usually the horizontal or the vertical axis; however, you can define any diagonal as the axis for a reflection. In Figure 1, the illustration has been flipped to create the illusion of a reflection in a mirror.

TIP The Reflect tool comes in very handy when you are drawing or tracing a symmetrical object, such as a spoon. Simply draw or trace half of the drawing, then create a flipped copy—a mirror image. Join the two halves, and you have a perfectly symmetrical shape…in half the time!

The Shear tool slants—or skews—an object on an axis that you specify. By definition, the Shear tool distorts an object. Of the five transform tools, you will probably use the Shear tool the least, although it is useful for creating a cast shadow or the illusion of depth.

Finally, the Free Transform tool offers you the ability to perform quick transformations and distort objects in perspective.

Figure 1 The Reflect tool flips an image horizontally or vertically

Defining the Point of Origin

All transformations are executed in relation to a fixed point. In Illustrator, this point is called the **point of origin**. For each transform tool, the default point of origin is the selected object's center point. However, you can change that point to another point on the object or to a point elsewhere on the artboard. For example, when a majorette twirls a baton, that baton is essentially rotating on its own center. By contrast, the petals of a daisy rotate around a central point that is not positioned on any of the petals themselves, as shown in Figure 2.

There are four basic methods for making transformations with the transform tools. First, select an object, then do one of the following:

- Click a transform tool, then click and drag anywhere on the artboard. The object will be transformed using its center point as the default point of origin.
- Double-click the transform tool, which opens the tool's dialog box. Enter the values you want to use to execute the transformation, then click OK. You may also click Copy to create a transformed copy of the selected object. The point of origin for the transformation will be the center point of the selected object.
- Click a transform tool, then click the artboard. Where you click the artboard defines the point of origin for the transformation. Click and drag anywhere on the artboard, and the selected object will be

transformed from the point of origin that you clicked.
- Click a transform tool, press [option] (Mac) or [Alt] (Win), then click the artboard. The tool's dialog box opens, allowing you to enter precise values for the transformation. When you click OK or Copy, the selected object

will be transformed from the point of origin that you clicked.

TIP If you transform an object from its center point and then select another object and apply the Transform Again command, the point of origin has not been redefined, and the second object will be transformed from the center point of the first object.

Figure 2 All transformations are executed from a point of origin

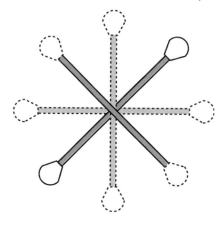

A baton rotating around its own center

Petals of a daisy rotate around a central point

Working with the Transform Again Command

An essential command related to transformations is Transform Again. Whenever you execute a transformation, such as scale or rotate, you can repeat the transformation quickly by using the Transform Again command. This is also true for moving an object. Using the Transform Again command will move an object the same distance and angle entered in the last step. The quickest way to use the Transform Again command is to press [command] [D] (Mac) or [Ctrl] [D] (Win). To remember this quick key command, think "D for *duplicate.*"

A fine example of the usefulness of the Transform Again command is the ease with which you can make incremental transformations. For example, let's say you have created an object to be used in an illustration, but you haven't decided how large the object should be. Simply scale the object by a small percentage—say 5%—then press the quick key for Transform Again repeatedly until you are happy with the results. The object gradually gets bigger, and you can choose the size that pleases your eye. If you transform again too many times, and the object gets too big, simply undo repeatedly to decrease the object's size in the same small increments.

Using the Transform Each Command

The Transform Each command allows you to transform multiple objects individually, as shown in Figure 3. The Transform Each dialog box offers options to move, scale, rotate, or

reflect an object, among others. All of them will affect an object independent of the other selected objects.

Without the Transform Each command, applying a transformation to multiple objects simultaneously will often yield an undesired effect. This happens because the selected objects are transformed as a group in relation to a single point of origin and are repositioned on the artboard.

Using the Free Transform Tool

When you click the Free Transform tool, an eight-handle bounding box appears around the selected object or objects. You can move the handles to scale or distort the object. You can click and drag outside the bounding box to rotate the selection. With the Free Transform tool, transformations always use the selected object's center point as the point of origin for the transformation.

Figure 3 Multiple objects rotated individually

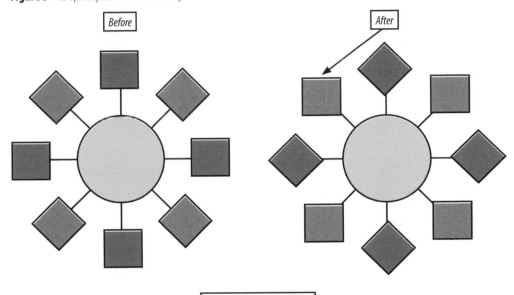

The eight squares are rotated on their own center points

In general, the role of the Free Transform tool is to make quick transformations by clicking and dragging; some designers prefer it to the individual Scale and Rotate tools, especially for making inexact transformations. However, the Free Transform tool has a powerful ability to distort objects in very interesting ways.

Moving the handles on the Free Transform tool in conjunction with certain keyboard commands allows you to distort an object or distort in perspective, as shown in Figure 4. You start by dragging any handle on the bounding box; then, to distort in perspective, you must apply the following *after* you start dragging a handle:

- Press and hold [shift] [option] [command] (Mac) or [shift] [Alt] [Ctrl] (Win) to distort in perspective.
- Press and hold [shift] [command] (Mac) or [shift] [Ctrl] (Win) to distort the selection.

When you click the Free Transform tool, the Free Transform toolbar appears, shown in Figure 5. The Free Transform toolbar offers four button controls to execute the transformations described before. If you click the top button, named Constrain, the object will be scaled in proportion. Note, however, that you can just hold the [shift] key when transforming to achieve the same result.

Figure 4 Use the Free Transform tool to distort objects in perspective

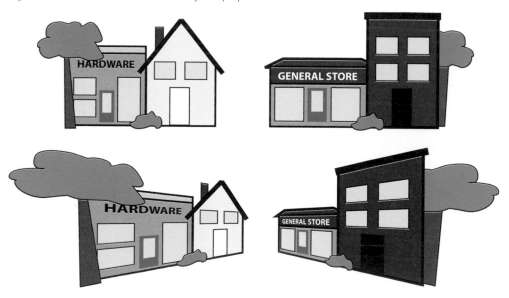

Figure 5 Free Transform toolbar

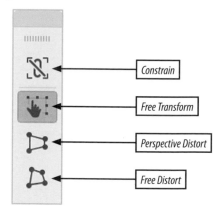

The second button, Free Transform, is the default setting. With this button selected, the Free Transform tool works as normal. The third button is Perspective Distort. When it is activated, the object will scale in perspective. The fourth button is called Free Distort. When it is activated, all four corner points move independently, allowing you to distort the object at will.

The method you use is up to you. Some designers like the simple ease of use that the tool buttons offer, while others like the hands-on use of alternating keyboard commands. In this lesson, you'll practice the keyboard commands, since that is the trickier method of the two.

Using the Transform Panel

The Transform panel displays information about the size, orientation, and location of one or more selected objects. You can type new values directly into the Transform panel to modify selected objects. All values on the panel refer to the bounding boxes of the objects, whether the bounding box is visible or not.

The Reference Point grid at the top-left corner of the panel determines the point of origin for any transformation you make. For example, if you click the center point on the grid and then scale a circle 200%, the circle will enlarge from its center point. Keep an eye on the Reference Point grid whenever you are using the Transform panel.

To flip an object vertically or horizontally using the Transform panel, click the Transform panel menu button, shown in Figure 6.

Figure 6 Transform panel

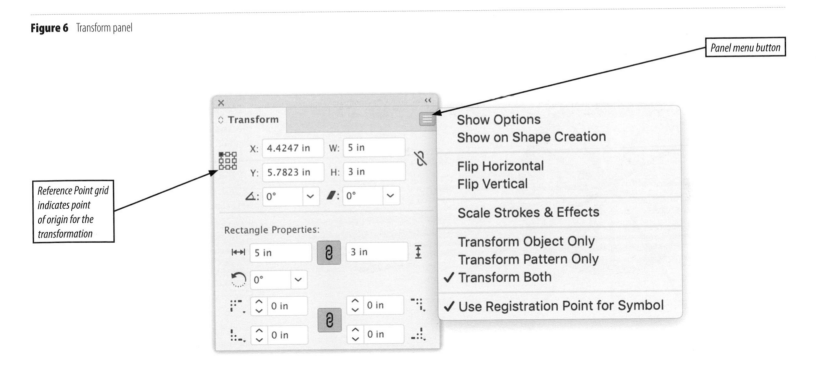

Rotate an object around a defined point

1. Open AI 4-1.ai, then save it as **Mod Clock**.

2. Click the **Selection tool** ▶ on the toolbar, click the **brown line**, then click the **Rotate tool** ↻.

3. Press and hold **[option] (Mac)** or **[Alt] (Win)**, then click the **bottom anchor point of the brown line** to set the point of origin for the rotation.

With a transform tool selected, pressing [option] (Mac) or [Alt] (Win) and clicking the artboard defines the point of origin and opens the tool's dialog box.

4. Enter **30** in the **Angle text box**, then click **Copy**.

5. Press **[command] [D] (Mac)** or **[Ctrl] [D] (Win)** 10 times so your screen resembles Figure 7.

TIP [command] [D] (Mac) or [Ctrl] [D] (Win) is the quick key for the Transform Again command.

6. Select all **12 lines**, group them, send them to the back, then hide them.

7. Select the **small orange circle**, click **View** on the menu bar, then click **Outline**.

8. Click the **Rotate tool** ↻ on the toolbar, press and hold **[option] (Mac)** or **[Alt] (Win)**, then click the **center point of the larger circle** to set the point of origin for the next rotation.

   The small circle will rotate around the center point of the larger circle.

TIP Outline mode is especially useful for rotations because center points are visible and easy to target as points of origin.

Figure 7 12 paths rotated at a point

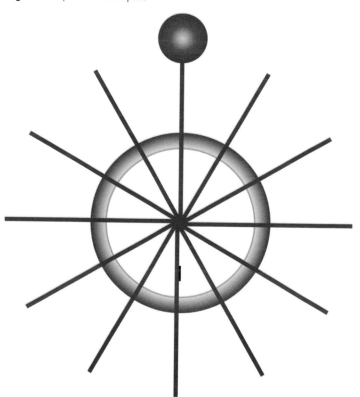

The X and Y coordinates of an object indicate the object's horizontal (X) and vertical (Y) locations on the artboard. These numbers, which appear on the Transform panel and the Control panel, represent the horizontal and vertical distance from the upper-left corner of the artboard. The current X and Y coordinates also depend on the specified reference point. Nine reference points are listed to the left of the X and Y Value text boxes on the Transform panel. Reference points are those points of a selected object that represent the four corners of the object's bounding box, the horizontal and vertical centers of the bounding box, and the center point of the bounding box.

9. Enter **30**, click **Copy**, apply the **Transform Again command** 10 times, then switch to **Preview mode**.

Your screen should resemble Figure 8.

10. Select the **small black vertical dash**, then apply the **Transform Again command** 11 times.

The dash is also rotated around the center point of the larger circle, since a new point of origin has not been set.

11. Unlock the **clock hands in the scratch area**, then move them onto the clock face.

12. Show all, then deselect all to reveal the 12 segments, as shown in Figure 9.

13. Save your work, then close the Mod Clock document.

You selected a point on the brown line, then rotated 11 copies of the object around that point. Second, you defined the point of origin for a rotation by clicking the center point of the larger circle, then rotated 11 copies of the smaller circle and the dash around that point.

Figure 8 12 circles rotated around a central point of origin

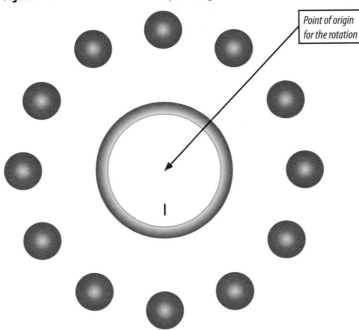

Point of origin for the rotation

Figure 9 Completed illustration

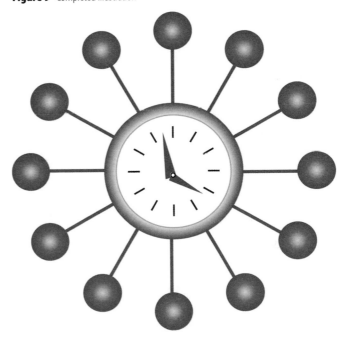

Use the Shear tool

1. Open AI 4-2.ai, then save it as **Shear**.

2. Select all, copy, paste in front, then fill the copy with the swatch named **Graphite**.

3. Click the **Shear tool** , on the toolbar.

TIP The Shear tool is hidden behind the Scale tool.

4. Press and hold **[option] (Mac)** or **[Alt] (Win)**, then click the **bottom-right anchor point** of the **letter R** to set the origin point of the shear and open the Shear dialog box.

5. Enter **45** in the **Shear Angle text box**, verify that the **Horizontal option button** is checked, then click **OK**.

   Your screen should resemble Figure 10.

6. Click the **Scale tool** on the toolbar.

7. Press **[option] (Mac)** or **[Alt] (Win)**, then click **any bottom anchor point** or **segment** on the **sheared objects** to set the point of origin for the scale and open the Scale dialog box.

8. Click the **Non-Uniform option button**, enter **100** in the **Horizontal text box**, enter **50** in the **Vertical text box**, then click **OK**.

9. Send the sheared objects to the back.

10. Apply a **1 pt. black stroke** to the **orange letters**, deselect, then compare your screen to Figure 11.

11. Save your work, then close the Shear document.

You created a shadow effect using the Shear tool.

Figure 10 Letterforms sheared on a 45° angle

The objects are sheared on a 45° angle in relation to a horizontal axis

Figure 11 Shearing is useful for creating a cast-shadow effect

The shadow is "cast" from the letters in the foreground

Use the Reflect tool

1. Open AI 4-3.ai, then save it as **Reflect**.

2. Select all, then zoom in on the **top anchor point**.

3. Click the **Reflect tool** 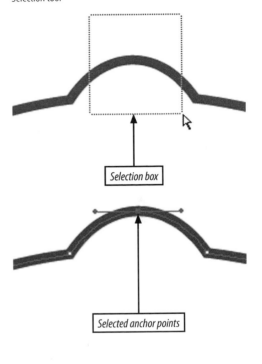 on the toolbar.

   The Reflect tool is hidden behind the Rotate tool.

4. Press **[option] (Mac)** or **[Alt] (Win)**, then click the **top anchor point** to set the point of origin for the reflection.

5. Click the **Vertical option button**, then click **Copy**.

   A copy is positioned, reflected across the axis that you defined, as shown in Figure 12.

6. Deselect all, then click the **Direct Selection tool** on the toolbar.

7. Using Figure 13 as a guide, drag a **selection box** around the **top two anchor points** to select them.

   TIP One of the anchor points is directly on top of the other because of the reflected copy.

8. Click **Object** on the menu bar, point to **Path**, click **Average**, click the **Both option button**, then click **OK**.

9. Click **Object** on the menu bar, point to **Path**, then click **Join**.

10. Select the **bottom two anchor points**, average them on both axes, then join them to close the path.

11. Save your work, then close the Reflect document.

You created a reflected copy of a path, then averaged and joined two pairs of open points.

Figure 12 Use the Reflect tool for illustrations that demand exact symmetry

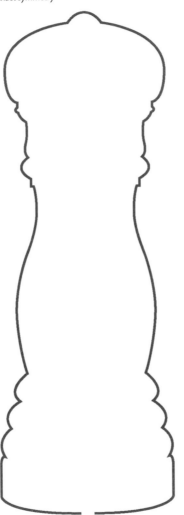

Figure 13 Selecting two anchor points with the Direct Selection tool

Selection box

Selected anchor points

Use the Free Transform tool to distort in perspective

1. Open AI 4-4.ai, then save it as **Distort in Perspective**.

2. Press **[command] [A] (Mac)** or **[Ctrl] [A] (Win)** to select all, then click the **Free Transform tool** on the toolbar.

3. Click and begin dragging the **upper-right handle** directly **to the right**; then, while still dragging, press and hold **[shift] [command] (Mac)** or **[shift] [Ctrl] (Win)** and continue dragging, releasing the mouse button when you are halfway to the edge of the artboard.

4. Compare your result to Figure 14.

   The illustration is distorted; the upper-right corner is moved to the right. The other three corners do not move.

5. Press **[command] [Z] (Mac)** or **[Ctrl] [Z] (Win)** to undo the last step.

Figure 14 Distorting the illustration

6. Click and start dragging the **upper-right handle** directly **to the right**; then, while still dragging, press and hold **[shift] [command] [option] (Mac)** or **[shift] [Ctrl] [Alt] (Win)** and continue dragging.

7. Release the mouse button when you are halfway to the edge of the artboard, then compare your result to Figure 15.

   The illustration is distorted with a different perspective.

8. Click and drag the **upper-left corner straight down**; then, while dragging, press and hold **[shift] [command] [option] (Mac)** or **[shift] [Ctrl] [Alt] (Win)** and continue dragging until your illustration resembles Figure 16.

9. Save your work, then close the Distort in Perspective document.

You used keyboard combinations first to distort the illustration, then to distort it in perspective.

Figure 15 Distorting the illustration in perspective

Figure 16 Illustration distorted in complex perspective

OFFSET AND OUTLINE PATHS

▶ *What You'll Do*

In this lesson, you will use the Offset Path command to create concentric squares and the Outline Stroke command to convert a stroked path into a closed path.

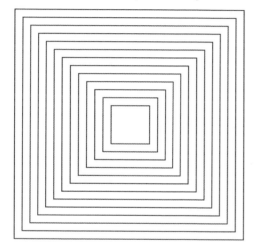

Using the Offset Path Command

Simply put, the Offset Path command creates a copy of a selected path set off by a specified distance. The Offset Path command is useful when working with closed paths—making concentric shapes or making many copies of a path at a regular distance from the original.

Figure 17 shows two sets of concentric circles. **Concentric** refers to objects that share the same center point, as the circles in both sets do. The set on the left was made with the Scale tool, applying an 85% scale and copy to the outer circle, then repeating the transformation 10 times. Note that with each successive copy, the distance from the copy to the previous circle decreases. The set on the right was made by offsetting the outside circle –.125", then applying the same offset to each successive copy. Note the different effect.

When you offset a closed path, a positive value creates a larger copy outside the original; a negative value creates a smaller copy inside the original.

Figure 17 Two sets of concentric circles

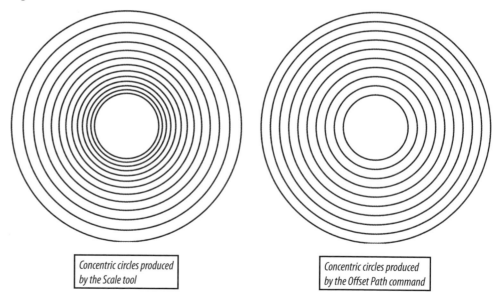

Concentric circles produced by the Scale tool

Concentric circles produced by the Offset Path command

Using the Outline Stroke Command

The Outline Stroke command converts a stroked path into a closed path that is the same width as the original stroked path.

This operation is useful if you want to apply a gradient to a stroke. It is also a useful design tool, allowing you to modify the outline of an object more than if it were just a stroke. Also, it is often easier to create an object with a single heavy stroke and then convert it to a closed path than it is to try to draw a closed path directly, as shown with the letter S in Figure 18.

Offset a path

1. Open AI 4-5.ai, then save it as **Squares**.

2. Select the **square**.

3. Click **Object** on the menu bar, point to **Path**, then click **Offset Path**.

4. Enter **−.125** in the **Offset text box**, then click **OK**.

   A negative value reduces the area of a closed path; a positive value increases the area.

TIP Be sure that your Units preference is set to Inches in the General section of the Units Preferences.

5. Apply the **Offset Path command** with the same value four more times.

TIP The Transform Again command does not apply to the Offset Path command because it is not one of the transform tools.

6. Deselect all, save your work, compare your screen to Figure 19, then close the Squares document.

You used the Offset Path command to create concentric squares.

Figure 18 The Outline Stroke command converts a stroked path to a closed object

Figure 19 Concentric squares created with the Offset Path command

Convert a stroked path to a closed path

1. Open AI 4-6.ai, then save it as **Outlined Stroke**.

2. Select the **path**, then change the **weight** to **36 pt**.

3. Click **Object** on the menu bar, point to **Path**, then click **Outline Stroke**.

   The full weight of the stroke is converted to a closed path, as shown in Figure 20.

4. Save your work, then close the Outlined Stroke document.

You applied a heavy weight to a stroked path, then converted the stroke to a closed path, using the Outline Stroke command.

Figure 20 The Outline Stroke command converts any stroked path into a closed path

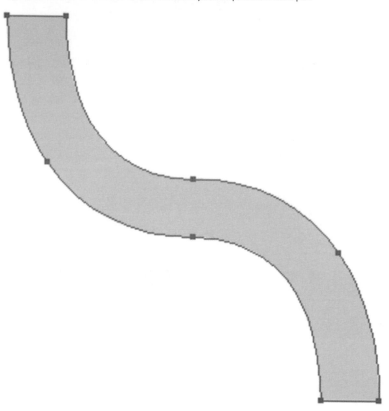

CREATE COMPOUND PATHS

Defining a Compound Path

Practically speaking, you make a compound path to create a "hole" or "holes" in an object. As shown in Figure 21, if you were drawing the letter D, you would need to create a hole in the outlined shape, through which you could see the background. To do so, select the object in back (in this case, the black outline that defines the letter) and the object in front (the yellow object that defines the hole), and apply the Make Compound Path command. When compounded, a "hole" appears where the two objects overlap.

Figure 21 The letter D is an example of a compound path

The overlapping object still exists, however. It is simply *functioning* as a transparent hole in conjunction with the object behind it. If you move the front object independently, as shown in Figure 22, it yields an interesting result. Designers have seized upon this effect and have run with it, creating complex and eye-catching graphics, which Illustrator calls compound shapes.

It is important to understand that when two or more objects are compounded, Illustrator defines them as *one* object. This sounds strange at first, but the concept is as familiar to you as the letter D. You identify the letter D as a single object although it is drawn with two paths—one defining the outside edge, the other defining the inside edge.

Compound paths function as groups. You can select and manipulate an individual element with the Direct Selection tool, but you cannot change its appearance attributes independently. Compound paths can be released and returned to their original component objects by applying the Release Compound Path command.

Create compound paths

1. Open AI 4-7.ai, then save it as **Simple Compound**.

2. Cut the **red circle** in the middle of the illustration, then undo the cut.

   The red circle creates the illusion that there's a hole in the life-preserver ring.

3. Select the **red background object**, then change its fill to the **Ocean Blue gradient** on the Swatches panel.

   The illusion is lost; the red circle no longer seems to be a hole in the life preserver.

4. Select both the **white "life preserver" circle** and the **red circle** in the center.

5. Click **Object** on the menu bar, point to **Compound Path**, then click **Make**.

   As shown in Figure 23, the two circles are compounded, with the top circle functioning as a "hole" in the larger circle behind it.

Figure 23 A compound path creates the effect of a hole where two or more objects overlap

Figure 22 Manipulating compound paths can yield interesting effects

6. Move the **background object left and right** and **up and down** behind the circles.

   The repositioned background remains visible through the compounded circles.

7. Deselect all, save your work, then close the Simple Compound document.

You selected two concentric circles and made them into one compound path, which allowed you to see through to the gradient behind the circles.

Create special effects with compound paths

1. Open AI 4-8.ai, then save it as **Compound Path Effects**.

2. Select all.

   The light blue square is locked and does not become part of the selection.

3. Click **Object** on the menu bar, point to **Compound Path**, then click **Make**.

4. Deselect, click the **Direct Selection tool**  on the toolbar, then click the **edge** of the **large blue circle**.

5. Click the **center point** of the circle, then scale the **circle 50%** so your work resembles Figure 24.

6. Click **Select** on the menu bar, then click **Inverse**.

7. Click **Object** on the menu bar, point to **Transform**, then click **Transform Each**.

8. Enter **225** in the **Horizontal** and **Vertical text boxes** in the Scale section of the Transform Each dialog box, click **OK,** then deselect all.

   Your work should resemble Figure 25.

9. Using the **Direct Selection tool**, click the **edge of the center circle**, click its **center point** to select the entire circle, then scale the circle **120%**.

10. Apply the **Transform Again command** twice, then compare your screen to Figure 26.

11. Deselect all, save your work, then close the Compound Path Effects document.

You made a compound path out of five small circles and one large circle. You then manipulated the size and location of the individual circles to create interesting designs.

Figure 24 A simple compound path

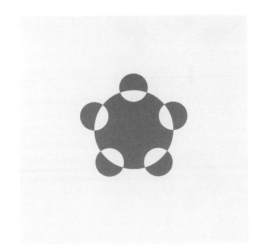

Figure 25 A more complex compound path

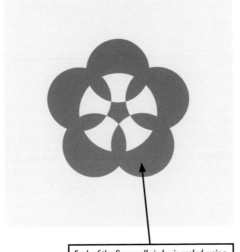

Each of the five small circles is scaled, using its own center point as the point of origin

Figure 26 Simple compound paths can yield stunning visual effects

WORK WITH THE PATHFINDER PANEL

▶ *What You'll Do*

In this lesson, you will use shape modes and pathfinders to create compound shapes from simple shapes.

Defining a Compound Shape

Like a compound path, a **compound shape** is two or more paths that are combined in such a way that "holes" appear wherever paths overlap.

The term "compound shape" is used to distinguish a complex compound path from a simple one. Compound shapes generally assume an artistic rather than a practical role. To achieve the effect, compound shapes tend to be composed of multiple objects. You can think of a compound shape as an illustration composed of multiple compound paths.

Understanding Essential Shape Modes and Pathfinders

Shape modes and **pathfinders** are preset operations that help you combine paths in a variety of ways. They are useful operations for creating complex or irregular shapes from basic shapes. In some cases, they are a means to an end in creating an object. In others, the operation they provide will be the end result you want to achieve. Shape modes and pathfinders can be applied to overlapping objects using the Effect menu or the Pathfinder panel.

For the purposes of drawing and creating new objects, familiarize yourself with the five essential shape modes and pathfinders shown in Figure 27.

Figure 27 Five essential shape modes and pathfinders

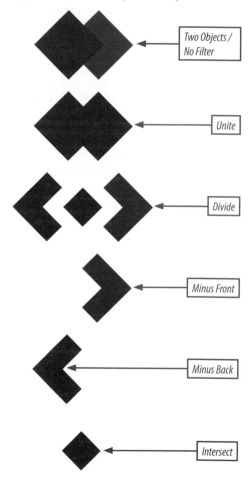

Two Objects / No Filter

Unite

Divide

Minus Front

Minus Back

Intersect

Unite shape mode Converts two or more overlapping objects into a single merged object.

Minus Front shape mode Where objects overlap, deletes the frontmost object(s) from the backmost object in a selection of overlapped objects.

Intersect shape mode Creates a single merged object from the area where two or more objects overlap.

Minus Back pathfinder The opposite of Minus Front; deletes the backmost object(s) from the frontmost object in a selection of overlapped objects.

Divide pathfinder Divides an object into its component-filled faces. Illustrator defines a "face" as an area undivided by a line segment.

Using the Pathfinder Panel

The Pathfinder panel contains 10 buttons for creating compound shapes, as shown in Figure 28. As you learned earlier, a compound shape is a complex compound path. You can create a compound shape by overlapping two or more objects, then clicking one of the four shape mode buttons in the top row of the Pathfinder panel, or clicking the Pathfinder panel list arrow, then clicking Make Compound Shape. The four shape mode buttons are Unite, Minus Front, Intersect, and Exclude. When you apply a shape mode button, the two overlapping objects are combined into one object with the same formatting as the topmost object in the group before the shape mode button was applied. After applying a shape mode button, the resulting objects in the compound shape can be selected and formatted using the Direct Selection tool. You can also press [option] (Mac) or [Alt] (Win) when you click a shape mode button. Doing so results in a compound shape whose original objects can be selected and formatted using the Direct Selection tool.

Figure 28 Pathfinder panel

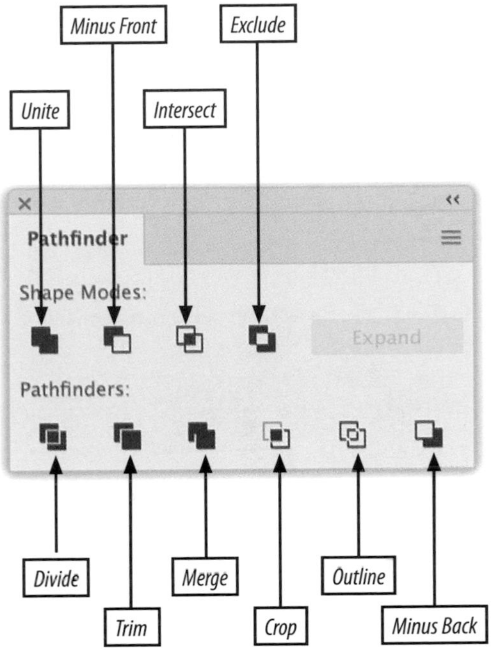

Applying Shape Modes

Figure 29 shows a square overlapped by a circle.

If you apply the Minus Front shape mode button, the resulting object is a compound shape, as shown in Figure 30. Notice the overlapped area is deleted from the square. The circle, too, is deleted. The result is a simple reshaped object.

If you took the same two overlapping shapes shown in Figure 29, but this time pressed [option] (Mac) or [Alt] (Win) when applying the Minus Front shape mode button, the circle would not be deleted but would function as a hole or a "knockout" wherever it overlaps the square, as shown in Figure 31. The relationship is dynamic: You can move the circle independently with the Direct Selection tool to change its effect on the square and the resulting visual effect.

Releasing and Expanding Compound Shapes

You can release a compound shape, which separates it back into individual objects.

To release a compound shape, click the Pathfinder panel menu button, then click Release Compound Shape. Expanding a compound shape is similar to releasing it, except that it maintains the shape of the compound object. You cannot select the original individual objects. You can expand a compound shape by selecting it, and then clicking the Expand button on the Pathfinder panel.

Figure 29 Two overlapping objects

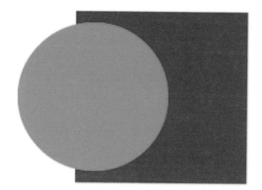

Figure 30 Applying the Minus Front shape mode without [option] (Mac) or [Alt] (Win)

Figure 31 Applying the Minus Front shape mode with [option] (Mac) or [Alt] (Win)

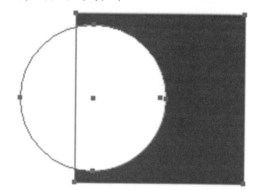

Apply the Unite shape mode

1. Open AI 4-9.ai, then save it as **Heart Parts**.

2. Click **Window** on the menu bar, then click **Pathfinder**.

3. Select **both circles**, then click the **Unite button** on the Pathfinder panel.

   The two objects are united.

4. Move the **diamond shape** up so it overlaps the united circles, as shown in Figure 32.

5. Click the **Delete Anchor Point tool** on the toolbar, then delete the **top anchor point of the diamond**.

6. Select all, press and hold **[option] (Mac)** or **[Alt] (Win)**, click the **Unite button** on the Pathfinder panel, then deselect all.

   Your screen should resemble Figure 33.

7. Remove the **black stroke**, then apply a **red fill** to the new object.

8. Draw a **rectangle** that covers the "hole" in the heart, then fill it with **black**, as shown in Figure 34.

9. Select all, press **[option] (Mac)** or **[Alt] (Win)**, then click the **Unite button**.

   The heart turns black.

10. Double-click the **Scale tool**, then apply a **non-uniform scale** of **90%** on the **horizontal axis** and **100%** on the **vertical axis**.

11. Save your work, then continue to the next set of steps.

You created a single heart-shaped object from two circles and a diamond shape using the Unite shape mode.

Figure 32 A diamond shape in position

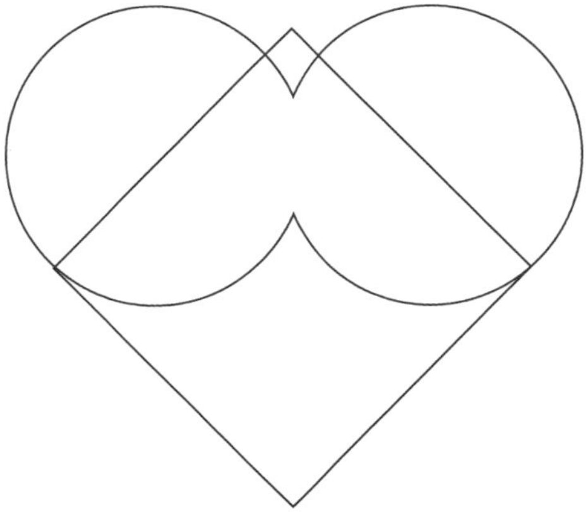

Figure 33 The diamond shape and the object behind it are united

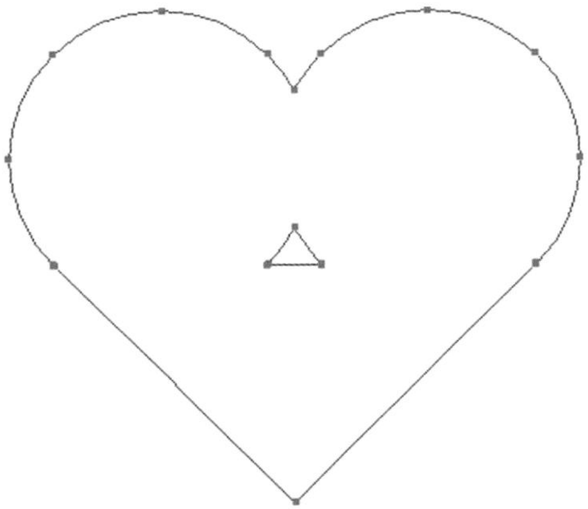

Figure 34 A heart shape created by applying the Unite shape mode to three objects

Apply the Minus Front shape mode

1. Rotate the **black heart shape 180°**, then hide it.

2. Create a **square** that is **1.5" × 1.5"** without a fill color and with a **1 pt. black stroke**.

3. Create a **circle** that is **1.75"** in width and height.

4. Switch to **Outline mode**.

5. Move the **circle** so it overlaps the square, as shown in Figure 35.

6. Verify that the **circle** is still selected, click the **Reflect tool** ▷◁ , press **[option] (Mac)** or **[Alt] (Win)**, then click the **center point** of the **square**.

7. Click the **Vertical option button**, click **Copy**, then arrange the three objects so your work resembles Figure 36.

8. Select all, then click the **Minus Front button** 🔳 on the Pathfinder panel.

9. Switch to **Preview mode**, then apply a **black fill** to the **new object**.

10. Show all, then overlap the **new shape** with the **black heart shape** to make a spade shape.

11. Select all, click the **Unite button** 🔳 on the Pathfinder panel, then deselect.

    Your work should resemble Figure 37.

12. Save your work, then continue to the next set of steps.

You overlapped a square with two circles, then applied the Minus Front shape mode to delete the overlapped areas from the square. You used the Unite button to unite the new shape with a heart-shaped object to create a spade shape.

Figure 35 Circle overlaps the square

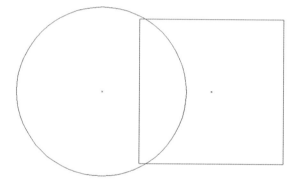

Figure 36 Right circle is a reflected copy of the left one

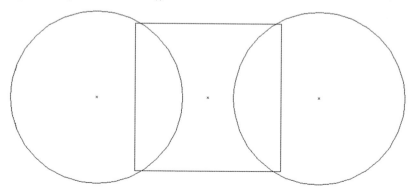

WORKING WITH THE ALIGN PANEL

The Align panel offers a quick and simple solution for aligning selected objects along the axis you specify. Along the vertical axis, you can align selected objects by their rightmost, leftmost, or center point. On the horizontal axis, you can align objects by their topmost, center, or bottommost point. You can also use the panel to distribute objects evenly along a horizontal or vertical axis. In contrasting the Align panel with the Average command, think of the Average command as a method for aligning anchor points and the Align panel as a method for aligning entire objects.

When you align and distribute objects, you have the choice of aligning them to a selection, a key object, or the artboard. If you want to align or distribute objects using the artboard, you must first define the artboard area using the Artboard tool on the toolbar. Click the Align To list arrow on the Align panel, then click Align to Artboard. Resize the artboard as desired. Finally, choose the alignment setting you need on the Align panel.

Figure 37 The final shape with all elements united

Apply the Intersect shape mode

1. Click the **Star tool** ☆ on the toolbar, then click the **artboard**.

2. Enter **1** in the **Radius 1 text box**, **3** in the **Radius 2 text box**, and **8** in the **Points text box**, then click **OK**.

3. Apply a **yellow fill** and no stroke to the **star**.

4. Use the **Align panel** to align the **center points of the two objects** so they resemble Figure 38.

5. Copy the **black spade**, then paste in front.

   Two black spades are now behind the yellow star; the top one is selected.

6. Press and hold **[shift]**, then click to add the **star** to the selection.

7. Click the **Intersect shape mode button** 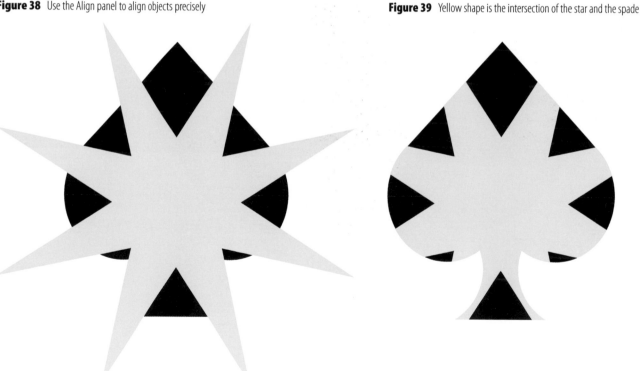 on the Pathfinder panel.

   The intersection of the star and the copied spade is now a single closed path. Your work should resemble Figure 39.

8. Save your work, then close Heart Parts.

You created a star, then created a copy of the black spade-shaped object. You used the Intersect shape mode button to capture the intersection of the two objects as a new object.

Figure 38 Use the Align panel to align objects precisely

Figure 39 Yellow shape is the intersection of the star and the spade

Apply the Divide pathfinder

1. Open AI 4-10.ai, then save it as **Divide**.

2. Select the **red line**, then double-click the **Rotate tool** ↻.

3. Enter **30** in the **Angle text box**, then click **Copy**.

4. Repeat the transformation four times.

5. Select all, then click the **Divide button** 🔲 on the Pathfinder panel.

    The blue star is divided into 12 separate objects, as defined by the red lines, which have been deleted. See Figure 40.

6. Deselect, click the **Direct Selection tool** ▷, select the **left half of the top point**, press **[shift]**, then select **every other object**, for a total of six objects.

7. Apply an **orange fill** to the selected objects.

8. Select the **inverse**, then apply a **yellow fill** so your work resembles Figure 41.

9. Save your work, then close the Divide document.

You used six lines to define a score pattern, then used those lines and the Divide pathfinder to break the star into 12 separate objects.

Figure 40   Blue star is divided into 12 objects by the Divide pathfinder

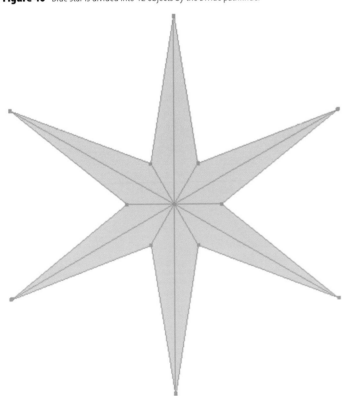

Figure 41   Divide pathfinder is useful for adding dimension

Create compound shapes using the Pathfinder panel

1. Open AI 4-11.ai, then save it as **Compound Shapes**.

2. Click **View** on the menu bar, then click **Yellow**.

3. Select the **two yellow circles**, press **[option] (Mac)** or **[Alt] (Win)**, then click the **Exclude button** on the Pathfinder panel.

   The area that the top object overlaps becomes transparent.

4. Deselect, click the **Direct Selection tool**, then move **either circle** to change the shape and size of the filled areas.

   Figure 42 shows one effect that can be achieved.

5. Click **View** on the menu bar, click **Green**, select the **two green circles**, press **[option] (Mac)** or **[Alt] (Win)**, then click the **Intersect button** on the Pathfinder panel.

The area not overlapped by the top circle becomes transparent.

6. Deselect, then use the **Direct Selection tool** to move **either circle** to change the shape and size of the filled area.

   Figure 43 shows one effect that can be achieved.

7. Save your work, then close the Compound Shapes document.

You applied shape modes to two pairs of circles, then moved the circles to create different shapes and effects.

Figure 42 An example of the Exclude shape mode

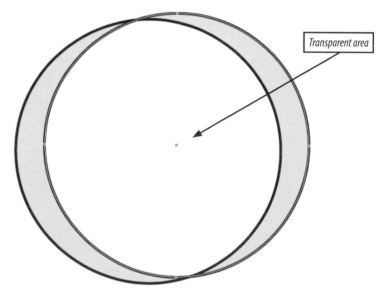

Transparent area

Figure 43 An example of the Intersect shape mode

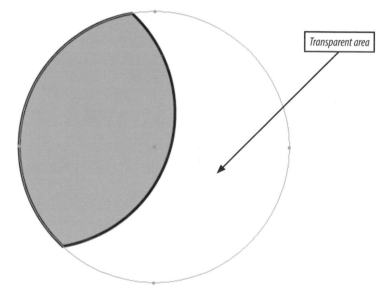

Transparent area

Create special effects with compound shapes

1. Open AI 4-12.ai, then save it as **Compound Shape Effects**.

2. Select all, press **[option] (Mac)** or **[Alt] (Win)**, then click the **Exclude button**  on the Pathfinder panel.

   Your work should resemble Figure 44.

3. Deselect all, click the **Direct Selection tool** on the toolbar, select the **three squares**, then move them **to the right**, as shown in Figure 45.

4. Drag and drop a **copy of the three squares**, as shown in Figure 46.

   TIP Use [shift] [option] (Mac) or [shift] [Alt] (Win) to drag and drop a copy at a 45° angle or in straight vertical or horizontal lines.

5. Scale **each circle 150%** using the **Transform Each command**.

6. Scale the **center circle 200%,** then bring it to the front of the stacking order.

7. Press **[option] (Mac)** or **[Alt] (Win)**, then click the **Intersect button** on the Pathfinder panel.

   Figure 47 shows the results of the intersection. Your final illustration may vary slightly.

   TIP The topmost object affects all the objects behind it in a compound shape.

8. Save your work, then close the Compound Shape Effects document.

You made three squares and three circles into a compound shape by excluding overlapping shape areas. You then manipulated the size and location of individual elements to create different effects. Finally, you enlarged a circle, brought it to the front, then changed its mode to Intersect. Only the objects that were overlapped by the circle remained visible.

Figure 44 A compound shape

Figure 45 A compound shape

Figure 46 A compound shape

Figure 47 A compound shape

APPLY ROUND CORNERS TO OBJECTS

▶ *What You'll Do*

In this lesson, you will apply round corners to the artwork using the Corners dialog box. You will also learn about the options in the Corners dialog box.

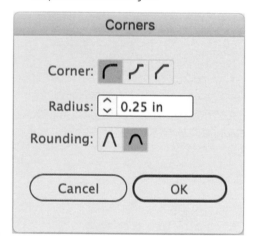

Applying Round Corners

Round corners are an essential component of any designer's tool kit. Figure 48 shows a five-point star, like one you'd see on the American flag. Note the five pointy points. This star is serious, and its points say "don't mess with me." With its mathematical basis and sharp points, a star is regal, which is why it's often used to convey majesty and supremacy.

Figure 49 shows the same star with round corners. The emotional effect of changing an object's corners from pointed to rounded is remarkable. Suddenly, the object is cute and playful. It's almost cartoonish, like an animated character or a sponge toy a child could play with in the bathtub.

Figure 48 Star with pointy points

Figure 49 Star with round corners

Round corners make objects fun, playful, comical, and cute. When you round corners in Illustrator, you are working with widgets, small circles that appear at every corner, as shown in Figure 50. To view widgets, you must select the object with the Direct Selection tool. If you do not see widgets, click the View menu and choose Show Corner Widget.

When you click and drag the widget, all the corners of the object are rounded as you drag. You may have a situation in which you only want to round one corner, not all of them, on a given object. To do so, first select *only* the anchor point of the corner you wish to round with the Direct Selection tool, then drag its associated widget. Using this method, you can apply differently rounded corners to every point on the object.

If you want to apply a specific corner radius to a point, rather than click and drag to create the rounded corner, simply double-click the widget. This opens the Corners dialog box, where you can enter a specific radius, as shown in Figure 51. You can also specify two other types of corners: Inverted Round and Chamfer.

Don't forget that you can apply round corners to type after you've converted the text to outlines. This is a great option for creating fun, friendly letter shapes.

TIP You can also enter a specific radius for a corner by clicking Corners on the Control panel.

Apply corners to an object

1. Open AI 4-13.ai, save it as **Round Corners**, click **View** on the menu bar, then click **Show Corner Widget**.

   If the command reads Hide Corner Widget, do nothing; the corner widget is already showing.

2. Click the **Direct Selection tool** on the toolbar, then click the **interior of the blue shape** to select the object.

   Corner widgets appear at every corner of the selected object.

TIP If you find corner widgets distracting, you can hide them by using the Hide Corner Widget command on the View menu.

3. Click and drag the **topmost corner widget** toward the center of the object.

   As you drag, all the corners on the object become increasingly rounded.

Continued on next page

Figure 50 Corner widgets visible on objects

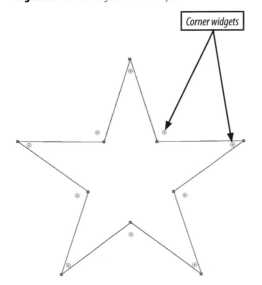

Figure 51 Corners dialog box with options for corners

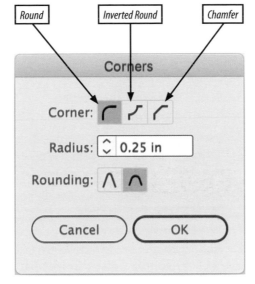

4. Drag until the object resembles Figure 52.

5. Press and hold **[option] (Mac)** or **[Alt] (Win)**, then click **any corner widget**.

   The round corners change to inverted round corners.

6. While still holding **[option] (Mac)** or **[Alt] (Win)**, click the **corner widget** again.

   As shown in Figure 53, the inverted round corners change to chamfer corners. Each time you press and hold [option] (Mac) or [Alt] (Win), and click a corner widget, the corner cycles through the three types of corner options in the Corners dialog box.

   TIP The word chamfer refers to a cut made in woodcutting and is similar to a beveled edge.

7. While still holding **[option] (Mac)** or **[Alt] (Win)**, click the **corner widget** again.

   The chamfer corners change to round corners.

8. Drag the **corner widget** away from the center of the object.

   The object is restored to its original shape.

9. Save your work, then continue to the next set of steps.

You dragged corner widgets with the Direct Selection tool to create round corners, then modified the corners from round to inverted round to chamfer. You then removed the specialized corners from the object.

Apply specific corner measurements to individual points on an object

1. Deselect all, then select the **top anchor point** on the **blue object** with the **Direct Selection tool** .

2. Click and drag the **top corner widget** toward the center of the object to create a round corner.

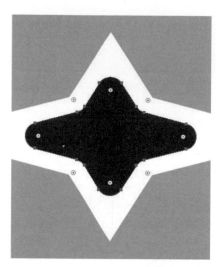

Figure 52 Round corners applied to the object

Note that the radius of the corner is identified in the Corners section of the Control panel.

3. Double-click the **top corner widget**.

   The Corners dialog box opens.

4. Enter **25** in the **Radius text box**, then click **OK**.

5. Select the **anchor point** at the **bottom of the blue object** with the **Direct Selection tool** .

6. Double-click the **corner widget**, enter **25** in the **Radius text box**, then click **OK**.

7. Select both the **orange objects**.

8. On the Control panel, enter **25** in the **Corners text box**, then press **[return] (Mac)** or **[Enter] (Win)**.

   All corners on the orange objects are rounded.

9. Select the **far left** and **far right anchor points** on the **blue object** with the **Direct Selection tool** .

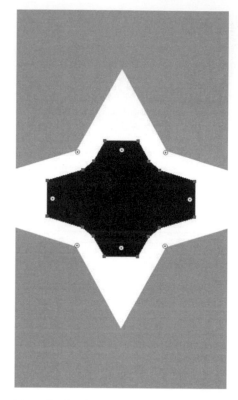

Figure 53 Chamfer corners applied to the object

10. On the Control panel, click the word **Corners** to open the Corners dialog box, click the **Inverted Round option** , then enter **25** in the **Radius text box**.

11. Deselect all, then compare your artwork to Figure 54.

12. Save your work, then close the Round Corners document.

You applied a corner to individual points on an object, then used the Corners dialog box to apply the exact same corner style to other points on the object and to other objects.

Figure 54 Final artwork with corners applied to all anchor points

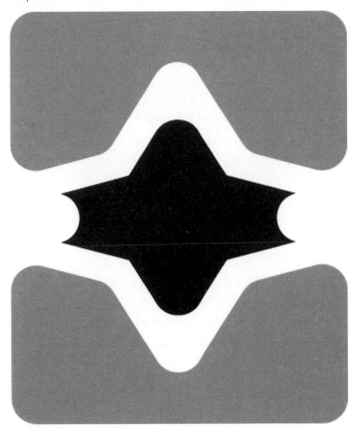

USE THE SHAPE BUILDER TOOL

▶ **What You'll Do**

In this lesson, you will use the Shape Builder tool to create new shapes from overlapping objects.

Understanding the Shape Builder Tool

The Shape Builder tool is grouped on the toolbar with the Live Paint Bucket. This makes sense because the tool functions in a similar manner to the Live Paint Bucket.

The Shape Builder tool is designed to help you create new objects from overlapping objects. Comparing it to the Live Paint Bucket (covered in Chapter 3) can help you understand its role. Where the Live Paint Bucket fills closed paths created by overlapping objects, the Shape Builder tool creates new closed paths from overlapping objects. From this perspective,

you can think of the Shape Builder tool as a combination of the Live Paint Bucket and the Pathfinder tools.

Figure 55 shows eight orange-filled circles overlapping. The Shape Builder tool is selected on the toolbar, and a pink fill and black stroke have been chosen on the toolbar. When the Shape Builder tool is selected, changing the fill or stroke color on the toolbar won't change the color of the selected objects. In the figure, closed objects are highlighted and outlined in red when the Shape Builder tool is dragged across them.

Figure 55 Specifying objects to be created with the Shape Builder tool

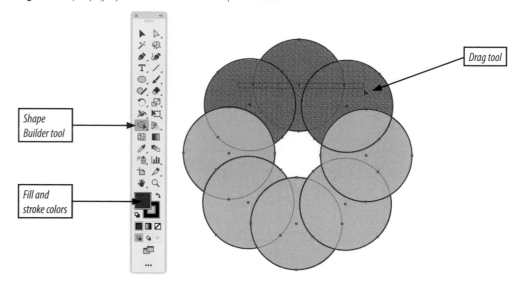

Shape Builder tool

Fill and stroke colors

Drag tool

In Figure 56, those objects are united into a single object with the pink fill and a black stroke. Note that this is not something you could do with the Unite pathfinder. The Unite pathfinder would have united the three whole circles, but, as shown in this example, the Shape Builder tool created a single object from overlapping components of the circles.

In Figure 57, the Shape Builder tool has been dragged to the negative space in the center so it will be added to the merged object.

Figure 56 New object created with the Shape Builder tool

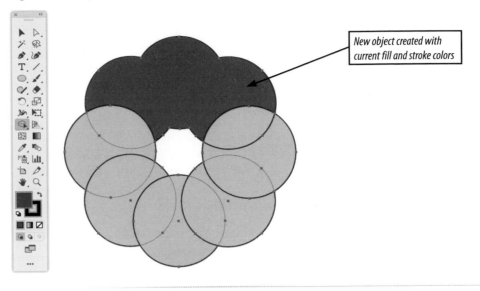

New object created with current fill and stroke colors

Figure 57 Adding the negative space to the object

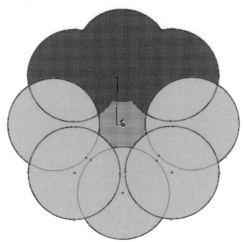

In addition to creating new objects, the Shape Builder tool also deletes closed paths from overlapping objects. To delete an object with the Shape Builder tool, press and hold [option] (Mac) or [Alt] (Win), then click or drag over the objects you want to delete. Note the minus sign beside the Shape Builder tool icon in Figure 58. Upon release, the objects are deleted, as shown in Figure 59.

Figure 58 Specifying objects to be deleted

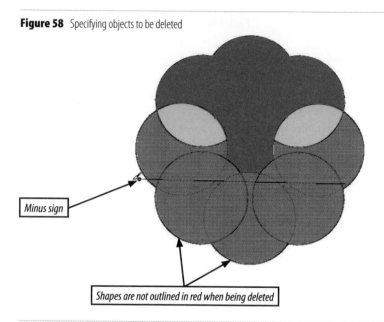

Minus sign

Shapes are not outlined in red when being deleted

Figure 59 Illustration after deletion

Create objects with the Shape Builder tool

1. Open AI 4-14.ai, then save it as **Shape Builder**.

2. Select all, then click the **Shape Builder tool** 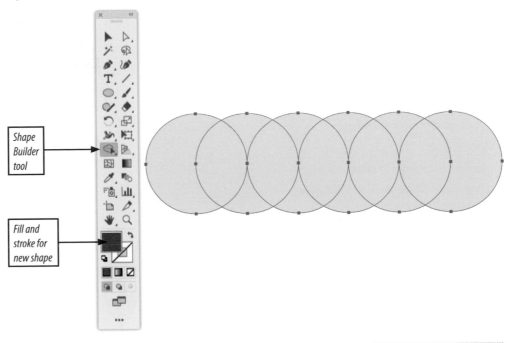 on the toolbar.

3. Set the **fill** and **stroke color** to **Pink** and **[None]**, respectively.

   Your artboard should resemble Figure 60. Even though the yellow circles are selected, when you set the foreground color to a different color, the circles don't change color.

4. Click and drag to highlight the **objects shown in Figure 61**.

   When you release the mouse button, the objects are united as a single object.

   Continued on next page

Figure 60 Selecting a fill color for the Shape Builder tool

Shape Builder tool

Fill and stroke for new shape

Figure 61 Highlighting objects to be merged into a new object

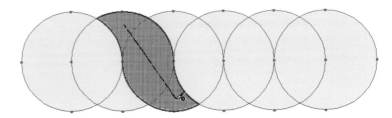

5. Click and drag to highlight the **objects shown in Figure 62**.

Because you included the first pink object, the objects are united into a single object, as shown in Figure 63.

6. Save your work, then continue to the next set of steps.

You dragged with the Shape Builder tool to create a new object.

Delete objects with the Shape Builder tool

1. Verify that the **entire illustration** is selected.

2. Press and hold **[option] (Mac)** or **[Alt] (Win)**, then drag the **Shape Builder tool**

over the objects shown in Figure 64.

When you release, the objects are deleted.

3. Press and hold **[shift] [option] (Mac)** or **[shift] [Alt] (Win)**, then drag the **Shape Builder tool**
over all the **yellow objects** to the right of the pink shape.

Adding the [shift] key to the combination allows you to drag a selection marquee to highlight more objects.

4. Press and hold **[option] (Mac)** or **[Alt] (Win)**, then click the **last remaining yellow object**.

Your result should resemble Figure 65.

5. Save your work, then close the Shape Builder document.

You used the Shape Builder tool to delete objects.

Figure 62 Adding more objects to the new shape

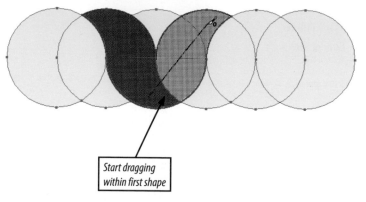

Start dragging within first shape

Figure 63 The new shape

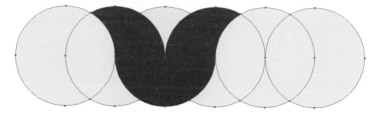

Figure 64 Highlighting shapes to be deleted

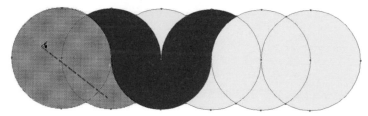

Figure 65 The final shape

CREATE CLIPPING MASKS

Defining a Clipping Mask

Clipping masks are used to yield a practical result. And as with compound paths, that practical result can be manipulated to create interesting graphic effects.

Practically speaking, you use a clipping mask as a "window" through which you view some or all the objects behind the mask in the stacking order. When you select any two or more objects and apply the Make Clipping Mask command, the *top object* becomes the mask and the object behind it becomes "masked." You will be able to see only the parts of the masked object that are visible *through* the mask, as shown in Figure 66. The mask crops the object behind it.

Figure 66 Clipping mask crops the object behind it

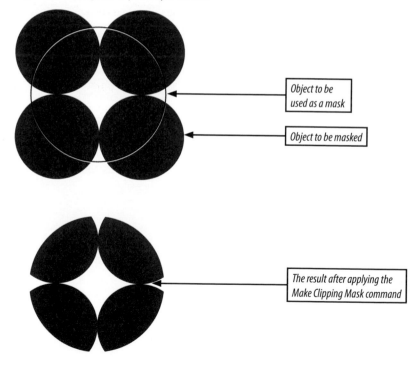

Object to be used as a mask

Object to be masked

The result after applying the Make Clipping Mask command

Using Multiple Objects as a Clipping Mask

When you select multiple objects and apply the Make Clipping Mask command, the top object becomes the mask. Since every object has its own position in the stacking order, it stands to reason that there can be only one top object.

If you want to use multiple objects as a mask, you can do so by first making them into a compound path because Illustrator regards compound paths as a single object. Therefore, a compound path containing multiple objects can be used as a single mask.

Creating Masked Effects

Special effects with clipping masks are, quite simply, fun! You can position as many objects as you like behind the mask and position them in such a way that the mask crops them in visually interesting (and eye-popping!) ways.

Using the Draw Inside Drawing Mode

The Draw Inside drawing mode does just what its name implies: it allows you to create one object within the perimeter of another object. For example, you can draw a square, click the Draw Inside button on the toolbar, then draw a circle that appears only inside the square. Drawing one object inside another is essentially the same thing as creating a clipping mask. The object that's drawn inside is clipped by the object that contains it. If you've drawn an object inside another and you want to remove the relationship between them, click Object on the menu bar, point to Clipping Mask, then click Release.

Create a clipping mask

1. Open AI 4-15.ai, then save it as **Simple Masks**.

2. Click **View** on the menu bar, then click **Mask 1**.

3. Move the **rectangle** so it overlaps the **gold spheres** as shown in Figure 67.

4. Apply the **Bring to Front command** to verify that the rectangle is in front of all the spheres.

5. Select the **seven spheres** and the **rectangle**.

6. Click **Object** on the menu bar, point to **Clipping Mask**, then click **Make**.

7. Deselect, then compare your screen to Figure 68.

Continued on next page

Figure 67 Masking objects must be in front of objects to be masked

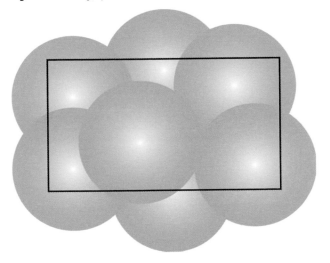

Figure 68 The rectangle masks the gold spheres

8. Click **View** on the menu bar, then click **Mask 2**.

9. Select the **three circles**, then move them over the "gumballs."

   The three circles are a compound path.

10. Select the **group of gumballs** and the **three circles**, click **Object** on the menu bar, point to **Clipping Mask**, then click **Make**.

11. Deselect, click **Select** on the menu bar, point to **Object**, then click **Clipping Masks**.

12. Apply a **1 pt. black stroke** to the masks.

   Your work should resemble Figure 69.

13. Save your work, then close the Simple Masks document.

You used a rectangle as a clipping mask. Then, you used three circles to mask a group of small spheres and applied a black stroke to the mask.

Apply a fill to a clipping mask

1. Open AI 4-16.ai, then save it as **Magnify**.

2. Move the **large text** over the **small text** so both letters *g* align as shown in Figure 70.

3. Select the **smaller text**, then hide it.

4. Select the **magnifying glass (circle)** and the **handle**, then drag them **over the letter g**, as shown in Figure 71.

Figure 69 A compound path used as a mask

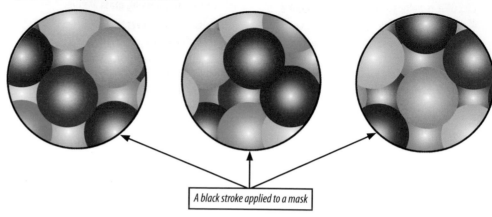

| A black stroke applied to a mask |

Figure 70 Lining up the letter g

Figure 71 Positioning the magnifying glass

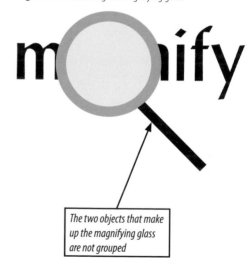

| The two objects that make up the magnifying glass are not grouped |

5. Deselect all, select only the **circle** and the **text**, click **Object** on the menu bar, point to **Clipping Mask**, then click **Make**.

The circle is the masking object. The blue fill disappears.

6. Deselect, click **Select** on the menu bar, point to **Object**, then click **Clipping Masks**.

7. Use the **Swatches panel** to apply a **light blue fill** and a **gray stroke** to the mask.

8. Change the **weight** of the stroke to **8 pt**. so your work resembles Figure 72.

9. Show all, deselect, then compare your screen to Figure 73.

10. Select the **mask** only, press and hold **[shift]**, then click the **magnifying glass handle.**

11. Press the **arrow keys** to move the magnifying glass.

As you move the magnifying glass left and right, it gives the illusion that the magnifying glass is enlarging the text. This would make for an interesting animation in a PDF or on a web page.

12. Save your work, then close the Magnify document.

You used the circle in the illustration as a clipping mask in combination with the large text. You added a fill and a stroke to the mask, creating the illusion that the small text is magnified in the magnifying glass.

Use text as a clipping mask

1. Open AI 4-17.ai, then save it as **Mask Effects**.

2. Select the **four letters** that make the word MASK.

3. Make the **four letters** into a **compound path**.

4. With the compound path still selected, select the **rectangle** behind it.

5. Apply the **Make Clipping Mask command**, then deselect.

6. Save your work, then continue to the next set of steps.

You converted outlines to a compound path, then used the compound path as a mask.

Figure 72 A fill and stroke are applied to a mask

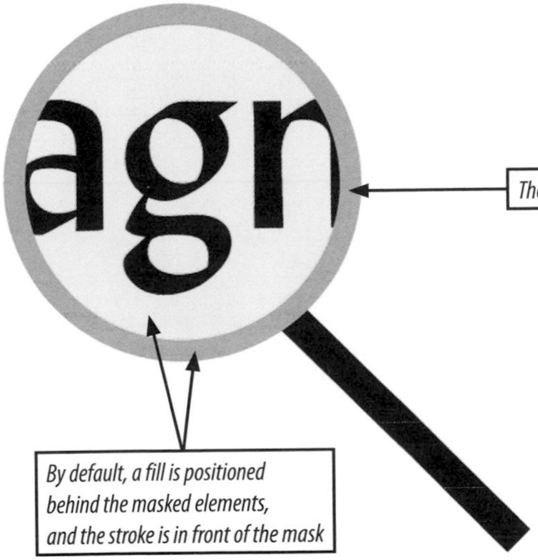

The mask

By default, a fill is positioned behind the masked elements, and the stroke is in front of the mask

Figure 73 Large text is masked by the magnifying glass

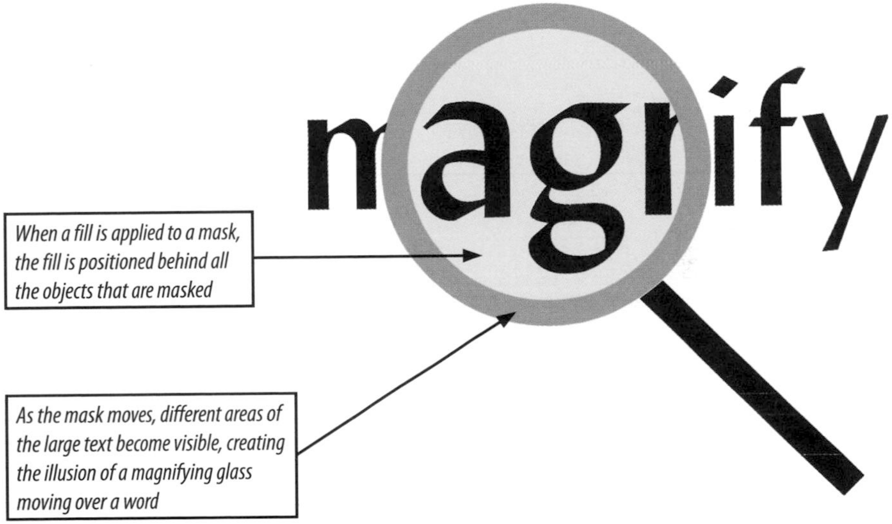

When a fill is applied to a mask, the fill is positioned behind all the objects that are masked

As the mask moves, different areas of the large text become visible, creating the illusion of a magnifying glass moving over a word

Use a clipping mask for special effects

1. Position the **curvy object** with the gradient fill over the mask, as shown in Figure 74.

2. Cut the **curvy object**.

3. Click **Select** on the menu bar, point to **Object**, then click **Clipping Masks**.

   The mask is selected.

4. Click **Edit** on the menu bar, click **Paste in Back**, then deselect so your screen resembles Figure 75.

   The object is pasted behind the mask and in front of the masked rectangle.

5. Click the **Selection tool** on the toolbar, select the **purple dotted line**, position it over the **letter K**, then cut the **purple dotted line**.

6. Click **Select** on the menu bar, point to **Object**, then click **Clipping Masks**.

7. Click **Edit** on the menu bar, then click **Paste in Back**.

8. Using the same technique, mask the other objects on the artboard in any way that you choose.

   When finished, your mask should contain all the objects, as shown in Figure 76.

TIP Add a stroke to the mask if desired.

9. Save your work, then close the Mask Effects document.

You created visual effects by pasting objects behind a mask.

Figure 74 Curvy object in position to be masked by the letters

Figure 75 Curvy object is masked by the letters

Figure 76 Pasting multiple objects behind a mask yields interesting effects

Use the Draw Inside drawing mode

1. Open AI 4-18.ai, save it as **Draw Inside**, click the **Selection tool** ▶, then select the **blue square** at the top of the document.

   When you select the blue square, by default the fill and stroke buttons on the toolbar take on the object's colors, which, in this case, are Blue and [None].

2. Click the **Draw Inside button** ⊚ at the bottom of the toolbar, then click the **Ellipse tool** ⬭.

   Because you must have an object selected to use the Draw Inside drawing mode, the object you draw will always be the same fill and stroke color as the object you're drawing into. You can make them different colors only after you draw inside.

3. Draw an **ellipse** that overlaps the **blue square**, making it approximately the same size as the **pink ellipse** already on the artboard.

4. With the **ellipse** still selected, change its **fill color** to **yellow**.

   Figure 77 shows one example of how the ellipse is drawn within the blue square. Dotted lines around the four corners of the blue square indicate that it is functioning as a mask for the ellipse. As long as you stay in Draw Inside drawing mode, any object you create will be drawn inside the blue square.

5. Click the **Draw Normal button** ⊚ on the toolbar, select the word **MASK**, click **Type** on the menu bar, then click **Create Outlines**.

6. With the **outlines** still selected, click **Object** on the menu bar, point to **Compound Path**, click

Make, then fill them with any **green swatch** on the Swatches panel.

   Defined as a compound path, the letter outlines are now a single object into which you can draw.

7. Select the **pink ellipse**, cut it, select the **MASK outlines**, then click the **Draw Inside button** ⊚.

   Dotted lines appear around the MASK outlines, indicated they can be drawn into.

8. Click **Edit** on the menu bar, click **Paste**, then move the **ellipse** so it overlaps the MASK outlines as shown in Figure 78.

9. Save your work, then close the Draw Inside document.

You used the Draw Inside drawing mode to create objects within other objects and within outlined text.

Figure 77 Drawing the yellow ellipse inside the blue square

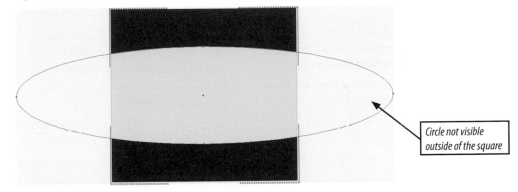

Circle not visible outside of the square

Figure 78 Drawing the pink ellipse inside the outlines via the Paste command

Transform objects

1. Open AI 4-19.ai, then save it as **Transform Skills**.
2. Select "DIVIDE."
3. Scale the text objects non-uniformly: Horizontal = 110% and Vertical = 120%.
4. Rotate the text objects 7°.
5. Shear the text objects 25° on the horizontal axis.
6. Save your work.

Offset and outline paths

1. Ungroup the text outlines.
2. Using the Offset Path command, offset each letter −.05".
3. Save your work.

Work with the Pathfinder panel

1. Select all.
2. Apply the Divide pathfinder.
3. Fill the divided elements with different colors, using the Direct Selection tool.
4. Select all, then apply a 2 pt. white stroke. Enlarge the view to see the effect better.
5. Save your work, compare your image to Figure 79, then close the Transform Skills document.

Create compound paths

1. Open AI 4-20.ai, then save it as **Compounded**.
2. Select all, press [option] (Mac) or [Alt] (Win), then click the Exclude button on the Pathfinder panel.
3. Deselect, then click the center of the small square with the Direct Selection tool.
4. Rotate a copy of the small square 45°.
5. Save your work, compare your image to Figure 80, then close the Compounded document.

Use the Shape Builder tool

1. Open AI 4-21.ai, then save it as **Shape Builder Skills**.
2. Select all, then set the fill color on the objects to [None] so you can see the shapes being created by the overlapping.
3. Click the Shape Builder tool.
4. Set the fill and stroke color to a shade of light blue and [None], respectively.
   Even though the circles are selected, when you set the foreground color to a different color with the Shape Builder tool, the circles don't change color.

Figure 79 Completed Skills Review, Part 1

Figure 80 Completed Skills Review, Part 2

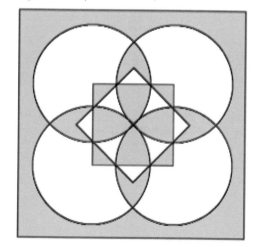

5. Click and drag to highlight the objects shown in Figure 81.

   When you release the mouse button, the objects are united as a single object.

6. Change the fill color on the toolbar to a shade of red.

7. Click and drag to highlight the remaining objects shown in Figure 82.

8. Click the Selection tool, then click the artboard to deselect both objects.

9. Click the top blue object, then drag it away from the red object.

10. Save your work, then close Shape Builder Skills.

Create clipping masks

1. Open AI 4-22.ai, then save it as **Masked Paths**.

2. Position any three of the letters on the right side of the canvas over the artwork on the left.

3. Hide the three letters you didn't choose.

4. Select the three letters over the artwork, click Object on the menu bar, point to Compound Path, then click Make.

5. Select everything on the artboard.

6. Click Object on the menu bar, point to Clipping Mask, then click Make.

7. Deselect all.

8. Click Select on the menu bar, point to Object, then click Clipping Masks.

9. Add a 1.5 pt. black stroke to the selection.

10. Compare your results to Figure 83, which shows one potential result.

11. Save your work, then close Masked Paths.

Figure 81 Highlighting with the Shape Builder tool

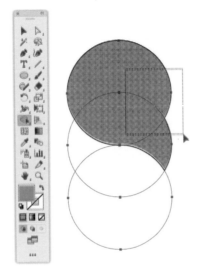

Figure 82 Highlighting the remaining shapes

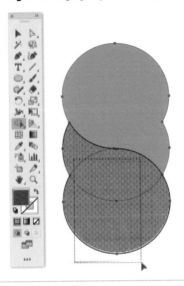

Figure 83 Completed Skills Review, Part 3

You are entering a contest to design a new stamp. You have decided to use a picture of Mark Twain, which you have placed in an Illustrator document. You have positioned text over the image. Now, to complete the effect, you want to mimic the perforated edges of a stamp.

1. Open AI 4-23.ai, then save it as **Mark Twain Stamp**.
2. Select all the circles, then make them into a compound path.
3. Add the rectangle to the selection.
   The rectangle is behind the circles in the stacking order.
4. Apply the Minus Front shape mode, then deselect all.
5. Save your work, compare your image to Figure 84, then close the Mark Twain Stamp document.

Figure 84 Completed Project Builder 1

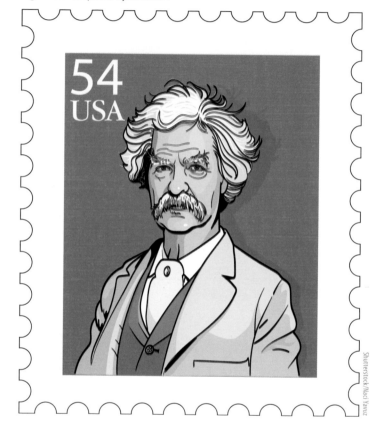

Shutterstock/Naci Yavuz

PROJECT BUILDER 2

You have been contracted to design the logo for Wired Gifts, which is an online gift site. Your concept is of a geometric red bow. You feel your idea will simultaneously convey the concepts of gifts and technology.

1. Open AI 4-24.ai, then save it as **Wired**.
2. Switch to Outline mode.
3. Select the small square, click the Rotate tool, press and hold [option] (Mac) or [Alt] (Win), then click the center of the large square.
4. Type **15** in the Angle text box, then click Copy.
5. Repeat the transformation 22 times.
6. Delete the large square at the center.
7. Switch to Preview mode.
8. Select all, then fill all the squares with Caribbean Blue.
   The color swatches on the Swatches panel in this file have been saved with names.
9. Apply the Divide pathfinder to the selection.
10. Fill the objects with the Red Bow gradient.
11. Delete the object in the center of the bow.
    Use the Direct Selection tool to select the object.
12. Select all, then remove the black stroke from the objects.
13. Save your work, compare your illustration with Figure 85, then close the Wired document.

Figure 85 Completed Project Builder 2

You are an illustrator for a small-town quarterly magazine. You're designing an illustration to accompany an article titled "A Walk Down Main Street." You decide to distort the artwork in perspective to make a more interesting illustration.

1. Open AI 4-25.ai, then save it as **Main Street Perspective**.
2. Select all the buildings on the left, then click the Free Transform tool.
3. Click and begin dragging the upper-right handle straight down.
4. While still dragging, press and hold [shift] [Ctrl] [Alt] (Win) or [shift] [command] [option] (Mac) and continue dragging until you like the appearance of the artwork.
5. Release the mouse button.
6. Click and drag the middle-left handle to the right to reduce the depth of the distortion.
   Figure 86 shows one possible result.
7. Using the same methodology, distort the buildings on the right in perspective.
   Figure 87 shows one possible solution.
8. Save your work, then close the Main Street Perspective document.

Figure 86 Distorting the left of the illustration

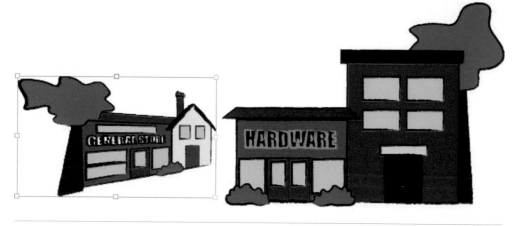

Figure 87 Completed Design Project

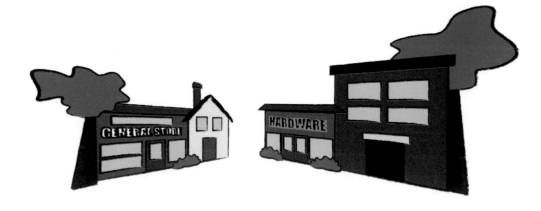

DESIGN PROJECT 2

You are the design department manager for a toy company, and your next project is to design a dartboard that will be part of a package of "Safe Games" for kids. The target market is boys and girls ages six to adult. You will design the board but not the darts.

1. Create a new document and name it **Dartboard**.

2. Search the Internet for pictures of dartboards.

3. Research the sport of throwing darts. What are the official dimensions of a dartboard? Is there an official design? Are there official colors?

4. Decide which colors should be used for the board, keeping in mind that the sales department plans to position it as a toy for both girls and boys.

5. Using the skills you learned in this chapter and Figure 88 as a guide, design a dartboard.

6. Save your work, compare your image to Figure 88, then close Dartboard.

Figure 88 Completed Design Project 2

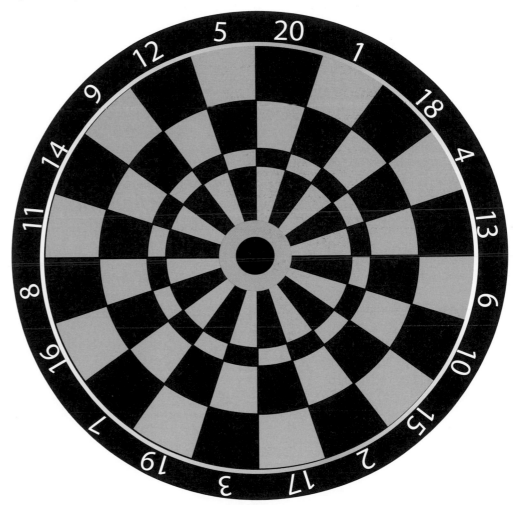

CAPTURING COMPLEXITY

Strangler Fig, a watercolor painting by Nirupa Rao, highlights the plant's unique role in its ecosystem.

Images courtesy of Nirupa Rao

DEVELOPING AN APPRECIATION

Growing up in Bengaluru, India, Nirupa Rao spent much of her childhood exploring the nearby jungle with her family. Their walks through the wild, tropical forest cultivated Nirupa's fondness for and appreciation of nature. Her granduncle, a field botanist, collected plant specimens from the jungle surrounding her grandfather's farm. Her mother's stories of this research inspired an air of adventure and excitement. A storyteller at heart, Nirupa enjoyed putting on plays for her family and also took an interest in creating handcrafted items, such as toys and books. Nirupa has carried her artistic talent and passion for nature into her career as a botanical illustrator. Her detailed works depict impactful stories about the unique behaviors of plants in India.

EDUCATION AND EARLY CAREER

With the exception of one online course, Nirupa is mostly a self-taught artist. While studying in Singapore, Nirupa had the opportunity to learn from other creatives and experiment with different mediums. Her interest grew when her cousin, a botanical researcher, shared photographs of plants and flowers with her. This inspired Nirupa to begin painting. She then took an internship in the children's division of a publishing house in the United Kingdom. While there, she learned about media research and further developed her creative skills using software programs such as Adobe Creative Suite. This helped Nirupa visualize her next step—providing children in India with similar content, so they, too, could learn about plants native to India.

CREATIVE PROJECTS AND PUBLICATIONS

In 2016, *National Geographic* awarded Nirupa a Young Explorers Grant to create an illustrated book of plant life in the Western Ghats of India. Published in 2019, *Hidden Kingdom—Fantastical Plants of the Western Ghats* sets Nirupa's colorful and intricately detailed illustrations to rhyme and helps open children's minds to the magical plants that exist in their own backyard. In addition to publishing other pieces, Nirupa's work has been displayed in the museum at Harvard's Dumbarton Oaks Museums. She collaborates with botanists and naturalists to ensure scientific accuracy in every illustration.

In Nirupa's book, *Hidden Kingdom*, she shares this watercolor painting titled *Strangler Fig*. The painting shows a tropical wild fig tree, which is part of the Ficus genus. This particular fig is often referred to as a strangler fig because of its unique behavior. This keystone species produces fruit throughout the year, providing food for birds, bats, and small mammals. In turn, birds drop strangler fig seeds on the branches of grown trees. The seeds germinate upon existing trees as a means to access sunlight more quickly. Over time, the roots of the strangler fig engulf the host tree, cutting off its access to sunlight and eventually strangling it to death with its roots.

Looking to capture this unique plant behavior, Nirupa created a watercolor painting of the strangler fig. Sitting low on the ground, she sketched the fig from below to capture the shapes of the branches, which she has described as "a hand grasping for sunlight." Nirupa often uses notes, photographs, and detailed sketches of the plants, which she then brings back to her studio to paint, scan, and manipulate using different software. Nirupa's process is very detail-oriented and thorough. She believes if you take the time to comprehend the complexity of an ecosystem, you can begin to understand how individual plants evolve, and what that communicates about the ecology of a place as a whole.

PROJECT DESCRIPTION

In this project, you will explore a plant within your community. Using pencil, paper, paints, or any art supplies available to you, you will create an illustration. Focus on capturing the details of the plant, such as the colors and textures. Include elements of the environment in which it grows. The goal of this project is to create a detailed botanical illustration of a plant and its environment within your community.

SKILLS TO EXPLORE

- Scribbling
- Smoothing and Shading
- Hatching and Cross-Hatching
- Creating Highlights
- Rough Sketching
- Finger Blending
- Stippling
- Working with Pencil, Pen, Paint
- Observation and Patience

SOFT SKILLS CHALLENGE

Host a round-table discussion with at least three classmates. The roundtable should focus on plant life in your community and the local environment as a whole. You will need to recruit classmates to take part in the discussion, write a script introducing the round-table topic and the people participating, and create an outline of the questions and talking points. It will be your job to facilitate the discussion, keep the conversation moving, and ensure everyone's opinion is being respected. The goals of this challenge are to think critically about the plant life in your community and connect it to a bigger picture. Find out what your peers think about the topic and use collaboration and conversation as a way to better understand the complexities of the topic.

ROUND-TABLE CHECKLIST

1. Group of three or more peers
2. Written script introducing the topic and each participant
3. Outline of questions and talking points
4. Safe space to facilitate respectful conversation

FOLLOW NIRUPA'S EXAMPLE

One of the many reasons Nirupa enjoys sketching is that it slows down your eye and helps you pick out small details of the subject you are looking at. This is very important when grasping the complexity of a plant and understanding how it behaves and interacts with other plants and wildlife in its natural environment.

Once you've chosen a plant to sketch, walk around it and look at it from different angles. Think about how much of the plant is visible and which vantage point gives you the best view. Keep your focus on the plant, but make sure you capture relevant surrounding plants and wildlife. Incorporate your prior knowledge about the plant as well. For example, if you were illustrating a purple coneflower, you might wait for a bee to land on the flower and sketch that as well, as the purple coneflower is a favorite for many pollinators.

Create a note-taking system. Consider a grid of notes so you can organize your observations and keep track of important details. Some categories could include: colors, textures, surrounding plant life, observed wildlife, movement over time, etc.

GETTING STARTED

Color	Texture	Movement	Location
Intense red color. Almost looks neon when sun is diectly on them. White tip in the middle of some flowers.

The buds and small/new petals look more pinkish. Some of the petals toward the bottom have turned a violet and light purple shade. | The fully bloomed petals look very soft like velvet, but the bud looks sharp. Almost like little spikes. | Petals don't move as loosely as they look like they would.

Petals are tightly held by the stem. With wind or when touched, whole flower moves together in a stiff motion. Looks delicate but holds well. | They don't seem to be by a lot of other flowers. Mostly by a lot of tall grass or Cardinals. |

To keep organized, the student created a grid system for notes. The student focused on the petals of the flower and how they compared to other flowers around it.

The student focused on illustrating the tree's leaves by experimenting with different lines and shading. The student then took photographs of the entire tree and surrounding environment for later reference.

PROJECT DESCRIPTION

In this project, you will use your plant illustration from the Design Project to create an infographic describing the different parts of the plant. You will need to either photograph and upload, or scan your illustration to your computer. Once you have your botanical illustration available on your computer, you will use Adobe Illustrator to refine, enhance, and add information to it. The goal of this project is to create a comprehensive infographic that educates viewers about the appearance, behavior, and environment of a local plant.

SKILLS TO EXPLORE

- Work with Basic Shapes
- Apply Fill and Stroke Colors to Objects
- Make Direct Selections
- Create Point Text
- Manipulate Text with the Touch Type Tool
- Create Gradients
- Draw Straight and Curved Lines
- Draw Elements of an Illustration
- Apply Attributes to Objects
- Use Image Trace
- Use the Live Paint Bucket Tool
- Transform Objects
- Offset and Outline Paths
- Create Compound Paths
- Work With the Pathfinder Panel
- Apply Round Corners to Objects
- Use the Shape Builder Tool
- Create Clipping Masks

SOFT SKILLS CHALLENGE

Write a blog post about the work you created and share it to a social media account. In your blog, include basic background information about your chosen plant, such as its behavior and characteristics. You will also want to write about why you chose the plant, what your creative process was when creating your composition, and some details of your illustration that a viewer might miss upon first glance. This is a great opportunity to explain your work to a wider audience and tell why you made some of your creative choices.

Don't forget to keep the conversation going. Respond to comments and interactions with your post. The goal of this challenge is for you to present your designs and use your work as a steppingstone to bigger conversations.

FOLLOW NIRUPA'S EXAMPLE

Take photographs. It can be hard to capture every detail in a sketch and even harder to remember the details once you've left the scene. Photographs are a great way to record a moment and refer back to it later. Sometimes photographs can even document elements you did not notice initially; for example, a nearby ant hill or the plant's shadow on the ground.

Use your resources. It can be helpful to know what you are looking for before you get there. Research local plants online, or better yet, find someone in your community to talk to. You might interview your science teacher or a friendly neighbor who enjoys gardening. Plants often have small details, such as colors and textures, that go unnoticed but communicate a lot about their behavior and health. If you do your research ahead of time, you will know what types of organisms are commonly found in your environment, and which are not. This will help you determine whether the plants you are seeing naturally occur in this ecosystem.

GETTING STARTED

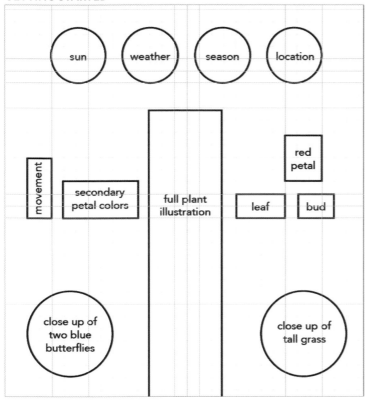

The student has a lot of information to include and fit into a single infographic. To keep it organized and cohesive, the student mapped out where each piece of information will go and eliminated information deemed less important to the story.

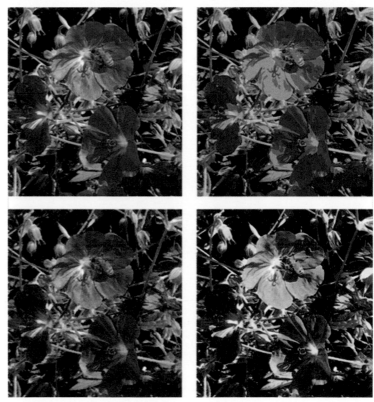

In order to enhance the illustration while maintaining authenticity, the student experimented with several techniques and effects in Illustrator to figure out which one felt the most authentic and original.

READY TO RETURN

The Basques were the master whalers of their day, but not all their ships weathered the voyages. Seamen's court testimony and insurance claims tell of a costly end to the *San Juan*: driven into the rocks by violent winds before departure in 1565. But the crew survived, many barrels were recovered, and the Basques dominated the hunting grounds of the north into the next century.

More than 2,000 miles
Red Bay ←→ Pasajes

CARGO 290 tons

Cider

PACKING THE WHALE OIL

Barrels were interlocked to prevent shifting and maximize space. On a typical return voyage, chalupas may have been left behind and some men given extra wages to winter in Red Bay to allow more room for oil.

Barrels of ship's biscuits, cod

Fifteen to 20 whales yielded enough oil to fill the cargo hold.

← WATER LEVEL

Bundles of baleen—in higher demand at the end of the 16th century—were stacked and bound.

1,000 barrels of whale oil

Whalers relieved themselves over the beakhead, with tarred rope as toilet paper.

During voyages, the crew cooked food in cauldrons over a stone-lined firebox.

Beakhead

Galley

Flensing operations

Crew's quarters

Barrels were floated from land to ships for loading.

Bottom of mast

16TH-CENTURY PROFIT SHARING

The ship's owners, outfitters, and crew each got a third of the cargo. The captain and master negotiated their share with the owners and outfitters, and the crewmembers' shares varied based on their position.

$10,000,000
total value of cargo in 2018 dollars

$10,000
per barrel

Owners and captain
Outfitters and master
Crew

Barrels per person

12	Harpooners
4	Seamen
3	Apprentices
8	Officers

FERNANDO G. BAPTISTA, RILEY D. CHAMPINE, DAISY CHUNG, AND EVE CONANT, NGM STAFF; PATRICIA HEALY, SHIZUKA AOKI, AND ELIJAH LEE; BIORENDER (BOWHEAD WHALE, INTERNAL ANATOMY). SOURCES: XABIER AGOTE AND MIKEL LEOZ AIZPURU, ALBAOLA BASQUE MARITIME HERITAGE ASSOCIATION; BRAD LOEWEN, UNIVERSITÉ DE MONTRÉAL; NINYA MIKHAILA AND JANE MALCOLM-DAVIES, THE TUDOR TAILOR; J. CRAIG GEORGE, DEPARTMENT OF WILDLIFE MANAGEMENT, UTQIAGVIK, ALASKA; ROSAULND ROLLAND, ANDERSON CABOT CENTER FOR OCEAN LIFE, NEW ENGLAND AQUARIUM; BRENNA FRASIER, SAINT MARY'S UNIVERSITY, NOVA SCOTIA; CINDY GIBBONS, PARKS CANADA

1978: RECOVERING THE SAN JUAN
Found under kelp and silt, the ship's flattened hull had been preserved for centuries by icy waters. The first plank brought up was oak, not native to the region but known to be used by the Basques. Red Bay is now a UNESCO World Heritage site.

feet
Reconstruction of remains
Actual remains
Seafloor
Original position of the shipwreck
Back view

Officers' quarters
Sandglass
Capstan
Compass box
Captain's cabin
Tiller
Crew's quarters
Sailors slept on straw-filled sacks.

Seamen passed the time weaving, playing checkers, and carving designs into baleen or the ship's hull.

Anchors attached by cables were hoisted onto the San Juan by the capstan.

When sailing, pilots carefully recorded distances, tides, and the ship's progress, guided by rudimentary instruments such as a sandglass—to measure time and speed—and a compass.

Rudder

Ready to Return is a realistic illustration of the Basques whaling ship, San Juan, which was recovered over 400 years after it was lost at sea in 1565.

Illustration by Fernando Baptista. From "On the Hunt with the Basque Whalers." *National Geographic Magazine*, Vol. 234, No. 2, August, 2018

CHAPTER 5

WORKING WITH LAYERS

1. Create and Modify Layers
2. Manipulate Layered Artwork
3. Manage Layers
4. Create a Clipping Set

Adobe Certified Professional in Graphic Design and Illustration Using Adobe Illustrator

2. Project Setup and Interface
This objective covers the interface setup and program settings that assist in an efficient and effective workflow, as well as knowledge about ingesting digital assets for a project.

2.3 Use non-printing design tools in the interface to aid in design or workflow.
  D Use views and modes to work efficiently with vector graphics.

3. Organize Documents
This objective covers document structure such as layers and tracks, for efficient workflows.

3.1 Use layers to manage design elements.
  A Use the Layers panel to modify layers.
  B Manage and work with multiple layers in a complex project.

3.2 Modify layer visibility using opacity and masks.
  B Create, apply, and manipulate clipping masks.

4. Creating and Modifying Visual Elements
This objective covers core tools and functionality of the application, as well as tools that affect the visual appearance of document elements.

4.3 Make, manage, and manipulate selections.
  B Modify and refine selections using various methods.

5. Publishing Digital Media
This objective covers saving and exporting documents or assets within individual layers or selections.

5.2 Export or save digital images to various file formats.
  C Export project elements.

CREATE AND MODIFY LAYERS

▶ What You'll Do

In this lesson, you will create new layers and explore options on the Layers panel for viewing, locking, hiding, and selecting layers and layered artwork.

Designing with Layers

When you're creating complex artwork, keeping track of all the items on the artboard can become a challenge. Small items hide behind larger items, and it may become difficult to find, select, and work with them. The Layers panel solves this problem because you can organize your work by placing objects or groups of objects on separate layers. Artwork on layers can be manipulated and modified independently from artwork on other layers. The Layers panel also provides effective options to select, hide, lock, and change the appearance of your work. In addition, layers are an effective solution for storing multiple versions of your work in one file.

Creating Layers and Sublayers

Layers are a smart solution for organizing and managing a complex illustration. For example, if you were drawing a map of your home state, you might put all the interstate freeways on one layer, the local freeways on a second layer, secondary roads on a third layer, and all the text elements on a fourth layer.

As the name suggests, the Layers panel consists of a series of layers. By default, every Illustrator document is created with one layer, called Layer 1. As you work, you can create new layers and move objects into them, thereby segregating objects and organizing your work. The first object that is placed on Layer 1 is placed on a sublayer and assigned a name based on its contents, such as <Path>, <Rectangle>, or <Group>. Each additional object placed on the same layer is placed on a separate sublayer.

On the Layers panel, each layer has a **thumbnail**, or miniature picture, of the objects on that layer. Thumbnails also display the artwork that is positioned on each of the individual sublayers of a layer. You can change the size of the rows on the Layers panel by choosing a new size in the Layers Panel Options dialog box. Click the Layers panel menu button, then click Panel Options. Layers and sublayers can also be given descriptive names to help identify their contents.

The stacking order of objects on the artboard corresponds to the hierarchy of layers on the Layers panel. Artwork in the top layer is at the front of the stacking order, while artwork in the bottom layer is in the back. The hierarchy of sublayers corresponds to the stacking order of the objects within a single layer.

Illustrator offers two basic ways to create new layers and sublayers. You can click the New Layer or New Sublayer command on the Layers panel menu, or you can click the Create New Layer or Create New Sublayer button on the Layers panel. Figure 1 shows a simple illustration and its corresponding layers on the Layers panel.

Duplicating Layers

In addition to creating new layers, you can duplicate existing layers by clicking the Duplicate command on the Layers panel menu or by dragging a layer or sublayer onto the Create New Layer button on the Layers panel.

When you duplicate a layer, all the artwork on the layer is duplicated as well. Note the difference between this and copying and pasting artwork. When you copy and paste artwork, the copied artwork is pasted on the same layer.

Setting Layer Options

The Layer Options dialog box offers a wealth of options for working with layered artwork, many of which are not available to you unless you are working with layers. You can name a layer, and you can also set a selection color for the layer. When an object is selected, its selection marks will be the same color as specified for the layer, making it easy to differentiate layers of artwork on the artboard.

TIP To quickly rename a layer, double-click its name, then type the new name.

Also in the Layer Options dialog box are options for locking, unlocking, showing, and hiding artwork on the layer. When you lock a layer, all the objects on the layer are locked and protected. When the Show check box is checked, all the artwork that is contained in the layer is displayed on the artboard. When the Show check box is not checked, the artwork is hidden.

Figure 1 Layers panel

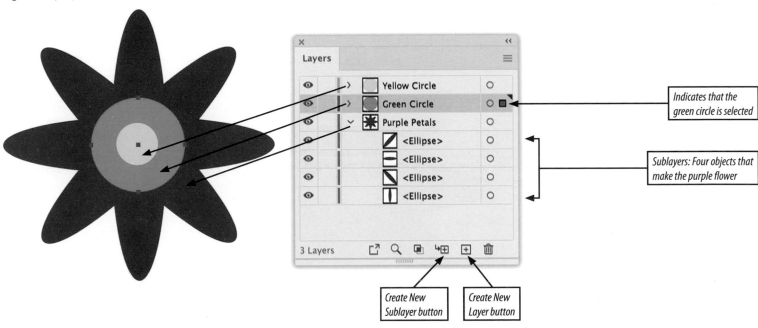

Indicates that the green circle is selected

Sublayers: Four objects that make the purple flower

Create New Sublayer button

Create New Layer button

The Preview option displays all the artwork on a layer in Preview mode. When the Preview option is not activated, the artwork is displayed in Outline mode. Thus, with layers, some elements on the artboard can be in Preview mode, while others are in Outline mode.

The Print option allows you to choose whether or not to print a layer. This feature is useful for printing different versions of the same illustration. The Dim Images to: option reduces the intensity of bitmap images that are placed on the artboard. Dimming a bitmap often makes it easier to trace an image.

Use the Template option when you want to trace the artwork on a layer to create a new illustration. By default, a template layer is locked and cannot be printed.

Buttons on the Layers panel represent ways to lock, unlock, hide, and show artwork on each layer, making it unnecessary to use the Layer Options dialog box to activate these functions. Clicking the Eye icon (the tool tip will display "Toggles Visibility" when you mouse over it) lets you hide and show layers, and the Lock icon lets you lock and unlock layers.

Selecting Artwork on Layers and Sublayers

The easiest way to select a layer is to click the layer name or the layer thumbnail. Selecting a layer is referred to as "targeting" a layer. When you select an object on the artboard, its layer is selected (highlighted) on the Layers panel, and the **Indicates Selected Art icon** (or **Selected art icon** for brevity) appears, as shown in Figure 2. Selecting a layer or sublayer on the

Layers panel does not select the actual artwork on that layer.

Changes you make to layers on the Layers panel affect the artwork on those layers. For example, if you delete a layer, the artwork on the layer will be deleted. The artwork on a layer will be duplicated if the layer is duplicated. Changing a layer's position in the layers hierarchy will move the artwork forward or backward in the stacking order.

Duplicating the artwork on the artboard does not duplicate the layer the artwork is on. If you delete all the artwork on a layer, you are left with an empty layer. *A layer is never automatically created, copied, or deleted because of something you do to the artwork on the layer.*

The same is *not* true for sublayers. If you delete or copy artwork that is on a sublayer, the *sublayer* is deleted or copied, respectively.

Selecting All Artwork on a Layer

The Select All command makes it easy to select every object on the artboard in one step. At times, however, you will want to select every object on a layer or sublayer, but not every object on the artboard. To select all the artwork on a single layer or sublayer, click the **target layer button**, shown in Figure 2. You can also press and hold [option] (Mac) or [Alt] (Win) and click the layer. All objects on that layer will become selected on the artboard.

Figure 2 Target layer button and Selected art icon

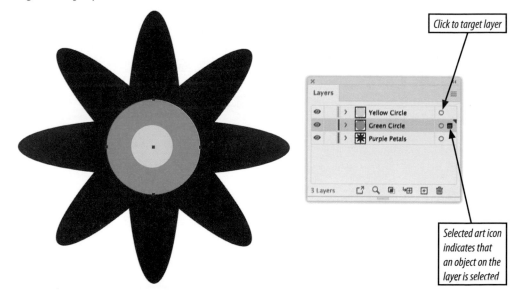

Click to target layer

Selected art icon indicates that an object on the layer is selected

Create a new layer

1. Open AI 5-1.ai, then save it as **Living Room**.

2. Open AI 5-2.ai, then save it as **Showroom**.

   You will work with two documents during this lesson.

3. Click the **Selection tool** ▶, select the **chair**, then copy it.

4. Click the **Living Room.ai document tab** to activate the Living Room document.

   TIP Using the Window menu is another way to switch between open documents.

5. Click **Window** on the menu bar, then click **Layers** if the panel is not already open.

   The Layers panel shows two layers. The Empty room layer contains the artwork you see on the artboard. The objects on the Foreground layer are hidden.

6. Click the **Create New Layer button** ⊞ on the Layers panel.

   A new layer named Layer 3 appears above the Foreground layer.

7. Click **Edit** on the menu bar, then click **Paste**.

   The chair artwork is pasted into Layer 3.

8. Position the **chair** on the artboard as shown in Figure 3.

9. Save your work, then continue to the next set of steps.

You created a new layer using the Create New Layer button on the Layers panel, then pasted an object onto that new layer.

Figure 3 Chair selected and positioned on its own layer

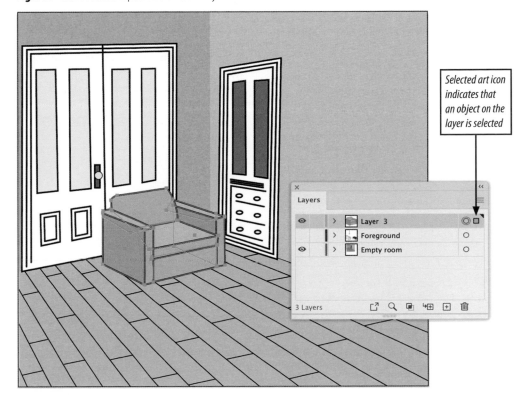

Selected art icon indicates that an object on the layer is selected

Name a layer and change a layer's selection color

1. Double-click anywhere inside the name **Layer 3**.

   "Layer 3" is highlighted.

2. Type **Chair** to rename the layer.

3. Double-click the **Chair layer thumbnail**.

   The Layer Options dialog box for the Chair layer opens.

4. Click the **Color list arrow**, click **Brick Red**, as shown in Figure 4, then click **OK**.

   Note that the selection marks on the chair are now red, reflecting the new selection color for the Chair layer.

5. Deselect the chair.

6. Save your work, then continue to the next set of steps.

You used the Layer Options dialog box to rename Layer 3 and assign it a new selection color.

Select items on a layer and lock a layer

1. Click the **Selection tool** ▶, then click the **chair**.

   Note that the Selected art icon appears on the Layers panel when the chair is selected, as shown in Figure 5.

TIP The Selected art icon is the same color as its layer.

2. Deselect the chair.

   The Selected art icon disappears.

3. Press **[option] (Mac)** or **[Alt] (Win)**, then click the **Chair layer** on the Layers panel.

   The chair artwork is selected.

4. Click either of the **two mauve walls** in the illustration.

   When an object is selected on the artboard, the layer on which the selected object is placed is highlighted on the Layers panel.

5. Double-click the **Empty room layer**, click the **Lock check box**, then click **OK**.

   The Lock icon 🔒 appears on the Empty room layer, indicating that all the objects on the Empty room layer are locked.

You noted the relationship between a selected item and its corresponding layer on the Layers panel. You activated the Selected art icon and selected the artwork on the Chair layer. You then locked the Empty room layer.

Figure 4 Layer Options dialog box

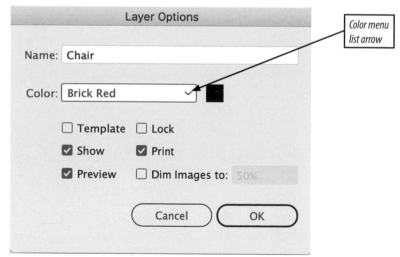

Figure 5 Selected art icon identifies the layer of a selected object

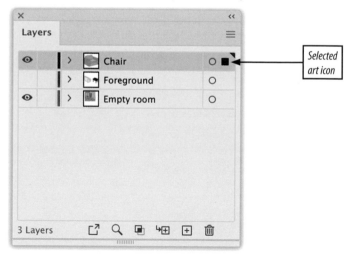

Show and hide layers

1. Double-click the **Foreground layer** to open its options dialog box.

2. Click the **Color list arrow**, then click **Grass Green**.

3. Click the **Show check box**, then click **OK**.

   The objects on the Foreground layer become visible, and the Eye icon 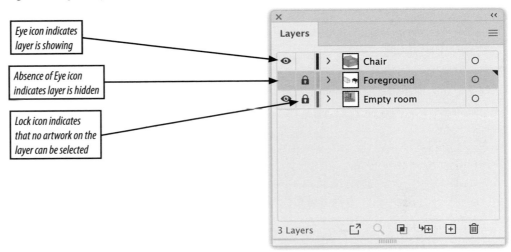 appears on the Foreground layer.

4. Click the **Eye icon** on the Foreground layer to hide the objects.

5. Click the **empty Eye icon box** on the Foreground layer to show the objects.

6. Click the **empty Lock icon box** on the Foreground layer.

   The Lock icon appears.

7. Click the **Eye icon** on the Foreground layer to hide the objects.

   Your Layers panel should resemble Figure 6.

8. Save your work, then continue to the next lesson.

You used the Eye icon on the Layers panel to toggle between showing and hiding the artwork on two layers. You also locked the Foreground layer.

Figure 6 Foreground layer is locked and hidden

Eye icon indicates layer is showing

Absence of Eye icon indicates layer is hidden

Lock icon indicates that no artwork on the layer can be selected

Layers

Chair
Foreground
Empty room

3 Layers

MANIPULATE LAYERED ARTWORK

▶ *What You'll Do*

In this lesson, you will learn methods for manipulating layers to change the display of layered artwork. You will change the order of layers on the panel, merge layers, work with sublayers, and move objects between layers.

Changing the Order of Layers and Sublayers

The hierarchy of the layers on the Layers panel determines how objects on the artboard overlap. All the objects on a given layer are behind the objects on the layer above it and in front of the objects on the layer beneath it. Multiple objects within a given layer overlap according to their stacking order, and you can reposition them with the standard stacking order commands.

To change the position of a layer or sublayer in the hierarchy, simply drag it up or down on the panel. A thick horizontal line identifies where the layer will be repositioned. When you reposition a layer, its sublayers move with it.

Merging Layers

After you have positioned artwork to your liking by using multiple layers and sublayers, you will often want to consolidate those layers to simplify the panel. First, you must select the layers you want to merge. Press [command] (Mac) or [Ctrl] (Win) to select multiple layers. Once you have selected the layers you want

to merge, apply the Merge Selected command on the Layers panel menu. When you merge layers, all the artwork from one or more layers moves onto the layer that was last selected before the merge.

Be careful not to confuse merging layers with condensing layers. Condensing layers is simply the process of dragging one layer into another. The repositioned layer becomes a sublayer of the layer into which it was dragged.

Defining Sublayers

Whenever you have one or more objects on a layer, you have **sublayers**. For example, if you draw a circle and a square on Layer 1, it will automatically have two sublayers—one for the square, one for the circle. The layer is comprised of its sublayers.

As soon as the first object is placed on a layer, a triangle appears to the left of the layer name, indicating that the layer contains sublayers. Click the triangle to expand the layer and see the sublayers, then click it again to collapse the layer and hide the sublayers.

Working with Sublayers

When you place grouped artwork into a layer, a sublayer is automatically created with the name <Group>. A triangle appears on the <Group> sublayer, which—when clicked—exposes the sublayers—one for every object in the group. In Figure 7, all the objects that make up the flower have been grouped. On the Layers panel, a sublayer named <Group> appears below the Green Flower layer. That <Group> sublayer contains a layer for every object that makes up the flower artwork.

Dragging Objects Between Layers

Sublayers are easy to move between layers; drag and drop a sublayer from one layer to another. Often, you'll want to move artwork from one layer to another. The Layers panel makes this easy to do. Select the artwork you want to move so the Selected art icon appears. Drag the Selected art icon to the destination layer, as shown in Figure 8, and the artwork will move with it.

If you drag the Selected art icon to a sublayer, the artwork is grouped with the object already on the sublayer.

You have two other options for moving objects between layers. You can cut and paste artwork from one layer to another by selecting the object you want to move, cutting it from the artboard, selecting the layer on which you wish to place it, then pasting. You can also use the Send to Current Layer command. Select the artwork you want to move, click the name of the destination layer to make it the active layer, click Object on the menu bar, point to Arrange, then click Send to Current Layer. Clearly, these two methods are more time consuming; your best option is to simply drag the Selected art icon.

Figure 7 <Group> sublayer on the Layers panel

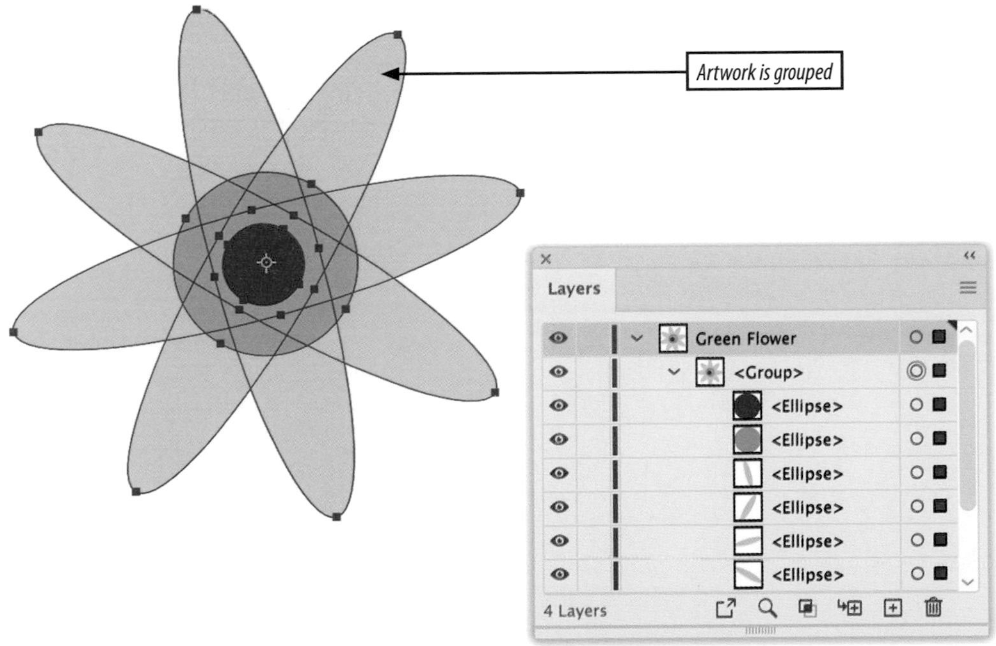

Artwork is grouped

Figure 8 Dragging selected artwork from one layer to another

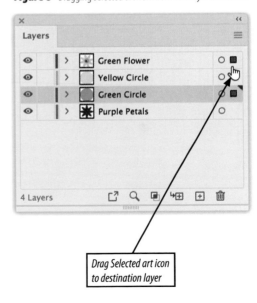

Drag Selected art icon to destination layer

Change the hierarchy of layers

1. Switch to the Showroom document, copy the **rug**, then return to the Living Room document.

2. Press **[command] (Mac)** or **[Ctrl] (Win)**, then click the **Create New Layer button**  on the Layers panel.

   Pressing [command] (Mac) or [Ctrl] (Win) creates a new layer at the top of the layer list.

3. Click **Edit** on the menu bar, then click **Paste**.

   The rug is pasted into the new layer because it is the active, or targeted, layer.

4. Name the new layer **Rug**, set the layer color to **Yellow**, then position the **rug artwork** with a corner of it hanging slightly off the artboard, as shown in Figure 9.

5. Click and drag the **Rug layer**; position it **below the Chair layer**, as shown

in Figure 10; then release the mouse button.

6. Save your work, then continue to the next set of steps.

   The rug artwork is now positioned below the chair artwork.

You created a new layer at the top of the Layers panel. You pasted artwork into that layer, then moved the layer below another layer in the hierarchy so the artwork on the two layers overlapped properly on the artboard.

Figure 9 The Rug layer is at the top of the layers hierarchy

Figure 10 Dragging the Rug layer below the Chair layer

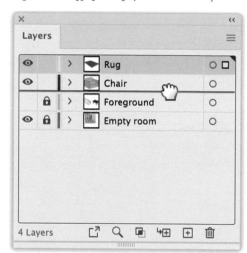

Merge layers

1. Switch to the Showroom document, copy the **sculpture**, then return to the Living Room document.

2. Press **[command] (Mac)** or **[Ctrl] (Win)**, then click the **Create New Layer button** ⊞ .

3. Paste the **sculpture** into the new layer, then name the layer **Sculpture**.

TIP Assign a unique color to this and all other layers you create in this lesson.

4. Show the **Foreground layer**, then position the **sculpture artwork** on the **brown end table**, as shown in Figure 11.

5. Deselect the sculpture, then drag the **Foreground layer above the Sculpture layer** on the Layers panel.

6. Unlock the Foreground layer.

7. Click the **Sculpture layer** to select it, press **[command] (Mac)** or **[Ctrl] (Win)**, then click the **Foreground layer**.

   When merging layers, the last layer selected becomes the merged layer.

8. Click the **Layers panel menu button** ≡ , then click **Merge Selected**.

   The objects from both layers are merged into the Foreground layer; the Sculpture layer is deleted.

TIP Layers must be showing and unlocked to be merged.

9. Compare your screen to Figure 12 and don't worry that your sculpture is temporarily behind the table.

10. Save your work, then continue to the next set of steps.

You merged the Sculpture and the Foreground layers.

Figure 11 Sculpture artwork positioned on top of the table

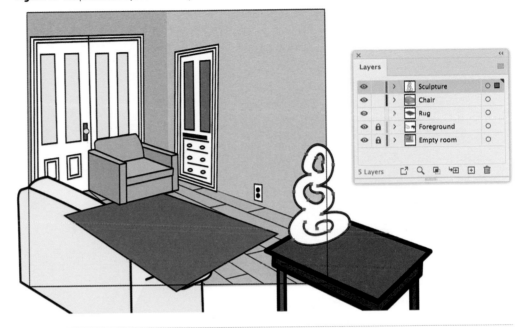

Figure 12 Foreground and Sculpture layers merged

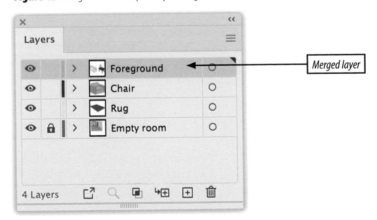

Merged layer

Work with sublayers

1. Expand the **Foreground layer** by clicking the **triangle** `>` to the left of the layer.

   Three sublayers, all named <Group>, are revealed.

2. Expand the **sofa <Group> sublayer** by clicking the **triangle** `>` to the left of it.

   The five paths that compose the sofa are revealed.

3. Select the **sofa artwork**.

   The Selected art icon appears for each of the selected paths, as shown in Figure 13.

4. Click the **triangle** `⌄` to the left of the **sofa <Group> sublayer** to collapse it, then deselect the **sofa**.

5. Double-click the **sofa <Group> sublayer**, then name it **Sofa**.

6. Name the sculpture sublayer **Sculpture**, then name the end table sublayer **End Table**.

7. Move the **Sculpture sublayer above the End Table sublayer** so your Layers panel resembles Figure 14.

   Notice that the sculpture artwork is on top of the end table.

8. Click the **triangle** `⌄` to the left of the **Foreground layer** to hide the three sublayers.

9. Hide the **Foreground layer**.

10. Save your work, then continue to the next set of steps.

You viewed sublayers in the Foreground layer. You then renamed the three sublayers in the Foreground layer and rearranged the order of the Sculpture and the End Table sublayers.

Figure 13 Each path in the sofa <Group> sublayer is selected

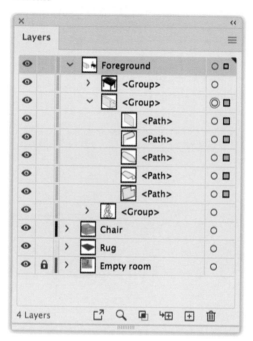

Figure 14 Sculpture sublayer moved above the End Table sublayer

Create new sublayers

1. Switch to the Showroom document, copy the **cabinet**, then return to the Living Room document.

2. Press **[command] (Mac)** or **[Ctrl] (Win)**, then click the **Create New Layer button** ⊞ .

3. Name the new layer **Entertainment**, select **Magenta** as the layer color, then click **OK**.

4. Paste the **cabinet artwork** into the new layer.

5. Copy the **plant** from the Showroom document, then paste the **plant artwork** into the Entertainment layer.

6. Position the **cabinet artwork** and the **plant artwork** as shown in Figure 15.

7. Deselect all, expand the **Entertainment layer**, then select the **plant artwork** on the artboard.

8. Double-click the **Reflect tool** ⋈ , click the **Vertical option button**, then click **Copy**.

   The reflected copy of the plant is placed on a new sublayer above the original plant sublayer.

9. Rename the new sublayer **Plant 2**.

10. Move the **Plant 2 sublayer** to the **bottom of the Entertainment sublayer hierarchy**, as shown in Figure 16.

11. Click the **Selection tool** ▶ , then move the **new plant artwork** into the position shown in Figure 17.

12. Scale the **new plant artwork 85%**, then delete or move some leaves on it so it's not an obvious copy of the original plant.

13. Save your work, then continue to the next set of steps.

You created and moved new sublayers.

Figure 15 Cabinet and plant are on the same layer

Figure 16 Moving the Plant 2 sublayer

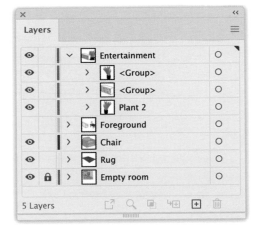

Figure 17 The reflected copy of the plant in position

Move objects between layers

1. Switch to the Showroom document, copy the **electronics images**, then return to the Living Room document.

2. Create a **new layer** at the top of the hierarchy, name it **Electronics**, then click **OK**.

3. Paste the **electronics** on the **Electronics layer**, then position the **electronics artwork** on the cabinet.

   The plant on the right needs to be positioned in front of the electronics for the visual to be realistic.

4. Name the top sublayer in the Entertainment layer **Plant 1**, then click the **Selected art icon** on the layer to select the **Plant 1 artwork** on the artboard.

   The Selected art icon is highlighted on the Plant 1 sublayer.

5. Drag the **Selected art icon** from the **Plant 1 sublayer** to the **Electronics layer**.

   The Plant 1 sublayer moves into the Electronics layer. The Plant 1 sublayer automatically becomes the top sublayer in the Electronics layer.

6. Switch to the Showroom document, copy the **Matisse**, return to the Living Room document, then create a new layer at the top of the hierarchy, named **Matisse**.

7. Paste the **Matisse artwork** into the new layer, then position it as shown in Figure 18.

8. Drag the **Matisse layer** on top of the **Electronics layer**.

Figure 18 The Matisse in position on its own layer

A white hand with a small rectangle appears when you drag the Matisse layer on top of the Electronics layer. As shown in Figure 19, the Matisse layer is moved into the Electronics layer as the topmost sublayer.

Figure 19 The Matisse layer relocated as a sublayer on the Electronics layer

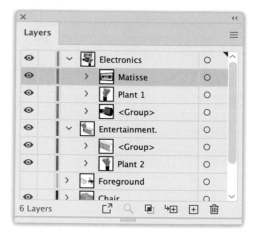

9. Create **new layers** for the **lamp** and the **table**, copy and paste the **lamp** and **table artwork** from the Showroom document to the new layers, then position the artwork so your illustration resembles Figure 20.

10. Save your work, then continue to the next lesson.

You created a new layer named Electronics and dragged the Plant 1 sublayer into the Electronics layer by dragging its Selected art icon to the Electronics layer. You then moved the Matisse layer into the Electronics layer by dragging it on top of the Electronics layer and created new layers for the table and the lamp.

Figure 20 The lamp and table in position

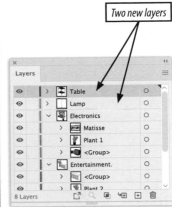

MANAGE LAYERS

Using the View Buttons on the Layers Panel

The view options, available on the Layers panel, make working with layers a smart choice for complex illustrations. You can target specific viewing options to each layer in the document. Without layers, options for viewing your work are limited to the Hide and Show All commands on the Object menu.

The Eye icon makes it easy to change what can be seen on the artboard. Clicking this icon once hides all the artwork on a layer, and the icon disappears. When you click the empty gray square where the icon was, all the artwork on the layer shows, and the Eye icon reappears. Pressing [option] (Mac) or [Alt] (Win) and clicking the Eye icon once shows all layers. Clicking a second time hides all layers except for the layer you clicked.

Pressing [command] (Mac) or [Ctrl] (Win) and clicking the Eye icon toggles between Outline and Preview modes, and all the artwork on the layer will switch between outlined and filled objects. Pressing [option] (Mac) or [Alt] (Win) and clicking the Eye icon switches all other layers between Outline and Preview modes.

Importing a Photoshop File with Layers

When you use the Open command to import a layered Photoshop file into Illustrator CC, you have the option to open that file with its layers intact. In the Photoshop Import Options dialog box that appears, click the Convert Layers to Objects option button, then click OK. Display the Illustrator Layers panel and you will see that Illustrator has preserved as much of the Photoshop layer structure as possible.

Locating an Object on the Layers Panel

With complex illustrations, layers and sublayers tend to multiply—so much so that you will often find it easiest to work with collapsed layers, those in which you hide the sublayers. Sometimes it can be difficult to identify an object's layer or sublayer, especially if there are multiple copies of the object in the illustration. The Locate Object command offers a simple solution. Select an object on the artboard, click the Layers panel menu button, then click Locate Object. The layers expand, revealing their sublayers, and the selected object's layer or sublayer is selected.

Reversing the Order of Layers

Another option the Layers panel offers for managing your artwork is the ability to reverse the order of layers. Select the layers whose order you want to reverse. Press [shift] to select multiple contiguous layers (those next to each other on the panel). Press [command] (Mac) or [Ctrl] (Win) to select multiple noncontiguous layers. Click the Layers panel menu button, then click Reverse Order.

Making Layers Nonprintable

The ability to choose whether or not to print the artwork on a specific layer is useful, especially during the middle stages of producing an illustration. For example, you could print just the text elements and give them to a copy editor for proofing. You could print just the elements of the illustration that are ready to be shown to the client, holding back the elements that still need work. See Figure 21 for the Print option in the Layer Options dialog box.

Another value of the Print option is the ability to print different versions of a document. Let's say you're working on the design of a poster

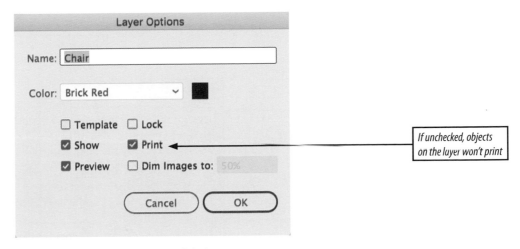

If unchecked, objects on the layer won't print

Figure 21 Print option in the Layer Options dialog box

for a client and you've finalized the artwork, but you're still undecided about the typeface for the headline after narrowing down the choices to five typefaces. You could create five layers, one for the headline formatted in each typeface. Then you would print the illustration five times, each with a different headline. This is a smart and simple way to produce comps quickly.

Exporting Illustrator Layers to Photoshop

You can export Illustrator layers to Photoshop. Click File on the menu bar, click Export As, then choose Photoshop (*.PSD) as the file format. When the Photoshop Export Options dialog box opens, verify that the Color Model is set to CMYK and that the Write Layers option button is selected. Click OK to export the layers to a Photoshop document.

Explore view options on the Layers panel

1. Collapse the **Electronics** and **Entertainment layers**, then hide them.

2. Press and hold **[option] (Mac)** or **[Alt] (Win)**, then click the **Eye icon**  on the Chair layer.

   All the layers are displayed.

3. Using the same keyboard commands, click the **Eye icon** on the **Chair layer** again.

   All layers except the Chair layer are hidden.

4. Using the same keyboard commands, click the **empty Eye icon box** on the **Chair layer** again so all the layers are displayed.

5. Move the **Foreground layer** to the top of the hierarchy.

6. Press **[command] (Mac)** or **[Ctrl] (Win)**, then click the **Eye icon** on the **Chair layer**.

   The artwork on the Chair layer switches to Outline mode.

7. Using the same keyboard commands, click the **Eye icon** on the **Chair layer** again.

8. Press **[option] [command] (Mac)** or **[Alt] [Ctrl] (Win)**, then click the **Eye icon** on the **Chair layer**.

   The artwork on every layer except for the Chair layer switches to Outline mode, as shown in Figure 22.

9. Press **[option] [command] (Mac)** or **[Alt] [Ctrl] (Win)**, then click the **Eye icon** on the **Chair layer** again.

10. Save your work, then continue to the next set of steps.

You learned keyboard commands to explore view options on the Layers panel.

Figure 22 The Chair layer shown in Preview mode and all other layers shown in Outline mode

Locate, duplicate, and delete layers

1. Select the **Plant 2 artwork** on the artboard.

2. Click the **Layers panel menu button** ≡, then click **Locate Object**.

   The Entertainment layer expands, as does the Plant 2 sublayer.

   TIP The Locate Object command is useful when you are working with collapsed layers or with many layers and sublayers.

3. Collapse the **Entertainment layer**.

4. Select the **Lamp layer**, then drag it on top of the **Create New Layer button** ⊞ on the Layers panel.

   The Lamp layer and its contents are duplicated onto a new layer that is created above the original Lamp layer. The copied lamp artwork is positioned directly on top of the original lamp artwork.

5. Position the **duplicated lamp artwork** on the artboard, as shown in Figure 23.

6. Drag the **Lamp copy layer** to the **Delete Selection button** 🗑 on the Layers panel.

7. Save your work, then continue to the next set of steps.

You used the Locate Object command to identify a selected object's position on the Layers panel. You duplicated a layer and then deleted it.

Figure 23 Positioning the second lamp

Dim placed images

1. Hide all layers, then create a **new layer** at the top of the hierarchy, named **Photo**.

2. Click **File** on the menu bar, then click **Place**.

3. Navigate to the drive and folder where your Chapter 5 Data Files are stored, click **Living Room Original.tif**, then click **Place**.

   The source for the illustration is placed on its own layer.

4. Align the **photo with the top-left corner of the artboard**, as shown in Figure 24.

5. Double-click the **Photo layer**, click the **Dim Images to: check box**, type **50** in the Dim Images to: text box, then click **OK**.

   The placed image is less vivid.

TIP Dimming a placed image is useful for tracing.

6. Save your work, then continue to the next set of steps.

You created a new layer, placed a photo on the new layer, then used the Layer Options dialog box to dim the photo 50%.

Figure 24 The source of the illustration, placed on its own layer

Exclude specific layers from printing

1. Create a **new layer** at the top of the hierarchy, named **Message**.

2. Using any font you like, type a message for the printer, as shown in Figure 25.

3. Convert the message text to outlines.

4. Double-click the **Message layer**, remove the check mark from the Print check box, then click **OK**.

   The Message layer will not print to any output device.

   TIP When a layer is set to not print, its name is italicized on the Layers panel.

5. Make the **Photo layer** nonprintable.

6. Hide the **Message** and **Photo layers**.

7. Make all the other layers visible.

8. Save your work, then continue to the next lesson.

You created a new layer called Message, typed a message for the printer, then designated the Message and Photo layers as nonprintable. You then displayed all the layers except for the Message and Photo layers.

Figure 25 Using a layer for a message to the printer

Printer: Use photo for reference if necessary. Thank you!
Call me at 555-1234 if any problems.

CREATE A CLIPPING SET

▶ What You'll Do

In this lesson, you will create a clipping mask on a sublayer that will mask the other sublayers in the layer.

Working with Clipping Sets

Adobe uses the terms "clipping mask" and "clipping path" interchangeably. The term **clipping set** is used to distinguish clipping paths used in layers from clipping paths used to mask nonlayered artwork. Essentially, the term "clipping set" refers to the clipping mask *and* the masked sublayers as a unit.

The following rules apply to clipping sets:

- The clipping mask and the objects to be masked must be in the same layer.
- You cannot use a sublayer as a clipping mask, unless it is a <Group> sublayer. However, the top sublayer in a layer becomes the clipping mask if you first select the layer that the sublayer is in, then create the clipping mask.

- The top object in the clipping set becomes the mask for every object below it in the layer.
- A <Group> sublayer can be a clipping set. The top object in the group will function as the mask.
- Dotted lines between sublayers indicate that they are included in a clipping set.

Flattening Artwork

When you apply the Flatten Artwork command, all visible objects in the artwork are consolidated in a single layer. Before applying the command, select the layer into which you want to consolidate the artwork. If you have a layer that is hidden, you will be asked whether to make the artwork visible so it can be flattened into the layer or delete the layer and the artwork on it.

Create clipping sets

1. Target the **Foreground layer**, click the **Rectangle tool** , then create a **rectangle** that is **6.5" wide** by **6" tall**.

2. Apply a **red fill** and **no stroke** to the rectangle.

3. Position the **rectangle** so it aligns exactly with the edges of the artboard.

4. Expand the **Foreground layer**.

   The rectangle is at the top of the sublayers. Note that the Foreground layer remains the targeted layer on the Layers panel.

5. Click the **Make/Release Clipping Mask button** on the Layers panel.

   The rectangle loses its red fill color and masks the sublayers below it on the Foreground layer. As shown in Figure 26, any path on the Foreground layer that is positioned off the artboard is masked. Therefore, the sofa, the end table, and the sculpture artwork no longer extend the artboard. The part of the rug that extends beyond the artboard is not masked because it is not in the same layer as the clipping path. The lamp, too, extends beyond the artboard and is not masked. The problem is that you can't move the rug to the Foreground layer, because it needs to be behind all the artwork in the file. So instead of moving it, you will create a copy of the clipping mask.

You created a rectangle, then used it as a clipping path to mask the sublayers below it in its layer.

Figure 26 Masking the artwork

Lamp artwork not masked

The rectangle will mask all the other sublayers on the Foreground layer. They will be visible only within the area of the rectangle.

Layers

Foreground
<Rectangle>
Sculpture
End Table
Sofa
Table
Lamp
Electronics
Entertainment.
Chair
Rug
Empty room

8 Layers

Rug artwork is not masked because it is not on the same layer as the <Rectangle>.

Copy a clipping mask

1. Click the **Target layer button** ○ on the **<Rectangle> sublayer** to select the artwork.

2. Click **Edit** on the menu bar, click **Copy**, click **Edit** on the menu bar again, then click **Paste in Front**.

   A new sublayer named <Rectangle> is created and can be used to mask other layers.

3. Drag the **Selected art icon** on the duplicated <Rectangle> sublayer down to the Rug layer, as shown in Figure 27.

4. Target the **Rug layer**, then click the **Make/Release Clipping Mask button** ▣ .

   The duplicated <Rectangle> sublayer now masks the Rug artwork.

5. Target the **Lamp layer** on the Layers panel, then drag it into the **Foreground layer below the Sofa sublayer**.

   The lamp artwork moves to the Foreground layer and is therefore masked.

6. Deselect the lamp and your illustration should resemble Figure 28.

7. Save your work, then continue to the next set of steps.

You made a copy of the rectangle, moved the copied rectangle to the Rug layer, then made it into a clipping path to mask the rug artwork. You then moved the Lamp layer below the Sofa sublayer on the Foreground layer, which masked the lamp.

Flatten artwork

1. Select the **Foreground layer**, click the **Layers panel menu button** ≡ , click **Flatten Artwork**, then click **Yes** when you are asked whether or not you want to discard the hidden art on the hidden layers.

2. Click **File** on the menu bar, click **Save As**, then save the file as **Living Room Flat**.

   Note that this saved the flattened version as a separate file from the layered Living Room.ai file. Whenever you flatten a layered document, save the flattened version as a copy so you can preserve your original layered file.

3. Close Showroom.ai and Living Room flat.ai, saving any changes if prompted.

You flattened all the artwork and then saved a copy of the file.

Figure 27 Moving the copy of the <Rectangle> to the Rug layer.

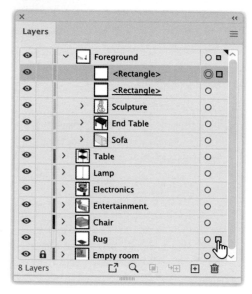

Figure 28 Completed layered illustration

Create and modify layers

1. Open AI 5-3.ai, then save it as **Gary**.
2. Create a new layer at the top of the layer hierarchy, named **Text**.
3. Create a new layer at the top of the layer hierarchy, named **Gary Garlic**.
4. Rename Layer 2 **Body Parts**.
5. Save your work.

Manipulate layered artwork

1. Move the picture of the garlic into the Gary Garlic layer.
2. Move the three text groups onto the Text layer.
3. Merge the Background layer with the Box Shapes layer so the Box Shapes layer is the name of the resulting merged layer.

TIP Click the Background layer, press [command] (Mac) or [Ctrl] (Win), click the Box Shapes layer, click the Layers panel menu button, then click Merge Selected.

4. Move the Body Parts layer to the top of the layer hierarchy.
5. Save your work.

Work with layered artwork

1. View each layer separately to identify the artwork on each.
2. Using Figure 29 as a guide, assemble Gary Garlic.
3. Merge the Gary Garlic and Body Parts layers so the resulting merged layer will be named Body Parts.
4. Select all the artwork on the Body Parts layer, then group the artwork.
5. Save your work.

Create a clipping set

1. Target the Box Shapes layer.
2. Create a rectangle that is 5" wide by 8" in height.
3. Position the rectangle so it is centered on the artboard.
4. With the rectangle still selected, expand the Box Shapes layer on the Layers panel.
5. Click the Make/Release Clipping Mask button on the Layers panel.
6. Reposition the masked elements (text and box parts) so your illustration resembles Figure 29.
7. Save your work, then close the Gary document.

Figure 29 Completed Skills Review

You are designing an outdoor sign for Xanadu Haircutters, a salon that recently opened in your town. You are pleased with your concept of using scissors to represent the X in Xanadu and decide to design the logo with different typefaces so the client can offer input into the final design.

1. Open AI 5-4.ai, then save it as **Xanadu**.
2. Create a new layer, then move the ANADU headline into that layer.
3. Make four duplicates of the new layer.
4. Change the typeface on four of the layers, for a total of five versions of the logo type.
5. Rename each type layer, using the name of the typeface you chose.
6. Rename Layer 1 **Xanadu Art**.
7. View the Xanadu Art layer five times, each time with one of the typeface layers, so you can see five versions of the logo.
8. Save your work, compare your illustration with Figure 30, then close the Xanadu document.

Figure 30 Completed Project Builder 1

You are the creative director for a Los Angeles design firm that specializes in identity packages for television networks. One of your most important projects this week is delivering the first round of comps for a new cable channel, Milty TV. Your art directors have come up with two concepts—one dark, one light. You decide to bring each to the client with two options for typography, for a total of four comps.

1. Open AI 5-5.ai, then save it as **Milty TV**.
2. Select the four pieces of artwork that comprise the television at the top of the artboard, then group them.
3. Group the four pieces of artwork at the bottom of the artboard, then cut them.
4. Create a new layer, name it **Orange**, then paste the artwork.
5. Position the orange artwork exactly on top of the blue artwork on the artboard so it is covered.
6. Rename Layer 1 **Blue**, then duplicate the layer and name it **Blue Two**.

Figure 31 Completed Project Builder 2

7. Duplicate the Orange layer, then name it **Orange Two**.
8. Deselect all, use the Direct Selection tool to select the large M on the Orange Two layer, change its typeface to any that you think works best, then hide the two Orange layers.
   The typeface in Figure 31 is Big Caslon Medium.
9. Select the Blue Two layer, change the M to Cooper Std, then hide it.
10. View each of the four layers separately.
11. You created two versions of each design.
12. Save your work, compare your Orange Two layer to Figure 31, then close Milty TV.

You are a freelance designer working out of your home. The owner of the town's largest plumbing company, Straight Flush, has hired you to redesign his logo. He gives you an Illustrator file with a design created by his son. You study the logo and decide that it lacks cohesion and focus.

1. Open AI 5-6.ai, then save it as **Straight Flush**.
2. Group together the elements of each playing card.
3. Create four new layers.
4. Move each card to the layer with the corresponding number in the layer name.
5. Select all the layers, click the Layers panel menu button, then click Reverse Order.
6. Reposition the cards on each layer so they are in order, directly behind the ace.
7. Adjust the layout of the cards to your liking to create a new layout for the logo.
8. Save your work, compare your illustration with Figure 32, then close the Straight Flush document.

Figure 32 Completed Design Project

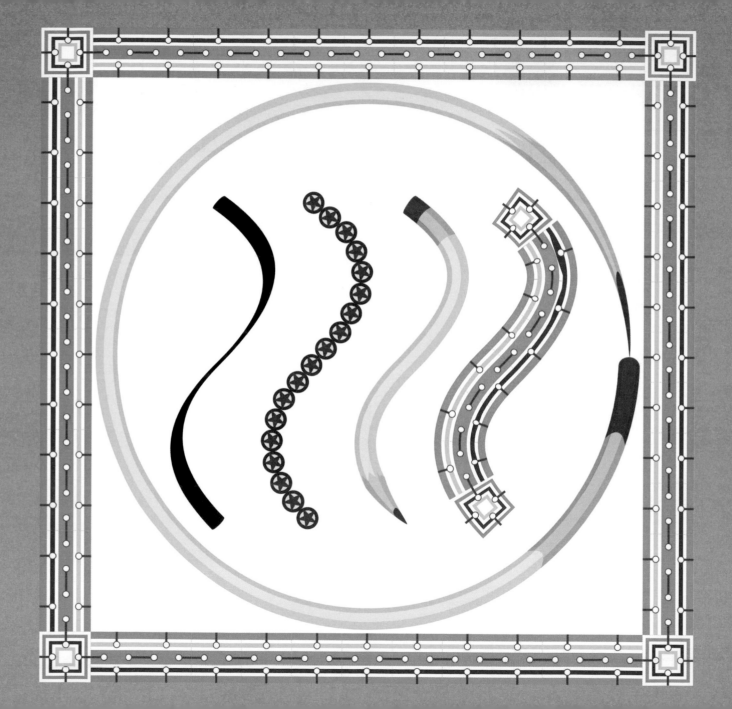

Ai **CHAPTER 6**

WORKING WITH
PATTERNS
AND BRUSHES

1. Use the Move Command

2. Create a Pattern

3. Design a Repeating Pattern

4. Use the Pattern Options Panel

5. Work with the Brushes Panel

6. Work with Scatter Brushes

7. Compare the Paintbrush Tool to the Blob Brush Tool

8. Enhance Artwork with Brushes and the Width Tool

CERTIFIED PROFESSIONAL

Adobe Certified Professional in Graphic Design and Illustration Using Adobe Illustrator

2. Project Setup and Interface

This objective covers the interface setup and program settings that assist in an efficient and effective workflow, as well as knowledge about ingesting digital assets for a project.

2.5 Manage colors, swatches, and gradients.

   C Create, manage, and edit swatches and swatch libraries.

2.6 Manage preset brushes, symbols, styles, and patterns.

   A Open and browse libraries of included brushes, symbols, graphic styles, and patterns.

   B Edit brushes, symbols, styles, and patterns.

4. Creating and Modifying Visual Elements

This objective covers core tools and functionality of the application, as well as tools that affect the visual appearance of document elements.

4.1 Use core tools and features to create visual elements.

   A Create graphics or artwork to create visual elements.

4.3 Make, manage, and manipulate selections.

   B Modify and refine selections using various methods.

4.4 Transform digital graphics and media.

   B Rotate, flip, and transform individual layers, objects, selections, groups, or graphical elements.

USE THE MOVE COMMAND

▶ What You'll Do

In this lesson, you will use the Move command to copy an object at precise offsets and create a simple pattern.

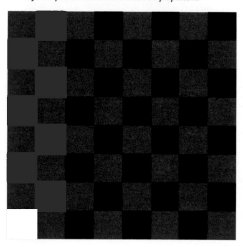

Using the Move Command

The word **offset** comes up when you explore the Move command. Quite simply, the term refers to the distance that an object is moved or copied from a starting location to an ending location. In a simple drop shadow, for example, you can describe the effect by saying, "The black copy behind the original has been offset three points to the left and three points down."

The Move command provides the most effective method for moving an object, or a copy of an object, at precise offsets. In the Move dialog box, you enter the horizontal distance and the vertical distance that you want to move a selected object. A positive value moves the object horizontally to the right, and a negative value moves it to the left. On a vertical axis, a positive value moves the object down, and a negative value moves it up. Be sure to make a note of that in Illustrator: down is positive, and up is negative.

An alternate (and uncommon) way to use the Move dialog box is to enter a value for the distance you want to move the object and a value for the angle on which it should move. Entering a distance and an angle is the same as specifying the move in horizontal and vertical values. When you enter values in the Distance and Angle text boxes, the Horizontal and Vertical text boxes update to reflect the move. Conversely, when you enter values

in the Horizontal and Vertical text boxes, the Distance and Angle text boxes update to reflect the move. The Move dialog box is shown in Figure 1.

Figure 1 Move dialog box

| Horizontal text box | Vertical text box | Distance text box | Angle text box |

Move

Position

Horizontal: 1 in

Vertical: –1 in

Distance: 1.4142 in

Angle: 45°

Options

☑ Transform Objects ☐ Transform Patterns

☐ Preview

(Copy) (Cancel) (OK)

Copy and move objects using the Move dialog box

1. Create a new 4" × 4" document, then save it as **Checkerboard**.

2. Click **Illustrator (Mac)** or **Edit (Win)** on the menu bar, point to **Preferences**, then click **Units**.

3. Verify that the **General** units of measure are **Inches**, then click **OK**.

4. Use the **Rectangle tool** , to create a **½-inch square**, apply a **red fill** and **no stroke**, then position it at the upper-left corner of the artboard.

5. Click **Object** on the menu bar, point to **Transform**, then click **Move**.

6. Enter **.5** in the **Horizontal text box**, press **[tab]**, enter **0** in the **Vertical text box**, then press **[tab]** again.

   TIP Values in the Distance and Angle text boxes automatically appear, based on the values entered in the Horizontal and Vertical text boxes.

7. Click **Copy**.

   A copy of the square is positioned immediately to the right of the original.

8. Change the **fill** on the second square to **Black**, select **both squares**, click **Object** on the menu bar, point to **Transform**, then click **Move**.

9. Enter **1** in the **Horizontal text box**, then click **Copy**.

10. Click **Object** on the menu bar, point to **Transform**, click **Transform Again**, then repeat this step.

    Your work should resemble Figure 2.

    TIP Press and hold [command] [D] (Mac) or [Ctrl] [D] (Win) to transform again.

11. Select all, open the **Move dialog box**, enter **0** in the **Horizontal text box**, enter **.5** in the **Vertical text box**, then click **Copy**.

12. Double-click the **Rotate tool** , enter **180** in the **Angle text box**, then click **OK**.

13. Select all, open the **Move dialog box**, enter **1** in the **Vertical text box**, then click **Copy**.

14. Apply the **Transform Again command** twice, then save your work.

    Your screen should resemble Figure 3.

15. Close the Checkerboard document.

Starting with a single square, you used the Move command to make multiple copies at precise distances to create a checkerboard pattern.

Figure 2 A simple pattern created using the Move command

Figure 3 A checkerboard created with a single starting square and the Move dialog box

CREATE A PATTERN

▶ *What You'll Do*

In this lesson, you will create a pattern from a simple illustration, add it to the Swatches panel, name it, and then fill an object with it.

Working with Patterns and Brushes

Artwork that you create in Illustrator is the result of your efforts in conceiving an image and rendering it using your skills and talents. However, as you become more familiar with Illustrator, you will also learn to use completed artwork as components of new illustrations.

Using patterns and brushes is a fine example of this working method. You can design artwork and then use it as a pattern to fill and stroke new artwork. This is useful if you are drawing things like flowers in a field, stars in a night sky, or trees on a mountainside.

The powerful options in Illustrator's Brushes panel extend this concept even farther. Using brushes, you can use completed artwork as a stroke, pattern, or freestanding illustration of greater complexity. For example, you could create a custom brush stroke, such as a leaf, and then use the Paintbrush tool to paint with the leaf as a brush stroke. Instead of being limited to filling or stroking an object with leaves, you could paint leaves anywhere on the artboard.

Creating Patterns

In Illustrator, you can design patterns to fill objects or stroke objects. You can design patterns that are simple or complex, abstract or specific, and you can save them for future use and applications. The Swatches panel comes preloaded with pattern swatches that you can modify.

To create a pattern, you first create artwork for the pattern, then drag that artwork into the Swatches panel, where it is automatically defined as a pattern swatch. You can use paths, compound paths, or text in patterns, but you cannot use gradients, blends, brush strokes, meshes, bitmap images, graphs, masks, or other patterns.

Designing a Pattern

Patterns repeat. A pattern fills an object by repeating the original pattern, a process called **tiling**. The word is used as an intentional reference to floor tiles. Illustrator creates pattern fills in much the same way you would use multiple tiles to cover a floor. Think of the pattern as the floor tile and the object to be filled as the floor.

You design fill patterns by designing one tile. For efficiency with previewing and printing, you should create a pattern tile between a ½" and 1" square. When you save it as a pattern and apply it as a fill, the tile will repeat as many times as necessary to fill the object, as shown in Figure 4.

Many times, you will create a pattern that contains no rectangular objects, such as a polka dot or line pattern. In these cases, you create a **bounding box** to define the perimeter of the pattern tile by positioning an unfilled, unstroked rectangular object at the back of the stacking order of the pattern tile. Illustrator will regard this as the bounding box. All the objects within the bounding box will be repeated as part of the pattern.

The pattern in Figure 5 is composed of lines only. The square is used as a bounding box. It defines the perimeter of the tile, and the pattern is created by repeating only the elements that fall within the bounding box. Again, a bounding box must have no fill and no stroke; it must be a rectangle or a square, and it must be the backmost object of the pattern tile.

Figure 4 The tile repeats to fill the object

Figure 5 Bounding box determines the perimeter of the pattern tile

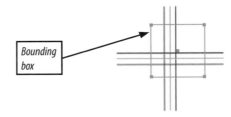

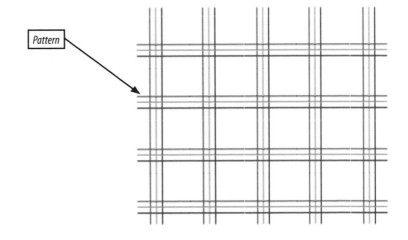

In Lesson 4, you will learn about the Pattern Options panel. The Pattern Options panel makes pattern creation easier by offering a dynamic preview of the pattern as you design the tile. It also presents many useful pattern layout options. In this lesson and Lesson 3, by learning the original method Illustrator used for generating patterns, you will better understand the basis of patterns and how the Pattern Options panel simplifies pattern design and generation.

Controlling How a Pattern Fills an Object

The way a pattern fills an object is a tricky concept. The pattern begins from the origin of the ruler, which is, by default, at the bottom-left corner of the artboard.

In other words, the pattern begins at the bottom-left of the artboard, *not* the bottom-left corner of the object.

When you move an object that is filled with a pattern, the pattern changes within the object. The pattern fill is easier to conceptualize if you understand the concept of a clipping mask. Think of it this way: The pattern covers the entire artboard, and the object that is filled with the pattern functions like a clipping mask—you can see the pattern only through the object.

The best method for controlling how a pattern appears within an object is to align the ruler origin with the bottom-left corner of the object. To do this, display the rulers, then position your cursor at the top-left corner of the window, where the two rulers meet. The cross hairs are the ruler origin. Drag the cross hairs

to the bottom-left corner of the filled object, as shown in Figure 6. Because the ruler origin and the bottom-left corner of the square are the same point, the first tile is positioned evenly in the corner. The pattern fills the object left to right, bottom to top.

Transforming Patterns

When an object is filled with a pattern, you can choose to transform only the object, only the pattern, or both the object and the pattern. For example, the Scale dialog box, shown in Figure 7, contains options for determining whether or not the transformation will affect a pattern fill.

Figure 6 Aligning the ruler origin with the bottom-left corner of the filled object

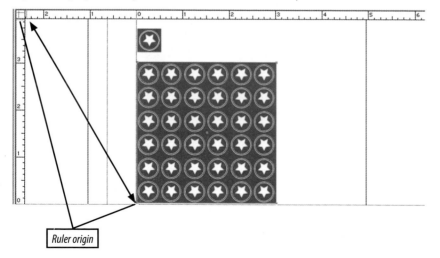

Ruler origin

Figure 7 Options for patterns in the Scale dialog box

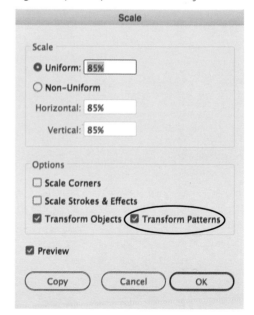

When you transform a pattern, all subsequent objects you create will be filled with the transformed pattern. To return a pattern fill to its appearance before it was transformed, fill an object with a different swatch, then reapply the pattern swatch.

Create a pattern swatch

1. Open AI 6-1.ai, then save it as **Starry Night**.
2. Position the **10 stars** randomly **over the black box**.

TIP Enlarge your view of the artboard.

3. Change the **fill color** of the **stars** to **White**.

Compare your screen to Figure 8.

4. Group the **white stars**.
5. Select all, then drag the **artwork** into the Swatches panel.

   The Swatches panel automatically identifies and defines artwork as a pattern swatch and lists it in the Pattern Swatches partition of the panel.

6. Deselect the artwork.
7. Double-click the **new swatch**.

   Double-clicking the swatch opens the Pattern Options panel, and the artboard changes to pattern editing mode, which shows a preview of the pattern.

8. Type **Starry Night** in the **Name text box**, then press **[return] (Mac)** or **[Enter] (Win)**.
9. Press the **Escape key [esc]** to escape pattern editing mode.
10. Delete all the artwork on the artboard.
11. Create a **circle** that is **4"** in diameter.
12. Apply the **Starry Night swatch** to fill the circle.

    Your screen should resemble Figure 9. The Starry Night swatch may have automatically been applied to your circle when you created it because it was still selected on the Swatches panel.

You created a 1" × 1" collection of objects, selected all of them, then dragged them into the Swatches panel. You named the new pattern swatch, then applied it as a fill for a circle.

Figure 8 Artwork to be used as a pattern swatch

Figure 9 Artwork applied as a pattern fill

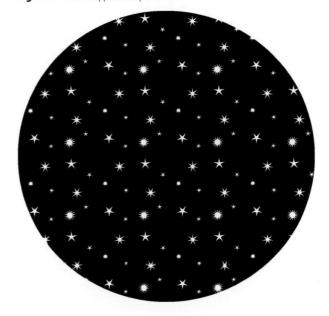

Transform pattern-filled objects

1. Select the **circle**, then double-click the **Scale tool**.

2. Type **50** in the **Scale Uniform text box**, verify that only the **Transform Objects check box** is checked in the Options section of the dialog box, then click **OK**.

   The object is scaled 50%; the pattern is not scaled.

3. Drag and drop a **copy above the original circle**.

4. Double-click the **Scale tool**.

5. Type **200** in the **Scale Uniform text box**, verify that only the **Transform Patterns check box** is checked, then click **OK**.

   The pattern is scaled 200%; the object is not scaled. Your screen should resemble Figure 10.

6. Save your work, then close the Starry Night document.

You experimented with options for scaling a pattern fill and an object independently using the Scale dialog box.

Figure 10 Patterns can be transformed independent of the objects that they fill

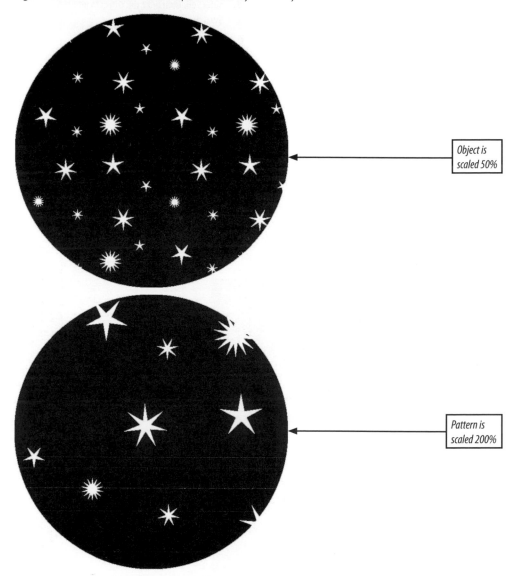

Object is
scaled 50%

Pattern is
scaled 200%

Create a pattern using open paths

1. Open AI 6-2.ai, then save it as **Line Pattern**.

2. Create a **1" square** with **no fill** and **no stroke**.

3. Position the **square over the lines**, as shown in Figure 11.

    Note that the rightmost vertical purple line is *within* the perimeter of the square so it will be included in the pattern.

4. Send the **square** to the back.

5. Select all, then drag the **objects** into the Swatches panel.

6. Hide the **objects** on the artboard.

7. Create a **4" square**, then fill it with the **new pattern**.

8. Create a **second 4" square**, fill it with **pale pink**, send it to the back, then position it behind the pattern, as shown in Figure 12.

The pink square is visible behind the pattern because the pattern is composed of lines only.

9. Save your work, then close the Line Pattern document.

You placed a 1" square with no fill or stroke behind a group of straight paths. You used all the objects to create a pattern swatch, with the square defining the perimeter of the pattern tile. You filled a square with the pattern, then positioned a pink square behind the square with the pattern fill, noting that you could see the pink background since the pattern was made of only lines.

Figure 11 Position a bounding box to define a pattern

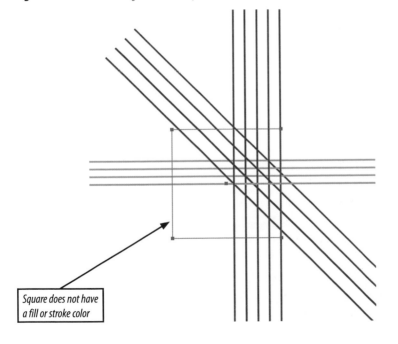

Square does not have a fill or stroke color

Figure 12 A pink square behind a line pattern

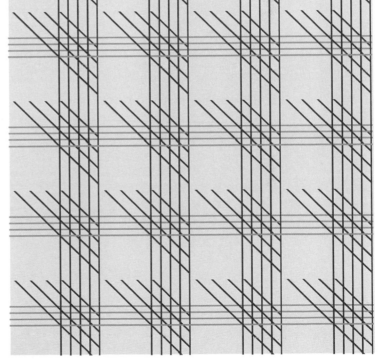

DESIGN A REPEATING PATTERN

▶ *What You'll Do*

In this lesson, you will design a visually repetitive pattern. You will then explore options for modifying the pattern after it has been applied as a fill.

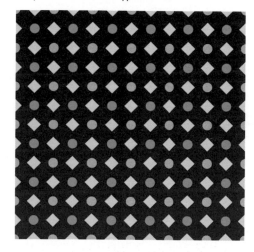

Planning Your Tiles

Simple patterns can be tricky to design. Understanding how tiles create patterns is important for achieving a desired effect. You will often be surprised to find the tile you designed does not create the pattern you had in mind.

In Figure 13, at first it seems logical that the tile on the left could produce the pattern below it. However, it requires the more complex tile on the right to produce what appears to be a "simple" pattern.

Figure 13 Only the top-right tile could create the pattern

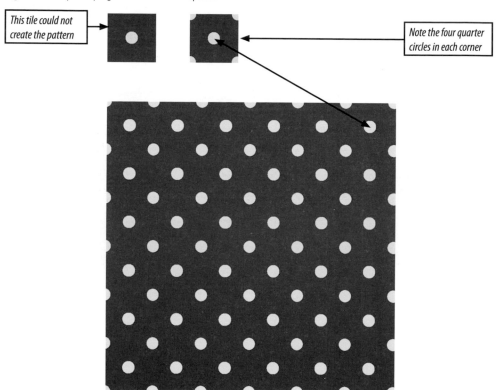

This tile could not create the pattern

Note the four quarter circles in each corner

Another consideration when designing patterns is whether you want the pattern to be apparent. If you were designing a plaid pattern, you would want the pattern to be noticed. However, if you were designing artwork for a field of flowers, you might want the pattern to be subtle, if not invisible. An invisible pattern is difficult to create, especially when it's based on a 1" tile!

In every case, precision is important when creating a pattern. If two objects are meant to align, be certain that they do align; don't rely on just your eye. Use dialog boxes to move and transform objects; don't try to do it by hand.

Modifying Patterns

You modify a pattern by editing the artwork in the pattern tile, then replacing the old pattern on the Swatches panel with the new pattern. When you replace the old pattern, any existing objects on the artboard that were filled with the old pattern will update automatically with the new pattern. Of course, you can always leave the original pattern as is and save the edited pattern as a new swatch. This is often a wise move because you may want to use the original pattern again sometime.

Create a repeating pattern with precision

1. Open AI 6-3.ai, then save it as **Repeating Pattern**.

2. Select the **lavender circle**, click **Object** on the menu bar, point to **Transform**, then click **Move**.

3. Enter **1** in the **Horizontal text box**, enter **0** in the **Vertical text box**, then click **Copy**.

   A copy of the lavender circle is created at the upper-right corner of the square.

4. Select both **lavender circles**, open the **Move dialog box**, enter **0** in the **Horizontal**

text box and **1** in the **Vertical text box**, then click **Copy**.

Your screen should resemble Figure 14.

5. Select the **light blue diamond**, then apply the **Transform Again command**.

   A copy of the blue diamond is created at the bottom edge of the square.

6. Select **both blue diamonds**, double click the **Rotate tool** , enter **90** in the **Angle text box**, then click **Copy**.

   Your work should resemble Figure 15.

Continued on next page

Figure 14 Work precisely when designing pattern tiles

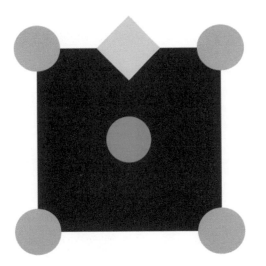

Figure 15 Use dialog boxes to make transformations when designing pattern tiles

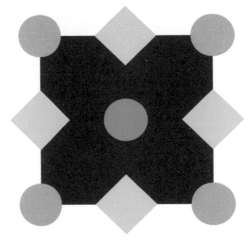

7. Select all, then click the **Divide button**  on the **Pathfinder panel**.

8. Deselect all, click the **Direct Selection tool** , then delete everything outside of the perimeter of the square so your design resembles Figure 16.

TIP Zoom in for a better view if necessary.

9. Click the **Selection tool** , select all, drag the **artwork** into the Swatches panel, then name the new pattern **Alpha Shapes**.

10. Delete the **artwork** on the artboard.

11. Create a **6" × 6" square**, fill it with the **Alpha Shapes pattern**, then center it on the artboard.

12. Compare your screen to Figure 17.

13. Save your work, then continue to the next set of steps.

You used the Move command to position multiple objects in a symmetrical pattern over a 1" square. You then used the Divide pathfinder, which allowed you to select and then delete the areas of objects that were positioned outside the square. You dragged the pattern into the Swatches panel. You named the pattern and then created a square with the pattern as its fill.

Figure 16 Designing pattern tiles can be tricky work

Figure 17 A "simple" pattern

Modify a pattern

1. Drag the **Alpha Shapes pattern** from the Swatches panel to the **pasteboard area** next to the artboard.

2. Click the **Direct Selection tool** ▷, click the **artboard** to deselect the pattern, then click the **royal blue section** on the pattern tile in the pasteboard area.

3. Change the **royal blue fill** to a **purple fill**.

4. Switch to the **Selection tool** ▶, then select the **entire pattern**.

5. Press and hold **[option] (Mac)** or **[Alt] (Win)**, then drag the **purple version of the pattern** on top of the Alpha Shapes pattern on the Swatches panel.

   The Alpha Shapes pattern is replaced on the Swatches panel, and the fill of the square is updated, as shown in Figure 18.

6. Using the **Direct Selection tool** ▷, select all the pieces in the pattern you dragged to the pasteboard area, except for the purple section.

7. Press and hold **[option] (Mac)** or **[Alt] (Win)**, then drag the **selected objects** on top of the Alpha Shapes swatch on the Swatches panel.

   Your screen should resemble Figure 19.

8. Save and close the Repeating Pattern file.

You dragged the Alpha Shapes pattern swatch out of the Swatches panel and onto the pasteboard to modify it. You changed a color in the pattern, then replaced the old pattern swatch with the new pattern. The object filled with the original pattern was updated to reflect the changes to the pattern. You modified the pattern again by dragging parts of it to the Swatches panel.

Figure 18 Changing the background color of the pattern

Figure 19 Updated pattern without the purple background

USE THE PATTERN OPTIONS PANEL

What You'll Do

In this lesson, you will use the Pattern Options panel to make patterns quickly and easily.

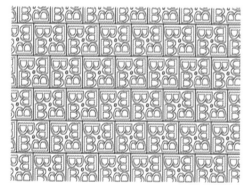

Using the Pattern Options Panel

Patterns can add enormous visual complexity to an illustration, but over the years, designers have found Illustrator's basic pattern creation process, which involves designing in a tile without a real sense of what the pattern will look like, too complex. If you talk to a few Illustrator users, you're likely to find that most haven't even tried it out.

The Pattern Options panel, a real game changer of a utility, makes pattern

generation easier, more interesting, and more fun.

To start working with the Pattern Options panel, select an object on the artboard, click the Object menu, point to Pattern, then click Make. This puts you into pattern editing mode. In pattern editing mode, any other objects on the artboard disappear. The Pattern Options panel, shown in Figure 20, appears and a pattern tile appears around the selected

Figure 20 Pattern Options panel

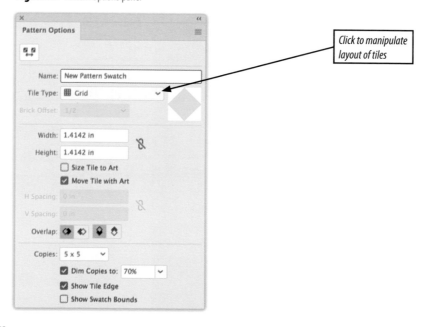

object, as shown in Figure 21. Immediately, the pattern is previewed outside of the tile. In this figure, the pattern outside of the tile is dimmed because the Dim Copies option in the panel is activated. Dimming copies makes it easier to see the artwork inside the pattern tile.

When you first enter pattern editing mode, the tile is automatically generated as a perimeter

around the selected object. That is just a default action; you can enter new sizes in the Width and Height text boxes on the Pattern Options panel to resize the tile. Figure 22 shows changes to the pattern after the tile was increased from a 0.25" to a 0.35" square.

As with traditional pattern creation, objects within the pattern tile define the whole

pattern. You can add objects to the tile to make the pattern more complex. Figure 23 shows the same basic diamond pattern made more complex with the additional diamonds, circles, and a grid. The pattern is dramatically more complex.

Figure 21 Pattern previewed outside of pattern tile

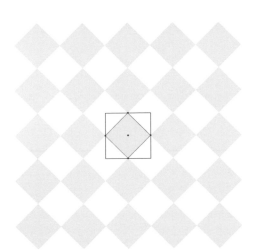

Figure 22 Changes to the pattern after increasing only the tile size

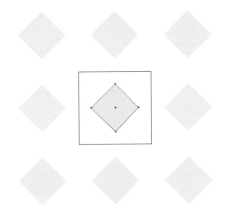

Figure 23 Adding elements to the pattern

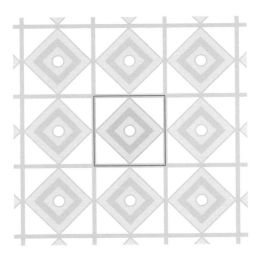

The Pattern Options panel has many built-in options that you can use to manage or modify the pattern you're creating. You can set the tile to move with the artwork—though you're usually better off leaving that option unchecked. Use the Copies list menu to specify how many rows of the pattern are previewed.

The Tile Type menu offers many layout options for the pattern, with the default being Grid.

Figure 24 shows the same pattern with the Brick by Row option activated. As opposed to Figure 23, the repeating tiles are now stacked in a brick pattern.

When you're working in pattern editing mode, keep in mind that all you're really doing is designing a pattern swatch, which is being constantly updated on the Swatches panel with every change you make. When you're done

designing, click the Done option at the top of the pattern editing window. The tile and the entire pattern preview will disappear, but that's only because you're back to the "real" artboard. Your pattern now exists as a pattern swatch on the Swatches panel. You can use that pattern to fill any object you create on the artboard. If you want to edit the pattern again, simply double-click the pattern swatch, which will put you back into pattern editing mode.

Figure 24 Choosing the Tile Type

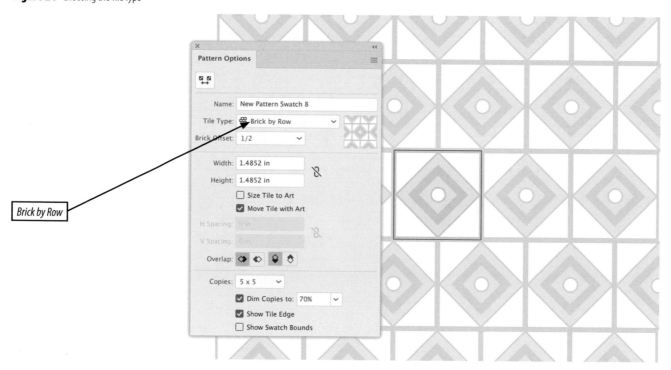

Brick by Row

Use the Pattern Options panel

1. Open AI 6-4.ai, then save it as **Pattern Options**.

2. Select the **letter B**, click **Object** on the menu bar, point to **Pattern**, then click **Make**.

   The artboard switches into pattern editing mode. As shown in Figure 25, the Pattern Options panel opens, a pattern tile appears around the letter B, and a preview of the pattern made by the letter appears. Note that the pattern outside the tile appears to be a lighter gray because the Dim Copies to: option on the Pattern Options panel is activated.

3. Verify that the settings on your Pattern Options panel match Figure 25.

4. Type **BBB** in the **Name text box**.

5. Compare your Swatches panel to Figure 26.

   As shown in the figure, a new pattern swatch has been added automatically to the panel. Any changes you make to the pattern will be updated to the swatch.

6. On the **Pattern Options panel**, change the **Width** and the **Height fields** to **1.5"**.

   The size of the pattern tile is increased. The Width and Height fields affect only the dimensions of the pattern tile.

7. Create a copy of the **B**, rotate it **180 degrees**, then position it in the **upper-right corner**.

8. Position the **original B** in the **lower-left corner**.

   Your pattern tile should resemble Figure 27.

   Continued on next page

Figure 25 The artboard in pattern editing mode

Figure 26 New pattern swatch added to the Swatches panel

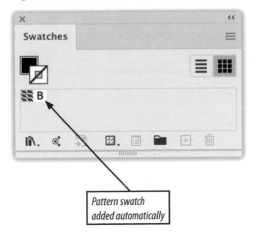

Pattern swatch
added automatically

Figure 27 Positioning the two letters

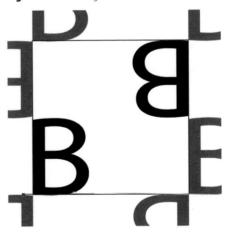

9. Select **both Bs**, double-click the **Rotate tool** 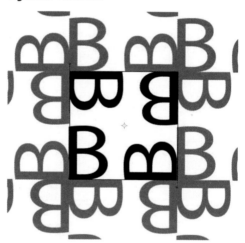, enter **90** in the **Angle text box**, then click **Copy**.

   Your tile and pattern should resemble Figure 28. Note that because the Bs are all touching the edge of the pattern tile, the Bs are all touching each other outside of the tile.

10. Use the arrow keys on your keyboard to move the **four Bs** toward the center of the pattern tile, as shown in Figure 29.

id="2"

Figure 29 Repositioning the Bs in the pattern tile

Figure 28 Four Bs total

id="1"

284 CHAPTER 6 WORKING WITH PATTERNS AND BRUSHES

11. Change the **fill color** on the four Bs to **[None]**, then apply a **1 pt. Black stroke**.

12. Deselect all.

13. Click the **Type tool** T, anywhere outside of the pattern, type an uppercase letter **O**, set its **font** to **Myriad Pro**, then set its **font size** to **14 pt**.

14. Position the **O** at the center of the Bs, as shown in Figure 30.

15. Deselect all, change the **fill color** to **[None]**, change the **stroke color** to **Black**, click the **Rectangle tool** , then draw a **rectangle** precisely on top of the pattern tile.

16. Deselect, fit all in window, then compare your pattern to Figure 31.

Continued on next page

Figure 30 Positioning the O

Figure 31 The pattern with the stroke applied

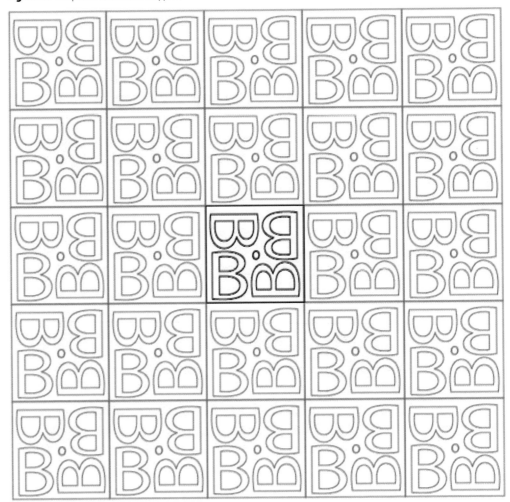

17. Uncheck the **Dim Copies to:** and **Show Tile Edge options** at the bottom of the panel.

The Dim Copies to: option dims the copies outside the pattern tile with the idea that it helps you view the artwork in the tile more clearly.

18. Click the **Tile Type list arrow**, then choose **Brick by Row**.

19. Click the **Brick Offset list arrow**, then click **1/2**.

Your pattern should resemble Figure 32.

20. At the top of the window, click **Done**.

Illustrator exits pattern editing mode. The artboard appears exactly as it did when you opened the document.

21. Delete the **B** on the artboard.

22. Create a **large rectangle** almost the size of the entire artboard.

23. Click the **BBB pattern swatch** on the Swatches panel.

The pattern fills the rectangle, as shown in Figure 33.

24. Save your work, then close the Pattern Options document.

You created a pattern from an object, used tools to modify the pattern, used the Pattern Options panel to change settings for the pattern, then saved the pattern.

Figure 32 Brick Offset option applied to the pattern

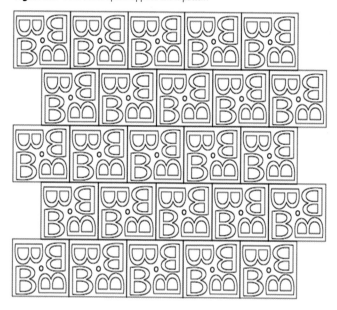

Figure 33 Rectangle filled with the pattern

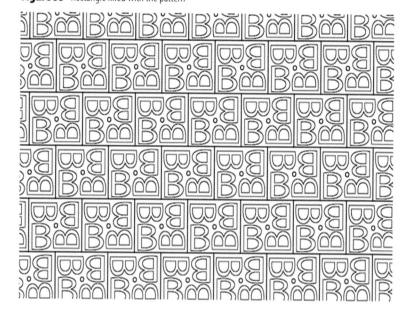

WORK WITH THE BRUSHES PANEL

Working with the Brushes Panel

The Brushes panel houses all the brush artwork with which you will work in Illustrator. The term **brush** refers to any artwork you can apply to paths or paint with using the Paintbrush tool.

The Brushes panel comes with standard brushes, but you can use your own Illustrator artwork as a brush. For example, you could create a star shape, then use it as brush artwork.

In that case, you'd be able to paint with the star using the Paintbrush tool, or you could apply the star artwork to an open path or a closed object.

Click the Brushes panel menu button, then point to Open Brush Library, and you'll see a list of preloaded brush libraries. It is worth your time to explore these preloaded brushes. Figure 34 shows a number of open brush libraries.

Figure 34 Brushes panel with preloaded brush libraries

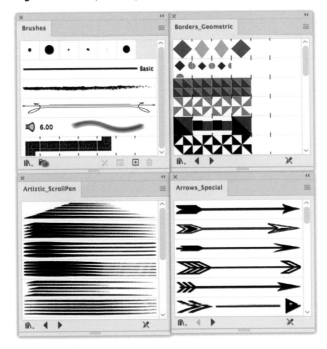

The Brushes panel houses five types of brushes:

Calligraphic brushes apply strokes that resemble those drawn with a calligraphic pen. Figure 35 is an example.

Scatter brushes disperse copies of an object along a path, as shown in Figure 36.

You can apply artwork—such as an arrow or a feather—to a path with an art brush.

Art brushes stretch an object along the length of a path, as shown in Figure 37.

Bristle brushes create brush strokes with the appearance of a natural brush with hairs and bristles.

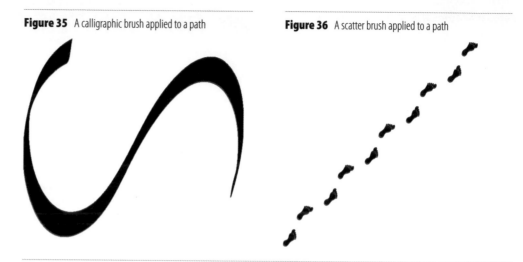

Figure 35 A calligraphic brush applied to a path

Figure 36 A scatter brush applied to a path

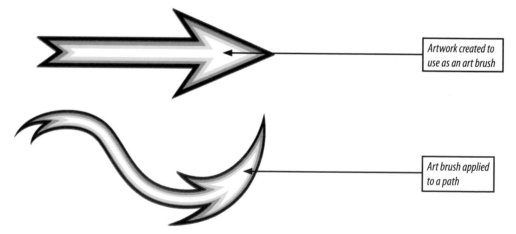

Figure 37 An art brush applied to a path

Artwork created to use as an art brush

Art brush applied to a path

Pattern brushes repeat a pattern along a path. Pattern brushes are made with tiles that you create. You can define up to five tiles as components of the pattern: one tile for the side, one for the inner corner, one for the outer corner, and one each for the beginning and ending of the path. Figure 38 shows five tiles and a pattern that was created with them.

You can create any of the five types of brushes. Artwork for brushes must be composed of simple paths, with no gradients, blends, mesh objects, masks, or other brush strokes. Art and pattern brushes cannot include text. You must convert text to outlines before it can be used as artwork for these types of brushes. Art, pattern, and scatter brushes can contain bitmap images, as long as they are not embedded.

Figure 38 Five tiles used for a pattern brush

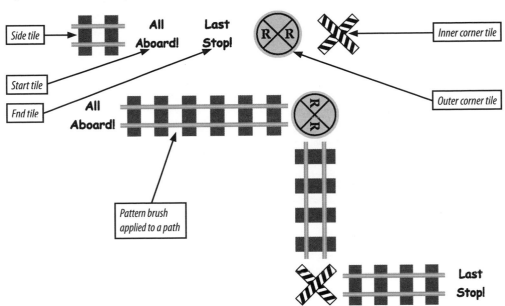

Side tile

Start tile

End tile

Inner corner tile

Outer corner tile

Pattern brush applied to a path

Applying Automatic Corners to Pattern Brushes

Illustrator's Pattern Brushes feature allows you to make corner tiles for pattern brushes. In previous versions, when you made a pattern for a pattern brush, you had to make separate artwork for the corners when the brush was applied to a shape with acute angles for corners.

You can still create your own artwork for corners, but if you don't, Illustrator automatically generates corner artwork based on the artwork you create for the pattern brush.

Illustrator generates four types of corner tiles that you choose from in the Pattern Brush Options dialog box:

- Auto-Centered: The edge tile bends around the corner and is centered on the path.
- Auto-Between: The edge tile is copied and extends to the corner.
- Auto-Sliced: The edge tile is sliced at an angle and mirrored, much like you'll see with a picture frame and its mitered corners.
- Auto-Overlap: The edge tile is copied and overlaps at the corner.

Figure 39 gives you an idea of what each of the four corner types does.

Figure 39 Four corner types

Auto-Centered corner

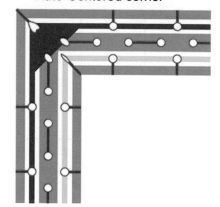

Auto-Between corner

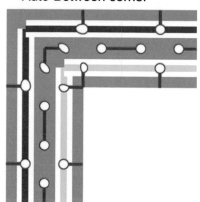

Auto-Sliced corner

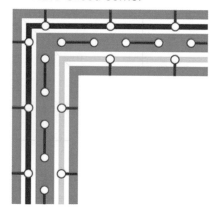

Auto-Overlap corner

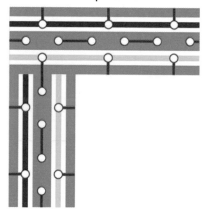

Create a calligraphic brush

1. Open AI 6-5.ai, then save it as **Four Brushes**.

2. Click **Window** on the menu bar, then click **Brushes** to display the Brushes panel.

3. Click the **Brushes panel menu button** ☰, then click **New Brush**.

4. Click the **Calligraphic Brush option button** in the New Brush dialog box, then click **OK**.

   The Calligraphic Brush Options dialog box opens, as shown in Figure 40.

5. Type **Twelve Points** in the **Name text box**, **45** in the **Angle text box**, and **12 pt** in the **Size text box**, then click **OK**.

   The Twelve Points brush is added to the Calligraphic brush section and is selected on the Brushes panel.

6. Click the **Selection tool** ▶, select the **first curved line** on the artboard, then click the **Twelve Points brush** on the Brushes panel.

7. Double-click the **Twelve Points brush** on the Brushes panel.

8. Change the **Roundness** to **20%**, noting the change in the Preview window, then click **OK**.

9. Click **Apply to Strokes** in the dialog box that appears.

   The curved line updates to reflect the changes.

10. Apply the **Twelve Points brush** to the **circle**, then deselect all.

   Your screen should resemble Figure 41.

You created and set the parameters for a new calligraphic brush, which you applied to a curved path and to a circle.

Figure 40 Calligraphic Brush Options dialog box

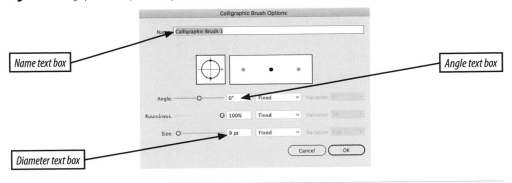

Figure 41 Applying a calligraphic brush to paths

Create a scatter brush

1. Select the **star target** in the lower-right corner of the artboard, click the **Brushes panel menu button** ≡ , click **New Brush**, click the **Scatter Brush option button**, then click **OK**.

2. Name the brush **Star Target**, type **20** in the **Size text box**, type **60** in the **Spacing text box**, then click **OK**.

   The Star Target brush is selected on the Brushes panel.

3. Hide the **star target artwork** on the artboard.

4. Apply the **Star Target brush** to the **second curved line**, then apply it to the **circle**.

TIP To remove a brush stroke from a path, select the path, then click the Remove Brush Stroke button ✖ on the Brushes panel.

5. Double-click the **Star Target brush**, change the **Spacing** to **20%**, click **OK**, then click **Apply to Strokes**.

6. Save your work, then compare your screen to Figure 42.

7. Continue to the next set of steps.

You used a group of simple objects as the artwork for a scatter brush, which you applied to a curved path and to a circle.

Figure 42 Applying a scatter brush to paths

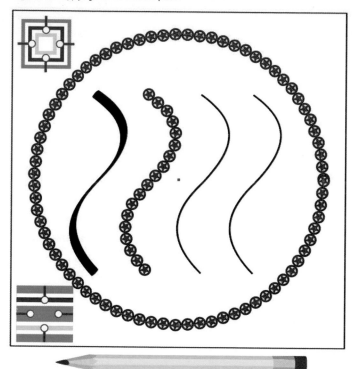

Create an art brush

1. Select the **pencil artwork**, click the **Brushes panel menu button** ≡ , click **New Brush**, click the **Art Brush option button**, then click **OK**.

2. Click the **Stroke From Right To Left button** ← in the Direction section of the Art Brush Options dialog box.

   The direction arrow in the preview window updates and points in the same direction as the point of the pencil.

3. Enter **75** in the **Width text box**, name the brush **Pencil**, then click **OK**.

4. Hide the **pencil artwork** on the artboard.

5. Apply the **Pencil brush** to the **third curved line**, then apply it to the **circle**.

6. Save your work, then compare your screen to Figure 43.

7. Continue to the next set of steps.

You used an illustration of a pencil as the art for an art brush. You defined the parameters of the art brush—its direction and its size—then applied the brush to a curved path and to a circle.

Figure 43 Applying an art brush to paths

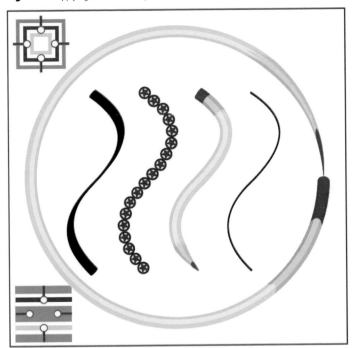

Create a pattern brush

1. Verify that your **Swatches panel** is visible.

2. Select the **artwork** in the **lower-left corner** of the artboard, then drag it into the Swatches panel.

3. Double-click the **swatch** to open the Pattern Options panel, type **Green Side** in the Name text box, press **[return] (Mac)** or **[Enter] (Win)**, then click **[esc]** on your keyboard.

4. Hide the **artwork** on the artboard used for the Green Side swatch.

5. Select the **artwork** in the **top-left corner**, drag it into the Swatches panel, then use the same method to rename the pattern **Green Corner**.

6. Hide the **artwork** used for the Green Corner swatch.

7. Click the **Brushes panel menu button** ≡, click **New Brush**, click the **Pattern Brush option button**, then click **OK**.

8. Name the new brush **Green Frame**.

9. Click the **Side Tile list arrow**, click **Green Side**, then compare your dialog box to Figure 44.

10. Click the **Outer Corner Tile list arrow**, then click **Auto-Between**.

    The preview window in the dialog box updates to show how the outer corner tile will appear. Note that the inner corner tile remains blank in the preview.

11. Click the **Inner Corner Tile**, click **Auto-Between**, then click **OK**.

Figure 44 Pattern Brush Options dialog box

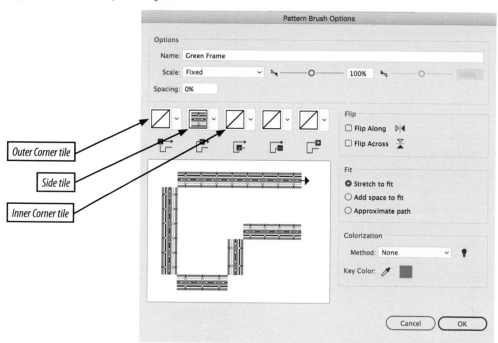

12. Select the **square frame** around the artwork, apply the **Green Frame brush**, then compare your frame to Figure 45.

As shown in the figure, the corner is not satisfactory. The white circles have morphed into ovals. Worse, the white, pink, and yellow lines are not aligned and form chipped corners.

13. Double-click the **Green Frame brush** on the Brushes panel to open the Pattern Brush Options dialog box.

14. Change the **Outer Corner Tile** and **Inner Corner Tile** to **Auto-Sliced**, click **OK**, then click **Apply to Strokes**.

As shown in Figure 46, the Auto-Sliced option is a successful choice and creates a clean corner with the white, pink, and yellow lines all meeting on an angle.

15. Double-click the **Green Frame brush** on the Brushes panel to open the Pattern Brush Options dialog box.

16. Change the **Outer Corner Tile** and **Inner Corner Tile** to **Green Corner**, click **OK**, then click **Apply to Strokes**.

As shown in Figure 47, the Green Corner artwork is a viable alternative to the Auto-Sliced option.

TIP You can use the Scale slider in the Pattern Brush Options dialog box to increase or decrease the width of the artwork on the frame.

17. Save your work, then continue to the next set of steps.

You dragged two pieces of artwork into the Swatches panel. You created a new pattern brush and then, in the dialog box, defined one piece of artwork as a side tile. You experimented with two automatic corners— Auto-Between and Auto-Sliced. Then you used the other artwork as corner art.

Figure 45 Green Frame pattern brush applied with Auto-Between corners

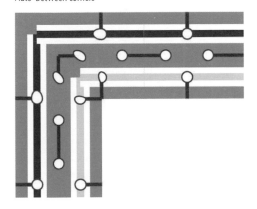

Figure 46 Green Frame pattern brush applied with Auto-Sliced corners

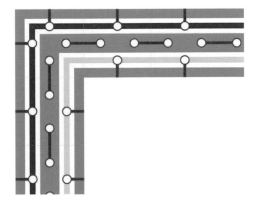

Figure 47 Green Corner artwork applied to corners

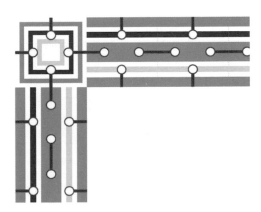

Modify a pattern brush

1. Apply the **Green Frame brush** to the **fourth curved line**, then apply it to the **square**.

   Your screen should resemble Figure 48.

2. Double-click the **Green Frame brush** on the Brushes panel.

3. Click the **Start Tile box**, then click **Green Corner** in the list of patterns.

4. Click the **End Tile box**, click **Green Corner** in the list of patterns, click **OK**, then click **Apply to Strokes**.

The curved line now begins and ends with the corner artwork, as shown in Figure 49.

5. Save your work.

6. Close the Four Brushes document.

You applied the pattern brush to a curved path and then added a Start and End tile to the pattern brush.

Figure 48 Applying the pattern brush to paths

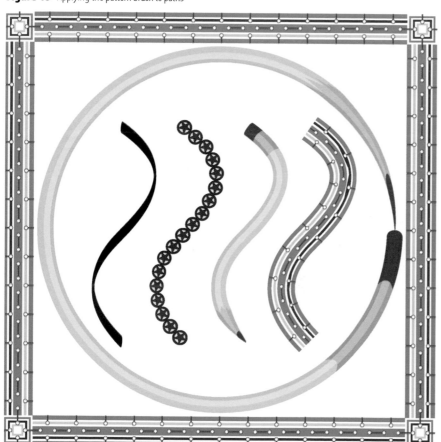

Figure 49 Adding a Start and End tile to the pattern brush

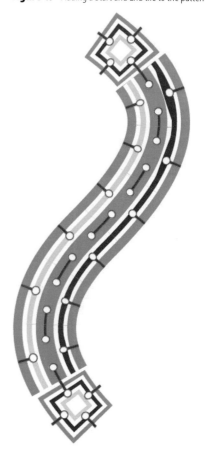

WORK WITH SCATTER BRUSHES

▶ *What You'll Do*

In this lesson, you will work with scatter brushes, enter fixed and random values in the Scatter Brush Options dialog box, and view how those values affect your artwork.

Working with Scatter Brushes

It is easy to underestimate the role of brushes in creating artwork. Many designers identify them as a method for creating really cool strokes and leave it at that. What they are missing is that brushes themselves can be the best option for creating an illustration.

Of the four types of brushes, the scatter brush best illustrates this point. For example, if you were drawing a pearl necklace, a scatter brush would be your smartest choice for creating the illustration, as opposed to dragging and dropping copies of a single pearl illustration along a path or creating a blend between two pearls.

Why? With the scatter brush, you can manipulate the path endlessly, with

precise control of the size, spacing, and rotation of the elements along the path. In addition, you can input a scatter value, which determines how far the objects can be positioned from the path, an option that blending does not offer.

The scatter brush is even more powerful for creating the effect of "randomness." Figure 50 shows a fine example of this effect using a flying beetle as the artwork for the scatter brush. In the Scatter Brush Options dialog box, you can apply a random range for Size, Spacing, Scatter, and Rotation and create the effect of a three-dimensional swarm of beetles flying in different directions—some of them closer to you and larger and some of them farther away and smaller.

Figure 50 A swarm of beetles created with a flying beetle scatter brush

For each setting in the Brush Options dialog box, you can choose fixed or random values. When you apply random settings to a scatter brush, the positioning of the objects on the path will be different every time you apply the brush.

TIP Click the Brush Libraries menu button on the Brushes panel to display a list of brush libraries. Each brush library opens in a new panel. For example, the Artistic Watercolor brush library includes 12 watercolor brush styles that offer the look and feel of real watercolor paint strokes.

Modify a scatter brush

1. Open AI 6-6.ai, then save it as **Random Beetles**.

2. Select the **circle**, then apply the **Flying Beetle brush**.

3. Double-click the **Flying Beetle brush** on the Brushes panel; click the **Preview check box** to add a check mark, if necessary; then move the Scatter Brush Options dialog box so you can see as much of the artboard as possible.

4. Click the **Size list arrow**, then click **Fixed**.

   The beetles become the same size.

TIP Press [tab] to see changes made to the artwork after you change a value in the dialog box.

5. Enter **50** in the **Size text box**.

The beetles are 50% the size of the original flying beetle artwork.

6. Click the **Scatter list arrow**, click **Fixed**, then enter **0** in the **Scatter text box**.

   The beetles are positioned on the path.

7. Click the **Spacing list arrow**, click **Fixed**, then enter **50** in the **Spacing text box**.

The beetles are evenly spaced along the path.

8. Click the **Rotation list arrow**, click **Fixed**, then enter **0** in the **Rotation text box**, as shown in Figure 51.

   The beetles rotate 360° as they move from the beginning to the end of the path.

Figure 51 Scatter Brush Options dialog box

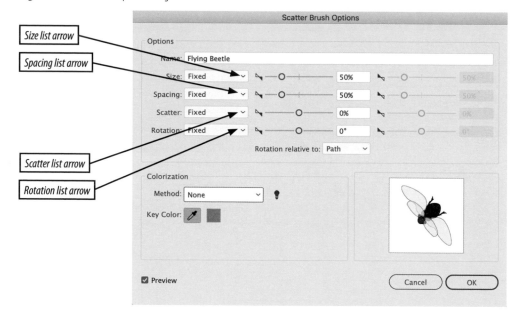

9. Click the **Rotation relative to list arrow**, then click **Page**.

The beetles no longer rotate along the path.

10. Click the **eyedropper button** ![eyedropper] in the Scatter Brush Options dialog box, then click the **black leg** of the **beetle artwork** in the preview window of the dialog box.

The Key Color box turns black.

11. Click the **Method list arrow**, then click **Tints**.

12. Click **OK**, then click **Apply to Strokes**.

The beetles are tinted with the new key color. Your work should resemble Figure 52.

13. Save your work, then continue to the next set of steps.

You explored the parameters that define a scatter brush. You started with scatter brush artwork that was random in size, spacing, scatter, and rotation. By removing the parameters that defined the randomness of the artwork, you gained an understanding of how those parameters created the random effects in the original artwork.

Figure 52 The Flying Beetle scatter brush, using fixed values

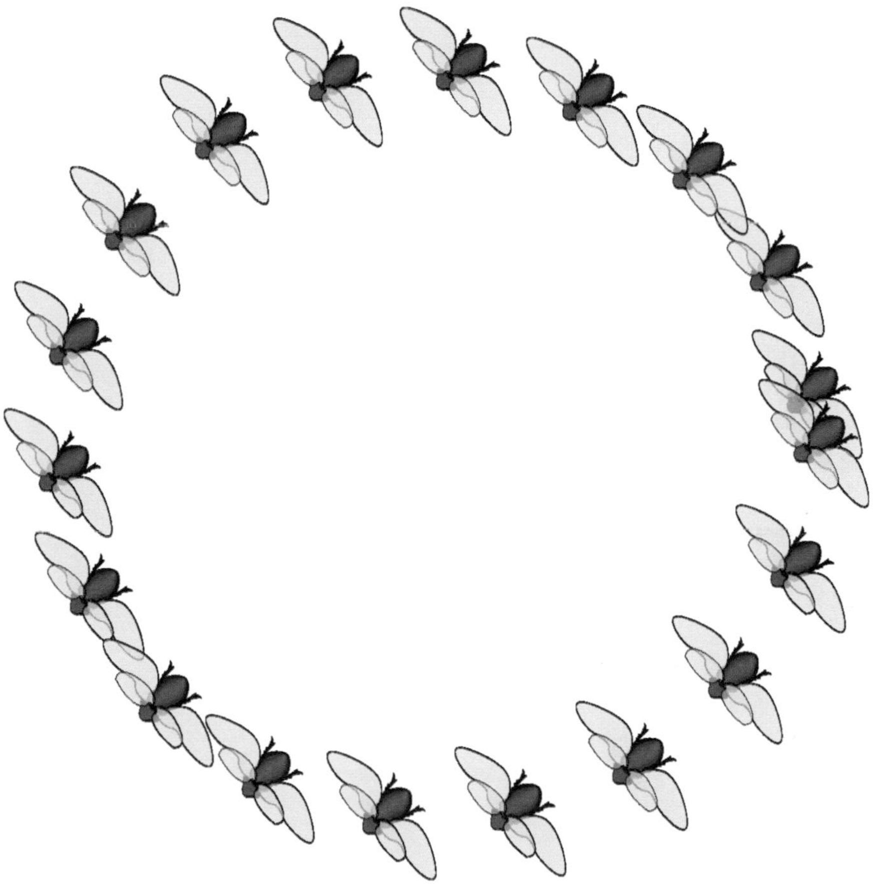

Manipulate random values in a scatter brush

1. Double-click the **Flying Beetle brush** on the Brushes panel.

2. Click the **Size list arrow**, click **Random**, then type **20** in the **first Size text box** and **100** in the **second Size text box**.

   The beetles will be randomly assigned a size anywhere between 20% and 100% of the original artwork.

3. Click the **Spacing list arrow**, click **Random**, then type **50** in the **first Spacing text box** and **200** in the **second Spacing text box**.

   The beetles are spaced randomly along the path within the set range of values.

4. Click the **Scatter list arrow**, click **Random**, then type **−100** in the **first Scatter text box** and **100** in the **second Scatter text box**.

   These values define the distance from each side of the path that the artwork can be positioned. In the case of a circular path, the first value determines how far into the circle the artwork can be positioned, and the second value determines how far outside the circle.

5. Click the **Rotation list arrow**, click **Random**, then type **−180** in the **first Rotation text box** and **180** in the **second Rotation text box**.

   The artwork can be rotated to any position within a full 360°.

6. Click the **Method list arrow**, click **None**, then compare your dialog box to Figure 53.

Figure 53 Scatter Brush Options dialog box

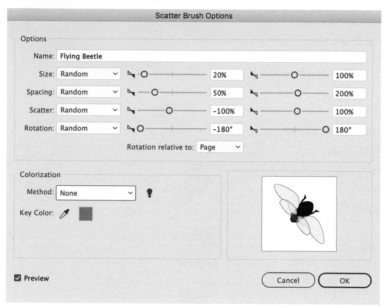

7. Click **OK**, then click **Apply to Strokes**.

   Figure 54 is an example of this brush setting.

8. Click the **Remove Brush Stroke button** ![X] on the Brushes panel, then reapply the **Flying Beetle brush**.

   The artwork will be different each time you reapply the brush because the values are determined randomly with each application.

   TIP To modify one of the beetles independently, click Object on the menu bar, then click Expand Appearance. The artwork will no longer be components of a brush. Each beetle can be selected and manipulated.

9. Save and close the Random Beetles document.

   Starting with symmetrical, evenly spaced scatter brush artwork, you manipulated parameters to create artwork that was random in size, spacing, scatter, and rotation values.

Figure 54 Scatter artwork using random values

COMPARE THE PAINTBRUSH TOOL TO THE BLOB BRUSH TOOL

In this lesson, you will make strokes with the Paintbrush tool and the Blob Brush tool, and then compare and contrast the results.

Working with the Paintbrush Tool

"Drawing" in Illustrator can be accomplished in many different ways. As you saw earlier in the book, one of the main methods of drawing is using the Pen tool to draw paths. As you saw earlier in this chapter, you can then apply brush strokes to paths. The Paintbrush tool accomplishes both tasks simultaneously. Working with the Paintbrush tool, you choose a brush from the Brushes panel, then simply "paint" on the artboard. The Paintbrush tool creates a path with the selected brush applied as a stroke. As with any path, you can change the brush style applied to the path at any time. You can also set options in the tool's dialog box that determine the smoothness of the stroke or the curve and how far the artwork can stray or scatter from the path you draw.

The main difference between using the Paintbrush tool and the Pen tool to create artwork is largely a measure of control. The Pen tool offers precision. As you draw, you can manipulate handles and anchor points to draw and position the path exactly where you want it and exactly how you want it to look. The Paintbrush tool, on the other hand, offers more of a "freehand" approach to drawing. You can use the Paintbrush tool to sketch out a drawing and create artwork that is more spontaneous and "hand-drawn."

Because both tools produce paths, you can manipulate the paths after you've drawn them. That's a big plus. Though you might use the tool to create more spontaneous strokes, you can always go back and manipulate anchor points and paths and perfect any paths that you make with the Paintbrush tool.

Comparing the Paintbrush Tool with the Blob Brush Tool

The essential difference between the Paintbrush tool and the Blob Brush tool is that the Paintbrush tool creates a stroked path, and the Blob Brush tool creates a closed filled object. Figure 55 shows two simple pieces of artwork. The top piece is made with the Paintbrush tool. The bottom piece is made with the Blob Brush tool. Figure 56 shows the same artwork in Outline mode. Note that the Blob Brush tool created the bottom artwork as a closed, filled object.

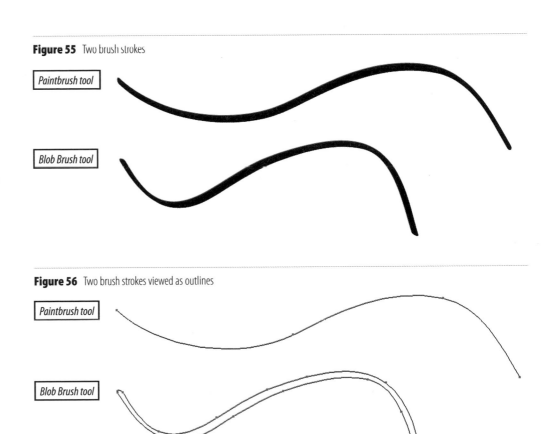

Figure 55 Two brush strokes

Paintbrush tool

Blob Brush tool

Figure 56 Two brush strokes viewed as outlines

Paintbrush tool

Blob Brush tool

Both the Paintbrush tool and the Blob Brush tool paint with color. The Paintbrush tool creates individual, unconnected paths with every stroke of the tool. The Blob Brush tool behaves differently. With the Blob Brush tool, if you overlap one stroke with a second stroke of the same color, the two strokes will be united as one object. Figure 57 shows a horizontal stroke and a vertical stroke created with the Blob Brush tool. Figure 58 shows the artwork in Outline mode, revealed as one closed object.

The Blob Brush tool is sensitive to color. Figure 59 shows a pink stroke crossed by a blue stroke, both created by the Blob Brush tool. Note that they are two separate filled objects. Because the second object was created with a different fill color, the Blob Brush tool does not unite the two objects.

This is an important feature of the Blob Brush tool. Let's say you were using the Blob Brush tool to paint a tree against a sky. You wouldn't want the "tree" to unite with the "sky." You'd want to keep them as separate objects. That's exactly what would happen if you painted the sky blue and the tree green—the Blob Brush tool would create them as two separate objects.

Figure 57 An "X" created with the Blob Brush tool

Figure 58 The "X" revealed as a single object

Figure 59 Two intersecting objects created with the Blob Brush tool

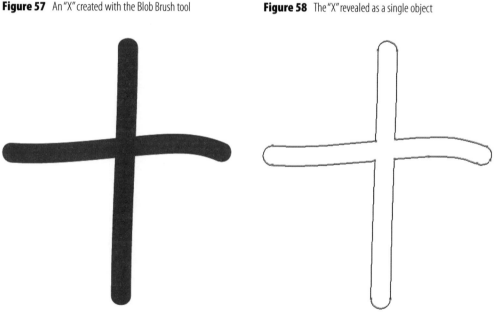

Use the Paintbrush tool

1. Open AI 6-7.ai, then save it as **Brush and Blob**.

2. Zoom in on the **top half of the artboard**, then click the **Paintbrush tool** 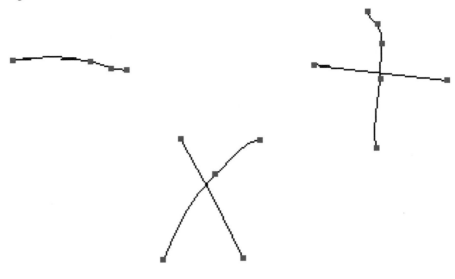 on the toolbar.

3. Verify that the **fill color** is set to **[None]** and the **stroke color** is set to **Black**, then click the **45 pt. Oval brush** on the Brushes panel.

4. Use the **Paintbrush tool** to trace the **single black dash** in the top section.

5. Make **two strokes** to trace the **black "plus" sign**.

6. Change the **stroke color** to **red**, then trace the **red component of the X**.

7. Change the **stroke color** to **blue**, then trace the **blue component of the X**.

8. Switch to **Outline mode** to see the results of your work.

   As shown in Figure 60, the Paintbrush tool created one open path for each stroke.

9. Switch back to **Preview mode**, then save your work.

10. Continue to the next set of steps.

You painted strokes with the Paintbrush tool and then switched to Outline mode to reveal that the tool creates simple paths.

Figure 60 Paths created with the Paintbrush tool

Use the Blob Brush tool

1. Zoom in on the **bottom half of the artboard**, then click the **Blob Brush tool** 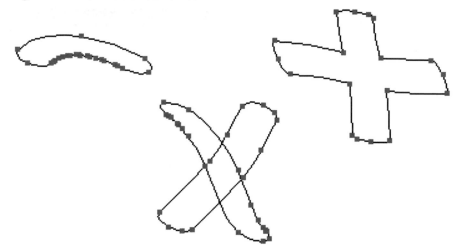 on the toolbar.

2. Verify that the **fill color** is set to **[None]** and the **stroke color** is set to **Black**, then verify that the **45 pt. Oval brush** on the Brushes panel is selected.

3. Use the **Blob Brush tool** to trace the **single black dash** in the bottom section.

4. Make **two strokes** to trace the **black "plus" sign**.

5. Deselect all, change the **fill color** to **[None]** and the **stroke color** to **red**, then trace the **red component** of the **X**.

6. Deselect all, change the **stroke color** to **blue**, then trace the **blue component** of the **X**.

7. Click **Object** on the menu bar, then click **Unlock All**.

   The placed image is unlocked and selected.

8. Click **Object** on the menu bar, point to **Hide**, then click **Selection**.

9. Select all, then switch to **Outline mode** to see the results of your work.

   Your artboard should resemble Figure 61. The Blob Brush tool created closed paths with a size the width of the diameter of the brush. Where two brush strokes of the same color overlap, the Blob Brush tool united the two closed paths into a single closed path. Where two different colors overlap, the two closed paths are not united.

10. Switch back to **Preview mode**, save your work, then close the Brush and Blob document.

You painted the same strokes, this time using the Blob Brush tool. Then you switched to Outline mode to compare the results of the Blob Brush tool to that of the Paintbrush tool.

Figure 61 Paths created with the Blob Brush tool

ENHANCE ARTWORK WITH BRUSHES AND THE WIDTH TOOL

▶ *What You'll Do*

In this lesson, you will use placed art, art brushes, the Bristle brush, and the Width tool to improve the appearance of artwork.

Improving Artwork with Brush Strokes

Figure 62 shows the "Snowball" drawing you created in Chapter 3. You drew all the objects that make up the illustration and assembled them. It's at this point that many designers hit a wall. What to do next?

The illustration at this point doesn't look great; it looks like a bunch of assembled illustrator objects. There's no flare, no nuance, nothing unique.

This is where brushes come in and convert your objects into artwork. In Figure 63, a simple charcoal art brush has been applied to the same artwork. Notice the dramatic effect it gives the illustration.

Figure 62 Objects with a simple stroke

Figure 63 Charcoal brush applied to artwork

Using Placed Art as Brushes

At some point, you might find yourself wanting brush artwork that's even more unique than what you can create with Illustrator's brushes or with Illustrator objects. One technique that designers use is to trace actual pencil, crayon, or marker sketches in Illustrator, then apply the artwork as a brush.

Figure 64 shows a placed bitmap graphic of a simple pencil stroke on paper. That bitmap art can be traced and then saved as a brush. When applied, it creates a unique effect, as shown in Figure 65.

Using the Bristle Brush

If you look at the arc of Adobe Illustrator from its debut in 1988 until now, with Creative Cloud, you see that Adobe has endeavored to make Illustrator more and more a drawing and painting tool. Adobe's challenge has been a tough one—to somehow devise and develop "computer tools" that mimic traditional art tools such as pens, brushes, crayons, and chalk.

The Bristle Brush represents a real step forward toward the goal. The Bristle Brush creates a natural brush stroke with the streaks and varying opacities you would find with an actual paint brush, allowing you to mimic the look and feel of traditional disciplines like watercolor or paint. As with the Paintbrush tool, the Bristle Brush creates open paths.

Figure 64 Artwork that will be used as a brush

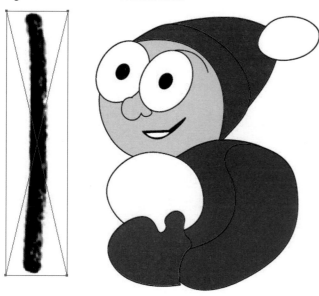

Figure 65 Artwork "brushed" with the placed art

When you paint with either brush, if you switch to Outline mode, you'll see a series of path segments. Therefore, colors you apply to those segments while painting with the brushes are applied as strokes. Figure 66 shows an illustration painted with the Bristle Brush.

To use the Bristle Brush, you first create a new brush on the Brushes panel, just as you would an art brush or a scatter brush, and then choose Bristle Brush as the type. This opens the Bristle Brush Options dialog box,

shown in Figure 67. You can choose from different brush shapes, like Round Fan or Flat Point, and you can specify the stiffness of the bristles. With the Bristle Brush though, you'll find that the many preferences are best experienced and understood by giving them a try.

To get the most effect out of working with the Bristle Brush, use a Wacom or other brand of pen tablet device. Depending on the device and the features available, the

pen will incorporate factors like pressure, angle, and rotation. If you use a mouse or non-tablet device, you can still use the Bristle Brush, but it will be like working with a brush fixed at a 45° angle.

The key word when working with the Bristle Brush is *experiment*. There are no specific sets of steps or specific approaches—you simply need to experiment. And don't forget about the many different brush shapes available to you as shown in Figure 68.

Figure 66 Snowball recreated with the Bristle Brush

Figure 67 Bristle Brush Options dialog box

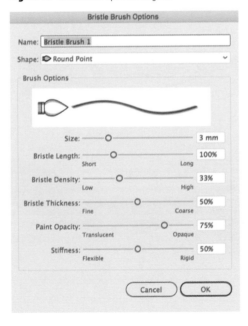

Figure 68 Shape menu for Bristle Brush

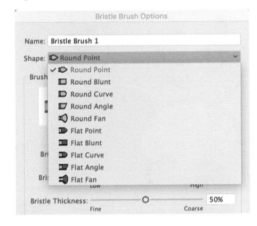

Using the Width Tool

In Chapter 3 of this book, you learned about making "pseudo-strokes" by creating black copies behind objects and distorting them to "peek" from behind the front object. Figure 69 shows the Snowball illustration you created in Chapter 3 with pseudo-strokes.

The Width tool offers you a method for quickly altering the width of a stroke by clicking and dragging on the stroke itself. In Figure 70, the top image shows a simple stroke, and the bottom image shows the same stroke being increased with the Width tool. With the Width tool, you simply position the tool over the stroke, then click and drag to increase the width of the stroke.

What's really great about the Width tool is that you can click and drag any area of a path, not just over an already-existing anchor point. This makes the entire path available for modification. Figure 71 shows the bottom stroke after it has been altered with the Width tool. Note that it is still simply a stroked path.

Figure 69 Pseudo strokes effect

Figure 70 Increasing the width of a stroke with the Width tool

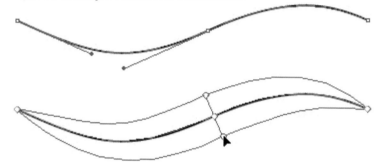

Figure 71 Stroke with an increased width

The Width tool provides a quick way to mimic the pseudo-strokes effect. Figure 72 shows the Snowball illustration after being altered with the Width tool. Compare this to the pseudo-strokes effect in Figure 69.

Figure 72 Snowball illustration with altered widths

Use placed art as a brush

1. Open AI 6-8.ai, then save it as **Flower Brushes**.

2. Evaluate the artwork in terms of shape, color, dimension, and its overall effect.

   The artwork has interesting shapes, and the colors work well together, but overall, the illustration is boring. It looks like what it is—a few Illustrator objects with color fills and a thin black stroke. The illustration is flat—it is not dynamic.

3. Click **File** on the menu bar, then click **Place**.

4. Navigate to where your Chapter 6 Data Files are stored, click the file named **Fat Charcoal**, then click **Place**.

   As shown in Figure 73, Fat Charcoal is a digital image of a line drawn with thick charcoal. The line has rough, uneven edges. The image was taken with a smartphone camera, brightened in Photoshop, then saved.

5. Click the **arrow button** next to the **Image Trace button** on the Control panel to expose the list of tracing presets, then click **Shades of Gray**.

   The artwork is traced and converted to filled Illustrator objects.

6. Click the **Expand button** on the Control panel, click the **Direct Selection tool** ▷, then delete the bounding box around the placed artwork.

   Deleting the bounding box leaves only the "charcoal" artwork for you to use.

7. Switch to the **Selection tool** ▶, and then drag the **traced artwork** into the gray area at the bottom of the Brushes panel.

   The New Brush dialog box opens.

8. Click the **Art Brush option button**, then click **OK**.

9. Type **Fat Charcoal** in the **Name text box**, then click **OK** to close the Art Brush Options dialog box.

   The Fat Charcoal brush appears on the Brushes panel.

10. Delete the placed charcoal artwork from the artboard.

11. Select all the artwork on the artboard, click **View** on the menu bar, then click **Hide Edges** if necessary.

Continued on next page

Figure 73 Fat Charcoal art placed

12. Click the **Fat Charcoal brush thumbnail** on the Brushes panel.

The Fat Charcoal brush is applied as a stroke to the selected objects. The brush strokes are too wide and need to be reduced.

13. Open the **Stroke panel**, then reduce the **weight** of the stroke to **.5 pt**.

Your artwork should resemble Figure 74.

14. Save your work, then close the Flower Brushes document.

You placed a graphic of a charcoal streak. You traced it, then created an art brush. You then applied the art brush to the flower artwork.

Use the Width tool

1. Open AI 6-9.ai, then save it as **Flower Width**.

2. Select the **vase**, then click the **Width tool** on the toolbar.

3. Click and drag to select **different areas of the vase path** to alter the width of the stroke.

Figure 75 shows one possible outcome.

4. Continue clicking and dragging **every path** in the illustration to create various widths and new shapes.

Figure 76 shows one example of the finished illustration.

5. Save your work, then close the Flower Width document.

You altered the width of the stroke on various parts of the vase using the Width tool.

Figure 74 Artwork with art applied as a brush

Figure 75 Applying the Width tool to the vase

Figure 76 Illustration modified with the Width tool

Create, apply, and modify a Bristle Brush

1. Open AI 6-10.ai, then save it as **Flower Bristles**.

2. Click the **Brushes panel menu button** ☰, then click **New Brush**.

3. Click **Bristle Brush**, then click **OK**.

4. Type **Flower Bristle Brush** in the **Name text box**, then click **OK** to accept the default settings for the brush.

5. Select **all the artwork** on the artboard, then change the **fill color** to **White**.

6. Click the **Flower Bristle Brush** on the Brushes panel, then compare your artwork to Figure 77.

7. Double-click **Flower Bristle Brush** on the Brushes panel.

   The Bristle Brush Options dialog box opens.

TIP Verify that Preview is checked.

8. Enter the settings shown in Figure 78, click **OK**, then click **Apply to Strokes** if prompted.

9. Deselect all, save your work, then continue to the next set of steps.

You created a new Bristle Brush and applied it to artwork. You then modified the brush with the artwork selected.

Figure 77 Artwork with Bristle Brush applied

Figure 78 New settings for the Bristle Brush

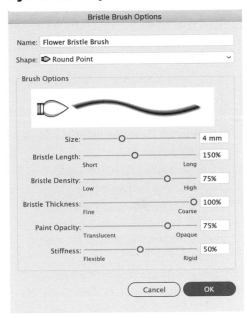

Paint with the Bristle Brush

1. Verify that the **flower artwork** is deselected, then open the **Layers panel**.

2. Click the **Create New Layer button** ⊞ on the Layers panel.

    You will paint with the Bristle Brush on the new layer.

3. Click the **Paintbrush tool** ✎ on the toolbar, then verify that **Flower Bristle Brush** is selected on the **Brushes panel**.

4. Set the **stroke color** to one of the **green swatches** on the Swatches panel.

5. Paint the **leaves and stems of the flower artwork**, setting your **stroke color** to various **shades of green**, then compare your results to Figure 79.

    Change the Size and Opacity of the Paintbrush tool on the Control panel as you like. Your results, obviously, will be unique. You can use the figure as one example of what can be done.

6. Continue painting with various colors to finish the illustration.

    Figure 80 shows one result.

Figure 79 Starting by painting the green areas of the flower

Figure 80 Applying paint to the entire illustration

7. Paint with a **white stroke** to add highlights to the artwork, as shown in Figure 81.

8. Paint with a **black stroke** to add shadows to the artwork and to strengthen the outlines of the artwork, as shown in Figure 82.

9. Save your work, then close the Flower Bristles document.

TIP If you get a dialog box warning you that the document you are currently saving contains multiple Bristle Brush Paths with transparency, click OK.

You painted artwork with the Bristle Brush.

Figure 81 Painting with a white stroke to add highlights

Figure 82 Painting with a black stroke to add shadows and detail

Use the Move command

1. Create a new 6" × 6" document, then save it as **Polka Dot Pattern**.
2. Create a 2" square, then fill it with a green fill, and remove any stroke if necessary.
3. Create a 0.25" circle, then fill it with White.
4. Align the circle and the square by their center points.

TIP Select both the circle and the square, then click the Horizontal Align Center button and the Vertical Align Center button on the Align panel.

5. Deselect all, select the white circle, click Object on the menu bar, point to Transform, then click Move.
6. Type **−.5** in the Horizontal text box, type **−.5** in the Vertical text box, then click Copy.
7. Keeping the new circle selected, click Object on the menu bar, point to Transform, then click Move.
8. Type **1** in the Horizontal text box, type **0** in the Vertical text box, then click Copy.
9. Select the two new circles, click Object on the menu bar, point to Transform, click Move, type **0** in the Horizontal text box, **1** in the Vertical text box, then click Copy.

    You moved a copy of the circles 1 inch below.
10. Fill the center circle with any blue swatch that you like.
11. Save your work.

Create a pattern

1. Select all the artwork, then drag it into the Swatches panel.
2. Double-click the new swatch on the Swatches panel, type **Green Polka Dot** in the Name text box of the Pattern Options panel, then press [esc] to escape pattern editing mode.
3. Delete the artwork on the artboard.
4. Create a 4" square, then fill it with the Green Polka Dot pattern.
5. Double-click the Scale tool, then scale only the pattern 25%.
6. Save your work.

Design a repeating pattern

1. Hide the 4" square.
2. Drag the Green Polka Dot pattern swatch from the Swatches panel onto the artboard.
3. Deselect the pattern swatch, draw a diagonal 1 pt. black line from the bottom-left corner to the top-right corner of the green square.
4. Change the stroke color of the line to a shade of green.
5. Deselect, select the line with the Selection tool, then rotate a copy of the line 90°, making sure the Objects check box in the Rotate dialog box is checked.
6. Click the Direct Selection tool, select the five circles, then cut them.
7. Click the Selection tool, select the two green lines, then paste in front.
8. Select the green square, click Object on the menu bar, point to Path, click Offset Path, type **−.5** in the Offset text box, then click OK.
9. Cut the new green square, then paste it in back of the blue circle.
10. Select all the artwork, press and hold [option] (Mac) or [Alt] (Win), then drag the artwork on top of the Green Polka Dot swatch to replace the old pattern with the new one.
11. Delete the artwork from the artboard.

12. Show all, then save your work.
    Your square should resemble Figure 83.

13. Close the Polka Dot Pattern document.

Use the Pattern Options panel

1. Open AI 6-11.ai, then save it as **Pattern Options Review**.

2. Select all four objects on the artboard, click Object on the menu bar, point to Pattern, then click Make.

3. Type **Lucky Shapes** in the Name text box.

4. On the Pattern Options panel, change the Width and the Height fields to 1".

5. Position the center of the green circle on the lower-left corner of the tile so only the top-right quadrant of the circle is inside the tile.

6. Delete the red diamond and the yellow square.

7. Move the star to the center of the pattern tile.

8. With the star still selected, double-click the Scale tool.

9. Enter **180** in the Uniform text box, then click Copy.

10. Set the fill color of the new star to [None], then apply a 1 pt. black stroke.

11. Deselect all, click the Rectangle tool, then draw a rectangle precisely on top of the pattern tile.

Figure 83 Completed Skills Review, Part 1

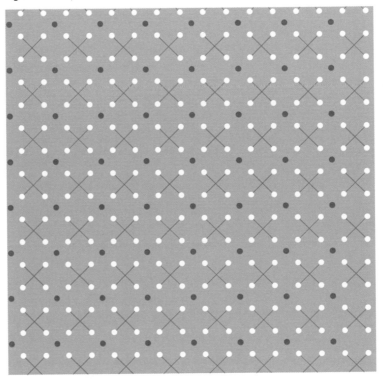

(continued)

12. Deselect, apply the Fit Artboard in Window command, then compare your pattern to Figure 84.
13. Uncheck the Dim Copies to: and Show Tile Edge options at the bottom of the panel.
14. Click the Tile Type list arrow, then choose Brick by Column.
15. Click the Brick Offset list arrow, then click 1/4.

16. At the top of the window, click Done.
17. Delete the four objects on the artboard.
18. Create a large rectangle almost the size of the entire artboard.
19. Make sure the fill button is activated on the toolbar, then click the Lucky Shapes pattern swatch on the Swatches panel.

    The pattern fills the rectangle, as shown in Figure 85.
20. Save your work, then close the Pattern Options Review document.

Work with the Brushes panel

1. Open AI 6-12.ai, then save it as **Brushes Review**.
2. Select the snowflake artwork on the artboard, click the Brushes panel menu button, then click New Brush.
3. Click the Scatter Brush option button, then click OK.
4. Name the new brush **Snowflake**.
5. Set the Size to 30%.
6. Set the Spacing to 40%, then click OK.
7. Hide the snowflake artwork on the artboard.

Figure 84 Pattern with the stroke applied

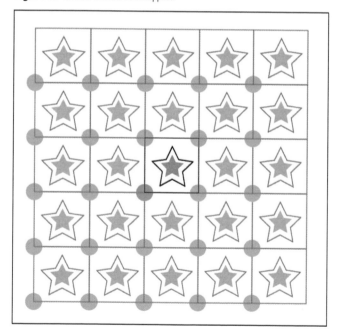

Figure 85 Rectangle filled with the pattern

8. Create a circle that is 4" in diameter, then apply the Snowflake brush to the circle.

9. Save your work.

Work with scatter brushes

1. Double-click the Snowflake brush on the Brushes panel.

2. Change all four categories from Fixed to Random.

3. Set the Size range from 15% to 46%.

4. Set the Spacing range from 10% to 45%.

5. Set the Scatter range from −55% to 114%.

6. Set the Rotation range from −90° to 90°.

7. Click OK, then click Apply to Strokes if prompted.

8. Save your work, deselect all, compare your screen with Figure 86, then close the Brushes Review document.

Compare the Paintbrush tool to the Blob Brush tool

1. Open AI 6-13.ai, then save it as **Brush Skills**.

2. Click the Paintbrush tool on the toolbar.

3. Verify that the fill color is set to [None] and the stroke color is set to red, then verify that the 15 pt. Round brush on the Brushes panel is selected.

4. Using the Paintbrush tool, make four strokes to trace the left object.

5. Click the Blob Brush tool on the toolbar, then make four strokes to trace the right object.

6. Click Object on the menu bar, then click Unlock All.

7. Click Object on the menu bar, point to Hide, then click Selection.

8. Select all, then switch to Outline mode to see the results of your work.

9. Switch back to Preview mode, save your work, then close the Brush Skills document.

Figure 86 Completed Skills Review, Part 2

Enhance artwork with brushes and the Width tool

1. Open AI 6-14.ai, then save it as **Dog Width**.
2. Select the "red beret," then click the Width tool.
3. Click and drag to select different areas of the beret path to alter the width.
4. Continue clicking and dragging every path in the illustration to create various widths and new shapes.
5. Select the six whiskers, then apply the Charcoal brush on the Brushes panel.
   Figure 87 shows one example of the finished illustration.
6. Save your work, then close the Dog Width document.

Figure 87 Completed Skills Review, Part 3

You work in the textile industry as a pattern designer. Your boss asks you to design a pattern for a new line of shower curtains. Her only direction is that the pattern must feature triangles and at least eight colors. (You can create the pattern using the Pattern Options panel if you prefer.)

1. Create a new 6" × 6" document, then save it as **New Curtain**.
2. Create a 1" square with a blue fill and no stroke.
3. Copy the square, paste in front, then fill the new square with green.
4. Click Object on the menu bar, point to Path, click Add Anchor Points, then click the Delete Anchor Point tool.

TIP The Delete Anchor Point tool is hidden beneath the Pen tool.

5. Delete the top-left corner, top-right corner, left side, and right side anchor points so the square is converted to a triangle.
6. Use the Move command to create a copy of the two shapes to the right, then two copies below so, altogether, the area of the four tiles is 2" × 2".
7. Change the colors in each tile.
8. Scale the four tiles 15%.
9. Make a new pattern swatch out of the four tiles, name it **Triangle Pattern**, then apply the pattern to a 4" square.
10. Save your work, then compare your pattern to Figure 88.
11. Close the New Curtain document.

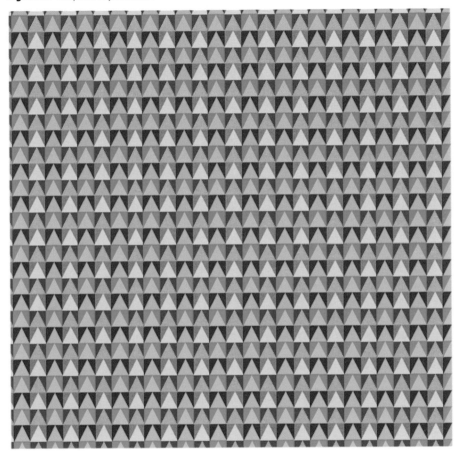

Figure 88 Completed Project Builder 1

You are a jewelry designer, and you've been hired to create the original design for a new line of necklaces that will be targeted to teenage girls. The necklaces will be made with flat, tinted metals, and you are asked to use bright colors. One catch: Your client tells you that he's unsure of what he's looking for and hints that he may make many changes to your design before he's satisfied.

1. Open AI 6-15.ai, then save it as **Jewelry**.
2. Create a new scatter brush with the artwork provided.
3. Name the new brush **Smile**.
4. Set the Size to 20%.
5. Set the Spacing to 25%.
6. Set the Rotation to Random.
7. Set the Rotation range from −92° to 92°, make it relative to the page, then click OK.
8. Hide the original artwork.
9. Draw a path resembling the arc of a necklace, then apply the Smile scatter brush to the path.
10. Save your work, then compare your pattern to Figure 89.
11. Close the Jewelry document.

Figure 89 Completed Project Builder 2

You own a gallery in Key West called Funky Frames. You are known for designing unusual and festive frames of various sizes. The process of designing the frames is complex, as you use many different kinds of materials. However, they all begin with a brush pattern that you create in Illustrator.

1. Open AI 6-16.ai, then save it as **Funky Frames**.
2. Select the left tile, drag it into the Swatches panel, then name it **Side Tile**.
3. Select the right tile, drag it into the Swatches panel, then name it **Corner Tile**.
4. Hide the artwork on the artboard.
5. Create a new pattern brush.
6. Name the new brush **Funky**.
7. Apply the Side Tile swatch as the side tile and the Corner Tile swatch as the outer corner tile.
8. Set the Scale value to 70%, then click OK.
9. Apply the Funky pattern brush as a stroke to a 6" white square.
10. Save your work, then compare your pattern to Figure 90.
11. Close the Funky Frames document.

Figure 90 Completed Design Project 1

You have been commissioned to design an original plaid pattern, which will be used to produce kilts for the wedding of a famous singer and her Scottish groom. Your only direction is that it must be an original pattern, and it must have at least three colors.

1. Create a new document, then save it as **Wedding Plaid**.
2. Research the history of plaid patterns and their association with specific groups, families, and organizations.
3. Search the Internet for plaid patterns.
4. Research the Burberry pattern, one of the most famous patterns ever created.
5. Create color swatches to compare and choose colors that work together, then design the pattern.
6. Fill a 6" × 6" square with the new pattern.
7. Save your work, then compare your pattern to Figure 91.
8. Close the Wedding Plaid document.

Figure 91 Completed Design Project 2

NATIONAL GEOGRAPHIC LEARNING | TRENT BUSAKOWSKI
SENIOR DESIGNER

For Trent Busakowski, print media has always been a source of inspiration. In high school, Trent was exposed to a variety of print and digital art classes, and was introduced to the Adobe Creative Suite, which he used as a form of creative expression. Trent took these skills with him to college, where he held internships and worked for the school paper. These experiences allowed him to figure out how to merge a conceptual idea into a practical, real-world design.

After designing for various firms, Trent now works as a Senior Designer for National Geographic Learning. Here, he enjoys the initial collaboration between design, editorial, and user experience teams to conceptualize the core identity of the product. Once the core is solidified, Trent enjoys playing with the design and adding his own creative flair.

In addition to time management, Trent places importance on communication skills. Although it may be easiest to complete a task yourself, "being able to effectively communicate how you want things done to achieve your vision is a skill that you continually need to work on," Trent shares. Being in a creative position also lends itself to critique. Learning how to receive feedback appropriately is an opportunity for growth.

While his job can be stressful, Trent likes to decompress by exploring Chicago neighborhoods on foot. He explains, "Constantly being curious about the world around you will help you in your work." Trent offers one more tidbit of advice to those looking to enter a creative field. "Don't take for granted the skill that is put into creative work. Oftentimes it gets siloed into work for passion when we're doing things that are bringing profit." In a nutshell, never sell yourself short.

PROJECT DESCRIPTION

In this project, you will create a graphic tree that displays and connects the important people and things in your life. You may choose to include family, friends, sentimental objects, memories, hobbies, foods, etc. The goal of this project is to design a visual representation of your values and priorities, and communicate how all of these different values connect. You are encouraged to share and present your graphic tree to classmates.

QUESTIONS TO CONSIDER

What stands out to you?

What questions would you ask?

What is important to convey in the graphic tree?

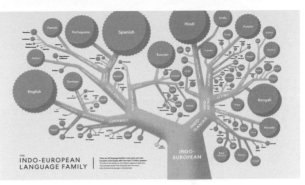

From Human Geography: A Spatial Perspective AP® Edition
© Cengage Learning, Inc.

GETTING STARTED

Your graphic tree should visually depict the people and things that are most important to you. Arrange the objects to clearly communicate your values and priorities. Begin by brainstorming a list of people that are closest to you. Then expand your list to include objects, memories, hobbies, foods, and other elements of your life or culture that carry meaning.

Rearrange your list to place the people and items in order of importance. You may choose to order them from left to right, or top to bottom. Now think about how you would like to represent each item on your graphic tree. Will they all get the same treatment? Will some words or images be larger than others? Applying a different design element to the items of greatest importance will help you to visually convey your priorities to others.

CHAPTER **7**

WORKING WITH
DISTORTIONS, GRADIENT MESHES, ENVELOPES, AND BLENDS

1. Edit Colors and Distort Objects
2. Work with Gradient Meshes
3. Work with Envelopes
4. Create Blends

Adobe Certified Professional in Graphic Design and Illustration Using Adobe Illustrator

2. Project Setup and Interface

This objective covers the interface setup and program settings that assist in an efficient and effective workflow, as well as knowledge about ingesting digital assets for a project.

2.5 Manage colors, swatches, and gradients.
   B Create and customize gradients.
   C Create, manage, and edit swatches and swatch libraries.

4. Creating and Modifying Visual Elements

This objective covers core tools and functionality of the application, as well as tools that affect the visual appearance of document elements.

4.4 Transform digital graphics and media.
   B Rotate, flip, and transform individual layers, objects, selections, groups, or graphical elements.

4.5 Use basic reconstructing and editing techniques to manipulate digital graphics and media.
   C Evaluate or adjust the appearance of objects, selections, or layers.

4.6 Modify the appearance of design elements using effects and graphic styles.
   A Use effects to modify images.
   C Expand the appearance of objects.

EDIT COLORS AND DISTORT OBJECTS

▶ *What You'll Do*

In this lesson, you will explore options for manipulating colors and basic shapes with effects.

Introducing Effects

Illustrator provides a number of effects to alter the shape of an object. These effects provide simple operations you can use to tweak your illustrations and give them a unique look. Of the many effects that modify shapes, some are essential operations you will want to have in your skills set.

The Pucker & Bloat effect adjusts the segments between an object's anchor points. With a Pucker effect, the segments are moved inward, toward the center of the object, while the anchor points are moved outward, as shown in Figure 1.

Figure 1 Pucker effect applied

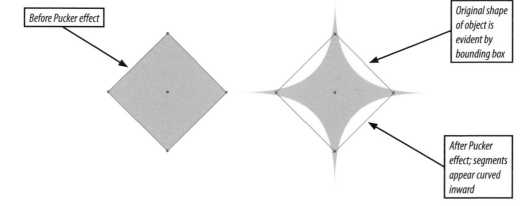

Before Pucker effect

Original shape of object is evident by bounding box

After Pucker effect; segments appear curved inward

The Bloat effect is achieved by moving the segments outward and the anchor points inward, as shown in Figure 2.

The Twist effect rotates an object more sharply in the center than it does at the edges, creating a whirlpool effect, as shown in Figure 3. With the Twist effect, it's often a good idea to use the Add Anchor Points command to add more anchor points to the object, because it makes the twist effect smoother.

The Pucker & Bloat and Twist exercises in this chapter are intended to familiarize you with these types of transformations, which are useful for designing artwork. In addition, these steps will serve as an introduction to effects.

The Pucker & Bloat and the Twist commands are applied as effects. Effects change only the appearance of the object. Note how in Figures 1, 2, and 3, the selected object does not change, even after the effect has been applied. This is evident by the bounding box.

Effects are controlled on the Appearance panel. You will study effects and the Appearance panel in-depth in Chapter 8. In this chapter, focus more on the Pucker & Bloat and Twist effects from a design perspective and how you might use them in your artwork.

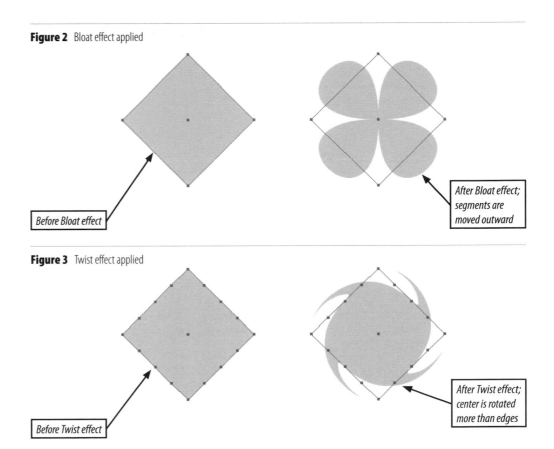

Figure 2 Bloat effect applied

Before Bloat effect

After Bloat effect; segments are moved outward

Figure 3 Twist effect applied

Before Twist effect

After Twist effect; center is rotated more than edges

Modifying Color with the Edit Colors Command

The Edit Colors commands are useful for quickly applying color changes to objects. With the Edit Colors commands, the changes are applied directly to the objects; they are not effects.

You can saturate an illustration, which makes colors more intense. Conversely, you can reduce the saturation of an illustration, making its colors duller, with a washed-out appearance. Use the Convert to Grayscale command to completely desaturate an illustration and create the effect of a black and white image.

You can also use the Edit Colors commands to make color blends between objects. The Blend Front to Back command creates a color blend through all the objects in the stacking order, using the frontmost object as the starting color and the backmost object as the ending color. This command is useful for adding the effect of color depth to an illustration.

Create a front to back blend

1. Open AI 7-1.ai, then save it as **Edit Colors**.
2. Select all, click **Object** on the menu bar, point to **Path**, then click **Outline Stroke**.

    The strokes are converted to closed paths.
3. Deselect, then fill the **smallest object** with **yellow**.
4. Select all, click **Edit** on the menu bar, point to **Edit Colors**, then click **Blend Front to Back**.

    A color blend is created from the frontmost to the backmost object in the stacking order.
5. Deselect, then compare your work to Figure 4.

TIP The Blend Front to Back command does not work on open paths.

6. Save your work, then close the Edit Colors document.

You converted stroked paths to outlines and then used the Blend Front to Back command to create the effect that objects lighten as they move from left to right.

Figure 4 Blending colors front to back

Saturate and desaturate an illustration

1. Open AI 7-2.ai, then save it as **Saturation**.

2. Select all, click **View** on the menu bar, then click **Hide Edges**.

3. Click **Edit** on the menu bar, point to **Edit Colors**, then click **Saturate**.

4. Click the **Preview check box** in the Saturation dialog box, drag the **Intensity slider** all the way to the right, then click **OK**.

Your work should resemble Figure 5.

5. Click **Edit** on the menu bar, point to **Edit Colors**, then click **Convert to Grayscale**.

Every object is filled with a shade of gray, as shown in Figure 6. Even though some of the objects have gone completely black, they can always be selected and modified individually. Therefore, you can think of the Saturate and Grayscale functions as a means to an end, not necessarily a one-time solution.

6. Click **View** on the menu bar, then click **Show Edges**.

7. Deselect all by clicking the artboard.

8. Save your work, then close the Saturation document.

You used the Saturate command to intensify the color of an image. You then used the Convert to Grayscale command to remove all chromatic color from the illustration, thereby creating a black and white illustration.

Figure 5 Illustration with saturated colors

Figure 6 Illustration with the Convert to Grayscale command applied

Apply the Pucker & Bloat and Twist effects

1. Open AI 7-3.ai, then save it as **Pucker and Bloat**.

2. Select the **large orange square**, click **Effect** on the menu bar, point to **Distort & Transform**, then click **Pucker & Bloat**.

3. Type **85** in the text box, then click **OK**.

   TIP A positive value produces a Bloat effect; a negative value produces a Pucker effect.

4. Select the **gray circle**, click **Object** on the menu bar, point to **Path**, then click **Add Anchor Points**.

5. Click **Effect** on the menu bar, point to **Distort & Transform**, then click **Pucker & Bloat**.

   The Pucker & Bloat dialog box opens with the settings last used.

6. Type **−75**, then click **OK**.

   Your work should resemble Figure 7.

7. Select the **blue circle**, then apply the **Add Anchor Points command** twice.

Figure 7 The orange shape is bloated, the gray circle is puckered

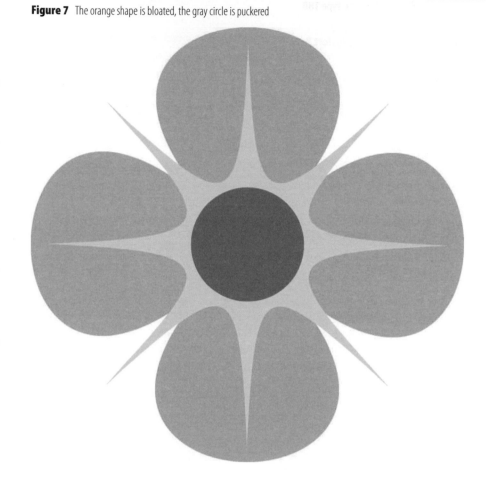

8. Open the **Pucker & Bloat dialog box**, type **180** in the text box, then click **OK**.

9. Click **Effect** on the menu bar, point to **Distort & Transform**, then click **Twist**.

10. Type **90** in the **Angle text box**, then click **OK**.

11. Deselect, then compare your work to Figure 8.

12. Save your work, then close the Pucker and Bloat document.

You applied the Pucker & Bloat effect in varying degrees to each object, producing three distinctly different effects. You also applied the Twist effect.

Figure 8 The blue circle with added anchor points and the Bloat and Twist effects applied

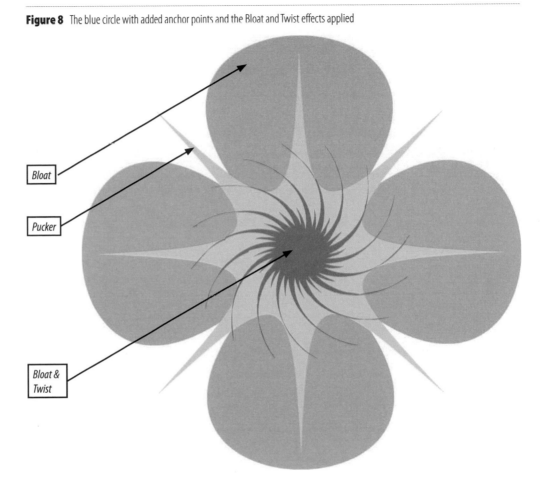

Bloat

Pucker

Bloat &
Twist

WORK WITH GRADIENT MESHES

▶ *What You'll Do*

In this lesson, you will create and manipulate a gradient mesh to add dimension to basic shapes.

Working with a Mesh Object

The Mesh tool and the Create Gradient Mesh command can be used to transform a basic object into a mesh object. A mesh object is a single, multicolored object in which colors can flow in different directions, and colors transition gradually from point to point. Meshes exceed the ability of simple radial and linear gradients for applying color blends to objects and are effective for adding contrast and dimension.

When you create a mesh object, multiple mesh lines crisscross the object, joined at their intersections by mesh points. Mesh points are diamond-shaped and work just like anchor points, with the added functionality of taking color assignments. When you assign a color to a mesh point, the color gradates outward from the point.

The area between four mesh points is a mesh patch. You can apply color to all four mesh points simultaneously by applying the color to the patch. Work with this method to apply broad color changes to the object.

Mesh points can be added, deleted, and moved along the mesh line without altering the shape of the mesh.

Anchor points are also part of the mesh, and they function as they do on simple paths. Just as with simple paths, you can manipulate the anchor points' direction lines to alter the shape of the mesh. Figure 9 shows an example of a mesh object.

Creating a Mesh Object

You can create a mesh object from any path. You cannot create a mesh object from compound paths or text objects. You can create a mesh object with the Mesh tool or by applying the Create Gradient Mesh command.

Generally, you'll be happiest creating a mesh object using the Create Gradient Mesh command, which creates a mesh object with regularly spaced mesh lines and mesh points. The Create Gradient Mesh dialog box is shown in Figure 10. The Mesh tool adds a mesh point and its intersecting mesh lines where you click. The tool is most effective when you want to add a particular mesh point, such as a highlight, to an existing mesh. The Create Gradient Mesh command is always the best choice when converting complex objects.

Once a mesh object has been created, it cannot be converted back into a simple path. Keep in mind that complex mesh objects are a memory drain and may affect your computer's performance. Also, it's better to create a few simple mesh objects than a single complex one.

Adding Transparency to a Gradient Mesh

You can apply opacity settings to any mesh point on a gradient mesh. Reducing the opacity allows you to make any mesh point or patch on a gradient mesh increasingly transparent, thus adding the option to create even more complex visual effects.

To affect opacity, select one or more points on the mesh, then drag the Opacity slider in the Transparency panel, Control panel, or Appearance panel. The ability to reduce the opacity on a single point or patch on the gradient mesh offers the powerful option of applying transparency effects to specific areas of the mesh without affecting other areas.

Figure 9 Elements of a mesh object

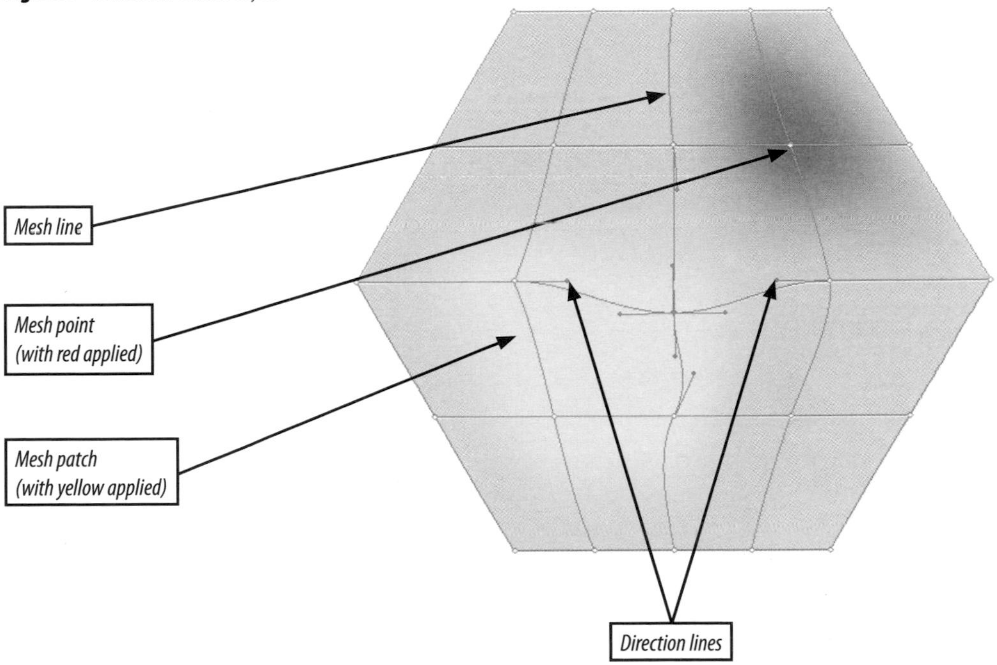

Mesh line

Mesh point
(with red applied)

Mesh patch
(with yellow applied)

Direction lines

Figure 10 Create Gradient Mesh dialog box

Create Gradient Mesh

Rows: 4

Columns: 4

Appearance: Flat

Highlight: 100%

☑ Preview   Cancel   OK

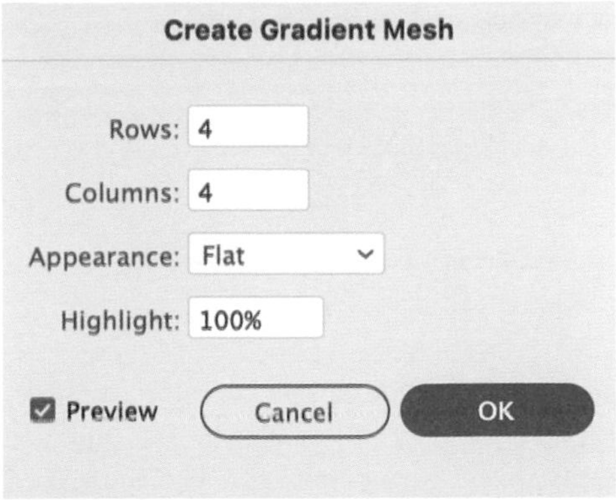

Create a gradient mesh

1. Open AI 7-4.ai, then save it as **Circle Mesh**.

2. Verify that the **Layers panel** is visible.

3. Select the **circle**, click **Object** on the menu bar, then click **Create Gradient Mesh**.

4. Type **2** in the **Rows text box** and **2** in the **Columns text box**, then click **OK**.

5. Deselect, then click the **edge of the circle** with the **Direct Selection tool** .

6. Select the **center mesh point**, then click a **yellow swatch** on the Swatches panel.

7. Move the **center mesh point** to the **green X**, as shown in Figure 11.

8. Move the **direction lines at the top, bottom, left, and right** of the circle's edge, as shown in Figure 12.

9. Click the **Mesh tool** on the toolbar, then click the **blue X**.

   A new mesh point is added to the mesh, and, by default, the same yellow fill has been applied to it.

   TIP Press [shift] while you click the Mesh tool to add a mesh point without applying the current fill color.

10. Click the **White swatch** on the Swatches panel to change the color of the mesh point to White.

Figure 11 Mesh points can be moved, just like anchor points

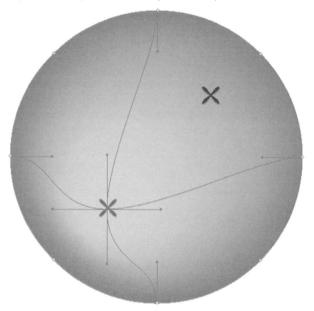

Figure 12 The shape of the mesh is manipulated by direction lines

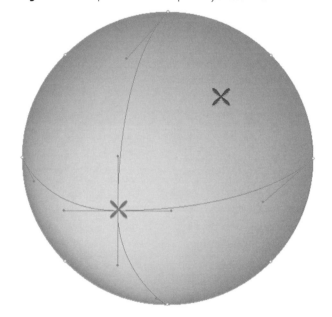

11. Hide **Layer 2** on the Layers panel, deselect all, then compare your artwork to Figure 13.

12. Save your work, then close the Circle Mesh document.

You applied a gradient mesh to a circle with the Create Gradient Mesh command, changed the color of a mesh point, then moved the mesh point. You then used the Mesh tool to expand the mesh. You changed the color of the new mesh point to white to add a highlight to the sphere.

Figure 13 Gradient meshes add dimension to an object

Manipulate a gradient mesh

1. Open AI 7-5.ai, then save it as **Heart Mesh**.
2. Select the **heart**, click **Object** on the menu bar, then click **Create Gradient Mesh**.
3. Type **4** in the **Rows text box** and **4** in the **Columns text box**, then click **OK**.
4. Deselect, then click the **edge of the heart** with the **Direct Selection tool** ▷.

5. Click the **mesh point in the upper-left section of the heart**, as shown in Figure 14, then change the mesh point color to **10% Black**, using the Color panel.

   The new color gradates out from the mesh point.

6. Click the **Mesh tool** 🔲 on the toolbar.
7. Press and hold **[shift]**, then drag the **mesh point** along the mesh path to the left, as shown in Figure 15.

8. Repeat Steps 5–7 for the **mesh point in the upper-right section of the heart**, then deselect so your work resembles Figure 16.
9. Click the **Direct Selection tool** ▷, press and hold **[shift]**, then select the **20 mesh points** and **anchor points** all around the edge of the heart.

TIP Mesh points appear as diamonds and have the same properties as anchor points, with the added capability of accepting color.

Figure 14 Selecting a mesh point

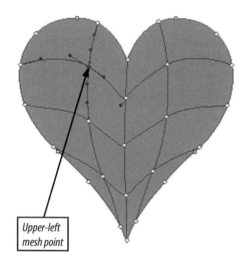

Upper-left mesh point

Figure 15 Mesh points can be moved without changing the shape of the mesh

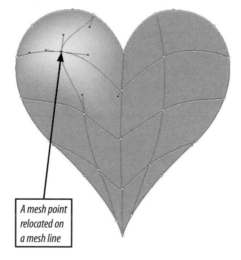

A mesh point relocated on a mesh line

Figure 16 The mesh reconfigured on both sides of the object

10. Apply a **black fill** to the selected mesh points.

The selected anchor points are unaffected. Your work should resemble Figure 17.

11. Deselect, select the **three interior mesh points** in the **lower third of the heart** as shown in Figure 18, then apply a **60% black fill** so your work resembles Figure 18.

12. Select the **mesh point** at the **center of the heart** between the two 10% black highlights.

13. Apply a **60% black fill**, deselect, then compare your work to Figure 19.

14. Save your work, then close the Heart Mesh document.

You applied a gradient mesh to a heart shape, then created highlights by changing the color of two mesh points. Next, you relocated the highlight mesh points without changing the shape of the mesh lines. You then darkened the color of other mesh points to add contrast and dimension to the artwork.

Figure 17 Selecting mesh points

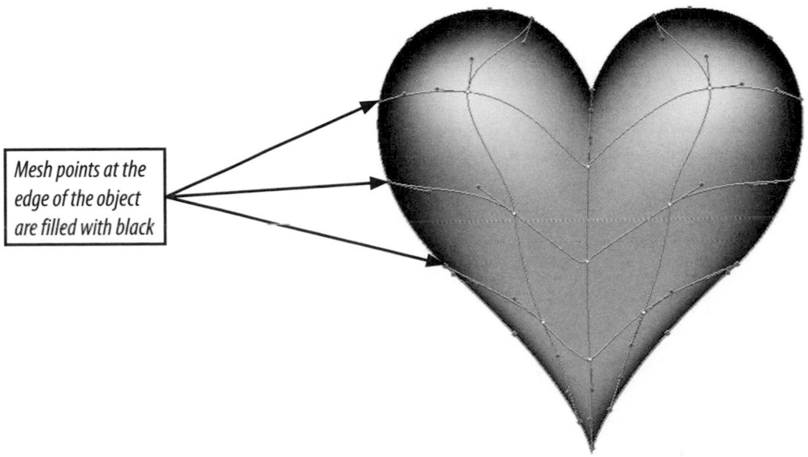

Mesh points at the edge of the object are filled with black

Figure 18 Mesh points are like anchor points with the added functionality of accepting color assignments

Figure 19 Meshes allow you to manipulate gradients precisely

Three interior mesh points, darkened

WORK WITH ENVELOPES

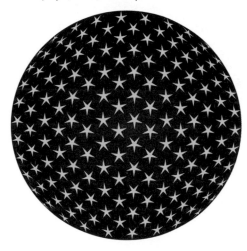

▶ *What You'll Do*

In this lesson, you will create envelope distortions using a top object, a mesh, and a warp.

Understanding Envelopes

Envelopes are objects that are used to distort other selected objects; the distorted objects take on the shape of the envelope object.

Imagine that you have purchased a basketball as a gift, and you want to wrap it in paper with a polka-dot pattern. If these were objects in Illustrator, the basketball would be the envelope object, and the sheet of wrapping paper would be the object to be distorted. Figure 20 is a good example of what an envelope distortion looks like.

You can make envelopes with objects you create, or you can use a preset warp shape or a mesh object as an envelope. You can use envelopes with compound paths, text objects, meshes, and blends. Using envelopes, you can add a lot of life to otherwise dull text. For example, you can create wavy text by applying the Wave or the Flag style in the Warp Options dialog box. Powerful effects can be achieved by applying envelopes to linear gradient fills or pattern fills.

Figure 20 An envelope created using a top object

Objects to be distorted   Object to be used as an envelope   Resulting envelope effect

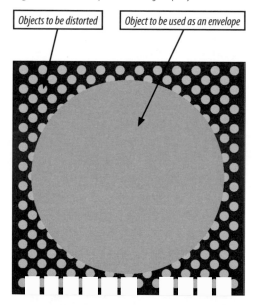
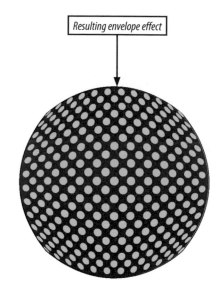

Creating Envelopes with Top Objects, Meshes, and Warps

You create an envelope by using the Envelope Distort command on the Object menu. The Envelope Distort command offers you three options for creating an envelope, which are Make with Warp, Make with Mesh, and Make with Top Object. The top object is the topmost selected object. Warps are simply 15 premade shapes to use as your top object. Warps are especially useful when you don't want to draw your own top object. The envelope in Figure 21 was created using the Flag warp. Meshes are the same as gradient meshes made with the Mesh tool. Creating an envelope with a mesh allows you to apply a mesh to multiple objects, which is not the case when you create a mesh using the Create Gradient Mesh command or the Mesh tool. The envelope in Figure 22 was created using a mesh.

Applying Envelopes to Gradient and Pattern Fills

Envelopes can be used to distort objects that have linear gradient fills or pattern fills, but you must first activate the option to do so. In the Envelope Options dialog box, you can check the Distort Linear Gradients or Distort Pattern Fills check box to apply an envelope to either of the fills. Figure 23 shows the options in the Envelope Options dialog box.

Figure 21 An envelope created using a warp

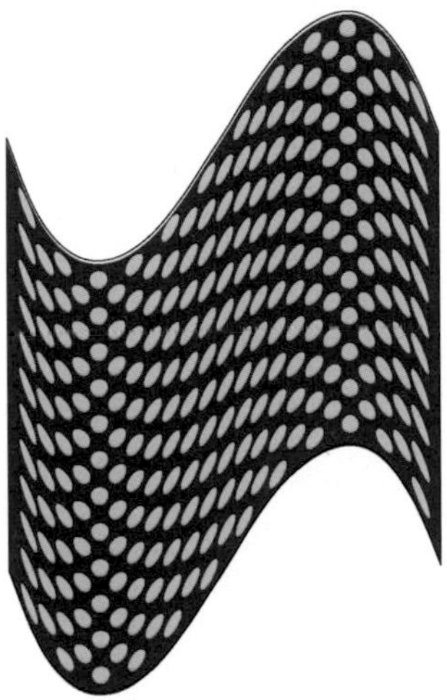

Figure 22 An envelope created using a mesh

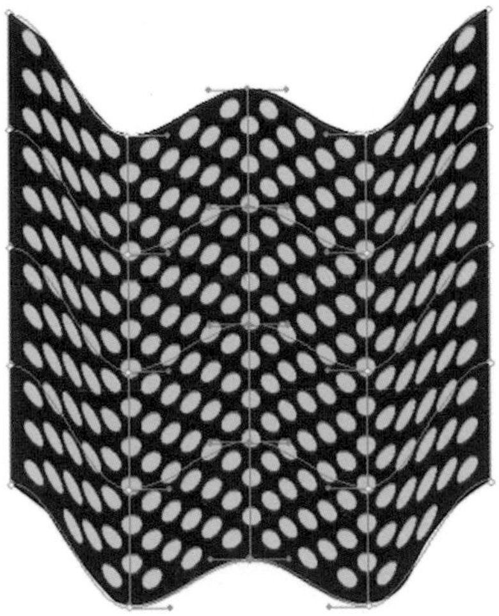

Figure 23 Envelope Options dialog box

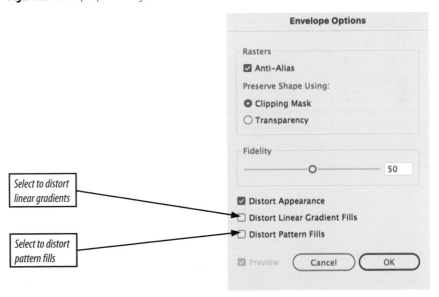

Select to distort linear gradients

Select to distort pattern fills

Create an envelope distortion with a top object

1. Open AI 7-6.ai, then save it as **Envelope Top Object**.

2. Copy the **yellow circle**, paste in front, then hide the copy.

3. Select all, click **Object** on the menu bar, point to **Envelope Distort**, then click **Make with Top Object**.

   Your work should resemble Figure 24.

4. Show all, then fill the **yellow circle** with the **Purple Berry gradient** on the Swatches panel.

5. Send the **circle** to the back so your work resembles Figure 25.

6. Save your work, then close the Envelope Top Object document.

You used a circle as the top object in an envelope distortion. Because you cannot apply a fill to the circle after it has been used to make the envelope, you filled a copy of the circle with a gradient, then positioned it behind the distorted objects to achieve the effect.

Figure 24 A round envelope distorting a flat star pattern

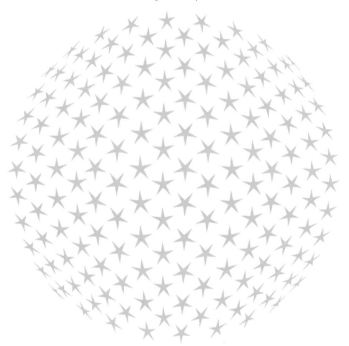

Figure 25 A radial blend enhancing the effect of an envelope distortion

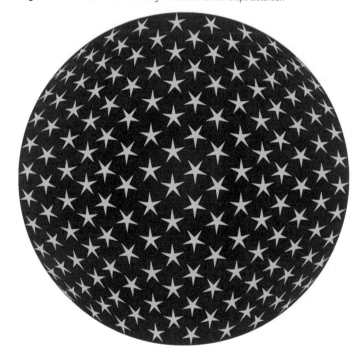

Create an envelope distortion with a mesh

1. Open AI 7-7.ai, then save it as **Envelope Mesh**.

2. Select all, click **Object** on the menu bar, point to **Envelope Distort**, then click **Make with Mesh**.

3. Type **4** in the **Rows text box** and **4** in the **Columns text box**, then click **OK**.

   There are five mesh points on each horizontal line.

4. Deselect, then select the **second and fourth columns of mesh points**, top to bottom, using the **Direct Selection tool** ▷ , as shown in Figure 26.

5. Press and hold **[shift]**, press **[↑]** two times, then release **[shift]**.

   Pressing an arrow key in conjunction with [shift] moves a selected item 10 keyboard increments.

TIP The keyboard increment value can be adjusted in the General Preferences dialog box.

6. Select the **middle column** of mesh points.

7. Press and hold **[shift]**, press **[↓]** two times, deselect, then compare your screen to Figure 27.

8. Save your work, then close the Envelope Mesh document.

You applied an envelope distortion with a mesh to a series of rectangles, then moved the mesh points to create a wave effect.

Figure 26 Select all of the mesh points in the second and fourth columns

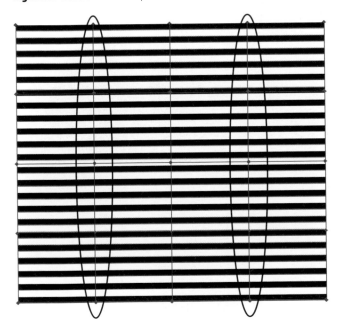

Figure 27 An envelope distortion created using a mesh

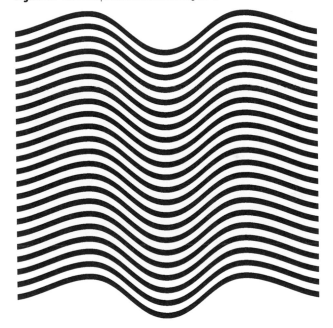

Create an envelope distortion with a warp effect

1. Open AI 7-8.ai, then save it as **Envelope Warp**.

2. Select all, click **Object** on the menu bar, point to **Envelope Distort**, then click **Make with Warp**.

3. Click the **Style list arrow**, click **Fish**, then click **OK**.

   Your screen should resemble Figure 28.

4. Undo the distort, then make **Layer 2** visible.

5. Select all.

USING THE WARP TOOLS

The Warp tool, found on the toolbar, applies a "warp effect" to objects on the artboard. Simply drag the Warp tool over an object and watch it change before your eyes. Objects do not have to be selected before you apply the tool. To adjust the Warp tool settings, double-click the Warp tool to open the Warp Tool Options dialog box. Hiding behind the Warp tool are six more tools offering you interesting ways to distort your text and graphics. As shown in Figure 29, these tools include Twirl, Pucker, Bloat, Scallop, Crystallize, and Wrinkle. Like the Warp tool, each has its own Options dialog box. Residing with the warp tools is the Width tool. The Width tool is used to modify the width of stroked paths and is covered in depth in Chapter 6.

Figure 28 An envelope distortion created using a warp

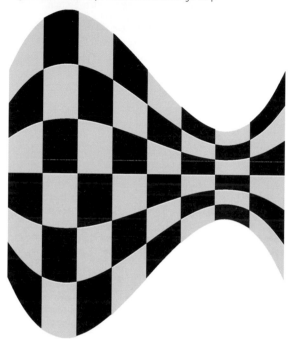

Figure 29 Warp tools panel

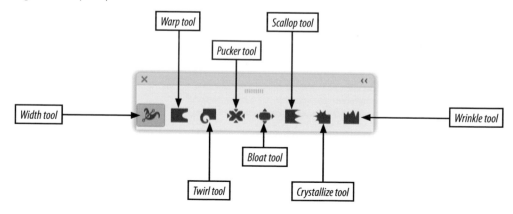

6. Click **Object** on the menu bar, point to **Envelope Distort**, then click **Make with Top Object**.

As shown in Figure 30, you get the same result as you did using the fish-style warp. The reason for this is that using the Envelope Distort feature with a warp is the same as using the feature with a top object. The difference is that warps are premade shapes rather than those you have made on your own.

7. Save your work, then close the Envelope Warp document.

You applied an envelope distortion with a Fish warp effect. You then used an object in the shape of the Fish warp as the top object in a new envelope, with the same result as in the first distortion. Through this comparison, you got a better sense of how Illustrator creates warp effects with envelopes.

Figure 30 An envelope distortion using a premade shape

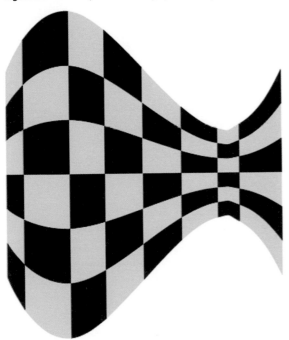

CREATE BLENDS

Defining a Blend

A **blend** is a series of intermediate objects and colors between two or more selected objects. If the selected objects differ in fill color, for example, the intermediate objects will be filled with intermediate colors. Therefore, in a blend, both shapes and colors are "blended." Figure 31 is an example of a blend using shapes and colors.

Blends are created with either the Blend tool or the Make Blend command. You can make blends between two open paths, such as two different lines. You can make blends between two closed paths, such as a square and a star. You can blend between objects filled with gradients. You can even blend between blends, as shown in Figure 32.

Figure 31 In a blend, both shapes and colors are blended

Figure 32 A blend between blends

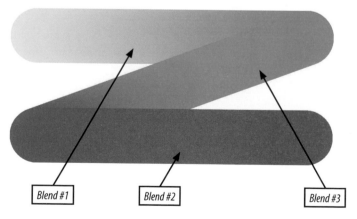

Blend #1   Blend #2   Blend #3

Specifying the Number of Steps in a Blend

The fewer the number of steps in a blend, the more distinct each intermediary object will be. At a greater number of steps, the intermediate objects become indistinguishable from one another, and the blend creates the illusion of being continuous or "smooth."

In the Blend Options dialog box, select from the following options for specifying the number of steps within a blend.

- **Specified Steps**: Enter a value that determines the number of steps between the start and the end of the blend.
- **Specified Distance**: Enter a value to determine the distance between the steps in the blend. The distance is measured from the edge of one object to the corresponding edge on the next object.
- **Smooth Color**: Illustrator determines the number of steps for the blend, calculated to provide the minimum number of steps for a smooth color transition. This is the default option, which poses a bit of a problem in that the minimum number of steps will not always give you the effect you desire, as shown in Figure 33.

Figure 33 Sometimes the Smooth Color option doesn't produce the blend effect you desire

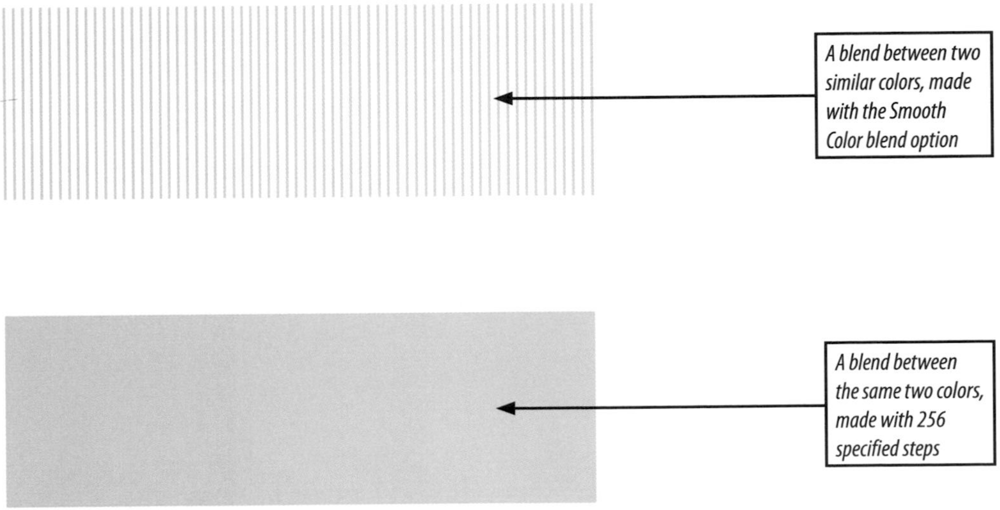

A blend between two similar colors, made with the Smooth Color blend option

A blend between the same two colors, made with 256 specified steps

Manipulating Blends

Once a blend is created, you can change its appearance by making changes to one or more of the original objects. For example, using the Direct Selection tool, you can select one of the original objects and then change its fill color, stroke color, or stroke weight. Illustrator will automatically update the appearance of the steps to reflect newly added attributes, thus changing the appearance of the entire blend. You can also change a blend by transforming one or more of the original objects—for example, by scaling, rotating, or moving them.

You can affect the appearance of a blend by manipulating its spine. When a blend is created, a path is drawn between the starting and ending objects. Illustrator refers to this path as the spine, but it can be manipulated like a path. For example, you can add anchor points to the spine with the Pen tool, then move them with the Direct Selection tool. The blend is updated when you alter the spine.

Figure 34 shows how a blend's spine can be manipulated.

One of the most stunning manipulations of a blend happens when you replace its spine. Draw any path with the Pen tool, then select it along with any blend. Apply the Replace Spine command, and the blend replaces its spine with the new path!

Figure 34 Manipulating the blend's spine changes the arc of the blend

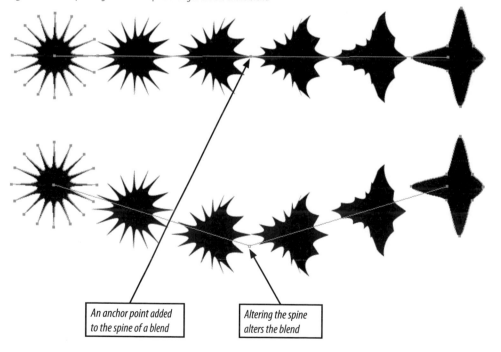

An anchor point added to the spine of a blend

Altering the spine alters the blend

RECORDING STEPS AS A REUSABLE ACTION

An **action** is a series of steps and commands you record and that are stored on the Actions panel. Once recorded, those steps are available to you to use over and over again on other objects or files. For example, let's say your work often calls for you to flatten a file, convert it to CMYK, then save it as an Illustrator EPS. You can record those steps as an action. Then, in the future, rather than step through the process every time, simply execute the action on the Actions panel, and the process will happen automatically. You can even "batch process" an action on multiple files all at once. The Actions panel functions like a tape recorder. Simply click New Action on the Actions panel menu, then click the Record button at the bottom of the panel. The Actions panel records the steps you are making. Once you are done, click the Stop Playing/Recording button. All the steps will be listed on the panel under the name you give to the action. Even after you close the file or quit Illustrator, the action remains and will be available when you start the program again.

Create blends between shapes

1. Open AI 7-9.ai, then save it as **Blend Tutorial**.

2. Double-click the **Blend tool**  to open its dialog box, click the **Spacing list arrow**, choose **Smooth Color**, then click **OK**.

3. Click the **Blend tool** anywhere on the **orange square**, then click anywhere on the **green square**.

   The orange square blends to the green square. You can click the Blend tool on two or more unselected objects to blend them.

4. Click the **Selection tool** , select the **red** and **blue squares**, then double-click the **Blend tool** .

5. Click the **Spacing list arrow**, click **Specified Steps**, type **5** in the **Spacing text box**, then click **OK**.

6. Click **Object** on the menu bar, point to **Blend**, then click **Make**.

   Five intermediary squares are created, as shown in Figure 35.

7. Switch to the **Selection tool** , then deselect all artwork.

8. Click the **Blend tool** , then click from left to right on each of the **three purple shapes**.

9. Keeping the **purple blend selected**, click **Object** on the menu bar, point to **Blend**, then click **Blend Options**.

   TIP You can also access the Blend Options dialog box by double-clicking the Blend tool .

Continued on next page

Figure 35 The red and blue objects blended with five steps

10. Click the **Spacing list arrow**, click **Specified Steps**, type **2** in the **Steps text box**, then click **OK**.

The intermediary steps between the blend objects are reduced to two.

11. Deselect the **purple blend**.

12. Click **View** on the menu bar, then click **Heart**.

13. Double-click the **Blend tool** 🐾, change the **Specified Steps** to **256**, then click **OK**.

14. Click the **heart**, click the **small pink circle** in the center of the heart, then deselect.

The 256 intermediary steps blend the heart to the circle in both color and shape. Your screen should resemble Figure 36.

15. Save your work, then close the Blended Shapes document.

You used the Blend tool to create a smooth blend and evenly distribute shapes between two sets of squares. You created a blend between differing shapes, then used the Blend Options dialog box to change the number of steps in the blend. You also used a smooth blend to add dimension to the heart.

Figure 36 Blends are effective for adding dimension to objects

Create a clockwise color blend

1. Open AI 7-10.ai, then save it as **Clockwise Blend**.

2. Double-click the **Blend tool** , click the **Spacing list arrow**, click **Specified Steps**, type **256** in the **Spacing text box**, then click **OK**.

3. Click the **top of the green line**, then click the **top of the yellow line** to create a blend, as shown in Figure 37.

TIP The Blend tool pointer turns black when it is successfully positioned over an anchor point.

4. Click the **remaining five lines**, ending with the green line, to make five more blends so your work resembles Figure 38.

5. Draw a **circle** over the blend that does not exceed the perimeter of the blend.

6. Select all, click **Object** on the menu bar, point to **Clipping Mask**, then click **Make**.

7. Click the **Selection tool** , deselect, then compare your image to Figure 39.

8. Save your work, then close the Clockwise Blend document.

You created blends among six lines. You specified the number of steps between each pair of paths to be 256, which resulted in a visually uninterrupted blend. You then masked the blend with a circle.

Figure 37 A blend between two open paths

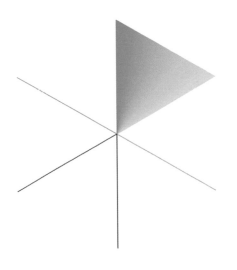

Figure 38 This color effect could not be reproduced with a gradient

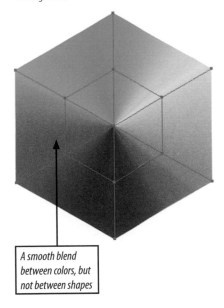

A smooth blend between colors, but not between shapes

Figure 39 The blended paths are masked by a circle

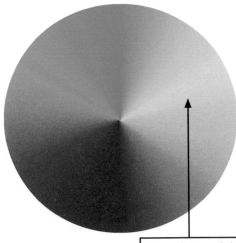

The use of 256 specified steps improves the appearance of the blend

Edit blends

1. Open AI 7-11.ai, then save it as **Blends on a Path**.

2. Click **Select** on the menu bar, then click **All** to select the blended objects and the path.

3. Click **Object** on the menu bar, point to **Blend**, click **Replace Spine**, then deselect.

   The curved path becomes the new spine for the blend, as shown in Figure 40.

4. Save your work, then close the Blends on a Path document.

You replaced the spine of a blend with a curved path.

Figure 40 Blends can be applied to paths

Create color effects with blends

1. Open AI 7-12.ai, then save it as **Chrome**.

2. Double-click the **Blend tool** , set the number of **Specified Steps** to **256**, then click **OK**.

3. Switch to **Outline mode**, click the **Selection tool** , then select the **five paths** at the bottom of the artboard.

   Two of the paths are stroked with white and cannot be seen in Preview mode.

4. Switch to **Preview mode**; click the **Blend tool** ; then, starting from the bottom of the artboard, create a **blend between each pair of paths** so your work resembles Figure 41.

5. Position the **text in front of the blend**.

6. Keeping the text selected, click **Object** on the menu bar, point to **Compound Path**, then click **Make**.

7. Select all, click **Object** on the menu bar, point to **Clipping Mask**, then click **Make**.

8. Deselect all, click **Select** on the menu bar, point to **Object**, then click **Clipping Masks**.

9. Apply a **2 pt. black stroke** to the mask.

10. Deselect, save your work, compare your screen to Figure 42, then close the Chrome document.

You selected five paths with the Blend tool, created a blend between each pair of paths, positioned text in front of the blend, then made a compound path. You selected all, made a clipping mask, then applied a 2 pt. black stroke to the mask.

Figure 41 A simple blend between open paths

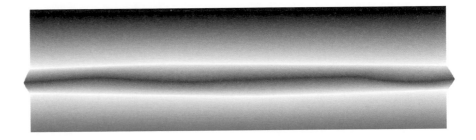

Figure 42 Chrome letters created with a blend and a mask

Create concentric blends

1. Open AI 7-13.ai, then save it as **Concentric Blends**.

2. Double-click the **Blend tool** on the toolbar, then type **10** in the **Specified Steps text box**.

3. Select **both circles** with the **Selection tool**.

4. Click the **Blend tool**, click the **top anchor point of the large circle**, then click the **top anchor point of the small circle**.

   A blend of concentric circles is created.

5. Change the **fill color** to **[None]**, then click the **artboard** to deselect all.

6. Click the **Direct Selection tool**, click the **edge of the small center circle** to show its anchor points, then click the **center anchor point** to select the entire small circle.

7. Drag the **small circle** left, halfway to the edge of the larger circle.

   Your blend should resemble Figure 43.

   TIP In the figure, the small circle is not shown as selected.

8. Drag the **small circle** to the upper-right corner.

   Your blend should resemble Figure 44.

9. Drag the **small circle** so its bottom edge is aligned with the bottom edge of the large circle.

   Your blend should resemble Figure 45.

10. Save your work, then continue to the next set of steps.

You blended two circles to create concentric circles. You then explored various blends by moving the small circle. Because you set the circles to have no fill, the blends produced dramatic geometric patterns.

Figure 43 First concentric blend

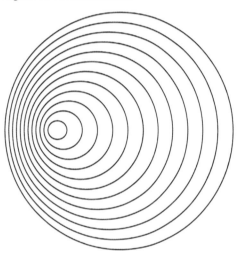

Figure 44 Second concentric blend

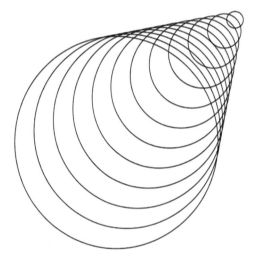

Figure 45 Third concentric blend

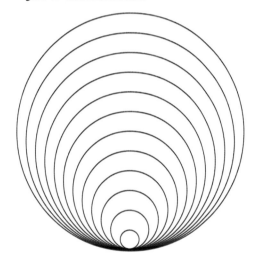

Expand and colorize blends

1. Drag the **small circle** straight up so it is close to the top edge of the artboard.

2. Click **View** on the menu bar, then click **Outline**.

   The blended circles disappear because they don't exist. The intermediary objects in blends are only virtual.

3. Click **Object** on the menu bar, then click **Expand**.

   The Expand dialog box appears.

4. In the **Expand dialog box**, make sure that only the **Object check box** is checked, then click **OK**.

   As shown in Figure 46, the intermediary objects are realized, and every circle is selected.

5. Switch to **Preview mode**.

6. Show the **Pathfinder panel**, then click the **Divide button** 🔳 .

7. Click **Object** on the menu bar, then click **Ungroup**.

8. Fill different objects with different fills.

   Figure 47 shows one example.

9. Save your work, then close the Concentric Blends file.

You expanded the blend to convert the intermediary objects from virtual to actual. You applied the Divide pathfinder, then colorized the artwork.

Figure 46 Expanded blend in Outline mode

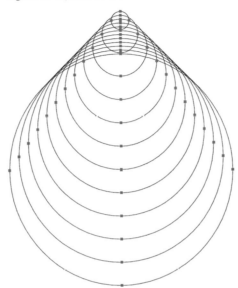

Figure 47 Divided and colorized artwork

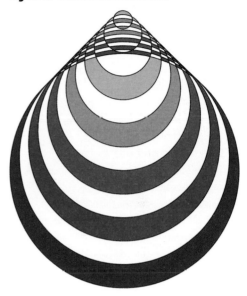

SKILLS REVIEW

Edit colors and distort objects

1. Create a new 6" × 6" CMYK Color document, then save it as **Distort Skills**.
2. Create a 4" circle with a yellow fill and no stroke.
3. Apply the Add Anchor Points command.
4. Apply the Bloat effect at 35%.
5. Apply the Twist effect at 50°.
6. Use the Scale Tool Options dialog box to make a 50% copy of the object.
7. Apply the Transform Again command twice.
8. With the top object still selected, fill it with a dark shade of blue.
9. Select all, then use the Edit Colors command to blend the objects from front to back.
10. Save your work, deselect, compare your illustration with Figure 48, then close the document.

Work with gradient meshes

1. Open AI 7-14.ai, then save it as **Mesh Skills**.
2. Select the yellow hexagon.
3. Apply the Create Gradient Mesh command with four rows and four columns.
4. Click the Direct Selection tool, deselect the hexagon, then click the edge of it.
5. Select the top row of mesh points, then click orange on the Swatches panel.

TIP Click and drag the Direct Selection tool on the artboard to create a selection box that includes the top row of mesh points.

6. Select the middle row of mesh points, then click red on the Swatches panel.

Figure 48 Completed Skills Review, Part I

7. Select the four mesh patches at the bottom of the hexagon, then click a shade of orange on the Swatches panel.

TIP Select each mesh patch one at a time.

8. Select the five mesh points at the bottom of the hexagon, then click a shade of red on the Swatches panel.

9. Save your work, deselect, then compare your mesh object with Figure 49.

10. Close the Mesh Skills document.

Work with envelopes

1. Open AI 7-15.ai, then save it as **Envelope Skills**.

2. Click Object on the menu bar, point to Envelope Distort, then click Envelope Options.

3. Verify that there is a check mark in the Distort Pattern Fills check box and in the Distort Appearance check box, then click OK.

4. Position a triangle in front of the square with the pattern fill.

TIP Click the Polygon tool, click the artboard, type **3** in the Sides text box, then click OK.

5. Scale the triangle so it covers most of the square behind it.

6. Select all, click Object on the menu bar, point to Envelope Distort, then click Make with Top Object.

7. Enlarge the size of the illustration if you like.

8. Save your work, deselect, compare your illustration to Figure 50, then close the Envelope Skills document.

Figure 49 Completed Skills Review, Part 2

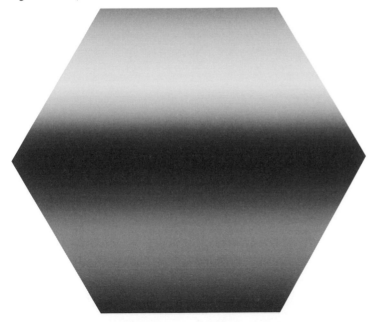

Figure 50 Completed Skills Review, Part 3

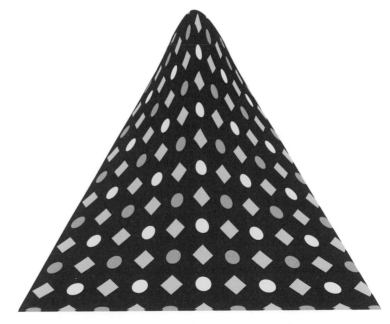

Create blends

1. Open AI 7-16.ai, then save it as **Star**.
2. Create a 15% copy of the star.
3. Fill the copy with White.
4. Double-click the Blend tool, then set the Specified Steps value to 256.
5. Blend the two stars.
6. Save your work, deselect, then compare your illustration to Figure 51.
7. Close the Star document.

Figure 51 Completed Skills Review, Part 4

The owner of Tidal Wave Publishing hires your design firm to redesign their logo. She shows you her original logo, which is a meticulous line drawing of a wave. She explains that the line drawing has been the firm's logo for more than 25 years, and she feels it's time for something more contemporary that has movement.

1. Create a new 6" × 6" document, then save it as **Tidal Wave**.
2. Create an ellipse that is 2.5" wide and 2.25" tall, then fill it with any color and no stroke.
3. Apply the Add Anchor Points command two times.
4. Apply the Pucker & Bloat effect at −80%.
5. Apply the Twist effect at 300°.
6. Deselect, save your work, see Figure 52 for one possible solution, then close the Tidal Wave document.

Figure 52 Completed Project Builder 1

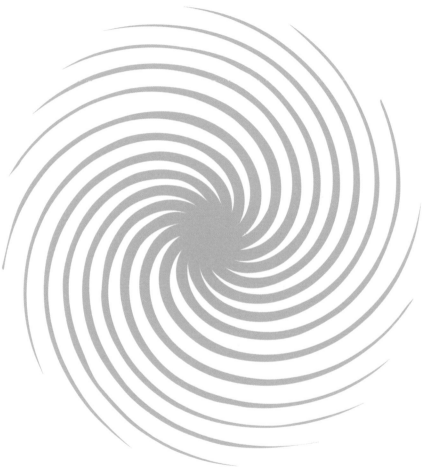

Miltie Berger, a famous journalist, commissions your design firm to create a logo for her new column. She explains that it will be a gossip column titled "Poison Pen."

1. Open AI 7-17.ai, then save it as **Poison Pen**.
2. Double-click the Blend tool, set the number of Specified Steps to 40, then click anywhere on the two white objects on the right side of the artboard to blend them.

TIP They do not need to be selected first.

3. Deselect, then click the Direct Selection tool.
4. Select only the bottom object of the blend, then change its fill color to Black and its stroke color to White.

TIP Refer to this new object as the "feather" blend.

5. Click the Selection tool, select the very narrow white curved stroke at the center of the artboard, copy it, paste in front, then hide the copy.
6. Select the white stroke again, click Object on the menu bar, point to Path, then click Outline Stroke.
7. Deselect all, double-click the Blend tool, change the number of steps to 256, then click OK.
8. Blend the white outlined stroke with the pointy black quill shape that is behind it.
9. Lock the new blend, then show all.
   The hidden white stroke appears and is selected.
10. Click the Selection tool, press and hold [shift], then click the "feather" blend to add it to the selection.
11. Click Object on the menu bar, point to Blend, then click Replace Spine.
12. Save your work, compare your illustration with Figure 53, then close the Poison Pen document.

Figure 53 Completed Project Builder 2

DESIGN PROJECT

You create graphics for a video game company. Your assignment for the morning is to create an illustration for a steel cup that will be used to store magical objects in a game.

1. Open AI 7-18.ai, then save it as **Steel Cup**.
2. Select the gray object, then apply the Create Gradient Mesh command using seven rows and three columns.
3. Deselect, then click the edge of the mesh object with the Direct Selection tool.
4. Press and hold [shift], then select the four mesh points shown in Figure 54.
5. Click the Color panel menu button, then click Grayscale if necessary.
6. Make sure the fill button is active on the toolbar, then drag the K slider on the Color panel to 15% to lighten the selected mesh points.
7. Select the top-right mesh patch and darken it, using the Color panel.
8. Select the mesh points along the left edge and the bottom edge of the "steel cup," then click Black.
9. Lock the gradient mesh object.
10. Click the edge of the black object with the Direct Selection tool, then select the five horizontal mesh points in the second row from the top.
11. Fill the mesh points with White.
12. Deselect, then unlock all.
13. Save your work, compare your steel cup with Figure 55, then close the Steel Cup document.

Figure 54 Click the mesh points indicated by the red ellipse

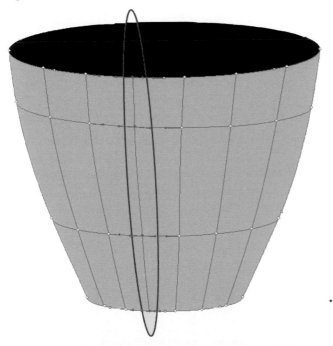

Figure 55 Completed Design Project

CHAPTER 8

WORKING WITH TRANSPARENCY, EFFECTS, AND GRAPHIC STYLES

1. Use the Transparency Panel and the Color Picker

2. Apply Effects

3. Use the Appearance Panel

4. Work with Graphic Styles

5. Use Opacity Masks

6. Recolor Artwork

Adobe Certified Professional in Graphic Design and Illustration Using Adobe Illustrator

1. Working in the Design Industry

This objective covers critical concepts related to working with colleagues and clients, as well as crucial legal, technical, and design-related knowledge.

1.4 **Demonstrate knowledge of key terminology related to digital graphics.**

    B   Demonstrate knowledge of how color is created in digital graphics.

2. Project Setup and Interface

This objective covers the interface setup and program settings that assist in an efficient and effective workflow, as well as knowledge about ingesting digital assets for a project.

2.3 **Use nonprinting design tools in the interface to aid in design or workflow.**

    D   Use views and modes to work efficiently with vector graphics.

2.5 **Manage colors, swatches, and gradients.**

    A   Set the active fill and stroke color.

    C   Create, manage, and edit swatches and swatch libraries.

    D   Use the Color Guide panel to select coordinated colors.

2.6 **Manage preset brushes, symbols, styles, and patterns.**

    B   Edit brushes, symbols, styles, and patterns.

3. Organize Documents

This objective covers document structure, such as layers and tracks, for efficient workflows.

3.2 **Modify layer visibility using opacity and masks.**

    A   Adjust the opacity of a layer.

4. Creating and Modifying Visual Elements

This objective covers core tools and functionality of the application, as well as tools that affect the visual appearance of document elements.

4.3 **Make, manage, and manipulate selections.**

    C   Group or ungroup selections.

4.5 **Use basic reconstructing and editing techniques to manipulate digital graphics and media.**

    C   Evaluate or adjust the appearance of objects, selections, or layers.

4.6 **Modify the appearance of design elements using effects and graphic styles.**

    A   Use effects to modify images.

    B   Create, edit, and save Graphic Styles.

    C   Expand the appearance of objects.

USE THE TRANSPARENCY PANEL AND THE COLOR PICKER

▶ **What You'll Do**

In this lesson, you will use the Transparency panel to change the opacity and blending modes of objects, and you will use the Color Picker to specify a new fill color.

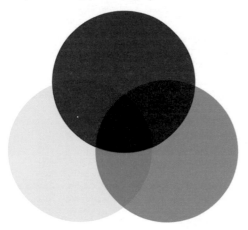

Understanding Opacity

The term "opacity" is a derivative of the word *opaque*. **Opacity** describes an object that is not transparent or translucent but, rather, impenetrable. Simply put—you cannot see through it. By default, objects in Illustrator are created with 100% opacity; they are opaque. Whenever one object overlaps another on the artboard, the top object hides all or part of the object behind it. If you were drawing a face behind a veil, clouds in a blue sky, or fish in a tinted goldfish bowl, having the ability to change the opacity of objects is critical to creating the illustration.

Figure 1 shows an example of opacity. The rectangle is set to 50% opacity, so the text behind it is visible *through* the rectangle.

Working with the Transparency Panel

The Transparency panel allows you to control the degree to which an object is transparent. You can change the opacity amount by dragging the Opacity slider in the panel. The Opacity slider works with percentages, with 100% being completely opaque and 0% being completely transparent, or invisible.

Working with Blending Modes

Blending modes are preset filters on the Transparency panel that vary the way the colors of objects blend with the colors of underlying objects when they overlap. You cannot determine the amount or intensity of a blending mode, but only choose whether or not to apply one. Thus, you will find yourself working with

Figure 1 Reducing opacity causes objects to appear translucent

Rectangle fill at 50% opacity

blending modes by trial and error, but it's fun experimenting with them. Apply a blending mode and if you like it, keep it. If not, try another.

Of all the blending modes, the most essential is Multiply. The Multiply blending mode makes the top object transparent and blends the colors of the overlapping objects in an effect that looks just like overlapping magic markers. Objects that overlap black become black, objects that overlap white retain their original color, and, as with magic markers, objects with color darken when they overlap other colors.

Imagine you spilled pink lemonade on a black, yellow, and blue tiled floor. You would see the tiled floor through the pink lemonade, but where the lemonade was spilled, you'd see different colors. Figure 2 presents that image using Illustrator objects. The pink object remains pink where it overlaps white, and it appears black where it overlaps the black tiles. Any color multiplied with black produces a black result. Where the pink overlaps yellow, the resulting color is orange. The resulting color is purple where the pink overlaps blue.

The Multiply blending mode is one of Illustrator's essential features for producing transparency effects. Don't forget it's there!

Working with the Color Picker

You use the Color Picker to specify new colors to be used as fills, strokes, or parts of effects, such as drop shadows. The easiest way to access the Color Picker is to double-click the fill or stroke button on the toolbar.

Figure 2 Multiply blending mode mimics the effect of overlapping transparent colors, like overlapping magic markers

In addition to choosing new colors, the Color Picker offers a valuable opportunity for studying the most fundamental color model, **HSB**, or Hue, Saturation, and Brightness.

The **hue** is the color itself. Blue, red, orange, and green are all hues. The Color Picker identifies hues based on the concept of a color wheel. Because there are 360 degrees to a circle, the hues on the color wheel are numbered 0–360. This is why you see a small degree symbol beside the H (hue) text box in the Color Picker dialog box. The color wheel is represented in the Color Picker by the vertical color slider. Move the triangles along the color slider and watch the number in the H (hue) text box change to identify the corresponding hue on the color slider.

Does this mean only 360 colors can be specified in the Color Picker? No, because each hue is modified by its saturation and brightness value.

Saturation refers to the intensity of the hue. A comparison of the colors of a tomato and a cranberry would be a fine illustration of different saturation values. Both have hues that fall within a "red" range. However, the tomato's red is far more intense, or saturated. In the Color Picker, 100% is the highest degree of saturation. A saturation value of 0% means there is no hue, only a shade of gray. A black and white photo, for example, has no saturation value.

The reds of the tomato and cranberry also differ in **brightness**, the degree of lightness of a color. The tricky thing about understanding the brightness component of the HSB color model is that the term "brightness" is so common it's difficult to know how it applies specifically to colors. A good example is a room with no windows filled with furniture and artwork. If you flood the room with light, all the colors of the objects in the room will appear at their most vivid. If you have only a single, dim light source (like a flickering candle), the colors will appear less vivid, and many hues will be indistinguishable from others. If there is no light source whatsoever, no colors would appear because in the absence of light there is no color.

In the Color Picker, 100% is the highest degree of brightness. A brightness of 0% is always black, regardless of the hue or saturation value specified. Thus, 100% saturation and 100% brightness produce a "pure" hue. Any

Figure 3 Color Picker dialog box

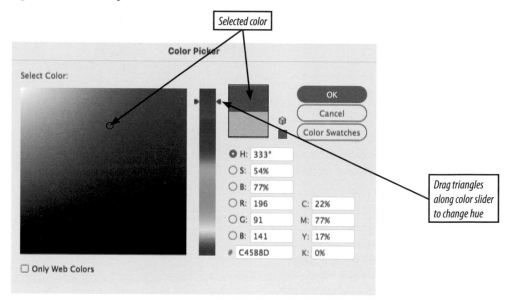

lesser amount of saturation or brightness is a degradation of the hue.

The Color Picker, shown in Figure 3, is made up of a large color field. The color field represents the current hue and all its variations of saturation and brightness. By dragging the circle around in the color field, you can sample different saturation and brightness values of the selected hue. Saturation values lie on the horizontal axis; as you move the circle left to right, the saturation of the color increases from 0 to 100%. Note that the colors along the left edge of the color field are only shades of gray. This is because the colors along the left edge have 0% saturation.

Brightness values lie on the vertical axis. All the colors at the bottom of the field are black (0% brightness). The color's brightness increases as you move up. Thus, the pure hue (100% saturation and 100% brightness) is at the top-right corner of the field.

For a hands-on example of these essential color concepts, you can drag the circle cursor around the color field. As the sampled color changes, you'll see the H (hue) number remains constant while the S (saturation) and B (brightness) numbers change. You can change the hue by dragging the triangles along the color slider.

Change the opacity and blending mode of objects

1. Open AI 8-1.ai, then save it as **Transparency**.

2. Click **Window** on the menu bar, then click **Transparency**.

3. Select both the **magenta circle** and the **letter** *T*.

   The selection appears on the Transparency panel.

4. On the Transparency panel, click the **Opacity list arrow**, then drag the **slider** to **50%**.

5. Select the **cyan and yellow circles**, click the **Opacity list arrow**, then drag the **slider** to **50%** so your screen resembles Figure 4.

6. Select the *T* and the **three circles**, then change the opacity to **100%**.

7. On the Transparency panel, click the **Blending Mode list arrow**, click **Multiply**, then deselect all so your screen resembles Figure 5.

8. Save your work, then close the Transparency document.

You changed the opacity of objects and applied the Multiply blending mode to overlapping objects.

Figure 4 The three circles and letter *T* at 50% opacity

Figure 5 The Multiply blending mode effect on overlapping objects

Use the Color Picker

1. Open AI 8-2.ai, then save it as **Comic Book Blast**.

2. Click **File** on the menu bar, point to **Document Color Mode**, then verify that **RGB Color** is checked.

3. Double-click the **fill button** on the toolbar to open the Color Picker.

4. Type **94** in the **H text box**, then press **[tab]**.

5. Type **64** in the **S text box**, then press **[tab]**.

6. Type **74** in the **B text box**, then press **[tab]**.

   The color circle identifies the new fill color, as shown in Figure 6.

7. Click **OK**, add the new color to the Swatches panel, then name it **POW Green**.

8. Double-click the **fill button** on the toolbar to open the Color Picker.

9. Type **239** in the **R text box**, type **76** in the **G text box**, type **35** in the **B text box**, then click **OK**.

10. Add the **new color** to the Swatches panel, then name it **POW Orange**.

11. Save your work, then continue to the next lesson.

You used the Color Picker to create new fill colors. You entered specific values for hue, saturation, and brightness and entered specific values for red, green, and blue. You then added the new colors to the Swatches panel.

Figure 6 Using HSB to specify color in the Color Picker

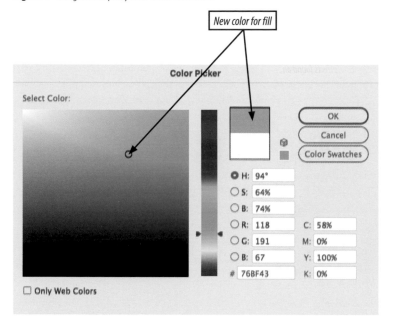

APPLY EFFECTS

▶ *What You'll Do*

In this lesson, you will work with a series of effects found on the Effect menu.

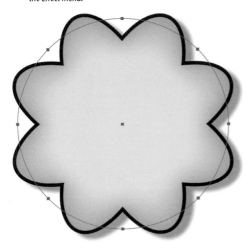

Working with Effects

The commands listed on the Effect menu can be applied to objects to alter their appearance without altering the objects themselves. You can apply effects, such as distort, transform, outline, and offset, without changing the original size, anchor points, and shape of the object. The object in Figure 7 is a simple square with some effects applied to it, creating the appearance of a complex illustration.

Figure 7 One square with multiple effects applied

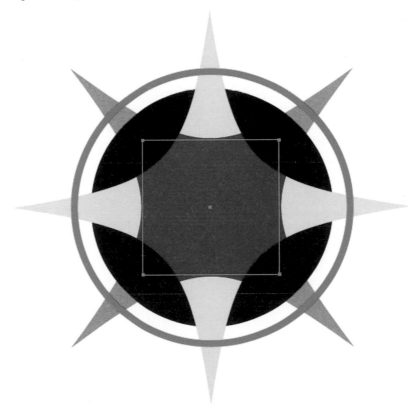

So what is the point of working with effects? The best answer is that working with effects offers you the ability to change your mind and change your work at any point because each effect can be easily edited or removed from an object without disturbing other effects that may be applied to it.

When you work with effects, all your actions are recorded and listed on the Appearance panel. You can, at any time, select an effect on the panel and modify its settings or delete it.

Another great benefit of working with effects is that the Appearance panel provides a record of what you've done to create an illustration.

Apply a Bloat effect

1. Click **Window** on the menu bar, then click **Appearance**.

2. Click the **Selection tool** ▶, select the **POW type**, then hide it.

3. Select the **blue circle**.

   The object is listed on the Appearance panel as Path. Its fill color and stroke color are also listed.

4. Double-click the **Stroke color icon** on the Appearance panel and change it to **12 pt. Black**.

5. Double-click the **Fill color icon** on the Appearance panel, then change the **fill color** to **POW Green**.

6. Click the **artboard** to deselect all, then click the **interior of the green circle** to select it.

7. Click the word **Path** on the Appearance panel.

8. Click the **Add New Effect button** *fx.* on the Appearance panel, point to **Distort & Transform**

in the Illustrator Effects section, then click **Pucker & Bloat**.

9. Type **19** in the text box, then click **OK**.

   The Pucker & Bloat item is listed on the Appearance panel. Even though the appearance of the object changes, the selection marks remain that of a circle, reflecting the fact that the original object has not actually been changed by the effect.

10. Click **Object** on the menu bar, point to **Path**, then click **Add Anchor Points**.

    As shown in Figure 8, the Bloat effect is updated to incorporate the change to the path. The

Add Anchor Points effect is not listed on the Appearance panel because it is not an effect. The Add Anchor Points command was applied directly to the path.

11. On the Appearance panel, hide and show the **Pucker & Bloat effect**.

12. When you are done, leave the **Pucker & Bloat effect** showing.

13. Save your work, then continue to the next set of steps.

You used the Appearance panel to apply a fill and a stroke to an object. You applied a Pucker & Bloat effect to the same object. You added anchor points to the path and then hid and showed the Pucker & Bloat effect on the Appearance panel.

Figure 8 Effect updates when anchor points are added

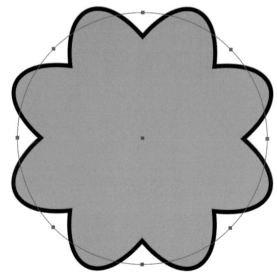

Apply an Inner Glow and a Drop Shadow effect

1. Target the word **Path** on the Appearance panel.

2. Click the **Add New Effect button** *fx.* on the Appearance panel, point to **Stylize** in the Illustrator Effects section, then click **Inner Glow**.

3. Enter the settings shown in Figure 9.

   Note that the color for the glow is set to white.

4. Click **OK**, then compare your results to Figure 10.

   Overlay is a lighten/darken blending mode. Choosing a white color for the glow causes the green fill color to be lightened. Had you chosen black, the green fill color would have been darkened.

5. Hide and show the **Inner Glow effect** on the Appearance panel.

6. When you are done hiding and showing the effect, keep the **Inner Glow effect** showing.

Continued on next page

Figure 9 Settings for Inner Glow

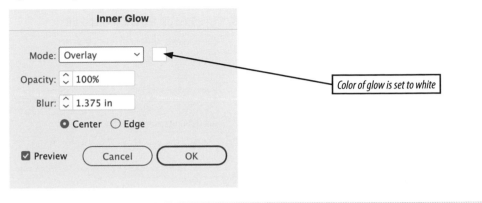

Color of glow is set to white

Figure 10 Inner Glow effect applied

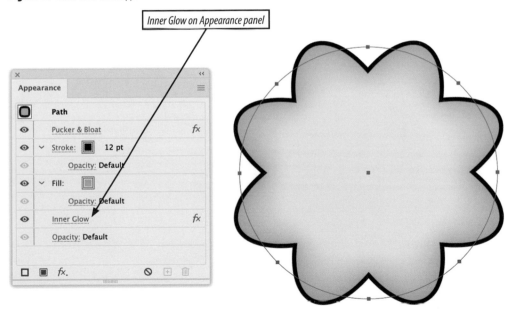

Inner Glow on Appearance panel

7. Click **Effect** on the menu bar, point to **Stylize** in the Illustrator Effects section, then click **Drop Shadow**.

8. Enter the settings shown in Figure 11.

9. Click **OK**, then compare your results to Figure 12.

   Drop Shadow is listed below Inner Glow on the Appearance panel.

10. Save your work, then continue to the next set of steps.

You applied an Inner Glow effect and a Drop Shadow effect to the artwork.

Figure 11 Settings for the Drop Shadow effect

Figure 12 Drop Shadow effect applied

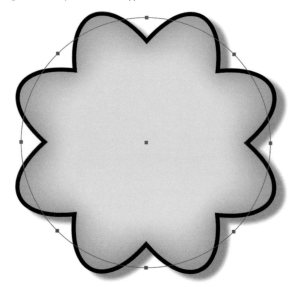

Apply a Transform effect

1. Click the word **Path** on the Appearance panel.

The hierarchy of effects on the Appearance panel can affect the artwork. For that reason, it's always a good idea to click the word Path when applying a new effect.

2. Click the **Add New Effect button** *fx.* on the Appearance panel, point to **Distort &** **Transform** in the Illustrator Effects section, then click **Transform**.

3. Enter the settings shown in Figure 13.

4. Click **OK**.

5. Click **Object** on the menu bar, then click **Show All**.

The hidden text appears and is selected.

6. Click **Edit** on the menu bar, click **Copy**, click **Edit** on the menu bar, then click **Paste in Front**.

7. Fill the **new text** with **POW Orange**.

8. Press and hold **[shift]**, press the **left arrow** on your keypad two times, then press the **up arrow** one time.

Your artwork should resemble Figure 14.

9. Save your work, then continue to the next set of steps.

You applied a Transform effect. You then duplicated and offset text.

Figure 13 Settings for Transform effect

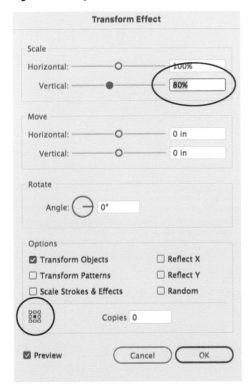

Figure 14 The transformed object behind the text

Apply an effect to text

1. Copy the **orange text**, click **Edit** on the menu bar, then click **Paste in Front**.

2. Click the **Add New Effect button** _fx._ on the Appearance panel, point to **Pixelate** in the Photoshop Effects section, then click **Color Halftone.**

3. Type **100** in the **Max. Radius text box**, then click **OK**.

4. On the Transparency panel, set the **blending mode** to **Overlay**.

5. Click **Edit** on the menu bar, then click **Paste in Front**.

   The orange text is pasted above the overlayed text.

6. Change the **fill color** to **[None]**, then apply a **12 pt. black stroke**.

   At this stage, the green bubble artwork is slightly too wide behind the text and needs to be transformed.

7. Click the **green bubble artwork** to select it.

8. Click the **Add New Effect button** _fx._ on the Appearance panel, point to **Distort & Transform**, then click **Transform**.

   The dialog box shown in Figure 15 appears. Because a Transform effect has already been applied, Illustrator is asking if you want to modify that first effect or if you want to apply a second instance of the effect.

9. Click **Apply New Effect**.

10. In the Transform Effect dialog box, enter the settings shown in Figure 16, then click **OK**.

    Your artwork should resemble Figure 17.

Figure 15 Info dialog box offering the option to apply a second instance of an effect

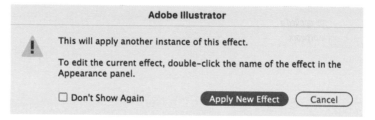

Figure 16 Transform Effect dialog box

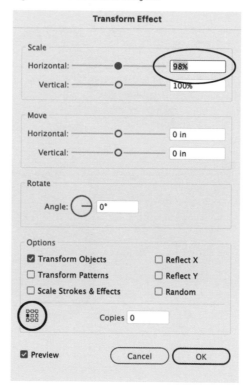

11. Save your work, then close the Comic Book Blast document.

You applied a Color Halftone effect to type, then you applied a second Transform effect to tweak the green bubble artwork.

Figure 17 Text with a Color Halftone effect overlayed

USE THE APPEARANCE PANEL

What You'll Do

In this lesson, you will explore the role of the Appearance panel in controlling the appearance attributes of objects.

Working with the Appearance Panel

The Appearance panel does far more than simply list appearance attributes. It is the gateway for controlling and manipulating all the appearance attributes of your artwork. The Appearance panel lists the fills, strokes, and effects that you have applied to artwork and offers you the ability to manipulate those attributes.

When you select an object on the artboard, the Appearance panel lists the associated attributes. Fills and strokes are listed according to their stacking order (front to back), and effects are listed in the order in which they are applied. You can double-click an effect on the Appearance panel to open the effect's dialog box, which will show the settings you used to apply the effect. This is an extremely valuable function of the panel. Imagine opening an illustration after six months and trying to remember how you built it! The Appearance panel provides all the information.

When you have applied a set of effects to an object and you then draw a new object, you can use the Appearance panel to decide whether you want the new object to be created with the effects with which you've been working. The Appearance panel has a setting called New Art

Has Basic Appearance. By default, this setting is checked and active. When it's active, any new object you create will have a "basic appearance," which means it will be a normal Illustrator object, with a simple fill and stroke but with no effects pre-applied.

If you remove the check mark next to New Art Has Basic Appearance, any new objects you create will "inherit" the effects you've applied to previous objects.

Removing Effects

To remove all appearances from an object, including the fill and stroke, click the Clear Appearance button on the Appearance panel. The object will take on the current fill and stroke colors on the toolbar.

If you want to remove effects but keep an object's current fill and stroke, choose the Reduce to Basic Appearance command on the Appearance panel menu.

Changing the Order of Appearance Attributes

You can change the order of attributes on the Appearance panel simply by dragging them up or down. The hierarchy of attributes might directly affect the appearance of the artwork.

Expanding Artwork with Effects

Once you've created artwork with effects, you might want to modify objects directly rather than modify them as effects. To do so, click Expand Appearance on the Object menu. Depending on the complexity of the artwork and the number of effects applied, Illustrator will create one or more objects to render the artwork as selectable objects.

Modify effects

1. Open AI 8-3.ai, then save it as **Comic Book Blast Expanded**.

2. Select the **green bubble artwork**.

3. On the Appearance panel, click the words **Drop Shadow**.

   The Drop Shadow dialog box opens.

4. Change the **Opacity** to **50%**.

5. Make the **X Offset value** negative by putting a **minus sign** in front of it.

6. Change the **Y Offset value** to **.375**, then click **OK**.

   Your artwork should resemble Figure 18.

7. Save your work, then continue to the next set of steps.

You modified the Drop Shadow effect on the artwork.

Figure 18 Modifying the Drop Shadow effect

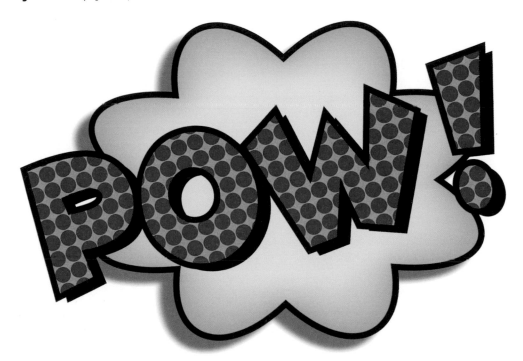

Expand effects

1. Select the **green bubble artwork**.

2. Click **Object** on the menu bar, then click **Expand Appearance**.

   Nothing appears to change, but the artwork is now composed of selectable objects and one bitmap image. Because it has a soft edge, the drop shadow is created with a bitmap image. All the components are grouped.

3. Click the **canvas** to deselect the artwork.

4. Click the **Direct Selection tool** 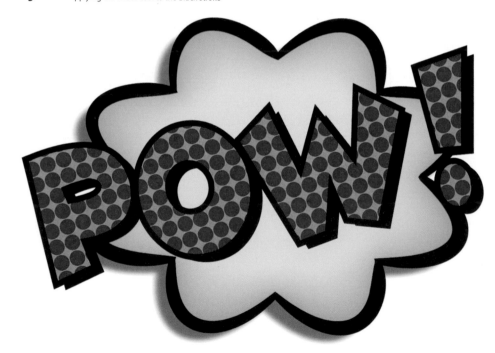, then click the **green bubble artwork**.

   The toolbar shows a white fill with no stroke; the Inner Glow artwork is selected.

5. Click **Object** on the menu bar, point to **Lock**, then click **Selection** to lock the selected Inner Glow artwork.

6. Click the **green artwork** again with the **Direct Selection tool**.

   The toolbar shows a green fill with no stroke; the green fill is selected.

7. Lock this selection, then click the **green artwork** again.

   The selection marks show a rectangle. The image of the bitmap drop shadow is selected.

8. Lock the selection.

9. Click the **black stroke on the green object** with the **Direct Selection tool**.

The toolbar shows a white stroke. This is an unexpected object created when the artwork was expanded.

10. Lock the selection.

11. Click the **black stroke on the green object** again.

    The toolbar shows a black stroke. The black stroke is selected.

12. Use the **Width tool** to enhance the black stroke.

Figure 19 shows an example of applying the Width tool to the black stroke.

13. Enhance the artwork in any way you wish using the skills you have learned so far.

    Figure 20 shows an example.

14. Save your work, then close the Comic Book Blast Expanded document.

You used the Expand Appearance command to make the artwork into selectable objects. You then used the Width tool to enhance the black stroke on the green bubble artwork.

Figure 19 Applying the Width tool to the black stroke

Figure 20 Final enhanced artwork

WORK WITH GRAPHIC STYLES

▶ *What You'll Do*

In this lesson, you will create and apply graphic styles.

Creating and Applying Graphic Styles

Working with various fills, strokes, gradients, and effects, you will eventually develop looks and appearances you will want to use repeatedly. For example, you might do something as simple as design a drop shadow for a headline and want to use that same drop shadow with those same settings repeatedly for other headlines. Or, you might design a complex appearance and want to use that for various other objects.

It's in these cases that graphic styles become quite useful. Graphic styles offer you the option to save different appearances for future use.

It's smart to associate graphic styles in your mind with effects and appearances. If there's a fill color or a gradient or a pattern you like

working with, it's not necessary to save them as a graphic style; you can just save them to the Swatches panel for future use. However, once you involve any effect, say a drop shadow or rounded corners or a distortion, that's when you use graphic styles as a method for saving that look.

To create a new graphic style, select the artwork on the artboard whose attributes you want to save as a style, then do one of the following:

- Click the New Graphic Style button on the Graphic Styles panel.
- Drag artwork from the artboard into the Graphic Styles panel.
- Drag an artwork thumbnail from the Appearance panel into the Graphic Styles panel.

A graphic style can include fills, strokes, effects, patterns, opacity settings, blending modes, and gradients. The Graphic Styles panel is shown in Figure 21.

When you apply a graphic style to an object, the new graphic style overrides any graphic style you previously applied to the object. When you apply a graphic style to a group, all objects in the group take on the graphic style's attributes.

Figure 21 Graphic Styles panel

Merging Graphic Styles

You can also create new graphic styles by merging two or more graphic styles on the Graphic Styles panel. To do so, [command]-click (Mac) or [Ctrl]-click (Win) to select all the graphic styles you want to merge, click the Graphic Styles panel menu button, then click Merge Graphic Styles. The new graphic style will contain all the attributes of the selected graphic styles and will be added to the Graphic Styles panel as a new graphic style.

Create and apply graphic styles

1. Open AI 8-4.ai, then save it as **Chrome Graphic Style**.
2. Click **Window** on the menu bar, then click **Graphic Styles**.
3. Select the **chrome square** at the top of the artboard, then note the Appearance panel.

   The square has a Drop Shadow effect applied and listed on the Appearance panel.
4. Click the **Add New Effect button** *fx.* on the Appearance panel, point to **Stylize**

in the Illustrator Effects section, then click **Round Corners**.

5. Enter **.125** in the **Radius text box**, then click **OK**.
6. On the Graphic Styles panel, click the **New Graphic Style button** ⊞ .

   The artwork is added as a new style.
7. Double-click the **new graphic style swatch**.

   The Graphic Style Options dialog box opens.
8. Type **Chrome Shadow** in the **Style Name text box**, then click **OK**.
9. Select the **black star** on the artboard, then change the **fill color** to **[None]**.
10. Click the **Chrome Shadow style** on the Graphic Styles panel.

    The star is filled with the chrome gradient, its corners are rounded, and the drop shadow appears.

TIP Theoretically, it is not necessary to remove an object's fill before applying a graphic style; the graphic style should override any fill or stroke already applied to the object. In practice, however, especially with multiple objects or outlined text, the pre-existing fill color may persist, which should not be the case. As a work-around, it's a good idea to first remove the fill and stroke from the object before applying the graphic style.

Continued on next page

11. Select the **headline text** on the artboard, change the **fill color** to **[None]**, then apply the graphic style.

    As shown in Figure 22, the style is applied to every letter in the headline.

12. Save your work, then continue to the next set of steps.

You applied the Round Corners effect to a square with a gradient fill and a Drop Shadow effect. You added the artwork to the Graphic Styles panel to create a new graphic style called Chrome Shadow. You then applied the Chrome Shadow graphic style to a star and outlined text.

Modify a graphic style

1. Select the **square** at the top of the artboard, then click the **Gradient tool** on the toolbar.

2. Click and drag from the **top edge of the square** to the **bottom edge** to reverse the direction of the gradient.

3. Click the **Selection tool**, then click the words **Drop Shadow** on the Appearance panel to open the Drop Shadow dialog box.

4. Change the **Opacity** to **75%**, then click **OK**.

5. Remove the **minus sign** in the **X Offset text box**.

6. Change the **color** of the drop shadow to a **burnt orange**, similar to the color in the chrome gradient.

    At this point, you could add this new look to the Graphic Styles panel to save it. Instead, you will overwrite and replace the Chrome Shadow style with this new look.

7. Press and hold **[option]** (Mac) or **[Alt]** (Win) on your keypad, drag the **square from the artboard** on top of the **Chrome Shadow swatch** on the **Graphic Styles panel**, then release the mouse button.

    As shown in Figure 23, the Chrome Shadow graphic style is updated in the Graphic Styles panel and the artwork on the artboard also updates with the modified style.

8. Save your work, then close the Chrome Graphic Style document.

You modified the gradient and the drop shadow effect on the square artwork, then used it to change the saved graphic style. When you did, the artwork on the artboard updated with the new style.

Figure 22 Applying the graphic style to letters and a star object

Figure 23 Updating the graphic style

USE OPACITY MASKS

What You'll Do

In this lesson, you will use an opacity mask to fade type in different directions.

Using Opacity Masks

Sometimes, rather than reducing opacity overall, you'll want to apply transparency precisely to specific areas of your artwork. That's when opacity masks come into play. You use an **opacity mask** and a **masking object** to alter the transparency of artwork in specific areas you choose.

Working with opacity masks involves the mask itself and the masking object. To make the opacity mask, select an object or objects, then click the Make Mask button on the Transparency panel to make the mask. By default, the mask is all black; a black mask makes the selected object invisible.

By default, the mask affects the entire artboard when the Clip option on the Transparency panel is activated. You use a masking object to apply the mask to specific areas of the artboard. The masking object is an object you create that defines which areas are transparent and the degree to which they are transparent. Where the opacity mask is white, the artwork is fully visible.

For example, if you add a white circle to the mask, the masked artwork will be visible on the artboard only in the area that corresponds to the white circle in the mask.

Think of masks and the masking object in terms of black, white, and shades of gray. Black hides the masked object completely; white shows it completely. Different shades of gray create different transparencies. Therefore, if you create a black to white fill for the masking object, the artwork will gradate from invisible to visible.

TIP You can move masks between Photoshop and Illustrator. Opacity masks in Illustrator convert to layer masks in Photoshop and vice versa.

You work with opacity masks by adding one or more masking objects to the mask that affect the transparency of the related artwork. When you click the mask on the Transparency panel, a black frame appears around the mask, indicating that the mask is targeted. With the mask targeted, any objects you create are created in the mask, and no objects on the artboard are selectable.

Figure 24 illustrates all these concepts. A pink star object was selected, and a mask was applied on the Transparency panel. Because the Clip option is activated, the mask extends to the entire artboard and would therefore make the entire star invisible or hidden. Three rectangular masking objects have been added to the mask. The top masking object has a white fill, so the star is 100% visible in that area. The second masking object has a gray fill, so the star is showing only partially. The bottom masking object has a dark gray fill that is nearly black, so the star is barely visible in that area.

TIP When working with complex artwork, group the artwork before applying the opacity mask.

Figure 24 Illustration of opacity mask concepts

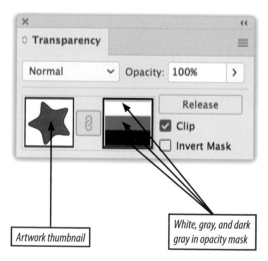

Artwork thumbnail

White, gray, and dark gray in opacity mask

Editing a Masking Object

Once you've added an opacity mask to an object and added a masking object to the opacity mask, you can edit a masking object to change the transparency of the mask. When you click the opacity mask (right thumbnail) on the Transparency panel, you can then select the masking object and modify its attributes, such as shape and color.

You can think of clicking the opacity mask on the Transparency panel as entering mask-editing mode because, once you have clicked it, everything you do will be done to the masking object. When you click the artwork (left thumbnail) on the Transparency panel, anything you do will affect the artwork itself. You can think of clicking the artwork thumbnail as exiting mask-editing mode.

You will often want to see the masking object as you are working. You can [option]-click (Mac) or [Alt]-click (Win) the opacity mask thumbnail to view the mask and the masking object.

If you want to hide and show the mask, press and hold [shift] and click the opacity mask thumbnail. When the opacity mask is deactivated, a red x appears over the mask thumbnail on the Transparency panel.

When you add an opacity mask to selected artwork, the artwork and the masking object are linked by default. This means if you move the artwork, the artwork and the masking object move together, and the relationship is maintained. This relationship is represented by the link icon on the Transparency panel between the artwork and opacity mask thumbnails. Click to remove the link, and then you can move the artwork and the masking object(s) independently of one another.

To remove an opacity mask, select the masked artwork, then click Release Opacity Mask in the Transparency panel menu. Removing the opacity mask does not delete the masking object. The masking object reappears on top of the objects that were masked.

Add an opacity mask to artwork

1. Open AI 8-5.ai, then save it as **Western Moon**.

   The illustration is of a horseman under a bright sun in a western environment. You will use opacity masks to make the illustration more complex and turn it into a night-time landscape.

2. Select the **tan rectangle background object**, copy, then paste in front.

3. Click the **Eyedropper tool** 🖊 , then click the **small blue square** at the top of the artwork.

   The copied rectangle fills with the blue color. You now have a blue rectangle above the original tan rectangle. Next, you will use an opacity mask to fade the blue background to the tan background.

4. With the **blue rectangle still selected**, click **Make Mask** on the Transparency panel.

   A black opacity mask is created on the Transparency panel and the blue background disappears from the artboard.

5. Click the **opacity mask thumbnail** on the **Transparency panel** to target it.

   A blue frame appears around the opacity mask indicating that it is targeted. Your Transparency panel should resemble Figure 25. With the opacity mask targeted, you can think of yourself as being in "mask mode." Original objects on the artboard are not selectable, and any objects you create at this point will be masking objects applied to the opacity mask itself.

Continued on next page

Figure 25 Targeting the opacity mask on the Transparency panel

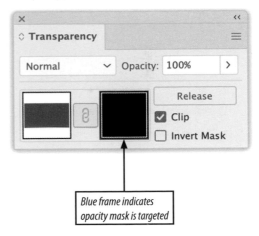

Blue frame indicates opacity mask is targeted

6. On the Swatches panel, click the **White swatch** to change the **fill color** on the toolbar to **white**.

7. Click the **Rectangle tool** ⬜, on the toolbar, then draw a **rectangle** on the artboard in the location shown in Figure 26.

The rectangle is a masking object. Because it is filled with white, the blue background is now 100% visible in that area, as shown in the figure.

8. Use the **Free Transform tool** 🔛 to extend the **white-filled rectangle** so it covers the **entire artboard**, making the blue background entirely visible.

9. Open the **Gradient panel** and click the **white to black linear gradient** at the top-left corner of the panel.

The gradient is used as a fill for the masking object.

Figure 26 Adding a white masking object to the opacity mask

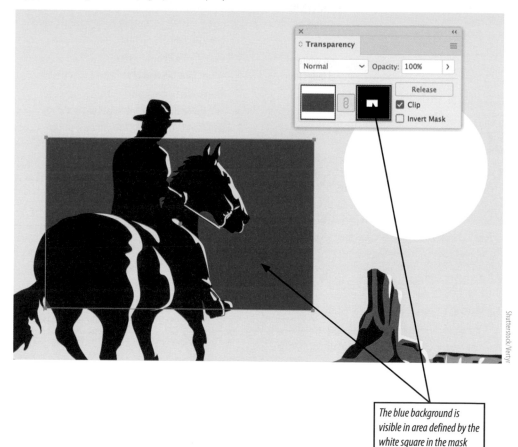

The blue background is visible in area defined by the white square in the mask

Shutterstock/Vertyr

10. Click the **Gradient tool** 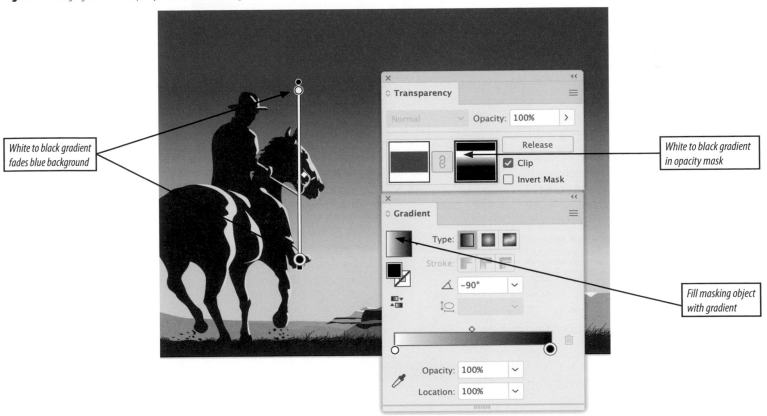 on the toolbar, then drag the **cursor** from the **top of the rider's hat** straight down to the **bottom of her shoe**, as shown in Figure 27.

The masking object now gradates from white to black. Therefore, the blue background fades from 100% blue to 0% blue.

11. Press and hold **[shift]**, then click the **opacity mask thumbnail** on the Transparency panel.

A red X appears on the mask thumbnail. The mask is disabled, and the solid blue background becomes visible.

12. **[shift]-click** the **opacity mask thumbnail** again.

The red X disappears, and the mask is enabled once again.

13. Save your work, then continue to the next set of steps.

You created an opacity mask and a masking object. You then used a white to black gradient to fade an object from 100% to 0%.

Figure 27 Using a gradient in an opacity mask to fade the background

White to black gradient fades blue background

White to black gradient in opacity mask

Fill masking object with gradient

Add multiple opacity masks to artwork

1. On the Transparency panel, click the **artwork thumbnail**.

 The artwork thumbnail is to the left of the opacity mask thumbnail. To select artwork on the artboard, it's necessary to target the artwork thumbnail.

2. On the Layers panel, show the **Clouds layer**.

3. Press **[option] (Mac)** or **[Alt] (Win)**, then click the **Clouds layer** to select all the artwork on the Clouds layer.

4. Click **Make Mask** on the Transparency panel.

5. Click the **opacity mask thumbnail** on the Transparency panel to target it.

6. On the Swatches panel, click the **white swatch** to change the **fill color** on the toolbar to **white**.

7. Click the **Rectangle tool** ▢ , then draw a **rectangle** anywhere on the artboard.

8. Use the **Free Transform tool** ⧉ to extend the white-filled rectangle so it covers the entire artboard and all the clouds are visible.

9. On the Gradient panel, click the **white to black linear gradient** as the fill for the masking object.

10. Click the **Gradient tool** ▮ , then drag from the **top of the canvas** to the **bottom**, as shown in Figure 28.

 The clouds fade, creating an illusion of depth and distance to the sky. Because you started the gradient at the top of the artboard, none of the clouds are 100% visible.

11. On the Transparency panel, click the **artwork thumbnail**.

12. Show the **Stars layer**, then delete the **Color Chip layer**.

13. Click the **Selection tool** ▶ , then select the **moon artwork** on the artboard.

14. On the Transparency panel, click **Make Mask**.

15. Click the **opacity mask thumbnail** to target it, then draw a **white rectangle** where the moon is located so it becomes visible.

TIP Use the Free Transform tool ⧉ to resize your rectangle as necessary.

16. Create a **new circle**, fill it with **Black**, then position it **over the moon** so it appears as a crescent moon, as shown in Figure 29.

17. Save your work, then close the Western Moon document.

You used a gradient in a mask to fade the clouds, then you used a black circle to mask a specific part of the moon.

Figure 28 Fading the clouds

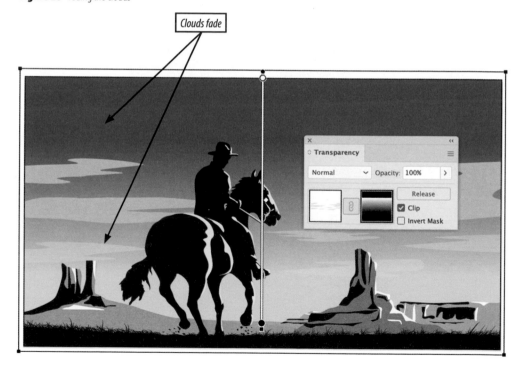

Clouds fade

Figure 29 Finishing the illustration

RECOLOR ARTWORK

Recoloring Artwork

The Recolor Artwork feature offers sophisticated color management options in Adobe Illustrator. It uses the Color Guide panel and the Recolor Artwork dialog box as an interface for dynamic color manipulation for an entire illustration. Rather than fill objects with various colors, you can drag sliders and watch the colors in your illustration change as you drag.

Recoloring artwork starts with the Color Guide panel, shown in Figure 30. The Color Guide panel uses harmony rules, which are based on color models with complementary colors, to help you select colors for your illustration that work well together.

Figure 30 Color Guide panel

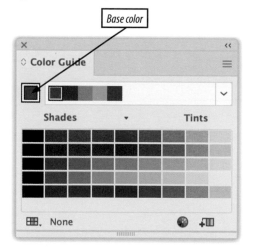

Note the base color in Figure 7. Whenever you click a swatch on the Swatches panel or a color on the Color panel, that color automatically becomes the base color for the current harmony rules in the Color Guide. Figure 31 shows some of the harmony rules available for the red base color.

Figure 31 Harmony rules available for the red base color

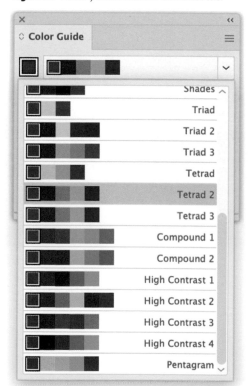

When you select an object on the artboard then choose a harmony rule in the Color Guide panel, the selected object does not change color. Instead, the Color Guide panel loads a group of swatches, called **variations**, based on the harmony rule. These swatches all work well together and can be used to color your illustration. In addition, you can modify any set of variations on the Color Guide panel menu by clicking Show Tints/Shades, Show Warm/Cool, and Show Vivid/Muted on the panel menu.

Assigning Color in the Recolor Artwork Dialog Box

You can access the Recolor Artwork dialog box by clicking the Edit or Apply Colors button on the Color Guide panel. If you do so with art selected, any changes you make in the Recolor Artwork dialog box will affect the selected art.

The Recolor Artwork dialog box functions based on two modes: Assign and Edit. Both have essentially the same effect, but they use different methods to manipulate color. Figure 32 shows the dialog box in Assign mode. When working in Assign mode, you choose a harmony rule, and that harmony rule alters the colors of the selected artwork.

In the figure, a harmony rule named Tetrad 2 has been loaded. The Current Colors column shows that the selected artwork contains six colors, including four chromatic colors plus black and white.

The New column shows each of the four colors from the Tetrad 2 harmony rule: tan, brown, green, and light blue. It's important to understand that each of the four New colors has been randomly assigned to one of the four current colors in the artwork. (By default, black and white are not affected.) For example, reading from left to right, you can see in the dialog box that tan colors in the original artwork have remained tan. Green colors have changed to brown. Turquoise colors are now green, and red colors have changed to light blue.

Figure 32 Recolor Artwork dialog box in Assign mode

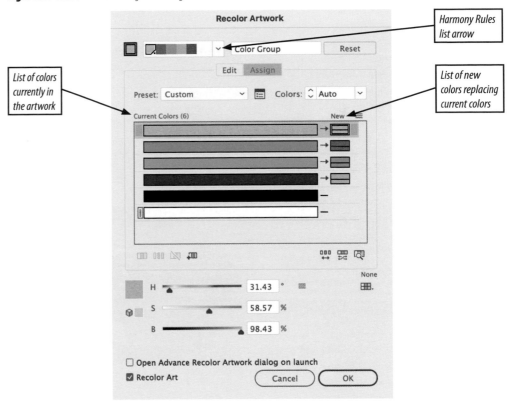

List of colors currently in the artwork

Harmony Rules list arrow

List of new colors replacing current colors

You can, at any time, reassign the new colors from the harmony rule to different current colors in the artwork simply by dragging and dropping them. For example, if you drag the light blue swatch in the New column on top of the tan swatch, their assignments will be switched in the artwork: Tan colors in the artwork will change to light blue, and red colors will be tan.

Your options for manipulating color in the Recolor Artwork dialog box are virtually unlimited, and that means you are not limited to using only the colors in the harmony rule you selected. Click any of the new colors in the new column, and then manipulate the sliders at the bottom of the dialog box to change that color to any color you choose. As you drag the sliders, you will see the color in the illustration change dynamically. You can also double-click any of the New color swatches to open the Color Picker dialog box and change the swatch to a new color.

> **TIP** Click the arrow button beside the sliders to change the mode the sliders use to specify color. For example, you can specify color in RGB mode.

Editing Color in the Recolor Artwork Dialog Box

As stated in the previous section, Edit and Assign modes in the Recolor Artwork dialog box essentially provide the same options for manipulating color but use different methods. However, Edit mode is so much more visually interesting and makes it so much easier to understand what's going on as you manipulate color.

Figure 33 shows the Recolor Artwork dialog box in Edit mode. The top illustration of the cat is the original, and the bottom illustration is the selected art being manipulated. When the Recolor Artwork dialog box is open, selection marks are automatically hidden for selected artwork on the artboard.

The six circles in the dialog box represent the five colors for the loaded Pentagram harmony rule, and each corresponds to one of the five chromatic colors in the original artwork. The circles are called color handles, and the color handle with the heavy border is the base color for the loaded harmony rule.

Figure 33 Recolor Artwork dialog box in Edit mode with before and after view of artwork

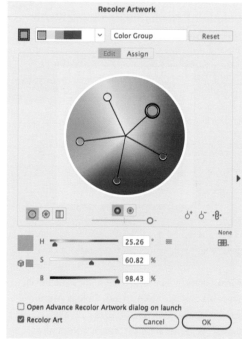

The big difference between Edit mode and Assign mode is that Edit mode does not show you a list of your current colors. Instead, when in Edit mode, the illustration on the artboard is your only reference to your current colors and how they're being affected.

In Edit mode, you adjust color by moving the color handles to different positions on the color wheel, and the corresponding colors in the artwork are affected. In Figure 34, the five colors have been rotated clockwise. Note the change to the illustration.

If you click the Unlink harmony colors button, you can move the color handles independently of one another. In addition, you can select any of the color tools, then modify that color with the color sliders at the bottom of the dialog box.

Reducing an Illustration's Colors in the Recolor Artwork Dialog Box

In most cases, when you select artwork and then choose a harmony rule in the Recolor Artwork dialog box, the harmony rule will not have the same number of colors as the number of colors in the selected artwork. When the harmony rule contains fewer colors than what is selected in the artwork, the color in the artwork must be reduced to whatever is available in the harmony rule. This is achieved with tints. For example, if you have artwork with six different colors and you choose a harmony rule that contains only three colors, each of the three colors in the harmony rule creates a second tint version of itself to assign to the three additional colors.

Figure 34 Recoloring the artwork by rotating the color handles

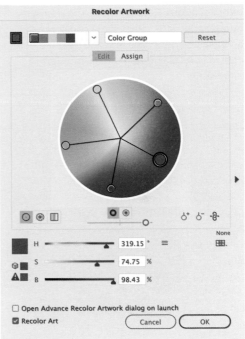

In Figure 35, the five current colors have been reduced to a harmony rule that contains only three colors. Thus, the illustration at the bottom is painted with only three colors, which are pink and light pink, blue and light blue, and yellow. Note the tints on the swatches in the New column.

Reducing Artwork to a Two-Color Job

Reducing the color results of multicolored artwork to a two-color job is probably the most practical feature offered in the Recolor Artwork dialog box. For example, it is common for designers to create "two-color jobs," which, in most cases, include black and a spot, or PANTONE, color. If the designer is working with artwork that has already been filled with multiple colors, the Recolor Artwork dialog box can convert those colors quickly to various shades of a spot color that you choose.

Figure 35 Five-color artwork reduced to a three-color harmony rule with two tints added

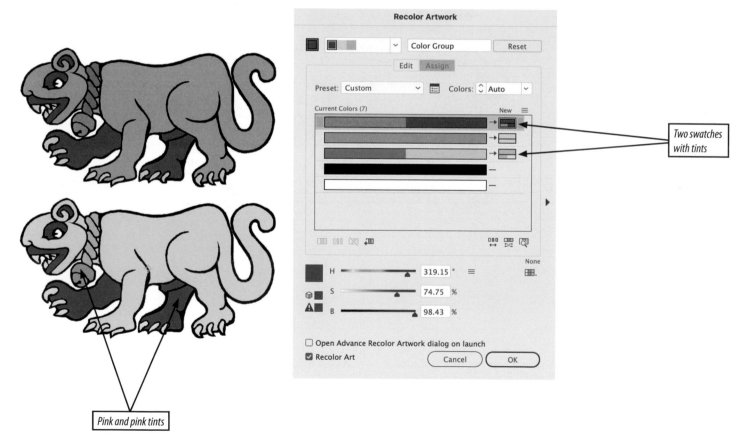

Using Isolation Mode

In addition to locking and unlocking or hiding and showing objects and layers, Isolation Mode is a feature that helps you select an object or a group of objects with ease. When you use Isolation Mode, the selected objects appear in full color, while all the remaining objects on the artboard are dimmed and not selectable. This allows you to access the isolated object or group of objects without any of the other objects getting in the way.

To work in Isolation Mode, select an object or a set of objects that has been grouped on the artboard. The Isolate Selected Object button appears on the Control panel. Click the button to enter Isolation Mode. When in Isolation Mode, the button changes to Exit Isolation Mode. Click it to return to the normal view of the artboard.

When you are in Isolation Mode, the Layers panel displays only the artwork in the isolated sublayer. You cannot access any other layers.

When you exit Isolation Mode, the other layers reappear on the Layers panel.

Explore the Color Guide panel

1. Open AI 8-6.indd, then save it as **El Gato**.

2. Click the **Magenta swatch** on the Swatches panel.

3. Open the **Color Guide panel**.

4. Click the **Harmony Rules list arrow**.

   As shown in Figure 36, the Color Guide panel contains a long list of harmony rules, all of which are sets of color swatches grouped together based on various established color models.

5. Note that the first color—the leftmost swatch—in all of the harmony rules is the Magenta swatch you clicked on the Swatches panel.

   Whenever you click a swatch on the Swatches panel, that swatch automatically becomes the base color on the Color Guide panel. All of the harmony rules in the current list use the Magenta swatch as the basis for their individual color groupings.

Figure 36 A list of harmony rules on the Color Guide panel

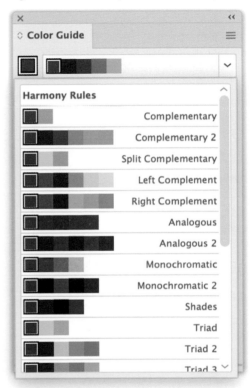

6. Click **Analogous** from the **Harmony Rules list** so your Color Guide panel resembles Figure 37.

The rows of swatches in the lower section of the Color Guide panel are referred to as the variation grid. The center column in the variation grid, as shown in the figure, contains the same colors from the Analogous harmony rule. The swatches to the left and right of this column are darker and lighter shades, all based on the same Analogous harmony rule.

TIP If the colors on your Color Guide panel differ from the figure, click the Color Guide list arrow, then verify that Show Tints/Shades is checked.

7. Apply various swatches from this variation grid to the various parts of the illustration of the lion.

Figure 38 shows one example.

8. Click **File** on the menu bar, then click **Revert** to remove the colors you applied to the illustration.

9. Continue to the next set of steps.

You explored the Color Guide panel, viewing various harmony rules. You then chose the Analogous harmony rule and applied swatches from that collection to the illustration. You then reverted the file to its original state.

Figure 37 Color Guide panel showing the Analogous harmony rule for a magenta swatch

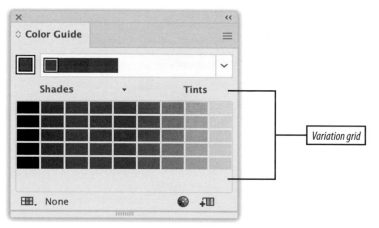

Figure 38 Lion illustration painted with swatches from the Analogous harmony rule

Set a base color and save a color group

1. Verify that the **Color Guide panel** is showing, verify that the **fill button** is active and in front of the stroke button on the toolbar, then click the **Pure Cyan swatch** on the Swatches panel.

   The Pure Cyan swatch becomes the base color on the Color Guide panel.

   TIP Whenever you click a swatch on the Swatches panel or click a color on the Color panel, that color automatically appears as the base color on the Color Guide panel.

2. Click the **Selection tool** , then click the **orange square** above the illustration.

3. On the Color Guide panel, click the **orange color swatch** to set it as the base color.

   The harmony rules update on the panel to reflect the new orange base color.

4. Click the **Harmony Rules list arrow**.

   As shown in Figure 39, the Color Guide panel and all the harmony rules update, with the orange from the selected item now functioning as the new base color.

5. Click the **Analogous 2 harmony rule**.

6. Click the **Save color group to Swatch panel button** on the Color Guide panel.

   As shown in Figure 40, the color group is saved on the Swatches panel.

7. Use the color group on the Swatches panel to paint the illustration as you like.

8. Save your work, then close the El Gato document.

   You clicked a swatch on the Swatches panel, noting that it automatically became the base color on the Color Guide panel. You then selected an object on the artboard and set it as the base color. You chose a harmony rule and then applied those colors to the illustration.

Figure 39 Color Guide panel with the new base color

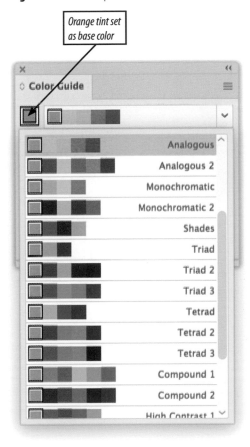

Orange tint set as base color

Use Isolation Mode to examine groups in an illustration

1. Open AI 8-7.ai, then save it as **Ancient Warrior**.

2. Verify that the **Control panel** is visible.

   The illustration features five colors plus black and white.

Figure 40 Saving a color group to the Swatches panel

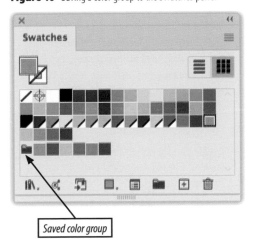

Saved color group

---

3. Click the **Selection tool** , then click one of the **turquoise blue jewels**.

   All the jewels are selected because they are grouped.

4. Click the **Isolate Selected Object button** on the Control panel.

   The selected artwork remains visible, but the selection marks disappear. All nonselected objects in the illustration are dimmed. Note that the jewels are the only objects in the illustration painted blue.

5. Click any of the **dimmed objects** in the illustration.

   In Isolation Mode, dimmed objects cannot be selected.

6. Click any one of the **blue jewels**.

   Only one jewel is selected. In Isolation Mode, grouped objects are selected individually.

Continued on next page

7. Click the **artboard** to deselect the jewel, then click the **Exit Isolation Mode button** on the Control panel.

8. Click **Illustrator (Mac)** or **Edit (Win)** on the menu bar, point to **Preferences**, then click **General**.

9. Verify that the **Double Click To Isolate check box** is checked, then click **OK**.

10. Double-click the **headdress**.

    Double-clicking isolates the group in Isolation Mode. The headdress and the eyelid are painted dark brown.

11. Click the **Exit Isolation Mode button** on the Control panel, then double-click the **gold wristband** to view the third color, Gold.

12. Click the **Exit Isolation Mode button** on the Control panel, then double-click the **gray belt** to view the fourth color, Gray.

13. Click the **Exit Isolation Mode button** on the Control panel, then double-click the **face** to view the fifth color, Tan.

14. Click the **Exit Isolation Mode button** on the Control panel.

15. Save your work, then continue to the next set of steps.

You used the Isolation Mode feature to view five groups in an illustration.

Assign colors with the Recolor Artwork dialog box

1. Select any area of the **warrior's face or body**, then click the **Set base color to the current color button** on the Color Guide panel.

2. Click the **Harmony Rules list arrow** on the Color Guide panel, then click **Analogous 2**.

Figure 41 Pentagram harmony rule applied to the artwork

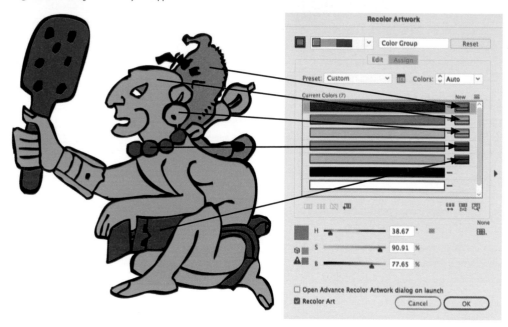

3. Select all the **artwork** on the artboard.

4. Click the **Edit or Apply Colors button** on the Color Guide panel.

    The Recolor Artwork dialog box opens.

5. Click the **Assign button** at the top of the Recolor Artwork dialog box.

    The Recolor Artwork dialog box is now in Assign mode.

6. Click the **Harmony Rules list arrow**, then experiment with different harmony rules, noting how each affects the art.

7. Click the **Pentagram harmony rule** from the list, then compare your art and your Recolor Artwork dialog box to Figure 41.

Like the illustration itself, the Pentagram harmony rule has five colors. In the Recolor Artwork dialog box, the list of colors on the left that includes five colors plus black and white represents the original colors used in the illustration. The smaller color squares to the right represent the new colors assigned with the Pentagram harmony rule. Because we chose a five-color harmony rule, the relationship between the original and the new colors is 1 to 1. For example, the turquoise used to paint the jewelry has now changed to purple, and the original gray on the belt and the paddle have now changed to red.

8. In the Recolor Artwork dialog box, click and drag the **red color box** in the New column up and release it on top of the **purple color box**.

   The swap is reflected in the art—the jewels are now red, and the belt and paddle are now purple.

9. Double-click the **green color box** in the New column.

   The Color Picker opens.

10. Type **237**, **184**, and **107** in the **R, G**, and **B text boxes**, respectively, then click **OK**.

    The Recolor Artwork dialog box and the artwork are updated with the change.

11. Click the **purple color box** in the New column to select it and drag the **H (hue) slider** at the bottom of the dialog box to **29°**.

    The purple components of the illustration are updated with the change to orange.

12. Click the **Show color group storage button** ▶ on the right side of the dialog box.

    The Recolor Artwork dialog box expands to show the color groups.

13. Click the **New Color Group button** 🖿 at the top of the Recolor Artwork dialog box.

    The new color group is saved. Note that this saved group is not the Pentagram harmony rule you first selected. The saved group is the Pentagram harmony rule with all the edits you made to it.

14. Click **OK**, then deselect the artwork.

15. Save your work, then continue to the next set of steps.

You used the Assign mode of the Recolor Artwork dialog box to assign a harmony rule to an illustration, then you modified the new colors in the Recolor Artwork dialog box to control how they affected the artwork.

Edit colors with the Recolor Artwork dialog box

1. Select **all artwork**, then click the **Edit or Apply Colors button** ● on the Color Guide panel.

2. Verify that the **Assign button** is active in the Recolor Artwork dialog box, click the **Harmony Rules list arrow**, then click **Pentagram**.

   This is the same harmony rule you applied in the previous lesson, but the colors have been applied differently because the base artwork was different when it was applied this time.

3. Click the **Edit button**, then reference Figure 42.

   In Edit mode, the Recolor Artwork dialog box shows you harmony rules in relation to a color wheel. In Figure 42, note how the Pentagram harmony rule has five handles on the color wheel, all of them equidistant from one another, just like a pentagram. The circle at the outside of each of the handles corresponds to a color in the illustration. The handle with the heavy circle is the base color of the active harmony rule.

   Continued on next page

Figure 42 Recolor Artwork dialog box in Edit mode

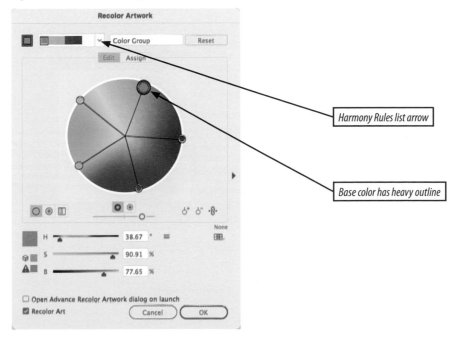

Harmony Rules list arrow

Base color has heavy outline

4. Click and drag the **base color handle** to the position shown in Figure 43.

All the colors in the illustration change dynamically with the movements in the dialog box. When you move the base color handle, the other color handles move with it, thus maintaining the original relationship established by the Pentagram harmony rule. The illustration in Figure 43 shows the result of the move; by definition, the new colors are all in mathematical harmony with one another, despite the change.

5. Click and drag the **base color handle** halfway to the **center of the color wheel**.

All the color handles move with the base color handle. The color in the illustration is desaturated because, on a color wheel, colors with the highest saturation are at the outside of the wheel.

6. Drag the **B (Brightness) slider** to **50**.

7. Drag the **B (Brightness) slider** to **100**.

The Hue, Saturation, and Brightness sliders offer you dynamic options for modifying colors in artwork.

8. Drag the **base color tool** back to the **outside edge of the color wheel**.

9. With the **base color handle** still selected, type **0**, **100**, and **100** in the **H**, **S**, and **B text boxes**, respectively.

10. Experiment with various hues by dragging the **H slider** to various locations.

Dragging the Hue slider with the base color handle selected is the same as dragging the base color handle by hand—all the color handles move with the base color handle and the relationships are maintained.

11. Drag the **H slider** back to **0**.

12. Click the **Unlink harmony colors button** .

The solid lines connecting the color handles become dotted, representing that the colors are no longer linked.

Figure 43 Repositioning the base color handle and the result on the artwork

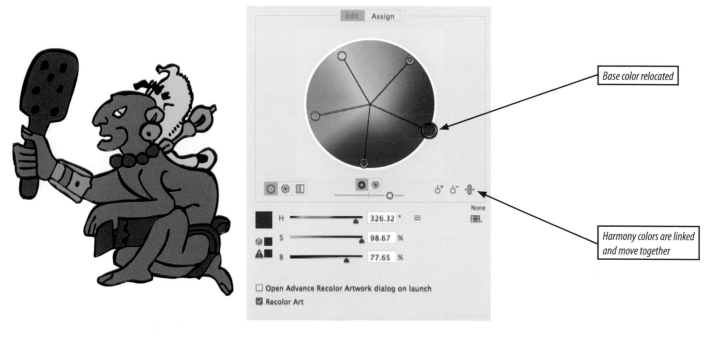

Base color relocated

Harmony colors are linked and move together

13. Click the **top (gold) color handle**, drag it to the location shown in Figure 44, then note the effect on the illustration.

Only the "skin" group is affected because the color handle you moved represents that group in the illustration.

14. Click the **Display segmented color wheel button** 🌐 in the Recolor Artwork dialog box.

15. Moving counterclockwise, reposition the other **handles** as shown in Figure 45.

Because you are moving the colors independently, you have abandoned the harmony selections and the colors are no longer necessarily in mathematical harmony.

16. Click the **Link harmony colors button** 🔗 .

The color handles are once again linked; moving one will move all. Note that the lines between them are solid once again.

Continued on next page

Figure 44 Moving a color handle independently of the others

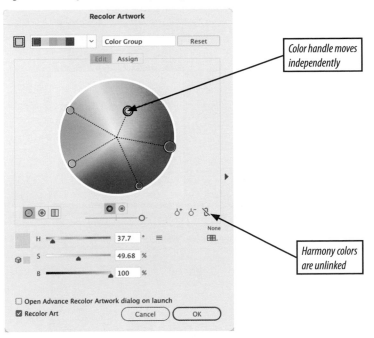

Color handle moves independently

Harmony colors are unlinked

Figure 45 Repositioning all handles

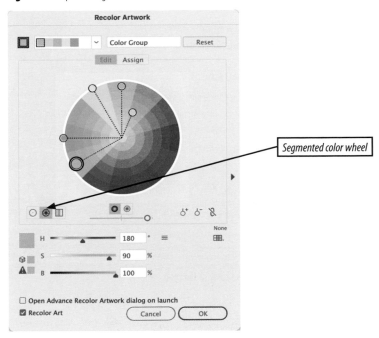

Segmented color wheel

17. Click the **green color handle** to select it, type **20** in the **H text box**, press **[tab]**, then compare your illustration to Figure 46.

18. Click **OK**, save your work, then close the Ancient Warrior document.

You edited the colors in the illustration using the Recolor Artwork dialog box.

Reduce colors in the Recolor Artwork dialog box

1. Open AI 8-8.ai, then save it as **Warrior Two**.

2. Select all, click the **Edit or Apply Colors button** on the Color Guide panel, then click the **Assign button** in the Recolor Artwork dialog box.

3. If necessary, click the **Show color group storage button** ▶ to expand the Recolor Artwork dialog box so the right-side section is visible.

4. Click **Test** in the Color Groups section.

The five original colors in the illustration correspond to each of the five colors in the Test harmony rule.

TIP This step is not necessary for reducing colors—you did this only so your illustration and dialog box are working with the same colors as the steps.

5. Click the **Hide color group storage button** ◀ to reduce the dialog box.

6. In the Current Colors column, drag the **fifth (bottom) color** in the list, which is dark green, **on top of the first (top) color** in the list.

The top color splits into two to accommodate both colors.

TIP Be sure to drag from the Current Colors column, not the New column.

Figure 46 Result of adjusting the hue of the green color handle

7. Drag the **remaining three colors** up to the top of the list so your dialog box and illustration resemble Figure 47.

    All five original colors in the illustration have been replaced by tints of the base color of the Test

harmony group. The black border lines and white eye remain untouched.

8. Click the **Limits the color group to colors in a swatch library button** ⊞ , point to **Color Books**, then click **PANTONE+ Solid Coated**.

Colors in the color group can now only be those found in the PANTONE+ Solid Coated swatch library.

9. Double-click the **top tan color box** in the New column to the right of the five combined colors, click **PANTONE Blue 072 C**, then click **OK**.

Continued on next page

Figure 47 Dragging four colors to the top color

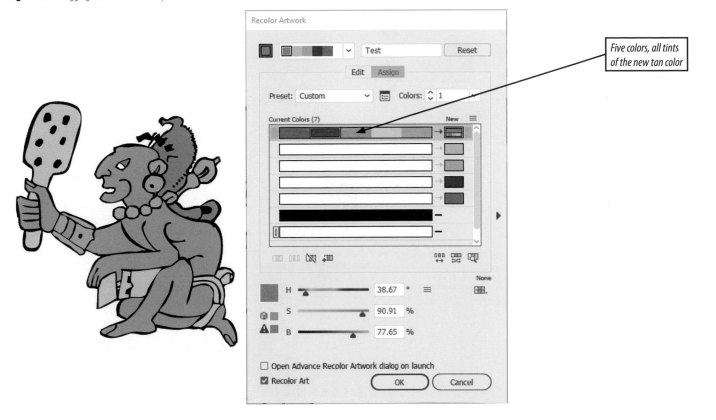

Five colors, all tints of the new tan color

10. Click **OK** to close the Recolor Artwork dialog box, save changes when prompted, then compare your illustration to Figure 48.

The five colors in the illustration are now all tints of PANTONE Blue 072 C. However, the tints are all very similar, making it difficult to distinguish various objects in the illustration.

11. Display the **Color panel**.

12. Deselect all, click the **Selection tool** , click the **face**, then note that the group is filled with an 80% tint of PANTONE Blue 072 C.

13. On the Color panel, drag the **slider** to **15%**.

14. Using this method, use the Color panel to distinguish the various objects in the illustration with tints of PANTONE Blue 072 C.

Figure 49 shows one outcome. This is two-color artwork: It could be printed with black ink and PANTONE Blue 072 C ink.

15. Save your work, then close the Warrior Two document.

You reduced the number of colors in the illustration using the Recolor Artwork dialog box.

Figure 48 Illustration with tints of PANTONE Blue 072 C

Figure 49 Final two-color illustration

Use the Transparency panel and the Color Picker

1. Open AI 8-9.ai, then save it as **Channel Z**.
2. Select the square on the artboard.
3. On the Transparency panel, change the Opacity of the square to 80%.
4. Save your work.

Apply effects to objects

1. With the square still selected, open the Appearance panel.
2. Click Fill on the Appearance panel.
3. Click Effect on the menu bar, point to Texture, click Grain, click the Grain Type list arrow, then click Regular.
4. Type **40** for the Intensity and **20** for the Contrast, then click OK.
5. Click the Stroke item on the Appearance panel, then change its weight to 2 pt. and its color to any blue swatch.
6. Click Effect on the menu bar, point to Path, click Offset Path, type **.1** in the Offset text box, then click OK.
7. Save your work.

Use the Appearance panel

1. Click the Fill item on the Appearance panel.
2. Click Effect on the menu bar, point to the first Stylize command, click Round Corners, type **.2** in the Radius text box, then click OK.
3. Save your work.

Work with graphic styles

1. Show the Graphic Styles panel if necessary.
2. Drag the Path thumbnail from the Appearance panel to the Graphic Styles panel.
3. Name the new graphic style **Channel Noise**.
4. Cut the square artwork from the artboard.
5. Click Object on the menu bar, then click Show All.
6. Deselect, then select only the text.
7. Change the fill on the text to [None].
8. Click the Graphic Styles panel menu button, then verify that Override Character Color is checked.
9. Apply the Channel Noise style to the text.

10. Expand the Stroke item on the Appearance panel, then change its color to Black.
    The artwork on the artboard is now different from the Channel Noise graphic style.
11. Update the Channel Noise graphic style with the new attributes by pressing [option] (Mac) or [Alt] (Wln) as you drag the thumbnail on the Appearance panel on top of the Channel Noise graphic style on the Graphic Styles panel.
12. Select only the black box under the text, then apply the Channel Noise graphic style.
13. Save your work, compare your screen to Figure 50, then close the Channel Z document.

Figure 50 Completed Skills Review, Part 1

Figure 51 Completed Skills Review, Part 2

Recolor artwork

1. Open AI 8-10.ai, then save it as **Jaguar**.
2. Double-click the orange nose to see the orange group in Isolation Mode.
3. Click the Exit Isolation Mode button on the Control panel.
4. Click the Eyedropper tool, sample the orange color from the nose, then notice that the orange color is now the base color on the Color Guide panel.
5. Select all, then click the Edit or Apply Colors button on the Color Guide panel.
6. Click the Assign button.
7. Click the Harmony Rules list arrow at the top of the Recolor Artwork dialog box, then choose the Pentagram harmony rule from the list.
8. Click and drag the red color box in the New column up and release it on top of the color box at the top of the column.
9. Double-click the green color box in the New column, type **237**, **184**, **107** in the R, G, & B text boxes respectively, then click OK.
10. Click the navy blue color box in the New column to select it, then drag the H (hue) slider at the bottom of the dialog box to 133°.
11. Click OK, deselect, then save your work.
12. Compare your illustration to Figure 51, then close the Jaguar document.

Use opacity masks

1. Open AI 8-11.ai, then save it as **Opacity Mask Skills**.
   The blue background square is locked.
2. Select all the text, then copy it.
3. Click Object on the menu bar, point to Lock,
   then click Selection.
4. Click Edit on the menu bar, then click Paste in Front.
5. Click the Eyedropper tool, then click the
   blue background.
   The copied text is filled with blue. You now have blue
   text over black text. However, there's a problem. If
   you zoom in, you can see a thin black line around
   the blue text. This is a known problem with Adobe
   Illustrator: If you paste one object exactly above
   another, a thin line shows from the object below.
   To remedy this, you're going to use the Offset Path
   command to make the blue text completely cover the
   black text.
6. With the blue text still selected, click Object on the
   menu bar, point to Path, then click Offset Path.
7. Enter 0.02 (inches) in the Offset text box, then
   click OK.
   The new text is slightly larger on all sides than
   the original text. However, this new text is a
   copy of the original, so you now have two groups of
   blue text. You will combine them in the next step.
8. Select all, then click the Unite pathfinder on the
   Pathfinder panel.
   You now have blue text that completely covers the
   black text below it.

9. Verify that the blue text is still selected, then click
   Make Mask on the Transparency panel.
   A black opacity mask is created on the Transparency
   panel and the blue text on the artboard disappears.
10. Click the opacity mask thumbnail on the
    Transparency panel to target it.
    A blue frame appears around the opacity mask
    indicating that it is targeted.

11. On the Swatches panel, change the fill color to White
    and the stroke color to [None].
12. Click the Rectangle tool, then draw a rectangle on the
    artboard as shown in Figure 52.
    The rectangle is a masking object. Because it is filled
    with white, it is white in the mask. On the artboard,
    the rectangle appears blue because the black text is
    not visible behind the blue text.

Figure 52 Adding a white masking object to the opacity mask

(continued)

13. Use the Free Transform tool to extend the rectangle so that it covers all the text.
14. Open the Gradient panel, then click the white to black linear gradient at the top of the Gradient panel to fill the blue box with the gradient.
15. Click the Gradient tool, then drag from the bottom of the text to the top of the text.
16. Deselect.

    As shown in Figure 53, the black text appears to fade out to the blue background. What's really happening, is that the blue text is visible at the bottom and gradually disappears as it moves upward. That's because the opacity mask gradates from white at the bottom to black at the top of the text.
17. Save your work, then close the Opacity Mask Skills document.

Figure 53 Using a gradient in an opacity mask to fade the blue text

The local VFW has contracted you to design their monthly newsletter. You are happy because it means a regular monthly payment. However, since their budget is modest, you want to streamline your work as much as possible. One design element of the newsletter that is used every month is a red and blue frame positioned around pictures. You decide to create this as a graphic style in Illustrator.

1. Open AI 8-12.ai, then save it as **Frame**.
2. Show the Brushes panel, then apply the 10 pt. Round brush to the square.
3. Click Effect on the menu bar, point to Stylize, then click Feather.
4. Accept the default settings in the Feather Radius text box, then click OK.
5. On the Appearance panel, duplicate the stroke, then change the duplicate stroke color to blue.
6. Click Effect on the menu bar, point to Path, click Offset Path.
7. Type **.18** in the Offset text box, then click OK.
8. Save the appearance attributes as a new graphic style on the Graphic Styles panel.
9. Name the new graphic style **Picture Frame**.
10. Save your work, compare your screen to Figure 54, then close the Frame document.

Figure 54 Completed Project Builder 1

You are a designer and have just finished a color illustration for a client who calls to tell you that the project is being changed. Because of budgetary constraints, it's going to be reduced from a four-color to a two-color job. The client tells you to use black ink plus any red PANTONE color you think will work best.

1. Open AI 8-13.ai, then save it as **2 Color Jaguar**.
2. Select all, click the Edit or Apply Colors button on the Color Guide panel, then click the Assign button.
3. Click the Harmony Rules list arrow, then choose the Pentagram harmony rule from the list.
4. Click and drag the fifth color in the Current Colors list, which is red, on top of the first color in the list.
5. Click and drag the remaining three colors up to the top of the list (don't move the black and white colors).
6. Click the Limits the color group to colors in a swatch library button 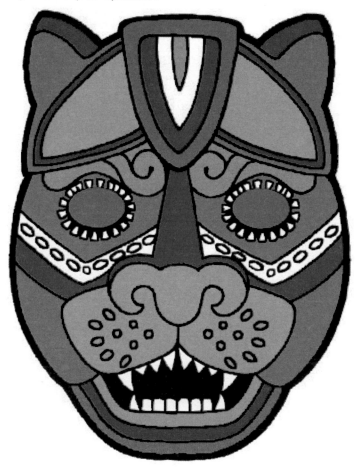, point to Color Books, then click PANTONE+ Solid Coated.
7. Double-click the color box in the New column to the right of the five combined colors, click PANTONE 200 C, then click OK.
8. Click OK to close the Recolor Artwork dialog box, save changes when prompted, then compare your illustration to Figure 55.
9. Save your work, then close the 2 Color Jaguar document.

Figure 55 Completed Project Builder 2

Burr Marina contacts your design firm for a consultation. They ask you to update their logo, which they've been using for a number of years. They tell you the logo can't really change because the look is already established. You tell them you can add some texture to provide some visual interest without dramatically changing the logo.

1. Open AI 8-14.ai, then save it as **Burr Marina**.
2. Verify that both the Transparency and Layers panels are displayed.
3. Click the Selection tool, click the royal blue shape, then copy it.
4. On the Layers panel, make the Swirls layer visible, then click the layer to target it.
5. Click the target on the Swirls layer to select the artwork on that layer.
6. Click the Make Mask button on the Transparency panel.
7. Click the opacity mask to activate it.
8. Paste in place.
9. Target the Swirls layer, then change its blending mode to Color Dodge.
10. Save your work, compare your screen to Figure 56, then close the Burr Marina document.

Figure 56 Completed Design Project

SEA SURVIVORS

Sea turtles have navigated the oceans since the time of the dinosaurs more than 100 million years ago. Today all seven species are under threat at every life stage because of human activities, from accidental capture in fishing nets to overharvesting of eggs and widespread plastic pollution.

HARD SHELL

Six of the seven species have hard shells fused to their ribs and overlaid with keratin scutes. They also have claws on their flippers.

Illustrations in approximate, relative scale

All sea turtles have glands around the eyes to remove excess salt from their bodies.

Interlocking scutes prevent water loss and cover flattened, fused ribs that separate at the tips.

Scute
1 in
Rib

Brain

Scute

Esophagus

Ribs

Lungs

Shell length
3.5 ft (maximum)

Stomach

Liver

The green turtle's serrated beak helps tear marine plants.

Fat

Claw

4 ft

CONSERVATION STATUS
◆ Critically endangered
◇ Endangered
◆ Vulnerable
◇ Insufficient data

PRIMARY ADULT DIET
Invertebrate
Marine plant
Horseshoe crab
Sponge
Crustacean
Mollusk
Fish

Adult males can be identified by their long tails, which hold sex organs.

Front flippers act as wings for propulsion. Rudder-like hind feet stabilize and steer.

2.1 ft

3.1 ft

Female

KEMP'S RIDLEY
Lepidochelys kempii
Accidental capture and egg overharvesting have made the smallest sea turtle the world's most threatened.

Diet   Maximum diving depth

160 ft

LOGGERHEAD
Caretta caretta
The most abundant sea turtle in the U.S. is named for its giant head. Its strong jaws can crack conch shells.

585 ft

FLATBACK
Natator depressus
The flatback makes the shortest migration: around Australian waters. It has a nearly flat body with flared edges.

200 ft

GREEN
Chelonia mydas
Named for a layer of green fat under their shell, green turtles start as omnivores before turning into herbivores.

500 ft

Nesting area

Range

Population at highest risk

PROJECT DESCRIPTION

In this project, you will explore informational blurbs about different sea turtles and create a poster to highlight one of the sea turtle species pictured. Your poster should use the information provided in the model spread to visually display the information about your chosen species in a new way. Consider the details that are most important to include, such as location, diet, and physical features. The goal of this project is to create a poster to represent existing information in a creative format.

SKILLS TO EXPLORE

- Create and Modify Layers
- Manipulate Layered Artwork
- Create a Clipping Set
- Use the Move Command
- Create a Pattern
- Design a Repeating Pattern
- Work with the Brushes Panel
- Work with Scatter Brushes

SOFT SKILLS CHALLENGE

Plan a TED-Ed Talk with at least three classmates to share information you have learned about the specific species of sea turtle you have chosen to research. Be sure to answer questions related to the survival of the species, the location in which it lives, its conservation status, its diet, and its migratory patterns. Include other information as appropriate. The goal of this project is to inform the audience about the importance of your topic and encourage them to take action. Be sure to share helpful tips that students can easily engage in to help protect your chosen sea turtle species. Leave time at the end of your talk for questions or comments.

TED-Ed TALK CHECKLIST

1. Group of three or more peers
2. Outline of main talking points
3. Safe space to facilitate respectful conversation

GETTING STARTED

Use a flow chart to capture important information from the model spread about your chosen sea turtle species.

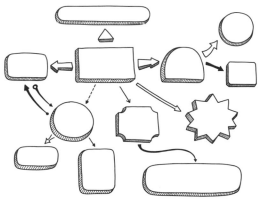

Bloomicon/Shutterstock

Create a flow chart to record information.

Sketch some of the elements of your poster to get a feel for how they might work together.

Dabeygoda/Shutterstock

Create a rough sketch of the sea turtle to show its important body parts.

Archelon (extinct)
This giant that roamed the seas 75 million years ago had unfused ribs, like its close relative, the modern leatherback.

Scute

Shell length: about 7 ft
Weight: up to 2 tons

The hawksbill is the only turtle with overlapping scutes and serrated edges on its shell.

3 ft

2.3 ft

FLEXIBLE SHELL
Leatherbacks are the only living species with unfused ribs, rubbery skin over layers of connective tissue, and a flexible shell of bony plates.

Skin   Bone

Fat

Waxy skin covers a shell of coin-size bony plates that can withstand the pressure of deep dives.

Migration cue
Pale skin lets light into the pineal gland, which can track day length and spur migration.

Brain   Salt glands

Ribs

Lungs

Stomach   Liver

Esophagus

Slippery diet
A long, barbed esophagus traps jellyfish and keeps them moving into the stomach.

4 ft

Artery warm blood   Vein cool blood

Transferring heat
Blood flowing to flippers warms returning cold blood, maintaining a warmer core than hard-shell turtles have.

◆ HAWKSBILL
Eretmochelys imbricata

Hawksbills' intricately patterned, translucent scutes have long been used to decorate jewelry and luxury items.

300 ft

◆ OLIVE RIDLEY
Lepidochelys olivacea

The most abundant species exits the sea en masse to nest, a safety-in-numbers strategy against predators.

835 ft

◆ LEATHERBACK
Dermochelys coriacea

The largest and deepest diving turtle makes the longest migrations and can weigh up to 2,000 pounds.

6,000 ft

MAP SOURCES: SCOTT BENSON, SOUTHWEST FISHERIES SCIENCE CENTER, NOAA; STATE OF THE WORLD'S SEA TURTLES (SWOT), OBIS-SEAMAP

PROJECT DESCRIPTION

In this project, you will build upon your Design Project and create a comprehensive infographic to convey information about a specific sea turtle species. Ask questions and conduct research to expand upon the information pictured in the model spread. Your infographic will consist of at least three different informational elements, such as location, conservation status, diet, migratory patterns, etc. The goal of this project is to provide viewers with a more in-depth look at a certain species of sea turtle.

SKILLS TO EXPLORE

- Edit Colors and Distort Objects
- Work with Gradient Meshes
- Work with Envelopes
- Create Blends
- Use the Transparency Panel and the Color Picker
- Apply Effects
- Use the Appearance Panel
- Work with Graphic Styles
- Use Opacity Masks

SOFT SKILLS CHALLENGE

An argumentative presentation is a speech given in support of a particular cause or claim. You will prepare an argumentative presentation to share your position on sea turtle conservation with an audience. Before doing so, be sure to conduct ample research on the conservation status of your chosen sea turtle species. Is this species critically endangered, endangered, vulnerable, or is there insufficient data to determine its status? Delve deeper to understand what that specific status means. Then look into the reasons for its conservation status. What puts this specific species at risk and why? This question may help focus your research on its diet or migratory patterns, or perhaps on pollution and/or poaching.

Be sure to document your findings and write down your main points before presenting. What argument are you trying to make? What supporting details would you like your audience to remember? Practice your speech so you are confident while presenting. You want your audience to view you as an expert on the topic.

GETTING STARTED

The planning and brainstorming step of your creative process can often be the most difficult and unstructured part, but it is also where you can be the most creative. Focus on exploring and researching your ideas without too many constraints. You might be surprised how one idea connects to another.

1. Find some inspiration. Search online, and look through books and your favorite magazines. Select imagery and photos you find visually appealing. Look for editing styles and visual effects that effectively communicate a message.

2. Do your research. Gather background information on the sea turtle species and its marine environment. What factors are harming this species? Think about the different perspectives you are reading about and decide whether you agree or disagree with their position(s). This will help you identify a story and create a composition that is authentic and well-informed.

3. Sketch out your ideas. Think about the elements you want to focus on and where they will sit on the page. Decide what role each piece will play in your story and how it will interact with other elements. Sketch out what you want each element to look like. Write down words and phrases that relate to your drawings.

◀ HOMERUS SWALLOWTAIL
Papilio homerus
Named after the Greek poet Homer. Featured on Jamaican postage stamps.

Ø Aristolochia dielsiana

Male

Female

NORTH AMERICA

JAMAICA

SOUTH AMERICA

Winged Desire

Of the planet's roughly 20,000 species of butterflies, swallowtails are especially intriguing to collectors. The more than 560 swallowtails include the world's largest butterflies—birdwings—and some of the most expensive and threatened (five are shown here). They face a triple menace of habitat loss, climate change, and poaching. Thanks to conservation programs and anti-poaching laws, swallowtails are surviving despite a black market where prices start in the pennies and run into the thousands for protected species.

Actual size of largest *O. alexandrae* on record.

All other butterflies shown at **half actual size.**

Ø **Host plant**
Hernandia catalpifolia

LUZON PEACOCK ▶ SWALLOWTAIL
Papilio chikae
Discovered in 1965; traders often mislabel this species to elude law enforcement.

Male

Female

Ø Euodia glauca

ASIA

PHILIPPINES

AUSTRALIA

ay eggs after
eaves with their
which have sensors
their target plant.

SENSORS

LEAF

◀ **QUEEN ALEXANDRA'S BIRDWING**
Ornithoptera alexandrae
The *O. alexandrae* is the
largest butterfly known to
scientists—its wingspan
can reach nearly 12 inches.

ASIA

PAPUA
NEW
GUINEA

AUSTRALIA

CLEAR
SCALE

DARK
SCALE

Female

Male

Microscopic scales scatter
light, creating iridescent
colors and patterns that
likely help attract mates.

Flying rarities

A coveted half-male, half-
female gynandromorph
can occur if a fertilized egg
unevenly divides into the
two cells that form each side
of a butterfly's body.

| UNIT 3 |

INCORPORATING ADVANCED TECHNIQUES

Winged Desire is a realistic illustration of some of the
world's largest butterflies, with inset locator maps.

Illustration by Monica Serrano. From "The Butterfly Catchers."
National Geographic Magazine, Vol. 234, No. 2, August, 2018

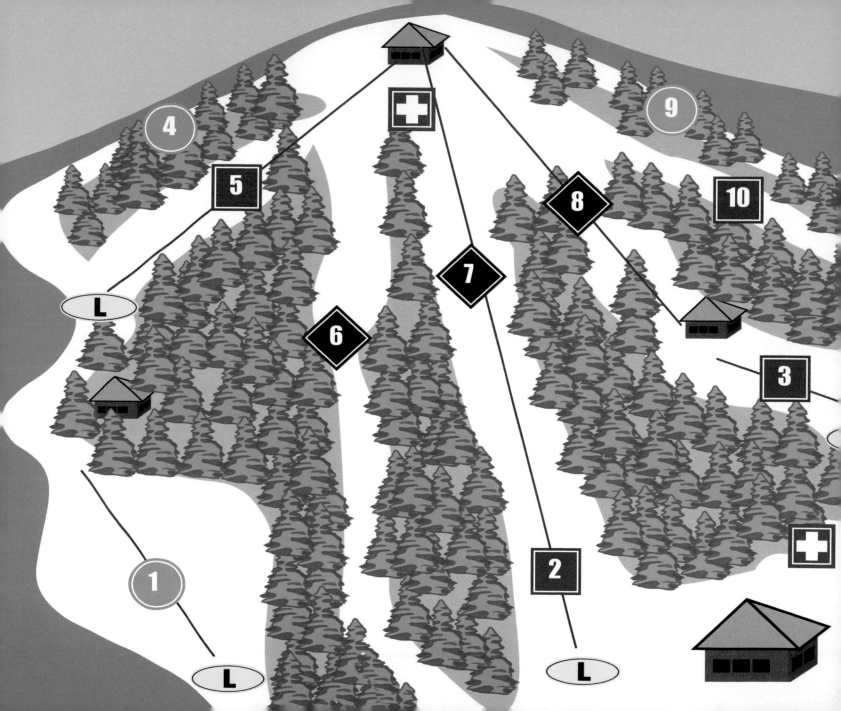

Ai CHAPTER **9**

DRAWING WITH
SYMBOLS

1. Create Symbols
2. Place Symbol Instances
3. Modify Symbols and Symbol Instances
4. Create Symbol Instance Sets
5. Modify Symbol Instance Sets

CERTIFIED
PROFESSIONAL

Adobe Certified Professional in Graphic Design and Illustration Using Adobe Illustrator

2. Project Setup and Interface

This objective covers the interface setup and program settings that assist in an efficient and effective workflow, as well as knowledge about ingesting digital assets for a project.

2.6 Manage preset brushes, symbols, styles, and patterns.

   A Open and browse libraries of included brushes, symbols, graphic styles, and patterns.

   B Edit brushes, symbols, styles, and patterns.

4. Creating and Modifying Visual Elements

This objective covers core tools and functionality of the application, as well as tools that affect the visual appearance of document elements.

4.6 Modify the appearance of design elements using effects and graphic styles.

   C Expand the appearance of objects.

5. Publishing Digital Media

This objective covers saving and exporting documents or assets within individual layers or selections.

5.2 Export or save digital images to various file formats.

   B Save images in appropriate formats for print or screen.

CREATE SYMBOLS

▶ What You'll Do

In this lesson, you will create symbols from Illustrator artwork and save them on the Symbols panel.

Working with Symbols

In Illustrator, the file size of a document is largely determined by the number and complexity of objects in the document. The greater the number of objects in the document, the greater the file size. A large number of objects with gradients, blends, and effects increases the file size greatly. When you are creating graphics for the Internet, file size becomes a serious concern.

Symbols are one solution for creating complex files while maintaining a relatively low file size. **Symbols** are graphic objects you create and store on the Symbols panel.

Imagine that you were drawing a field of flowers, and you have drawn a pink, a blue, and a yellow flower. Each flower has a radial gradient in its center and color blends to add dimension to the petals and green leaves. Now imagine that you must drag and drop 200 copies of each to create your field of flowers! Along with a cramp in your hand, you would have an unusually large Illustrator file.

With the three flowers defined as symbols, you can create 200 symbol instances of each flower symbol quickly and easily. The key is that you haven't actually added the complex artwork multiple times because the instances don't really exist as artwork. A **symbol instance** is a reference to the original symbol artwork on the Symbols panel. Symbol instances function only to show the positioning of the symbol artwork on the artboard.

Symbolism tools allow you to edit large numbers of symbol instances quickly and effectively. Whenever you are using the same artwork multiple times in a document, consider using symbols to save time and reduce file size.

Creating Symbols

You can create symbols from any Illustrator artwork, including text, compound paths, and grouped paths. Symbols may also include blends, effects, brush strokes, gradients, and even other symbols.

The Symbols panel, shown in Figure 1, is a great place to store artwork that you plan to use again. When you use symbol artwork, you can modify the symbol instance on the artboard without affecting its original appearance on the panel. In this way, you can think of the Symbols panel as a database of your original art.

TIP Illustrator comes loaded with hundreds of symbols for you to use. Click the Symbol Libraries Menu to see all the available choices.

Figure 1 Symbols panel

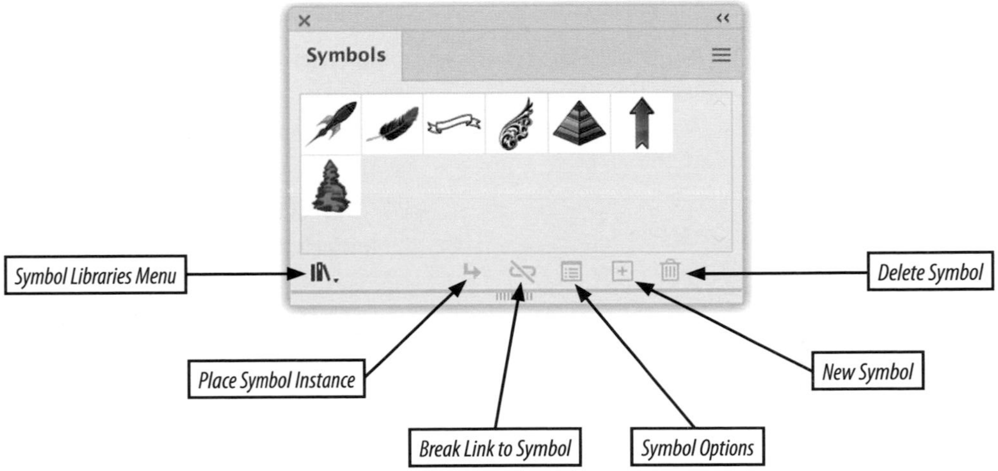

Symbol Libraries Menu

Place Symbol Instance

Break Link to Symbol

Symbol Options

New Symbol

Delete Symbol

Create symbols

1. Open AI 9-1.ai, then save it as **Ski Trail Map**.
2. Open the **Symbols panel**.
3. Select the **brown house artwork** in the scratch area outside the artboard.
4. Click the **Symbols panel menu button** 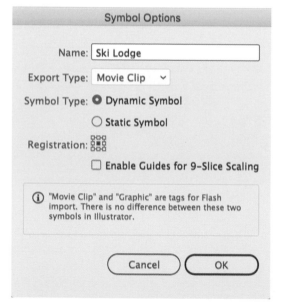, then click **New Symbol**.

   The Symbol Options dialog box opens.
5. Type **Ski Lodge** in the Name text box, note that Movie Clip is the Export Type, by default, then compare your Symbol Options dialog box to Figure 2.

Symbols are often used with animation on websites. Sticking with the default Movie Clip type has no effect on symbols in Illustrator.

6. Click **OK** to add the Ski Lodge symbol to the Symbols panel.
7. Select the **green circle artwork**, then drag it into the Symbols panel.

   The Symbol Options dialog box opens.
8. Type **Novice** in the **Name text box**, then click **OK**.
9. Add the **blue square artwork** to the Symbols panel, then name it **Intermediate**.

10. Add the **black diamond artwork** to the Symbols panel, then name it **Expert**.
11. Add the **red square artwork** to the Symbols panel, then name it **First Aid**.
12. Add the **orange oval artwork** to the Symbols panel, then name it **Chairlift**.

    Your Symbols panel should resemble Figure 3.
13. Delete the Ski Lodge, Novice, Intermediate, Expert, First Aid, and Chairlift icons on the artboard, then save your work.

You created new symbols by using the Symbols panel menu and by dragging and dropping artwork to the Symbols panel.

Figure 2 Symbol Options dialog box

Figure 3 Symbols panel with new symbols added

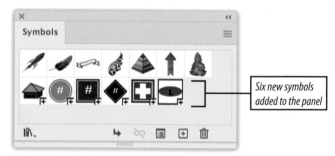

Six new symbols added to the panel

PLACE SYMBOL INSTANCES

▶ *What You'll Do*

In this lesson, you will place symbol instances on the artboard.

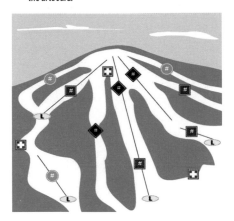

Placing Instances of Symbols

If a symbol is artwork stored on the Symbols panel, then the artwork, when used in the document, is called a symbol instance. You can place a symbol instance on the artboard by first selecting the symbol on the Symbols panel, then dragging it to the artboard, or by selecting it, then clicking the Place Symbol Instance button on the Symbols panel, as shown in Figure 4. You can also use the Place Symbol Instance command on the Symbols panel menu.

Symbol instances are "linked" to their corresponding symbols on the panel. This relationship introduces powerful functionality when you work with symbol instances. Imagine an illustration showing a field with hundreds of flowers, all of them yellow. If the flowers were all symbol instances, you could change the single symbol to pink, and all the yellow instances would update immediately.

Figure 4 Placing a symbol instance

Symbol instance placed on artboard

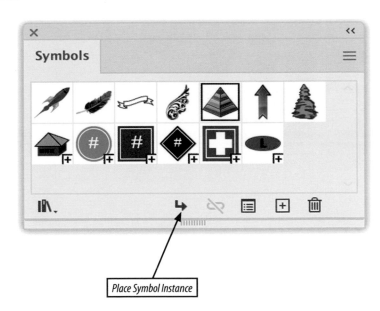

Place Symbol Instance

Place instances of a symbol

1. Click the **Novice symbol** on the Symbols panel.

2. Click the **Symbols panel menu button** ≡, then click **Place Symbol Instance**.

   A single Novice symbol instance appears on the artboard.

3. Drag the **green Novice symbol instance** to the location shown in Figure 5.

4. Click the **Intermediate symbol** on the Symbols panel, then drag it to the artboard above the Novice symbol instance.

5. Drag a **symbol instance** of the **Expert**, **First Aid**, and **Chairlift symbols** onto the artboard, then position them as shown in Figure 5.

6. Click the **Chairlift symbol instance** on the artboard, press and hold **[option] (Mac)** or **[Alt] (Win)**, then drag and drop **three copies** as shown in Figure 6.

7. Copy and reposition the **Novice**, **Intermediate**, **Expert**, and **First Aid symbol instances** so your screen resembles Figure 7.

Figure 5 Positioning symbol instances

Figure 6 Positioning copies of the Chairlift symbol instance

Figure 7 Positioning the Novice, Intermediate, Expert, and First Aid symbol instances

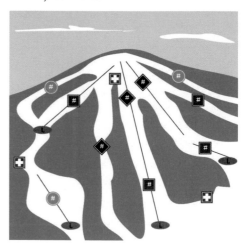

You can either drag the symbols from the Symbols panel and place them, or you can drag and drop copies of the existing symbols already on the artboard.

8. Save your work, then continue to the next set of steps.

You placed symbol instances of five symbols on the artboard. You then duplicated the symbol instances and positioned them on the artboard.

Edit a symbol

1. Double-click the **Chairlift symbol** on the Symbols panel.

   When you double-click a symbol on the Symbols panel, Illustrator switches to Isolation mode and the symbol is isolated on a blank artboard. A white cross hatch appears at the center of the artwork.

2. Click the **Direct Selection tool** ▷, then select the **orange fill background** of the symbol.

3. Change the **fill color** to **Yellow**.

4. Press **[esc]** to exit Isolation mode.

5. Compare your screen to Figure 8.

   All instances of the Chairlift symbol instance are updated with the yellow fill.

6. Save your work, then continue to the next set of steps.

You modified a symbol on the Symbols panel, noting that all instances on the artboard automatically update.

Explore symbol libraries

1. Click the **Symbol Libraries Menu button** ▥ on the Symbols panel.

Figure 8 Chairlift symbol instances updated

A menu of libraries is revealed. Together, these libraries contain thousands of royalty-free symbols for you to use.

2. Click **Mad Science**.

   The Mad Science symbol library opens as a panel, as shown in Figure 9.

You showed the Symbol Libraries Menu on the Symbols panel. You then opened the Mad Science symbol library to see symbol artwork available for you to use.

Figure 9 Mad Science symbol library

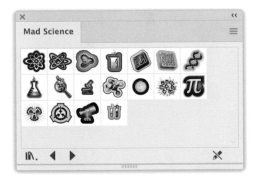

MODIFY SYMBOLS AND SYMBOL INSTANCES

What You'll Do

In this lesson, you will modify both symbol instances and the symbols themselves.

Modifying Symbol Instances

When working with symbol instances, approach them as you would any other Illustrator artwork. You can transform symbol instances by using commands on the Object menu or by using any of the transform tools. You can cut, copy, and drag and drop copies of symbol instances. You can perform any operation from the Transparency, Appearance, and Graphic Styles panels. For example, you can reduce the opacity of a symbol instance and you can apply effects, such as a drop shadow or a distortion.

Symbols are most often composed of multiple objects, such as you would expect to find in a drawing of a butterfly or a flower. When you select a symbol instance on the artboard, its selection marks show only a simple bounding box, as shown in Figure 10; the individual elements of the artwork are not selected.

You can, however, select the individual components of a symbol instance by using the Expand command on the Object menu. The bounding box disappears, and the individual elements of the artwork are available to be selected (and modified), as shown in Figure 11.

Figure 10 When you select a symbol instance, the individual elements of the artwork are not selected

Figure 11 The Expand command allows you to select the individual elements of the artwork

Redefining Symbols

Once you have modified a symbol instance, you can use the modified artwork to redefine the associated symbol on the panel by replacing the original symbol. When you do so, all existing symbol instances are updated and reflect the changes to the symbol.

If you don't want a particular symbol instance to be updated, you can select the instance and break the link to the symbol. The symbol instance will no longer be associated with the symbol.

You can also modify a symbol instance on the artboard and use it to create a new symbol without affecting the original symbol on which it is based. Thus, the Symbols panel is useful for storing subtle or dramatic variations of artwork. For example, if you are drawing a landscape that features a wind farm, you can draw a single windmill, save it as a symbol, rotate the blades on the original artwork, then save a new symbol, and so forth.

TIP Symbols, ideal for web graphics, can be output as Scalable Vector Graphics (SVG) files. To output your symbol artwork as SVG, click File on the menu bar, click Save As, then click SVG from the Save as type list arrow.

Edit symbol instances

1. Using the **Selection tool** ![cursor], select the **green Novice symbol instance** in the lower-left corner of the artboard.

   A bounding box identifies the selection. The elements of the artwork cannot be selected individually.

2. Click **Object** on the menu bar, then click **Expand**.

TIP If you receive a message saying, "You are about to edit the Symbol definition. Any edits to the symbol will be applied to all its instances. Do you want to continue?" click OK.

3. In the Expand dialog box, verify that the **Object check box** is checked, and the **Fill check box** is not checked, then click **OK**.

   The elements of the symbol instance are selected individually.

4. Deselect the symbol instance, click the **Type tool** ![T], highlight the **# sign** in the symbol instance, then type **1**.

   Your screen should resemble Figure 12.

TIP If you receive a message stating that the text was created in a previous version of Illustrator, click OK.

5. Using the same method, expand the **Novice**, **Intermediate**, and **Expert symbol instances**, then change their numbers to those shown in Figure 13.

6. Select **every symbol instance** and **each of the blue chairlift lines** on the artboard, then hide them.

7. Save your work, then continue to the next set of steps.

You used the Expand command to allow you to select individual elements of a symbol instance and edit those elements.

Figure 12 Editing a symbol instance

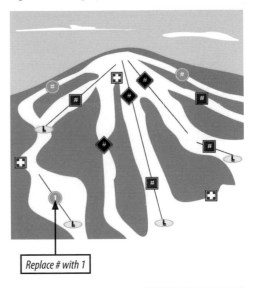

Replace # with 1

Figure 13 Adding numbers to symbol instances

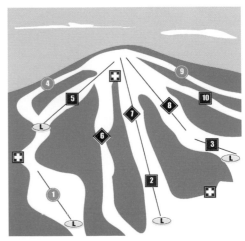

Edit a symbol

1. Position **four symbol instances of the Ski Lodge symbol**, as shown in Figure 14.

2. Select the **bottom-right Ski Lodge symbol instance**, then click the **Break Link to Symbol button** on the Symbols panel.

3. Select the **top Ski Lodge symbol instance**, then click the **Break Link to Symbol button**.

4. Scale the **top ski lodge artwork 50%.**

5. Press and hold **[option] (Mac)** or **[Alt] (Win)**, then drag the **scaled artwork** on **top of the Ski Lodge symbol** on the Symbols panel.

   The three symbol instances of the Ski Lodge symbol are updated, as shown in Figure 15. The bottom ski lodge artwork does not change.

6. Click the **Sequoia symbol**, then place one instance of the symbol in the scratch area.

7. Click the **Break Link to Symbol button**.

8. Reduce the artwork **50%.**

9. Press and hold **[option] (Mac)** or **[Alt] (Win)**, then drag the **edited tree artwork on top of the Sequoia symbol** on the Symbols panel.

10. Delete the **Sequoia symbol instance** in the scratch area.

11. Save your work, then continue to the next set of steps.

You edited symbols by modifying instances, then replaced the original symbols with the edited artwork. You protected a symbol instance from modification by breaking its link.

Figure 14 Positioning four symbol instances of the Ski Lodge symbol

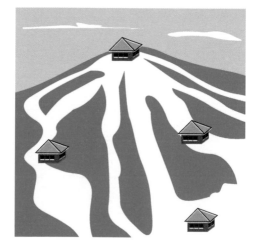

Figure 15 Updated instances of the Ski Lodge symbol

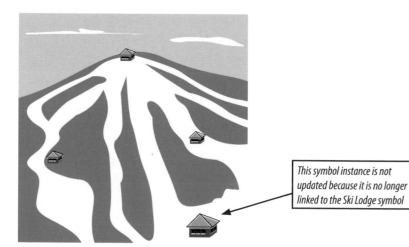

This symbol instance is not updated because it is no longer linked to the Ski Lodge symbol

Transform symbol instances

1. Select the **six green objects** within the snow area of the artboard, change their fill color to a **light gray**, then position **an instance of the Sequoia symbol** so your screen resembles Figure 16.

TIP Use the Color panel to mix a new light gray color if necessary.

2. Drag and drop **nine copies of the Sequoia symbol instance** on the artboard, so your screen resembles Figure 17.

3. Verify that the **Sequoia symbol** is still selected on the Symbols panel, click the **Symbols panel menu button** ☰ , then click **Select All Instances**.

All instances of the Sequoia symbol are selected on the artboard.

4. Scale the symbol instances **75%**.

5. Drag and drop **14 copies of the newly scaled Sequoia symbol instance** to the opposite side of the artboard, as shown in Figure 18.

TIP Press [option] (Mac) or [Alt] (Win) while dragging to create copies.

6. Save your work, then continue to the next set of steps.

You positioned one instance of a symbol on the artboard, then copied it nine times. You used the Select All Instances command to select the 10 instances of the symbol quickly, scaled them 75%, then positioned 14 copies of the scaled symbol instance.

Figure 16 Positioning the Sequoia symbol instance

Figure 17 Positioning nine copies of the Sequoia symbol instance

Figure 18 Positioning 14 copies of the Sequoia symbol instance

CREATE SYMBOL INSTANCE SETS

▶ *What You'll Do*

In this lesson, you will use the Symbol Sprayer tool to create sets of symbol instances and mixed symbol instance sets.

Creating a Symbol Instance Set

Instead of creating symbol instances one at a time using the Symbols panel, you can use the Symbol Sprayer tool to create multiple symbol instances quickly. Imagine that you have a symbol of a star and you want to draw a night sky filled with stars. The Symbol Sprayer tool would be a good choice for applying the star symbol multiple times.

Symbol instances created with the Symbol Sprayer tool are called **symbol instance sets**. Incorporate the term "set" into your work with symbols to differentiate the multiple symbol instances created with the Symbol Sprayer tool from individual instances of a symbol that you create using the Symbols panel.

To create a symbol instance set, click the symbol that you want to use on the Symbols panel, then drag the Symbol Sprayer tool where you want the symbols to appear on the artboard.

Working with Symbol Instance Sets

When you create a symbol instance set with the Symbol Sprayer tool, the entire set of symbols is identified within a bounding box, as shown in Figure 19. If the set is selected and you begin dragging the Symbol Sprayer tool again, the new symbol instances will be added to the selected set—even if the new symbol instances are outside of the existing set's bounding box. (The bounding box will expand to encompass the new symbol instances.)

Figure 19 A symbol instance set created with the Symbol Sprayer tool

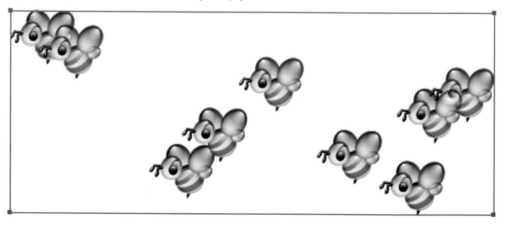

You can also create mixed symbol instance sets. Mixed symbol instance sets include symbol instances based on more than one symbol. To create a mixed symbol instance set, make your first set of symbol instances, click a different symbol on the Symbols panel, then drag the Symbol Sprayer tool where you want the new symbols to appear on the artboard. The new symbol instances will be added to the existing set, as shown in Figure 20.

Even though a symbol instance set, by definition, appears as multiple objects, it is best to think of it as a single object. A symbol instance set can be modified and transformed (as a whole). Figure 21 shows a symbol instance set that has been reflected using the Reflect tool.

Setting Options for the Symbol Sprayer Tool

The Symbol Sprayer tool has many options to help you control the dispersion of symbol instances. You can access these options in the Symbolism Tools Options dialog box by double-clicking the Symbol Sprayer tool on the toolbar.

The Diameter setting determines the brush size of the tool. Use a larger brush size to disperse symbol instances over a greater area of the artboard. Note that the brush size does not determine the size of the symbol instances themselves.

The Intensity setting determines the number of instances of the symbol that will be sprayed. The higher the intensity setting, the greater the number of symbol instances that will be dispersed in a given amount of time.

Figure 20 A mixed symbol instance set

Figure 21 A symbol instance set transformed with the Reflect tool

The Symbol Set Density setting determines how closely the symbol instances will be positioned to each other. The higher the density setting, the more closely packed the instances will appear. Figure 22 shows a symbol instance set with a high symbol set density, and Figure 23 shows a symbol instance set with a low symbol set density.

Figure 22 A symbol instance set with a high symbol set density

Figure 23 A symbol instance set with a low symbol set density

Expanding a Symbol Instance Set

It is best to think of the Symbol Sprayer tool as a way to quickly disperse symbol instances but not as a tool to position symbols precisely.

Once you have created a symbol instance set that contains roughly the number of symbol instances with which you want to work and have positioned them roughly where you want them to be on the artboard, you can then apply the Expand command to release the set into individual symbol instances. Figure 24 shows a symbol instance set expanded into individual symbol instances.

The power of this operation cannot be overstated. Once expanded, all the symbol instances of the set can be transformed, repositioned, duplicated, or deleted. Expand the individual symbol instances to be able to select their component parts.

Figure 24 A symbol instance set expanded into individual symbol instances

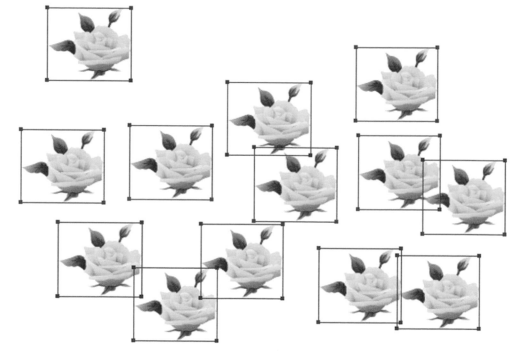

Use the Symbol Sprayer tool

1. Click the **Sequoia symbol** on the Symbols panel if it is not already selected.

2. Double-click the **Symbol Sprayer tool** 🖭 on the toolbar.

3. Type **.5** in the **Diameter text box**, type **3** in the **Intensity text box**, type **5** in the **Symbol Set Density text box**, then click **OK**.

4. Click and drag the **Symbol Sprayer tool** 🖭 to spray **instances of the Sequoia symbol over the gray areas** so your artboard resembles Figure 25.

TIP Don't try to create all the instances in one move. Click and drag the Symbol Sprayer tool 🖭 multiple times in short bursts. Your results will vary from the figure.

5. Press and hold **[option] (Mac)** or **[Alt] (Win)**, then click the **Symbol Sprayer tool** 🖭 over symbol instances that you do not want to include to remove them.

6. With the entire set still selected as a unit, click **Object** on the menu bar, click **Expand**, verify that only the **Object check box** is checked, then click **OK**.

7. Deselect, then using the **Direct Selection tool** ▷, move the **individual Sequoia symbol instances** so your work resembles Figure 26.

Figure 25 Instances of the Sequoia symbol created with the Symbol Sprayer tool

Figure 26 Moving and deleting symbol instances from the set

You may also copy and/or delete instances as necessary.

8. Click **Object** on the menu bar, click **Show All**, then, while the hidden objects are still selected, bring them to the front, then deselect.

   Your screen should resemble Figure 27.

9. Save your work, then close the Trail Map document.

You defined the diameter, the intensity, and the symbol set density for the Symbol Sprayer tool. You then used the Symbol Sprayer tool to create a set of Sequoia symbols.

Figure 27 The majority of the trail map artwork is created with symbol instances

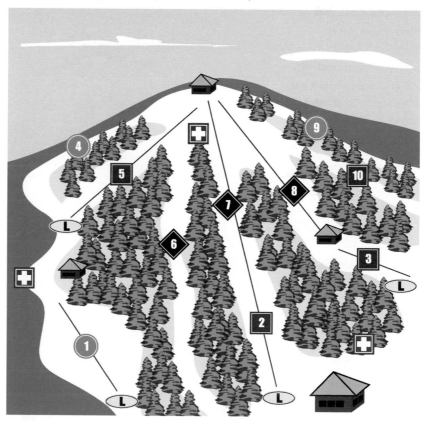

Create a mixed symbol instance set

1. Open AI 9-2.ai, then save it as **Fish Tank**.

2. Click the **Red Stone symbol** on the Symbols panel.

3. Double-click the **Symbol Sprayer tool** 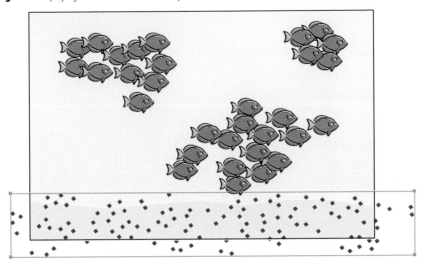 .

4. Type **1** in the **Diameter text box**, type **8** in the **Intensity text box**, type **5** in the **Symbol Set Density text box**, then click **OK**.

5. Click and drag the **Symbol Sprayer tool** over the "sand," as shown in Figure 28.

6. Click the **Purple Stone symbol**, then drag the **Symbol Sprayer tool** over the "sand," as shown in Figure 29.

   The Purple Stone symbols are added to the set, creating a mixed symbol instance set.

Continued on next page

Figure 28 Spraying instances of the Red Stone symbol

Figure 29 Spraying instances of the Purple Stone symbol

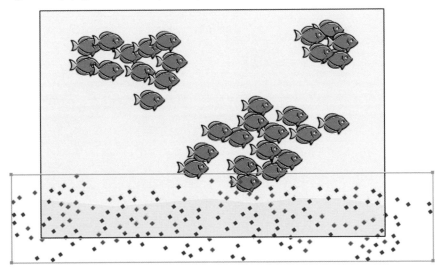

7. Add the **Green Stone**, **Orange Stone**, and **Tan Stone symbols** to the set, so your screen resembles Figure 30.

8. Select the **sand object**, copy it, paste in front, then bring the copy to the front.

9. Press and hold **[shift]**, then click the **mixed symbol instance set** so the **sand** and the **set of rocks** are selected.

10. Click **Object** on the menu bar, point to **Clipping Mask**, click **Make**, deselect, then save your work.

    The sand acts as a mask to hide the rocks that extend beyond the sand object, as shown in Figure 31.

You used five different symbols and the Symbol Sprayer tool to create a mixed set of symbol instances.

Figure 30 Spraying instances of the Green Stone, Orange Stone, and Tan Stone symbols

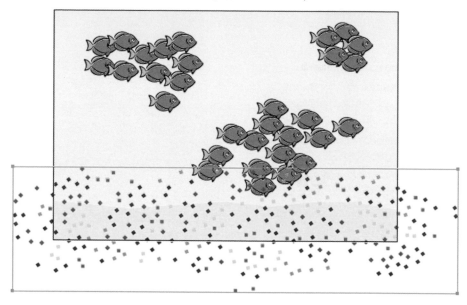

Figure 31 Masking the mixed symbol instance set

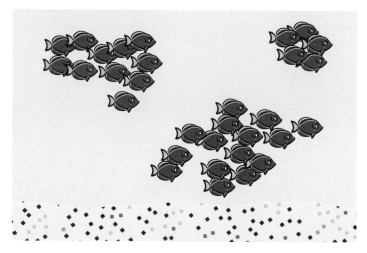

MODIFY SYMBOL INSTANCE SETS

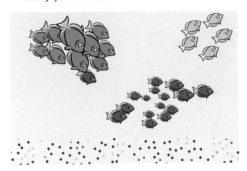

Using Symbolism Tools

Illustrator offers eight symbolism tools that you can use to modify symbol instances or sets of symbol instances. You will most often use the symbolism tools to affect symbol instances within a set, since individual symbol instances are easy to select and modify directly with transform tools and menu commands. Table 1 lists each symbolism tool and its function.

TABLE 1: SYMBOLISM TOOLS	
Symbolism tool	**Function**
Symbol Sprayer tool	Places symbol instances on the artboard
Symbol Shifter tool	Moves symbol instances and/or changes their stacking order in the set
Symbol Scruncher tool	Pulls symbol instances together or apart
Symbol Sizer tool	Increases or decreases the size of symbol instances
Symbol Spinner tool	Rotates symbol instances
Symbol Stainer tool	Changes the color of symbol instances gradually to the current fill color on the toolbar
Symbol Screener tool	Increases or decreases the transparency of symbol instances
Symbol Styler tool	Applies the selected style on the Graphic Styles panel to symbol instances

Figure 32 shows an illustration of a symbol instance set with each tool applied to the set.

When you apply symbolism tools to mixed symbol instance sets, each corresponding symbol must be selected on the Symbols panel in order for each type of symbol instance to be modified by the tool. For example, imagine you have created a mixed symbol instance set of four types of flowers—such as daisies, tulips, roses, and lilies—and only the daisy symbol is selected on the Symbols panel. If you apply a symbolism tool to the mixed symbol instance set, only the instances of the daisy symbol will be modified.

Figure 32 Applying the symbolism tools

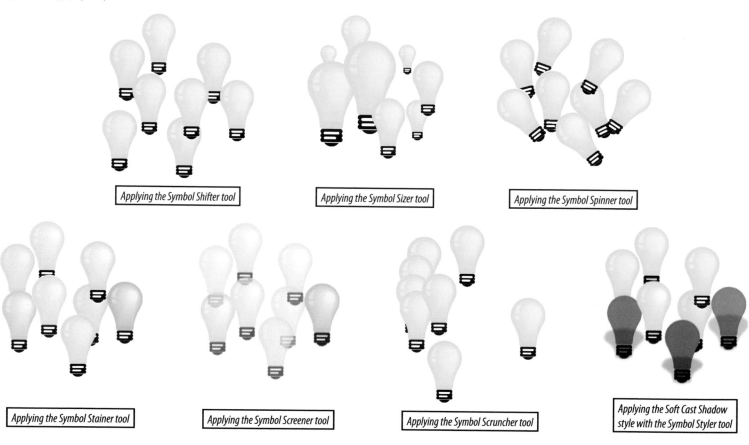

Applying the Symbol Shifter tool

Applying the Symbol Sizer tool

Applying the Symbol Spinner tool

Applying the Symbol Stainer tool

Applying the Symbol Screener tool

Applying the Symbol Scruncher tool

Applying the Soft Cast Shadow style with the Symbol Styler tool

When working with symbolism tools, it is also important that you set realistic goals. The symbolism tools are particularly useful if you have created a symbol set that is intended to appear random. For example, if you use symbol instances to render multiple stars in the night sky, the symbolism tools will be an excellent choice for modifying their orientation on the artboard. However, if your goal is to position symbol instances precisely in your artwork, you should expand the symbol set and use the selection tools and transform tools to modify each instance directly.

Use the Symbol Stainer tool

1. Click **Object** on the menu bar, then click **Unlock All**.

2. Change the **fill color** on the toolbar to **green**.

3. Click the **Symbol Stainer tool** ⬚ on the toolbar.

   The Symbol Stainer tool ⬚ is hidden beneath the Symbol Sprayer tool ⬚ .

   TIP Press and hold the current Symbol tool until you see all the Symbol tools, then click the tearoff tab at the end of the row of tools to create a floating Symbol tools panel.

4. Click and drag the **Symbol Stainer tool** ⬚ over the **11 fish symbol instances** in the upper-left region of the artboard so your work resembles Figure 33.

   TIP Using the Symbol Stainer tool ⬚ results in increased file size and may tax your computer's performance.

5. Position the **Symbol Stainer tool** ⬚ over the **bottom-most fish symbol instance** in the same group.

6. Press and hold **[option] (Mac)** or **[Alt] (Win)**, then press and hold the **mouse button** for approximately two seconds.

   Pressing [option] (Mac) or [Alt] (Win) while using the Symbol Stainer tool ⬚ gradually removes color applied by the Symbol Stainer tool ⬚ . The symbol instance that you clicked returns to its original blue color. The surrounding symbol instances are not affected as directly; their color changes toward the original blue color but remains somewhat green. Your results may vary.

7. Change the **fill color** on the toolbar to **yellow**.

8. Drag the **Symbol Stainer tool** ⬚ over the **five fish symbol instances** in the upper-right region of the artboard, so your work resembles Figure 34.

   You used the Symbol Stainer tool to modify the color of symbol instances within a set.

Figure 33 Applying the Symbol Stainer tool with a green fill

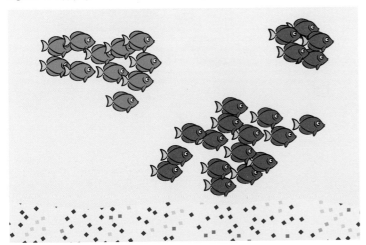

Figure 34 Applying the Symbol Stainer tool with a yellow fill

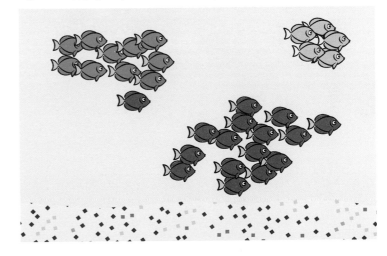

Use the Symbol Shifter tool

1. Double-click the **Symbol Shifter tool** 🐟 to open the **Symbolism Tools Options dialog box**.

   The Symbol Shifter tool 🐟 is hidden beneath the current symbolism tool if you did not create a tearoff Symbol tools panel.

2. Type **.25** in the **Diameter text box**, then click **OK**.

3. Position the **Symbol Shifter tool** 🐟 over **any of the green fish**, press and hold **[shift]**, then click the **fish instance**.

The symbol instance is brought to the front of the set.

TIP It's usually a good idea to enter a small diameter setting when you want to affect the stacking order of instances in a set. A larger brush will affect the stacking order of surrounding instances.

4. Press and hold **[shift] [option] (Mac)** or **[shift] [Alt] (Win)**, then click a **green fish**.

   The symbol instance is sent to the back. Figure 35 shows an example of the green fish instances after the stacking order has been affected by the

Symbol Shifter tool 🐟 . Compare your choices and results.

5. Change the **Diameter setting** of the **Symbol Shifter tool** 🐟 to **2.5**.

   Click and drag the **Symbol Shifter tool** 🐟 over the **yellow fish** until they no longer touch each other, as shown in Figure 36.

   Your results may vary.

You used the Symbol Shifter tool to change the stacking order of instances within the symbol set and to move symbol instances within the set.

Figure 35 Using the Symbol Shifter tool to change the stacking order of instances in a set

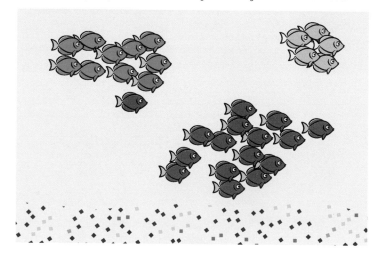

Figure 36 Using the Symbol Shifter tool to reposition instances within the set

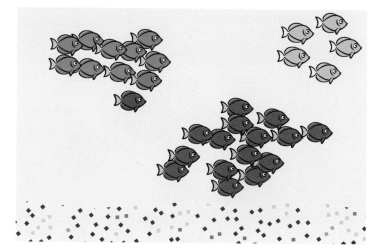

Use the Symbol Spinner tool

1. Double-click the **Symbol Spinner tool** on the toolbar.

2. Type **2.6** in the **Diameter text box**, type **10** in the **Intensity text box**, then click **OK**.

3. Position the **Symbol Spinner tool** over the **center of the green fish group**.

4. Click and drag **slightly to the right**, so the fish rotate, as shown in Figure 37.

   Your results may vary.

TIP The blue arrows that appear when you click and drag the Symbol Spinner tool are not always reliable predictors of the final rotation of the symbol instances. The Diameter and Intensity settings and the location of the tool in regard to the instances all affect the impact of the rotation.

5. Position the **Symbol Spinner tool** over the **center of the yellow fish group**.

6. Click and drag **slightly to the upper-left** so the yellow fish rotate, as shown in Figure 38.

   Your results may vary.

You used the Symbol Spinner tool to rotate symbol instances within the set.

Figure 37 Using the Symbol Spinner tool on the green fish

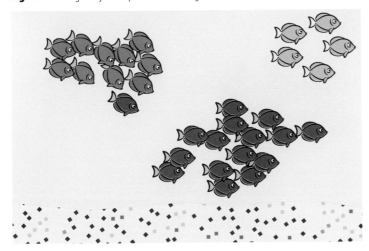

Figure 38 Using the Symbol Spinner tool on the yellow fish

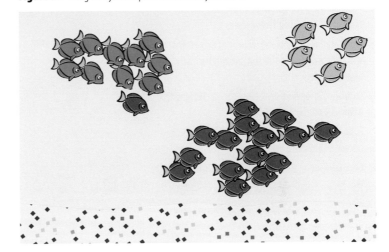

Use the Symbol Sizer tool

1. Double-click the **Symbol Sizer tool**.

2. Type **2** in the **Diameter text box**, type **8** in the **Intensity text box**, then click **OK**.

3. Position the **Symbol Sizer tool** over the **center of the green fish group**.

4. Press and hold the **mouse button** for approximately two seconds so your work resembles Figure 39.

   Your results may vary.

5. Position the **Symbol Sizer tool** over the **center of the blue fish group**.

6. Press and hold **[option] (Mac)** or **[Alt] (Win)**, then press and hold the **mouse button** for approximately three seconds.

7. Click the **Selection tool**, then click the **fish artwork** on the artboard to select it.

   A single frame appears around all the symbols because they are a set.

8. Click **Object** on the menu bar, then click **Expand**.

   The Expand dialog box opens.

9. Check only the **Object option**, then click **OK**.

The single symbol set is expanded. Each individual symbol now has its own frame and is selectable.

10. Using the **Direct Selection tool**, select **individual symbols**.

11. Use the **Free Transform tool** to scale or rotate the artwork to your liking.

12. Deselect all, then save your work.

    Figure 40 shows one possible result.

13. Close the Fish Tank document.

You used the Symbol Sizer tool to change the size of symbol instances within the set.

Figure 39 Using the Symbol Sizer tool to enlarge symbol instances

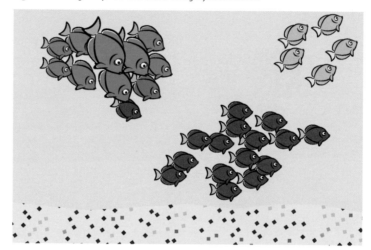

Figure 40 Final artwork

Create symbols

1. Open AI 9-3.ai, then save it as **Winter Ball Fun**.
2. Show the Brushes panel, then drag the Radiant Star brush onto the artboard.
3. Verify that the Symbols panel is displayed, then drag the Radiant Star artwork into the Symbols panel.
4. Name the new symbol **Snowflake**.
5. Delete the Radiant Star artwork from the artboard.

Place symbol instances

1. Click the Snowflake symbol on the Symbols panel.
2. Click the Place Symbol Instance button on the Symbols panel.
3. Position the symbol instance between the words *ball* and *December*.

Modify symbols and symbol instances

1. Scale the Snowflake symbol instance 35%, then reposition the Snowflake symbol instance if necessary.
2. Click Effect on the menu bar, point to Distort & Transform, click Pucker & Bloat, type **50** in the text box, then click OK.
3. Change the Opacity of the symbol instance to 75%.
4. Click the Break Link to Symbol button on the Symbols panel.

5. Press [option] (Mac) or [Alt] (Win), then drag the modified snowflake artwork directly on top of the Snowflake symbol on the Symbols panel.

Create symbol instance sets

1. Double-click the Symbol Sprayer tool.
2. Enter **1** for the Diameter, **2** for the Intensity, and **1** for the Symbol Set Density in the Symbolism Tools Options dialog box.
3. Spray approximately 25 symbol instances of the Snowflake symbol evenly over the artboard.

Modify symbol instance sets

1. Use the Symbol Sizer tool to enlarge and reduce symbol instances.
2. Expand the symbol set.
3. Move or delete symbols to your liking.
4. Save your work, then see Figure 41 for one possible solution.
5. Close the Winter Ball Fun document.

Figure 41 Completed Skills Review

You work in the design department of a major Internet portal site. As part of the promotion of this year's Hooray for Hollywood Awards, your site will link to the Awards' site. You are asked to create a banner that says "click here to meet the stars" against a starry sky.

1. Open AI 9-4.ai, then save it as **Hollywood Stars**.
2. Double-click the Symbol Sprayer tool.
3. Enter **2** for the Diameter, **1** for the Intensity, and **10** for the Symbol Set Density.
4. Click the 5 Point Star symbol on the Symbols panel, then drag the Symbol Sprayer tool across the gradient-filled rectangle.
5. Repeat Step 4, using the 8 Point Star symbol on the Symbols panel.
6. Expand the symbol set.
7. Use the Symbol Shifter tool to move symbol instances that overlap each other.
8. Use the Symbol Sizer tool to enlarge and reduce symbol instances to add depth and variety.
9. Show all to reveal the semitransparent text.
10. Save your work, compare your illustration to Figure 42, then close the Hollywood Stars document.

Figure 42 Completed Project Builder 1

You work at a busy design firm. Your boss emails you an Illustrator file. He tells you the file contains a symbol of the American flag that he saved some months ago. Your boss wants you to update the existing symbol on the Symbols panel so the flag is scaled 25% and the opacity of the flag is 50%. He also wants the new symbol to show the flag waving.

1. Open AI 9-5.ai, then save it as **American Flag Symbol**.
2. Show the Symbols panel if necessary, then place an instance of the American Flag symbol on the artboard.
3. Break the link between the symbol instance and the symbol.
4. Click Object on the menu bar, point to Envelope Distort, then click Make with Warp.
5. Click the Style list arrow, then click Flag.
6. Type **–35** for the Bend value, then click OK.
7. Scale the artwork 25%.
8. On the Transparency panel, change the Opacity of the artwork to 50%.
9. Replace the original American Flag symbol with the modified artwork, then remove the flag artwork from the artboard.
10. Save your work, compare the flag artwork in your Symbols panel with Figure 43, then close the American Flag Symbol document.

Figure 43 Completed Project Builder 2

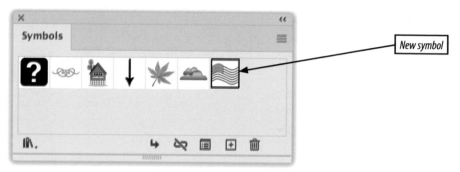

New symbol

DESIGN PROJECT

A member of the local Chamber of Commerce has created a poster for this year's Memorial Day parade and asks you if you could jazz it up. Since your firm is very busy, your improvements must be quick and simple. You email a file containing a symbol of the American flag to an employee with instructions for updating the symbol. He emails the file back to you with the updated symbol, and you paste the parade text into the file.

1. Open AI 9-6.ai, then save it as **Memorial Day Parade**.
2. Fill the black rectangle with orange, then hide it.
3. Select all the elements on the artboard, then hide them.
4. Place an instance of the American Flag symbol in the lower-left corner of the artboard.
5. Create a pattern out of the American Flag symbol instances that covers the entire artboard, referring to Figure 44 for ideas.
6. Select all the symbol instances, group them, then send them to the back.
7. Show all, then deselect all.
8. Select the orange rectangle and the symbol instances, then make a clipping mask.
9. Click Select on the menu bar, point to Object, then click Clipping Masks.
10. Apply a 10% Cyan fill and a 3-pt. black stroke to the clipping mask.
11. Save your work, compare your screen to Figure 44, then close the Memorial Day Parade document.

Figure 44 Completed Design Project

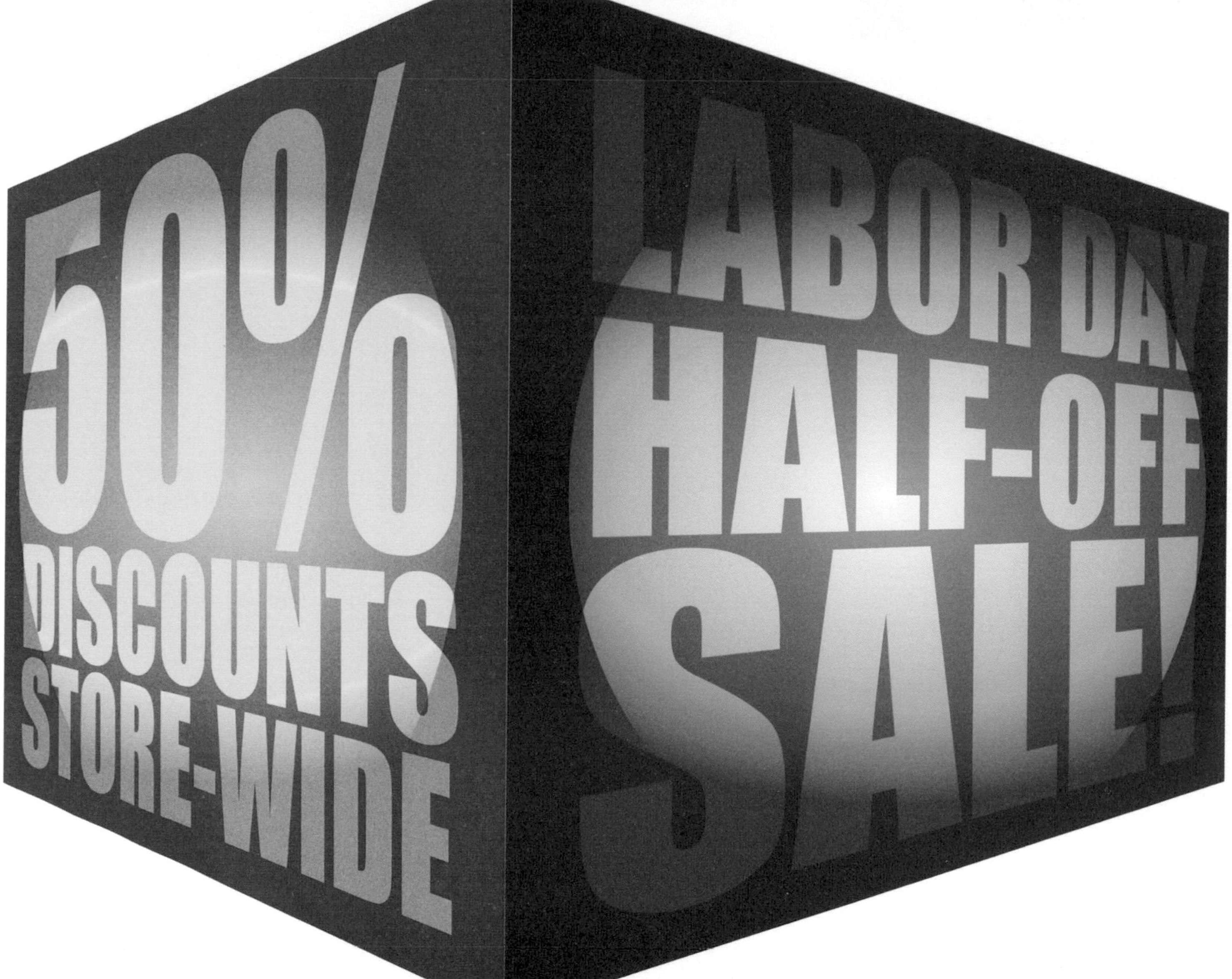
50%
DISCOUNTS
STORE-WIDE
LABOR DAY
HALF-OFF
SALE!

CHAPTER 10

CREATING 3D OBJECTS

1. Extrude Objects
2. Revolve Objects
3. Manipulate Surface Shading and Lighting
4. Map Artwork to 3D Objects
5. Work with a Perspective Grid

Adobe Certified Professional in Graphic Design and Illustration Using Adobe Illustrator

2. Project Setup and Interface
This objective covers the interface setup and program settings that assist in an efficient and effective workflow, as well as knowledge about ingesting digital assets for a project.

2.3 Use nonprinting design tools in the interface to aid in design or workflow.

    C Use guides and grids.

4. Creating and Modifying Visual Elements
This objective covers core tools and functionality of the application, as well as tools that affect the visual appearance of document elements.

4.4 Transform digital graphics and media.

    B Rotate, flip, and transform individual layers, objects, selections, groups, or graphical elements.

4.6 Modify the appearance of design elements using effects and graphic styles.

    A Use effects to modify images.

EXTRUDE OBJECTS

▶ *What You'll Do*

In this lesson, you will use the 3D Extrude & Bevel effect to extrude objects.

Extruding Objects

Illustrator's **Extrude & Bevel effect** makes two-dimensional objects three-dimensional. A two-dimensional object has two axes, which are the X axis representing the width and the Y axis representing the height. When you **extrude** an object, you add depth to an object by extending it on its Z axis, as shown in Figure 1. An object's Z axis is always perpendicular to the object's front surface.

Figure 2 shows four 2D objects before and after being extruded. Note the changes to each object's fill color on the front surface and the light and dark shadings on the other surfaces. These shadings create the 3D effect and are applied automatically when the Extrude & Bevel effect is applied.

TIP 3D effects may produce fills with flaws. These are usually screen aberrations that are an issue with your monitor and don't show when you print the document.

Figure 1 Identifying the Z axis on an extruded object

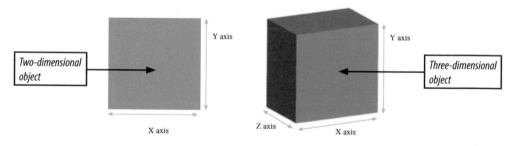

Figure 2 Four objects before and after being extruded

You determine the degree of extrusion by changing the Extrude Depth value in the 3D Extrude & Bevel Options dialog box, shown in Figure 3. Extrusion depth is measured in points. The greater the value, the more the object is extended on its Z axis, as shown in Figure 4.

Figure 3 3D Extrude & Bevel Options dialog box

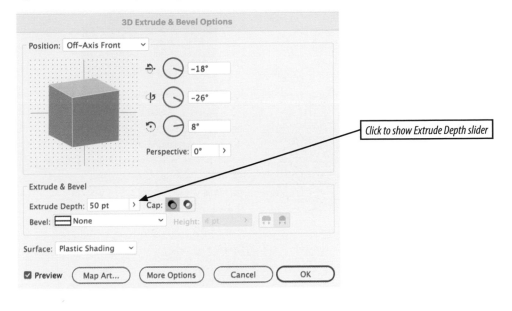

Click to show Extrude Depth slider

Figure 4 Two objects extruded to different depths

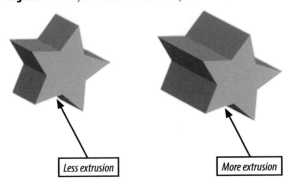

Less extrusion

More extrusion

Use the Cap buttons in the 3D Extrude & Bevel Options dialog box to make extruded objects appear solid or hollow. The Solid cap button is the default setting. It produces an object in which the front and back faces (surfaces) are solid, as shown in Figure 5. The Hollow cap button makes the front and back faces invisible, producing an object that appears hollow, as shown in Figure 6.

Figure 5 Activating the Solid cap button

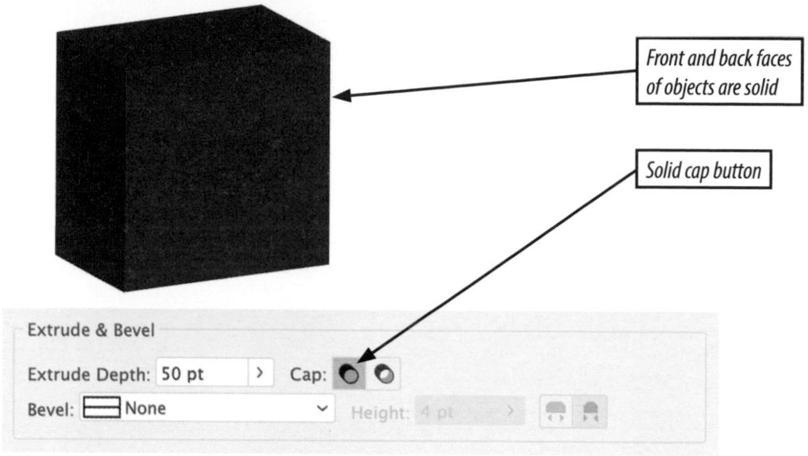

Front and back faces of objects are solid

Solid cap button

Extrude & Bevel

Extrude Depth: 50 pt > Cap: ⬤ ◯

Bevel: None Height: 4 pt >

Figure 6 Activating the Hollow cap button

Front and back faces of objects are hollow

Hollow cap button

Extrude & Bevel

Extrude Depth: 50 pt > Cap: ◯ ⬤

Bevel: None Height: 4 pt >

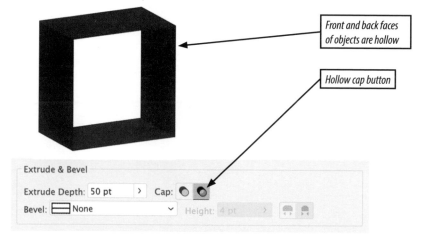

Rotating 3D Objects

The 3D Extrude & Bevel Options dialog box offers controls for rotating extruded objects. You can rotate the object manually by dragging the rotation cube, shown in Figure 7. The three text boxes to the right of the cube represent the selected object's X, Y, and Z axes. When you rotate the cube, the values in these text boxes update to reflect the changes you make. You may also enter values in these text boxes to rotate the selected object at specific angles.

Once an object has been extruded, you can use the rotation cube to view any surface of the object, such as the front, back, left, or right. The surface shading will update whenever you rotate an object.

Figure 7 Options for rotating 3D objects

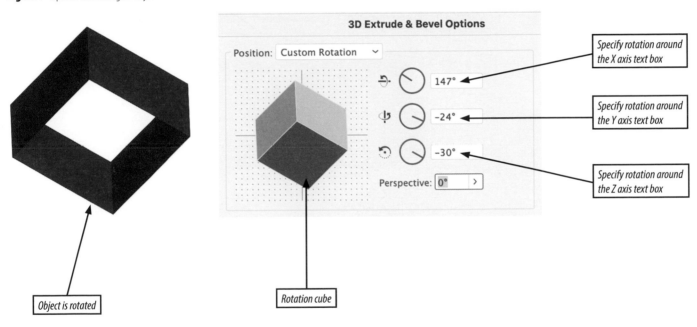

Applying a Bevel Edge to an Extruded Object

A **bevel** is the angle that one surface makes with another when they are not at right angles. The Bevel menu offers 10 predefined bevel shapes that you can apply to the edges of extruded objects. The width of the bevel edge is controlled by the Height slider. Figure 8 shows six objects, each with a different bevel shape applied to its edge. Each bevel has a width of 4 points.

As shown in Figure 9, text can be extruded without first having to convert it to outlines. Once extruded, you can add a bevel edge to text.

Figure 8 Six objects with bevel shapes applied to edges

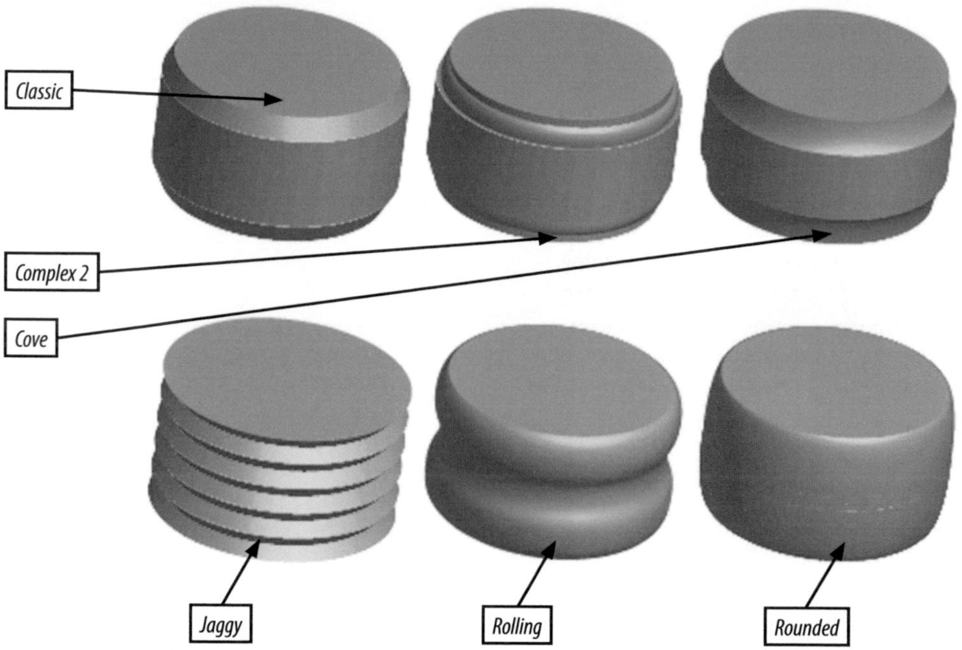

Classic

Complex 2

Cove

Jaggy

Rolling

Rounded

Figure 9 Extruding text

Because many letters are complex shapes, applying a bevel to extruded text often causes problems. Simply put, the shapes are too intricate to be rendered with a bevel edge. In Figure 10, the Classic bevel shape has been applied, but it isn't rendered properly.

Whenever Illustrator is having difficulty rendering an object with a bevel edge, a warning appears in the 3D Extrude & Bevel Options dialog box reading "Warning, self-intersection may have occurred." When problems do occur, your best bet is to reduce the extrusion depth, reduce the width of the bevel, or change the rotation of the object. Sometimes, you won't be able to solve the problem using the dialog box. In those cases, your only solution is to render the graphic, expand it, then repair the flaws using traditional tools.

When you apply a bevel shape to an object's edge, you can decide how the bevel will be applied to the object using the Bevel Extent In and Bevel Extent Out buttons in the 3D Extrude & Bevel Options dialog box. The Bevel Extent In button produces a bevel edge that carves away from the edge of the existing object. The Bevel Extent Out button adds the bevel edge to the object. Figure 11 shows the Bevel Extent Out and Bevel Extent In buttons. In general, the Bevel Extent In option is the better choice because it stays within the already-established boundaries of the object.

Figure 10 Identifying problems with a bevel edge

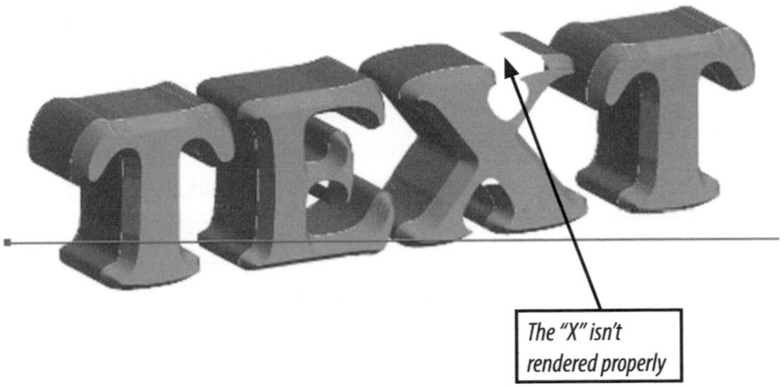

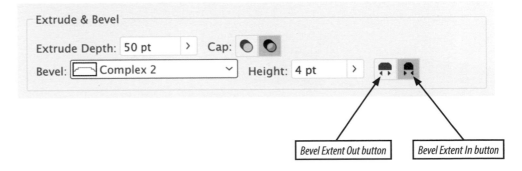

The "X" isn't rendered properly

Figure 11 Bevel Extent Out and Bevel Extent In buttons

Extrude & Bevel

Extrude Depth: 50 pt > Cap: ◓ ◓

Bevel: Complex 2 ∨ Height: 4 pt >

Bevel Extent Out button   Bevel Extent In button

Extrude an object

1. Open AI 10-1.ai, then save it as **Extrude Objects**.

2. Click **View** on the menu bar, then click **Blue Square**.

3. Click the **Selection tool** ▶, select the **blue square**, click **View** on the menu bar, then click **Hide Edges**.

4. Click **Effect** on the menu bar, point to **3D and Materials**, point to **3D (Classic)**, then click **Extrude & Bevel (Classic)**.

5. Position the 3D Extrude & Bevel Options dialog box so it is not blocking the blue square on the artboard, then click the **Preview check box** if it's not checked.

   As shown in Figure 12, the blue square is extruded 50 points on the Z axis.

6. Click the **Extrude Depth list arrow**, drag the **slider** to **96 pt.**, then click **OK**.

7. Open the **Appearance panel**.

   As shown in Figure 13, the Appearance panel lists the 3D Extrude & Bevel effect applied to the object.

8. Click **3D Extrude & Bevel** on the Appearance panel to open the dialog box.

9. Click the **Hollow cap button** ◑.

   The object's front and back "capping faces" become transparent, making the object appear hollow.

10. Click **OK**, save your work, then continue to the next set of steps.

You applied the 3D Extrude & Bevel effect to a selected object, increased the depth of the extrusion, then changed the cap so the 3D object would appear hollow.

Figure 12 Applying the 3D Extrude & Bevel effect

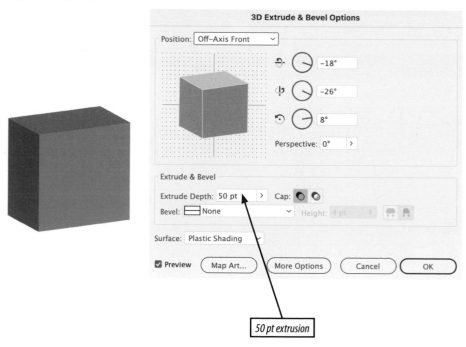

50 pt extrusion

Figure 13 The effect is listed on the Appearance panel

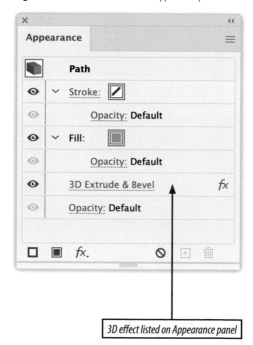

3D effect listed on Appearance panel

Extrude and rotate an object

1. Click **View** on the menu bar, then click **Orange Star**.

2. Hide edges for this object and objects in all remaining lessons in this chapter.

3. Click the **star**, click **Effect** on the menu bar, point to **3D and Materials**, point to **3D (Classic)**, then click **Extrude & Bevel (Classic)**.

4. Change the **Extrude Depth value** to **60 pt**.

5. Position your cursor over the **top-front edge of the rotation cube** so a rotate cursor appears, as shown in Figure 14.

6. Click and drag to rotate the **cube**, noting that the value in the **Specify rotation around the X axis text box** is the only value that changes as you drag.

7. Experiment with different rotations by dragging the **rotation cube** from all sides and note the changes to the **orange star object** in the document window.

8. Double-click the **Specify rotation around the X axis text box**, as shown in Figure 15, to select its contents, type **149**, making sure you have deleted the negative sign that was there, then press **[tab]**.

9. Type **0** in the **Specify rotation around the Y axis text box**, press **[tab]**, type **103** in the **Specify rotation around the Z axis text box**, press **[tab]**, then compare your dialog box to Figure 15.

10. Click **OK**, save your work, then continue to the next set of steps.

You applied the 3D Extrude & Bevel effect to a star-shaped object, then manipulated the rotation cube to rotate the object.

Figure 14 Manipulating the rotation cube manually

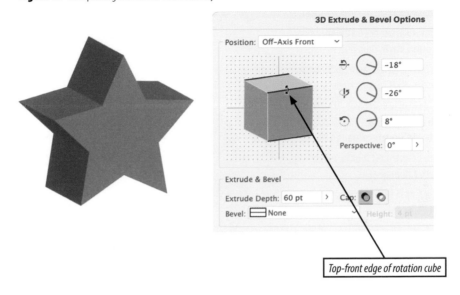

Top-front edge of rotation cube

Figure 15 Entering rotation values

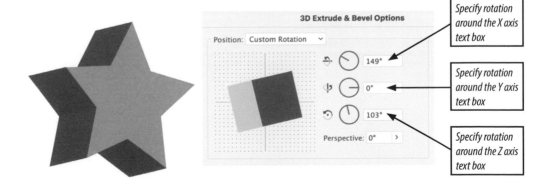

Specify rotation around the X axis text box

Specify rotation around the Y axis text box

Specify rotation around the Z axis text box

Extrude a compound path

1. Click **View** on the menu bar, then click **Target**.

2. Select the **circles**, click **Object** on the menu bar, point to **Compound Path**, then click **Make**.

3. Click **Effect** on the menu bar, point to **3D and Materials**, point to 3D **(Classic)**, then click **Extrude & Bevel (Classic)** to open the 3D Extrude & Bevel Options dialog box.

4. Change the **Extrude Depth value** to **100 pt**.

5. Experiment with different rotations by dragging the **rotation cube** from all sides.

6. Double-click the **X axis text box**, make sure the **negative sign** is also selected, type **28**, then press **[tab]**.

7. Type **–26** in the **Specify rotation around the Y axis text box**, press **[tab]**, type **8** in the **Specify rotation around the Z axis text box**, then press **[tab]**.

8. Click **OK**, then save your work.

9. Compare your work to Figure 16, then continue to the next set of steps.

You created a compound path, applied the 3D Extrude & Bevel effect, then rotated the graphic, all the time noting the visual effect created by applying the effect to a compound path.

Figure 16 Viewing the 3D Extrude & Bevel effect applied to a compound path

Apply a bevel shape to an object's edge

1. Click **View** on the menu bar, then click **DOG**.

   The text has been converted to outlines and made into a compound path.

2. Click the **Selection tool** ▶, click **any letter of the text**, click **Effect** on the menu bar, point to **3D and Materials**, point to **3D (Classic)**, then click **Extrude & Bevel (Classic)**.

3. Change the **Extrude Depth value** to **25 pt**.

4. Click the **Choose bevel shape list arrow**, click **Classic**, then verify that the **Height value** is set to **4 pt**.

5. Note that the **Bevel Extent In button** 🔧 is pressed, click the **Bevel Extent Out button** 🔧, then note the change to the graphic, as shown in Figure 17.

6. Note the warning in the dialog box: "Bevel self-intersection may have occurred," and note the problem with the graphic circled in the figure.

7. Click the **Bevel Extent In button** 🔧, click the **Choose bevel shape list arrow**, then click **Complex 2**.

   Your graphic should resemble Figure 18.

8. Click **OK**, save your work, then close the Extrude Objects document.

You applied two bevel shapes to extruded text outlines. You also experimented with the Bevel Extent In and Bevel Extent Out buttons.

Figure 17 Identifying a self-intersection problem

Problem

Figure 18 Viewing the Complex 2 bevel

REVOLVE OBJECTS

▶ ***What You'll Do***

In this lesson, you will use the 3D effect to revolve objects.

Revolving Objects

Revolving is another method Illustrator provides for applying a 3D effect to a 2D object. Imagine taking a large, hardcover book and opening it so much that its front and back covers touch. The pages would fan out from one cover to the other, all of them with their inside edges adhering to the spine of the book. This example is similar to what happens when the Revolve effect is applied to an object.

Revolving an object "sweeps" a path in a circular direction around the Y axis. Figure 19 shows a familiar shape—the letter E—before and after the Revolve effect is applied. The blue selection marks show the original path, and the left edge of that path is the Y axis around which the path was revolved. The surface shading is applied automatically with the effect.

Figure 19 The letter E before and after being revolved

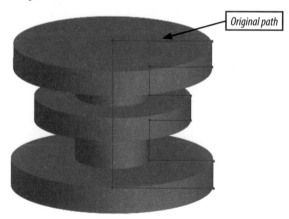

Original path

The 3D Revolve Options dialog box offers the option to revolve the object from its left or right edge. By default, an object is revolved around a vertical axis that represents its leftmost point. An example of this is shown in Figure 20. Revolving the object from its right edge yields an entirely different result, as shown in Figure 21.

Because a revolution occurs around a vertical axis, in most cases, the starting path will depict half of the object you want to revolve. This is more easily explained with examples. Figure 22 shows the original path and the result of applying the Revolve effect to that path. Note how the original path is a two-dimensional half of the revolved three-dimensional object.

Once revolved, an object can be rotated by manipulating the rotation cube in the 3D Revolve Options dialog box. This feature is extremely powerful with a revolved graphic. You can use the rotation cube to present all surfaces of the graphic.

Figure 20 Revolving an object around its left edge

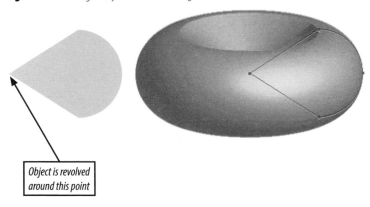

Object is revolved around this point

Figure 21 Revolving an object around its right edge

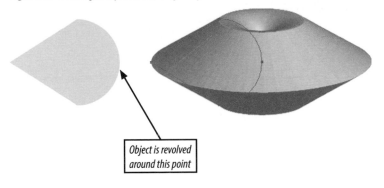

Object is revolved around this point

Figure 22 Identifying the path used to produce the revolved 3D graphic

Revolving Multiple Objects

You can apply the Revolve effect to multiple paths simultaneously, and you can revolve open or closed paths. As shown in Figure 23, when you apply the Revolve effect to multiple paths, each path is revolved around its own axis. For this reason, it is often best to align the left edges of multiple paths on the same Y axis, as shown in Figure 24.

As the figure shows, aligning separate paths on the same Y axis can be useful when revolving. However, unwanted results can occur when rotating those paths, even when they are aligned on the same Y axis. Figure 25 shows the same two paths being rotated. Note that because they are separate paths, they rotate separately, each on its own axis. This problem can be resolved by grouping the paths.

Figure 23 Multiple paths revolved on their own axis

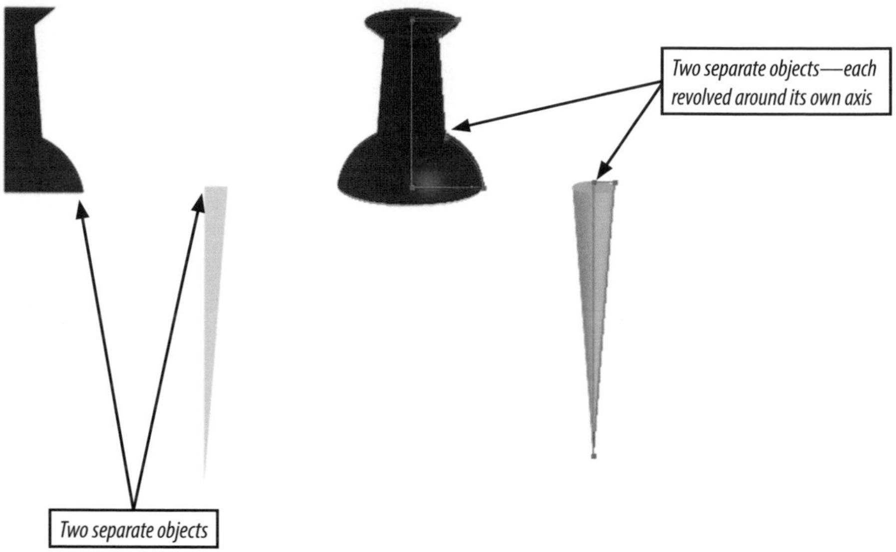

Two separate objects—each revolved around its own axis

Two separate objects

Figure 24 Multiple paths aligned, then revolved

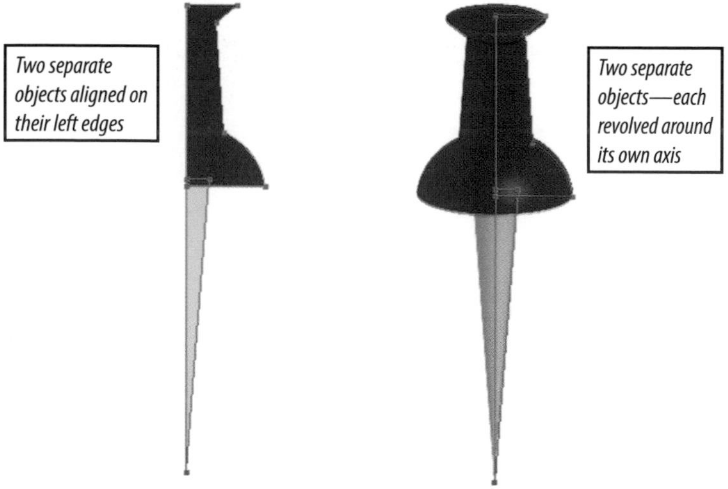

Two separate objects aligned on their left edges

Two separate objects—each revolved around its own axis

Figure 25 Multiple paths rotated on their own axis

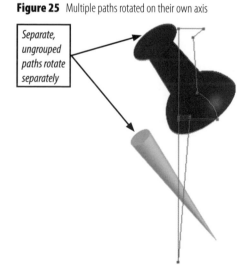

Separate, ungrouped paths rotate separately

Revolving Grouped Objects

When grouped, multiple paths are revolved around a single axis. This can yield unexpected results. In Figure 26, the two paths (left) are grouped, but they don't share the same Y axis.

When revolved, both paths revolve around the leftmost axis.

When multiple paths are grouped and revolved, they will also rotate together. Figure 27 shows four versions of two grouped and revolved

paths after they have been rotated in the 3D Revolve Options dialog box. In every case, the two paths rotate together because they are grouped. Compare this to Figure 25, in which the two ungrouped paths rotated separately, each on their own axes.

Figure 26 Two grouped paths revolved around a single Y axis

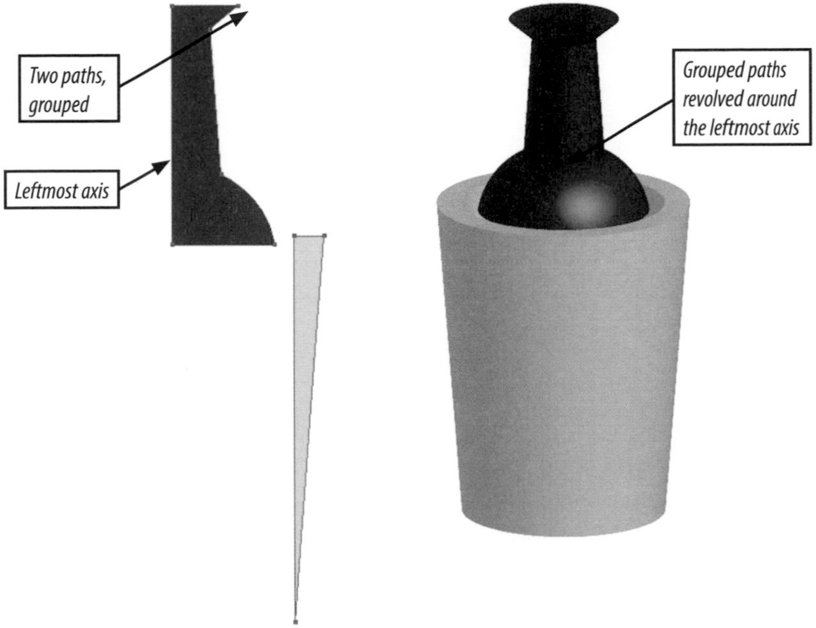

Two paths, grouped

Leftmost axis

Grouped paths revolved around the leftmost axis

Figure 27 Four grouped paths after being revolved and rotated

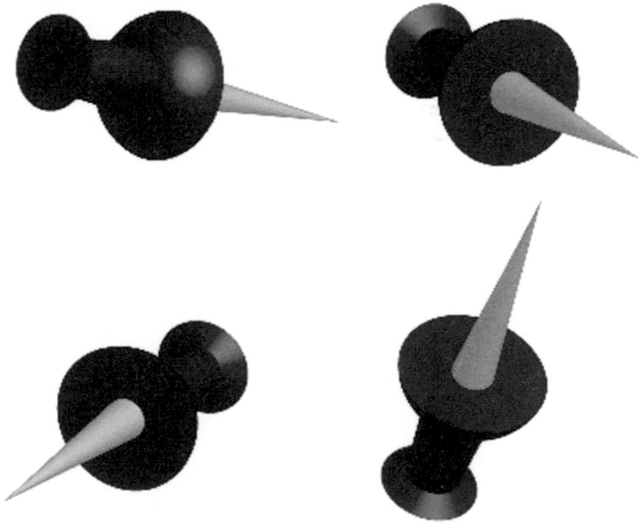

Applying an Offset to a Revolved Object

By default, an object is revolved around a vertical axis that represents its leftmost point. Figure 28 illustrates this point. Increasing the Offset value increases how far from the Y axis the object is revolved. Figure 29 shows the same revolved object with a 90-point offset value. The path revolves around the same Y axis, but it does so at a distance of 90 points. Figure 30, in which the object has been rotated, shows the offset more clearly. Try to visualize that the object is a series of half circles rotated around a single vertical axis—90 points from that vertical axis.

Figure 28 Object revolved around its leftmost point

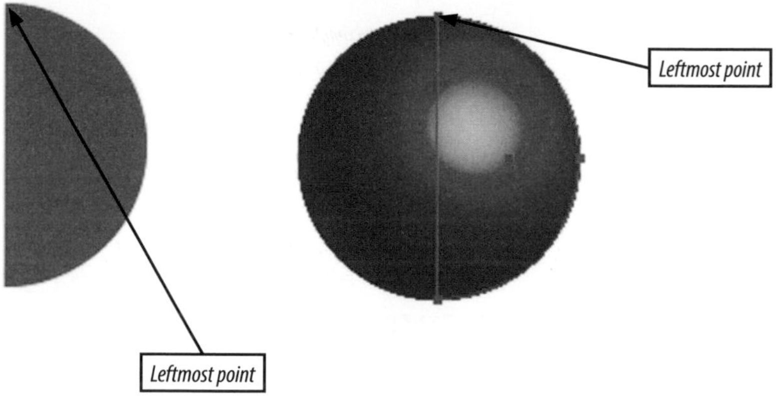

Leftmost point

Leftmost point

Figure 29 Object revolved with a 90-point offset from its Y axis

Figure 30 Rotated object shows 90-point offset more clearly

Revolve an object

1. Open AI 10-2.ai, then save it as **Green Bottle**.

2. Click the **Selection tool** ▶, click the **green object**, click **View** on the menu bar, then hide edges if necessary.

3. Click **Effect** on the menu bar, point to **3D and Materials**, point to **3D (Classic)**, then click **Revolve (Classic)**.

   As shown in Figure 31, the object is revolved on its axis and appears as a bottle. Highlights and shadows are applied automatically.

4. Click **OK**, save your work, then close the Green Bottle document.

You revolved a simple object to produce a three-dimensional graphic.

Revolve multiple objects

1. Open AI 10-3.ai, then save it as **Revolve Objects**.

2. Select the **second row of blue objects**, then open the **3D/Revolve dialog box**.

3. Click the **Preview check box**.

   Each object revolves on its own axis.

4. Click **OK**, then compare your work to Figure 32.

   The graphic on the left has a hard edge because the original object was a rectangle. The round edge of the original object on the right produced a 3D graphic that also has a round edge.

Continued on next page

Figure 31 Revolving an object

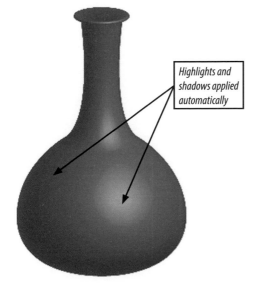

Highlights and shadows applied automatically

Figure 32 Revolving multiple objects

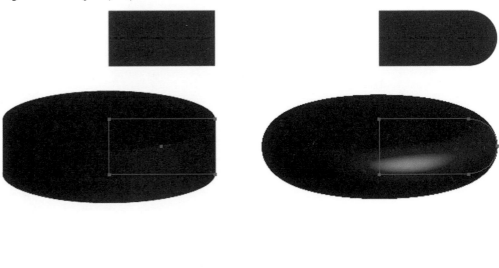

5. Select the **second row of red objects**, then open the **3D/Revolve dialog box**.

6. Click **OK**, deselect all, then compare your work to Figure 33.

The first two graphics produced spheres when revolved, but only the middle graphic is a perfect sphere. Because they face in opposite directions, the two crescent shapes produce two drastically different results when revolved.

7. Select the **rightmost red object**, click **3D Revolve (Classic)** on the Appearance panel, manipulate the **rotation cube** to rotate the graphic any way that you like, then click **OK**.

Figure 34 shows one possible result.

8. Save your work, then close the Revolve Objects document.

You selected multiple objects, applied the 3D Revolve effect, then noted that each object revolved on its own axis. You compared the results with the original objects, then rotated one of the revolved objects.

Figure 33 Revolving three objects

Figure 34 Rotating a revolved object

Revolve grouped objects

1. Open AI 10-4.ai, then save it as **Push Pins**.

2. Click **View** on the menu bar, click **Green Pin**, then select the two objects in the Green Pin view.

TIP The two objects in Green Pin view are not grouped.

3. Click **Effect** on the menu bar, point to **3D and Materials**, point to **3D (Classic)**, then click **Revolve (Classic)**.

4. Note the effect on the objects on the page.

5. Manipulate the **rotation cube** in any direction.

   As shown in Figure 35, the two objects are each rotated on their own axis and the illustration is no longer realistic.

TIP Because your rotation will differ, your results will differ from the figure.

6. Click **OK**, click **View** on the menu bar, click **Red Pin**, click **one of the objects in the Red Pin view**.

TIP The two objects are grouped.

7. Open the **3D/Revolve dialog box**.

   As shown in Figure 36, because the two objects are grouped, they are both revolved around the same axis.

Continued on next page

Figure 35 Rotating revolved objects that are not grouped

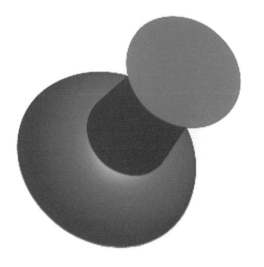

Figure 36 Two grouped objects revolved around the same axis

8. Click **OK**, click **View** on the menu bar, click **Blue Pin**, select the **two objects**, click **Object** on the menu bar, then click **Group**.

9. Open the **3D/Revolve** dialog box.

   As shown in Figure 37, the two grouped objects are revolved around the same axis. Because they both share the same axis (their left edge), the illustration is realistic.

   TIP The selection edges are showing in the figure so you can see the left edge that both graphics share.

10. Manipulate the **rotation cube** in any direction you like.

    Figure 38 shows one possible result.

11. Click **OK**, save your work, then close the Push Pins document.

You explored the results of revolving grouped and ungrouped objects. With the green pin, you noted that ungrouped objects cannot be rotated together. With the red pin, you noted that grouped objects are revolved around the same axis. With the blue pin, you noted that grouped objects can be rotated together.

Figure 37 Two grouped objects revolved around the same axis

Figure 38 Rotating revolved objects that are grouped

Offset a revolved object

1. Open AI 10-5.ai, then save it as **Desk Lamp**.

2. Select the **silver object**, click **Effect** on the menu bar, point to **3D and Materials**, point to **3D (Classic)**, click **Revolve (Classic)**, then click **OK**.

3. Select the **gold diagonal line**, then open the **3D/Revolve** dialog box.

   As shown in Figure 39, the object's leftmost point is the axis around which it is revolved.

4. Double-click the **value** in the **Offset text box**, type **50**, press **[tab]**, then compare your work to Figure 40.

   The object is revolved at a radius that is 50 points from its axis.

5. Click **OK**, save your work, then close the Desk Lamp document.

You used an increased offset value to manipulate how an object is revolved in relation to its axis.

Figure 39 Revolving an object around its leftmost point

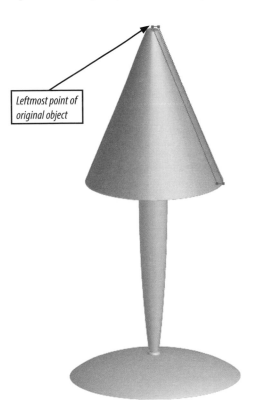

Leftmost point of original object

Figure 40 Revolving an object with a 50-pt offset from its axis

50-pt offset from leftmost point

MANIPULATE SURFACE SHADING AND LIGHTING

▶ *What You'll Do*

In this lesson, you will familiarize yourself with the controls that allow you to manipulate the highlight effects of a 3D object.

Applying Surface Shading

When the Extrude & Bevel effect or the Revolve effect is applied to an object, surface shading and lighting are applied automatically. However, you can manipulate these effects.

Surface shading controls how the object's surface appears. When an object is revolved, four surface shadings are available: Wireframe, No Shading, Diffuse Shading, and Plastic Shading. Examples of all four are shown in Figure 41.

Plastic shading is the default surface shade. With plastic shading, the object reflects light as though it were made of a shiny plastic material. Distinct highlight areas appear on the surface of an object.

Diffuse shading offers a surface that reflects light in a soft, diffuse pattern. With Diffuse Shading, no distinct highlights appear on the surface of the object.

The Wireframe option makes all surfaces transparent and shows the object's geometry.

The No Shading option, as its name suggests, applies no new shading to the object. Its surface is identical to that of the 2D object.

Manipulating Lighting Controls

When you choose Diffuse Shading or Plastic Shading, a number of lighting controls are available for you to manipulate the lighting effects that are applied to the object automatically.

Lighting Intensity controls the strength of the light on the object. The range for lighting intensity is 0–100, with 100 being the default.

Ambient Light determines how the object is lit globally. The range for Ambient Light is 0–100. Any changes that you make with the Ambient Light slider affect the brightness of the object uniformly, though the effect is much more pronounced in the shadow areas than in the highlight areas. Decreasing the ambient light noticeably makes the shadow areas darker, which increases the overall contrast of the object, from shadow to highlight.

Highlight Intensity controls how intense a highlight appears. The more intense the highlight, the whiter it appears.

Highlight Size controls how large the highlights appear on the object.

Blend Steps controls how smoothly the shading appears on the object's surface and is most visible in the transition from the highlight areas to the diffusely lit areas. The range for blend steps is 1–256, with higher numbers producing more paths and therefore smoother transitions. If your computer can handle it, use 256 blend steps, but be aware that the higher the number, the more computer memory will be required to render the object.

Figure 41 Four surface shading choices

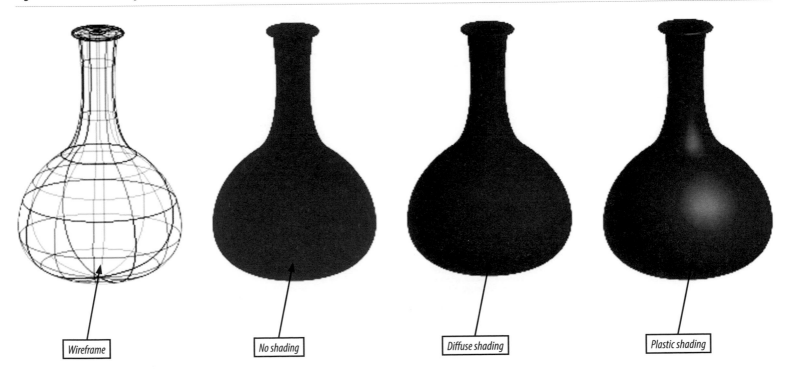

Wireframe

No shading

Diffuse shading

Plastic shading

Manipulating Light Sources

In addition to manipulating lighting controls, you can manipulate the light itself. When you choose Diffuse Shading or Plastic Shading as the surface shading, a default light source, shown in Figure 42, is applied. You can drag the light source to a new location to light the object from a different angle, as shown in Figure 43. This can be effective for manipulating the overall lighting of the object.

In addition to relocating the default light source, you can add additional light sources by clicking the New Light button. By default, the new light source appears at the center of the lighting key, but you can relocate it as well. You can apply different light intensity values to individual light sources. It is often a good idea for one light source to be more dominant than the other(s).

To delete a light source, select it and then click the Delete Light button. The Move selected light to back of object button moves the light source to the back of the object. This is most effective when there's a background object that allows the back light to be more apparent.

Figure 42 Viewing default light source settings

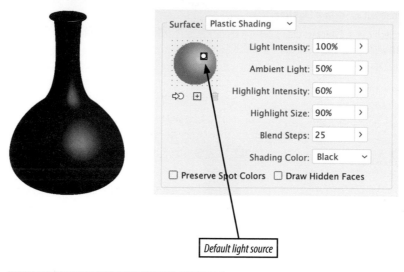

Default light source

Figure 43 Relocating a light source

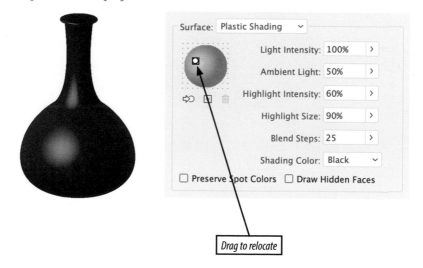

Drag to relocate

Apply surface shading to a 3D object

1. Open AI 10-6.ai, then save it as **Surface Lighting**.

2. Click the **object** to select it, click **Effect** on the menu bar, point to **3D and Materials**, point to **3D (Classic)**, then click **Revolve (Classic)**.

3. Click the **Surface list arrow**, then click **Diffuse Shading**.

4. Click the **Surface list arrow**, then click **No Shading**.

5. Click the **Surface list arrow**, then click **Wireframe**.

6. Click the **Surface list arrow**, click **Plastic Shading**, then compare your artwork to Figure 44.

7. Save your work, then continue to the next set of steps.

You examined four types of surface shadings as applied to a revolved object.

Manipulate lighting controls

1. Click **More Options** in the dialog box.

2. Click the **Ambient Light list arrow**, then drag the **slider** to **20**.

3. Click the **Highlight Intensity list arrow**, then drag the **slider** to **75**.

4. Click the **Highlight Size list arrow**, then drag the **slider** to **75**.

5. Click the **Light Intensity list arrow**, drag the **slider** to **50**, note the change in the object, then drag the **slider** to **100**.

6. Click the **Blend Steps list arrow**, then drag the **slider** to **128**.

   The range of color is smoothed from highlight to shadow. Color stepping between colors is no longer visible. With more steps added to the blend, the color transitions more smoothly.

7. Click **OK**, then compare your artwork to Figure 45.

8. Save your work, then continue to the next set of steps.

You manipulated five surface shading controls, noting their effect on a 3D object.

Figure 44 Plastic Shading surface applied

Figure 45 Manipulating surface shading

Manipulate light sources

1. Verify that the **gold object** is selected, then click **3D Revolve (Classic)** on the Appearance panel.

2. Drag the **light** to the **top center of the sphere**, as shown in Figure 46.

Figure 46 Relocating a light

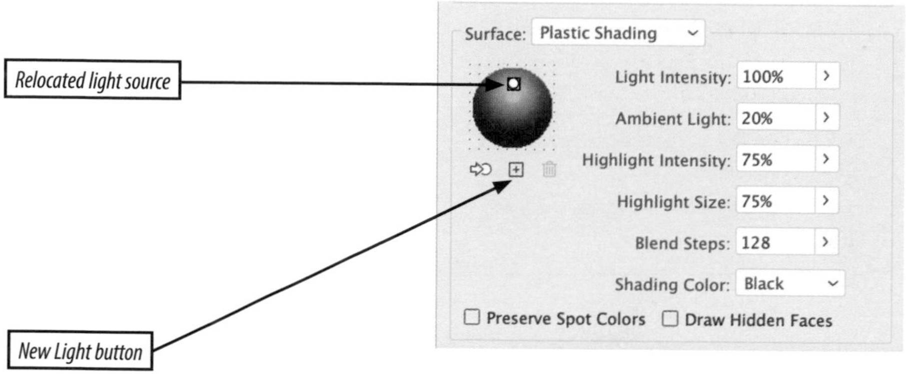

Relocated light source

New Light button

Surface: Plastic Shading

Light Intensity: 100% >
Ambient Light: 20% >
Highlight Intensity: 75% >
Highlight Size: 75% >
Blend Steps: 128 >
Shading Color: Black

☐ Preserve Spot Colors ☐ Draw Hidden Faces

3. Click the **New Light button** ⊞ to add a second light.

TIP By default, a new light is positioned at the center of the sphere.

4. Drag the **new light** to the **top-right corner of the sphere**, as shown in Figure 47.

5. Click the **New Light button** ⊞ to add a third light, then move it to the location shown in Figure 48.

6. Click **OK** and compare your work to Figure 49.

7. Save your work, then close the Surface Lighting document.

You added and positioned lights to modify the lighting effects applied to the 3D object.

Figure 47 Positioning a new light

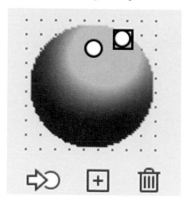

Figure 48 Positioning a third light

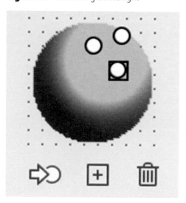

Figure 49 The object with three lights

MAP ARTWORK TO 3D OBJECTS

▶ **What You'll Do**

In this lesson, you will map 2D artwork to a 3D object.

Mapping Artwork

Once you have created a three-dimensional object, you can "map" two-dimensional artwork to the three-dimensional object. A good example of this concept is a soup can and a soup label. The two-dimensional soup label is designed and printed. It is then wrapped around the three-dimensional soup can.

The process of mapping a 2D object to a 3D object first includes converting the 2D object to a symbol. Figure 50 shows a revolved 3D object and 2D artwork that will be mapped to it.

Figure 50 Viewing 3D object and 2D artwork to be mapped

2D Illustrator artwork

3D object

To map the artwork, you first select the 3D object, then click Map Art in the 3D Revolve Options dialog box. In the Map Art dialog box, you must first choose the surface to which you intend to map the art. When you click the surface buttons, the active surface is shown in red wireframe on the 3D object. In this example, we are mapping the wrapping paper to surface 1 of 4, which is shown in Figure 51.

The grid pattern represents the *complete* surface of surface 1 of 4. Understand that this means not only the front surface that you see, but the entire surface, all the way around. For this exercise, we're interested in mapping the wrapping paper to the front surface that we can see. In Figure 52, the wrapping paper artwork covers that area. Note that you can scale the artwork and see a preview on the artboard of how it will wrap to the selected 3D object.

Figure 51 Identifying the surface to be mapped

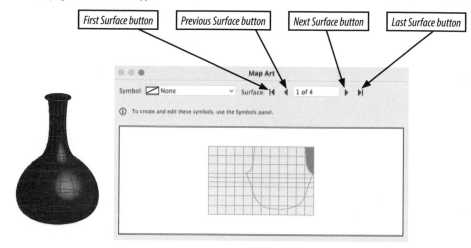

Figure 52 Positioning the symbol artwork

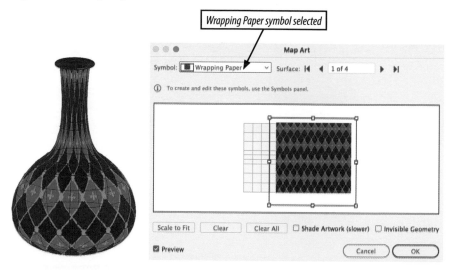

Artwork that you want to map to an object must first be converted into a symbol on the Symbols panel. Drag the artwork onto the Symbols panel and the Symbol Options dialog box opens, allowing you to name the symbol and identify it as a graphic. Symbols are covered extensively in Chapter 9. Once you have chosen the surface, you then choose the symbol to be mapped by clicking the Symbol list arrow in the Map Art dialog box and selecting the appropriate symbol. When you do so, the symbol artwork is centered on the grid. In this example, the symbol is named Wrapping Paper. For this exercise, we drag the artwork so it completely covers the curved lines that represent the front face.

Once the artwork is mapped, it reshapes itself to the three-dimensional object, as shown in Figure 53.

Prepare a document for mapped artwork

1. Open AI 10-7.ai, then save it as **Tea Can**.
2. Select all, click **Effect** on the menu bar, point to **3D and Materials**, point to **3D (Classic)**, then click **Revolve (Classic)**, click **OK**, then deselect all.
   Your artwork should resemble Figure 54.
3. Open AI 10-8.ai, select all, click **Edit** on the menu bar, click **Copy**, close the document, then return to the Tea Can document.
4. Open the Symbols panel, click **Edit** on the menu bar, click **Paste**, then drag the **pasted artwork** onto the Symbols panel.

The Symbol Options dialog box opens.

5. Name the new symbol **Elephant Rectangle**, click the **Type list arrow**, click **Graphic**, then click **OK**.
   The artwork is added as a symbol on the Symbols panel.
6. Delete the pasted artwork from the artboard.
7. Open AI 10-9.ai, select all, copy the artwork, close the document, return to the Tea Can document, then paste the artwork.

Figure 53 Viewing the mapped art

8. Drag the **pasted artwork** onto the Symbols panel, name it **Elephant Circle**, click the **Type list arrow**, click **Graphic**, then click **OK**.
9. Delete the pasted artwork from the artboard.
10. Save your work, then continue to the next set of steps.

You used the 3D Revolve effect to create the artwork to which the 2D artwork will be mapped. You then created two symbols, one for each part of the 2D artwork.

Figure 54 Creating the "tea can" and "lid"

Map rectangular artwork

1. Click the **Selection tool** ▶, click the **silver object**, then press the **up arrow** [↑] on your keypad eight times so the **silver artwork** is fully "under" the purple lid.

2. Click **3D Revolve (Classic)** on the Appearance panel to open the 3D Revolve Options dialog box, then click **Map Art**.

3. Note that the **Surface text box** reads **1 of 3** and that a red line indicates that surface on the object, as shown in Figure 55.

4. Click the **Next Surface button** two times so the **Surface text box** reads **3 of 3**.

   The light gray areas of the layout grid represent the visible area of the silver object at this viewing angle.

5. Click the **Symbol list arrow**, then click **Elephant Rectangle**.

6. Drag the **top-left** and **bottom-right resizing handles** on the symbol's bounding box so the artwork fits into the light gray areas of the layout grid, as shown in Figure 56.

   Note that as you resize and move the artwork in the dialog box, it is updated on the artboard.

7. Drag the **bottom-middle resizing handle** up slightly so the silver "can" will show beneath the "elephant label."

8. Click the **Shade Artwork (slower) check box**.

Figure 55 Viewing surface 1 of 3 in the Map Art dialog box

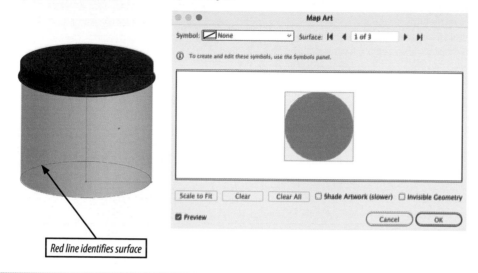

Red line identifies surface

Figure 56 Positioning the elephant label artwork on the side of the can

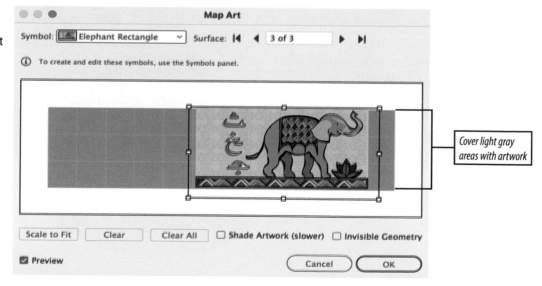

Cover light gray areas with artwork

9. Click **OK**, click **More Options** if they are not already showing, change the **Ambient Light setting** to **65%**, change the **Highlight Intensity setting** to **80%**, change the **number of blend steps** to **128**, then move the **light** to the location shown in Figure 57.

10. Click **OK**, deselect all, then compare your work to Figure 58.

11. Save your work, then continue to the next set of steps.

In the Map Art dialog box, you selected the symbol that you wanted to map and the surface to which you wanted to map it. You resized the symbol artwork so it fit onto the surface properly, then you activated the shading option to make the artwork appear more realistic as a label. You modified surface shading settings and lighting to improve the appearance of the artwork.

Figure 57 Adjusting surface shading and lighting

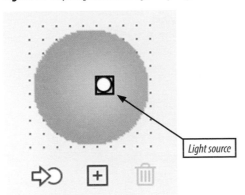

Light source

Figure 58 Viewing the mapped art

Map round artwork

1. Click the **purple "cover" object**, click **3D Revolve (Classic)** on the Appearance panel, then click **Map Art**.

2. Click the **Next Surface button** once so the **Surface text box** reads **2 of 5**.

3. Click the **Symbol list arrow**, then click **Elephant Circle**.

4. Point to the **upper-right resizing handle** until a rotate cursor appears, then drag to rotate the graphic to the position shown in Figure 59.

5. Click **OK** to close the Map Art dialog box, click **OK** again, deselect all, then compare your artwork to Figure 60.

6. Save your work, then continue to the next set of steps.

You mapped a circular piece of 2D artwork to an oval 3D object.

Figure 59 Rotating the mapped art

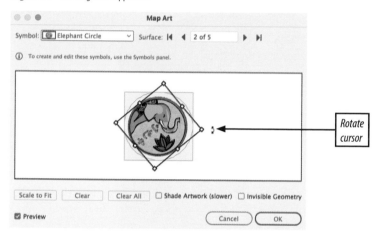

Rotate cursor

Figure 60 Viewing the mapped art

Map texture artwork

1. Open AI 10-10.ai, select all, copy the artwork, close the document, then return to the Tea Can document.

2. Verify that the **Symbols panel** is visible, click **Edit** on the menu bar, click **Paste**, then drag the **pasted artwork** onto the Symbols panel.

3. Name the new symbol **Cover Texture**, click the **Type list arrow**, click **Graphic**, then click **OK**.

4. Delete the pasted artwork from the artboard.

5. Click the **purple "cover" object**, click **3D Revolve (Classic) (Mapped)** on the Appearance panel, then click **Map Art**.

6. Click the **Next Surface button** until the **Surface text box** reads **5 of 5**.

7. Click the **Symbol list arrow**, then click **Cover Texture**.

8. Position the **symbol artwork** so it covers the entire light gray area, as shown in Figure 61.

9. Click **OK** to close the Map Art dialog box, then drag the **light** to the location shown in Figure 62.

10. Click **OK**, deselect all, then compare your work to Figure 63 on the following page.

11. Save your work, then close the Tea Can document.

You mapped artwork to the front face of a 3D object to add texture.

Figure 61 Positioning the artwork

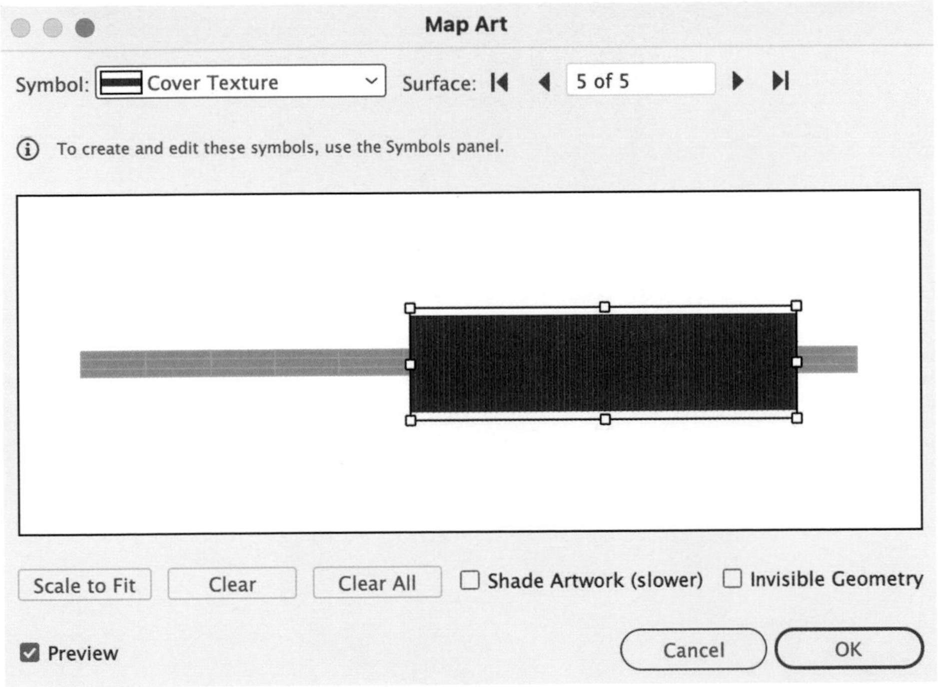

Map Art

Symbol: [■■■] Cover Texture ⌄ Surface: |◀ ◀ 5 of 5 ▶ ▶|

ⓘ To create and edit these symbols, use the Symbols panel.

Scale to Fit | Clear | Clear All | ☐ Shade Artwork (slower) | ☐ Invisible Geometry

☑ Preview   (Cancel)   (OK)

Figure 62 Relocating the light

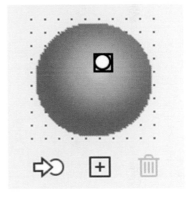

Figure 63 The finished mapped art project

WORK WITH A PERSPECTIVE GRID

Working with the Perspective Grid

Illustrator features a powerful **perspective grid** feature that you can use to draw and create objects in perspective. Like guides, the default perspective grid is listed on the View menu, where you can choose to hide or show it. But the perspective grid is more than just a visual guide—it's a drawing tool. When you're working with the perspective grid, it's like you're working in "perspective mode." The grid allows you to draw, copy, and transform objects in perspective.

It even adjusts the shape of the object to keep it in perspective as you move it around the artboard.

There are three types of grids: One Point Perspective, Two Point Perspective, and Three Point Perspective, as shown in Figure 64. The term "point" refers to vanishing points. So, for example, a Two Point Perspective grid has two vanishing points. Of the three types of grids, Two Point Perspective is most applicable for most types of Illustrator artwork and is therefore the default grid.

Figure 64 1, 2 & 3-point perspective grids

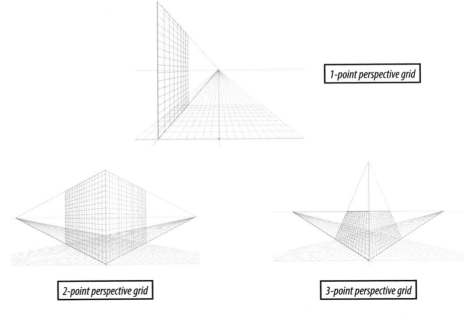

1-point perspective grid

2-point perspective grid

3-point perspective grid

You access the Perspective Grid by selecting to show it in the View menu or by clicking the Perspective Grid tool on the toolbar. When you do, the default Two Point Perspective grid appears, as shown in Figure 65. You can resize and reshape the grid by clicking and dragging the handles, known as widgets. When you've resized and reshaped the grid to your liking, you can save the modified grid as a **Perspective Grid Preset**. When you do, the saved grid is available in the View menu for future use. You can also edit the preset after saving it by clicking the Edit menu, then clicking Perspective Grid Presets.

Figure 66 shows a modified perspective grid. Note the change in shape, size, color, and opacity. Many users like to use a reduced opacity for the grid, making it a bit easier to see the artwork as you draw on the grid.

Figure 65 Default Two Point Perspective grid

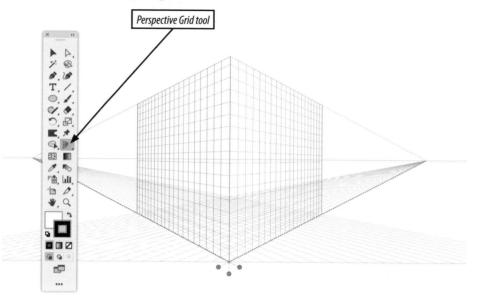

Perspective Grid tool

Figure 66 Modified grid

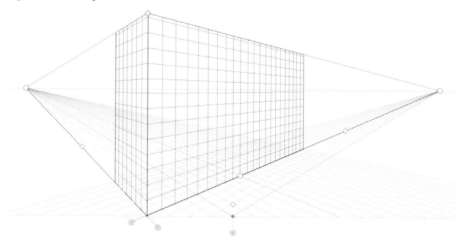

Drawing in Perspective

When you click the Perspective Grid tool and the grid becomes visible, the basic shape tools such as the Rectangle, Ellipse, and Star tools function differently, allowing you to draw objects in perspective.

When drawing in perspective, you should first specify on which perspective plane you want to draw by clicking one of the faces on the Plane Switching Widget that appears with the perspective grid.

Figure 67 shows three views of the widget for a Two Point Perspective grid. Figure 68 shows a rectangle drawn in perspective on the left plane. Figure 69 shows a rectangle drawn on the right plane.

You can also use the number keys on your keypad to specify the plane on which you want to draw. For example, you can type 1 to draw on the left plane, 2 to draw on the bottom plane, and 3 to draw on the right plane.

Figure 67 Plane Switching Widget in three modes

Figure 68 Drawing on the left plane

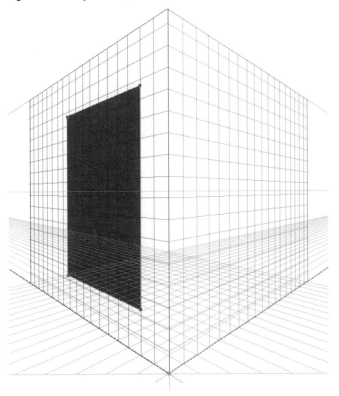

Figure 69 Drawing on the right plane

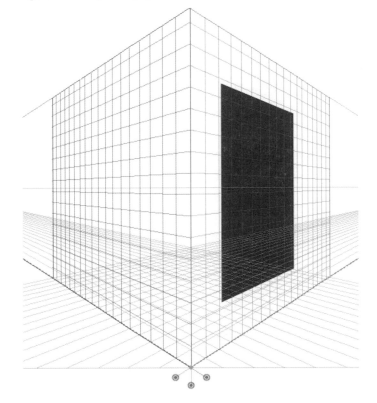

Using the Perspective Selection Tool

Once you've drawn objects in perspective, the Perspective Selection tool allows you to move and modify the objects in perspective. Let us not mince words here—this is a really cool tool! When you click and drag an object with the Perspective Selection tool, it moves in perspective. Figure 70 shows an ellipse in perspective on the left plane. Figure 71 shows three copies of the ellipse dragged and dropped with the Perspective Selection tool. Note how they automatically reduce in perspective as they move toward the left vanishing point.

You can also use the Perspective Selection tool to move an object or multiple objects between different planes on the grid. While dragging an object, type the number of the plane to which you want to move it. For example, let's say you have an object on the left plane. If you drag it with the Perspective Selection tool, press the number 3 on your keypad while dragging, and the object will be redrawn in perspective on the right plane.

Figure 70 Ellipse in perspective on the left plane

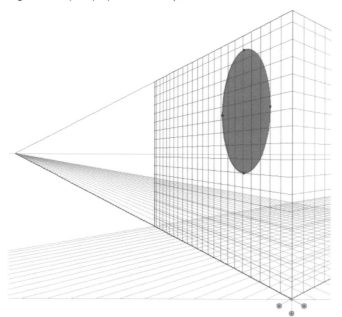

Figure 71 Three copies of the ellipse dragged and dropped with the Perspective Selection tool

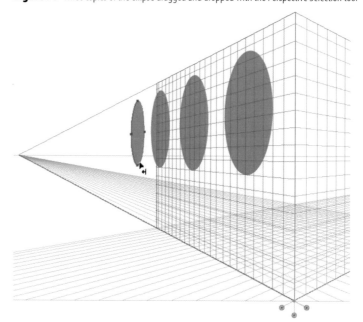

Draw on a perspective grid

1. Open AI 10-11.ai, then save it as **Basic Planes**.

2. On the toolbar, set the **fill color** to **[None]**, set the **stroke color** to **Black**, then set the **stroke weight** to **3 pts**.

3. Click **View** on the menu bar, point to **Perspective Grid**, point to **Two Point Perspective**, then click **[2P-Normal View]**.

4. Click the **Perspective Grid tool** ⬚.

   When you click the Perspective Grid tool ⬚, the default perspective grid appears on the page, along with the Plane Switching

Widget. The default perspective grid is a two-point perspective grid, blue on the left, orange on the right, with both planes being equal size.

TIP The Perspective Grid tool ⬚ might be hidden behind the Perspective Selection tool ⬚.

5. On your keypad, press the **numbers 1, 2,** and **3** repeatedly and note that it toggles among three planes on the Plane Switching Widget.

6. Press the **number 1** on the keypad.

7. Click the **Rectangle tool** ⬚, position it near the **top-center of the perspective grid**,

then click and drag to create a **rectangle** that resembles Figure 72.

The Rectangle tool ⬚ draws an object on the same plane that is active in the Plane Switching Widget.

8. Press the **number 3** on your keypad, then position the cursor at the **top-center of the grid** again.

9. Click and drag to draw a **second rectangle** similar to the one shown in Figure 73.

   The rectangle is drawn on the active plane in the widget.

Continued on next page

Figure 72 Drawing the first rectangle

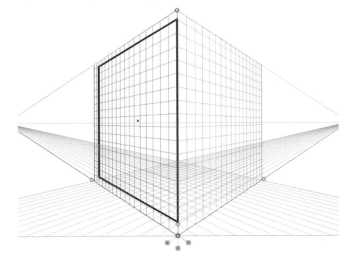

Figure 73 Drawing the second rectangle

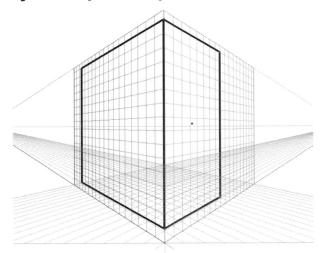

10. Press the **number 2** on your keypad, position your cursor over the **bottom-center intersection of the two rectangles**, then draw a **third rectangle** as shown in Figure 74.

TIP Pressing 4 on your keypad is the "no plane" option for the Plane Switching Widget, allowing you to draw objects without perspective.

11. Using the same steps, draw **two more rectangles** so your screen resembles Figure 75.

12. Click **View** on the menu bar, point to **Perspective Grid**, then click **Hide Grid**.

13. Save your work, then close the Basic Planes document.

You used the perspective grid to draw multiple rectangles in perspective on different planes.

Figure 74 Drawing the third rectangle

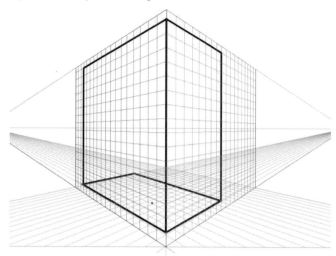

Figure 75 Drawing two more rectangles

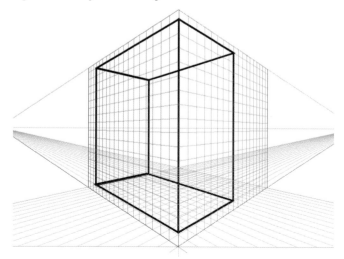

Modify and save a perspective grid

1. Open AI 10-12.ai, save it as **Receding Rectangles**, then verify that guides are showing.

   The artboard has a single rectangular guide.

2. Click the **Perspective Grid tool** 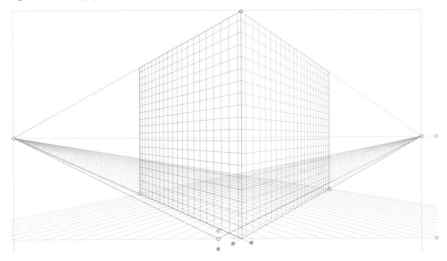 on the toolbar.

3. Drag the **left vanishing point handle** (on the center horizontal guide) left to the vertical guide.

   The perspective grid changes shape as you drag.

4. Drag the **right vanishing point handle** right, to the vertical guide.

5. Drag the **top diamond handle** up to the guide.

   Your perspective grid should resemble Figure 76. Note the three small circles are all touching the guides.

6. Click **View** on the menu bar, point to **Guides**, then click **Hide Guides**.

   The rectangular guide is hidden, but the perspective grid remains visible.

7. Click **View** on the menu bar, point to **Perspective Grid**, then click **Save Grid as Preset**.

8. Change the name to **Receding Rectangles**.

   The values in the Save Grid As Preset dialog box reflect the specifics of the grid as it was created by default and as you modified it. You can continue to modify the grid within this dialog box.

9. Click the **Left Grid list arrow**, choose **Brick Red**, click the **Right Grid list arrow**, then choose **Dark Blue**.

   Your dialog box should resemble Figure 77.

Continued on next page

Figure 76 Moving right and top handles

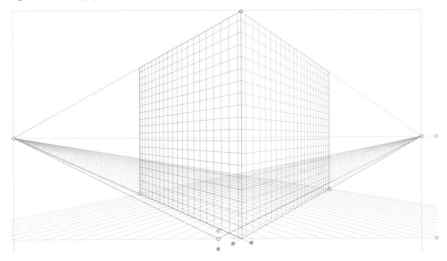

Figure 77 Save Grid As Preset dialog box

10. Click **OK**.

The perspective grid does not change.

11. Click **View** on the menu bar, point to **Perspective Grid**, point to **Two Point Perspective**, then click **Receding Rectangles**.

The perspective grid you edited, named, and saved is loaded.

12. Click **View** on the menu bar, point to **Perspective Grid**, point to **Two Point Perspective**, then click **[2P-Normal View]**.

The default Two Point Perspective grid is loaded. The Receding Rectangles perspective grid preset can be further edited.

13. Click **Edit** on the menu bar, then click **Perspective Grid Presets**.

The Perspective Grid Presets dialog box opens.

14. In the (top) Presets window, click **Receding Rectangles**, then click the **Edit button** ✎.

15. Reduce the **Opacity setting** to **30**, click **OK** to close the dialog box, then click **OK** again to close the Perspective Grid Presets dialog box.

16. Click **View** on the menu bar, point to **Perspective Grid**, point to **Two Point Perspective**, then click **Receding Rectangles**.

The Receding Rectangles grid is reloaded and appears to have faded, reflecting the reduction in opacity.

17. Save your work, then continue to the next set of steps.

You modified the size and shape of the default two-point perspective grid. You saved it as a preset, named it, and changed its colors. You loaded it to make it the active perspective grid on the artboard. You loaded the default two-point perspective grid, then edited the Receding Rectangles preset, reducing its opacity.

Use the Perspective Selection tool

1. On the toolbar, set the **fill color** to **Black** and the **stroke color** to **[None]**.

2. Press the **number 1** on your keypad, click the **Rectangle tool** ▭, then draw a **rectangle** as shown in Figure 78.

3. Click the **Perspective Selection tool** , then click and drag the **rectangle** around the artboard.

The rectangle remains in perspective anywhere you drag it. It enlarges as you drag to the right and reduces as you move it left and closer to the vanishing point.

4. Drop the **rectangle** anywhere, then undo the move so the rectangle is returned to its original position.

Figure 78 Creating a rectangle

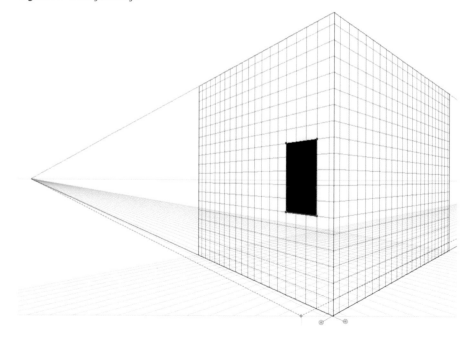

5. Press and hold **[shift] [option] (Mac)** or **[Shift] [Alt] (Win)**, then drag and drop a **copy of the rectangle** to the left of the first.

6. Press **[command] [D] (Mac)** or **[Ctrl] [D] (Win)** seven times to repeat the transformation.

   Each copy gets smaller as it moves left toward the vanishing point.

7. Select all, then drag and drop a **copy of the rectangles** above the first row, as shown in Figure 79.

   The copies are in perspective on the same plane as the original and recede toward the vanishing point.

8. Drag and drop a **copy of the rectangles** below the original row, as shown in Figure 80.

9. Select all the **rectangles**, verify that the **Perspective Selection tool** ▸⊙, is active, then click and drag the **rectangles** toward the right of the artboard, then, while still dragging, press the **number 3** on your keypad once, but *do not release* the mouse button.

   When you press the number 3, the rectangles' perspective changes to that of the right plane.

10. Continue dragging, then press and hold **[option] (Mac)** or **[Alt] (Win)**.

11. Position the **copied rectangles** as shown in Figure 81.

12. Save your work, then close the Receding Rectangles document.

You used the Perspective Selection tool to move objects in perspective, to drag and drop copies of objects in perspective, and to copy objects from one plane to another.

Figure 79 Creating the top copy of rectangles

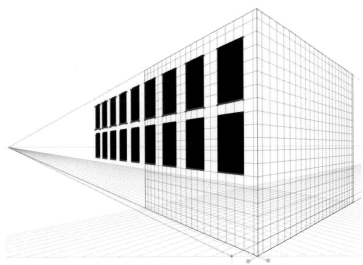

Figure 80 Creating the bottom copy of rectangles

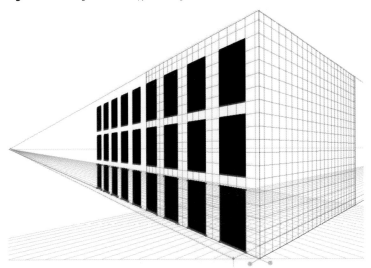

Figure 81 Moving a copy of rectangles onto the right plane

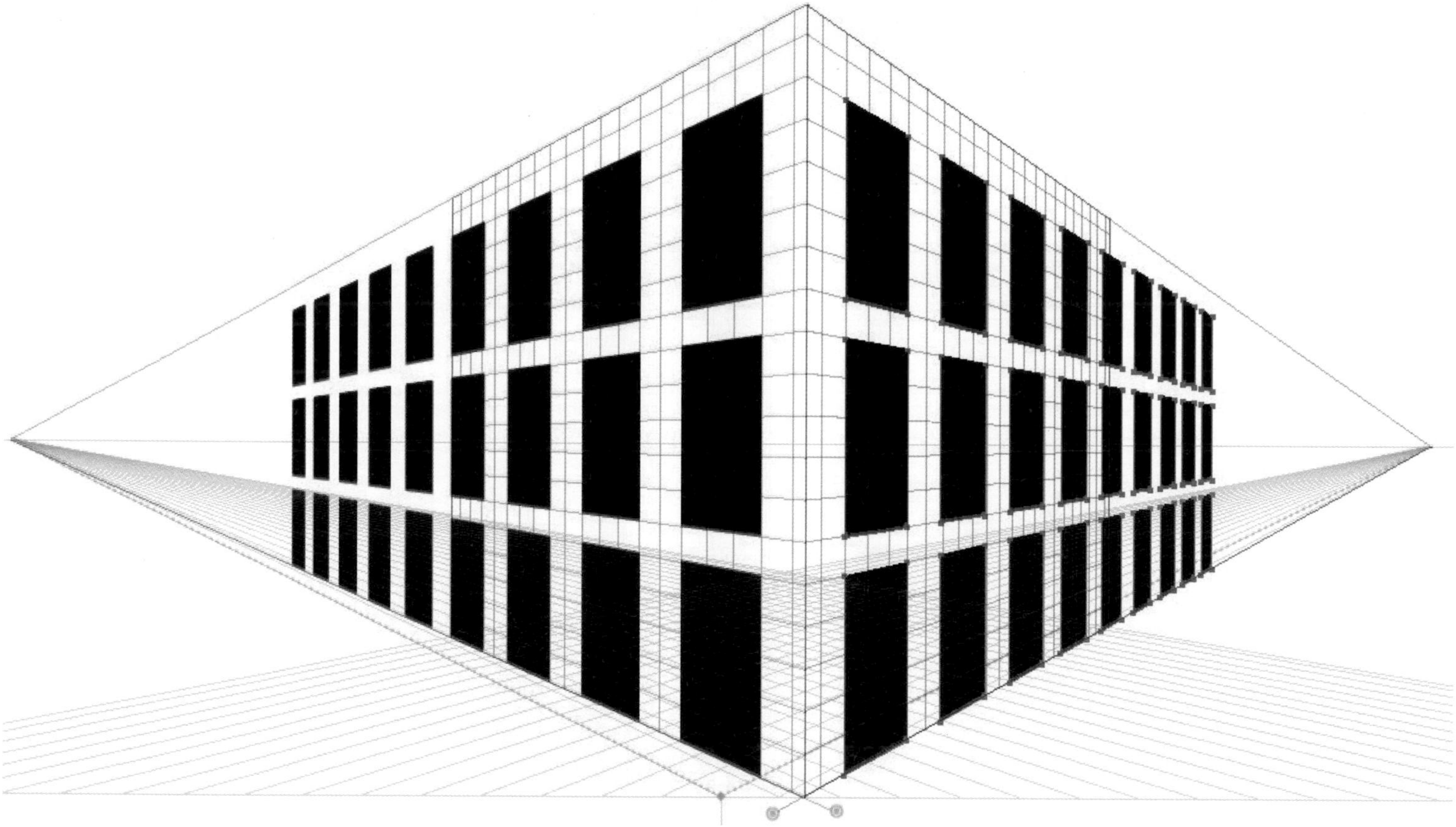

Add text and composed artwork to a perspective grid

1. Open AI 10-13.ai, save it as **Perspective Text**, then verify that guides are showing.

   The artboard has a single rectangular guide.

2. Click the **Perspective Grid tool** .

3. Drag the **left vanishing point handle** left to the guide.

4. Drag the **right vanishing point handle** right to the guide.

5. Click **View** on the menu bar, point to **Guides**, then click **Hide Guides**.

6. Click **View** on the menu bar, point to **Perspective Grid**, point to **Two Point Perspective**, then click **[2P-Normal View]**.

7. Click **Object** on the menu bar, then click **Show All**.

8. Click the **Perspective Selection tool** , move the **red illustration** onto the grid, and then scale the artwork and position it so your artboard resembles Figure 82.

   TIP The figures in this chapter show the artwork with selection marks hidden.

9. Press the **number 1** on your keypad.

10. Click the **Perspective Selection tool** , then drag **over the artwork** and position it as shown in Figure 83.

11. Press the **number 3** on your keypad.

12. Using the same methodology, position the **blue artwork** in perspective on the right plane so your artwork resembles Figure 84 on the following page.

13. Save your work, then close the Perspective Text document.

You used the Perspective Selection tool to position flat artwork and text in perspective on the perspective grid.

Figure 82 Scaling and positioning the artwork to be distorted in perspective

Figure 83 Positioning the artwork on the perspective grid

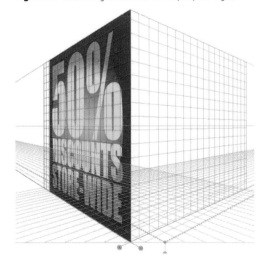

Figure 84 The completed illustration

Extrude objects

1. Open AI 10-14.ai, then save it as **Extrude & Bevel Skills**.
2. Click the Selection tool, select the blue octagon, click View on the menu bar, then click Hide Edges.
3. Click Effect on the menu bar, point to 3D and Materials, point to 3D (Classic), then click Extrude & Bevel (Classic).
4. Click the Extrude Depth list arrow, then increase the Depth to 75 pt.
5. Click the Hollow cap button, then click OK.
6. Select the orange letter H, click Effect on the menu bar, point to 3D and Materials, point to 3D (Classic), then click Extrude & Bevel (Classic).
7. Click the Preview check box, then change the Extrude Depth value to 60 pt.
8. Double-click the Specify rotation around the X axis text box to select its contents, type **17**, then press [tab].
9. Type **–17** in the Specify rotation around the Y axis text box, press [tab], type **–31** in the Specify rotation around the Z axis text box, then click OK.
10. Select the green octagon and the two objects inside it, click Object on the menu bar, point to Compound Path, then click Make.
11. Open the 3D/Extrude & Bevel dialog box.
12. Experiment with different rotations by clicking and dragging the rotation cube from all sides.
13. Double-click the Specify rotation around the X axis text box, type **26**, then press [tab].
14. Type **–9** in the Specify rotation around the Y axis text box, press [tab], then type **5** in the Specify rotation around the Z axis text box.

15. Click OK.
16. Select the hollow blue octagon at the top of the artboard, then click 3D Extrude & Bevel (Classic) on the Appearance panel.
17. Click the Solid cap button.

18. Click the Bevel list arrow, click Complex 3, then drag the Height slider to 6.
19. Click the Bevel Extent Out button, click OK, then compare your work to Figure 85.
20. Save your work, then close the Extrude & Bevel Skills document.

Figure 85 Completed Skills Review, Part 1

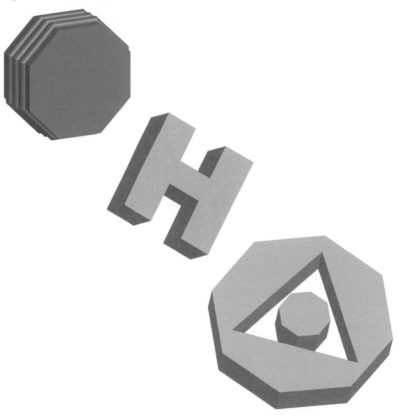

Revolve objects

1. Open AI 10-15.ai, then save it as **Gold Urn**.
2. Click the Selection tool, select all, click View on the menu bar, then click Hide Edges if it is not already selected.
3. Click the Horizontal Align Left button on the Align panel.
4. Open the 3D/Revolve dialog box.
5. Manipulate the rotation cube in any direction, note that the three objects all rotate on their own axes, then click Cancel.
6. Click Object on the menu bar, then click Group.
7. Open the 3D/Revolve dialog box.
8. Manipulate the rotation cube in any direction.
9. Click Cancel.
10. Open the 3D/Revolve dialog box.
11. Click the Offset list arrow, change the offset value to 48, then click OK.

Manipulate surface shading and lighting

1. Click 3D Revolve (Classic) on the Appearance panel.
2. Click the Preview check box, click the Surface list arrow, then click No Shading.
3. Click the Surface list arrow, then click Diffuse Shading.
4. Click the Surface list arrow, then click Plastic Shading.
5. Click More Options if they are not already displayed, click the Ambient Light list arrow, then drag the slider to 45.
6. Drag the light to the top center of the sphere.
7. Click the New Light button to add a second light.
8. Drag the Light Intensity slider to 30.

Map artwork to 3D objects

1. Drag the Offset slider to 0, then click Map Art.
2. Click the Next Surface button until the Surface text box reads 8 of 16.
3. Click the Symbol list arrow, then click Wrapping Paper.
4. Click OK.
5. Click OK, then compare your work to Figure 86.
6. Save your work, then close the Gold Urn document.

Work with a perspective grid

1. Open AI 10-16.ai, save it as **Receding Circles**, then verify that guides are showing.
2. Click the Perspective Grid tool.
3. Drag the left vanishing point handle left to the guide.
4. Drag the right vanishing point handle right to the guide.
5. Drag the top diamond handle up to the guide.

Figure 86 Completed Skills Review, Part 2

(continued)

6. Click View on the menu bar, point to Guides, then click Hide Guides.
7. Click View on the menu bar, point to Perspective Grid, then click Save Grid as Preset.
8. Change the name to **Receding Circles**.
9. Click the Left Grid list arrow, choose Grass Green, click the Right Grid list arrow, then choose Dark Blue.
10. Click OK.
11. Click View on the menu bar, point to Perspective Grid, point to Two Point Perspective, then click Receding Circles.

12. Click Edit on the menu bar, then click Perspective Grid Presets.
13. In the (top) Presets window, click Receding Circles, then click the Edit button.
14. Increase the Opacity setting to 100, click OK to close the dialog box, then click OK again to close the Perspective Grid Presets dialog box.
15. Click View on the menu bar, point to Perspective Grid, point to Two Point Perspective, then click Receding Circles.
16. On the toolbar, set the fill color to Black and the stroke color to [None].
17. Press the number 1 on your keypad, click the Ellipse tool, press and hold [shift], then draw an ellipse as shown in Figure 87.

18. Switch to the Perspective Selection tool if necessary, press and hold [shift] [option] (Mac) or [Shift] [Alt] (Win), then drag and drop a copy of the ellipse to the left.
19. Enter [command] [D] (Mac) or [Ctrl] [D] (Win) seven times to repeat the transformation.
20. Select all, then drag and drop a copy above them.
21. Drag and drop a copy below the original row.
22. Click and drag the ellipses toward the right of the artboard and, while still dragging, press the number 3 on your keypad once.
23. Continue dragging, then press and hold [option] (Mac) or [Alt] (Win).
24. Position the copied ellipses as shown in Figure 88.
25. Save your work, then close the Receding Circles document.

Figure 87 Positioning the first ellipse

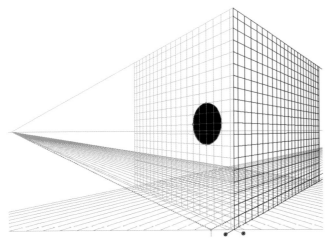

Figure 88 Completed Skills Review, Part 3

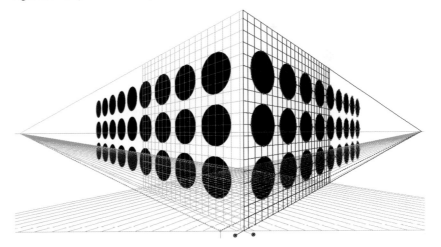

You are a freelance illustrator, and you have been hired to draw an old-fashioned lava lamp to be part of a montage. To begin work on the illustration, you decide to draw three paths, then use the 3D Revolve effect.

1. Open AI 10-17.ai, then save it as **Lava**.
2. Click the Selection tool, then drag the three path segments so they are aligned with the blue guide.
3. Hide the guides.
4. Select all, click Effect on the menu bar, point to 3D and Materials, point to 3D (Classic), then click Revolve (Classic).
5. Note the results, then click Cancel.
6. Group the three paths, then apply the Revolve effect again.
7. Click More Options if necessary, apply Plastic Shading as the surface shading, then drag the Ambient Light slider to 45.
8. Click OK, deselect all, then compare your work to Figure 89.
9. Save your work, then close the Lava document.

Figure 89 Completed Project Builder 1

You are a designer for a game company, and you are designing the packaging for a chess game. You decide to use basic shapes and the 3D Revolve effect to create a graphic for the cover art.

1. Open AI 10-18.ai, then save it as **Chess**.
2. Click the Selection tool, then align each shape with the black rules.
3. Hide the Assembled layer, then verify that the Pawn Parts layer is targeted.
4. Select all on the Pawn Parts layer, then hide edges.
5. Open the 3D/Revolve dialog box.
6. Note the results, then click Cancel.
7. Click the Horizontal Align Left button on the Align panel.
8. Press and hold [option] (Mac) or [Alt] (Win), then click the Unite button on the Pathfinder panel.
9. Open the 3D/Revolve dialog box.
10. Select the contents of the Specify rotation around the X axis text box, type −57, then click OK.
11. Click the White Pawn swatch on the Swatches panel, then compare your work to Figure 90.
12. Save your work, then close the Chess document.

Figure 90 Completed Project Builder 2

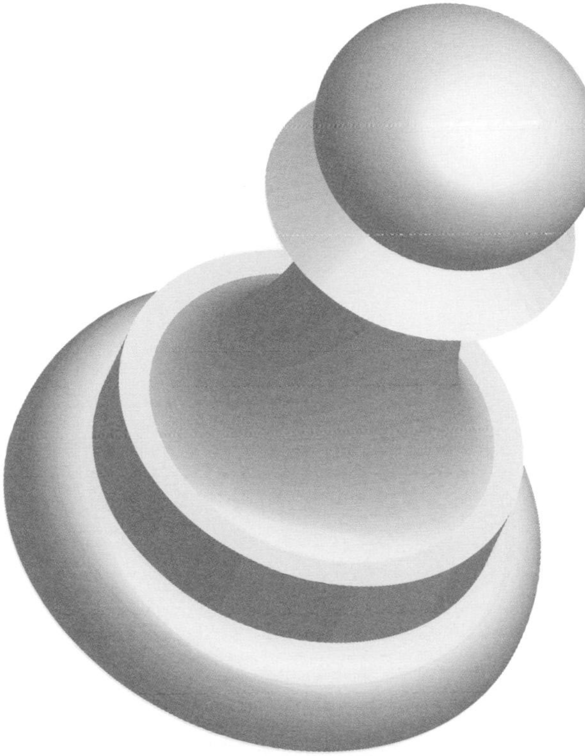

DESIGN PROJECT

This design project is designed to challenge your ability to visualize simple paths and how they will appear when the 3D Revolve effect is applied. You will look at nine graphics, all of which are simple paths to which the 3D Revolve effect has been applied. Use a piece of paper and a pencil and try to draw the simple path that is the basis for each graphic. Note that for each 3D graphic, no rotation or offset has been applied—each is the result of simply applying the 3D Revolve effect to a simple path. Note also that two of the simple paths are open paths and the other seven are all closed paths.

1. Refer to Figure 91.
2. Look at Graphic #1 and try to visualize what it would look like if the 3D Revolve effect were removed.
3. Using a pencil and paper, draw the original path that was used to create the graphic.
4. Do the same for the remaining eight graphics.
5. Open AI 10-19.ai, then save it as **Mystery Shapes**.
6. Select each graphic, then delete the 3D Revolve effect from the Appearance panel.
7. Compare your pencil drawings to the graphics in the file.
8. Save your work, then close the Mystery Graphics document.

Figure 91 Reference for Portfolio Project

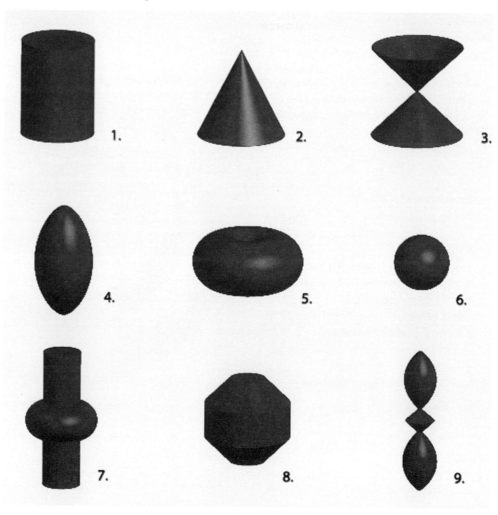

NATIONAL GEOGRAPHIC LEARNING

NATIONAL GEOGRAPHIC **LEARNING** | KATIE SLOVICK **SENIOR DESIGNER**

Katie Slovick has always had an affinity toward printed materials, such as comic books and magazines. In college, this drew her to the school newspaper and later, a graphic design job at a magazine where she created many infographics. But Katie's love of design started much earlier than college. Katie recounts influential elementary and middle school teachers who supported her path into the arts.

In college, Katie worked with professors to hone her design skills. Critique is a major component of art school. As someone who tends to judge herself harshly, Katie learned to lean on the advice of a former teacher: "Not everything you create is going to be perfect."

Katie brings that perspective to her job as a Senior Designer at National Geographic Learning. She also sees value in the group process. Katie likes to bounce ideas off of her colleagues to see which resonate best. But the team doesn't always agree, which leads to a lot of discussion. Sometimes, other factors—like usability—come into play and change the direction of the design. Being flexible and able to switch gears—from one idea to another and one project to another—is key.

Work can present its challenges, so Katie leaves room for fun. Drawing comics, baking treats, and playing creative video games helps her avoid burnout and expand her design knowledge. Katie shares, "When I was first drawing, I struggled with perfectionism. I could see my eraser marks on paper. But those don't exist in the digital space. It's important to find the right tool for the job."

PROJECT DESCRIPTION

In this project, you will create a comprehensive infographic about a place of interest to you. This could be your favorite place to vacation, a hangout spot with friends, or even a place you'd like to visit. Consider the who, what, when, where, why, and how of your location. The goal of this project is to combine images and words in a way that fully explain the details of your chosen location.

QUESTIONS TO CONSIDER

Who or what makes this location important?

When did you visit and why?

Where is this place located and how might you get there?

GETTING STARTED

An infographic is a powerful visual tool utilizing information and graphics to convey a message or tell a story.

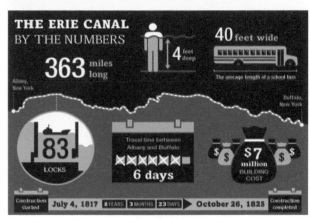

From U.S. History American Stories Beginnings to World War 1
© Cengage Learning, Inc.

Begin by conducting an Internet search for "infographic". Compare the various infographics that pop up. Choose one that your eye is drawn to. Study the colors, typography, and layout. Focus on the relationship between words and images. Which element plays a bigger role? How do the words help support the images?

Brainstorm places of interest. Consider the reasons these locations are important. Narrow your focus to one key location. Conduct an Internet search to locate facts (cultural events, demographics, weather data) on that location. Then consider your layout. What information is most important to convey? Where should it be placed? How will you use images and words to explain the importance of this location?

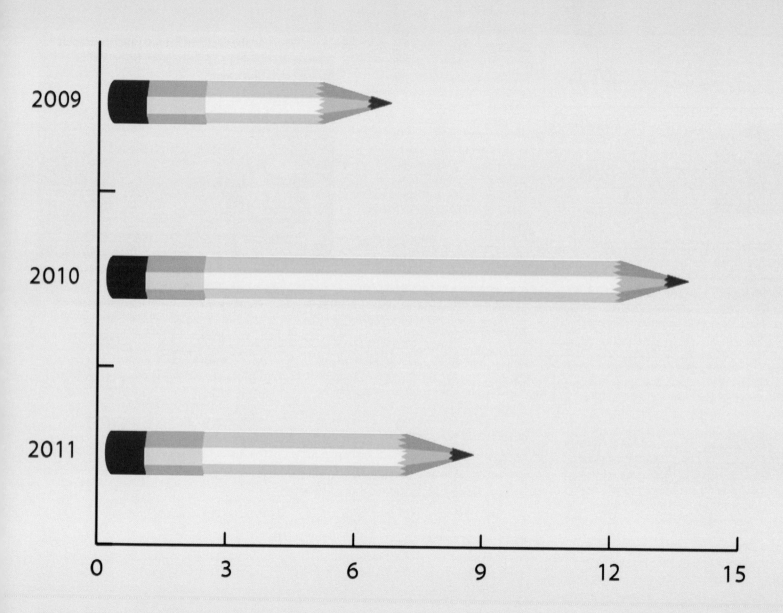

CREATING AND DESIGNING GRAPHS

1. Create a Graph
2. Edit a Graph Using the Graph Data Window
3. Use the Group Selection Tool
4. Use the Graph Type Dialog Box
5. Create a Combination Graph
6. Create a Custom Graph Design
7. Apply a Custom Design to a Graph
8. Create and Apply a Sliding-Scale Design

Adobe Certified Professional in Graphic Design and Illustration Using Adobe Illustrator

2. Project Setup and Interface

This objective covers the interface setup and program settings that assist in an efficient and effective workflow, as well as knowledge about ingesting digital assets for a project.

2.3 Use nonprinting design tools in the interface to aid in design or workflow.
  C Use guides and grids.

4. Creating and Modifying Visual Elements

This objective covers core tools and functionality of the application, as well as tools that affect the visual appearance of document elements.

4.3 Make, manage, and manipulate selections.
  B Modify and refine selections using various methods.
  C Group or ungroup selections.

CREATE A GRAPH

▶ *What You'll Do*

In this lesson, you will enter data and create a column graph.

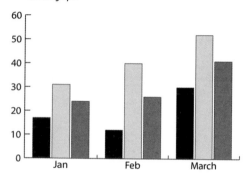

Working with Graphs

When you think of graphs, you may think of those standard, premade, click-a-button graphs that you can make with any presentation or financial software package. As a designer, you'll be excited by the graphs you can create with Adobe Illustrator. You can enter the data directly into Illustrator and have all of its design and drawing power at your fingertips.

For the right project, visually interesting and smartly designed graphs are a powerful tool for conveying information. Rather than using "canned" graphs from business software, think instead of using Illustrator graphs as an opportunity for expressing data artistically. Since people naturally pay more attention to a well-designed graph than to blocks of text, using graphs in a presentation will help you make your points more persuasively. And using Illustrator graphs will make your presentations one-of-a-kind.

Defining a Graph

A graph is a diagram of data that shows relationships among a set of numbers. A set of data can be represented by a graphic element, such as a bar, line, or point. Different types of graphs are used to emphasize different aspects of the data. The right type of graph can help you simplify complex data and communicate a message more effectively.

Illustrator offers nine types of graphs:

- Column
- Stacked column
- Bar
- Stacked bar
- Line
- Area
- Scatter
- Pie
- Radar

Illustrator creates the graph you specify and allows you to modify the graph objects to create unique artwork. You can also easily convert one type of graph into another type and create custom designs you can then apply to the graph.

Creating a Graph

Before you create a graph, it is important to understand how data is plotted in Illustrator's Graph Data window. The first column (vertical axis) of the Graph Data window is reserved for category labels, while the first row (horizontal axis) is reserved for legend labels. See Figure 1.

Category labels describe non-numeric data, such as the months of the year, the days of the week, or a group of salespersons' names.

Legend labels describe numeric data that may change, such as weekly sales totals, payroll amounts, or daily temperatures; they appear in a box next to the graph, called the legend.

The legend, like a map legend, contains the legend labels and small boxes filled with colors that represent the columns on the graph.

Figure 1 Entering category labels and legend labels

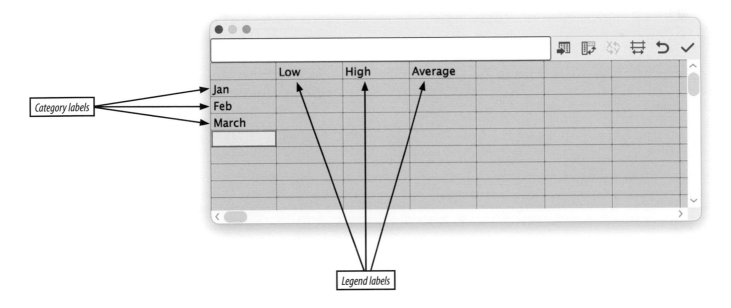

Create a column graph

1. Open AI 11-1.ai, then save it as **Combination Graph**.

2. Verify that you are using **inches** as your unit of measure by checking the **General setting** in the **Units category** of **Preferences**.

3. Click the **Column Graph tool** 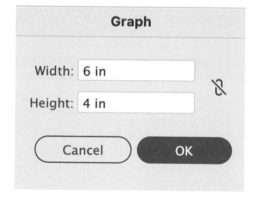, then click the **center of the artboard**.

4. Type **6** in the **Width text box** and **4** in the **Height text box**, as shown in Figure 2, then click **OK**.

The Graph Data window appears in front of the graph and consists of rows and columns. The intersection of a row and a column is called a **cell**. The first cell, which is selected, contains the number 1.00 as sample data to create a temporary structure for the graph. The appearance of the graph will change after you enter data.

5. Press **[delete]**, then press **[tab]** to remove the 1.00 from the first cell and select the next cell in the first row.

6. Type **Low**, press **[tab]**, type **High**, press **[tab]**, then type **Average**.

   You have entered three legend labels.

7. Click the **second cell** in the first column, type **Jan**, press **[return] (Mac)** or **[Enter] (Win)**, type **Feb**, press **[return] (Mac)** or **[Enter] (Win)**, type **March**, then press **[return] (Mac)** or **[Enter] (Win)**.

   You have entered three category labels. Compare the positions of your labels with those shown in Figure 3.

Figure 2 Graph dialog box

Figure 3 Graph Data window

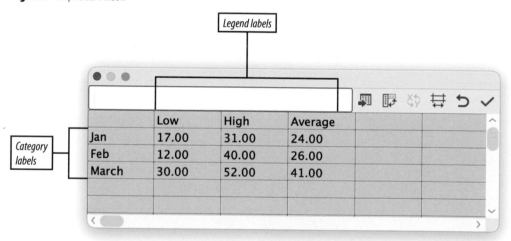

TIP Category labels are listed vertically, and legend labels are listed horizontally in the Graph Data window. If you enter your labels incorrectly, you can click the Transpose row/column button 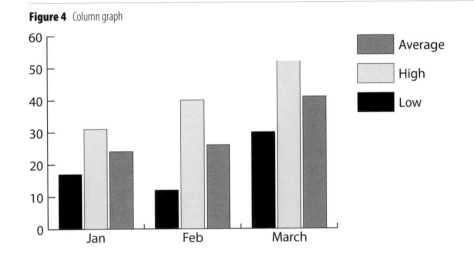 in the Graph Data window to switch them.

8. Enter the remaining data shown on the artboard, using **[tab]** and **[return] (Mac)** or **[Enter] (Win)** and the **four arrow keys** on your keyboard to move between cells.

TIP Often you will want to create labels that consist of numbers, such as a zip code or the year. Since these labels are meant to describe categories, they must be set in quotes

("2021") so Illustrator will not mistake them for data that should be plotted.

9. Close the Graph Data window, saving the changes you made, then using the **Selection tool** ▶, reposition the **graph** on the artboard if it is not centered.

10. Deselect, save your work, then compare your graph to Figure 4.

11. Continue to the next lesson.

You defined the size of the graph, then entered three legend labels, three category labels, and numbers in the Graph Data window.

Figure 4 Column graph

Average

High

Low

EDIT A GRAPH USING THE GRAPH DATA WINDOW

▶ *What You'll Do*

In this lesson, you will change the data that is the basis of the column graph, then update the graph to reflect the new data.

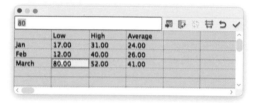

Editing Data and Graphs

A project that calls for a graph often calls for edits to the graph. Fortunately, it is easy to make changes to the data that defines the graph and just as easy to update the graph. For every graph in Illustrator, the data you used to plot it is stored in the Graph Data window. This data is editable. If you make changes, you can preview them by clicking the Apply button in the Graph Data window.

When you create text and data in another program that you want to use in an Illustrator graph, the document must be saved as a text-only file with commas separating each number from the next. If you are importing an Excel worksheet, it must be saved as a tab-delimited text file for Illustrator to support it. To import data from Word or Excel, you must have the Graph Data window open and selected. Click the Import data button. You will then be prompted to open the file you wish to import.

Edit data in a graph

1. Click **View** on the menu bar, then click **Hide Print Tiling** if it is not already activated.

2. Click the **Selection tool** 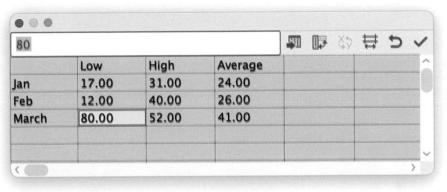, then select and delete the text at the top of the artboard.

3. Click the **graph**, click **Object** on the menu bar, point to **Graph**, then click **Data**.

TIP The separate objects that make up the graph are automatically grouped when the graph is created.

4. Click the **cell that contains the number 30.00**, type **80**, press **[return] (Mac)** or **[Enter] (Win)**, then compare your screen to Figure 5.

   When you click a cell, the number in the cell becomes highlighted in the Entry text box of the Graph Data window, allowing you to change it to a new number.

5. Click the **Apply button** ✓ in the Graph Data window, then compare your graph to Figure 6.

   The numbers on the left edge extend up to 80. The black graph for March is updated and is now tall enough to reach the 80-mark.

6. Change the **number 80.00 to 34**, click the **cell that contains the number 41.00**, type **43**, then press **[return] (Mac)** or **[Enter] (Win)**.

7. Close the Graph Data window, then save changes when prompted.

8. Continue to the next lesson.

TIP To remove data from cells in the Graph Data window, select the cells from which you want to delete the data, click Edit on the menu bar, then click Clear.

You edited the graph's data in the Graph Data window, then clicked the Apply button to view the changes to the graph.

Figure 5 Changing data in the Graph Data window

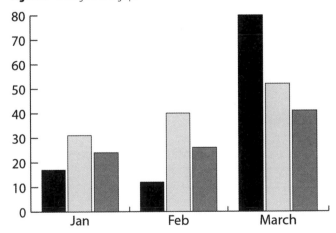

	Low	High	Average		
Jan	17.00	31.00	24.00		
Feb	12.00	40.00	26.00		
March	80.00	52.00	41.00		

Figure 6 Viewing the new graph

USE THE GROUP SELECTION TOOL

▶ What You'll Do

In this lesson, you will use the Group Selection tool to select different areas of the graph for modification.

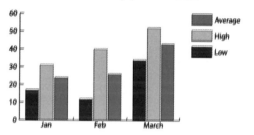

Using the Group Selection Tool

Graphs are grouped objects, consisting of many individual groups grouped together. Each set of colored columns represents an individual group within the larger group. For example, all the black columns in Figure 7 represent the low temperatures for each month. The gray columns are the average-temperature group, and the light gray columns are the high-temperature group.

The Group Selection tool allows you to select entire groups within the larger group for the purpose of editing them with the Illustrator tools and menu commands.

Figure 7 Individual groups within a group

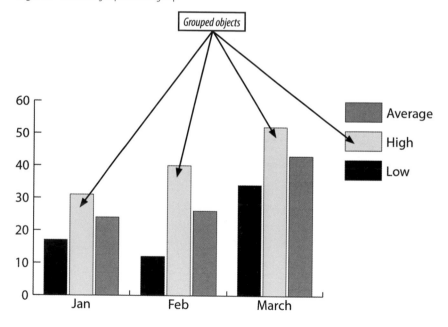

Use the Group Selection tool

1. Click the **artboard** to deselect the graph.

2. Click the **Group Selection tool** .

TIP The Group Selection tool .is hidden beneath the Direct Selection tool .

3. Click the **first black column** above the Jan label, then click it again.

   The first click selects the first black column, and the second click selects the two remaining black columns.

4. Click the **first black column** a third time to select the Low temperature legend box.

   If you click too many times, you will eventually select the entire graph instead of an individual group. In that case, deselect and try again.

5. Change the **fill color** of the selected columns to **red**, as shown in Figure 8.

Continued on next page

Figure 8 Changing the color of the Low temperature group to red

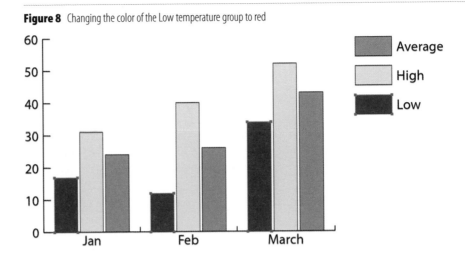

6. Click the **first light gray column** above the Jan label, click it again, click it a third time, then change the **fill color** of the High temperature columns and legend box to **yellow**.

7. Select the **gray columns** and **legend box**, change the **fill color** to **green**, then deselect all.

   Your graph should resemble Figure 9.

8. Save your work, then continue to the next lesson.

TIP The text labels, value axis labels, and legend labels are also individual groups within the larger graph group. Click twice to select them, then change their font, size, or color as desired.

You used the Group Selection tool to select groups within the graph, then changed the colors of the columns and the legend boxes.

Figure 9 Column graph with new colors applied

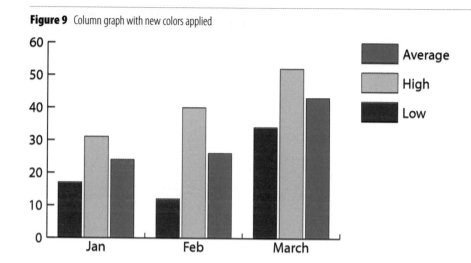

USE THE GRAPH TYPE DIALOG BOX

▶ *What You'll Do*

In this lesson, you will modify the graph using the Graph Type dialog box.

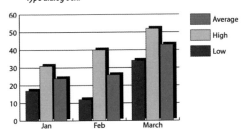

Using the Graph Type Dialog Box

The Graph Type dialog box provides a variety of ways to change the look of your graph. For example, you can add a drop shadow behind the columns in a graph or change the appearance of the tick marks.

Tick marks are short lines that extend out from the value axis, which is the vertical line to the left of the graph. Tick marks help viewers interpret the meaning of column height by indicating incremental values on the value axis. You can also move the value axis from the left side of the graph to the right side or display it on both sides.

Values on the value axis can be changed, and symbols such as $, %, and ° can be added to the numbers for clarification.

CHOOSING A CHART TYPE

Keep in mind the following guidelines when choosing a chart type:

- Pie or column charts are typically used to show quantitative data as a percentage of the whole.
- Line or bar charts are used to compare trends or changes over time.
- Area charts emphasize volume and are used to show a total quantity rather than to emphasize a portion of the data.
- Scatter or radial charts show a correlation among variables.

Use the Graph Type dialog box

1. Click the **Selection tool** ▶, then click the **graph**.

   The entire graph must be selected to make changes in the Graph Type dialog box.

2. Click **Object** on the menu bar, point to **Graph**, then click **Type**.

3. Click the **Add Drop Shadow check box**, as shown in Figure 10.

4. Click the **Graph Options list arrow**, then click **Value Axis**.

   All the options in this window now refer to the value axis, which is the vertical line located to the left of the columns on the graph.

5. Click the **Length list arrow** in the Tick Marks section of the window, click **Full Width**, compare your Graph Type dialog box to Figure 11, then click **OK**.

Figure 10 Graph Type dialog box

Figure 11 Choosing options for the value axis

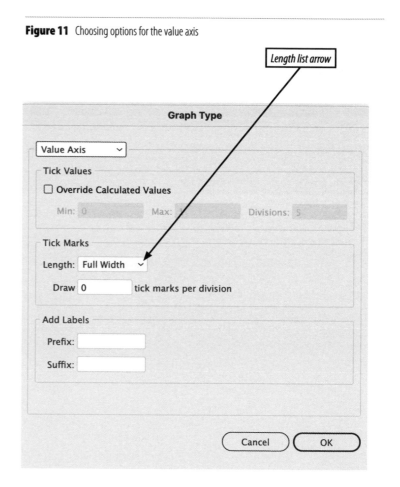

Graph types ↓

Graph Type

Graph Options ⌄

Type

▮▮▮ ▮▮▮ ▬ ▬ ⟋ ⟋ ⠿ ◗ ◉

Value Axis: On Left Side ⌄

Style

☑ Add Drop Shadow   ☐ First Row in Front

☐ Add Legend Across Top   ☑ First Column in Front

Options

Column Width: 90%

Cluster Width: 80%

Cancel   OK

Length list arrow ↘

Graph Type

Value Axis ⌄

Tick Values

☐ Override Calculated Values

Min: 0   Max: Divisions: 5

Tick Marks

Length: Full Width ⌄

Draw 0   tick marks per division

Add Labels

Prefix:

Suffix:

Cancel   OK

---

516   CHAPTER 11   CREATING AND DESIGNING GRAPHS

6. Deselect the graph, save your work, then compare your graph to Figure 12.

7. Continue to the next lesson.

TIP The Graph Type dialog box does not provide an option for displaying the number or value that each column in the graph represents. For example, it will not display the number 32 on top of a column that represents 32°. If you want to display the actual values of the data on the chart, you must add those labels manually, using the Type tool.

You used the Graph Type dialog box to add a drop shadow to the graph and to extend the tick marks to run the full width of the graph.

Figure 12 Graph with full-width tick marks and a drop shadow

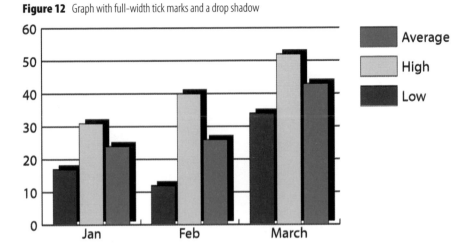

CREATE A COMBINATION GRAPH

▶ *What You'll Do*

In this lesson, you will create a combination graph to show one set of data as compared to other data.

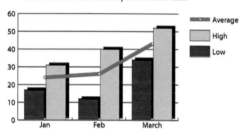

Defining a Combination Graph

A **combination graph** is a graph that uses two graph styles to plot numeric data. This type of graph is useful if you want to emphasize one set of numbers in comparison to others. For example, if you needed to create a column graph showing how much more paper than glass, plastic, or aluminum is recycled in a major city over a one-year period, you could plot the paper recycling data as a line graph, leaving the other recycling categories as columns. Your audience would be able to compare how much more paper is recycled than the other three products by looking at the line in relationship to the columns on the graph.

Create a combination graph

1. Click the **Group Selection tool** 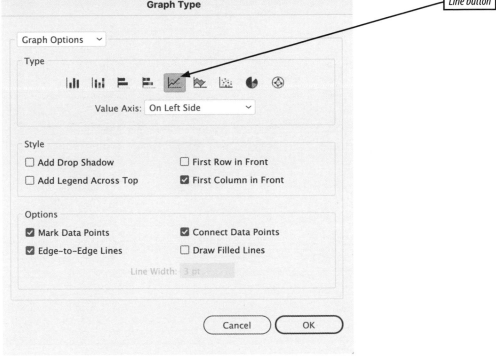, then select all **four items of the Average (green) group**.

2. Click **Object** on the menu bar, point to **Graph**, then click **Type**.

3. In the Graph Type dialog box, click the **Line button** , then uncheck the **Add Drop Shadow check box**.

4. Click the **Edge-to-Edge Lines check box**, make sure there are **check marks** in the **Mark Data Points** and **Connect Data Points check boxes**, as shown in Figure 13, then click **OK**.

    The four green columns are replaced by four small square markers.

5. Click the **artboard** to deselect the graph.

Continued on next page

Figure 13 Graph Type dialog box

6. Click the **Group Selection tool** 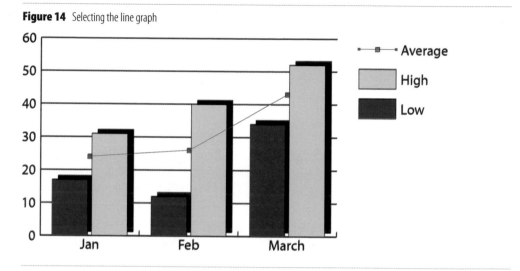, then click the **first line segment connecting the markers** three times to select the entire line and the corresponding information in the legend, as shown in Figure 14.

7. Click **Object** on the menu bar, point to **Arrange**, then click **Bring to Front**.

8. Change the **stroke weight** to **10 pt.**, the **fill color of the line** to **[None]**, the **stroke color of the line** to **green**, and the **cap** to a **round cap**.

9. Deselect, select the **four gray markers** using the **Group Selection tool** , change their **fill color** to **White**, then deselect again.

10. Save your work, compare your graph to Figure 15, then close the Graph document.

You created a combination graph.

Figure 14 Selecting the line graph

Figure 15 Formatting the line graph

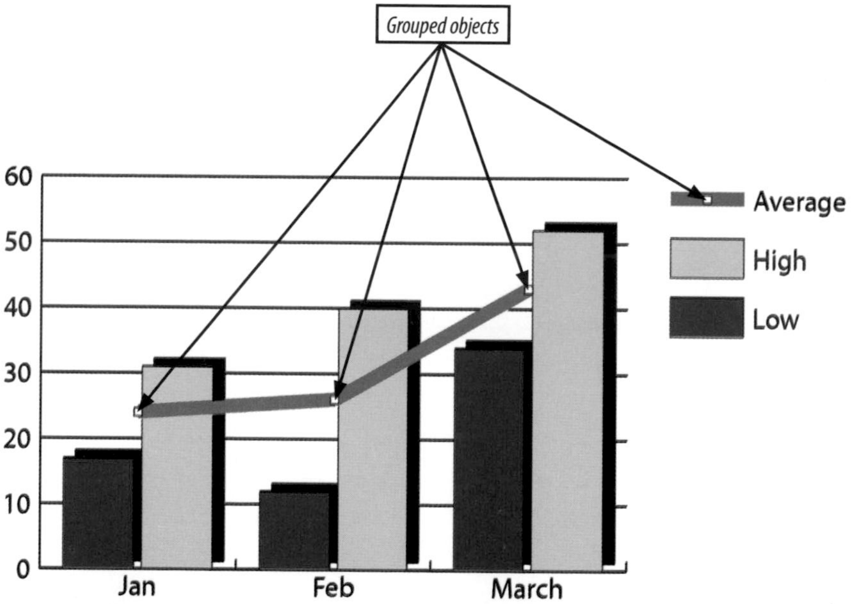

CREATE A CUSTOM GRAPH DESIGN

▶ What You'll Do

In this lesson, you will define artwork for a custom graph.

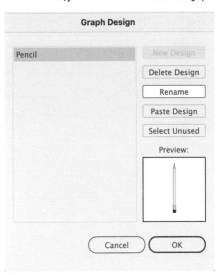

Creating a Custom Graph Design

This is where Illustrator really shines as a design tool for graphs. A **custom graph design** is a picture of something used to replace traditional columns, bars, or markers in Illustrator graphs. For example, when reporting on financial news, newspapers such as *USA Today* often print graphs made with custom designs of coins or dollars instead of columns and bars.

Only vector-based objects can be used for custom graph designs, however. You cannot use bitmaps, objects created with the Paintbrush tool, or objects filled with gradients.

Create a custom graph design

1. Open AI 11-2.ai, then save it as **Pencil**.
2. Click **View** on the menu bar, then click **Pencil**.
3. Click the **Selection tool** ▶, drag a **selection marquee** around the **entire pencil** to select all of it, then group it.
4. Show the rulers if they are hidden, then align two guides with the top and bottom of the pencil, as shown in Part A of Figure 16.

Continued on next page

Figure 16 Creating a custom graph design

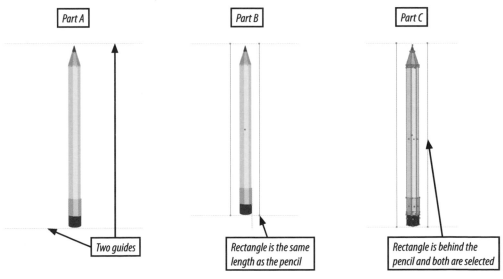

5. Deselect the pencil, then change the **fill** and **stroke colors** to **[None]** on the toolbar.

6. Click the **Rectangle tool** 🔲 , then create a **rectangle around the pencil** that snaps to the top and bottom guides, as shown in Part B of Figure 16.

 The height of the rectangle should exactly match the height of the custom artwork to ensure that data values are represented correctly on the graph.

7. While the rectangle is still selected, click **Object** on the menu bar, point to **Arrange**, then click **Send to Back**.

 The rectangle must be behind the illustration.

8. Select both the **rectangle** and the **pencil**, as shown in Part C of Figure 16, click **Object** on the menu bar, point to **Graph**, then click **Design**.

9. Click **New Design**, click **Rename**, name the design **Pencil**, then click **OK**.

 The pencil design appears in the Graph Design dialog box, as shown in Figure 17.

10. Click **OK** to close the Graph Design dialog box.

11. Save your work, then continue to the next lesson.

You created a custom design for graphs using the Graph Design dialog box.

Figure 17 Graph Design dialog box

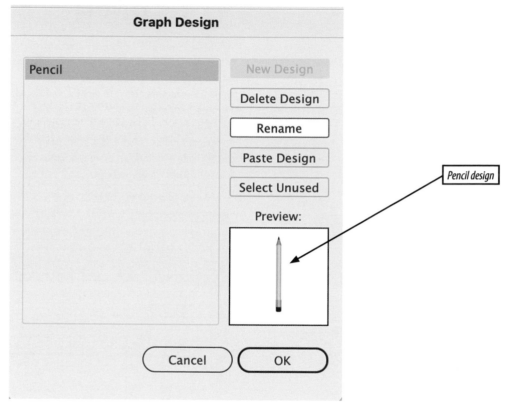

APPLY A CUSTOM DESIGN TO A GRAPH

What You'll Do

In this lesson, you will apply the Pencil custom design to a graph.

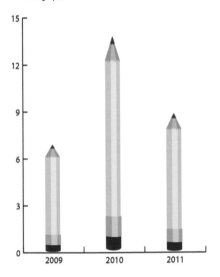

Applying a Custom Design to a Graph

Custom designs are typically applied to column graphs and line graphs. Illustrator provides four options for displaying custom designs on a graph: uniformly scaled, vertically scaled, repeating, and sliding.

Uniformly scaled designs are resized vertically and horizontally, whereas vertically scaled designs are resized only vertically. Figure 18 shows an example of a uniformly scaled design, and Figure 19 shows an example of a vertically scaled design. Repeating designs assign a value to the custom design and repeat the design as many times as necessary. For example, if the pencil is assigned a value of one school, three pencils would represent three schools. Sliding-scale designs allow you to define a point on the custom design from which the design will stretch, so everything below that point remains uniform.

Figure 18 A uniformly scaled custom design

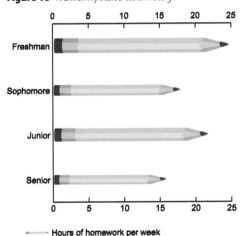

Hours of homework per week

Figure 19 A vertically scaled custom design

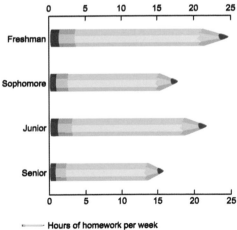

Hours of homework per week

Apply a custom graph design

1. Click **View** on the menu bar, then click **Fit Artboard in Window**.

2. Click the **graph** with the **Selection tool** 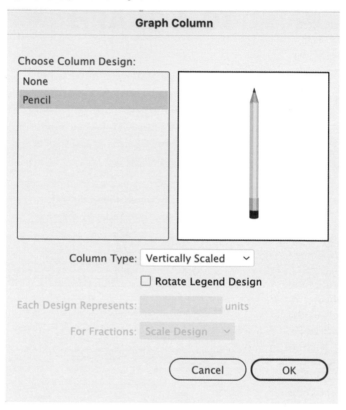.

3. Click **Object** on the menu bar, point to **Graph**, then click **Column**.

    The Graph Column dialog box shows a list of custom designs you can apply to your graph.

4. Click **Pencil**, then verify that **Vertically Scaled** is selected for the Column Type and the **Rotate Legend Design check box** is *not* checked, as shown in Figure 20.

Figure 20 Graph Column dialog box

5. Click **OK**, click the **artboard** to deselect the graph, then compare your work to Figure 21.

The three columns on the graph are replaced with pencils that are each a different length, indicating how many scholarships were given out. Note, however, that the erasers and the points on the pencils are all inconsistent. This is because the artwork is being stretched vertically to different sizes.

6. Save your work, then continue to the next lesson.

You selected a custom design in the Graph Design dialog box, you selected Vertically Scaled for the column type, and then you applied the custom design to a graph. The artwork is scaled vertically to represent the graph data.

Figure 21 Pencil custom design applied to the graph

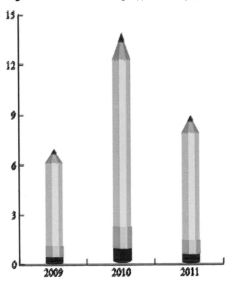

USING THE GLYPHS AND OPENTYPE PANELS TO OBTAIN SPECIAL CHARACTERS

OpenType is a type of font formatting. OpenType fonts often come with alternative characters. For example, when the letter f is followed by the letter i, an OpenType font might offer you a ligature character that is one character of the f and i combined. Click Window on the menu bar, point to Type, then click OpenType to specify your preferences for applying alternate characters in OpenType fonts. For example, you can specify that you want to use standard ligatures for a given font, or you could choose to use dingbat characters to make check boxes or radio buttons. Note that the OpenType panel works hand-in-hand with the Glyphs panel. You can view all the characters in any given font using the Glyphs panel.

CREATE AND APPLY A SLIDING-SCALE DESIGN

▶ *What You'll Do*

In this lesson, you will define the area on the Pencil design that will be affected by a sliding-scale design. Then you will apply a sliding-scale design to the existing graph.

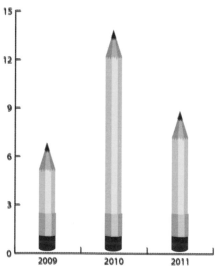

Creating and Applying a Sliding-Scale Design

When you apply a vertically scaled design style to a column graph, the entire design stretches to accommodate the value assigned to it. This expansion may present a problem if the custom design needs to maintain an aspect ratio. For example, a custom logo design might become unreadable if it is stretched too far. For this reason, a vertically scaled design can sometimes be unsatisfactory.

The answer to the problem is the sliding-scale design, which allows you to define a point on the custom design from which the graph will stretch. Thus, a portion of the design can be specified to remain at its original size and not stretch. Figure 22 shows an example of a sliding-scale design. Note how only the handles lengthen in the graph, while the "shovels" at the bottom are not scaled.

Figure 22 A sliding-scale design

Create and apply a sliding-scale design

1. Click **View** on the menu bar, then click **Pencil**.

2. Click **View** on the menu bar, point to **Guides**, then click **Clear Guides**.

3. Set the **stroke color** to **Black** on the toolbar.

4. Using the **Line Segment tool** , draw a **black line** across the pencil, as shown in Figure 23, Part A.

5. Click the **Selection tool** , select the entire line, click **View** on the menu bar, point to **Guides**, then click **Make Guides**.

   The black line turns into a guide, as shown in Figure 23, Part B.

6. Click **View** on the menu bar, point to **Guides**, then verify that **Lock Guides** is *not* checked.

7. Select the **pencil**, the **rectangle**, and the **guide**, so all three objects are selected, as shown in Figure 23, Part C.

TIP Drag a selection marquee around the pencil to make sure you select the rectangle too, or switch to Outline view to see the outline of the rectangle. Because the rectangle has no fill or stroke, it is "invisible" in Preview.

Continued on next page

Figure 23 Creating a sliding-scale design

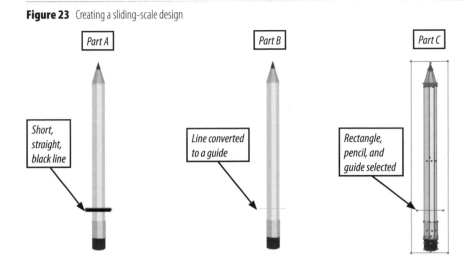

Part A — Short, straight, black line

Part B — Line converted to a guide

Part C — Rectangle, pencil, and guide selected

8. Click **Object** on the menu bar, point to **Graph**, then click **Design**.

9. Click **New Design**, click **Rename**, name the design **Sliding Pencil**, click **OK**, then click **OK** again to close the Graph Design dialog box.

10. Hide the guides, fit the artboard in the window, then select the **graph**.

11. Click **Object** on the menu bar, point to **Graph**, then click **Column**.

12. Click **Sliding Pencil**, click **Sliding** from the Column Type list, as shown in Figure 24, then click **OK**.

13. Deselect, then save your work.

    Notice that the metal and the eraser tip of the three pencils and the pencil points remain unscaled and identical despite the varying lengths, as shown in Figure 25.

14. Close the Pencil document.

You created a guide on top of the pencil design to identify the area of the artwork that will not be scaled in the graph. You then saved the new artwork as a new sliding-scale design.

Figure 24 Graph Column dialog box

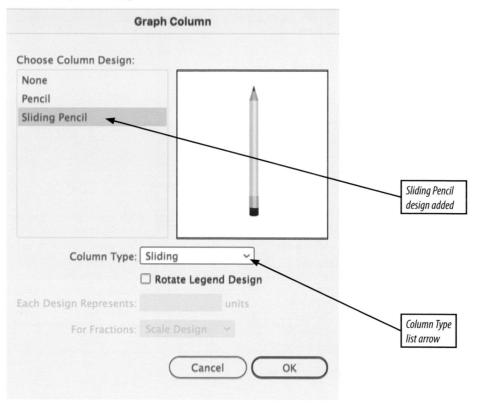

Figure 25 Completed graph

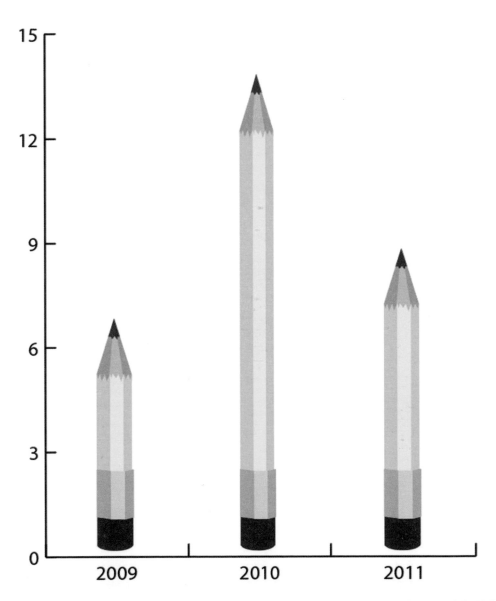

Create a graph

1. Open AI 11-3.ai, then save it as **Nice Weather**.
2. Click the Column Graph tool, then click the artboard.
3. Type **6** in the Width text box, type **4** in the Height text box, then click OK.
4. Delete the number 1.00 from the first cell in the Graph Data window.
5. Press [tab] to select the next cell in the first row.
6. Type **Rain**, press [tab], type **Sun**, press [tab], type **Clouds**, then press [tab].
7. Click the second cell in the first column, type **June**, press [return] (Mac) or [Enter] (Win), type **July**, press [return] (Mac) or [Enter] (Win), type **August**, then press [return] (Mac) or [Enter] (Win).
8. Enter the rest of the data that is supplied in the upper-left corner of the artboard to fill in the cells underneath Rain, Sun, and Clouds.
9. Close the Graph Data window, saving your changes to it.
10. Move the graph onto the artboard if it is not fully on it.

Edit a graph using the Graph Data window

1. Delete the text at the top of the artboard.
2. Click the graph to select it.
3. Click Object on the menu bar, point to Graph, then click Data.
4. Click the cell that contains the number 7 and change it to 8.
5. Click the cell that contains the number 20 and change it to 19.
6. Drag the Graph Data window down slightly to view the artboard, then click the Apply button in the Graph Data window.
7. Close the Graph Data window.
8. Save your work.

Use the Group Selection tool

1. Deselect the graph, then click the Group Selection tool.
2. Click the first black column above the June label, click a second time, then click a third time to select the Rain group.
3. Change the fill color of the selected columns to green.
4. Change the fill color of the Sun group to yellow.

5. Change the fill color of the Clouds group to a shade of blue.
6. Save your work.

Use the Graph Type dialog box

1. Click the Selection tool, then click the graph.
2. Click Object on the menu bar, point to Graph, then click Type.
3. Click the Add Drop Shadow check box if it is not already selected to add a drop shadow.
4. Click the Graph Options list arrow, then click Value Axis.
5. Click the Length list arrow in the Tick Marks section of the window and click Full Width if it is not already selected.
6. Click OK.
7. Save your work.

Create a combination graph

1. Deselect the graph, then, using the Group Selection tool, select the entire Sun group.
2. Click Object on the menu bar, point to Graph, then click Type.
3. Click the Line button.

4. Click the Add Drop Shadow check box to deselect the option.
5. Click the Edge-to-Edge Lines check box.
6. Verify that both the Mark Data Points and Connect Data Points check boxes are checked, then click OK.
7. Click the artboard to deselect the graph.
8. Using the Group Selection tool, select the line that connects the markers and the small corresponding line in the legend.
9. Change the stroke weight of the line to 10 pt.
10. Remove the fill color from the line, then change the stroke color of the line to yellow.
11. Save your work, compare your graph to Figure 26, then close the Nice Weather document.

Create a custom graph design

1. Open AI 11-4.ai, then save it as **Flower Graph**.
2. Click View on the menu bar, then click Flower.
3. Click View on the menu bar, then click Show Rulers if they are not already showing.
4. Drag two guides from the horizontal ruler. Position one at the very top of the flower and the other at the bottom of the stem.
5. Lock the guides, then set the fill and stroke colors to [None] on the toolbar.

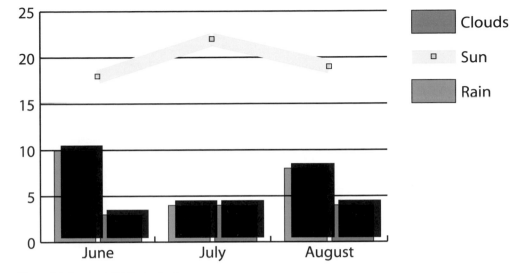

Figure 26 Completed Skills Review, Part 1

6. Create a rectangle that is slightly wider than the width of the flower and that snaps to the top and bottom of the guides.
7. Send the rectangle to the back.
   If you deselect the rectangle and cannot see it, switch to Outline view, repeat Step 7, then switch back to Preview view.
8. Select the flower and the rectangle.
9. Click Object on the menu bar, point to Graph, then click Design.
10. Click New Design, click Rename, name the design **Flower**, click OK, then click OK again.
11. Delete the flower artwork at the top of the document window, then hide the guides.

(continued)

Apply a custom design to a graph

1. Click View on the menu bar, then click Graph.
2. Select the graph with the Selection tool.
3. Click Object on the menu bar, point to Graph, then click Column.
4. Click Flower, then make sure that Vertically Scaled is chosen for the Column Type.
5. Click the Rotate Legend Design check box to remove the check mark, then click OK.
6. Click the artboard to deselect the graph.

7. Using the Direct Selection tool, carefully drag the legend text and flower below the graph. (You may want to create a selection marquee around the small flower to select all its pieces.)
8. Save your work, then compare your graph to Figure 27.

Create and apply a sliding-scale design

1. Click the graph with the Selection tool.
2. Click Object on the menu bar, point to Graph, then click Column.
3. Click the Column Type list arrow, then click Repeating.

4. Type **10** in the units text box next to "Each Design Represents."
5. Verify that there is not a check mark in the Rotate Legend Design check box.
6. Click the For Fractions list arrow, then click Chop Design.
7. Click OK, then save your work.
8. Deselect the graph, then with the Direct Selection tool, carefully select the legend text and flower and drag them below the chart.
9. Compare your graph to Figure 28, then close the Flower Graph document.

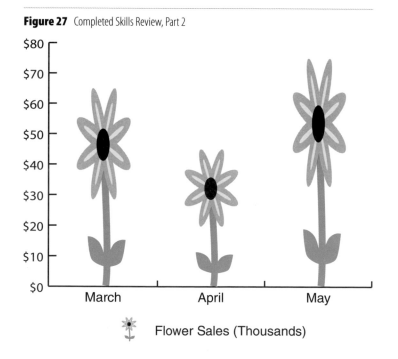

Figure 27 Completed Skills Review, Part 2

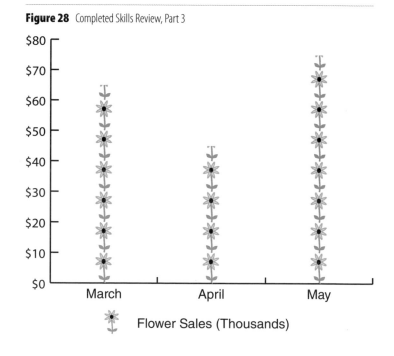

Figure 28 Completed Skills Review, Part 3

PROJECT BUILDER 1

Your apartment is heated and cooled electrically, and your monthly bills vary month to month. You decide to create a graph to get an idea of which months are most costly.

1. Open AI 11-5.ai, then save it as **Electrical Expenses**.
2. Create a 6" wide by 4" tall column graph.

3. Delete 1.00 from the first cell, then press [tab].
4. Type **Monthly Electrical Expenses**. Don't worry if the title is not in full view.
5. Enter the data as shown in Figure 29.
6. Close the Graph Data window, saving your changes to the data.
7. Change the fill color of the graph columns and legend box to the Jade swatch.
8. Place a drop shadow behind the columns.

9. Click Object on the menu bar, point to Graph, click Type, click the Graph Options list arrow, click Value Axis, type **$** in the Prefix text box, then click OK.
10. Click Object on the menu bar, point to Graph, click Type, click the Graph Options list arrow, click Value Axis, click the Length list arrow under Tick Marks, click Full Width, then click OK.
11. Compare your graph to Figure 30, save your work, then close the Electrical Expenses document.

Figure 29 Graph data

	Monthly...	
Jan	400.00	
Feb	200.00	
Mar	85.00	
Apr	25.00	
May	30.00	
Jun	130.00	
Jul	90.00	

Figure 30 Completed Project Builder 1

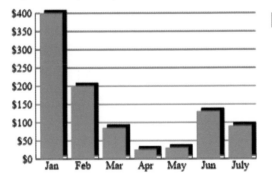

PROJECT BUILDER 2

You own an independent market research consulting business that specializes in the television industry. You have recently conducted a survey of 1,000 people who describe their television-watching habits as "regularly watch television." The question they were asked was, "What is your favorite TV program?" Your research assistants have tabulated the data and supplied the breakdown to you as a column graph in an Illustrator file. You note that the words under the columns are running into each other, and you decide the graph would work better as a pie chart.

1. Open AI 11-6.ai, then save it as **Television**.
2. Create a 6" wide by 4" tall column graph.
3. Delete 1.00 from the first cell, then press [tab].
4. Type **What is your favorite TV program?**
5. Using the information at the top of the artboard, enter the rest of the data.
6. Close the Graph Data window, saving your changes to the data.
7. Verify that the graph is selected, click Object on the menu bar, point to Graph, then click Type.

8. Click the Pie button, remove the check mark in the Add Drop Shadow check box if necessary, then click OK.
9. Click Object on the menu bar, point to Graph, then click Data.
10. Click the Transpose row/column button  in the Graph Data window.
11. Close the Graph Data window, save changes, then delete the information at the top of the artboard.
12. Choose colors that you like for each section of the pie graph and the corresponding legend box.
13. Save your work, compare your graph to Figure 31, then close the Television document.

Figure 31 Completed Project Builder 2

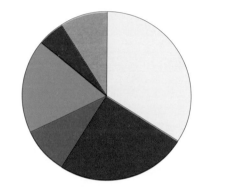

What is your favorite TV program?

- Soap Opera
- Game Show
- Sports
- News
- Comedy
- Drama

DESIGN PROJECT

You are a freelance designer and you are hired by a small market research company that specializes in television. They are submitting an annual report to one of their network clients. The report contains many pie charts. They want you to design a look that is more eye-catching.

1. Open AI 11-7.ai, then save it as **Designer Pie**.
2. Click the Group Selection tool, then click the largest wedge two times.
   The largest wedge and the Drama legend box are selected.
3. Change the fill of the two objects to any shade of red.
4. Moving clockwise, fill the remaining wedges and legend boxes with any of the orange, yellow, green, blue, and violet swatches, respectively.
5. Deselect all, click the Direct Selection tool, drag a marquee to select the pie chart only, then scale the chart 150%.
6. Deselect, click the Type tool, type **34%** on top of the red wedge, change the font size to 27 pt., then set the fill color to White.
7. Moving clockwise, type the following percentage values on the remaining wedges: **25**, **9**, **18**, **5**, and **9**.

TIP Change the fill color of the values on top of the yellow and orange wedges to Black.

8. Using the Direct Selection tool, move each word from the legend over its corresponding wedge.

The words "Game Show" and "Soap Opera" must be positioned outside of their corresponding wedge because they are too long.

9. Change the fill color of Sports and Drama to White.
10. Hide the legend boxes, then reposition the "What is your favorite TV program?" text and any other objects if necessary.
11. Select only the wedges of the graph, using the Direct Selection tool.
12. Click Effect on the menu bar, point to Stylize, click Round Corners, type **.139**, then click OK.
13. Apply a 2 pt. Black stroke to the pie wedges.
14. Save your work, compare your graph to Figure 32, then close the Designer Pie document.

Figure 32 Completed Design Project

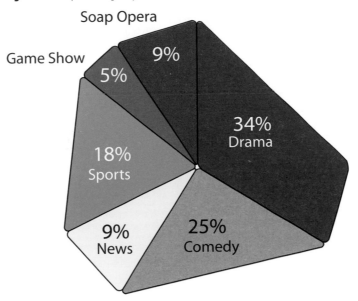

What is your favorite TV program?

Roy G. Biv
Vice President, Sales

Roy G. Biv
Vice President, Sales

Roy G. Biv
Vice President, Sales

Roy G. Biv
Vice President, Sales

Roy G. Biv
Vice President, Sales

Roy G. Biv
Vice President, Sales

Roy G. Biv
Vice President, Sales

Roy G. Biv
Vice President, Sales

Roy G. Biv
Vice President, Sales

Roy G. Biv
Vice President, Sales

Roy G. Biv
Vice President, Sales

Roy G. Biv
Vice President, Sales

CHAPTER **12**

PREPARING FILES FOR PREPRESS, PRINTING, AND THE WEB

1. Explore Color Theory and Resolution Issues
2. Work in CMYK Mode
3. Specify Spot Colors
4. Create Crop Marks
5. Create Bleeds
6. Save a File as a PDF
7. Prepare Files for the Web

CERTIFIED PROFESSIONAL

Adobe Certified Professional in Graphic Design and Illustration Using Adobe Illustrator

1. Working in the Design Industry
This objective covers critical concepts related to working with colleagues and clients, as well as crucial legal, technical, and design-related knowledge.

1.1 Identify the purpose, audience, and audience needs for preparing designs and artwork.
  B Identify requirements based on how the designs and artwork will be used, including video, print, and Web.

1.4 Demonstrate knowledge of key terminology related to digital graphics.
  B Demonstrate knowledge of how color is created in digital graphics.

2. Project Setup and Interface
This objective covers the interface setup and program settings that assist in an efficient and effective workflow, as well as knowledge about ingesting digital assets for a project.

2.1 Create a document with the appropriate settings for mobile, Web, print, film and video, or art and illustration.
  A Set appropriate document settings for printed and onscreen artwork.

2.3 Use nonprinting design tools in the interface to aid in design or workflow.
  C Use guides and grids.
  D Use views and modes to work efficiently with vector graphics.

2.5 Manage colors, swatches, and gradients.
  A Set the active fill and stroke color.
  C Create, manage, and edit swatches and swatch libraries.

4. Creating and Modifying Visual Elements
This objective covers core tools and functionality of the application, as well as tools that affect the visual appearance of document elements.

4.6 Modify the appearance of design elements using effects and graphic styles.
  A Use effects to modify images.
  C Expand the appearance of objects.

5. Publishing Digital Media
This objective covers saving and exporting documents or assets within individual layers or selections.

5.1 Prepare images for export to Web, print, and video.
  A Verify project specifications.

5.2 Export or save digital images to various file formats.
  A Save in the native file format for Illustrator (.ai).
  B Save images in appropriate formats for print or screen.
  C Export project elements.
  D Package an Illustrator project.

EXPLORE COLOR THEORY AND RESOLUTION ISSUES

▶ *What You'll Do*

In this lesson, you will learn basic color theory to gain an understanding of the role of CMYK ink in offset printing.

Using Illustrator for Page Layout, Prepress, and Printing

Illustrator is so widely praised for its excellence as a drawing tool, it's easy to forget that the application is also a top-notch page layout solution. Illustrator is a powerhouse print production utility, a state-of-the-art interface with the world of professional prepress and printing. Everything you need to produce an output-ready document is there—crop marks, **trim marks,** reliable **process tints**, the full PANTONE library of non-process inks—all backed by a sophisticated color separations utility. If you are new to the world of prepress and printing, Illustrator makes for an excellent training ground, with straightforward, easy-to-use panels and dialog boxes. If you are experienced, you will admire how Illustrator seamlessly transitions from design and drawing to layout and output, thoughtfully

and thoroughly encompassing the gamut of a printer's needs, demands, and wishes.

Exploring Basic Color Theory

All the natural light in our world comes from the sun. The sun delivers light to us in waves. The entirety of the sun's light—the electromagnetic spectrum—contains an infinite number of light waves, some which are at high frequencies, some which are at low frequencies—many of which will sound familiar to you. X-rays, gamma rays, and ultraviolet rays are all components of the electromagnetic spectrum.

The light waves we see in our world are only a subset of the electromagnetic spectrum. Scientists refer to this subset—this range of wavelengths—as **visible light**. Because this light appears to us as colorless (as opposed to, say, the red world of the planet Mars), we refer to visible light as **white light**.

From your school days, you may remember using a prism to bend light waves to reveal what you probably referred to as a rainbow. It is through this bending, or "breaking-down" of white light, that we see color. The rainbow with which we are all so familiar is called the visible spectrum, and it is composed of seven distinct colors: red, orange, yellow, green, blue, indigo, and violet. Though the colors are distinct, the color range of the visible spectrum is infinite. For example, there's no definable place in the spectrum where orange light ends and yellow light begins.

Colors in the visible spectrum can themselves be broken down. For example, because red light and green light, when combined, produce yellow light, yellow light can, conversely, be broken down, or reduced, to those component colors.

Red, green, and blue (RGB) light are the **additive primary colors** of light, as shown in Figure 1. The term "primary" refers to the fact that red, green, and blue light cannot themselves be broken down or reduced. The term "additive" refers to the fact that

these same colors combine to produce other colors. For example, red and blue light, when combined, produce violet hues. As primary colors, red, green, and blue light are the irreducible component colors of white light. Therefore, it logically follows that when red, green, and blue light are combined equally, they produce white light.

Finally, you'll note that nowhere in this paradigm is the color black. That is because, in the natural world, there is no such color as black. True black is the absence of all light.

Figure 1 Red, green, and blue are the additive primary colors of light

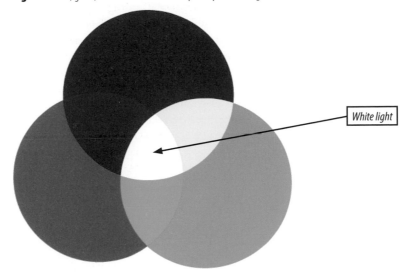

White light

Understanding Subtractive Primary Colors

Three things can happen when light strikes an object: the light can be reflected, absorbed, or transmitted, as shown in Figure 2.

Reflection occurs when light strikes an object and "bounces" off the object. Any object that reflects all the light that strikes it appears as pure white.

Absorption occurs when light strikes an object and is not reflected, but instead is absorbed by the object. Any object that absorbs all the light that strikes it appears as pure black.

Transmission occurs when light strikes an object and passes through the object. Any object that transmits all the light that strikes it becomes invisible.

There are no truly invisible objects in our world (only some gasses are invisible). Nor are there any purely white or purely black objects. Instead, depending on the physical properties of the object, varying amounts of light are reflected, absorbed, and transmitted.

If an object absorbs some light, it logically follows that not all the white light that strikes the object will be reflected. Put another way, red, green, and blue light will not be reflected in full and equal amounts. What we perceive as the object's color is based on the percentages of the red, green, and blue light that are reflected and the color that combination of light produces.

An object appears as cyan if it absorbs all the red light that strikes it and also reflects or transmits all of the green and all of the blue light. An object that absorbs all the green light that strikes it and also reflects or transmits all of the red and all of the blue light appears as magenta. An object that absorbs all the blue light that strikes it and also reflects, or transmits, all of the red and all of the green light appears as yellow, as shown in Figure 3.

Cyan, magenta, and yellow are called **subtractive primary colors**. The term "subtractive" refers to the fact that each is produced by removing or subtracting one of the additive primary colors and overlapping all three pigments would absorb all colors.

Figure 2 Visual representations of reflection, absorption, and transmission

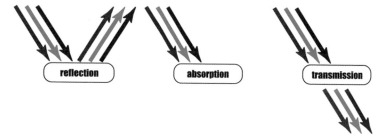

reflection   absorption   transmission

Figure 3 Printers often refer to cyan as "minus red," magenta as "minus green," and yellow as "minus blue"

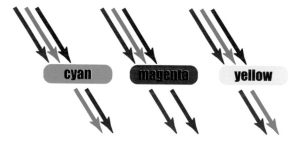

cyan   magenta   yellow

Understanding the Theory of Four-Color Process Printing

Color printing uses the three subtractive primary colors (plus black) to produce a color image or tint. To understand this, read the two points below carefully:

■ The standard color for paper is white. The paper appears as white because it is manufactured to reflect RGB light in equal amounts.

■ Cyan, magenta, and yellow inks are transparent—they are manufactured so that light passes through them. For example, cyan ink is manufactured to absorb red light and transmit green and blue light.

Here is the key to the whole theory: the color you see when you look at a printed page is not reflected off the inks, it is light reflected off the paper. The light that is reflected off the paper is that which has not been absorbed (or subtracted) by the inks. Figure 4 demonstrates this concept.

If all this color theory talk is making your head spin, don't worry about it. Working in Illustrator and producing a printed project does not require that you have these theories in your head. As you become more experienced with the printing process, these concepts will make more sense. Until then, remember the two essential points of this discussion: the offset printing process uses transparent CMYK inks, and the color you

see on a printed page is reflected off the paper, not the inks.

Understanding CMYK Inks

CMYK inks are called process inks. Process inks are manufactured by people, so they're not perfect. For example, no cyan ink can be manufactured so that it absorbs 100% of the red light that strikes it. Some is reflected and some is transmitted, as shown in Figure 5. Perfect magenta and yellow inks cannot be manufactured either. In addition, an ink's ability to transmit light is not perfect. That same cyan ink should, if it were a true cyan, transmit both blue and green light. Manufactured cyan inks actually absorb a small percentage of blue and green light.

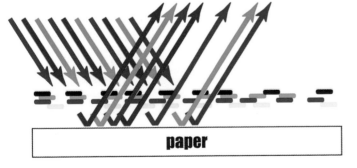

Figure 4 The color of the printed image is reflected off the paper, not the inks

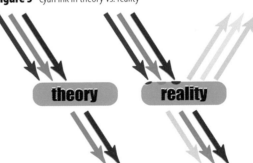

Figure 5 Cyan ink in theory vs. reality

These imperfections become crucial when you try to use cyan, magenta, and yellow (CMY) to print dark areas of an image. In theory, if you overlapped all three inks, the area would appear black because each would absorb an additive primary, and no light would be reflected off the paper, as shown in Figure 6.

Because, in reality, the inks are unable to achieve 100% absorption and some light gets through and is reflected off the paper, CMY inks are unable to produce satisfactory shadows and dark areas of an image, as shown in Figure 7.

Figure 6 If "perfect" inks were overlapped, no light would be reflected; the area of the overlap would appear black

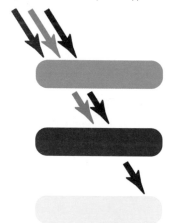

Figure 7 In reality, CMY inks are insufficient to produce black areas

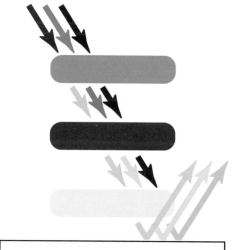

To compensate, black ink is used to produce deep shadows and fine detail. Printers refer to black ink as "K." They do not refer to it as "B" because "B" could be confused with blue, and blue could be confused with cyan. Also, printers have long referred to black as the "key" for aligning (registering) the four colors. Thus, the K in CMYK, though not a subtractive primary, is nevertheless essential to the subtractive printing process, as shown in Figure 8.

Rasterizing a Vector Graphic

Illustrator is a vector-based drawing program; the graphics you create are called vector graphics. Vector graphics do not have pixels. Thus, they have no resolution. Graphics professionals refer to vector graphics as being **resolution independent**. This means that when you place an Illustrator graphic into a layout, you can use it at any size—tiny or enormous—without concern for quality. An Illustrator graphic will print with the same level of quality at any size.

Note, however, that Illustrator is not exclusively vector-oriented, nor are Illustrator graphics limited to vectors. If your illustration is very complex, you may wish to convert a vector graphic into a bitmap graphic by a process called **rasterization**. Sometimes output devices have trouble with complex vector graphics and effects, such as gradient meshes and transparent objects. If you rasterize the vector graphic, you will immediately see if the effects translated properly. If so, the artwork is ready to print, as a simple, standard bitmap image.

Figure 8 The image on the left was printed with only CMY inks; black ink adds contrast and depth to the image on the right

Photo courtesy of Chris Botello

Understanding Bitmap Graphics

A bitmap image is comprised of a rectangular grid of colored squares called **pixels**. Because pixels (a contraction of "picture elements") can render subtle gradations of tone, they are the most common medium for continuous tone images—what you perceive as a photograph on your computer.

All scanned images are composed of pixels. All "digital images" are composed of pixels. And all rasterized Illustrator images are composed of pixels. Figure 9 shows an example of a bitmap image. The enlarged section shows you the pixels that compose the image.

Figure 9 Bitmap graphic

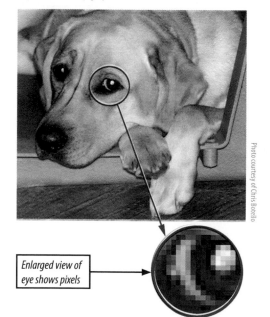

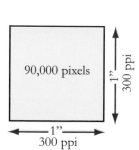

Enlarged view of eye shows pixels

Photo courtesy of Chris Botello

Understanding Bitmap Image Resolution

The number of pixels in an inch is referred to as the image's **resolution**. To be effective, pixels must be small enough to create an image with the illusion of continuous tone. The standard resolution for images for the Web is 72 pixels per inch (ppi). For images that will be professionally printed, the standard resolution is 300 ppi.

The term **effective resolution** refers to the resolution of a placed image based on its size in the layout. The important thing to remember about bitmap images in relation to printing is that the size of the image has a direct effect on the image's resolution. Think about it—if you rasterize an image you create in Illustrator, converting it from a vector graphic to a bitmap graphic, and then increase its size, the pixels

that make up the image are spread out over a larger area. Thus, the effective resolution of the image goes down because there are now fewer pixels per inch. This decrease in resolution will have a negative impact on the quality of an image when it is printed.

Let's use a clear example to illustrate this. Let's say you have a bitmap image that is 1" × 1" at 300 ppi. (300 ppi is the resolution of the image.) The image contains a total of 90,000 pixels (300 × 300 = 90,000).

Now, let's say you place the image into a 2" × 2" frame in a layout application, like InDesign, and enlarge the image 200% to fill the frame. Those same 90,000 pixels are spread out to fill a 2" × 2" frame. Thus, the effective resolution is 150 (ppi)—too low for professional printing. Figure 10 illustrates this example.

Figure 10 Illustration of effective resolution

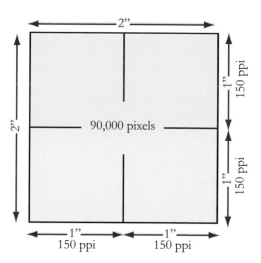

Enlarging a bitmap graphic beyond 10% results in a loss of quality, even if you do it in a program like Photoshop. That's because interpolated data is only duplicated data—inferior to the original data that you get from a scan or a digital image that you download from your digital camera.

In a nutshell, you should try your best to create bitmap graphics at both the size and resolution that they will be used at the final output stage. When rasterizing a vector graphic for output, whether for high-resolution printing or to appear on the Internet, you must determine the resolution (the number of pixels per inch) that the resulting bitmap will contain. You can input the desired resolution for the resulting bitmap file in the Document Raster Effects Settings dialog box, which you can open by clicking Document Raster Effects Settings on the Effect menu.

Remember, nothing in this discussion applies to basic vector graphics, graphics you create in Illustrator. Vector graphics are resolution independent. You can enlarge and reduce vector graphics to your heart's content.

TIP Reducing a bitmap graphic is not a problem because you increase the effective resolution of the bitmap graphic (the same number of pixels in a smaller area means more pixels per inch).

Misused Resolution Terminology

The misuse of the terms "resolution" and "DPI" by designers, printers, and even software programmers has resulted in some confusion over this concept. In general, when the term "resolution" is used, it is in reference to the number of pixels per inch in a bitmap image, or PPI. Unfortunately, many people use the term DPI instead of PPI; PPI is the only correct term for the resolution of a bitmap image. DPI stands for "dots per inch," which is the resolution of an output device. Dots are dots, and pixels are pixels; they are mutually exclusive.

The resolution of your laser printer is probably 600 dpi or 1200 dpi, which is a satisfactory number of printing device dots to print text and lines that appear to be smooth. For bitmap images and blends, a minimum resolution of 2400 dpi is required for the output device to produce the smooth transitions of tone.

Add to this confusion a third type of resolution—the resolution of a printed document. Lines per inch, LPI, or "line screen" is the number of lines of halftone dots (ink dots) in a printed image (professionally printed, not output from a desktop printer). Many printers refer to this resolution as, you guessed it, DPI. Lines are lines, and dots are dots. LPI is the correct term for the resolution of a printed image. Standard line screens for color printing are 133 lpi and 150 lpi.

Standard Resolutions for Rasterized Images

A fluency with resolution terminology will help you in Illustrator when you want to rasterize a vector graphic (convert it to a bitmap image).

When doing so, you must determine the resolution of the resulting bitmap image, or the PPI. The PPI for a bitmap graphic that will be used on the Internet is 72 ppi. The PPI for a bitmap graphic that will be printed is twice the LPI and is usually 300 ppi for a high-resolution graphic.

Printing Transparent Artwork

Whenever you have a document with transparent objects (objects with blending modes applied or whose opacity is set to less than 100%), you can check the transparency preferences before printing the file. When you print or save artwork that contains transparency, Illustrator performs a process called flattening. When flattening, Illustrator identifies transparent artwork, then isolates the areas that are overlapped by the transparent object by dividing the areas into components. Illustrator then analyzes those components to determine if they can be output with vector data or if they must be rasterized (converted to pixels). The flattening process works very well in most cases. However, if you are unsatisfied with the appearance of the high-resolution output, you may want to step in and rasterize the artwork yourself. Before outputting the file, you can use Illustrator's Overprint Preview mode (found on the View menu), which approximates how transparency and blending will appear in the color-separated output.

WORK IN CMYK MODE

In this lesson, you will use Illustrator's Color Picker, Color panel, and print options in CMYK Color mode.

Understanding Color Gamut

RGB, CMYK, and HSB are each known as a **color model**. Color models are essentially mathematical algorithms that computers use to calculate and manage the color you see on your monitor. The **color mode** determines the color model used to display and print Illustrator documents. Illustrator offers two color modes for documents: RGB and CMYK.

As we've discussed, offset color printing is based on the CMYK color model. All light-emitting devices, such as your television or your monitor, produce color based on the RGB color model. If you flick a drop of water at your television screen, you will be able to see that the image is composed of very small red, green, and blue pixels. The full range of color that you perceive when you watch TV is the result of the additive properties of light; the red, green, and blue light are combining to produce the image.

Color gamut refers to the range of colors that can be printed or displayed by a given color model. A good monitor, based on the RGB color model, can produce a color gamut of more than 16 million colors. However, the spectrum of colors that can be viewed by the human eye is wider than any man-made method for reproducing color.

SETTING UP COLOR MANAGEMENT

Illustrator's Color Settings dialog box simplifies the goal of setting up a color-managed workflow by bringing most of the standard color management controls to a single place. Click Edit on the menu bar, then click Color Settings to open the Color Settings dialog box. You can choose predefined RGB or CMYK configurations designed to help you achieve color consistency in a production workflow.

The CMYK color model is substantially smaller than the RGB color model. Therefore, when you are creating computer graphics, remember that some colors that you can see on your monitor cannot be reproduced by the CMYK printing process.

Illustrator addresses this reality in different ways. For example, if you are working in RGB mode and choosing colors in the Color Picker or the Color panel, Illustrator will warn you if you have chosen a color that is "out-of-gamut"—that is, a color that cannot be printed. Also, if you have created an image in RGB mode and you convert to CMYK mode, Illustrator will automatically replace the out-of-gamut colors applied to images with their closest CMYK counterparts.

As shown in Figure 11, the colors in RGB that are out-of-gamut for the CMYK color model are the brightest, most saturated, and most vibrant hues.

Don't despair. As you have certainly noted from looking at art books, posters, and even some high-quality magazines, the CMYK color model can be used to reproduce stunning color images. (*Note*: Because this book is a printed product and therefore based on the CMYK color model, we are unable to show you examples of out-of-gamut colors.)

Specifying CMYK Tints

Tints are, quite simply, colors that you print by mixing varying percentages of CMYK inks. The lighter colors are produced with smaller percentages of ink, and darker colors are produced with higher percentages. You can purchase process tint books that show you, with a high degree of fidelity, a large number of the color combinations available in the CMYK gamut.

In Illustrator, you specify CMYK tints by entering percentages in the Color Picker and the Color panel, as shown in Figure 12. If this idea is setting off alarms in your head . . . good for you! All the color produced by your monitor is based on the RGB color model so you cannot "see" the CMYK color model (or real CMYK tints, for that matter) on your monitor.

In the early days of desktop publishing, this contradiction generated enormous fear in the hearts of print professionals and created an entire cottage industry of color calibration hardware and software. Despite the dire warnings, however, color calibration problems

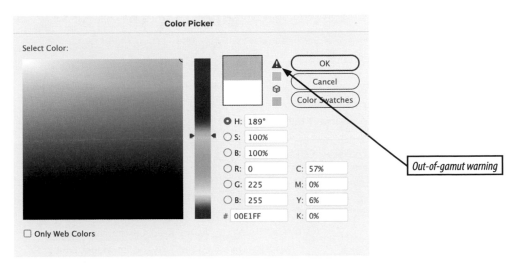

Figure 11 The CMYK color model is unable to reproduce the brightest and most saturated hues you can see on your screen

turned out to be a phantom menace. Simply put, the majority of print work produced is not so color-critical that variation in color is a problem (if the variation is even noticed).

Practically speaking, you must accept that the colors in your illustration on-screen will never be an exact match to the printed version. However, the numbers that you enter when specifying percentages of CMYK are exactly the percentages that will be output when the illustration goes to the printer. Therefore, if you must have a specific tint, find the color in a process tint book, and enter the percentages as specified. Then, don't worry about how the tint looks on your screen. If it looks close, that's great. If not, it doesn't matter. The printer is contractually responsible to be able to reproduce the tint you specified.

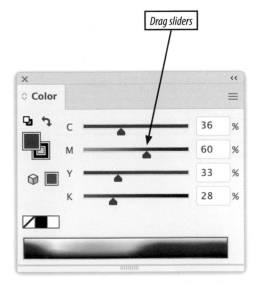

Figure 12 Specifying a process tint on the Color panel

The easiest way to mix process tints on the Color panel is to start out by double-clicking the C text box to select the current value, then enter the percentage of cyan that you want for the new tint. Press [tab] to advance to the next text box, enter the new percentage, and so on. After you have entered the percentage in the K (black) text box, be sure to press [tab] again. If you want to reverse direction, press and hold [shift] while tabbing.

When working in Illustrator, you have the option to specify a fill or a stroke to overprint. However, in most cases, only separation devices support overprinting. When you print to a composite, or when your artwork contains overprinted objects that interact with transparent objects, you need to choose what to do with the objects you have set to overprint. You can choose to simulate the overprint or to discard the overprint altogether. Choose File on the menu bar, then click Print. Select Advanced on the left side of the Print dialog box. Select Simulate or Discard from the Overprints list arrow.

Specify process tints in the Color Picker

1. Open AI 12-1.ai, then save it as **Oahu**.

2. Select the **placed image**, then hide it.

3. Double-click the **fill button** or **stroke button** on the toolbar to open the Color Picker, then type **189** for the H (hue), **100** for the S (saturation), and **100** for the B (brightness).

   The out-of-gamut warning icon **⚠** appears, as shown in Figure 13.

4. Click the **blue square** under the out-of-gamut warning icon **⚠**.

   The closest process color is specified as the new fill color.

5. Click **OK** to close the Color Picker dialog box.

6. Add the **new color** to the Swatches panel, then name it **Maverick**.

You chose a color in the Color Picker that was out-of-gamut for CMYK. You chose the process match that the out-of-gamut warning offered as a new fill color, then added it to the Swatches panel.

Figure 13 Out-of-gamut warning in the Color Picker

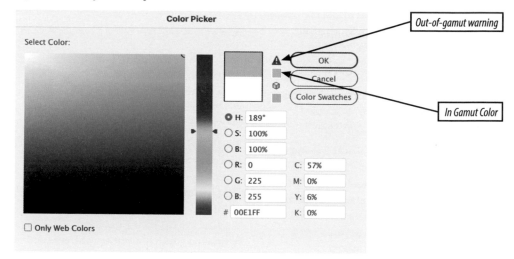

Mix process tints on the Color panel

1. Open the Color panel if necessary.

2. Click the **Color panel menu button** ≡ , then click **CMYK** if it is not already selected.

3. Using the sliders on the panel, mix a process tint that is **5C/70M/100Y**, then press **[return] (Mac)** or **[Enter] (Win)**.

   In standard notation for process tints, zero is not specified. As there is no black in this tint, the K percentage is not noted.

   TIP You will not see the new color on the Color panel if the cursor is still flashing in the text box in which you last entered a new value. Pressing [tab] advances your cursor to the next text box.

4. Add the new color to the Swatches panel, then name it **Living**.

5. Mix a new process tint that is **5C/40M/5Y**.

6. Add the new color to the Swatches panel, then name it **Amazing**.

7. Mix a new process tint that is **30M/100Y**.

8. Add the new color to the Swatches panel, then name it **Twist**.

9. Apply the **four new tints** that you have added to the Swatches panel to the artwork, as shown in Figure 14.

10. Save your work, then continue to the next lesson.

You mixed three different process tints on the Color panel, saved them on the Swatches panel, then applied the four tints you created so far in this chapter to the artwork.

Figure 14 Applying process tints to the artwork

SPECIFY SPOT COLORS

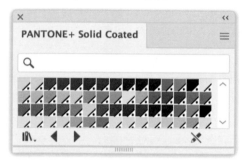

Understanding Spot Colors

Though printing is based on the four process colors CMYK, it is not limited to them.

Imagine that you are an art director designing the masthead for the cover of a new magazine. You have decided that the masthead will be an electric blue, vivid and eye-catching. If you were working with process tints only, you would have a problem. First, you would find that the almost-neon blue that you want to achieve is not within the CMYK gamut and can't be printed. Even if it could, you would have an even bigger problem with consistency issues. You want that blue to be the same blue on every issue of the magazine, month after month. But process tints will vary on press. As the cover is printed, the blue color in the masthead will shift in tone, sometimes sharply.

Designers and printers use non-process inks to solve this problem. Non-process inks are special premixed inks that are printed separately from process inks. The color gamut of non-process inks available far exceeds that of CMYK. Non-process inks also offer consistent color throughout a print run.

The print world refers to non-process inks by a number of names:

Spot color refers to the fact that non-process inks print on the "spots" of the paper where the process inks do not print.

Fifth color refers to the fact that the non-process ink is often printed in addition to the four process inks. Note, however, that non-process inks are not necessarily the "fifth" color. For example, many "two-color" projects call for black plus one non-process ink.

PANTONE color refers to "Pantone" as a manufacturer of non-process inks.

PMS color is an acronym for PANTONE Matching System.

Loading Spot Colors

In Illustrator, you use the Swatch Libraries menu item to select from a range of color systems (or libraries), including PANTONE, which is the standard library for non-process inks. When you import the PANTONE library, it appears as a separate panel, as shown in Figure 15.

TIP To access the PANTONE color library in Illustrator, click the Swatch Libraries Menu button 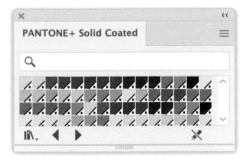 on the Swatches panel, point to Color Books, then choose a PANTONE library.

Outputting Documents with Spot Colors

All spot colors in the PANTONE library have a process match, which is of course a misnomer: if the process tint matched the spot color, there would be no need for the spot color in the first

place. Some process tints—especially in the yellow hues—can come close to matching a spot color. Others—especially deep greens and blues—don't even come close.

When a four-color document is printed on a printing press, each of the four colors is printed separately: first yellow, then magenta, then cyan, then black. When an Illustrator document is output for printing, the document must be output as separations. Separations isolate each of the four process colors on its own "plate."

When a color document is printed with four colors and a spot color, the spot color requires its own plate on the printing press so that the non-process ink can be laid down separately from the process inks.

In Illustrator, all spot colors you use in a document can be output as spot colors or as process tints. Specify this by checking or unchecking the Convert All Spot Colors to Process check box in the Output section of the Print dialog box. See Figure 16.

Figure 16 Spot colors are converted to their process match when separated

Figure 15 PANTONE+ Solid Coated library appears as a separate panel

Import and apply spot colors

1. On the Swatches panel, click the **Swatch Libraries Menu button** 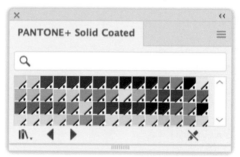, point to **Color Books**, then click **PANTONE+ Solid Coated**.

   The PANTONE+ Solid Coated panel appears with small sample colors of each color in the library, as shown in Figure 17.

Figure 17 PANTONE+ Solid Coated library

TIP You can purchase PANTONE swatch books from the Pantone website at *www.pantone.com*.

2. In the PANTONE+ Solid Coated panel, click in the **Find text box**.

TIP If the Find text box is not available, click the PANTONE+ Solid Coated panel menu button ☰, then click **Show Find Field**.

3. Type **663** in the **Find text box**.

   Color number 663 C is selected on the PANTONE+ Solid Coated panel.

TIP To display the number for each PANTONE color, click the PANTONE+ Solid Coated panel menu button ☰, then click Small or Large View.

4. Click the **OAHU letters**, then click the **PANTONE 663 C color swatch**.

   The PANTONE 663 C color swatch is added to the standard Swatches panel.

5. Double-click the **PANTONE 663 C swatch** on the Swatches panel.

6. In the Swatch Options dialog box that opens, click the **Color Mode list arrow**, then click **CMYK**.

7. Note that **Spot Color** is listed as the **Color Type** in the Swatch Options dialog box, then note the **CMYK values**.

   The CMYK values represent the values you would use to create the closest possible match of PANTONE 663 C with process inks.

8. Click **Cancel** to close the Swatch Options dialog box.

9. Change the **fill of the red frame** to **PANTONE 663 C**.

10. Show all, then send the placed image to the back.

    Your work should resemble Figure 18.

11. Save your work, then close the Oahu document.

You displayed the PANTONE+ Solid Coated library of swatches. You then applied a spot color to artwork.

Figure 18 Spot color applied to the artwork

Image Courtesy of Chris Botello

CREATE CROP MARKS

In this lesson, you will set up documents to print with crop marks.

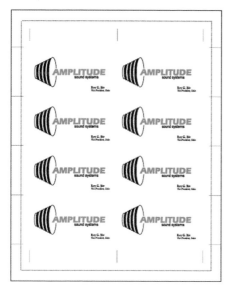

Creating Crop Marks

The **trim size** of a document refers to the size of the finished document. By default, Illustrator crops the artwork at the size of the artboard, which you specify when you create the document. The document size is the trim size. **Crop marks** are short, thin lines you can use to define areas of the page that you want trimmed after the document is printed. Figure 19 shows crop marks around a graphic. When the trim size and the document size (the size of the artboard) are the same, you don't need to create your own crop marks.

You can create custom-sized crop marks on the artboard by drawing a rectangle that is precisely the same size as the document's trim size. Then, keeping the rectangle selected, click Effect on the menu bar, then click Crop Marks in the Illustrator Effects section of the menu. Crop marks will be added, representing the same size as the selected rectangle.

Illustrator adds crop marks as effects. Like all effects, crop marks are listed on the Appearance panel.

Figure 19 Crop marks define the trim size of the artwork

Editing Crop Marks

Once you've created crop marks, you cannot directly select them to edit them. Because they are added as effects, you must first expand the appearance to select and edit the crop marks. Click Object on the menu bar, then click Expand Appearance.

Creating Multiple Crop Marks for Multiple Objects

You can select multiple objects of different sizes on a page and create crop marks for each of those objects. The method is the same as for a single object: select the objects, click Effect on the menu bar, then click Crop Marks.

This situation often occurs when you "gang up" artwork on a page. For example, when printing business cards, printers use a standard-sized 8.5" × 11" sheet of paper. Printing a single business card on that size paper would be a waste, so printers position multiple copies of the card on one sheet. Each of those copies must be trimmed, as shown in Figure 20.

When you apply the Crop Marks effect to multiple objects, you will often find that the effect creates redundant and/or overlapping crop marks. Simply expand the appearance and remove the crop marks you don't need.

Creating Templates

Templates are used to save time in creating documents like business cards that require common settings such as size, layout, design elements, and crop marks. To create a template, open a new or existing document. Set up the document the way you want it, add artwork or other elements, and delete any existing swatches, styles, brushes, or symbols you don't want to retain. Click File on the menu bar, then click Save as Template.

Figure 20 Multiple crop marks define marks for multiple cuts

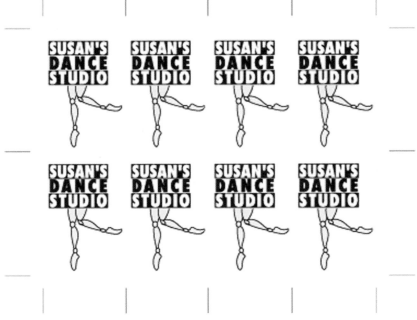

Create crop marks

1. Open AI 12-2.ai, then save it as **Crop Marks**.

2. Click **View** on the menu bar, then click **Business Card**.

3. Select the **2" × 3.5" rectangle**.

   2" × 3.5" is the standard size for business cards.

   TIP Switch to Outline mode if you have trouble selecting the rectangle.

4. Click **Effect** on the menu bar, then click **Crop Marks**.

   The rectangle remains; crop marks appear that define the trim size as that of the rectangle. Your screen should resemble Figure 21.

   TIP Switch back to Preview mode, if necessary, to see the crop marks.

5. Save your work, then close the Crop Marks document.

   You selected a rectangle, then you applied the Crop Marks effect.

Figure 21 Applying crop marks

When you overlap objects, Illustrator allows you to create transparency effects, as though you are seeing one object through another. For example, if you overlap a blue circle with a yellow circle with a transparency effect, the overlapped area will appear green.

When you are viewing transparency effects on your monitor, everything looks great. It's when you print a document that unexpected colors can result from transparency effects.

If your document or artwork contains transparency, it usually needs to undergo a process called flattening before being output. To understand flattening, it helps to think of overlapping areas as separate shapes with their own fills. To use the above example, think of the green overlapped area not as a section of the blue object overlapped by the yellow object, but as a separate object with a green fill. That's how Illustrator—through flattening—manages overlapped areas with transparency effects. Flattening divides the artwork into vector-based areas and rasterized areas.

Click the Refresh button on the Flattener Preview panel to get a preview of artwork affected by flattening. You can use this preview to verify that your output artwork will output the way you expect.

Use the Crop Marks effect

1. Open AI 12-3.ai, then save it as **Multiple Crop Marks**.

2. Select all.

   The artwork is locked. Only the eight rectangles that represent each business card are selected.

3. Click **Effect** on the menu bar, click **Crop Marks**, then deselect.

   Crop marks appear for each rectangle.

4. Note that **Crop Marks** is listed on the **Appearance panel**.

5. Select all, click **Object** on the menu bar, then click **Expand Appearance**.

   The rectangles are deleted. All the crop marks become selectable.

6. Deselect all, then use the **Direct Selection tool** ▷ to select the **crop marks** shown in Figure 22.

   All these crop marks are redundant; they all define the same cuts that are defined by the crops outside of the artwork.

7. Delete the selected crops.

8. Save your work, then close the Multiple Crop Marks document.

You applied crop marks to eight objects, expanded the appearance of the effect, then deleted the redundant crop marks.

Figure 22 Delete crop marks that lie on trim lines

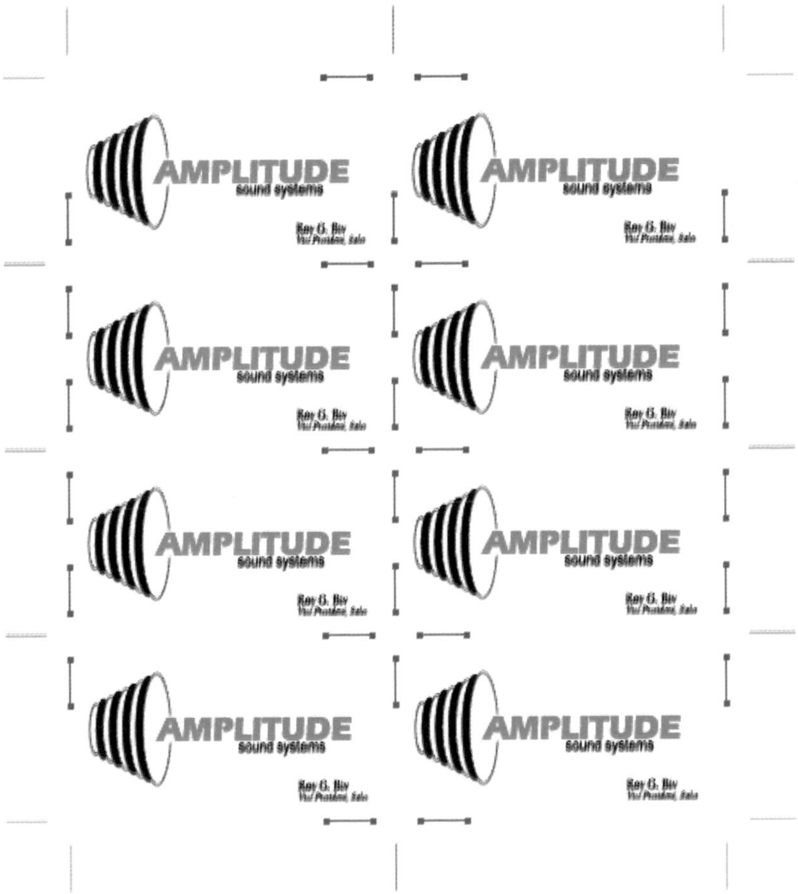

CREATE BLEEDS

▶ What You'll Do

In this lesson, you will modify artwork to accommodate bleeds.

Creating Bleeds and Safety Guides

Artwork that extends to the trim is referred to as a "bleed" element, or simply a **bleed**. Based on printer lingo, this means that to print correctly, the ink must bleed off the page.

Imagine that you have designed a business card that shows white lettering against a black background. You have used the Crop Marks effect so that the marks define the "live area" as 2" × 3.5". When the cards are trimmed, if the cutter is off by the slightest amount, 1/10 of an inch, for example, your black business card will have a white line on one edge.

To accommodate variations in trimming, a printer will ask you to "build a bleed." What the printer is asking you to do is to extend bleed artwork so that it exceeds the cropped area by a minimum of .125". This is something you do manually to the artwork on the artboard. Artwork can bleed off any one or all four sides of the trim. Two of the most straightforward ways of doing this are to create a bleed object with the Offset Path command or to extend the existing artwork off the artboard using the Move command for precision. Figure 23 shows an example of using bleeds.

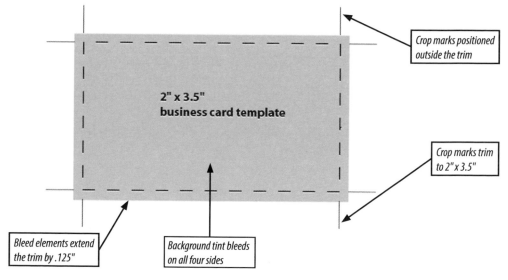

Figure 23 Bleeds extend the crop marks to accommodate variations when trimming

Crop marks positioned outside the trim

2" x 3.5" business card template

Crop marks trim to 2" x 3.5"

Bleed elements extend the trim by .125"

Background tint bleeds on all four sides

In Illustrator you can specify a bleed amount in the New Document dialog box when you create the document. If you don't know the bleed size you're planning to use, or if you've already created the document and now want to apply a bleed (which will often be the case), you can specify the bleed setting in the Document Setup dialog box. When you input a bleed amount in these dialog boxes, it doesn't actually *create* bleeds in the document. However, the information for the bleed amount is saved with the file.

In addition to bleeds, as a designer you should be conscious of your safety margin. All elements that aren't designed to bleed should be kept a minimum of .125" from the trim edge. This practice is known as maintaining safety or type safety. As with bleeds, safety guides anticipate variations in the trim cut and are designed to keep artwork from being accidentally trimmed off the page.

Create a bleed using the Offset Path command

1. Open AI 12-4.ai, then save it as **Oahu Bleed**.
2. Click **File** on the menu bar, then click **Document Setup**.
3. Enter **.125** in **all four Bleed text boxes**, then click **OK**.

   Red guides appear around the artboard indicating the bleed area.
4. Switch to the **Selection tool** ▶, then select the **frame of the artwork** that is filled with PANTONE 663 C.

5. Click **Object** on the menu bar, point to **Path**, then click **Offset Path**.
6. Type **.125** in the Offset text box, then click **OK**.

   The Offset Path command creates a new object, in this case, a bleed object that extends the artboard .125" on all sides. Your artwork should resemble Figure 24.

7. Verify that the **new bleed object** is still selected, then send it to the back.
8. Save your work, but *don't* close the Oahu Bleed document.

You used the Offset Path command to extend the edges of a bleed object .125".

Figure 24 A bleed object created with the Offset Path command

.125" bleed

Create a bleed using the Move command

1. Open AI 12-5.ai, then save it as **Three-Sided Bleed**.

2. Click **View** on the menu bar, then click **Business Card**.

3. Select the **black-stroked rectangle**, click **Effect** on the menu bar, then click **Crop Marks**.

4. Click **Object** on the menu bar, click **Expand Appearance**, deselect all, then use the **Direct Selection tool** ▷, to delete the **black rectangle**.

5. Still using the **Direct Selection tool** ▷, click the **bottom edge of the blue rectangle**.

6. Click **Object** on the menu bar, point to **Transform**, click **Move**, type **0** in the **Horizontal text box**, type **.125** in the **Vertical text box**, then click **OK**.

7. Select the **left edge** of the **blue rectangle** with the **Direct Selection tool** ▷.

8. Click **Object** on the menu bar, point to **Transform**, click **Move**, type **−.125** in the **Horizontal text box**, type **0** in the **Vertical text box**, then click **OK**.

9. Select the **right edge** of the **blue rectangle** with the **Direct Selection tool** ▷, click **Object** on the menu bar, point to **Transform**, click **Move**,

type **−.125** in the **Horizontal text box**, type **0** in the **Vertical text box**, then click **OK**.

The blue rectangle bleeds on all three sides, as shown in Figure 25.

10. Select only the **left anchor point of the black line**, then move the point **−.125"** horizontally.

11. Select only the **right anchor point of the black line**, then move the point **.125"** horizontally, so that your work resembles Figure 26.

12. Save your work, then close the Three-Sided Bleed document.

You extended individual lines and anchor points outside the crop marks as bleeds.

Figure 25 Three sides of the blue rectangle must bleed

Figure 26 The rule must also bleed

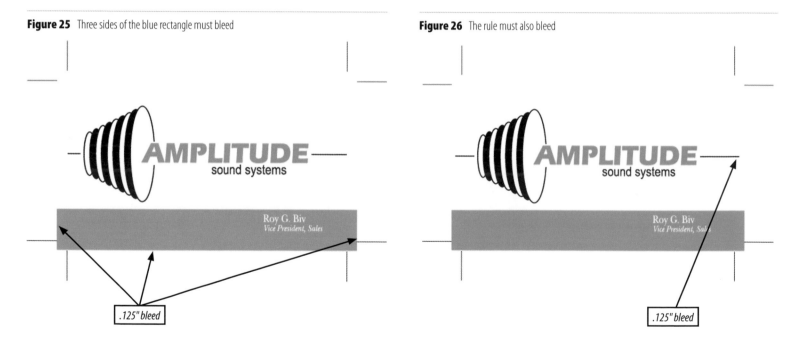

SAVE A FILE AS A PDF

What You'll Do

In this lesson, you will save an Illustrator file as a PDF for both print and email.

Saving a PDF for Print and Email

PDF (portable document format) is one of the most common export formats for emailing documents and printing high-res output. The key to the relationship between Illustrator and PDF is that, as a PDF, the Illustrator document is complete and self-contained. Issues with placed graphics and fonts become nonissues. The PDF file includes all imported graphics and fonts. The recipient of the file does not need to have the document fonts loaded to view the file correctly.

The self-contained nature of PDFs, and the issues that it solves, makes PDF the format of choice for both printing and emailing documents. In advertising and design agencies, it's standard procedure to export an InDesign document as a PDF to email to the client for approval. For professional printing, it's becoming more and more the case that, rather than asking for an InDesign document packaged with all the supporting graphics and fonts, printers just ask for a single "high-res" PDF. If you're using Illustrator as your layout software, the PDF format offers the same options.

When a layout includes placed graphics, especially high-resolution, large-file-size Photoshop images, how you save the PDF affects how the document is compressed to reduce the resulting file size.

When emailing a layout as a PDF, you will save the document with compression utilities activated to reduce the file size for email. These compression utilities will compress the file size of placed images. Figure 27 shows the Save Adobe PDF dialog box with compression utilities activated.

When sending a layout to a printer for professional printing, you won't want the placed graphics to be compressed. In this case, you'll export the PDF with compression utilities turned off. The resulting PDF will likely be too large to email, but it will remain high quality for printing.

Creating a PDF Preset

PDF settings are not only used for conserving file size. The PDF format offers a number of useful options. You can choose whether or not the resulting PDF shows crop marks and printer marks, for example, or you can choose whether the filename and the date and time of the creation of the PDF is listed at the top. You also specify whether the resulting file will be in the CMYK or RGB color space.

Most users rely on predefined presets in the PDF dialog box. Most predefined presets are shared across Adobe Creative Cloud components, including InDesign, Illustrator, Photoshop, and Acrobat. However, you can always create and save your own unique settings as new presets.

Figure 27 Save Adobe PDF dialog box

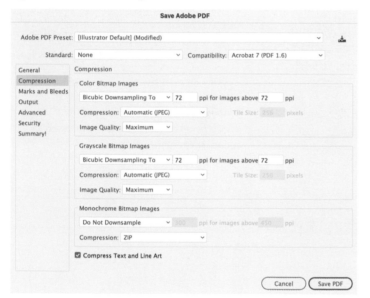

CREATING PRINT PRESETS

You can also save print presets. Choose File on the menu bar, click Print, adjust print settings, then click the Save Print Preset button next to the Print Preset list arrow. Type a name or use the default, and then click OK. With this method, the preset is saved in the preferences file. Or you can choose Edit on the menu bar, click Print Presets, and then click New to set up a new print preset.

Save a compressed PDF for email

If you do not have Adobe Acrobat on your computer, you will be able to step through most of this exercise but will not be able to save your file as a PDF at the end.

1. Return to the Oahu Bleed.ai document, click **File** on the menu bar, then click **Save a Copy**.

2. In the Save a Copy dialog box, name the file **Oahu for Email**.

3. Click the **Format list arrow (Mac)** or **Save as type list arrow (Win)**, click **Adobe PDF**, then click **Save**.

4. In the Save Adobe PDF dialog box, enter the **General settings** as shown in Figure 28.

These are default settings for saving a PDF for general use.

5. Click **Compression** on the left side of the dialog box, then enter the settings shown in Figure 29.

The settings indicate that, for both color and grayscale images, Illustrator will use JPEG compression with High Image quality to reduce the file size. The settings also indicate that Illustrator will use Bicubic Downsampling (standard pixel interpolation) to reduce to 72 pixels per inch any color or grayscale graphics that are over 72 pixels per inch. Downsampling refers to reducing the resolution of a bitmap

image. Thus, a 300 ppi PSD graphic in the layout will be reduced to a 72 ppi JPEG with High quality in the PDF.

6. Click **Marks and Bleeds** on the left side of the dialog box and verify that **all check boxes in the Marks and Bleeds sections** are *not* checked.

Note that the word (Modified) now appears after [Illustrator Default] in the Adobe PDF Preset box at the top of the dialog box. This indicates that the Illustrator Default preset has been modified because you changed the compression settings.

Continued on next page

Figure 28 General settings for the PDF

Figure 29 Compression settings for the PDF

7. Click the **Save Preset as button** 🔽 in the upper-right corner, type **Use for Email** in the Save Adobe PDF Settings As dialog box, then click **OK**.

These new settings are now saved and will be available in the Preset list for any future PDFs that you want to email.

8. Click **Save PDF**.

The PDF will open in Acrobat for you to view. The exported PDF file size is less than 5MB. If you do not have Adobe Acrobat installed on your computer, you will receive an error message and will not be able to save the PDF you created.

You exported the Oahu Bleed document as an Adobe PDF file with a file size small enough to email. You entered settings

for JPEG compression and for reducing the resolution of placed images. You then saved a preset for the settings you entered.

Export an uncompressed PDF

If you do not have Adobe Acrobat on your computer, you will be able to step through most of this exercise but will not be able to save your file as a PDF at the end.

1. Return to the Oahu Bleed.ai document, click **File** on the menu bar, then click **Save a Copy**.

2. In the Save a Copy dialog box, name the file **Oahu for Hi-Res Print**.

3. Click the **Format list arrow (Mac)**, or the **Save as type list arrow (Win)**, click **Adobe PDF**, then click **Save**.

4. In the Save Adobe PDF dialog box, enter the same **General settings** shown in Figure 28.

5. Click **Compression** on the left side of the dialog box, then enter the settings shown in Figure 30.

The settings indicate that no compression or downsampling will be applied to any of the images in the layout. Thus, if this document were built for professional printing, with high-resolution images, the images would not be affected.

6. Click **Marks and Bleeds** on the left side of the dialog box, then enter the settings shown in Figure 31.

Printer's marks include crop marks and color bars. Note that Use Document Bleed Settings is checked. The bleed you created in Illustrator will be represented in the final PDF.

Figure 30 Do Not Downsample and Compression options deactivated

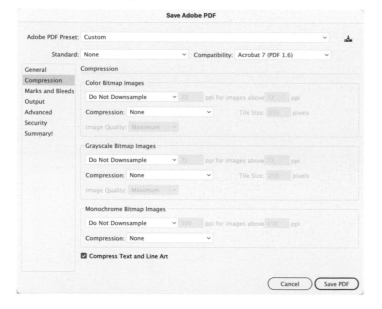

Figure 31 Marks and Bleeds settings

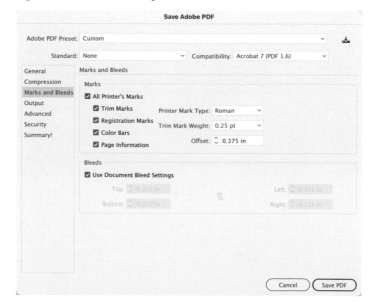

7. Click the **Save Preset button** 🖳 in the upper-right corner, type **No Compression** in the Save Adobe PDF Settings As dialog box, then click **OK**.

These new settings are now saved and will be available in the Preset list for any future PDFs that you want to export with no compression.

8. Click **Save PDF**.

The PDF will open in Acrobat as shown in Figure 32. The OAHU image has not been affected in any way since being placed in Illustrator. If you do not have Adobe Acrobat installed on your computer, you will get an error message and your PDF will not be created.

9. Save your work, then close all open documents.

You exported the Oahu Bleed document as an Adobe PDF file with no compression.

Figure 32 Exported PDF with no compression and with printer's marks and bleed and slug

PREPARE FILES FOR THE WEB

▶ What You'll Do

In this lesson, you will use the Save for Web and Export for Screens commands to optimize artwork for the Web.

Working with Web-Safe Colors

Given all the variables that might affect color display on the Internet, such as different monitors with different settings, different web browsers with different settings, as well as many other conditions, you can never be certain that the colors you specify in your document will appear the same way when viewed as a web page. You can't even be certain that they'll be consistent from computer to computer. To alleviate this problem to some degree, Illustrator offers a Web Safe RGB mode on the Color panel and a Web swatch library. The Web swatch library contains predefined colors that are coded to be recognized by most computer displays and by the common web browser applications. When color is critical, it is best to think of the Web-safe gamut as a safe bet for achieving reasonable consistency, understanding that a guarantee might be too much to expect.

Optimizing Artwork for the Web

Most artwork requires optimization. **Optimization** is a process by which the file size is reduced through standard color compression algorithms.

Illustrator offers a number of optimization features to save artwork in different web graphics file formats. Your choice of a file format will have the greatest effect on the optimization method that is performed on the artwork.

The Save for Web dialog box presents many options for previewing images. The tabs at the top of the image area define the display options. The Original display presents the artwork with no optimization. The Optimized display presents the artwork with the current optimization setting applied. The 2-Up display presents two versions of the artwork—the original and the optimized version—side by side.

Optimizing with the GIF File Format

GIF is a standard file format for compressing images with flat color, which makes it an excellent choice for many types of artwork generated in Illustrator. GIFs provide effective compression for the right type of artwork, especially line art and logos. GIFs maintain excellent quality with crisp detail. In many cases, the compression has no noticeable effect on the image.

GIF compression works by lowering the number of colors in the file. The trick with GIFs is to lower the number of available colors as much as possible without adversely affecting the appearance of the image. Generally, if the number of colors is too low, problems with the image are obvious, as shown in Figure 33.

Optimizing with the JPEG File Format

JPEG is a standard file format for compressing continuous-tone images, gradients, and blends. JPEG compression relies on "lossy" algorithms—"lossy" refers to a loss of data. In the JPEG format, data is selectively discarded.

You choose the level of compression in the JPEG format by specifying the JPEG's quality setting. The higher the quality setting, the more detail is preserved. Of course, the more detail preserved, the less the file size is reduced.

When JPEG compression is too severe for an image, the problems with the image are obvious and unappealing, as shown in Figure 34.

Figure 33   A GIF file with too few colors available to render the image adequately

Figure 34   Problems with JPEGs are obvious and unappealing

Optimizing with the PNG File Format

PNG (Portable Network Graphics) is a bitmap graphics file format that supports lossless data compression. PNG was created as an improvement over the GIF and was designed for transferring images on the Internet. It supports palette-based and full-color non-palette-based RGB images (with or without alpha channel). PNG is the most used lossless image compression format on the Internet.

Exporting for Screens

The Export for Screens command is another method available for exporting Illustrator artwork for screen use. This command gives you the option to export entire artboards or assets (individual items) on an artboard. Note that you may export all artboards in an Illustrator document or choose a range of artboards to export. The Export for Screens feature works hand in hand with the Asset Export panel. In fact, you can open the Asset Export panel directly from the Export for Screens dialog box. The Asset Export panel is an organizational tool for you to specify which assets you wish to export and how you want to export them. Once your asset list is populated, you can choose settings for each individual asset, such as the file type, quantity, name, and suffix. For example, imagine you have an illustration of a garden on your artboard. The garden artwork includes flowers, herbs, and vegetables and you only want to export the flower images. To do so, you would simply drag each flower type that you wish to export into the Asset Export panel. As assets are dragged into the panel, they are automatically named Asset 1, Asset 2, and so on. You can rename each asset by clicking its default name and typing a new name, such as Rose, Tulip, or Daffodil. You can choose to export all assets with the same settings by selecting all of them before choosing export settings or select one at a time and choose individual settings. You can also export multiple copies of each asset and scale them as needed.

Optimize an image as a JPEG

1. Open AI 12-6.ai, then save it as **Montag for the Web**.

2. Click **File** on the menu bar, point to **Document Color Mode**, then click **RGB Color Mode**.

   RGB Color Mode is the correct color mode for onscreen graphics.

3. Click **File** on the menu bar, point to **Export**, then click **Save for Web (Legacy)**.

   The Save for Web dialog box opens.

4. Click the **Optimized tab** if it is not active.

The Optimized view shows you the artwork with the current optimization settings applied.

5. In the Save for Web dialog box, click the **Optimized file format list arrow**, then click **JPEG**.

6. Under the JPEG setting, click the **Compression quality list arrow**, then click **Very High**.

   Your Save for Web dialog box should resemble Figure 35.

7. Click the **Preview button** in the lower left corner of the Save for Web dialog box.

   The artwork opens in your default browser. Here you can check the quality of its appearance on the

Web. If you are not satisfied with the quality, you can go back and modify settings in the Save for Web dialog box.

TIP For a transparent background, you must choose the GIF or PNG file format.

8. Click the **Save button** in the Save for Web dialog box, navigate to the location where you store your solution files, then click **Save**.

9. Close the Montag for the Web document.

You exported an Illustrator file using the Save for Web dialog box, you chose JPEG as the file type and Very High as the Compression quality, then previewed the graphic in a browser before exporting it.

Figure 35 Save for Web dialog box

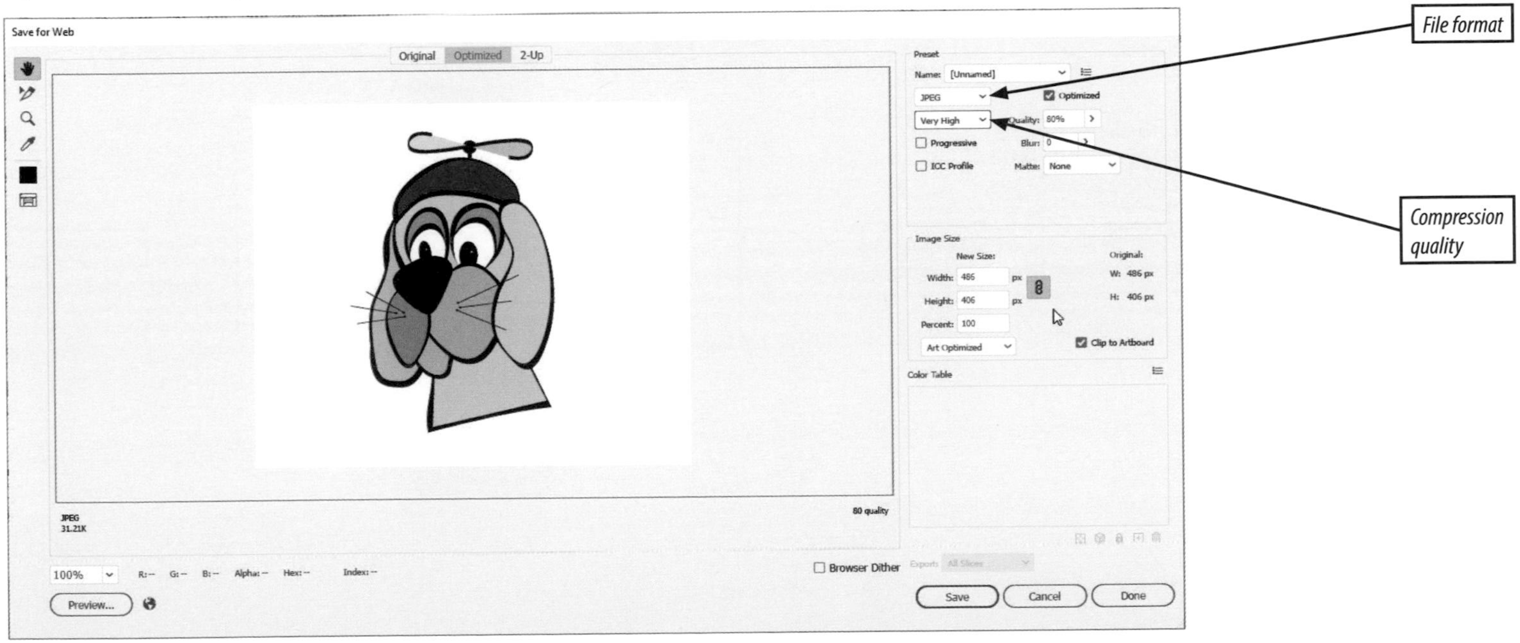

Use the Export for Screens command and the Asset Export panel

1. Open AI 12-7.ai, then save it as **Fish Assets**.

   The document has been created in RGB Color mode.

2. Click **File** on the menu bar, point to **Export**, then click **Export for Screens**.

   The Export for Screens dialog box opens.

3. Notice that **Artboards** is selected at the top of the dialog box and a thumbnail of the fish artboard is selected and named Artboard 1.

4. Click **Assets** next to Artboards at the top of the dialog box.

   Choosing Assets allows you to export individual pieces of artwork on an artboard.

5. Click the **Asset Export Panel button** in the middle of the Export for Screens dialog box.

   The Asset Export panel opens.

6. Click the **Selection tool** ▶, then drag the **largest green fish** onto the Asset Export panel.

   The green fish, now named Asset 1, appears as a thumbnail in the Asset Export panel, as shown in Figure 36.

Figure 36 Asset Export panel

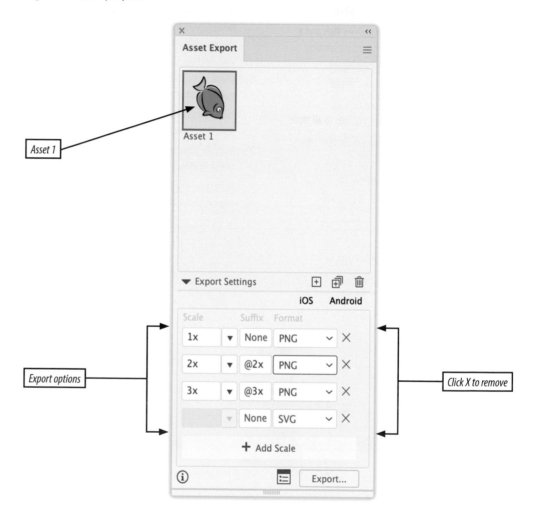

7. Click the **Asset 1 name**, type **Green Fish**, then press **[return] (Mac)** or **[Enter] (Win)**.

8. Repeat Steps 6 and 7 to add a **yellow fish** and a **purple fish** to the Asset Export panel, naming them **Yellow Fish** and **Purple Fish**.

9. Press and hold **[shift]** to select all **three fish assets**.

   You will apply the same export settings to all three assets. You will export the three assets as PNG, which is already chosen.

10. Click the **Launch the Export for Screens dialog button** [icon] at the bottom of the Asset Export panel.

    The Export for Screens dialog box comes back into view and the three fish assets are selected in the window. You can choose to export assets from this window or the Asset Export panel. The two utilities are interactive.

11. Click the **Cancel button** in the Export for Screens window to return to the Asset Export panel, then click **Export**.

12. Navigate to the folder where you save your files, then click **Select Folder**.

    The files are exported.

13. Open the folder named **1x** to view the three exported assets.

14. Close the Fish Assets document.

You opened an Illustrator document and exported three individual assets from the artboard as PNG files.

Explore color theory and resolution issues

1. List the seven distinct colors of the visible spectrum.
2. What are the three additive primary colors?
3. What are the three subtractive primary colors?
4. When red, green, and blue light are combined equally, what color light do they produce?
5. Explain the term "subtractive" in terms of the subtractive primary colors.
6. Explain the term "transmission" in terms of light striking an object.
7. Which additive primary color would be 100% absorbed by a perfect cyan ink?
8. Which additive primary color would be 100% absorbed by a perfect magenta ink?
9. Which additive primary color would be 100% absorbed by a perfect yellow ink?
10. What is the fourth color in the four-color printing process, and why is it necessary?
11. What is the difference between a vector graphic and a bitmap graphic?
12. What does effective resolution mean?
13. Why are Illustrator graphics called resolution independent?

Work in CMYK mode

1. Open AI 12-8.ai, then save it as **Sleep Center**.
2. Using the Color panel, create a new process tint that is 55M/75Y.
3. Save the process tint on the Swatches panel as **text color**.
4. Fill the words THE SLEEP CENTER with the text color swatch.
5. Deselect the text, then save your work.

Specify spot colors

1. On the Swatches panel, click the Swatch Libraries Menu button **IN.**, point to Color Books, then click PANTONE+ Solid Coated.
2. Select the object with the gradient on the artboard.
3. Select the black color stop on the gradient slider on the Gradient panel.
4. Press [option] (Mac) or [Alt] (Win), then click a purple swatch in the PANTONE+ Solid Coated panel.
5. Save your work.

Create crop marks

1. Click Effect on the menu bar, then click Crop Marks.
2. Click Object on the menu bar, then click Expand Appearance.
3. Save your work.

Create bleeds

1. Deselect, then click the left edge of the rectangle with the Direct Selection tool.
2. Click Object on the menu bar, point to Transform, then click Move.
3. Type —**.125** in the Horizontal text box, type **0** in the Vertical text box, then click OK.
4. Select the top edge of the rectangle.
5. Open the Move dialog box, type **0** in the Horizontal text box, type —**.125** in the Vertical text box, then click OK.
6. Select the right edge of the rectangle.

7. Open the Move dialog box, type **.125** in the Horizontal text box, type **0** in the Vertical text box, then click OK.
8. Save your work, then compare your illustration to Figure 37.

Save a file as a PDF

1. Click File on the menu bar, then click Save a Copy.
2. In the Save a Copy dialog box, name the file **Sleep Center for Email**.
3. Click the Format list arrow (Mac) or the Save as type list arrow (Win), click Adobe PDF, then click Save.
4. In the Save Adobe PDF dialog box, accept the default settings.
5. Click Compression on the left side of the dialog box, then accept the default settings.
6. Click Marks and Bleeds on the left side of the dialog box and verify that nothing is checked.
7. Click Save PDF.
   The PDF will open in Acrobat for you to view. If you do not have Acrobat, you will receive a warning message and will not be able to save the file as a PDF.
8. Save changes, then close the Sleep Center document.

Figure 37 Completed Skills Review

You work in the computer department at a small print shop. Your boss brings you an Illustrator file for a business card for USAchefs, a company that works with the top chefs and restaurants in the city. Your boss asks you to create a print proof, which she will show to the customer. She asks you to create it with a rich black, add crops, and build a bleed, then says, with a wink, "But not necessarily in that order." You realize that she's challenging you to figure out the right order in which to get all three processes accomplished.

1. Open AI 12-9.ai, then save it as **USAchefs**.
2. Select the black rectangle, click Effect on the menu bar, then click Crop Marks.
3. Click Object on the menu bar, then click Expand Appearance.
4. Use the Offset Path command to offset the black rectangle path .125" on all four sides.
5. Keeping the rectangle selected, increase the cyan portion of its fill color 50% to create a rich black.
6. Save your work, then compare your illustration to Figure 38.
7. Close the USAchefs document.

Figure 38 Completed Project Builder 1

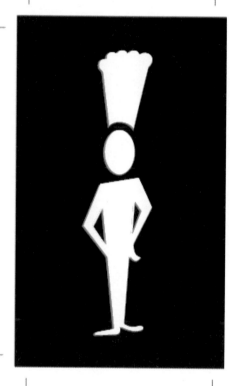

You own a design firm in a small town. A new client delivers his logo to you on a flash drive, telling you that it has two colors: PANTONE 255 C and 70% PANTONE 5767 C. He tells you, "It's all set to go." You know that this client knows only enough to be dangerous. You open his file and, sure enough, you note immediately that all of the tints are process tints. You must change the fills and strokes to the proper PANTONE colors. Because this is a complex logo, and because you know that your client's knowledge of Illustrator is limited, you are aware that you must be very careful not to miss any elements.

1. Open AI 12-10.ai, then save it as **City Square**.
2. Apply the Show All command, just to avoid any potential surprises.
3. Delete the green letters.
4. Display the PANTONE+ Solid Coated panel and verify that the Find field is showing.

TIP If the panel isn't displaying the Find field, open it using the Panel options menu.

5. Select the letter C in the center of the logo.
6. Click Select on the menu bar, point to Same, then click Fill Color.
7. Apply PANTONE 255 C to the fill, then hide the selection.

TIP If the Find Field text box does not work, you'll have to scroll around to find the correct swatch.

8. Select the top white rectangle.
9. Click Select on the menu bar, point to Same, then click Stroke Color.

10. Apply PANTONE 255 C to the stroke, then hide the selection.
11. Click the green square in the center, then change the black stroke to PANTONE 255 C.
12. Click Select on the menu bar, point to Same, then click Fill Color.
13. Apply PANTONE 5767 C to the fill.

14. Display the Color panel, if necessary, then drag the slider to 80%.
15. Hide the selection.
16. Select all and note that all the remaining items have a white fill.
17. Show all, save your work, then compare your illustration with Figure 39.
18. Close the City Square document.

Figure 39 Completed Project Builder 2

You are the head of the film output department for a small printer. You receive an Illustrator file for the business card for USAchefs. The file is complete with a rich black, crop marks, and bleeds. With so many years' experience, you know how best to lay out and print standard-sized business cards for maximum cost-effectiveness. However, you have a group of six new workers whom you hired for the third shift, and you realize that the issues involved with preparing this job would make for a great lesson.

1. Open AI 12-11.ai, then save it as **Chef Output**.

TIP The single card is 2" wide by 3.5" tall. The document is 8.5" by 11".

2. What would be the most cost-efficient layout for the card on an 8.5" × 11" sheet? How many cards can be positioned on the sheet while still keeping a minimum .25" margin from the edge of the sheet?
3. Once you have calculated the number of cards that can fit on the page, calculate the size of the total area (without bleeds) covered by the artwork.
4. Use the Move dialog box to position 12 cards (four across, three down) centered on the 8.5" × 11" page.
5. Select just the black rectangles, copy them, paste in front, then bring them to the front.
6. Open the Pathfinder panel, then click the Unite button.

TIP The 12 rectangles are united as one rectangle.

7. Hide the new rectangle.
8. Select just the black rectangles again, click Effect on the menu bar, then click Crop Marks.
9. Click Object on the menu bar, then click Expand Appearance.
10. Deselect, then use the Direct Selection tool to move the outside crop marks onto the 8.5" × 11" document.

TIP Move the crop marks close to the black rectangles, but don't let them touch.

11. Select the black rectangles, then hide them.
12. Delete all the redundant interior crop marks so that your document resembles Figure 40.
13. Reveal the hidden objects, then deselect.

Figure 40 Interior crop marks deleted

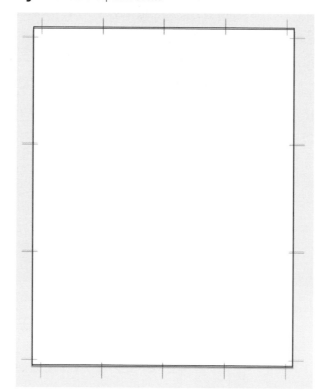

14. Select the large black rectangle, click Object on the menu bar, point to path, then click Offset Path.
15. Type **.125** in the Offset text box, then click OK.
16. Click Object on the menu bar, point to Arrange, then click Send to Back.
17. Deselect all, click the center of the large black triangle to select it, then delete it.
18. Compare your results to Figure 41, save your work, then close the Chef Output document.

Figure 41 Completed Portfolio Project

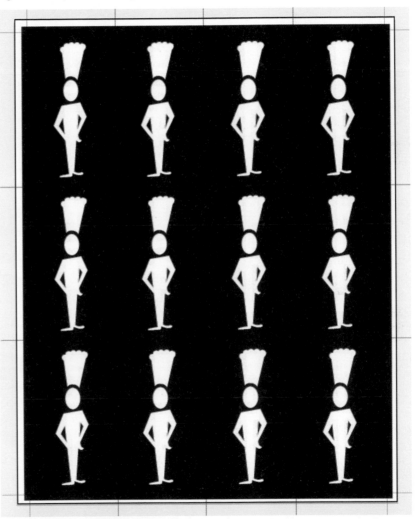

Adobe Certified Professional in Graphic Design and Illustration Using Adobe Illustrator

3. Organize Documents

This objective covers document structure, such as layers and tracks, for efficient workflows.

3.1 Use layers to manage design elements.
- **A** Use the Layers panel to modify layers.
- **B** Manage and work with multiple layers in a complex project.

3.2 Modify layer visibility using opacity and masks.
- **A** Adjust the opacity of a layer.

4. Creating and Modifying Visual Elements

This objective covers core tools and functionality of the application, as well as tools that affect the visual appearance of document elements.

4.1 Use core tools and features to create visual elements.
- **A** Create graphics or artwork to create visual elements.

4.3 Make, manage, and manipulate selections.
- **A** Select objects using a variety of tools.
- **B** Modify and refine selections using various methods.
- **C** Group or ungroup selections.

4.4 Transform digital graphics and media.
- **B** Rotate, flip, and transform individual layers, objects, selections, groups, or graphical elements.

4.5 Use basic reconstructing and editing techniques to manipulate digital graphics and media.
- **B** Repair and reconstruct graphics.
- **C** Evaluate or adjust the appearance of objects, selections, or layers.

4.6 Modify the appearance of design elements using effects and graphic styles.
- **A** Use effects to modify images.
- **C** Expand the appearance of objects.

CREATE A COMPLEX ORIGINAL ILLUSTRATION

▶ *What You'll Do*

In this lesson, you will trace a placed image to create an illustration.

Drawing an Illustration from Scratch

It's difficult to find anything in Illustrator as rewarding as creating your own illustration from scratch. When you're done, it's your artwork, your drawing, created from a blank canvas.

That phrase "from scratch" can be a little tricky though. It's certainly possible to create an illustration in Illustrator using nothing but Illustrator tools. In fact, many of the illustrations in this book were generated that way. Figures 1 and 2, for example, were generated in Illustrator using only Illustrator tools.

Figure 1 Masked artwork

Figure 2 Rotation illustration

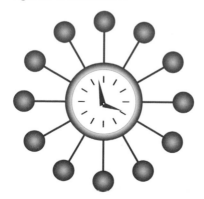

When you move on to portraits and still lifes, however, trying to draw "from scratch" in Illustrator can be difficult and may even be impractical. Instead, tracing from a photo or from a hand-drawn sketch is often a far better route to take. For example, both Figures 3 and 4 were traced from original artwork. The dog in Figure 3 was traced in Illustrator from a pencil sketch and the room in Figure 4 was traced from a photograph.

Figure 3 Illustration based on a pencil sketch

Figure 4 Illustration based on a photograph

When doing a portrait, you will need to think strategically what to trace and what not to trace. Specifically, you can't be afraid to overlap objects. Figure 5 shows an image of a woman and how it can be traced. You can't just draw the mouth and the eyes and the nostrils and the eyebrows—your illustration will have no character. You also need to include some shadows to add dimension. All the blue outlines are objects that will be shadows. Note how they overlap the red lines.

In Figure 6, the head object is filled and the hair object overlaps it, but note how the hair object goes outside of the head object. Using the Intersect pathfinder, the hair aligns perfectly with the head in Figure 7.

Figure 5 Strategies for tracing an image of a face

View Stock on Offset/Shutterstock

Shadow object overlaps head object

Figure 6 Hair object overlapping head shape

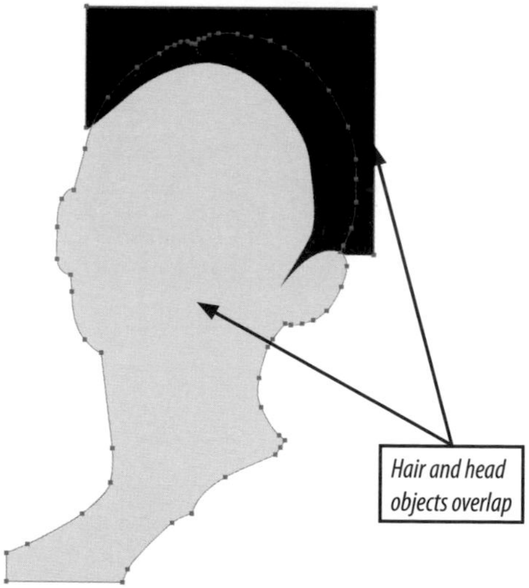

Hair and head objects overlap

Figure 7 Hair object aligns perfectly with head object

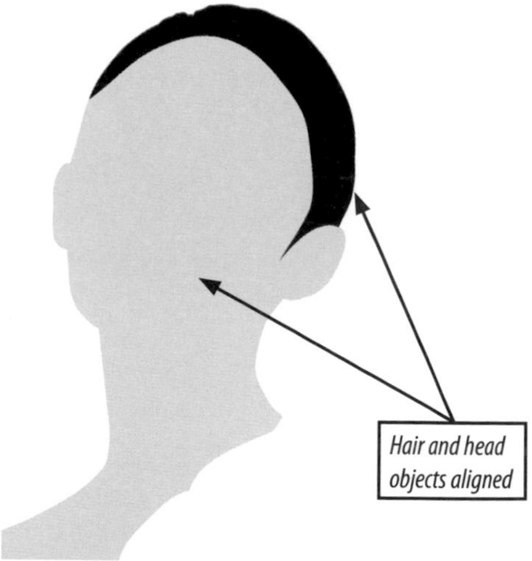

Hair and head objects aligned

In Figure 8, the shadow object overlaps the head and neck. Again, with the Intersect pathfinder, the shadow aligns perfectly in Figure 9. Keeping in mind all that you can do with the Pathfinder tools, you should feel confident to trace and overlap any area of an image you want to work with.

Figure 10 shows a working sketch based on the trace lines shown in Figure 5. What's really amazing is that, with just a very few objects to work with, the illustration expresses genuine emotion and character. It's also interesting to consider the subtle difference in expression. The woman in the photo is serene and tranquil. The woman in the illustration has a slightly different expression. There's a little less tranquility and a little bit of an edge. This would be a solid foundation upon which a truly compelling illustration could be finished.

Figure 8 Shadow object overlaps head object

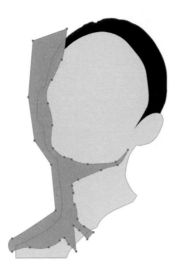

Figure 9 Shadow object aligns perfectly with the head and neck

Figure 10 Foundations for a portrait illustration

Crop an image for hand tracing

1. Open AI 13-1.ai, then save it as **Carly Part 1**.

2. Verify that guides are showing, then select the **image of the woman**.

   The file contains a placed image of a woman smiling. A guide has been positioned vertically down the middle of her face. For this illustration, we will use a technique that involves drawing just one half of her face and then creating a mirror image to complete her face. To do so, we will first crop the image vertically in half.

3. Set the **fill color** on the toolbar to **White** and the stroke to **[None]**.

4. Select the **image**, then click **Make Mask** on the Transparency panel.

5. Click the **opacity mask thumbnail** on the Transparency panel to activate it.

6. Click the **Rectangle tool** , then drag a **box** anywhere on the artboard.

7. Use the **Free Transform tool** to position the rectangle over **just the right half of the image**, with the left edge aligned exactly to the vertical guide.

   Your result should resemble Figure 11.

   TIP If you do not see the Free Transform tool on the toolbar, press [E] to access the Free Transform tool or click Window on the menu bar, point to Toolbars, then click Advanced.

8. Click the **artwork thumbnail** on the Transparency panel.

9. On the Layers panel, double-click **Layer 1**.

   The Layer Options dialog box opens.

10. Click the **Dim Images to: check box**, type **25** in the text box, then click **OK**.

11. Save your work, then continue to the next set of steps.

   You used the Transparency panel to mask an image so only the right half is visible.

Figure 11 Cropping the image

Woman: santypan/Shutterstock, Sunglasses: Rohappy/Shutterstock

Hand-trace elements of a placed image

1. Select the **image of the woman**, then enter **[command] [2] (Mac)** or **[Ctrl] [2] (Win)** to lock it.

2. Change the **fill color** to **[None]** and the **stroke color** to a **shade of red**.

3. Click the **Pen tool** 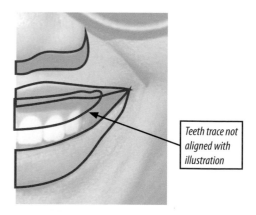, then trace the **face** as shown in Figure 12.

   Note that the left edge of the face trace is a straight line that aligns to the vertical guide as closely as possible. In the figure, the trace has no fill and a red stroke. The stroke in the figure is heavy so you can see it. Your stroke should be just one point or less in size.

4. Trace the **sunglass frame** and **lens**, as shown in Figure 13.

TIP To keep your screen from getting cluttered, feel free to hide individual shapes after creating them.

5. Trace the **top lip**, **bottom lip**, **nose shadow**, and **earring**, as shown in Figure 14.

TIP The model has a beautiful smile, so take the time to trace the lips accurately. Draw the top lip first, lock it, then draw the bottom lip. Try to align the right corners of both lips at the same location. Verify that the top lip is unlocked when you're finished.

6. Using Figure 15 as a reference, draw an object for the **teeth**.

Figure 12 Tracing the face

Figure 13 Tracing the frame and lens

Figure 14 Tracing the top lip, bottom lip, nose shadow, and earring

Figure 15 Drawing an object for the teeth

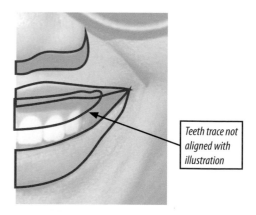

Teeth trace not aligned with illustration

This is the first instance in which you will "freehand" a trace. Trying to draw each individual tooth would be too much detail for this illustration. Instead, you created a single object that you will fill with white to represent the top row of her teeth. Note the positioning—the object overlaps with the top lip and does not align with the actual teeth in the image. If you're asking yourself, "How would I have known to do the teeth this way?" the answer is, you likely wouldn't have. This solution comes with experience of producing many illustrations for many faces.

7. Draw the **mouth shadow** and **sunglasses shadow**, as shown in Figure 16.

The mouth shadow will be a black-filled object representing the interior of the mouth behind the lips and teeth. The sunglasses shadow should be below the sunglass frame trace you drew; it is a shadow cast down from the frames.

8. Draw the **brow** and the **neck**, as shown in Figure 17.

The brow is completely imagined because no brow is visible in the artwork. The neck intentionally doesn't align with the neck in the image; the rectangle is taller and narrower.

9. Add the **shoulders** and the **chin shadow**, as shown in Figure 18.

Note that the shoulders overlap the neck. Also note that the chin shadow is aligned left with the neck, but it extends the neck on the right.

10. Click **Object** on the menu bar, then click **Show All** if you have hidden objects along the way.

11. Unlock the image of the woman, then hide it, so all your tracings are visible.

Your results should resemble Figure 19.

12. Save your work, then close the Carly Part 1 document.

You used the Pen tool and referenced figures to trace various elements from the image.

Figure 16 Drawing the mouth shadow and sunglasses shadow

Figure 17 Drawing the brow and neck

Figure 18 Drawing the shoulders and the chin shadow

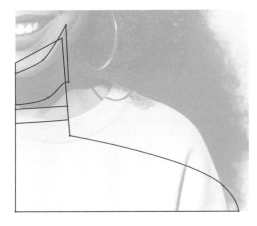

Figure 19 All the tracings showing

Align anchor points and flip artwork with the Reflect tool

1. Open AI 13-2.ai, then save it as **Carly Part 2**.

   The document opens in Outline mode.

2. Switch to **Outline mode** if you are in Preview mode, then zoom in on the artwork.

   No matter how you try, it's difficult to get all the artwork to align on its left edge just by drawing. You could use the Align panel, but that would move objects and alter the relationships between some objects, such as the frame and the lens. Instead, you will make a quick selection of all the leftmost points.

3. Click the **Direct Selection tool** 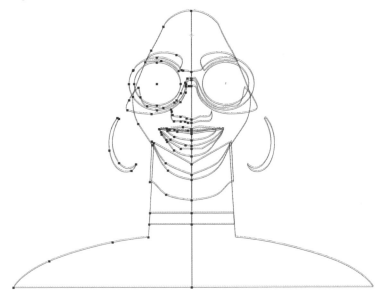, then, starting at the top-left corner of the artwork, drag a **selection marquee** around **all the leftmost anchor points** that are meant to be positioned on the vertical guide.

   You want to select only the leftmost anchor points on each object. After selecting, you might want to zoom in to be sure you have the selection you intend to.

4. Click **Object** on the menu bar, point to **Path**, then click **Average**.

5. Click the **Vertical option button**, then click **OK**.

6. Zoom in on the **center of the face** to **200%**, select all, then click the **Reflect tool** on the toolbar.

7. Press and hold **[option] (Mac)** or **[Alt] (Win)**, then click as precisely as possible on the **vertical line that is the left edge of the face**.

   The Reflect tool dialog box opens.

8. In the Axis section, click **Vertical**, then click **Copy**.

   As shown in Figure 20, a reflected copy is created. The copy is selected. You will now merge the two halves of each object. To do so, you want to be sure they are overlapping slightly.

9. Press the **right arrow key** on your keypad one time.

If you clicked the vertical line precisely when you made the reflection, moving the artwork one increment with the arrow key will be enough to overlap all reflected objects that meet at the vertical center.

10. Switch to **Preview mode**, save your work, then continue to the next set of steps.

You selected the leftmost anchor points of objects meant to be aligned on the left edge. You used the Average dialog box to align those points. You created a reflected copy across the vertical axis, then you pressed the right arrow on your keypad one time to be sure the two halves overlapped.

Figure 20 Reflecting the artwork

Use Pathfinders to build an illustration and align shadow artwork

1. Select the **two halves of the shoulders**, then click the **Unite pathfinder**.

2. Click the **Eyedropper tool**, then click the **navy blue color chip** below the artboard.

3. Use the **Unite pathfinder** to unite all the overlapping mirrored objects.

   This means you will unite ten mirrored sets of two. Starting from the top, unite the two halves of the face, then the sunglasses frames, the sunglasses shadow, the nose shadow, the top lip, the teeth, the mouth shadow, the bottom lip, the chin shadow, and the neck. When you are done, you will no longer see a vertical line through the artwork because all the mirrored halves have been united as shown in Figure 21.

4. Show the **Hair Start layer** on the Layers panel.

5. Using the method from Step 2, use the **Eyedropper tool** to colorize the artwork as shown in Figure 22.

   You will need to rearrange the stacking order to match the figure.

6. Select the **neck artwork**, copy, then paste in front.

   Only the pasted copy is selected.

7. Add the **chin shadow artwork** to the copied neck selection, then click the **Intersect button** on the Pathfinder panel.

   The left and right edges of the chin shadow artwork are trimmed so they align with the edges of the original neck artwork.

8. Select the **face artwork**, copy, then paste in front.

   Only the pasted copy is selected.

Figure 21 Uniting and colorizing the shoulders

Figure 22 Colorizing the illustration

Shadow objects extend the face and neck

9. Add the **sunglasses shadow artwork** to the selection, then click the **Intersect button**  on the Pathfinder panel.

Your artwork should resemble Figure 23. Consider how these shadows were drawn originally with the plan to intersect them to fit with the artwork.

10. Save your work, then continue to the next set of steps.

You used the Unite pathfinder to create one object from every pair of mirrored objects. You used the Intersect pathfinder to overlap the shadow artwork exactly with the artwork beneath it. You applied color fills to the artwork.

Figure 23 Using the Intersect pathfinder to align the shadows with the face and neck

Apply a Zig Zag effect

1. Unlock the **Hair start layer**.

2. Select the **hair**, click **Effect** on the menu bar, point to **Distort & Transform**, then click **Zig Zag**.

3. Enter the settings shown in Figure 24, then click **OK**.

Your artwork should resemble Figure 25.

4. Click **Object** on the menu bar, then click **Expand Appearance**.

5. Click **Object** on the menu bar, point to **Transform**, then click **Move**.

6. Enter **1.25 in** in the Horizontal text box, enter **−1.25 in** in the Vertical text box, then click **Copy**.

7. Enter **[command] [D] (Mac)** or **[Ctrl] [D] (Win)** to repeat the transformation.

There are now three overlapping "hair" objects on the artboard.

Figure 24 Zig Zag settings

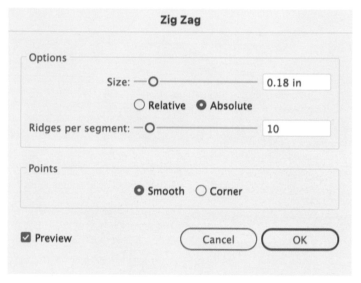

Figure 25 The Zig Zag effect applied

8. Select the **three "hair" objects**, click the **Shape Builder tool** , press and hold **[option] (Mac)** or **[Alt] (Win)**, then delete the **two objects demarcated with an "x"** in Figure 26.

9. Delete the small objects circled in Figure 27.

When you are done, the Zig Zag effect should be smooth and unbroken.

10. Show the **Background layer**.

11. Fill the remaining hair segments, as shown in Figure 28.

12. Hide the **Color Chips layer**.

13. Save your work, then close the Carly Part 2 document.

You applied a Zig Zag effect, then expanded the appearance. You offset two copies, then used the Shape Builder tool to remove extra segments. You then colorized the shapes in the hair.

Figure 26 Two segments to delete

Figure 27 Areas containing small objects to be deleted from the hair shape

Figure 28 Final artwork at this stage

Apply blending modes to an illustration

1. Open AI 13-3.ai, then save it as **Carly Part 3**.

2. Copy the **face object**, paste in front, then fill the **copy** with a **white to black gradient** from **top to bottom**, as shown in Figure 29.

3. Click the **Selection tool** ▶, then on the Transparency panel, change the **blending mode** to **Overlay**.

   Overlay is a brightening/darkening mode. White overlayed produces the most brightening, black overlayed produces the most darkening, and 50% gray overlayed produces no effect. Thus, the gradient from top to bottom on the face fades from brighter to darker. In this case, it is too dark at the bottom, so you will change the gradient fill with the Gradient tool ▮.

4. Click the **Gradient tool** ▮, then drag from top to bottom, as shown in Figure 30.

Continued on next page

Figure 29 Applying a gradient to the face copy

Figure 30 Adjusting the gradient overlay

5. Select the **purple hair**, copy it, then paste in front.

6. Fill the copy with a **linear gradient** that resembles Figure 31.

7. Click the **Selection tool** ▶, then set the object's **blending mode** to **Overlay**.

8. Using the same method, overlay a **white to black linear gradient** over the **blue hair segment** so your artwork resembles Figure 32.

Figure 31 Applying a gradient to the hair

Figure 32 Applying a gradient to the hair

For the blue segment, apply the white to black gradient from right to left so the right side of the blue hair is the brightest.

9. Apply the gradients shown in Figure 33.

- White to black vertical linear gradients are used in the sunglass frames, on the bottom lip, and on the two earrings. The gradients move from white at the top to dark gray at the bottom of those objects.
- Radial gradients are used in the lenses and on the top lip.
- For the teeth, create a black to white to black linear gradient. Note that the center is white and the left and right sides of the teeth are dark.

TIP Don't feel pressured to recreate these gradients exactly. Also, remember that they can be edited repeatedly as you build the illustration.

Figure 33 Applying gradients to multiple objects

10. On the Transparency panel, apply the **Overlay blending mode** to the gradients in the **lips** only.

11. Use Figure 34 as a reference for the three gradients in the remaining steps.

Figure 34 Applying gradients to the shoulders, neck, and hair

12. Create a **white to black linear gradient** over the **shoulders**, then set its blending mode to **Overlay**.

13. Create a **white to black radial gradient** over the **neck** (but behind the chin shadow), set its **blending mode** to **Overlay**, then reduce its **Opacity** on the Transparency panel to **60%**.

14. Apply a **blue to black radial gradient** to the **black hair** and keep the **Normal blending mode**.

15. Save your work.

16. Double-click the **fill color** on the toolbar to open the Color Picker dialog box, then enter **255/135/181** in the **R**, **G**, and **B text boxes** (respectively), then click **OK**.

17. Copy the **pink background**, paste in front, fill the copy with a **large radial gradient**, then overlay it.

18. Duplicate the **gradient** to double the effect.

    Your artwork should resemble Figure 35.

19. Save your work, then close the Carly Part 3 document.

You copied different objects of the illustration, filled them with gradients, then applied blending modes to the gradient-filled objects to add complexity, nuance, and dimension to the illustration.

Figure 35 Completing the gradient effects

Apply effects to an illustration

1. Open AI 13-4.ai, then save it as **Carly Part 4**.
2. Click the **face** to select it.

   You will automatically select the overlayed face copy with the gradient fill.
3. On the Appearance panel, click the **Add New Effect button** *fx.*, point to **Stylize**, then click **Drop Shadow**.
4. Enter the settings shown in Figure 36, then click **OK**.

5. Select the **rightmost hair object**.

   You will automatically select the overlayed copy with the gradient fill.
6. On the Appearance panel, click the **Add New Effect button** *fx.*, point to **Stylize**, click **Drop Shadow**, enter the settings shown in Figure 37, then click **OK**.

   Note that the Opacity is at 50%.
7. Apply the **same drop shadow** at **75% Opacity** to the **middle hair object** and at **100% Opacity**

to the **leftmost hair object**, then compare your results to Figure 38.

The illustration now has four objects with drop shadow effects. Keep these four objects in mind as you finish the illustration.

8. Save your work but keep the Carly Part 4 document open. You will use this file for the final illustration.

You applied drop shadow effects to four objects in the illustration.

Figure 36 Settings for the face drop shadow

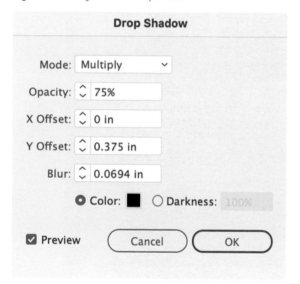

Figure 37 Settings for the hair drop shadow

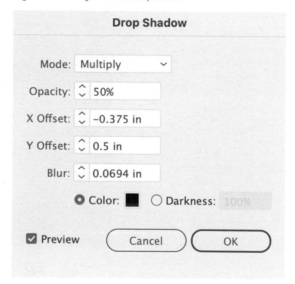

Figure 38 Finishing the shadows on the illustration

Divide an illustration

1. Open AI 13-5.ai, then save it as **Carly Divided**.

   This is a simplified version of the illustration without drop shadow effects or gradient overlays.

2. On the Layers panel, show the **Divide Lines layer**.

3. Select all, then click the **Divide button** 🔲 on the Pathfinder panel.

   The illustration is divided. The preference would have been to divide the working illustration, however, the overlayed gradient objects and the drop shadow effects make that illustration too complex for the Divide pathfinder. Therefore, you used this simplified version to create the divided artwork.

4. Using the **Direct Selection tool** ▷, select **individual components**, then use the **Eyedropper tool** ✐ to select colors from the squares on the right side of the artboard to colorize the divided components, as shown in Figure 39.

   All the colors in the illustration are available in the color squares to the right of the artboard.

5. When you are done colorizing, simplify the illustration by uniting **adjacent color objects** with the **Unite pathfinder** ▪.

   For example, the bright pink hair object at the top left of the illustration was divided in two with the Divide pathfinder, then united into one pink object to simplify the illustration.

6. Select all, then **copy the selection**.

7. Save your work, then close the Carly Divided document.

You applied the Divide pathfinder to a version of the illustration without shadows or gradients.

Figure 39 Colorizing the divided image

Finish the illustration

1. Return to the **Carly Part 4 file**.

2. Click the **Layers panel menu button** ≡, then click **Paste Remembers Layers** to add a check mark (if it is not already checked).

3. Target the **Components layer**, click **Edit** on the menu bar, then click **Paste in Place**.

   The divided artwork is pasted on a new layer in exactly the location of the underlying artwork.

4. Target the **two top layers** on the Layers panel, click the **Layers panel menu button** ≡, then click **Merge Selected**.

   Except for the background, all the components of the illustration are on one layer. To keep things clear, the illustration contains four types of artwork: the original color-filled objects, the gradient overlay objects, the four objects with drop shadows, and the divided objects. The goal now is to move the divided objects downward in the layer hierarchy so the drop shadow and gradient overlay effects become visible.

5. Deselect all, then click the **Direct Selection tool** ▷.

6. Select the **three objects that make up the woman's shoulders** (not the "collar").

7. Cut the **objects**, select the **gradient overlay over the shoulders**, click **Edit** on the menu bar, then click **Paste in Back**.

   As shown in Figure 40, the divided shoulder objects are positioned behind the gradient overlay.

Figure 40 Pasting the divided shoulder objects behind the gradient overlay

8. Delete the **teeth** and the **two lenses in the glasses** so the gradient fills beneath them are visible.

9. Delete the **largest segments of the earrings** so the gradient fills beneath them are visible.

10. Select and lock the **five divided pieces** identified in Figure 41.

11. Cut each of the **unlocked divided hair objects** and paste each **behind the objects with drop shadow effects**.

    This step can feel a little confusing because there are so many layers of objects involved and it might not be obvious which one you're selecting and pasting behind. With some trial and error you will be able to successfully paste behind the shadows with little or no difficulty.

12. Cut the **divided face objects**, then paste them **behind the gradient that overlays the entire face**.

13. Cut the **chin shadow objects**, then paste them **behind the drop shadow at the bottom of the face**.

14. Continue with this method of cutting and pasting any other objects (such as the lips) below the

Figure 41 Identifying five pieces to be locked

gradient overlay objects. If you don't like the color change, undo the move.

Figure 42 shows a final version of the illustration.

15. Save your file as **Carly Final**, then close it.

You pasted the divided objects at the top of the layer stack. You then moved or pasted the divided objects behind the shadows and gradient overlays to create a vibrant and visually complex illustration with divided color effects.

CREATE MULTIPLE DIMENSIONS WITH THE SHAPE BUILDER TOOL

▶ *What You'll Do*

In this lesson, you will create a unique design starting with a simple shape using the Move dialog box and the Shape Builder tool.

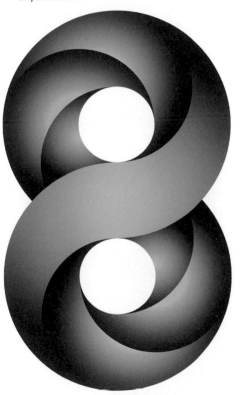

Drawing an Illustration from Scratch

Don't underestimate the power of the Shape Builder tool. It would be easy to regard the tool as just a different expression of the Pathfinder operations because the Shape Builder tool essentially either unites or subtracts shapes created by overlapping paths. However, the fact that you can execute those functions by clicking and dragging with the Shape Builder tool elevates the function and makes it something of a drawing tool. Also, unlike the Pathfinders, the Shape Builder tool does not create compound paths when applied to overlapping objects. When you are done working, you are left with individual objects that you can select independently from one another.

With some practice, you will find that overlapping simple shapes can produce complex and stunning results after editing them with the Shape Builder tool. Figure 43 shows a simple ellipse rotated 20 times. Applying the Shape Builder tool produces a new pattern, as shown in Figure 44, and adding gradients creates an even more dynamic effect, as shown in Figure 45.

Align artwork with precision

1. Open AI 13-6.ai, then save it as **Infinity Icon**.

2. Click the **Ellipse tool** 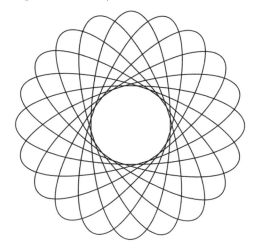, then click the artboard to open the tool's dialog box.

3. Create a **3"× 3" circle** with a **Black fill** and **no stroke**.

4. Switch to **Outline mode**.

   This illustration calls for perfect precision in terms of layout and relationships between objects. Thus,

you will work in Outline mode and rely heavily on the Align panel for positioning and the Move dialog box to relocate the object.

5. Create a **second circle** at 2" × 2", then create a **third circle** at 1" × 1".

6. Select all **three circles**, then, on the Align panel, click the **Horizontal Align Center button**, and then click the **Vertical Align Center button**.

Figure 43 Rotated ellipse

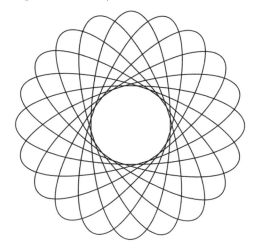

Figure 44 Pattern created with the Shape Builder tool

Figure 45 Gradient adds dimension

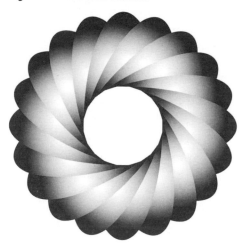

All three circles are aligned at their centers. Every aligned point, either on the horizontal or vertical axis, is ½" apart.

7. Select all, then move the **artwork** to the **top half of the artboard**.

8. Select the **2" circle**, copy it, then apply the **Paste in Front command** two times.

   You now have three 2" circles on the artboard. One needs to be moved straight up, one straight down, and one straight left.

9. Click **Object** on the menu bar, point to **Transform**, then click **Move**.

10. Enter the **settings in Figure 46**, then click **OK**.

    The circle moves straight up, and the top anchor points of the two circles are perfectly aligned at the exact same spot.

11. Select the **second 2" circle at the center**, open the Move dialog box, then move it **.5" left**.

TIP Enter −.5 in the Horizontal text box and 0 in the Vertical text box.

12. Select the **remaining 2" circle at the center**, open the Move dialog box, then move it **.5"** down.

TIP Enter 0 in the Horizontal text box and .5 in the Vertical text box.

Your artwork should resemble Figure 47.

Continued on next page

Figure 46 Settings in the Move dialog box

Move

Position

Horizontal: 0 in

Vertical: −0.5 in

Distance: 0.5 in

Angle: 90°

Options

☑ Transform Objects   ☐ Transform Patterns

☐ Preview

Copy   Cancel   OK

Figure 47 The three 2" circles aligned precisely with the 3" circle at the top, left, and bottom

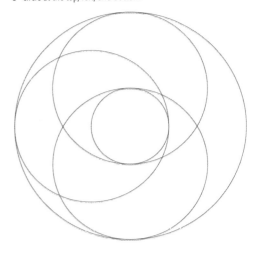

13. Select all, open the **Move dialog box**, enter the settings shown in Figure 48, then click **Copy**.

14. Compare your results to Figure 49.

With a 2" move vertically down, the top anchor point of the new 1" circle is aligned exactly with the bottom anchor point of the original 3" circle.

15. Select the **leftmost 2" circle in the copied artwork**, then use the Move dialog box to move it **1"** to the right.

Your results should resemble Figure 50.

16. Deselect, then note how the precise alignment has created many interesting

shapes that can be accessed with the **Shape Builder tool** 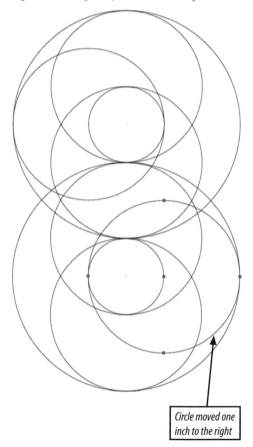.

17. Save your work, then continue to the next set of steps.

You created three circles at specific sizes. You duplicated and aligned the circles to create a result with complex interior shapes.

Figure 48 Settings to move a copy of the artwork

Figure 49 Copied artwork aligned precisely

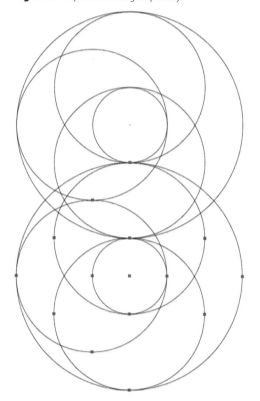

Figure 50 Moving the copied left circle to the right

Circle moved one inch to the right

Unify shapes and colorize them

1. In the Infinity Icon.ai document, verify that you are still in **Outline mode**, then select all.

2. See Figure 51.

   You will continue to work in Outline mode. Figure 51 has been colorized to help you visualize the shapes you will create with the Shape Builder tool 🔲. Use Figure 51 as a reference as you create the shapes.

3. Click and drag the **Shape Builder tool** 🔲 to create the shapes shown in Figure 51.

4. Switch to **Preview mode**, then colorize the artwork as shown in Figure 51.

   Note that as you united shapes with the Shape Builder tool 🔲, Illustrator created additional 1" circles at the top and bottom of the artwork. These must be deleted.

5. Select and delete the **ten 1" circles** to create two negative-space "holes" in the artwork.

6. Select all, click the **Eyedropper tool** ✐, then click the **center of the blue square** at the top-left of the artboard.

   Your artwork should resemble Figure 52.

   Continued on next page

Figure 51 Shapes to be created

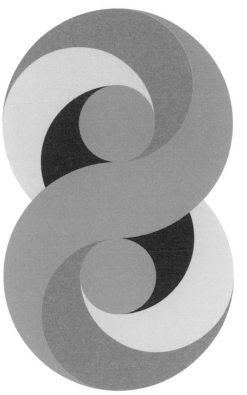

Figure 52 Shapes filled with a gradient

7. Click the **Radial Gradient button** ⬛ on the Gradient panel.

   The illustration is essentially a mirror image, top and bottom, and each individual shape is mirrored top and bottom. Note that the gradient fills each pair identically. The goal now is to achieve the best gradient fill possible in each of the pairs while keeping the fill identical in each of the pairs.

8. Select the **two shapes that were filled with orange** in Figure 51.

   The gradient at the inner edge of both can be brighter.

9. On the Gradient panel, drag the **left color stop** to the right until the Location text box reads **40%**.

Because the two shapes were filled at the same time with the same gradient, the edit on the Gradient panel affects the two objects the same way.

10. Select the **two shapes that were painted yellow** in Figure 51, then repeat Step 8.

11. Select the **two shapes that were filled with pink** in Figure 51.

12. On the Gradient panel, drag the **Gradient Slider** (the diamond-shaped slider between the color stops) to the right until the Location reads **60%**.

13. Select the **center shape**, then drag the **Gradient Slider** to the right until the Location reads **70%**.

14. Select all, double-click the **Rotate tool** ↻, enter **90** in the **Angle text box,** then click **OK**.

Your artwork should resemble Figure 53. Consider the role precision played in achieving the graphic. The shapes could only have been built and mirrored with exact alignment. Also remember how the Gradient panel was able to modify the gradient in different shapes in the same way.

15. Save your work, then close the Infinity Icon document.

You used the Shape Builder tool to combine shapes within the artwork and create a mirror image between the two halves. You applied the same radial gradient to each individual shape, then modified the gradient on the Gradient panel, which allowed you to make the same modifications simultaneously to mirrored pairs.

Figure 53 The final illustration

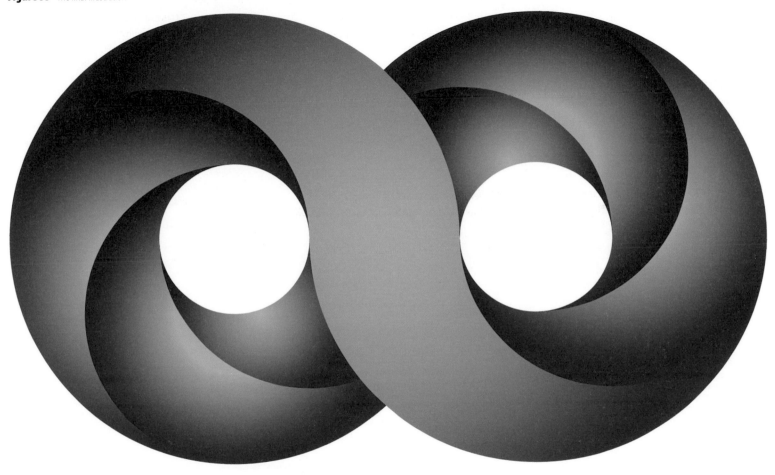

CREATE TESSELLATING PATTERNS

▶ *What You'll Do*

In this lesson, you will create a tessellating pattern and then apply it to a jigsaw puzzle in Photoshop.

Understanding Tessellation Patterns

The definition of the verb "to tessellate" is to form a pattern of squares, like a mosaic or a checkerboard. If you've ever entered a public building and seen a checkerboard floor pattern, you've seen tessellation.

Tessellating patterns can be far more complex than simple checkerboards. Figure 54 shows a pattern composed of two squares and one octagon. It's been positioned in Illustrator so anchor points and paths are available to show you the tile that repeats. Consider how it can repeat forever and note how the white line on all four edges is split in half between the tiles.

Figure 54 A tessellating pattern based on a repeating tile

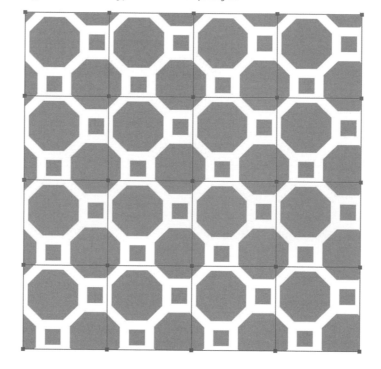

The tile patterns we studied earlier in the book are tessellating patterns by definition because the pattern can be repeated to infinity by duplicating the tile. But tessellating patterns aren't only based on tiles. They can be based on irregular-shaped objects as well. Figure 55 shows an object composed of three intersecting right-angle shapes. In Figure 56, that object has been repeated to form a tessellating pattern.

Figure 55 Irregular-shaped object

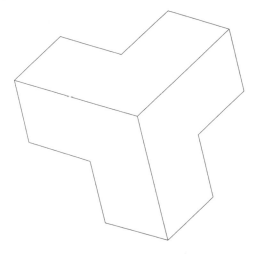

Figure 56 Tessellating pattern

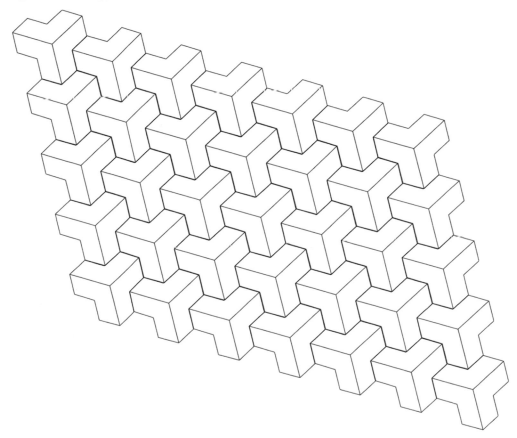

Similarly, Figure 57 shows you what you can do with a simple arrow.

The key to tessellation is working with objects whose opposite sides are the same shape.

Figure 58 shows a basic square that has been modified with two points. In order for it to tessellate, the opposite sides must have the same points, as shown in Figure 59. As odd as that shape is, mathematically it must tessellate.

Figure 57 Tessellating pattern with arrow

Figure 58 Square shape with two sides altered

Figure 59 Square shape with duplicate opposite sides

You can have a lot more fun with the interiors of tessellating objects. If you design a shape that will tessellate, you can draw any image you like inside of the object to add to the pattern. Figure 60 shows a simple cube. Look at the perimeter of the total shape. It's composed of six sides and three pairs of parallel lines. Since each side has an exact opposite, it will tessellate.

Figure 61 shows basic artwork drawn in the interior of the shape. Because it's in the interior, it can't affect the object's ability to tessellate. However, once the object is multiplied, as shown in Figure 62, the interior becomes something magical. Note that you can see it as an abstract pattern or as a repeating face. Note also that the original cube shape is no longer all that recognizable because of the blue pattern, which itself becomes its own abstract shape.

Tessellating patterns are a lot of fun, and they are fascinating to pretty much everybody. Be careful! They can be addictive. If you start designing one in Illustrator, you might find yourself still working 12 hours later trying to make it perfect.

Figure 60 Cube shape that will tessellate

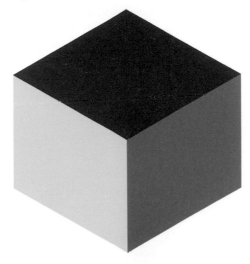 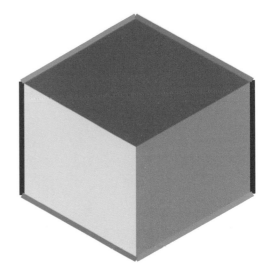

Figure 61 Any cube shape will tessellate

Figure 62 Cube object tessellating with artwork

Build a complex tessellation jigsaw pattern

1. Open AI 13-7.ai, then save it as **Jigsaw Build**.

   The green and red grid is locked. Each box in the grid is exactly 1". There are six puzzle-shaped edges that are also 1" in length.

2. Switch to **Outline mode** so you can work accurately.

3. Press **[option] (Mac)** or **[Alt] (Win)** and drag the **puzzle-shaped lines** on the artboard to make copies of them, then position them at the top and left of the grid, as shown in Figure 63.

4. Select the **top three puzzle-shaped lines**, click **Object** on the menu bar, point to **Transform**, then click **Move**.

   The Move dialog box opens.

5. Enter **0** in the **Horizontal text box**, enter **3** in the **Vertical text box**, then click **Copy**.

6. Move a **copy** of the **three left edges** to the right so your grid resembles Figure 64.

The entire outer perimeter will tessellate.

7. Using Figure 65 as a guide, position copies of the lines to create the middle puzzle pieces.

   The middle pieces do not need to tessellate with any other pieces, so they provide an opportunity to create edges that don't repeat in the way the top and bottom or the left and right edges must repeat.

8. Unlock the **grid**, delete it, then delete any **extra puzzle-shaped lines** at the left of the artboard.

Continued on next page

Figure 63 Positioning the top and left-edge pieces

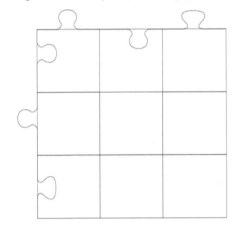

Figure 64 Finishing the perimeter

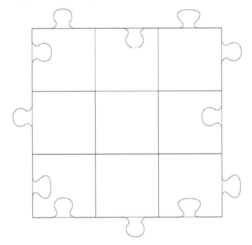

Figure 65 Interior puzzle pieces have randomly shaped sides

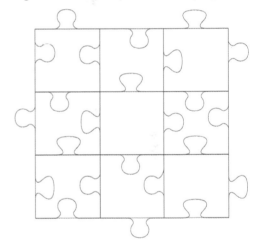

9. See Figure 66.

   The red circles indicate 16 points on the grid where anchor points intersect. To use the Live Paint Bucket tool  to fill the puzzle pieces, all the intersecting points must be in exactly the same location to create a closed area. You will use the Average command to achieve this.

10. Use the **Direct Selection tool** ▷, to select the **two top-left anchor points**, press and hold **[option] [command] (Mac)** or **[Alt] [Ctrl] (Win)**, then press the **letter [J]** on your keypad.

    The Average dialog box opens, shown in Figure 67.

11. Click the **Both option button**, then click **OK**.

    The two anchor points are positioned at the exact same location, but they are not joined. You will now join them.

12. With the two points still selected, press and hold **[command] [J] (Mac)** or **[Ctrl] [J] (Win)**.

    The points are joined.

13. Repeat Steps 10–12 to average and join the **top-right**, **bottom-left**, **and bottom-right anchor points**.

14. Using the same method from Steps 10 and 11, use the **Average dialog box** to average **all the intersecting anchor points** identified in Figure 66.

Unlike the four corners, the interior intersecting points do not need to be joined. However, where they meet, they must be at the exact same location.

15. Switch to **Preview mode**, select all, click **Object** on the menu bar, point to **Live Paint**, then click **Make**.

16. Press the **letter [K]** to access the **Live Paint Bucket tool** , then fill the **puzzle pieces** with **different colors**.

This will not work for you if there are gaps in the grid. For example, if a line is supposed to touch the perimeter but there's a small gap, the Live Paint Bucket tool  won't see that area as a single puzzle piece. If you encounter difficulty at this step, undo Step 15. Zoom in and make sure there are no gaps anywhere on the grid. Then, redo Step 15, and the Live Paint Bucket tool  will fill each "piece" individually.

Figure 66 Identifying intersecting anchor points on the grid

Figure 67 Average dialog box

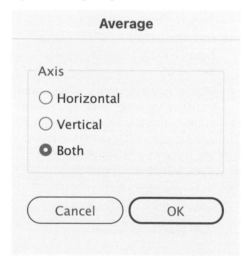

17. Remove the stroke, then compare your results to Figure 68.

It's interesting to keep in mind the power of the Live Paint feature and the role it's playing here. These puzzle pieces are not closed paths, but because the points are all accurately averaged, the Live Paint Bucket tool is able to fill them each with color. Prior to the advent of the Live Paint feature, you would have had to create closed paths of each object to have filled it.

18. Duplicate the tessellating pattern to fill the artboard.

Remember, the base pattern is exactly 3" × 3," so you can use the Move tool to create the duplicates. Don't try to click and drag!

19. Select all, click **Object** on the menu bar, click **Expand** to open the dialog box, click only **Fill**, then click **OK**.

When you expand the artwork, Illustrator creates closed objects of each puzzle piece. Think about that: each puzzle piece automatically becomes a closed path with joined points at the corners. This is a major step that would have been very time-consuming to do on your own.

20. Use the **Direct Selection tool** to change the **colors** in all the pieces to hide the repetitive pattern.

Figure 69 shows one example.

TIP In order to select individual pieces with the Selection tool , you'll need to ungroup artwork multiple times.

21. Click the **Delete Anchor Point tool** , then use it to remove the **curved anchor points** along the top edge.

The best way to get this done is to delete every smooth anchor point one by one. When you are done, you should have straight edges to the puzzle, as shown in Figure 70.

22. Save your work, then close the Jigsaw Build document.

You created a jigsaw puzzle pattern using individual paths. You created the outer pattern so it would tessellate. You created the inner pattern randomly because it doesn't need to tessellate. You averaged and joined anchor points, then colorized the pieces with the Live Paint Bucket tool. You expanded the artwork so each piece became an individual object. You duplicated the tessellated pattern to fill the artboard, then you straightened the outer pieces to create straight-line edge pieces.

Figure 68 Filling the pieces with color

Figure 69 Colorizing all the pieces in the puzzle

Figure 70 Creating edge pieces for the puzzle

Apply a jigsaw tessellation pattern to an image in Photoshop

1. Open AI 13-8.ai.

2. Select all, then change the **fill color** to **[None]**.

3. Apply a **3-point black stroke** to the artwork.

4. Click **Object** on the menu bar, point to **Path**, then click **Outline Stroke**.

5. Copy the artwork, then close AI 13-8.ai without saving changes.

6. Switch to Photoshop, open AI 13-9.psd, then save it as **Montag Jigsaw Puzzle**.

7. Click **Edit** on the menu bar, then click **Paste**.

   The Paste dialog box opens.

8. Click **Pixels**, click **OK**, then press **[return] (Mac)** or **[Enter] (Win)**.

   Your artwork should resemble Figure 71.

9. On the Layers panel, rename the new layer **Puzzle**, then click it to target it.

10. Click **Select** on the menu bar, click **Load Selection**, enter the settings shown in Figure 72, then click **OK**.

    A selection of the pasted Illustrator artwork is created.

11. Hide the **Puzzle layer**, then target the **Montag layer**.

Continued on next page

Figure 71 Positioning the pasted artwork over the dog image

Figure 72 Loading a selection of the pasted Illustrator artwork

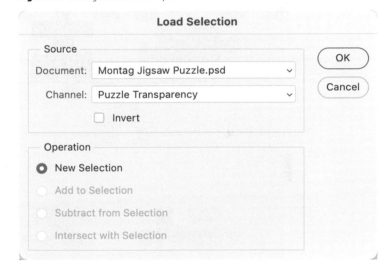

12. Copy the **artwork**, click **Edit** on the menu bar, point to **Paste Special**, then click **Paste in Place**.

A new layer is created.

13. Hide the **Montag layer** so that you can see what is on the new layer.

14. Name the new layer **Emboss**, then click it to target it.

15. Click **Layer** on the menu bar, point to **Layer Style**, then click **Bevel & Emboss**.

16. Click the words **Bevel & Emboss** on the left column, then enter the settings shown in Figure 73.

17. Click **OK**, then show the **Montag layer**.

Your artwork should resemble Figure 74.

18. Verify that the **Options panel** is showing at the top of the Photoshop window.

TIP If you do not see the Options panel, click Window on the menu bar, then click Options.

Figure 73 Settings for the Bevel & Emboss

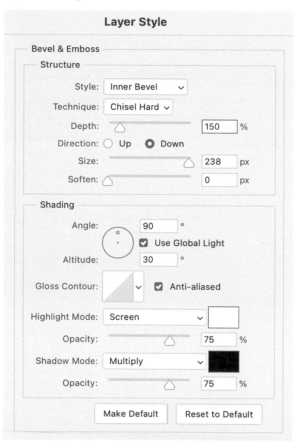

Figure 74 Bevel & Emboss effect applied

19. Click the **Magic Wand tool** 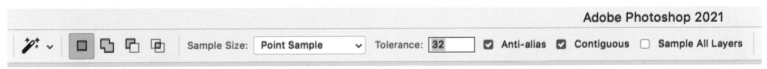 on the toolbar, then enter the settings shown in Figure 75.

20. Verify that the **Emboss layer** is targeted, click the **Magic Wand tool** on the **center of the puzzle piece** that is **two over and two down from the top-left corner of the puzzle**.

The puzzle piece is selected.

21. Click **Select** on the menu bar, point to **Modify**, then click **Expand**.

22. Type **6** in the Expand By text box, then click **OK**.

The selection expands to include the embossed effect on the puzzle piece.

23. Click **Edit** on the menu bar, then click **Copy Merged**.

24. With the **Emboss layer** still targeted, press the **[delete] key**.

The embossed effect is deleted.

25. Target the **Montag layer**, then press the **[delete] key**.

The puzzle piece image is deleted.

TIP If you're an experienced Photoshop user, you can use layer masks to hide these elements rather than delete them.

26. Click **Edit** on the menu bar, then click **Paste**.

The puzzle piece you copied with the Copy Merged command is pasted on a new layer.

Continued on next page

Figure 75 Settings for the Magic Wand tool

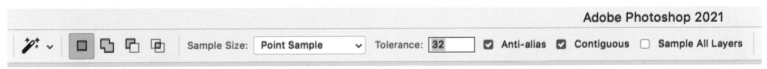

27. Click the **Move tool** , then move the **pasted piece** into the left margin, as shown in Figure 76.

28. Using the same method, repeat steps 18–27 to move two additional pieces into the margins.

29. Target the **Montag layer**, click **Layer** on the menu bar, point to **Layer Style**, then click **Drop Shadow**.

30. Click the words **Drop Shadow** on the left column, enter the settings shown in Figure 77, then click **OK**.

31. Copy the **drop shadow** to the **individual puzzle piece layers** by pressing **[option] (Mac)** or **[Alt] (Win)** and dragging the **layer style icon** 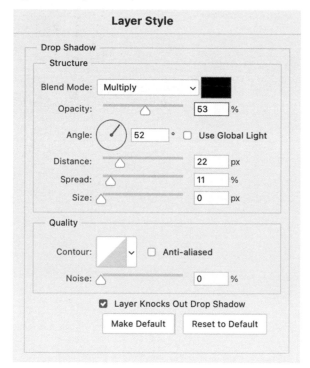 from the **Montag layer** to those layers.

32. Compare your work to Figure 78.

33. Save your work, then close all open files.

You removed the fill and applied a stroke to the jigsaw pieces then used the Outline Stroke command. You then copied the puzzle artwork into Photoshop and positioned it over an image. You used the Illustrator artwork only to copy and paste a layer of the image in the shape of puzzle pieces. You then applied a Bevel & Emboss layer style to that copied artwork, thus creating the impression of a jigsaw puzzle. With strategic selections, copies, and moves, you created artwork of puzzle pieces outside of the puzzle.

Figure 76 Positioning the piece outside the puzzle

Figure 77 Settings for the Drop Shadow

Figure 78 The final illustration

Build an illustrated tessellation pattern

1. Open AI 13-10.ai, then save it as **Tessellating Birds**.

2. Switch to **Outline mode**.

   The square is an exact 1" square.

3. Select the **square**, click **Object** on the menu bar, point to **Path**, then click **Add Anchor Points**.

4. Apply the **Add Anchor Points command** two more times.

   There is a ⅛" space between each anchor point.

5. Zoom in to see a larger view of the square, then click the **Direct Selection tool** ▷.

6. Deselect, select and move the **two anchor points** as shown in Figure 79, then click **OK** in the Move dialog box.

7. Select and move the **two anchor points** as shown in Figure 80.

Figure 79 Moving two points up and to the right

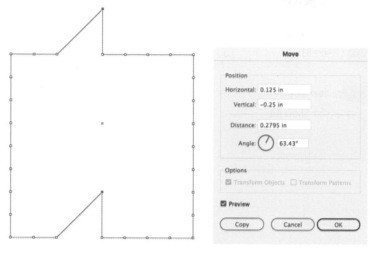

Figure 80 Moving two points down and to the left

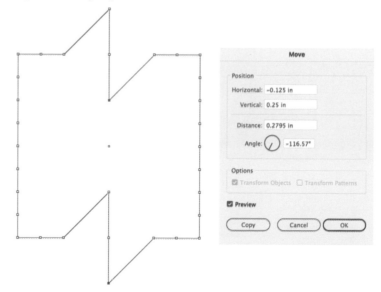

8. Select all, double-click the **Rotate tool** 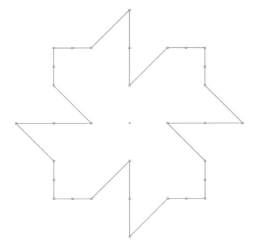 to open its dialog box, enter **90** in the **Angle text box**, then click **OK**.

9. Repeat Steps 6, 7, and 8 on the top and bottom edges so your artwork resembles Figure 81.

All four sides are identical.

10. Save your work, then switch to **Preview mode**.

11. Click **Object** on the menu bar, then click **Show All**.

The interior artwork appears, making the object that of a bird.

12. Select all, click **Object** on the menu bar, point to **Live Paint**, then click **Make**.

13. Click the **Live Paint Bucket tool** , then fill the artwork as shown in Figure 82.

14. Open the **Move dialog box**, then make a **copy of the artwork** exactly **1" to the right**.

15. Select **both birds**, then make a copy exactly **1" down**.

Your artwork should resemble Figure 83.

16. Click the **Selection tool** , then select the **top-right** and **bottom-left bird**.

17. Click **Edit** on the menu bar, point to **Edit Colors**, then click **Recolor Artwork**.

Continued on next page

Figure 81 Applying the same modifications to all four sides

Figure 82 Adding color to the artwork

Figure 83 Positioning the four objects

18. Drag the **large circle-handle** to the location shown in Figure 84, then click the **artboard** to close the Recolor Artwork dialog box.

19. Save your work.

20. Select the **top-right bird**, double-click the **Rotate tool** ↻, type **–90** in the **Angle text box**, then click **OK**.

21. Select the **bottom-right bird**, then rotate it **–180 degrees**.

22. Select the **bottom-left bird**, then rotate it **–270 degrees**.

Your artwork should resemble Figure 85.

23. Use the Move dialog box to make multiple copies of the pattern and fill the artboard, as shown in Figure 86.

24. Save your work, then close the Tessellating Birds document.

You modified a square to have the same pattern on all four sides. You then added interior artwork to make the shape into that of a bird. You created a tessellating pattern of four rotated birds, each at a different angle. From that point, you duplicated the pattern to fill the artboard.

Figure 84 Recoloring two of the objects

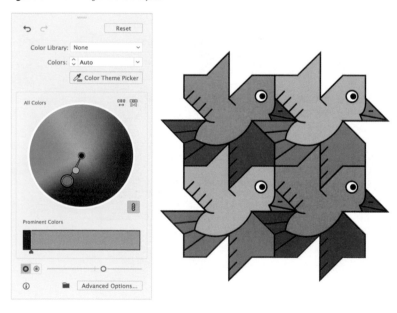

Figure 85 The quartet with each rotated

Figure 86 The final illustration

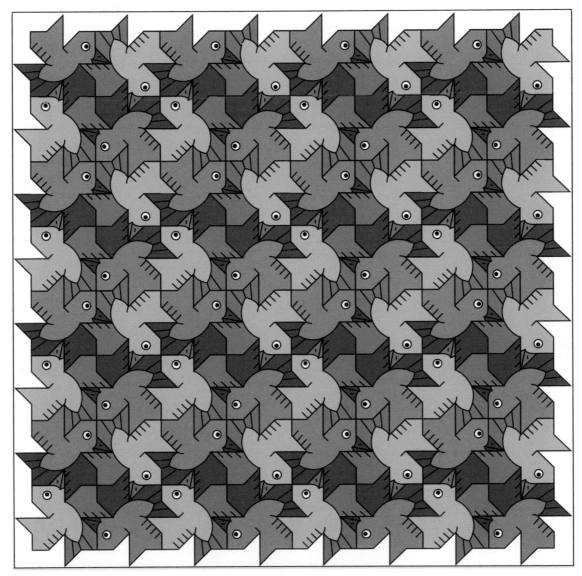

USE ILLUSTRATOR ARTWORK AS THE BASIS FOR A PHOTOSHOP ILLUSTRATION

▶ **What You'll Do**

In this lesson, you will use the Offset Path command with type to make a complex type design.

Using the Offset Path command with Type

Offset Path is one of the more powerful commands in Illustrator. You used it in Chapter 4 to create concentric circles and squares. In this chapter, you'll use it with type.

Figure 87 shows simple type set in Illustrator. Applying the Offset Path command three times produced the result shown in Figure 88. For such a simple operation, the results have a big WOW factor. The shapes are fun and exaggerated and the type comes to life, which is why this is a classic and much-used look for type.

Figure 87 Starting type in Illustrator

Figure 88 Three offset outlines of the starting type produced with the Offset Path command

It's when you bring offset type paths into Photoshop that things can get really eye-popping. In Figure 89, the blue and green objects in the illustration have been brought into Photoshop and filled with a silver color. The blue artwork has a Bevel & Emboss layer style applied to it, and the green has an Inner Shadow layer style. Together, they look like one piece of metal with a bevelled edge and negative space cut into the interior. Using the same method produces the stunning illustration in Figure 90. Overlay the same image into each of the four styled layers, and you get the even-more-stunning illustration in Figure 91.

Here's the big takeaway: The base art in this illustration is from Adobe Illustrator, not Photoshop. Even though the artwork is in Photoshop, it couldn't have been done without Illustrator. The reason this illustration is likely not typical of one you see very often is because many Photoshop designers do not know how to base their work on Illustrator. Therefore, when you're proficient with Illustrator, you can leverage Photoshop in ways that make you different and allow you to really stand out from the crowd.

Figure 89 Blue and green offset paths with layer styles in Photoshop

Figure 90 The base art with Photoshop effects and lighting

Figure 91 Photoshop artwork based on Adobe Illustrator

Offset Paths

1. Open AI 13-11.ai, then save it as **Offset Path**.

2. Select all, click **Object** on the menu bar, point to **Path**, then click **Offset Path**.

3. Type **.25"** in the **Offset text box**, then click **OK**.

4. Open the Pathfinder panel, then click the **Unite button** .

5. On the Swatches panel, click a **light orange swatch**.

6. Click **Object** on the menu bar, point to **Arrange**, then click **Send to Back**.

Your artwork should resemble Figure 92.

7. Click **Object** on the menu bar, point to **Path**, then click **Offset Path**.

8. Type **.25"** in the **Offset text box**, then click **OK**.

9. Click the **Unite button** on the Pathfinder panel.

10. Click a **green swatch** on the Swatches panel.

11. Apply the **Send to Back** command.

12. Click **Object** on the menu bar, point to **Path**, then click **Offset Path**.

13. Enter **.25"** in the **Offset text box**, then click **OK**.

14. Click the **Unite button** on the Pathfinder panel.

15. Click a **blue swatch** on the Swatches panel.

16. Apply the **Send to Back** command.

Your artwork should resemble Figure 93.

17. Save your work, then continue to the next set of steps.

You used the Offset Path command to create three offset copies of the original text.

Figure 92 Positioning the Orange offset path behind the pink type

Figure 93 The finished illustration with three offset paths

Export layers to Photoshop

1. Select all the artwork on the artboard.

   The artwork is all on the same single layer.

2. Create **four layers** on the Layers panel, then name them **Blue**, **Green**, **Orange**, and **Pink** (from bottom to top).

3. Select all the **pink objects**, then move them to the **Pink layer**.

4. Move all the **orange objects** to the **Orange layer**, all the **green objects** to the **Green layer**, and all the **blue objects** to the **Blue layer**.

5. Delete the original, empty layer.

   Your Layers panel should resemble Figure 94.

6. Save your work.

7. Click **File** on the menu bar, point to **Export**, then click **Export As**.

8. Type **Offset Path Layers.psd** in the **Save As text box**, choose **Photoshop (.psd)** from the **Format menu**, then click **Export**.

   The Photoshop Export Options dialog box opens.

9. Enter the settings shown in Figure 95, then click **OK**.

10. Switch to Photoshop.

Figure 94 Moving each color of the illustration onto separate layers

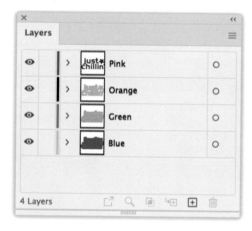

Figure 95 Settings for exporting layers

11. Open the file you just exported: **Offset Path Layers.psd**, then view the Layers panel.

   Your Layers panel should resemble Figure 96. Your Layers panel might be slightly different (e.g., some layers might be in folders), but you will have all the elements from the Illustrator file layered in the Photoshop file.

12. Close the Offset Path Layers.psd document.

You separated artwork onto four layers in Illustrator then exported the file as a high-resolution .psd file with layers. You opened the file in Photoshop and saw that the layered artwork and layers had transferred.

Figure 96 Illustrator artwork on layers in Photoshop

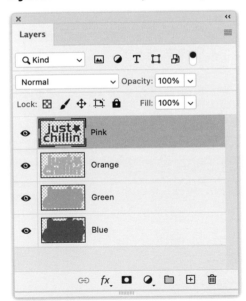

Apply Photoshop effects to Illustrator artwork

1. Open AI 13-12.psd in Photoshop, then save it as **Offset Path Effects**.

2. Hide the **Pink** and **Orange layers**, then target the **Blue layer**.

3. Click **Layer** on the menu bar, point to **Layer Style**, then click **Bevel & Emboss**.

4. Enter the settings shown in Figure 97, then click **OK**.

   When you click OK, a small *fx* icon appears on the layer indicating that a layer style has been applied. The Bevel & Emboss effect is not available in Adobe Illustrator.

Continued on next page

Figure 97 Settings for the Bevel & Emboss effect

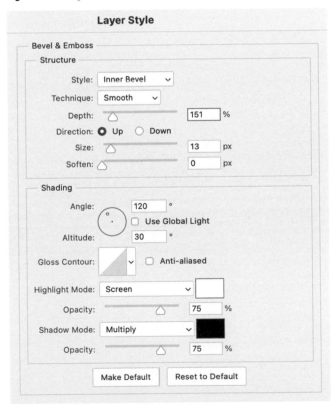

5. Press and hold **[option] (Mac)** or **[Alt] (Win)**, then drag the  *fx* icon from the **Blue layer** to the **Green layer**.

The Bevel & Emboss effect is copied to the Green layer.

6. Show the **Orange layer**, then copy the effect from the **Green layer** to the **Orange layer**.

7. Target the **Orange layer**, click **Layer** on the menu bar, point to **Layer Style**, then click **Drop Shadow**.

8. Enter the settings shown in Figure 98, then click **OK**.

9. Show the **Pink layer**, click **Layer** on the menu bar, point to **Layer Style**, then click **Inner Shadow**.

The Inner Shadow effect is not available in Adobe Illustrator.

10. Enter the settings shown in Figure 99, then click **OK**. Your artwork should resemble Figure 100.

11. Save your work, then close the Offset Path Effects document.

You applied the Bevel & Emboss, Inner Shadow, and Drop Shadow effects in Photoshop to the Illustrator artwork to produce an effect that couldn't have been achieved in Illustrator.

Figure 98 Settings for the Drop Shadow

Figure 99 Settings for the Inner Shadow

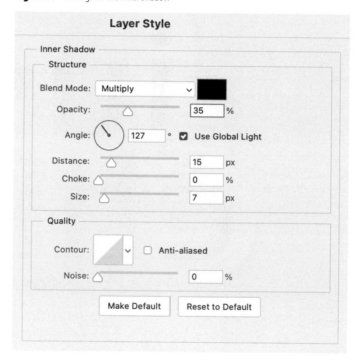

Figure 100 The final illustration

LESSON 5

DESIGN NEON ILLUSTRATIONS

▶ *What You'll Do*

In this lesson, you will create a complex neon effect using multiple fill and stroke appearances on a single object.

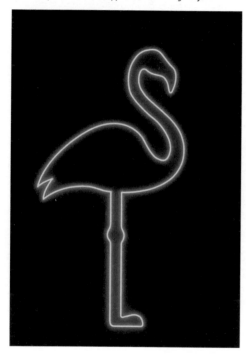

Utilizing Multiple Fill and Stroke Appearances on a Single Object

It's tricky to consider the idea that a single object can have multiple strokes and fills, but that's exactly what you can do if the fills and strokes are appearances applied on the Appearance panel.

Figure 101 shows a single circle with two strokes; the blue stroke is aligned to the inside of the circle and the orange stroke to the outside. Both strokes are listed on the Appearance panel. The word Path at the top of the panel indicates that this is a single object.

Figure 101 A circle with two stroke appearances

Multiple strokes are useful when creating neon effects. In Figure 102, the NEON type has three different color strokes at three different weights. Adding Gaussian Blur effects and reducing opacity results in a glowing neon effect, as shown in Figure 103. The multiple stroke appearance makes it possible for this text object to have three different blurs applied to it.

Figure 102 Type with three strokes

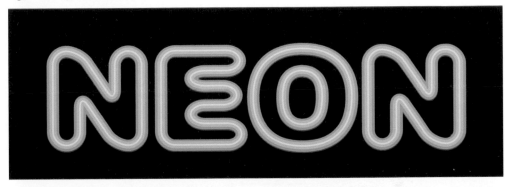

Figure 103 Effects and opacity shifts applied to create a glowing neon effect

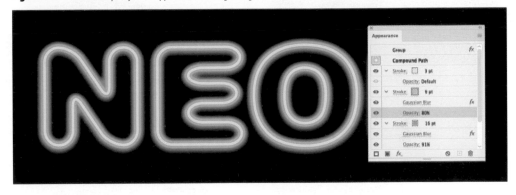

Designing Freeform Gradients

When you apply a gradient fill to an object, the Gradient panel offers you linear and radial gradients along with the freeform gradient. A freeform gradient is used to create graduated blends of colors inside a shape.

Figure 104 shows a freeform gradient applied to a circle. When you click the Freeform Gradient button on the Gradient panel, default color stops appear in the interior of the object. Each color stop represents a color in the gradient. You can click to select a color stop and apply a color to it using a swatch or the sliders on the Color panel. You can move a color stop to any location inside the object, and you can click and drag the perimeter around the color stop to enlarge or reduce the size of it. To remove a color stop, either press [delete] or simply drag it outside of the object.

You can also add additional color stops to the object by clicking the interior of the object.

When you deselect an object with a freeform gradient fill, the next time you select it the color stops will not automatically appear. You must first click the Edit Gradient button on the Gradient panel.

Figure 104 Circle with freeform gradient fill

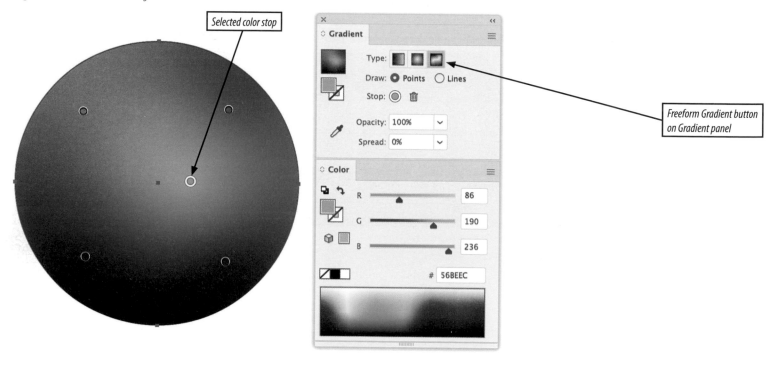

Selected color stop

Freeform Gradient button on Gradient panel

Design with the Appearance panel

1. Open AI 13-13.ai, then save it as **Pink Flamingo**.

   Note that the black background is on its own layer and is locked.

2. Open the Swatches panel.

   As shown in Figure 105, a group of six swatches has been saved on the Swatches panel: dark pink, dark yellow, dark blue, light pink, light yellow, and light blue. These are the colors that will be used for this illustration.

3. Select all the artwork.

   The yellow and blue paths end in butt caps. The pink and blue paths have miter joins, which are pointed corners. Real-world neon lights are made with glass tubes, so they don't have sharp or pointed corners. They also end in rounded ends.

4. On the Stroke panel, click the **Round Cap button** , click the **Round Join button** , then deselect.

5. Open the Appearance panel, select the **Flamingo**, then hide the selection marks.

   The object is listed as Path on the Appearance panel, and the pink stroke and [None] fill are listed separately.

6. On the Appearance panel, click **Stroke** to target it, click the **Appearance panel menu button** , then click **Duplicate Item**.

7. Target the **bottom Stroke** on the Appearance panel, then increase its **Stroke Weight** to **2 pts**.

8. Target the **top Stroke**, then change its color to **light pink**.

   Your Appearance panel should resemble Figure 106.

9. Zoom in on the **flamingo** so you can see the strokes.

   The goal is to see the darker pink stroke slightly outside of the lighter pink stroke. The idea is that the two hard-edged strokes are the neon tube itself. The lighter stroke is the "hot" brighter "inside" of the tube. At this size, the 2-pt. stroke is not thick enough to really be visible.

10. Increase the size of the **bottom Stroke** to **3 pts**.

    At 3 pts. the stroke is too much larger than the 1 pt. stroke. The relationship needs to be subtle but visible.

11. Change the size of the **bottom Stroke** to **2.25 pts**.

    Your artwork should resemble Figure 107.

    Continued on next page

Figure 105 Swatches group

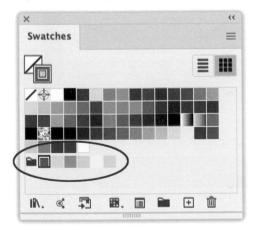

Figure 106 Two strokes on the Appearance panel

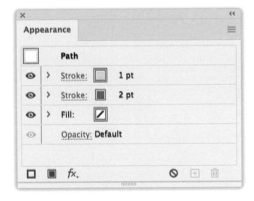

Figure 107 Two strokes drawing the flamingo

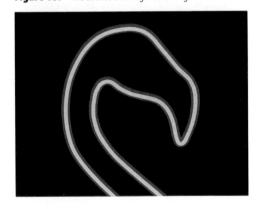

12. With the **bottom Stroke** still targeted, click the **Duplicate Selected Item button** ⊞ on the Appearance panel.

13. Target the **new bottom Stroke**, then increase its **Stroke Weight** to **4 pts**.

14. On the Appearance panel, click the **Add New Effect button** *fx.*, point to **Blur**, then click **Gaussian Blur**.

15. Type **4** in the **Radius text box**, then click **OK**.

Your blur will likely be pixelated. You will fix that in the next two steps. If it's not pixelated, skip the next two steps.

16. Click **Effect** on the menu bar, then click **Document Raster Effects Settings**.

17. Set the **Resolution** to **High (300 ppi)**, then click **OK**.

18. Verify that the **bottom Stroke** is targeted on the Appearance panel, then duplicate it to create a **fourth stroke**.

The Gaussian Blur effect is also doubled and therefore becomes brighter.

19. Target the **bottom Stroke**, then increase its **Stroke Weight** to **6 pts**.

20. Click the **arrow** › to expand the **bottom Stroke** on the Appearance panel.

21. Click **Gaussian Blur**, increase the **Radius** to **18 pts.**, then click **OK**.

22. Click **Opacity**, set it to **80**, then keep your **artwork selected**.

Your artwork should resemble Figure 108. Consider that the flamingo artwork is selected on the

artboard, and the word Path is at the top of the Appearance panel. The word Path indicates that only one path is selected. There are not four pink strokes on the flamingo, just one. However, that one stroke has four appearances applied to it: four strokes, two with a Gaussian Blur effect.

23. Save your work, then continue to the next set of steps.

You applied Round Caps and Round Joins to paths intended to mimic neon tubes. You used the Appearance panel to duplicate a stroke three times, change its weight, add a Gaussian Blur effect, and modify its Opacity setting.

Figure 108 Neon effect applied to the flamingo artwork

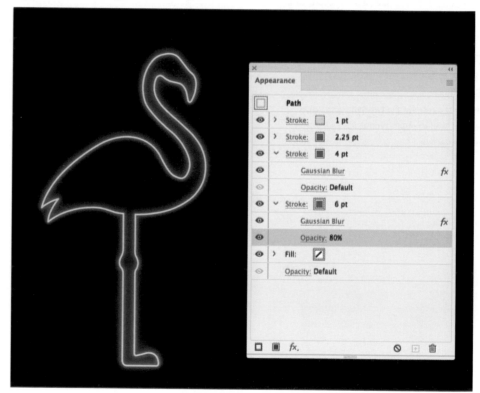

Copy complex appearances between objects

1. Verify that the **flamingo artwork** is selected on the artboard.

2. On the Appearance panel, note the **thumbnail artwork** to the left of the word Path.

3. Drag the **thumbnail** from the Appearance panel to the **yellow "sun" circle** on the artboard, then release the mouse pointer when you see a **plus sign** added to the cursor.

   The appearance is copied to the circle.

4. Click the **artboard** to deselect all, then select the **circle**.

5. Change the **color** of the **top Stroke** to **light yellow**, then change the other **three Strokes** to **dark yellow**.

This is the same color pattern used for the pink flamingo. Because the yellow is such a brighter color, the inner "hot" tube doesn't look much different from the surrounding colors.

6. Change the **color** of the **top Stroke** to **White**, then increase its **Stroke Weight** to **1.25 pts**.

   This change helps to differentiate the top stroke from those behind it, but it's still hard to see.

7. Click the **Eye icon** 👁 on the second stroke to hide it.

   Simplifying the artwork makes the top stroke read better as the white "hot" tube at the center of the yellow neon. However, there's an optical illusion happening in which the yellow neon appears much thicker than the pink. Again, this is because the white inner tube isn't as visible.

8. Reduce the **Stroke Weight** on the **third Stroke** to **3 pt**.

9. Deselect all, then select the **pink flamingo artwork**.

10. Copy the **appearance** from the Appearance panel to **one of the blue waves**.

11. Copy the **appearance** from the Appearance panel to the **other blue wave**.

12. Click the **Selection tool** ▶ on **one of the waves**.

    Because the two waves are grouped, both are selected. The Appearance panel indicates that more than one path is selected by listing the word Group at the top of the panel.

Continued on next page

13. Double-click the word **Contents** on the Appearance panel.

The Appearance panel shows the appearance settings for the two objects.

14. Change the color of the **top Stroke** to **light blue**, then change the other **three Strokes** to **dark blue**.

15. Compare your artwork to Figure 109.

16. Save your work, then continue to the next set of steps.

You copied the total appearance from the flamingo to the sun and the waves, then modified them to suit the illustration.

Figure 109 Neon effect copied to other elements and modified

Finish the neon effect

1. Deselect all on the artboard, then open the Layers panel.

2. Duplicate the **Artwork layer**, rename the new layer **Reflection**, then drag it down **below** the **Artwork layer**.

3. Lock the **Artwork layer**, then select **all the artwork** on the artboard.

4. Press the **right arrow key** on your keypad four times.

A copy of the artwork is offset to the right of the original. The bright areas on the copy are not as bright because they are behind the two blurs of the original.

5. On the Transparency panel, reduce the **Opacity** to **60%**.

6. Compare your artwork to Figure 110.

7. Save your work, then close the Pink Flamingo document.

TIP When designing neon effects, keep in mind that the document color mode has a huge effect on the final product. You should always work in RGB mode, but your destination will define the ultimate color mode. If you're printing your neon effects, as we do in this book, the colors will be substantially muted once the file is converted to CMYK and printed. They'll still appear as neon effects, but they won't be nearly as vivid as what you see on your screen. That's why neon effects are so good for web graphics. The file remains in RGB mode and none of the color intensity is lost.

You duplicated the layer containing the neon artwork to create a reduced-opacity copy to function as a reflection.

Figure 110 Reflection copy with reduced opacity

Design a freeform gradient

1. Open AI 13-14.ai, then save it as **Hand-Drawn Neon**.

   The first goal is for you to recreate the gradient colors supplied with the file. This can be done with a gradient mesh, which we explored in Chapter 7. It can also be done with a freeform gradient, which is what you'll do in this set of steps.

2. Lock the **Supplied Freeform Gradient layer**, then show and target the **Freeform Gradient layer** above it.

3. Verify that the **fill button** is active on the toolbar, select the **black square** on the artboard, open the **Gradient panel**, then click the **Freeform Gradient button** 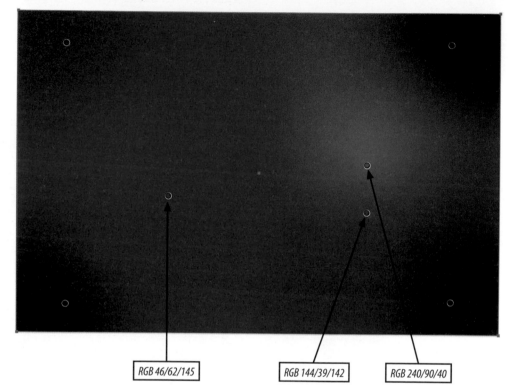.

   The rectangle fills with a gradient, and four color stops appear in each corner.

4. Select **each color stop**, then click **Black** on the Swatches panel to change each to black.

5. Refer to Figure 111 to add **three new color stops** using the locations and colors shown in the figure.

   Use the Color panel or the Color Picker to colorize the stops. The artwork will require more black at the edges, so you will add more black color stops.

Figure 111 Three new color stops

RGB 46/62/145

RGB 144/39/142

RGB 240/90/40

6. Add **six black color stops**, as shown in Figure 112.

At the end of the project, you might need to add more black stops to make the neon effect its most vivid. Use this same method to do so. It's not a problem if your gradient doesn't match the figure exactly; at the end of the project you can use the supplied gradient if you want your results to match the figures in the book as closely as possible.

TIP If you add one stop and colorize it black, every subsequent stop you create will automatically be black.

7. Save your work, then continue to the next set of steps.

You used the Freeform Gradient button on the Gradient panel to create three gradating colors in a black rectangle.

Figure 112 Six new black color stops

Explore the Color Dodge blending mode

1. Verify that the **Freeform Gradient layer** is targeted.

2. Create a **thin rectangle** over the middle of the gradient, then fill it with **White**.

3. On the Transparency panel, change the rectangle's **blending mode** to **Color Dodge**.

You will see no change. Any white object remains white with the Color Dodge blending mode.

4. Change the **fill color** on the rectangle to a **medium gray**, then compare your result to Figure 113.

With the Color Dodge blending mode, the gray rectangle brightens any area of the artwork below it. You will use this blending mode to create the neon glow effects in the artwork.

5. Delete the **rectangle**, then lock the **Freeform Gradient layer**.

6. Save your work, then continue to the next set of steps.

You used a rectangle with a medium-gray fill to explore how the Color Dodge gradient can be used to brighten artwork in specific areas.

Figure 113 Color Dodge blending mode brightening the underlying freeform gradient

Preparing a template for a neon illustration

1. Show and target the **3D Type layer**, then select the **NEON text** on the artboard.

2. Click **Effect** on the menu bar, point to **3D and Materials**, point to **3D (Classic)**, then click **Extrude & Bevel (Classic)**.

3. Enter the settings shown in Figure 114, then click **OK**.

   The 3D type will not show in the final artwork. It is a template for the hand-drawn neon effects that you will create. You will need to harness the front face of each letter separately, so you will do that by first expanding the appearance.

4. Click **Object** on the menu bar, then click **Expand Appearance**.

   The 3D artwork is expanded, which means you have access to select its component parts.

5. Create a **new layer above the 3D Type layer**, then name it **Front Face Type**.

6. Click the **Direct Selection tool** ▷, select the **N, E, O, and N shapes** on the **3D Type layer**, copy, then paste in front.

7. Move the **pasted artwork** to the **Front Face Type layer**.

8. Show the **2 Brushes layer**.

   Artwork for two custom brushes becomes visible. The top one is a rounded oval, and the bottom one comes to a point on both sides.

9. Drag the **top brush** into the **Brushes panel**.

   The New Brush dialog box opens.

10. Click **Art Brush**, click **OK**, name the brush **Larger Brush**, then click **OK**.

11. Drag the **bottom brush** into the **Brushes panel**, click **Art brush**, click **OK**, name the brush **Smaller Brush**, then click **OK**.

12. Hide the **2 Brushes layer**, save your work, then continue to the next set of steps.

You created 3D type to be used as a template. You expanded the 3D effect to be able to select components of the artwork. You duplicated the front face letters and saved the copies to a new layer. You created two new art brushes from simple artwork.

Figure 114 Settings for the Extrude & Bevel effect

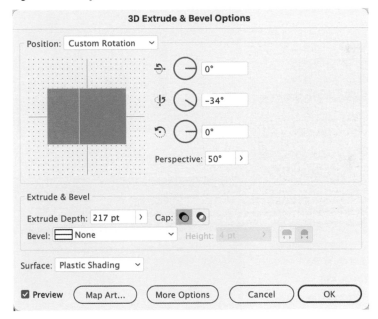

DESIGN NEON ILLUSTRATIONS   LESSON 5   **647**

Hand-draw strokes for a neon effect

1. Create a **new layer** above the **Front Face Type layer**, then name it **Larger Brush Strokes**.

2. Click the **Pen tool** 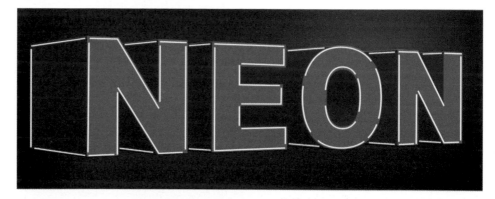, then set the **fill color** to **[None]** and the **stroke** to **1 pt. White**.

3. Use the **Pen tool** to draw the **paths** shown in Figure 115.

   The strokes in the figure are slightly thicker than 1 pt. so you can see them more easily. They should be slightly inside the edge of each letter, and they should be parallel to each edge.

4. Select **all the strokes** on the **Large Brush Strokes layer**, then click the **Larger Brush** on the **Brushes panel**.

   The Larger Brush artwork is too large at this size.

5. On the **Stroke panel**, reduce the **Weight** to **.25 pts.**, then change the stroke color from White to **60% Gray**.

TIP Click the swatch on the Swatches panel whose name is C=0 M=0 Y=0 K=60.

6. Create a **new layer**, then name it **Smaller Brush Strokes**.

7. Click the **Paintbrush tool**, click the **Smaller Brush** on the **Brushes panel**, then, on the **Control panel**, set the **Weight** to **.5 pt**.

8. Use the **Paintbrush tool** to paint the same strokes as you did in Step 3, all of them slightly inside of the existing strokes.

   Your artwork should resemble Figure 116. These strokes should be unique and appear to be

"freehand." They should not be too straight or too curvy.

9. Save your work, then continue to the next set of steps.

You used the Pen tool to create straight strokes, then applied the Larger Brush to those paths. You then used the Paintbrush tool to hand-draw strokes with the Smaller Brush. You painted all strokes with 60% Gray.

Figure 115 Paths drawn inside the letter forms

Figure 116 Drawing freehand brush strokes

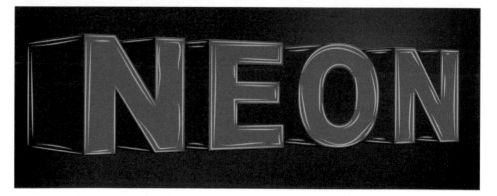

Use the Color Dodge blending mode to create neon effects

1. Hide the **3D Type layer**.

2. Select the **four letter objects** on the **Front Face Type layer**, then, on the Transparency panel, change their blending modes to **Color Dodge**.

3. Select **all the brush strokes**, then change their **blending modes** to **Color Dodge**.

   Compare your artwork to Figure 117. Even though most of the strokes appear to be white, remember that they are all gray and are all brightening the artwork underneath. Note that the strokes between the O and N are pink at the bottom and orange at the top.

4. Hide and show the **Freeform Gradient layer**.

   When the layer is hidden, you're seeing the Supplied Freeform Gradient artwork beneath it. The supplied gradient artwork is likely a bit darker, which makes the neon effects a bit more vivid.

5. Show the **Freeform Gradient layer**, unlock it, then select the **rectangle** on the layer.

6. On the Gradient panel, click the **Edit Gradient button**.

7. Working from the outside in, add **additional black color stops** that get closer to the brush strokes. As you add black color stops, the neon effects will become more vivid. It's a delicate balance; if you go too far, you will darken the illustration too much.

   Figure 118 shows four new black color stops added to the freeform gradient. The color stop to the left of the letter N is black and greatly influences the blue color in the left half of the N. Move it left to show more color.

Continued on next page

Figure 117 Neon effect produced with the Color Dodge blending mode

Figure 118 Four black color stops added

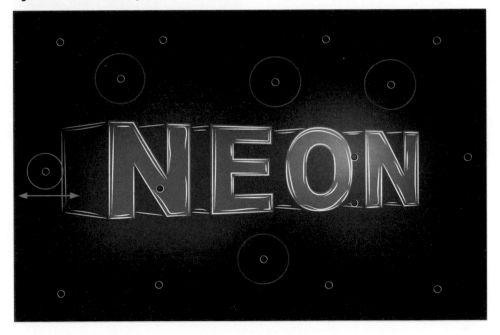

8. Save your work.

9. Create a **new layer above the Smaller Brush Strokes layer**, then name it **Flares**.

10. Draw a **small circle** anywhere on the artboard, then fill it with a **white to black radial gradient**.

11. Set its **blending mode** to **Color Dodge**, then position it **over a stroke** in the artwork.

12. Press **[option] (Mac)** or **[Alt] (Win)** and **drag** the **flare** to duplicate it, click the **Free Transform tool** , then stretch it vertically so that it is substantially taller than it is wide.

Figure 119 shows a round flare and a stretched flare in position.

13. Using the same methods, position round and stretched flares throughout the illustration, then create one very large wide flare and position it at the bottom edge of the letters to create a shiny "floor" for the artwork.

Use Figure 120 as a guide.

14. Save your work, then close the Hand-Drawn Neon document.

You used the Color Dodge blending mode to make the strokes and the Front Face type to brighten the freeform gradient. You created radial gradients and used the Color Dodge blending mode to create light flares on the illustration.

Figure 119 Round flare and stretched flare

Figure 120 Positioning the large "floor" flare

The ultimate tessellation patterns are those that repeat what appears to be a freeform illustration. Given that it tessellates, the image is more strategically designed than it appears at first glance. This Project Builder will teach you how to recreate a classic tessellation pattern of a happy bird that goes on to infinity.

1. Open AI 13-15.ai, then save it as **Repeating Road Runner**.
2. Zoom in on the 1" × 1" blue square.
3. On the toolbar, set the fill color to [None] and the stroke color to Black.
4. On the Stroke panel, set the Weight to .5 pt.
5. Target the Top Trace layer on the Layers panel, then use the Pen tool to trace the yellow line.
6. When you are done tracing, hide the Top Trace layer.
7. Target the Right Trace layer, then trace the pink line.
8. Hide the three bottom layers.
9. Show the Top Trace layer.
10. Select the black line on the Top Trace layer, then use the Move dialog box to make a copy exactly 1" down.
11. Select the black line on the Right Trace layer, then use the Move dialog box to make a copy exactly 1" to the left.
12. Switch to Outline mode, then join the overlapping points that are circled in Figure 121.

TIP Select a pair of points with the Direct Selection tool ▷, then enter [command] [J] (Mac) or [Ctrl] [J] (Win).

13. Show the Interior layer.
14. On the Layers panel, target the top three layers, click the Layers panel menu button, then click Merge Selected.
15. Rename the resulting layer **Road Runner**.
16. Fill the bird shape with light yellow.
17. To give some character to the line work, select all, then apply a brush that you like from the Brushes panel or the Brushes library on the Brushes panel menu.
18. Select all the artwork, then group it.
19. Use the Move tool to create a copy exactly 1" to the right.
20. Fill the copy with a different color.
21. Create the pattern shown in Figure 122.
22. Save your work, then close the Repeating Road Runner document.

Figure 121 Points to be joined

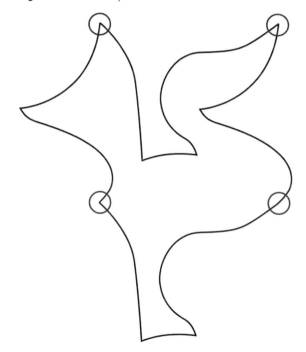

Figure 122 The tessellated pattern

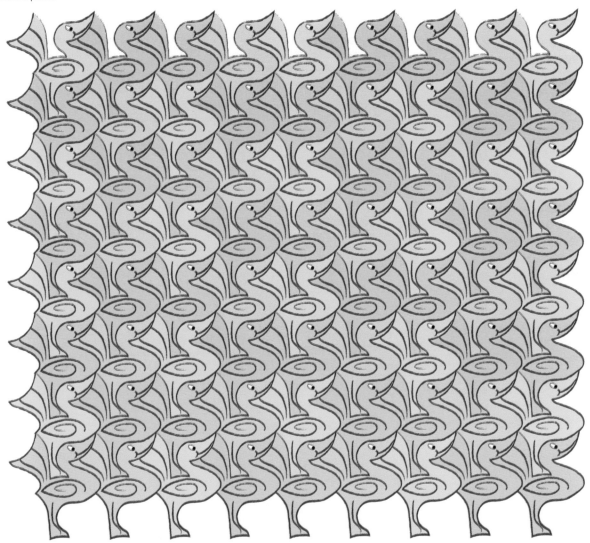

This Project Builder is a variation of the neon effect you used for the flamingo illustration. In that illustration, the neon effect was a very thin bright "tube" surrounded by a much thicker glow. In this illustration, there will be no differentiation between the glowing element and the tube itself; instead, the result will be a single, glowing thick glass tube. You will also explore how shadows and blending modes can interact with a neon effect.

1. Open AI 13-16.ai, then save it as **Neon Burger**.
2. Select all the strokes on the Outer Tube layer, then increase the Weight to 12 pts.
   The increased thickness represents the thickness of the glass neon tube. The challenge now is to give it dimension and make it glow as though it is lit up.
3. Show the Inner Tube layer.
   The strokes on the Inner Tube layer are each a lighter color.
4. Select all the strokes on the Inner Tube layer, then increase the Weight to 8 pt.
5. Apply a 4-pixel Gaussian Blur effect to the Inner Tube and Outer Tube artwork.
6. Show the Glow layer, then select all the strokes on that layer.
   The Glow layer is a copy of the Outer Tube layer before you increased the stroke weight and added the blur.
7. Increase the Weight to 20 pt., then add a 20-pixel Gaussian Blur to the selection.
8. Show the Brick Wall layer.
   The introduction of the brick wall takes the illustration from abstract to real-world. The brick wall brings with it opportunities for shadows and color reflections. The brick artwork is deliberately darkened to create the opportunity for the neon lights to brighten it up.
9. Duplicate the Outer Tube layer, rename the copy **Shadow**, then drag it down below the Glow layer.
10. Select all the strokes on the Shadow layer, then change them to Black.
    You won't see the change because the artwork is behind the glow.
11. Press and hold [shift], then press the down arrow on your keypad two times.
12. Change the blending mode on the Shadow artwork to Multiply.
13. Duplicate the Glow layer, rename the copy **Reflection**, then drag it down below the Shadow layer.
    From this point on, the work becomes experimenting with different sizes, blending modes, and layer interactions. With each move, you will work your way toward a final look.

14. Change the stroke weight on the Reflection artwork to 55 pt.

   This large glow is intended to be the diffuse light emanating from the neon and colorizing and reflecting off the brick wall.

15. Change the blending mode to Color Dodge.

   Color Dodge is a logical first choice because it's the blending mode you used in a previous lesson. It's not right for this illustration.

16. Change the blending mode to Overlay.

   This is a move in the right direction, but the color is still too "hot" to be a reflection off a brick wall— especially in the yellow areas. You could choose to reduce the opacity but changing the blending mode is a better choice.

17. Change the blending mode to Soft Light.

   When you become experienced with blending modes, you know that Soft Light is a less intense version of Overlay. In this case, it produces the perfect effect and is completely believable as a reflection of the neon light against the brick.

18. On the Appearance panel, open the Gaussian Blur effect then increase the Radius of the blur to 30 pixels.

   The edge of the reflection blur is no longer so distinct.

19. Hide the Glow layer.

   The illustration is improved. The "tubes" read more clearly as neon tubes, and the shadow is more visible. Removing the glow reveals that the shadow artwork is too opaque – we can't see the wall through it.

20. Target the Shadow layer, then reduce its Opacity to 65%.

   Remember that the shadow artwork was applied not as an effect on the Appearance panel, but as actual strokes painted black. To reduce the Opacity, you'll need to use the Transparency panel.

21. Show the Glow layer.

   The glow is definitely too much for the artwork. The question is whether or not it can play a diminished role.

22. Select the Glow artwork, then reduce its Opacity to 25%.

23. Compare your artwork to Figure 123.

   If you compare this to the flamingo illustration (Figure 110) you can see the variation of the design. The flamingo is a thin white neon tube surrounded by a much larger glow. In this cheeseburger illustration, the glow and the tube are essentially the same one object. The *other* glow in this artwork is the larger blur "reflecting" off the wall, which is simultaneously subtle and the "wow" aspect of the illustration.

24. Save your work, then close the Neon Burger document.

Figure 123 "Large tube" neon illustration

Brick wall: OlegRi/Shutterstock

DESIGN PROJECT

The illustration of "Carly" in Lesson 1 of this chapter is the culmination of all the skills you've learned in this book. It includes gradients, fills, blending modes, transparency, effects, and pathfinders, among other strategies. Your challenge in this Design Project is to create your own version of the illustration.

1. Take multiple pictures of a friend, then choose one to be your illustration.
2. Place the image in Illustrator, then crop it so only one half is visible.
3. Trace the face components and the shadows on the face.
4. Reflect all the tracings, then unite the ones that overlap.
5. FIll the objects with color to create the first version of the illustration.
   Use Figure 28 as a guide for your goal.
6. Save this iteration with the name **First Flat**. This will be the version you will use with the Divide pathfinder to create the final pattern effect.
7. Copy components of the illustration, fill them with gradients, then overlay the gradients to add dimension and complexity to the illustration.
8. Apply drop shadows where they are possible to add further dimension and complexity to the image.
   Use Figure 35 as a guide for your goal.
9. Open the First Flat file you created, then divide it with the Divide pathfinder.
10. Colorize the divided parts of the illustration as you like.
11. Copy the divided illustration to the top of the working illustration.
12. Copy and paste the divided parts of the illustration below the shadows and overlays you created.
13. Use Figure 42 as a guide.

STEPS TO AN HERBAL REMEDY

1 DIAGNOSE PATIENT
A practitioner identifies a patient's ailment through an extensive examination that can include checking the pulse and tongue.

2 GATHER INGREDIENTS
Each patient is unique: People suffering from the same symptoms may receive significantly different prescriptions.

3 PROCESS PRESCRIPTION
Depending on the prescription, an herb may be processed in various ways to extract its healing properties in their proper potency.

4 TREAT PATIENT
A traditional prescription is designed to target specific parts of the body and to bring the patient's entire system back into balance.

君 **Monarchs**
These principal ingredients target the immediate cause and symptoms of the disease.

臣 **Ministers**
These herbs are said to enhance the monarch's effects and also target underlying symptoms.

佐 **Assistants**
These treat secondary symptoms, eliminate toxins, and optimize the effects of the other herbs.

使 **Guides**
Not always necessary in prescriptions, these herbs help deliver ingredients to targeted areas.

The Paozhi (processing) stage distills herbs to their essence by crushing, roasting, burning, or frying to eliminate impurities.

Medicine grinder

• Acupuncture point
Meridian Pathway in the body where energy is said to flow

HERBS SCIENTIFICALLY SHOWN TO
Fight infection
Reduce inflammation
Reduce fever

Licorice root

Forsythia fruit
FLAVOR
PROPERTY

Burdock fruit

Reed rhizome

Bamboo leaf

Fermented soybean

Balloon flower

Honeysuckle flower

Schizonepeta spike

Mint leaf

YINQIAO FORMULA

Traditional and artisanal
The medicine is consumed in a broth or tea of reed roots or applied as a patch at acupuncture points.

The grinder is sometimes used on soft herbs, like mint, the mortar and pestle on hard ones.

Mortar and pestle

Patch

Tea

The herbs are steadily boiled, often for hours, causing a chemical change believed to blend their healing properties.

Premade and standardized
Generic remedies can be sold as pills or in packets, but some say teas from raw herbs are more effective.

Boiling pot

Pills

Powder

Traditional Treatment

Herbal prescriptions, many dating back millennia, are a big part of traditional Chinese medicine. Formulas may consist of a single herb or many and are customized based on a patient's condition, age, gender, and body type. The recipe for mixing Yinqiao, a 10-herb treatment for the common cold, is shown here.

ANCIENT THEORIES
One belief is that the body consists of opposite but complementary qualities, or yin and yang, that maintain its healthy balance. Treatments following the four properties and five flavors are thought to promote balance.

FOUR PROPERTIES
Herbs are labeled hot or cold for their ability to treat ailments considered related to either cold (yin) or heat (yang).

| Cold | Cool | Neutral | Warm | Hot |

Yin (cold) herbs treat yang (hot) ailments, such as swelling.

Yang (hot) herbs treat yin (cold) conditions, such as chills.

FIVE FLAVORS
Different flavors are believed to have specific healing properties and the ability to target specific body areas and organs.

Spicy Stimulates sweating, blood circulation

Salty Aids bowel movements

Bitter Reduces heat

Sweet Relieves pain

Sour Stops sweating, coughing, and diarrhea

MONICA SERRANO AND DAISY CHUNG, NGM STAFF; MANYUN ZOU; MEG ROOSEVELT. ART: JIWOON PAK. CALLIGRAPHY: JAMIE WU. SOURCES: NATIONAL CENTER FOR BIOTECHNOLOGY INFORMATION; ZHANG WEI, INSTITUTE OF CHINESE MATERIA MEDICA, CHINA ACADEMY OF CHINESE MEDICAL SCIENCES; LINN YEH CHING

PROJECT DESCRIPTION

In this project, you will explore different herbs and their uses in traditional Chinese medicine. You will then choose one of the herbs that is of interest to you and create a poster illustrating the "life cycle" of the herb. Be sure to include the following points: how the herb is grown, harvested, processed, and then used as a treatment. Conduct research as necessary to fill in the missing information. The goal of this project is to give a more in-depth look into one of the Chinese herbs pictured in the spread.

SKILLS TO EXPLORE

- Create Symbols
- Place Symbol Instances
- Modify Symbols and Symbol Instances
- Create Symbol Instance Sets
- Modify Symbol Instance Sets
- Extrude Objects
- Revolve Objects
- Manipulate Surface Shading and Lighting
- Map Artwork to 3D Objects
- Work with a Perspective Grid
- Create a Graph
- Edit a Graph Using the Graph Data Window
- Use the Group Selection Tool

SOFT SKILLS CHALLENGE

Engage in a pair discussion activity with a classmate to share information on the specific Chinese herb you have chosen. Be sure to highlight the main points of your research, including the name of the herb, its growth patterns, preparation methods, and its traditional uses. Allow your partner time to ask related questions. When your part is complete, turn the tables and allow your partner time to present. After hearing the presentation and asking your own questions, compare the two herbs.

What information was most powerful or surprising to your audience? What would you or your partner like to learn more about? The goal of this project is to inform your partner about your chosen herb using strong conversational skills. This conversation should help you determine the information that is most important to convey in your infographic.

PAIR DISCUSSION CHECKLIST

1. Partner
2. Outline of main talking points
3. Safe space to facilitate respectful conversation

GETTING STARTED

As you begin to create your "life cycle" poster, explore all aspects of traditional Chinese medicine. Allow yourself to be creative, without restraint. Imagine using nature as a remedy for various ailments and symptoms. Keep an open mind as you research traditional treatments.

1. Conduct research. Look online or search through books to discover traditional herbs that might be of interest to you. Then study the image of traditional treatments and choose one herb to focus on. Think about why this particular herb piqued your interest. Find out what the herb is used to treat and how it is prepared. Highlight or list the important information you want to share about the herb.

2. Start a conversation. Conversations are often stepping stones to new ideas. Use the people around you as a creative resource to delve into new avenues of research. And remember—herbs are food. In the same way your ancestors might have treated a stomach ache with mint leaves, Chinese herbs are used for healing.

3. Map out your poster. Create a pencil sketch of a grid and visually place the elements of your composition on the grid. Mapping out your poster will help you achieve balance in your composition. Consider the hierarchy of the page. Decide how you want each individual element of your composition to attract attention. Create a layout that catches the viewer's eye in an effective manner.

PROJECT DESCRIPTION

In this project, you will build upon your Design Project to create an infographic of a traditional Chinese herb used to treat a certain ailment or illness. Your infographic must convey information about the herb; where it is grown; how it is harvested, dried, and processed; and what condition(s) it is used to treat. If possible, include information about its efficacy, or its studied results, and what it smells and/or tastes like. The goal of this project is to provide viewers with a comprehensive look at an herb used as a form of traditional treatment in Chinese culture.

SKILLS TO EXPLORE

- Use the Graph Type Dialog Box
- Create a Combination Graph
- Create a Custom Graph Design
- Apply a Custom Design to a Graph
- Create and Apply a Sliding-Scale Design
- Explore Color Theory and Resolution Issues
- Work in CMYK Mode
- Specify Spot Colors
- Create Crop Marks
- Create Bleeds
- Create Multiple Dimensions with the Shape Builder Tool
- Create Tessellating Patterns

SOFT SKILLS CHALLENGE

Reflection is an important component to continued learning. When you reflect on what you've learned, you give yourself the opportunity to think deeply about the topic and focus on the important elements of your research. In the art world, self-reflection is critical. Reflecting on your process and your final result gives you the opportunity to improve upon your design skills for the future.

In this challenge, you will reflect upon the necessary steps to complete your project. Look back at your pencil sketch and your research. Does your sketch allow for room to convey all of the important information you have highlighted or listed?

Now envision a layout for your infographic. What text or visuals will you add and how will they enhance your composition? Remember, more isn't always better. Will simplifying your graphics or text allow for better balance and visual representation? Take a few moments to reflect on these questions.

GETTING STARTED

Inspiration is everywhere! Many natural ingredients are used in cosmetics. The sketches show the plants or foods, as well as the way they are processed into beauty products.

lenaalyonushka/Shutterstock

1. Find your own source of inspiration. It can be hard to explore new ideas and concepts, especially when you are just getting used to what you previously learned. Help yourself break out of your comfort zone by exploring more expressive and abstract visuals that might spark some ideas. Since traditional treatments come from nature, look to the outdoors for inspiration.

2. Add and share. Jot down ideas or enhance your sketch to help expand upon your layout. Remember: your words and images should work together to tell a story. Then share your direction with a classmate or group of peers. Group brainstorming sessions often lead to new ideas as creative people bounce concepts off of each other. Try to see your design from a new perspective. How can your group's feedback inspire you to take a new direction?

3. Avoid perfectionism. It's not uncommon for creatives to want their work to be absolutely perfect. In this project, perfection is not the goal, or even an objective. Let yourself pursue your concept relentlessly and try to tell the story of your chosen herb using whatever visuals necessary, no matter how abstract they might seem. This is a great opportunity to take some creative risks.

| GLOSSARY |

A

Absorption Occurs when light strikes an object and is absorbed by the object.

Additive primary colors Refers to the fact that red, green, and blue light cannot be broken down themselves but can be combined to produce other colors.

Ambient light Determines how an object is lit globally.

Area text Text that is created inside an object.

Art brush Brush style that stretches an object along the length of a path.

Attributes Formatting that has been applied to an object that affects its appearance.

B

Bevel Angle that one surface makes with another when they are not at right angles.

Bitmap images Graphics created using a grid of colored squares called pixels.

Bleed Artwork that extends to the trim and must extend the trim size by .125-inch to allow for variations when trimmed.

Blend Series of intermediate objects and colors between two or more selected objects.

Blend steps Controls how smoothly shading appears on an object's surface and is most visible in the transition from the highlight areas to the diffusely lit areas.

Blending modes Preset filters that control how colors blend when two objects overlap.

Brightness Degree of lightness of a color.

Bristle brush Brush style that mimics traditional media such as watercolors.

Butt caps Squared ends of a stroked path.

C

Calligraphic brush Brush style that applies strokes that resemble those drawn with a calligraphic pen.

Caps Ends of stroked paths.

Clipping set Term used to distinguish clipping paths used in layers from clipping paths used to mask nonlayered artwork.

Color gamut Range of colors that can be printed or displayed within a given color model.

Color mode Illustrator setting determining the color model of a document: RGB or CMYK.

Color model System used to represent or reproduce color.

Color stops Small circles on the gradient slider that represent the colors used in the gradient.

Combination graph Graph that uses two graph styles to plot numeric data; useful for emphasizing one set of data in comparison to others.

Compound shape Two or more paths that are combined in such a way that "holes" appear wherever paths overlap.

Concentric Objects that share the same center point.

Corner point Anchor point joining two straight segments, one straight segment and one curved segment, or two curved segments.

Crop marks Short, thin lines that definewhere artwork is trimmed after it is printed.

Custom graph design Artwork used to replace traditional columns, bars, or markers in Illustrator graphs.

D

Direction lines Lines that emanate from an anchor point and determine the arc of a curved segment.

E

Edge Similar to a stroke, an edge is a new shape or area created by the overlap of Illustrator objects when the Live Paint Bucket tool is applied.

Effective resolution Resolution of a placed image based on its size in the layout.

Envelopes Objects that are used to distort other objects into the shape of the envelope object.

Extrude To add depth to an object by extending it on its Z axis. An object's Z axis is always perpendicular to the object's front surface.

Extrude & Bevel effect 3D effect that applies a three-dimensional effect to two-dimensional objects.

G

GIF Standard file format for compressing images by lowering the number of colors available to the file.

Gradient/gradient fill Graduated blend between two or more colors used to fill an object or multiple objects.

H

Highlight Intensity A setting that controls how intense a highlight appears.

Highlight Size A setting that controls how large the highlights appear on an object.

Hue Name of a color, or its identity on a standard color wheel.

I

Insertion mode Drawing mode in Illustrator that allows you to add a new object to a live paint group. A gray rectangle surrounding a live paint group indicates Insertion mode is active.

J

Joins Define the appearance of the corner where two paths meet.

JPEG Standard file format for compressing continuous tone images, gradients, and blends.

K

Kerning Increasing or decreasing the horizontal space between any two text characters.

L

Layers Solution for organizing and managing a complex illustration by segregating artwork.

Leading Vertical space between baselines.

Lighting Intensity A setting that controls the strength of the light on an object. The range for lighting intensity is 0–100, with 100 being the default.

Live paint group A group of objects that maintain a dynamic relationship with each other. When one object in the group is moved, the overlapping areas change shape and fill accordingly.

M

Midpoint Point at which two colors meet in equal measure.

Miter limit Determines when a miter join will be squared off to a beveled edge.

O

Objects Individual pieces of artwork created in Illustrator.

Offset Distance that an object is moved from a starting location to a subsequent ending location.

Opacity Degree to which an object is transparent.

Opacity mask Function that allows selective control of where an object is transparent.

Optimization Process by which a file's size is reduced through standard color compression algorithms.

P

Pathfinders Preset operations that combine paths in a variety of ways; useful for creating complex or irregular shapes from basic shapes.

Pattern brush Brush style that repeats a pattern along a path.

Perspective Grid Grid and functionality that allows you to draw and copy objects in a fixed perspective.

Pixels Picture element; small, single-colored squares that compose a bitmap image.

PNG (Portable Network Graphics) Bitmap graphics file format that supports lossless data compression.

Point of origin Point from which an object is transformed; by default, the center point of an object, unless another point is specified.

Preferences Specifications you can set for how certain features of an application behave.

Process tints Colors that can be printed by mixing varying percentages of CMYK inks.

Projecting caps Squared edges that extend the end anchor point of a path at a distance that is one-half the stroke weight.

R

Reflection When light strikes an object and "bounces" off the object.

Region Similar to a fill, a region is a new shape or area created by the overlap of Illustrator objects; created when the Live Paint Bucket tool is applied.

Resolution Number of pixels in a given inch of a bitmap graphic.

Resolution-dependent Graphics that should not be scaled when brought into other programs.

Resolution-independent Graphics that can be scaled with no impact on image quality.

Revolving Method for applying a 3D effect to a 2D object by "sweeping" a path in a circular direction around the Y axis of the object.

Round caps Rounded ends of a stroked path.

S

Saturation Intensity of a hue.

Scatter brush Brush style that disperses copies of an object along a path.

Shape modes Preset operations that combine paths in a variety of ways; useful for creating complex or irregular shapes from basic shapes.

Smart guides Nonprinting words that appear on the artboard and identify visible or invisible objects, page boundaries, intersections, anchor points, etc.

Smooth points Anchor points created by clicking and dragging the Pen tool; the path continues uninterrupted through the anchor point.

Stacking order The order of how objects are arranged in front and behind other objects on the artboard.

Subtractive primary colors Cyan, magenta, and yellow; the term subtractive refers to the concept that each is produced by removing or subtracting one of the additive primary colors and that overlapping all three pigments would absorb all colors.

Symbol instance Reference to the original symbol artwork on the Symbols panel; functions only to show the positioning of the symbol artwork on the artboard.

Symbol instance set Symbol instances created with the Symbol Sprayer tool.

Symbols Graphic objects you create and store on the Symbols panel.

T

Thumbnail Miniature picture of the objects on a layer.

Tick marks Short lines that extend out from the value axis of a graph and aid viewers in interpreting the meaning of column height by indicating incremental values on the value axis.

Tiling Process of repeating a tile as a fill for a pattern.

Tracking Process of inserting or removing uniform spaces between text characters to affect the width of selected words or entire blocks of text.

Transmission Occurs when light strikes an object and passes through the object.

Trim marks Like crop marks, they define where a printed image should be trimmed.

Trim size Size to which artwork or a document is to be cut.

V

Variations Groups of swatches loaded by the Color Guide panel when you select an object on the artboard and then choose a harmony rule.

Vector graphics Resolution-independent graphics created with lines, curves, and fills.

Visible light Light waves that are visible to the human eye.

W

White light Concept that natural light on Earth appears to people as not having any dominant hue.

Workspace Positioning of panels on an artboard or computer monitor; Illustrator includes preset workspaces targeted for specific types of work, such as typography and painting.

INDEX